Playing the Indian Card

Everything You Know about Canada's "First Nations" Is Wrong

STEPHEN K. RONEY

ISBN: 1775267814
ISBN-13: 978-1775267812

Bonsecours Editions London, Ontario

DEDICATION

This book is dedicated to Saint Catherine (Kateri) Tekakwitha, a light in my childhood.

CONTENTS

ACKNOWLEDGMENTS

With many thanks to Michael D. Roney for financial support. Lovely cover by BG Communications; editing by Cy Strom, who knows everything. Just to annoy him, I went back and added in some mistakes after he had finished. And for the help and support of my wife Vaneza in a thousand ways.

1 SIR JOHN A. MACDONALD, GENOCIDAL MANIAC

An oddly appropriate memorial. *Library and Archives Canada.*

To celebrate Canada's Sesquicentennial in 2017, a Kitchener-Waterloo citizens group proposed a sculpture park, to feature likenesses in bronze of Canada's prime ministers. Funded by private subscription, it was to grace Kitchener's Victoria Park. Nice gift to the city: it might have become a tourist attraction.

Kitchener City Council torpedoed the project. Such gift horses were not acceptable. The proposed sculpture park was offered instead to the Waterloo campus of Wilfrid Laurier University. The first statue, of Sir John A. Macdonald, was accordingly unveiled.

In February 2016, WLU withdrew its support, and actually had the Macdonald statue pulled up and hauled away.

The stated reason, according to an online petition, was that it was "politically insensitive (if not offensive) to celebrate and memorialize all Canadian Prime Ministers … on land that traditionally belongs to the Neutral, Anishnawbe and Haudenosaunee peoples." [1]

"It's disingenuous to make a commitment to indigeneity and recognize that land belonged to First Nations people and then go and erect statues of leaders who took the land away from them, and were responsible for policies of genocide," added

Jonathan Finn, the chair of the department of communication studies, who started the petition and who introduced the motion to the university's senate cancelling the project. [2]

The city of Kitchener had backed out on the grounds that it did not reflect the "diversity" of the region.

Celebrating Canada in Canada, on Canadian land, is offensive? Are we Canadians not entitled to our own land and our own history?

The online petition opposing the installation refers readers to a web page outlining similar protests in the United States, against statues of Southern Civil War figures.[3]

This helps explain the otherwise seeming non sequitur of statues of our prime ministers being somehow offensive to aboriginals: if something is happening in the United States, we must imitate it in Canada, whether the case is comparable or not. If big brother does something, little brother must do it too. Not having had slavery to any extent plausibly worth mentioning, we need to hold something against our early prime ministers.

Most and probably all Canadian prime ministers have been rather easygoing and ethnically inclusive in their attitudes and policies. You pretty much have to be, if you are going to get to be prime minister of Canada. This is part of the Canadian experience, if only due to the circumstance of being a half anglophone, half francophone, half Catholic, half Protestant nation run as a democracy. While politicians are by their trade not always entirely to be admired, it is absurd to see Kim Campbell or John Turner as war criminals. This is beyond anything even Godwin foresaw. But then, it is just as absurd to accuse Sir John A. Macdonald.

It is Sir John A. who seems to be singled out for condemnation by the social justice league of Canada. It was his statue that was physically uprooted in Waterloo. In Kingston, on January 11, 2015, Macdonald's 201st birthday, somebody slashed the tires of the man organizing a commemorative ceremony and splashed his car with red paint. Presumably symbolizing blood. They also apparently, in eerie if unintentional echo of KKK traditions, burned a Canadian flag on the man's lawn. One of the local "activists" (what might you prefer to call them?) is quoted by the papers referring to Macdonald as a "genocidal maniac."

In previous years, the anniversary has been celebrated by nocturnal spraypainting—again with red paint—of the John A. statue in Kingston's city park with the phrases "This is stolen land," "Murderer," and "Colonizer." An Idle No More protester explained: "Would people commemorate the crimes that Hitler did? Because this is basically the same principle."

On the eve of Canada's 150th year, in response to Prime Minister Justin Trudeau's New Year address, one activist writes:

> In praise of 150 years of the consolidation of this colonial-settler state, it [the address] ignores the very ground we're presently occupying in common. Ground, land, that belonged to the Indigenous peoples of what is now called Canada. A colonial "success story" always involves conquest, assimilation, dispossession, inter-generational trauma, inequality and countless other injustices. The type of things Liberal prime ministers don't include in their New Year's messages, especially when kicking off things like Canada 150 celebrations. … The starting point for understanding the history of Canada is the colonial project, the theft of land, and the dispossession of and attempt to extinguish the Indigenous nations. [4]

Macdonald's unspeakable crimes, and those of all Canadians, are apparently these:

1. as per the Kingston graffito, that we stole Indian land;

2. that we deliberately killed Indians;

3. that we and he, through the residential schools system, waged "cultural genocide" on Indian traditions as well as enabling widespread child abuse;

4. that we and he waged active war against the Indians in 1885.[5]

That seems to be the full bill of indictment. Let's deal with the charges in turn.

One: We stole Indian land

Everyone supposes so; it is not so. Kid brother syndrome to the contrary, the history of aboriginal-government relations is different in Canada and the United States. Which is why the US-Canada border was known among plains Indians as the Medicine Line. Which is why, in both the Revolutionary War and the War of 1812, Indians rallied to British/Canadian colours in great numbers. The favourable treatment of Indians, in fact, protecting them from wildcat European settlement beyond the Appalachians, was one of the causes of the American Revolution, cited obliquely in the Declaration of Independence.[6] Here was no Trail of Tears. Here was no Wounded Knee. Here, negotiated treaty settlements, notably the numbered treaties that began under Macdonald, preceded any major land settlement, and here we sent out the NWMP/RCMP to preserve peace and order—another initiative of Sir John A.'s. The Mounties' first mandate was to protect the natives against the predations of treacherous non-aboriginal traders.

This policy of negotiated treaties and compensation for any lands deeded to non-native Canadians was largely due as well to Sir John A. Not everyone at the time felt it necessary. After all, Indians held and used land in a manner foreign to European norms. They were nomadic, in a sense never more than visitors, and their use of and therefore natural claim on any particular parcel of land was ephemeral. Their population was tiny; they had no need for so much land, nor were they using most of it. Boundaries between tribes were constantly shifting. (Note that, in the bill of indictment in Kitchener-Waterloo, the same land is assigned historically to the "Anishnawbe [Algonquin] and Haudenosaunee [Iroquois] peoples." The two were for most of recorded history mortal enemies; and they were far from the only groups who passed through here. The Neutrals are also mentioned—wiped out by the Haudenosaunee.) Oliver Mowat, premier of Ontario for much of Macdonald's tenure, held that the Indians had no strictly legal rights in the matter, and their claims were purely moral. A celebrated Ontario court judgment of the time held the same.[7]

Macdonald and his government instead adhered to earlier British policies respecting native claims, setting a precedent honoured by future Canadian governments and prime ministers, without exception.

If someone sells you his house, you did not steal it. Especially when he held no clear title in the first place. If he comes back years later and demands more money, he is not an upright fellow. He certainly has no say if you choose to put a statue on your lawn.

Some natives have recently insisted that the Indian oral understanding of the original treaties was different from the government's written documents; that they, being non-literate, were lied to and conned by the government agents. They had intended to cede ownership of the land "only to the depth of a plough blade."[8] Their fellow Canadians therefore now owed them trillions in past resource revenue.

There are several problems with such claims.

First, there is a reason for the invention of writing. The original reason was to keep accurate records in case of dispute. Oral records can be reliable, if it is in everyone's interest to preserve them intact. But they can also be altered at any time by either party, and are therefore not of great evidentiary value. Written evidence preserves the matter beyond dispute. As a result, there is every reason to give written records absolute priority.

Second, this claim goes against the written text. In the words of Treaty Three, which become legal boilerplate for subsequent agreements: "[the Indian signatories] do hereby cede, release, surrender and yield up to the Government of the

Dominion of Canada for Her Majesty the Queen and Her successors forever, all their rights, titles and privileges whatsoever, to the lands included." There is no ambiguity there. To accuse the government agents of misleading the Indians on this point requires accusing them of a truly breathtaking mendacity. Yet we assume without evidence the Indians must always be telling the truth?

Third, a large part of the very point of the treaties from the government's point of view was to allow for mineral extraction. To go back on that now would be unfair to that signatory.

Fourth, the native cultures were still in the stone age. They did not mine metals. They would have had little idea of value of any sort buried underground, little use for it, and little reason to think anything of interest was down there. It seems unlikely they would have made any such reservation, even in their own minds.

Fifth, this being so, the government agents would have gained nothing by having lied on this point. It would have done nothing to improve their bargaining position.

Sixth, surprisingly enough, the issue actually did come up in treaty negotiations, and Alexander Morris, negotiating for the government, made clear that mineral rights were included in the cession.

Two: We killed Indians

To the second charge, then, in the bill of indictment: Macdonald and we non-native Canadians generally killed Indians by deliberate starvation. No doubt we would have used blankets infected with smallpox, too, if the smallpox vaccine had not become readily available by Confederation.

The essential bit of evidence usually given here is Macdonald's boast in the Commons, "[We] are doing all we can by refusing food until the Indians are on the verge of starvation."

But note this: "on the verge." At worst possible interpretation, Macdonald is saying that Indians may be hungry, but to the best of his knowledge, nobody is starving. Nevertheless, Dennis Gruending, for example, writing for *Rabble*, accuses Kingston's favourite son of creating "the conditions for a tuberculosis epidemic in aboriginal communities."[9]

This is a bit of a stretch, since tuberculosis has been a major problem in aboriginal communities both before and after Sir John. It is currently at 31 times the rate found among the general Canadian population.[10]

Now, the words immediately before that "on the verge" are significant. A fuller quote is "We cannot allow them to die for want of food. We are doing all we can, by refusing food until the Indians are on the verge of starvation, to reduce the expense."

That gives a little context. Simply on the face of it, there was no policy to starve the Indians, no genocide. Macdonald said these words in 1882. Canada was then in the middle of the "Long Depression," which lasted until the beginning of the 20th century. Funds were scarce. The opposition was challenging the government policy of sending food aid to the Indians as extravagant. Macdonald was defending against this attack. Canada at this time had no welfare payments, no disability pensions, no child allowance, no old age pension. Other Canadians were left to sink or swim, as far as the government was involved. Yet this group was being helped out, by taking funds from other Canadians who might have needed it badly themselves.

Note too that there was no treaty obligation to send food. Treaty One, Two, Three, Four, Five, and Seven say nothing about the government being responsible for sending aid in any circumstances. Aboriginals were given seed, large tracts of land, and farm implements, and expected thenceforth to look after themselves. The wording of Treaty Six alone, of all the treaties in effect during Macdonald's time, gives a mandate for aid, but is ambiguous and leaves wiggle room:

That in the event hereafter of the Indians comprised within this treaty being overtaken by any pestilence, or by a general famine, the Queen, on being satisfied and certified thereof by Her Indian Agent or Agents, will grant to the Indians assistance of such character and to such extent as Her Chief Superintendent of Indian Affairs shall deem necessary and sufficient to relieve the Indians from the calamity that shall have befallen them. (Treaty Six)

At the discretion of the government, then-although it would have violated the spirit of Treaty Six to have done nothing.

Now consider what the government was being told by its Indian agents: that some Indian bands had stopped hunting, yet had not begun farming. They were under the impression that, now that they had treaties, the Great White Mother had an obligation to look after them.

The Indian Affairs Branch writes at the time: "When the Deputy-Superintendent-General of Indian Affairs was on his reserve, in 1883, he found Poundmaker engaged in the not very praiseworthy occupation, for a chief, of dissuading his band from working at all, though they got full rations when they worked. He informed them that the Government was bound to feed them all the same, whether they worked or not."[11]

This put the government in an awkward position. "In this effort to encourage them to become self-supporting the Government is placed between two fires of hostile criticism. On the one hand it is charged with wasting the public money in feeding a lot of idle vagabonds. On the other band, if it stints the rations of the lazy and the thriftless, it is charged with starving the poor Indians."[12]

Three: We waged cultural genocide

Charge number three from our bill of indictment: Macdonald was guilty of "cultural genocide" for founding the residential schools system.

All of the numbered treaties included the requirement that the government set up schools and pay for teachers.

> And further, Her Majesty agrees to maintain a school on each reserve hereby made whenever the Indians of the reserve should desire it. (*Treaty One, Treaty Two*)
>
> And further, Her Majesty agrees to maintain schools for instruction in such reserves hereby made as to Her Government of Her Dominion of Canada may seem advisable whenever the Indians of the reserve shall desire it. (*Treaty Three*)
>
> Further, Her Majesty agrees to maintain a school in the reserve allotted to each band as soon as they settle on said reserve and are prepared for a teacher. (*Treaty Four*)
>
> And further, Her Majesty agrees to maintain schools for instruction in such reserves hereby made as to Her Government of the Dominion of Canada may seem advisable, whenever the Indians of the reserve shall desire it. (*Treaty Five, Treaty Six*)
>
> Further, Her Majesty agrees to pay the salary of such teachers to instruct the children of said Indians as to Her Government of Canada may seem advisable, when said Indians are settled on their Reserves and shall desire teachers. (*Treaty Seven*)

At whose insistence was this? Not the government's. Its priority was to spare expense, and this was an expense. It was at native request, and was one of their chief goals in signing the treaties-negotiating treaties 3 through 6, Lieutenant-Governor Alexander Morris reports a "universal demand" for teachers.[13] They could see that their traditional way of life was less desirable than that of the Europeans. They wanted the next generation to learn to farm or follow a trade, and to integrate. The treaties specified that schools would be built only where and when the Indians wanted; when they were, the majority of aboriginal children were always educated at day schools. The residential schools were for children whose homes were too remote or their parents' lifestyle too nomadic to support a local school-or, in many cases, for orphans and the abandoned. The government did not want to pay for a residential school if it did not have to: it increased the costs per student. And good or bad, chosen or not, the fact that only a minority of native children were educated in residential schools makes mockery of the claim, often heard, that the residential schools are to blame for the ills of Indian society even today.

The basic idea of the residential schools, counter to the familiar claim, was not to eliminate native culture or to promote integration. This is common sense: if the objective were integration, the obvious step would be to integrate Indian children into the public school system. This was the program advocated for American blacks by Martin Luther King and the civil rights movement of the US South. If this in turn was "cultural genocide," Martin Luther King is a criminal against humanity.

No doubt there was child abuse in the residential schools. It is a tragic certainty that those inclined to bully will want to choose careers, like teacher or palliative care nurse, which make this avocation easier to pursue. They will seek defenseless prey. They will, if possible, sign up for locations, like remote residential schools, where supervision is minimal.

Pedophiles are going to want jobs that put them in close contact with children, ideally without much supervision, for long periods of the day and night. Better if the pedophiles are in some formal relationship of control.

There are few ways to protect against this hazard; probably the best is to turn such positions over to those who have a clear religious or moral reason for wanting to be there, as this may explain their presence without assuming predatory instincts. Better still if they have some sort of moral supervision by a religious society and superior. Probably a vow of celibacy is even better.

This is the path the residential schools took. If it was not 100 percent effective, nothing is. In recent years, we have been gradually realizing that this problem is pandemic in schools of all sorts; there is nothing special about, and certainly nothing intentional in the design of, residential schools, in this regard. Ironically, the very richest strata of society have traditionally insisted on paying large sums for the privilege of sending their children into the same circumstances considered abusive when students are aboriginal.

In 2006-07, a settlement of $2 billion was mandated by the courts-the largest class action settlement in Canadian history-to anyone who had gone to a residential school. Not just those who could demonstrate abuse-anyone. This was a huge transfer of wealth from fellow Canadians who obviously had nothing to do with the residential schools. Other than having to pay for them.

Four: We made war on the Indians, in 1885

We did not. This seems to be another imitation of big brother America. It trou^bles some Canadians, it seems, that Canada had no Indian Wars.

The reference is to the Northwest Rebellion. The Indians, or rather a small group of Indians, made war on the Canadian government. A minority of Métis also made war.

Did they have valid grievances? So we usually hear, but this rationale warrants questioning. We seem always to get the Métis side, never the position of the government of the day. Everybody wants to believe in the purity of the motives of the noble savages. But the Canadian government had not, they insisted, ignored or denied their concerns. They had already agreed to recognize Métis ownership of their claimed land plots, and to survey in accord with Métis traditions-generally the matter cited as the main complaint behind the rebellion. This seems generous enough, given that these same Métis had already been awarded land in Manitoba.

Lord Minto writes:

> To these claims and assertions Ottawa answers that a commission had already been appointed to inquire into half-breed [i.e., Métis] claims, that it was in the power of any half-breed legally entitled to obtain a patent for his farm by following the ordinary legal process, that the claims put forward for the Manitoba settlement [to be repeated in Saskatchewan] are made by the very men who were already settled with in 1870, and that the Government form of survey can and will be, if required, so arranged as not in any way to interfere with the river frontages and farms—in fact, that "the breeds" have no case at all.[14]

Of the four Métis who went to Montana to ask Riel to return and lead them, three had already been given government positions by the time the rebellion broke out—only months later. That looks conciliatory, and hardly like foot-dragging. Louis Riel sent his petition to Ottawa on December 16, 1884. The federal cabinet struck a three-man commission to review and settle Métis claims on January 28, 1885. Nevertheless, without waiting for word from the commission, and without any democratic mandate, Riel and his followers proclaimed a provisional government on March 19 and seized hostages. Riel threatened a "war of extermination" on March 21.

As to the Indians, Theresa Delaney, who lived among the Cree and whose husband was killed at Frog Lake, insists:

> But there is one thing I do know and most emphatically desire to express and have thoroughly understood and that is the fact, the Indians have no grievances and no complaints to make. Their treatment is of the best and most generous kind. The government spares no pains to attempt to make them adopt an agricultural life, to teach them to rely upon their own strength, to become independent people and good citizens.
>
> Many an English, Scotch or Irish farmer, when he comes poor to Canada and strives to take up a little farm for himself, if he had only one half the advantages that the government affords to the Indians, he would consider his fortune forever made. They need never want for food. Their rations are most regularly dealt out to them and they are paid to clear and cultivate their own land. They work for themselves and are, moreover, paid to do so and should a crop fail they are certain of their food, anyway. I ask if a man could reasonably expect more?[15]

Even if there were real grievances, does this rebellion seem like a sensible way to get them resolved? Could Métis land claims and Indian hunger have been the true motives?

Not according to the testimony of Wandering Spirit, the Cree war chief who launched the aboriginal element of the rebellion with a massacre at Frog Lake. While awaiting execution, he explained to William Cameron, a survivor, in the presence of another witness:

> Four years ago we were camped on the Missouri River in the Long Knives' land [the United States]. Riel was there, trading whiskey to the Indians. He gave us liquor and said he would make war on this country [Canada]. He asked us to join him in wiping out all Canadians.... Last fall Riel sent word to us that when the leaves came out the half-breeds would rise and kill all whites. The Long Knives [Americans] would come. They would buy the land, pay the Indians plenty money for it, and afterwards trade with them. All the tribes who wished to benefit must rise, too, and help rid the country of Canadians.[16]

Perhaps it was indeed attempted genocide, then. But not quite in the way we have been led to believe.

Lending credibility to the idea that it was all about plunder, two witnesses testified at his trial that Louis Riel had offered to forget the whole thing for a personal payment from the Canadian government of $35,000.[17]

Macdonald had the natural right of self defense, as well as the public duty to keep the country together and in possession of its territory, and to protect the lives and property of its citizens. What else could he responsibly do?

After a conventional trial and benefit of law, eight aboriginal leaders were hanged for murder, along with Louis Riel. Maybe they did not deserve it; but it was not really Macdonald's call. It was the decision of a duly constituted judge and jury, confirmed by the Provincial Supreme Court and an extraordinary review panel. Macdonald could have exercised mercy; but past experience surely argued against it. He had been magnanimous after the Red River Rebellion, and the upshot of that, after all, was another rebellion. He did extend a general amnesty within the year. The chief government response in the aftermath was to send more food aid to the Western reserves.

If this is the worst that can be brought against Canada's leaders, Canada stands as the most tolerant of nations. We ought to be celebrating this. How about a sculpture park?

Instead, Canada gets its land claimed and its traditions banned. If there is such a thing as cultural genocide, call that cultural genocide.

That is why you hold this book in your hands.

2 THERE ARE NO ABORIGINAL CANADIANS

A few tardy Vikings arrive in Chicago harbour for the Word Exposition, hoping to rape and pillage.

Listen to me, as when ye heard our father
Sing long ago the song of other shores—
Listen to me, and then in chorus gather
All your deep voices as ye pull the oars;
Fair these broad meads—these hoary woods are grand;
But we are exiles from our fathers' land.

From the lone shieling of the misty island
Mountains divide us, and the waste of seas—
Yet still the blood is strong, the heart is Highland,
And we in dreams behold the Hebrides.
Fair these broad meads—these hoary woods are grand;
But we are exiles from our fathers' land.

We ne'er shall tread the fancy-haunted valley,
Where 'tween the dark hills creeps the small clear stream,
In arms around the patriarch banner rally,
Nor see the moon on royal tombstone gleam.
Fair these broad meads—these hoary woods are grand;
But we are exiles from our fathers' land.

When the bold kindred, in the time long-vanished,
Conquered the soil and fortified the keep,
No seer foretold the children would be banished,
That a degenerate lord might boast his sheep.
Fair these broad meads—these hoary woods are grand;
But we are exiles from our fathers' land.

Come foreigner rage—let Discord burst in slaughter!
O then for clansmen true, and stern claymore—
The hearts that would have given their blood like water
Beat heavily beyond the Atlantic roar.
Fair these broad meads—these hoary woods are grand;
But we are exiles from our fathers' land.

—*Anonymous,* Canadian Boat Song

What is an aboriginal?

In 1960, in a remote cove at the northern tip of Newfoundland, the husband and wife archaeological team of Helge and Anne Ingstad uncovered the remains of a Norse settlement dating to roughly AD 1000. It is now confirmed that Europeans have been in Canada for at least a thousand years.

The Norse also encountered non-European inhabitants, "aboriginals" or Indians, if you like, whom they called skraelings. But these skraelings were probably not any native group now in Canada. More likely, they were representatives of the Dorset culture, which has since disappeared. They were supplanted in their lands by the Inuit. The Inuit (Eskimos) only began moving into Canada from Asia through Alaska in about AD 1300, seven hundred years ago.

In other words, although they left and came back later, Europeans were in Canada before the Inuit. Who then rightly gets to be called "native" or "aboriginal"?

Consider now the Iroquois of the Grand River and Bay of Quinte in Ontario. They arrived in Canada in the 1780s with other United Empire Loyalists. They had left their homes in upstate New York out of loyalty to the British Crown. The land in Canada was purchased for them by the British government from the Mississauga Indians of the area, just as it was for other UE Loyalists. They are immigrants from another country; they immigrated at the same time as many Europeans, and after other Europeans. How is the one group "native" or "aboriginal," and not the other? What is the rule here?

Consider, too, the Assiniboine of southern Manitoba and Saskatchewan. In 1640, the *Jesuit Relations* placed them in present-day Minnesota. Some time between then and 1806, they moved to the Assiniboine River Valley. They arrived in Canada centuries after the first Europeans. Why are they aborigines, and the French of Quebec or Irish of Newfoundland are not?

The Blackfoot, the quintessential plains tribe, similarly, arrived on the prairies in the 18th century, apparently coming from an earlier home in the northeastern United States.

At Treaty Six negotiations (covering the central portions of Alberta and Saskatchewan), one of the groups present were the Chippewa/Ojibway, who had only arrived in the region within the previous few hundred years. When they insisted on their aboriginal status, Alexander Morris, treaty negotiator for the Canadian government, called them on it:

"I will not sit here and hear such words from the Chippewas. Who are you?" Morris was indignant that this group of Saulteaux, whose ancestors had migrated from Ontario into the North-West only within the last few hundred years, asserted that other newcomers had no right to the land. "You come from my country [Ontario] and you tell me the Queen has cheated you; it is not so."[18]

When the Saulteaux chief Peguis signed the Red River Treaty with Lord Selkirk in 1817, ceding the land that would form the Red River settlement, his people had been in the area only since the 1790s. They had, within his lifetime, lived in Ontario and then Minnesota.[19]

Even within the first few years of the Presbyterian mission at Prince Albert, Saskatchewan, in the later 19th century, the local Indian population changed. "It was found curiously enough that the haunts in the neighborhood of the town so long frequented by the Cree Indians, were now being appropriated by a wandering band of Sioux who came in the first place from Dakota."[20]

Let us grant, for argument's sake, that the Iroquois were aboriginal to their lands in upstate New York. Surrounded by Algonquin speakers, clues suggest they migrated there from areas further south in fairly recent times. But allow it for now. Even so, surely the Europeans who came to Canada before and since they did are just as native or aboriginal to the homes they left to come here—Ireland, France, Scotland, England, Germany, Poland, Italy, indeed any country you might mention. Why is upstate New York to be privileged here? Both came to Canada, or to the lands that they currently occupy, from elsewhere. If the distance they came makes a difference, why?

Lost lands

Does a group perhaps qualify as aboriginal because their original lands were taken? Because some other group—"non-aboriginal"—muscled in?

Fair enough. A large proportion of the Europeans who have come to Canada came because their ancestral lands were taken by other groups; they are aboriginal, then. They have legitimate land claims, generally of a rather more serious nature than do Canadian Indians, who mostly signed off on their land claims a century or more ago for an agreed payment. Begin with the United Empire Loyalists, the original settlers in most of eastern English Canada. They arrived here, often penniless, because their lands were taken in the United States.

Throughout the 19th century, the largest group of immigrants to Canada were the Irish. Their descendants remain by some counts the largest ethnic grouping in Canada after the French, although many, probably most, now identify themselves on census forms as simply "Canadian." Their land was taken from them, both as a culture and as individuals. It is not just that Irish sovereignty was blotted out, and Ireland assimilated involuntarily into the larger Kingdom of Great Britain; the Irish themselves were legally forbidden, if Catholic, to own any of their land. Reduced to being tenants, hustled "to Hell or Connaught," commonly evicted, to likely starvation. This is something the Indians or Inuit of Canada never suffered at European hands.

An estimated 10 percent of Canadian francophones, beginning with Jacques Cartier, are not French, but Breton[21], an ethnically distinct Celtic nation taken over by France just two years before Cartier sailed. They were understood even by the Indians in Acadia to be a separate nationality: "Now they call all the French 'Normans,' except the Malouins (Bretons), whom they call Samaricois, and the Basques, Bascua."[22] Since then, the Bretons and the Basques have undergone forced assimilation of the very sort Canadian Indians claim to have experienced. Consider too that proportion of French Canada that is Acadian, famously evicted from their farms in Nova Scotia by the British in 1755-64; the current population is mostly returnees forced in later years to clear new land in remote areas of New Brunswick. And of the balance of French Canada, forty percent are estimated to have Irish blood.

Then there are the Scots, Canada's third or fourth largest ethnic group. The Highland Scots had their tenant lands taken from them in the Clearances, and were forced into exile in, notably, Cape Breton, Antigonish, Prince Edward Island, and Glengarry County, Ontario.

Many other groups sought refuge in Canada largely or entirely because their lands were taken from them: the Kashubians of Ontario, the Doukhobors of British Columbia, and the German and Russian Mennonites, to name three. Western Canada was largely settled by Poles and Ukrainians, nationalities that also know a history of conquest and forced assimilation by larger neighbours—and real genocide, in the case of the Ukrainians. Even most German-Canadians came originally from Eastern Europe, not Germany: places where they were a minority, forced after 1881 to assimilate if they remained. Not that they escaped that fate, of course, by coming to Canada. Many also arrived as refugees from the Russian Revolution and the forced nationalization of their properties that followed. Lost their land? Precisely.

In sum, many if not most Canadians are "aboriginals" in the sense that their ancestors had their lands taken from them by other groups; it comes close to being the common Canadian experience. That's why we are here. Given the culturally dominant influence of the UE Loyalists and the francophone Québécois, not to mention the Scottish and Irish, the sense of a lost homeland is near the core of the Canadian identity. The native tribes of Canada are, if anything, the exception to this rule. They are the only Canadian group who have been able to remain in their ancestral lands.

And did I mention the Jews?

How wrong is it, then, if the descendants of those who have actually had their lands taken from them, are now asked to pay some sort of ongoing compensation to groups whose ancestors had some of their land bought and paid for?

Which lands?

There are other considerations. When Cartier came down the St. Lawrence in 1534-35, he found Indian settlements—around 3,000 inhabitants each—at Quebec City and Montreal (Stadacona and Hochelaga, respectively). When he returned six years later, in 1541, Hochelaga had disappeared. When Champlain arrived in 1608, Stadacona had vanished as well. Indeed, the entire Indian culture Cartier encountered, now called the "St. Lawrence Iroquois," had gone without a trace.

Any Indian group that claims aboriginal ownership of this land, the St. Lawrence Valley, in succession to the St. Lawrence Iroquois, has in fact been in the area for less time than the French. Are they truly aboriginal?

In 1650-53, during the Beaver Wars, the Iroquois wiped out their Southern Ontario neighbours, the Neutrals, the Petun, and the Huron. They cleared the entire native population of the area, to allow themselves unrestricted access to the French trading posts of the St. Lawrence Valley. Some time later, the Mississauga Indians moved in from their previous lands around Manitoulin Island, northern Lake Huron, and Lake Superior.

The French built Fort Frontenac, modern Kingston, in 1673. They settled at Detroit and Windsor by 1701. This being so, the Indian group from which the British purchased the lands of Southern Ontario was perhaps less, perhaps only marginally more, "aboriginal" there than the French.

These examples—more could be given—expose a truth of Indian history that is often forgotten or misunderstood. Until the British or Canadian authorities arrived with their muscular rule of law to end the game of musical territories, nobody held anywhere for long. The various Indian tribes were in a state of more or less constant warfare, and lands constantly changed hands.

On top of this, despite limited agriculture by some groups, most Indian tribes in Canada were nomadic. They would think little of pulling up stakes—literally—and moving a thousand kilometres inland to new hunting grounds.

In other words, "ancestral lands" did not really form part of the Indian experience. No one was anything like original to the territories they happened to be in when they signed treaties with the Europeans. They were much less rooted to their lands than were the settled Europeans, whose borders and traditional land use tended to be more stable, both in North America and in Europe.

The perpetual motion of Amerindian tribes only increased with early European contact. Tribes who lived close to the European line of settlement suddenly developed an overwhelming military and economic advantage over their neighbours. First, they had access to the wealth of the fur trade; they could then trade with more remote tribes for furs at a healthy markup. Second, they had preferential access to iron weapons, far superior to the bows and arrows with which more remote groups were obliged to defend themselves. Third, they also had preferential access to horses, guns, and gunpowder, all militarily devastating. Fourth, they were often able to form military alliances with the yet more powerful Europeans, who had an interest in defending and supporting their trading partners.

In the areas beyond European settlement, these tribes were conquering and expanding more or less at will—until the turkey shoot ended with the signing of treaties, after which they could rely on the Europeans to preserve their gains for them. And the remnants of their neighbours could now rely on the Europeans to protect them.

The Cree, for example, had the good fortune to find themselves at the southern end of Hudson Bay when the Hudson's Bay Company first set up posts there in 1668. Because they were the first to get modern weapons and held a monopoly for a time over the Northwest fur trade, they were able to spread west in a conquering wave as far as the Peace River in present-day Alberta. They became the largest single cultural group among Canada's Indians. The Iroquois had a similar advantage: the Dutch set up trading posts at the eastern edge of their territory in upstate New York. This gave them the wealth and muscle to take the American Midwest as far as the Mississippi, and as far south as Virginia and Kentucky, as their hunting grounds.

It is therefore ironic for native groups to accuse the Europeans of having "stolen" their land. In most, if not all, cases, the Indians themselves "stole" the land, that is, took it by conquest, and then bartered it to the Europeans at good terms.

Note too once again that the realities of a nomadic lifestyle meant that Indian groups did not have the same relationship to the land that European settlers did. This was obvious to the first French settlers: "they are wanderers, with nothing to attach them to a place, neither homes or relationship, neither possessions nor love of country."[23] So much for the popular illusion, often invoked, that native Indians have some special attachment to the land. They were essentially tourists wherever they went, or like gypsies or itinerant tinkers; hunting grounds were variable month by month, year by year, and generation by generation. No particular Indian owned any particular land. It was entirely possible for different Indian groups to pass through and use the same hunting ground in the same year. Describing his band in the 1800s, Reverend Peter Jones writes:

> The Ojebway nation is found scattered in small bodies in the country extending from the River St. Lawrence, thence along the northern shores of lakes Ontario, Erie, St. Clair, Huron, both sides of Lake Superior, and on to Hudson's Bay territory, and the head waters of the Mississippi. A few of the same people are also found inter-mingled with the Ottawas and others on the south shore of Lake Huron, and in the vicinity of Lake Michigan. Within the range of the same tract of country are to be found several other nations of Indians, as the Six Nations, of whom are the following: Mohawks, Onondagas, Senecas, Oneidas, Cayugas, Tuscaroras; and also Delawares, Mimceys, Minominees, Wayandots, Ottawas, and Pottawatamees, &c.[24]

So who then owns that land? Who is aboriginal or native to it? All of them? What if one group had one family in the area for seven weeks last year, and the other one seven families for four? Do we work out percentages? On what basis? Do I, part Mohawk, have a legal claim on Algonquin Park because I once summered there?

Of course, all this is not to mention the most obvious relevant fact. As a matter of science, "aboriginal" is nonsensical anywhere outside of Africa. Many Indian groups claim to be autochthonous in their own legends, it is true. Many others do not: Vine Deloria, Sioux historian, claims lots of tribes have legends of coming to America: "they remember that we came across the Atlantic as refugees from some struggle, then came down the St. Lawrence River, and so forth."[25] Louis Lesage, a representative of the Huron/Wendat, says their tradition is that they came from a "great salt lake" to the east.[26] Father LeClercq discovered such a legend among the Micmac.[27] Alexander Mackenzie discovered a legend among the Chipewyan, that they had come from afar across a vast lake.[28] But the bottom line is this: the best current science holds that humans are not native to the Americas. The Western

Hemisphere was the last large bit of land to be settled by humankind. The earliest inhabitants were immigrants, coming from Asia across the Bering Sea or land bridge about 14,000 years ago.

Calling a spade an excavation implement

So what is going on here? What do we mean by calling some Canadians "aboriginal"?

In 2007, the United Nations General Assembly passed the Declaration on the Rights of Indigenous Peoples. Oddly, nowhere in that document is the term "indigenous peoples" defined. And for good reason: it could be embarrassing. If attempted, it produces odd results. The term is really a political construct, applied usually and arbitrarily to specific groups in Canada, the United States, Australia, and New Zealand. The Norse, Welsh, Irish, Basque, or Bretons, not to mention the English, French, Germans, or Italians, do not qualify, although they were certainly in possession of their own "ancestral lands" much longer than were the Inuit; or, for that matter, just about any of the Canadian "First Nations." The Sami of Scandinavia, on the other hand, are generally referred to as aboriginal. So are the Ainu of Japan.

It seems that we have managed to confuse ourselves through use of a euphemism. What we really mean when we call a group "aboriginal," "indigenous," "native," or "First Nations" is not that they are "aboriginal," but that they are "primitive"; that is, that their culture is significantly technologically backward in comparison with the culture nearby. The idea that they are somehow "indigenous" is perhaps a reference of their lack of any written history—they don't know where they came from. Probably no truly consistent definition is possible, but what really distinguishes most groups called "aboriginal" or "indigenous" seems to be that they live, or lived recently, by hunting and gathering, had no permanent dwellings, and had no writing system. They are, more properly speaking, "primitives" or "savages." "Uncivilized" might be most accurate. But to say so could wound feelings. And so we say "aboriginal."

This avoidance of the facts has led to two strands of silliness: first, the "aboriginal" concept has come to seduce us, thanks to a lot of free-floating romanticism, into thinking such cultures have special, semi-spiritual ties to the land, hence some kind of special and eternal ownership. Second, we have obscured the vital fact that their traditional culture is, in a word, backward. Hence the idea that it is a public obligation to preserve it, and to encourage individuals to cling to it. Which is a perfect way to consign them to relative poverty. Obviously enough: when a tool is not doing the job, the wise response is to get a new tool.

Given the common-sense if politically incorrect proposition that cultures can be better or worse at doing what cultures are created to do, it follows that any individual stuck with an "aboriginal" culture is at a disadvantage. Accordingly, it is perverse and cruel to support such cultures. It is to consign some of our citizens to a human zoo.

3 NOBODY HERE BUT US INDIANS

A typical gathering of Canadians.

On April 14, 2016, the Supreme Court issued a long-awaited decision in *Daniels v. Canada*, regarding aboriginal status. Métis and non-status Indians across Canada celebrated what they saw as a great victory. (Non-status Indians being those with Indian blood not covered by treaty.) David Chartrand, president of the Manitoba Métis Federation, had trouble finding the right word to describe his emotions, writes the *Globe and Mail*: "Ecstatic, excited, happy, pleased." Gabriel Daniels, son of the man who launched the court case back in 1999, said he was "overwhelmed and ecstatic." Métis leaders were "screaming" with excitement in the lobby of the Supreme Court. The *Toronto Star* headlined "Supreme Court recognizes rights of Métis, non-status Indians."

I suspect their celebration may be premature. The ultimate effect of the current decision may be to make the concept of "Indian," and the special status it entails, untenable.

At first glance at the ruling, in fact, the Métis mostly lost. They asked the court to affirm three things: "(1) that Métis and non-status Indians are 'Indians' under s. 91(24) of the Constitution Act, 1867; (2) that the federal Crown owes a fiduciary duty to Métis and non-status Indians; and (3) that Métis and non-status Indians have the right to be consulted and negotiated with." The court ruled against them on two out of these three claims, and these were the two parts that involved any additional rights for Métis. All they agreed on with the plaintiffs was the definition of "Indian" as it appears in the British North America Act of 1867. Yes, "Indians" includes Métis and non-status Indians.

And all the BNA Act says about "Indians" is that they are a federal, not a provincial, responsibility.

The ruling therefore implicitly denies that this entails any new rights. It explicitly says that it sees no obligation on the part of the federal government to pass any new legislation.

Nevertheless, there is a history here, and you can understand why the Métis and non-status leaders think the gravy train is soon to arrive at their door. Long before Canada was confederated, in the Royal Proclamation of 1763, the British Crown asserted a fiduciary responsibility for the interests of Canadian Indians. This, from the beginning, set us loyalists apart from the Americans, and indeed was one of the causes of both the American War of Independence and the War of 1812. Unlike the American hooligans, the British held that Indians had corporate rights, specifically land rights. They could not be simply displaced piecemeal by new arrivals; the entire matter had to be dealt with by negotiation and agreement, and rather than being adversary, the government should seek to be a fair arbiter between two parties of its subjects. With, indeed, a special care for the Indians, supposed to be less able to stand up for themselves.

The Supreme Court ruling would seem, therefore, to be self-contradictory. If Indians are a federal responsibility, the Canadian Crown implicitly continues to have this fiduciary responsibility toward them, inherited in 1867 from the British Crown, even though this is denied in the ruling. And this fiduciary responsibility would seem logically to include making some effort to be aware of their concerns, and to meet them—the third proposition.

This already seems to be the tack taken by the Trudeau government.

But, given this reading, this expansion of the meaning of the term "Indian" is troublesome. It adds a huge new federal liability. Status Indians get special benefits. Granted, these new "Indians" have no treaties, and so the government owes them no treaty benefits. On the other hand, doesn't this mean that their aboriginal land rights remain unextinguished, and so the government is obliged to negotiate new treaties with them to settle their title?

According to official figures, there are about as many non-status Indians and Métis again as there are status Indians. The federal budget estimates a current annual expenditure on Indians of around $8.1 billion. The real figure is probably higher; virtually every arm and operation of government has added special programs for aboriginals, the costs of which do not necessarily appear in this line item. For example, Health Canada spends $1 billion per year on health benefits for Indians not available to other Canadians.[29] Whatever the real cost is, it must now presumably be doubled, as the number of eligible people of "Indian" status doubles. In the face of a budget deficit.

But that may not end the problem. The real tin of bait may be much bigger. Is the official count complete?

The realization that this was an issue is probably why the Supreme Court tried to sidle slowly away from the second and third parts of the plaintiffs' submission. The Supreme Court surely realized that applying these principles would make the entire concept of "aboriginal rights" economically ruinous.

But the concept was always mad. And the most the Supremes are really doing here, I suspect, is avoiding blame for the dénouement.

The problem starts, if not with the Royal Proclamation, then with the Indian Act, in 1876. The very notion of an Indian Act implies that different rules will apply to different sorts of Canadians. That obviously violates basic democratic and liberal principles. At the time the Act was passed, this seemed only a temporary situation. The overt purpose of the original treaties was assimilation. On election as Canada's first prime minister, Sir John A. Macdonald declared his government's desire to "do away with the tribal system, and assimilate the Indian people in all respects with the inhabitants of the Dominion."[30] The Indians were assigned land to farm, farm implements, and education for their children in farming and trades. There should have been no call, beyond a generation or two, to worry about treaty rights. Individual Indians should have all moved on to unhyphenated Canadianness, and left the jurisdiction of the original band. With no members, the band ceases, and the treaty collects dust in the archives.

Wait—weren't the Indians told the treaties were for as long as the grass grows and the sun shines?

That is the assertion, for example, of the Truth and Reconciliation Commission, which cites as evidence the medals struck and given to the chiefs. Pointing to the image of a rising or setting sun behind the European figure depicted, they explain, "The sun rising on the horizon indicated that the treaties were meant to last forever."[31]

No, not exactly. Might the image more clearly imply a new dawn? For that matter, a sun has been a conventional bit of iconography on British medals since at least the time of Charles II.[32]

At the Treaty Eight negotiations, Keenooshayo, speaking for the assembled Indians, asked Lieutenant Governor Laird exactly this.

> Are the terms good forever? As long as the sun shines on us?
> ... Are you willing to give means to instruct children as long

> as the sun shines and water runs, so that our children will grow up ever increasing in knowledge?

Laird responded:

> About treaties lasting forever, I will just say that some Indians have got to live so like the whites that they have sold their lands and divided the money. But this only happens when the Indians ask for it.[33]

Dr. P.H. Bryce, commissioned by the federal government to report on health conditions in the residential schools in 1922, recommends that schools teach Indians using the regular provincial curriculum, since "it was assumed that as the bands would soon become enfranchised and become citizens of the Province they would enter into the common life and duties of a Canadian community."[34]

Unfortunately, the Indian Act required the setting up of a bureaucracy to oversee Indian affairs. A bureaucracy every member of which had a vested interest in making sure that Indians did not assimilate. No Indians, no job.

Even as the treaties were autographed, it was clear that Indian status was, and was going to be, a vexed question. After all, the Métis were already an established group. Were they Indians, or European Canadians? In the natural course of things, just like other Canadians, Indians were not always going to marry into their own ethnicity. Unless there are either laws or strong social taboos involved, love is going to find a way. The English are averse to marrying out. But Catholics—the French, the Irish, the Highland Scots, as were commonly employed by the fur trading companies—are not. And neither are the Indians. Witness the thorough mixing of races in Mexico, or points south.

Indian tribes commonly married out and adopted into the tribe. "It was the policy of the Iroquois to incorporate the nations, especially those of their own stock, which they conquered; and the modern Iroquois are descended from Hurons, Eries, Neutrals, and Conestogas as well as from the Six Nations."[35] "The injunction of [longtime Inspector General for Indian Affairs Sir John] Johnson against intermarriage with whites has not been effective, and the New York Iroquois show to the most superficial observer their strong infusion of white blood."[36] In 1917, General Pratt observes of American tribes, "[t]he Indians by amalgamation have been bleaching out and the full bloods decreasing rapidly, some tribes having scarcely a full-blood left."[37]

Remnants of the Huron located near Quebec City in 1656. "[H]ere, to this day," writes Francis Parkman in 1867, "the tourist finds the remnant of a lost people ... the Huron blood fast bleaching out of them, as, with every generation, they mingle and fade away in the French population around."[38] By now, the Indians of Quebec are thoroughly interbred with the surrounding population.

In other words, the framers of the Indian Act were mostly right. This process of assimilation, just as Macdonald and the framers expected, is real and ongoing. Indian leaders themselves predict (and lament) that, of the current generation, more than half who still consider themselves Indians have married or will marry non-natives. Left to itself, Indianness as a distinct identity, if not kept alive by artificial means, might have died out well before now, or should soon die out. We would all return to being equals.

In the meantime, the Indian Act did make an attempt to deal with the issue. What if an Indian marries a non-Indian? Do the children, and their children, count as Indians under the treaties, or are they ordinary Canadians, on the other side in the original bargain?

The Act specified that, if an Indian man married a non-Indian woman, the woman too became legally Indian. Their children were Indian. The male children might again marry non-Indians, generation after generation, all of them officially remaining status Indians.

Inevitably, nature taking its course, by now many status Indians are mostly European. Wikipedia puts the matter delicately: "Indigenous Amerindians experienced two very distinctive genetic episodes; first with the initial peopling of the Americas, and secondly with European colonization of the Americas." Modern Ojibway turn out to be 50 percent to 90 percent European in the male line. Dogrib are 40 percent.[39]

This is in the male line, the easiest to trace genetically, and it is so despite the fact that, since the Indian Act was passed, if an Indian woman married a non-Indian man, the children lost their Indian status. So in theory, there should be no European blood at all in the male line. It seems likely that the average Indian has far more European ancestry than this in the female line.

By now, concurrently, just as many Canadian Indians have become largely European, many non-Indian Canadians are largely Indian by ancestry—the descendants of mixed marriages involving a European man and an Indian woman.

In the minds of the authors of the Indian Act, status Indians would naturally want to lose Indian status as soon as they could. Call them crazy; but then, call Martin Luther King crazy, too. Although being a status Indian had benefits, like the right to hunt and fish on untilled land, so did becoming a citizen. One got to vote, to run for office, to drink alcohol, to own property, and so forth. In remaining on reserve and retaining status, Indians were accepting being taken care of in a sort of perpetual childhood. Surely all would eventually want to grow up.

According to the original Indian Act, if any Indian earned a university degree, qualified for a profession, or served in the armed forces, that person "lost" Indian status. Its framers surely did not think that any such provision would deter Indians from earning a degree, learning a profession, or serving in the armed forces. Citizenship was their reward. Women who married out were in the same class. If there was sexual discrimination in the original act, it was in favour of Indian women and against Indian men.

Unfortunately, the nature of the Indian Act has altered, or reversed, over time. Doubtless with the enthusiastic advice of all Indian-Act-associated bureaucrats, aided and abetted by an always-present popular sentiment in favour of the Noble Savage. With the civil rights movement in the US South, anything that seemed to put status Indians at a disadvantage as compared with other Canadians was dropped. They were given the vote and the right to hold office. They were allowed to buy alcohol. But the treaty benefits remained untouched; indeed, they were vastly augmented. A provision in one treaty to supply reserves with a chest of medicines became a commitment to free medical care. A provision to hire teachers became an obligation to fund any education for any Indian at any level. Nothing in most treaties says the government is required to fund band organizations, or even send food in case of famine, let alone provide a basic income. Yet these obligations are now taken for granted. At the same time, the goal of assimilation into the mainstream and becoming self-supporting, has been lost. What was meant as a temporary leg up has become a permanent status—a status of permanent if comfortable dependency. A second-class citizenship. An underclass.

As the benefits of remaining a status Indian grew, and the benefits of assimilation were suppressed, perceptions naturally changed. Gradually, a lot of people awoke to the benefits of Indian status. Rather than trying to assimilate, everyone suddenly wanted to be recognized as Indian. Here the real problem begins. Because, as noted, a lot of Canadians have a legitimate claim to be "Métis" or "non-status Indians," now that the broader definition has been affirmed in court.

The Métis turn

In 1985, the Mulroney government changed the Indian Act to make it sex-neutral. Indian women no longer lost their status if they married out. Nor did their children. Indians also no longer waived their treaty status by getting an education or serving in the army.

But making the Indian Act sex-neutral opened up a huge new government liability. What about all those who had lost their status through marriage and female descent in the past? If they were now properly status Indians, the government had suddenly doubled the number of Indians, by their own estimate.

In fact, the real problem is greater than that. By making Indian status seem financially attractive, we have thrown centuries of assimilation into reverse. Many who could have claimed Indian status before, but were happy to see themselves as simply Canadian, now had reason to change their minds.

No doubt recognizing this problem, and especially an unsupportable additional liability, the government tried in 1985 to retain a distinction. The descendants of Indian men were always Indians. The children and grandchildren of Indian women who married out were still Indians; but after two generations, their descendants no longer were. A limited amount of new liability was thus accepted; people could not resort to genealogical appeals.

But the full can of worms was not yet opened. For how was this fair? It was just moving the injustice two generations down the family tree.

So, if Métis and non-status Indians are now legally Indians, who is Métis? Who is Indian? So long as "Indian" was understood as limited to status Indians, the situation was relatively manageable, if already morally awkward. The Department of Indian Affairs, its predecessors, and its successors kept an actual list of those it considered to have Indian status. Children were enrolled at birth, based on parentage.

Now we have to go back to the general population and create a new list. How to do this reliably and fairly?

An earlier ruling, *R. v. Powley* (2003) offered this definition: A Métis is someone who (1) self-identifies as a Métis, (2) has an ancestral connection with the Métis community, and (3) is accepted as a member by that community.

The current court ruling threw out the third part of that "test." One can understand why. First, the Métis associations are themselves self-selected groups. Who is to say these groups are representative of the Métis community? If they get to choose their own members, we'll never know. Why can't I form such a group, and name my buddies? Second, this test penalizes anyone whose ancestors tried in good faith to assimilate, and rewards those who did not. Perhaps assimilation is now a dirty word, but it is unfair to punish descendants.

The only way to avoid this was and is to be as inclusive in the definition as possible. Anyone with any Indian ancestry is Métis.

Unfortunately, this increases the government's liability quite a bit. Genetic studies suggest that more than half of the current population of Western Canada has Indian blood. Estimates are that one-half to three-quarters of Québécois do.[40] Figures may be greater or less for the rest of Canada.

To give some idea of the pending avalanche, witness what happened in Newfoundland when, in 2011, the federal government allowed for the establishment of a new Micmac (Mi'kmaq) band. This did not involve any land treaty. Nevertheless, members got Indian status and Indian cards, legal proof of this status. By 2012, the original deadline, the band had received over 100,000 applications. The deadline had to be extended, and as of this writing, four years later, applications are still apparently coming in. It is now projected to become the largest Indian band in Canada.

This is from an overall Newfoundland population of 500,000. In a part of Canada in which the original native population has commonly been considered extinct.

We would seem to have two choices. First, we could rely on a genetic test: a given proportion of Indian genetic makeup qualifies you as Indian or Métis. But this is obviously troublesome for being too racially based. Nobody wants that. Perhaps sensing this pending quagmire, the Royal Commission of 1996 inserts a passage into its report, à propos of nothing, saying, "we believe strongly that membership in Aboriginal nations should not be defined by race. Aboriginal nations are political communities, often comprising people of mixed background and heritage. Their bonds are those of culture and identity, not blood. Their unity comes from their shared history and their strong sense of themselves as peoples."[41]

Second, we can rely, as the recent Daniels ruling indeed implies, on "self-identification" and "an ancestral connection." But that, in turn, cannot mean official records. After all, aboriginal groups do not keep written records. Traditions are oral. And other recent Supreme Court rulings say that aboriginal oral traditions have the same weight in court as official records. So, in sum, anyone who attests to a "strong sense of themselves" being aboriginal, and to a family tradition of being aboriginal, which need not be substantiated by any other group calling itself aboriginal, is presumably legally aboriginal. With all its rights and privileges.

Canada may have to declare bankruptcy. The Great White Mother will need to nursemaid all of us.

No matter which way we turn, the present Indian policy, our policy on aboriginal people, is nonsensical. It is financially unsustainable. It enshrines two levels of citizenship, and discriminates based on race. But madder still, it cannot be made coherent. Unless you extend the same deal to all Canadians, you are always favouring some over others on a random basis. Part-Indians are paying out to other part-Indians for no services rendered.

4 CALLING AN INDIAN AN INDIAN

Redmen: politically corrent version.

We need to settle on terminology.

Apparently, this is important. It has become a minefield for anyone writing on First Nations/indigenous people/native people/aboriginals/Inuit/and so on. We would hate to give offence. In a previous life, I was the designated editor for the Centre for World Indigenous Knowledge at Athabasca University. Most of the first-year course in the offered major in Indigenous Studies was devoted to the matter of what to call people. Native? Indigenous? Aboriginal?

And this only in the Canadian context. The concept of "indigenous" becomes wholly incoherent beyond the borders of North America and Australia.

But using the correct terms has apparently become a big deal. When you're oppressed, little things mean a lot. Like peas under the mattress.

So I guess "redskins" is out?

I'm not sure why.

Any reference at all to Indians in the names of sports teams is now considered offensive.

To my mind, nothing could be more offensive than the claim that a common name for an ethnicity, not itself pejorative in its meaning, is "offensive." Especially when it was considered inoffensive when coined. That is, in the end, a claim that there is something offensive about being a member of that group. How else would the term have gotten a bad reputation?

If that is the problem, changing words will do nothing. Other than to endorse the proposition that there is something wrong with being an X. Over time, the new word will just gain all the associations of the old. Once, it was polite to say "coloured." Soon that sounded pejorative, and you had to say "negro." Then that started to sound offensive, and thoughtful people said "black." Then that sounded rude, and you started to say "African American." And now you have to say "person of colour." Almost a perfect circle. Something else will come along soon; we are just dogs chasing our mangy tails. Nothing is accomplished, other than signalling your membership in the privileged, better-educated upper class who knows the proper current term.

Odd too that "redskin" and "black" are now both considered offensive, yet nobody complains about "white." Similarly, one can say "Westerner," but not "Oriental," "Caucasian," but not "Mongoloid" or "Negroid"; "Brit" or "Yank" or "Canuck," but not "gook," "gypsy," or "Paki." McGill University has been able to preserve the traditional name of its sports teams, the "Redmen," because it was able to convince the public that the original "red men" referred to were not Canadian Indians, but Scots—because of their red hair. A bit of a racial stereotype. But apparently Scots deserve whatever they get.

"Redskin" was apparently originally coined by Indians themselves to describe their racial group, in distinction to the white skins and black skins of their fellow Americans. In their 1968 "Red Paper"—note the name—the Alberta Chiefs as a matter of course used the term "redmen" to refer to themselves.[42]

Granted, their skin is not really red. My skin is not really white. Barack Obama's skin is not really black. Scottish hair is never red. A certain amount of poetic license seems to be allowed here.

The term "redskin" was later adopted by the French, and finally the English.[43]

It is actually a useful term, to refer to American Indians as a group. We have struggled with every alternative, in one way or another.

Nevertheless, to use the term "redskin" now appears provocative. In any case, it counts as an informal term, in English, not the standard one. That would be "Indian." It is the one we prefer in this book.

Indians

Almost nobody in Canada uses "Indian" any more. This is a bit unfortunate, because "Indian" has a legal definition, thanks to the Indian Act, and none of the alternative terms do. There is, again, nothing in the term "Indian" itself that is pejorative or insulting. If it were, we would be equally concerned about using it to refer to natives of the Indian subcontinent, or the West Indies. The objection can only be that it is inaccurate. At first glance, it preserves a geographical error on the part of Columbus and the early European explorers, the notion that they had reached India.

Granted, we see no similar problem with the geographical designation "West Indies." But in that case, the addition of the qualifier "west" might make the difference.

Yet objecting to "Indian" on these grounds still seems a bit of a quibble, if not an anachronism. When Columbus and the Spanish located the Americas, there was no country called "India." My grandparents' atlas, only a couple of generations ago, clearly marked the big pink British South Asian possession as "Hindoostan."

So there was no question of Columbus thinking mistakenly that these people were "Indians" in the modern sense, residents of that country squeezed between Pakistan and Myanmar, Nepal and Sri Lanka. He need not have supposed he had reached Chennai. In Columbus's day, and until recently, "India" was any place past the Indus River, from the perspective of Europe. "Indians" were any people who lived there. Filipinos were also called "Indians," as were Indonesians. When Hermann Hesse sailed to "India" in 1911, documenting the trip for a German audience, his ports of call were Penang, Singapore, and Borneo. When, in 1537, Pope Paul III published the bull *Sublimus Dei*, he referred to "the Indians of the West and the South," including sub-Saharan Africans in that designation.[44] In practical terms, the word until recently meant little more than "non-Europeans."

Granted, it seems wrong to us to see North America as to the east of the Indus River. But here again, the ground has shifted beneath us since Columbus lost his sea legs. If you accept the fiction of the Greenwich meridian being the centre of the world, zero degrees longitude, and determine east and west from there, it is true, the Indians of North America are west, not east, of Europe. The map as based on Greenwich divides neatly down the middle of the Pacific Ocean.

However, the world is round—you would have thought Columbus had made the point—and so any designation of west and east is ultimately arbitrary. You travel east from China to reach the Far West. And the Greenwich meridian was not proposed until 1831. If you sail east from Europe, passing the Indus River on the way, you will indeed eventually arrive at North America. It is to the east of the Indus River—very far east. But not so far that the Spanish did not administer the Philippines from their regional capital in Mexico.

So what might look like a misnomer in modern context, was a reasonable term when first applied. It is less a misapprehension than, for example, the designation

"Canada" or "Canadian." Canada is not a small village, after all—and that is what the term apparently means. Yet we make no fuss about that.

Yes, there is some awkward ambiguity since the creation of the state of India. But that, after all, is nothing as compared to the ambiguity we face with "American." When used, does it refer only to the United States, or to all of the Americas?

"Indian" is still generally acceptable in the United States. But here in Canada, where we have fewer natural antibodies to the PC virus, it has been mostly supplanted by "First Nations."

First Nations

This is, for several reasons, a worse term.

First, the Indian tribes are not "nations." *Oxford* defines nation as "a large aggregate of people united by common descent, history, culture, or language, inhabiting a particular country or territory."[45] *Webster's Revised Unabridged* 1913 (before modern political considerations might have crept in) gives "the body of inhabitants of a country, united under an independent government of their own."[46]

Neither definition applies here. Indian "nations" are usually a few thousand people or fewer, despite a population explosion in recent decades. There were fewer Indians at the time of treaty signing. Most Indian reserves in Canada even today have fewer than a thousand residents. Whether they ever occupied a particular territory for any period or in a meaningful sense is, as noted in another chapter, debatable. They are all subject to the Canadian government, and before that the French and British, not independent. It would, after all, be impractical for a group of a few thousand people to be sovereign.

Recent dictionaries may give "Indian tribe" as an alternative definition of "nation"; this is under the influence of the political correctness we are challenging. Even here, it is given as a separate meaning; it would be grossly misleading to suggest that Indian bands are "nations" in the same sense as is England or France.

But the term "First Nations" does that implicitly. If there is a First, there has to be a second, at least, perhaps a third. Who else is that?

To use the term is also to sidestep an important debate: it implicitly asserts that the Indian group has a claim to territory, and to its own government. By definition, after all. This we ought not to allow without examining the premises. Otherwise, I might simply define myself as King of Portugal, and be done with it.

In *Guns, Germs, and Steel,* Jared Diamond makes a useful anthropological distinction.

He gives four levels of social organization, from least to most complex: band, tribe, chiefdom, and state (which last I think we can take to approximate our "nation"). Bands, generally one extended family, have typical populations of dozens. Peace within the band is kept with little supervision or direction from above, because everybody not only knows one another, but is related. No government is necessary, in other words, and no government exists. Tribes, also kinship based, can be hundreds of people. Still, peace can be maintained organically, because everybody knows one another well. Chiefdoms group thousands.[47] They require a definite leader and a bureaucracy, because members can be strangers. As groups grow larger, you need a more developed social organization, a stronger government, to keep social order.

Accordingly, a state or nation is a very different critter from a band or tribe. And considerably more developed or organized.

The various Indian or Inuit groups in Canada all fall in the lower range in terms of size and social organization: they are bands, tribes, or, at a stretch, chiefdoms. None are nations. The Iroquois, with an on-reserve population in the tens of thousands, come closest. They also have the strongest social organization of any Canadian tribe, the celebrated Six Nations Confederacy.

The term "First Nations" emerged in the 1980s, and seems to have been a deliberate response to the idea that Canada was composed of "two founding nations," anglophone and francophone. This is no doubt why the term never gained similar currency in the United States. If this is so, the intent from the outset was to deceive. "First Nations" would then set up the various tiny Indian bands or tribes as equivalent in significance, organization, and strength to France or Britain. This is using the term "nation" in two senses as if they were the same. It is, like "aboriginal," an attempt to disguise the fact that traditional Indian culture is much less developed than the mainstream.

Worse, it seems to posit the various Indian bands and tribes as having priority over Britain and France in the Canadian fabric. The "Two Nations" formulation of Canadian identity suggests equality between the two. The "First Nations" add-on implies a priority for this third element.

If "First" here is merely a chronological assertion, it is dubious, but not offensive. However, "First" also carries a suggestion of "best," "most important," or some other form of precedence. One comes first in class; one travels First Class. In the United States, the "First Lady" is the president's wife. If this were not intended, "Earliest Nations," or rather, "Early Tribes," would have been better. Or, as a matter of fact, "Primitive Tribes." (*Merriam-Webster*: "Primitive: of or relating to the earliest age or period."[48] *Oxford*: "Relating to, denoting, or preserving the character of an early stage in the evolutionary or historical development of something."[49]) This is probably what we actually mean; the rest is euphemism. If "first" in the sense of "ahead" or "better" is intended, it is offensive nonsense.

So let's discard "First Nations."

How about the oft-heard alternative "Native Peoples"?

Native Peoples

This is almost as bad. Anyone born in Canada, by proper definition, is a "native person." I am a Canadian native. In a nation still welcoming a large number of immigrants, that is a meaningful distinction, and ought not to be lost. And, as we have seen, none of the "aboriginal" groups is "native" in any deeper sense. All originally came from somewhere else, so far as we can determine. If they developed a distinct culture while in Canada, so has Canada.

"Aboriginal" and "indigenous" have the same problems: no people outside of Africa, if any there, are either indigenous or aboriginal.

An alternative now gaining popularity is to speak of the different Indian cultural groups individually by name, rather than using any generic term. This is better, because the different Indian cultures were distinct, not all one thing. Not only were the Algonquins' languages linguistically unrelated to the Iroquois'; the two tribes were mortal enemies. Calling them all "Indians" is like calling all Europeans "Europeans" or all Asians "Asians." It is confusing.

Except that we do that.

And, in those cases, consider it no big deal. Obviously, Canadian Indians here have some special privilege.

This use of individual tribe designations also probably appeals for the same reason all this politically correct language appeals: showing you know the terminology marks you off as well educated and in attendance at all the right cocktail parties. It is a marker of class. Nothing to do with the interests of the average Inuit.

For most Indian groups, we then have a choice of two names: either the name they call themselves, or the name their neighbours call them.

Those guys

Let's start with the latter; it is the more common case. Historically, anglophones and francophones were usually first introduced to a new native cultural group through interviews with their near neighbours already contacted. From them, we got our first report of the tribe over the next hill. So our familiar, traditional name for each is usually from their neighbours' language.

Bad luck: the term used by their neighbours often involves a pejorative. Not our doing, as anglophones, not our fault, but that's the way Indian societies tended to roll. The Indians did not know enough of our future politics to be politically correct. In many, indeed most cases, they were at constant genocidal war with nearby tribes, so tolerance and fellow-feeling were not in great supply.

"One of the main difficulties which the Christian missionary has to encounter in planting the gospel amongst the aborigines of North America," explains Rev. Peter Jones, Ojibway chief and missionary, "arises from their unwillingness to believe what is taught in the unerring Word of God, that the whole human race originally sprang from one pair."[50] What a wild idea! According to them, "every nation speaking a different language is a separate creation."[51] The Inuit thought the same: "Upon first acquaintance, the Eskimos usually treated Europeans in an utterly contemptuous manner, calling them dogs and barbarians."[52] This is typical of primitive societies everywhere: they do not see anyone outside the tribe as human. It is on the Biblical concept that all men are descended from Adam that Locke based the doctrine of human rights.

Their names for their neighbours tend to betray this Indian prejudice.

"Iroquois," for example, is apparently from the Innu for "terrible man." "Slave" (Dene) is a translation of the Cree name for their neighbours in the Mackenzie Valley. The word describes them in terms of their functional value. "Blood" Indians were given that name with the intended meaning "bloodthirsty." "Sarcee" means "stubborn."

"Ojibway" is less offensive. It means, in Cree, "people who stammer." That is, they do not speak proper Cree. It is cognate to the Greek term "barbarian": unlearned peoples who make sounds like birds ("bar, bar") instead of speaking good Greek.

One well-known name given by nearby tribes is not pejorative: "Eskimo." Contrary to legend, it simply means, in the Cree language, "a person who laces a snow shoe." Yet, based on a false etymology that it means "cannibal," this is the one everyone "knows" is insulting, and avoids using. Probably someone, knowing how things usually are, just assumed it was so, and so objected to it.

Us guys

Growing aware of this problem, enlightened social justice warriors have increasingly come to insist instead upon the terms the various Indian groups use for themselves. The recent protesters over the proposed sculpture park at Wilfrid Laurier University honouring Canadian prime ministers, for example, wrote that it was being built "on land that traditionally belongs to the … Anishnaube and Haudenausanee peoples...." That's Algonquin and Iroquois, to the lower class.

So why not? Why not use the terms these groups use among themselves? After all, isn't it better to use the names people prefer for themselves, instead of imposing our own names on them?

That, after all, is why we call the Germans "Deutsch," or the Greeks "Ellinika." Right?

Or not.

Once again, the courtesy only extends, it seems, to Indians.

This approach, however, has the notable advantage of requiring the unwashed to learn a whole new terminology introduced to English only over the last few years, so as not to be revealed as being lower class. Anything they remember from high school will no longer serve. "Slave" becomes "Dene," "Montagnais" becomes "Innu," "Eskimo" becomes "Inuit," and so forth.

But still we have a problem. What do these terms actually mean? "Dene," in the Dene language, literally means "people," "human beings." So does "Micmac"—the new spelling "Mi'kmaq" is unjustifiable, as the original "Micmac" accurately reflects the sounds in English, and the source language, having no traditional writing system, has no traditional orthography. Not that there would be any reason anyway for Micmac orthography to influence English.

"Innu" also means "human." So does "Haida." So does "Inuit." "Anishinaabe," the Algonquin term for Algonquins, is a bit more specific. It means "good people." As opposed to Iroquois.

This might strike you as merely quaint. But it is less innocent than that. If you refer to your own cultural group as "the humans," the implication is necessarily that anyone not of your own group is not human. You owe them no consideration, any more than you do any animal. You may, say, kill them on sight, rustle their horses, torture them, rape them, take their land, exterminate them, eat them if you are hungry. Recall that the Nazis referred to non-members of their own racial group as "*untermenschen*," "subhuman." This gave them license to do rather naughty things to them.

This is an unfortunate attitude toward their fellow-Canadians to encourage and endorse with our own language. Why do it?

Related to this is the modern insistence on using the original names in the original languages in place of more familiar English names for individuals. "Poundmaker" must no longer be called "Poundmaker." He is now the unpronounceable if impressive "Pîhtokahanapiwiyin." The Queen Charlotte Islands are now "Haida Gwaii."

This is wrongheaded. We have English names for Vienna and Leonard Cohen, too. We do not feel obliged, when speaking English, to refer to them as Wien or Eliezer, do we, because those are their traditional names in their original language? Heck, my own last name, "Roney," is an Anglicization from the Irish "O'Ruanaidh." Sorry, the Gaeilge.

Why special consideration for Indians here? Most of whom speak English or French as their first language?

So let us be clear: from this point onward, this book will freely and recklessly use the terms "Indian" and "Eskimo." This is not because we have never been to the right schools, or been invited to the best cocktail parties. Although perhaps we have not. It is because they are the most politically neutral, least prejudiced terms. And because we consider ourselves, too, human.

5 GOT WHEEL?

Old World caribou.

We must understand one basic concept: cultures are not equal. Why would they be? A culture is a tool made by men for a certain purpose. Not all tools are equal, are they? A laptop computer is rather more useful, in the end, than a block and pulley. Although they have different virtues, this is surely true in an absolute sense. In the same way, culture A can be superior to culture B, even if, cultures being more complex tools, this is not always so immediately evident.

Our task, then, is to settle the matter: is the mainstream Canadian culture clearly superior to the various Indian and Eskimo cultures? If not, Indians and Eskimos are better off sticking with their traditions. And we should all become Indians and Eskimos. But if it is, Indians and Eskimos are better off taking what is worthwhile in their original culture, sharing it with the rest of us, and, for the most part, assimilating.

Recently, some Saskatchewan Indians began wearing t-shirts with the slogan: "Got Land? Thank an Indian."[53]

Kate McMillan, proprietress of the *Small Dead Animals* blog, also in Saskatchewan, responded with a t-shirt that kind of spoiled the effect: "Got Wheel?"[54]

Here is our first clue that mainstream culture might indeed be superior to the native competition: the latter never developed the wheel.

Does it matter?

Ask yourself: how many modern Canadian Indians today are doing without it?

Jared Diamond, in *Guns, Germs, and Steel*, absolves the Indians of cultural backwardness in this, by arguing that they had no use for wheels, not having any large domestic animals for haulage. "That seems incredible to us, until we reflect that ancient Mexicans lacked domestic animals to hitch to their wheeled vehicles, which therefore offered no advantage over human porters."[55]

Okay. But wait. First, the wheel is not only good for hauling wagons. Notably, besides pulleys and gears and such, it is invaluable for turning pottery. This actually seems to have been its first use.

Most Canadian Indian societies had not invented pottery, either.[56] Unfortunate, because almost any other cooking or eating container they could come up with had a leaking problem.

And never mind not inventing pottery. Never mind not inventing the wheel. Why did they never domesticate large animals? After all, these would have been a reliable source of meat, milk, and leather or wool for clothing, as well as hauling carts, or performing other tasks requiring, if you will, horsepower. Milling, sawing, raising roofbeams, drawing water.

Diamond excuses this technological failure, in turn, by suggesting that there were no suitable local wild species. But his primary evidence for this is simply that none of them were, in fact, domesticated: "Surely, if some local wild animal species of those continents had been domesticable, some Australian, American, and African people would have domesticated them and gained great advantage from them."[57] This is a perfectly circular argument. They might have gained just such an advantage by inventing the wheel, or pottery, or metal. They didn't.

And, inconveniently for Diamond's argument, before Columbus disembarked, North America was choking, festering, chock-a-block, with caribou. They ranged historically from the Yukon to Newfoundland, from Baffin Island to Idaho. Their herds numbered in the hundreds of thousands, thundering through the tundra and across the plains. It would be hard for most Canadian tribes to miss them. Many made their living following the herds, cutting down stragglers.

Caribou, as it happens, are also called, in Europe, reindeer. As in, reined deer. As in, Santa's sleigh. Reindeer and caribou are the same species, *Rangifer tarandus*. Successfully domesticated in Eurasia, and proven good for milk, meat, and haulage.

Visiting the then-unknown interior of Newfoundland, Europeans found the opportunities obvious:

> Were the agriculturalists of the coast to come here, they would see herds of cattle, fat on natural produce of the

> country, sufficient for the supply of provision to the fisheries, and the same animal fit, with a little training, to draw sledges at the rate of twenty miles an hour. Nature has liberally stocked Newfoundland with herds, finer than which Norway and Lapland cannot boast. Some of the reindeer here attain the size of six or seven hundred pounds weight, and even upwards. These natural herds are the best adapted for this climate and pasture; and it is evident on witnessing their numbers, that all that is required to render the interior, now in waste, at once a well-stocked grazing country, could be done through the means of employing qualified herdsmen, who would make themselves familiar with, and accompany these herds from pasture to pasture, as is done in Norway and Lapland with the reindeer there, and in Spain with the sheep. When taken young these deer become very domestic and tractable. Were the intelligent resident inhabitants of the coast, who have an interest in advancing the country internally, to adopt a plan for effecting this object, under their own vigilance, benefits and comforts now unthought of could be realized.[58]

Of course, when the intelligent inhabitants of the coast did move inland, they preferred their familiar bovine cattle and horses.

There are other obvious North American candidates for the barnyard. Canadian Indians never domesticated the turkey, although they were successfully raised in captivity in Mesoamerica and the US Southwest. They never domesticated bighorn sheep, although the latter seem remarkably tame even in the wild. They are, after all, sheep. They never domesticated muskoxen, whose coats produce a very fine wool, qiviut; although they have been successfully domesticated in modern times.[59] They never domesticated moose, or bison. They never domesticated the pigeon, a steady source of meat elsewhere, although the skies were dark with passenger pigeons when the first settlers came. Or the rabbit. Or the prairie chicken, or pheasant, or duck, or goose, or any number of other native fowl.

Diamond argues that some—obviously not all—of these species were not suitable because of a "nasty disposition." Yet he allows that people will adopt almost any wild animal as a pet: he mentions kangaroos, possums, flycatchers, ospreys, eagles, cheetahs, gazelles, hartebeests, cranes, giraffes, elephants, bears, and hyenas.[60] And he ignores the possibility that a nasty disposition can be bred out of domestic stock over time. After all, the Pekinese is descended from the wolf. And, if people are able to tolerate a nasty disposition in a pet, why not in livestock, until it was bred out?

Yet American Indians had only dogs.

They did not invent the arch, let alone the flying buttress: other than earthen mounds, they built no permanent structures. They had no writing. Aside from the odd meteor, and copper for ornament, they knew nothing of metal. When the first Europeans came, Indians were in the Stone Age; they were a Neolithic people. They also do not seem to have come up with the lever, the screw, the inclined plane, the pulley, or the wedge.

Diamond admits—indeed, he insists—that some cultures are more innovative than others. He takes this, oddly, as evidence of his thesis. Surely, then, he argues, some American Indian cultures must have been innovative. So it cannot be the fault of the cultures if they did not innovate as much as Europe.

Yet that does not follow; the opposite does. It is entirely possible that all Canadian Indian cultures were simply very conservative and resistant to new ideas, in comparison to at least one Eurasian or African Neolithic culture, which then swept the field. QED.

This inevitably left the Indians materially poor. Indian culture produces poverty. When Columbus encountered the natives of San Salvador, almost his first impression was, "It appeared to me to be a race of people very poor in everything."[61] The *Jesuit Relations* record of the Whitefish Indians near Quebec, "these good people, concealed in the depth of the forests, have not great opportunities for Sin. Luxury, ambition, avarice, or delights, do not come near their country; poverty, sufferings, cold, and hunger, banish from it those monsters."[62]

Lucky them.

So it is simply so that the average Canadian Indian or Eskimo/Inuit is much better off materially, incomparably richer, because of European contact. The average status Indian may still, for whatever reason, be poorer than the average Canadian. And that may breed resentment. But they have not lost; they have gained. Land may come to the rest of us from the Indians; or it may not. But they did nothing to create it or much to improve it themselves; and they were nevertheless compensated for it, so that the rest of us could also use it. The wheel—that took thought, enterprise, and was a general boon, freely available to all mankind.

And hey, for that matter, who invented t-shirts?

Culture shock

Granted, man does not live by bread alone. Material comfort is not the only source of happiness. There are attractions to a conservative culture; so much so that most of the world's cultures have been traditionalist and conservative, certainly more conservative than Canadian culture is. We even know of cultures, once innovative, that have pulled back and become traditionalist: late Medieval China, or the Muslim world.

Innovation, despite its benefits, requires sacrifice. Change is painful; it produces what economists call "creative destruction," the loss of ways and means once familiar, to which we may have developed emotional attachment. And so we grow nostalgic over "simpler times," over steam trains, home milk delivery, vinyl 45s, the lost savour of the strawberries of our youth. Innovation also leads to the need for more decisions, more stress, and more opportunity for personal failure.

It produces what Alvin Toffler termed "future shock." Our innovative culture is constantly shifting under our feet; there is no solid ground on which to stand. The cursive writing we learned in school is suddenly pointless; now we type with our thumbs. Things we learned in high school have been proven wrong by later experiment.

And culture shock is no minor thing. At full strength, it can produce depression, even psychosis. Some retreat into alcohol or drugs; you see them at any expat bar. Some start to behave outrageously, thinking there are no longer any rules. Some stop caring for themselves. Some just become relentlessly critical and gloomy. It is far more humane, more comfortable, to know that familiar things are not going to change, that you are going to live about the same life as your grandparents. That is something you can reasonably prepare for.

Besides producing poverty, though, cultural conservatism only delays the inevitable. To remain unchanged, in the end, you must shut out the rest of the world with its foreign ways; to be traditionalist is to be xenophobic. "As for strangers," the *Jesuit Relations* reports to their readership in France of the North American Indians, "they have a great contempt for them."[63] Sooner or later, though, the rest of the world comes knocking at the door. Most likely, at the door are the most restless, most innovative among those outlanders. And then the reckoning comes. All the culture shock you have been avoiding for centuries, or millennia, hits you at once. And you have no experience with it. You discover you are far behind everyone else, that you are poorer, that you cannot do things they can do. They have planes delivering cargo; all you can do is pray. You may be vulnerable to new diseases to which you have developed no immunity. If you physically survive, nothing makes sense any more. Your culture is likely to collapse, as everything is thrown in question.

Does all this sound familiar? Haven't we just described the North American Indian experience? No European malice need be involved. It was going to happen.

Remains of the day

Without anyone else's assistance, then, traditional Indian culture collapsed, for it always bore within it its own destruction. It is questionable how much of it remains. Since Indians had no written records, most of what we—and they—know of aboriginal culture comes from European sources. Or from Hollywood movies. A Métis relative not long ago presented me a postcard of Iroquois elders meeting in Tyendinaga in the 1950s. All were wearing impressive feather headdresses.

Only the Indians of the plains ever wore such headdresses, and it followed a strict protocol. The Iroquois of the picture, like any of us, were recreating what they imagined Iroquois culture to be.

There is no path back to traditional Indian life in its isolation, its innate conservatism. That ship sailed with the *Niña*, the *Pinta*, and the *Santa Maria*. Our forefathers, aboriginal and pale, up until about the 1970s, saw the only way forward as abandonment, however regretful, of an obsolete culture, and gradual assimilation to the mainstream.

Our ancestors were right.

The idea that all cultures are equal, that on balance they all have equivalent strengths and weaknesses, is no doubt attractive to many. Like the similar doctrine that all people have equal talents, just in different areas—the "multiple intelligences" theory, beloved by the educational establishment. In reality, though, both ideas are impossibly romantic.

The idea that all men are equal is a religious idea. It means created equal, that is, equal in worth in the eyes of God. It does not mean that they are equally smart, equally hardworking, equally talented, equally brave, or, indeed, equally moral.

Nor, as any reader of the Old Testament must know, are their cultures. Yahweh was not keen on the Egyptians, or Canaanites, or Philistines, or Babylonians, or Sodom and Gomorrah, as cultural entities.

So much for cultural relativism. We have the right and the duty to judge cultures, just as we would judge any other human invention. Culture belongs to man, not man to his culture.

Leave aside the probability that, given the nature of traditionalist culture, preserving or restoring the Indian or Eskimo/Inuit culture is simply impossible, that its core value of resistance to change was long ago defeated by contact. Even if cultural relativism is true, even supposing that all cultures are equally useful, differing only in their areas of accomplishment or expertise, it does not follow that it is wise to artificially sustain cultures and seek segregation. It does not justify keeping anyone isolated from the rest of us on, shall we say, a reserve. Or, to use a roughly parallel term, in a concentration camp. Even if their own culture has some unique advantages, to do so is to deny such individuals any comparative advantages of any culture not their own. It denies them the choice. It would make sense only if their original culture was absolutely superior to all others in every way. And if it were, why on earth would it need such protection?

Human zoos

Cultural relativism of this sort would—does—condemn some Canadians to life as museum exhibits.

Yet we seem to be heading in that mad misdirection with our new and accelerating faith in segregation. Last time I visited Sainte-Marie among the Hurons, you could see an Indian woman sitting, looking bored, in a reconstructed longhouse. I doubt she had any better idea than I did how to build one. This sort of thing is now politically "progressive," even though we still, not noticing any contradiction, condemn the "human zoos" of the early 20th century. For fifty years we worked hard to end apartheid, as demeaning and rendering some less than human. Now we condemn those who fought apartheid and segregation, and are working hard to reverse their efforts.

Imagine instead, if you will, that people are individuals, each with free will. This is, granted, for many, counterintuitive; it is the very opposite of the colonialist mentality. In the natural course of things, if left alone by their imagined betters, each will tend to adopt from other cultures that which he or she finds best, while keeping what is best from his or her own culture. No outside intervention is required, and nobody's culture should or need be subsidized by others.

If some then choose to cling, to the limited extent they can, to a traditionalist, xenophobic culture, that too is their business. Good luck with it. We may believe they are chasing a wisp of swamp gas, but that is not our concern. So long as they do not expect the rest of us to subsidize them in this preference.

Multiculturalism, dividing Canada into colourful little ghettos, was lately fashionable, but was always a bad idea. For many reasons, probably too obvious to most of us now to mention. Visited the ISIS tent at Folkfest recently?

The current attitude to aboriginal peoples is in many ways the last vestige of this failed segregationist approach. But Canada's great strength is that, having invited the world to our banquet, we can each choose from the best the planet has to offer.

We eat spaghetti, donairs, and maple syrup, and watch anime; we listen to African music, and many of us worship a Middle Eastern Jew. Similarly, we paddle canoes and kayaks, hike on snowshoes, push our kids on toboggans, and play lacrosse. Why deny ourselves any of these things? Through these many individual choices, over time, the many cultures naturally converge, as they all adopt the best of all. This is Canada, or what Canada ought to be. Increasingly, this is the world.

Unfortunately, as noted, change is painful for many. These things create their own undertow, an invincible nostalgia for some simpler time. Hence the romantic turn. Those who suffer from such nostalgia—in the end, to some extent, all of us—have naturally taken the traditional Indian cultures as their mascot. This has been true just about for as long as European and American native cultures have been in contact. It is useful for them—for us—emotionally to romanticize Indian culture as some lost Eden when things were simpler and more right. This is the "Noble Savage" myth, which fogs all our thinking about Canadian Indians. It is in the end not helpful either to those who self-identify as Indians or to the rest of us. Not least because isolationism and trying to moonwalk backwards into the past do not work well with things like physics and logic.

Cultural appropriation

Isolationist, romantic forces have embraced the Indian as their vehicle. And they seek to impose their rainbow-tinted childhood-nostalgic, xenophobic, lost boys preferences on the rest of us; often, ironically, under the banner of "diversity." Not only do they want to prevent any transfer of culture from non-natives to natives. They also want to inhibit any transfer of native culture to non-natives. This is now a matter of "cultural appropriation."

In spring 2017, Hal Niedzviecki was forced to resign as editor-in-chief of *Write!* Magazine for an op-ed in which he wrote "I do not believe in cultural appropriation." The Writers Union of Canada, *Write!*'s publisher, issued a public apology, saying they "deeply regret the pain and offence caused by" the article.[64] In September, 2017, the Canada Council for the Arts announced they would henceforth screen for and refuse to fund any art involving "cultural appropriation."[65] The matter is, in Canada, no longer debatable.

Common heritage of mankind be damned.

The recent United Nations Declaration on the Rights of Indigenous Peoples, among its provisions, requires (Article 11: 2) that:

> States shall provide redress through effective mechanisms, which may include restitution, developed in conjunction with

> indigenous peoples, with respect to their cultural, intellectual, religious and spiritual property taken without their free, prior and informed consent or in violation of their laws, traditions and customs.

Note the mention of "intellectual property." What can this mean? This normally involves patents and copyrights. It has nothing to do with one's ethnicity. Is there "Jewish science"? Aboriginal or not, all may submit the details of their new idea to the patent office; in the case of copyright, in Canada, it is automatic. Just write something; just create something.

Go ahead, then. Do it.

Instead, this provision seems to introduce a novel idea: that aboriginal cultures hold a joint and perpetual patent or copyright to anything their culture has developed.

An Australian government site explains:

> In conventional western legal terms, intellectual property rights refers to copyright, patents, trademarks, designs and trade secret laws, and breach of confidence. To Aboriginal and Torres Strait Islander peoples, however, the cultural products, forms and expressions for which protection is sought do not strictly conform to the limited provisions of intellectual property laws.... Indigenous peoples also consider that they have rights in the substance that underlies these cultural products. That is, the knowledge, innovations and practices that give rise to cultural products and expressions are significant elements of their culture.... Indigenous knowledge is also essential to Indigenous peoples' rights and interests in medicinal substances, biological diversity, land and ecosystem management, and sacred sites and objects, as well as arts and other cultural expressions. The performance aspects of Indigenous cultures, such as language use, story, song, dance and ceremony are vital to Indigenous identity and cultural expression....[66]

One can see why this view might be attractive to a traditionalist, isolationist, and communistic culture: hands off, universe! Nevertheless, it is incompatible with the idea of human equality, brotherly love, individual rights, or human progress. Theoretically, by this doctrine, we have no right, if we are not aboriginal, to play lacrosse or paddle our own canoe or wear a pair of moccasins. Or eat a potato. At best, if we are going to do so, we owe everyone who is "aboriginal," for all that they had nothing to do with it, some sort of payment. On racial grounds. After, of course, we have asked for permission.

Now consider if this principle were applied equally. As it must be, if humans are equal. That would mean aboriginal people would owe something to the rest of us every time they used a wheel. They—and most of the rest of us—would owe anyone who is ethnically English some payment any time we spoke English; those of Greek ancestry any time we cited Plato. We would owe Jews if we cracked open the Bible. A vast legal industry would be needed to work out precise ethnic contributions for all innovations. For a transfer of wealth to people who did nothing to deserve it.

Indians, with a backward culture, would be worse off than anyone, surely.

Got wheel?

6 THE BOUNTY OF EDEN

Skibbereen, by James Mahoney. Irish during the Great Hunger

> *And the Lord God planted a garden eastward in Eden; and there he put the man whom he had formed.*
> *And out of the ground made the Lord God to grow every tree that is pleasant to the sight, and good for food; the tree of life also in the midst of the garden, and the tree of knowledge of good and evil.*
> *And a river went out of Eden to water the garden; and from thence it was parted, and became into four heads.*
>
> *– Genesis 2: 8-10, KJV*

It ought to be a no-brainer.

As we have seen, traditional Indian culture was materially impoverished. It was, at least in this regard, simply inferior to the mainstream Canadian culture.

Yet there is a counter-argument that must be addressed. Sure, Indians had little. But, proponents of hunter-gatherer societies argue, they got it with little work. It was a conscious trade-off. Why work, when you are surrounded by the bounties of nature? Who needs wheels anyway, when every tree bows low with fruit?

Look closely, and I think you see here traces of the Garden of Eden story. Agriculture is the result of the fall: now man must earn his bread by the sweat of his brow.

True, no doubt, in a spiritual sense, but I suspect it did not actually happen as a matter of history in North America.

Primitive culture generally was, we read from time to time in the anthropological literature, "the original affluent society." People had all they needed. They were healthier, and they had lots more free time.

It seems we civilized miscreants have impoverished the Indians.

According to Jared Diamond, he of *Guns, Germs, and Steel*, settled agriculture was, to use the title of a celebrated 1987 article he wrote for *Discovery* magazine, "the worst mistake in the history of the human race"[67]

So how, barring some fall from grace and an angel with flaming sword barring the passage back, were we so stupid in the rest of the world to give up the lives of happy Indians for wage slavery?

"Archaeologists studying the rise of farming," Diamond explains, "have reconstructed a crucial stage at which we made the worst mistake in human history. Forced to choose between limiting population or trying to increase food production, we chose the latter and ended up with starvation, warfare, and tyranny."[68]

Okay—we know this script. There are too many people. Here we see, in scientific disguise, the notion of original sin. It really was the fall, after all. People are morally bad by their very existence. Good thing we don't know any personally.

Any such concept of an original fall from grace needs to address the problem of evil: if life was so much better then, how did we end up worse off? And, as explanations for evil go, Diamond's seems weak. We made a collective decision to sacrifice an easier, better-fed, healthier life in order to have more children? Unselfishness was our first mistake?

> [R]ecent discoveries suggest that the adoption of agriculture, supposedly our most decisive step toward a better life, was in many ways a catastrophe from which we have never recovered. With agriculture came the gross social and sexual inequality, the disease and despotism, that curse our existence.[69]

Agriculture, it seems, brought sexual inequality, despotism, starvation, warfare, and bad dental hygiene. The essential claim, and the living nub of Diamond's argument, is this: before agriculture, man was able to satisfy his wants with very little actual work. "[T]he average time devoted each week to obtaining food," Diamond says, "is only 12 to 19 hours for one group of Bushmen, 14 hours or less for the Hadza nomads of Tanzania."[70] And if that were not enough, it seems the items on the modern menu, although more costly, are worse for our health:

> At Dickson Mounds, located near the confluence of the Spoon and Illinois rivers, archaeologists have excavated some 800 skeletons that paint a picture of the health changes that occurred when a hunter-gatherer culture gave way to intensive maize farming around A.D. 1150. Studies by George Armelagos and his colleagues then at the University of Massachusetts show these early farmers paid a price for their new-found livelihood. Compared to the hunter-gatherers who preceded them, the farmers had a nearly 50 per cent increase in enamel defects indicative of malnutrition, a fourfold increase in iron-deficiency anemia (evidenced by a bone condition called porotic hyperostosis), a threefold rise in bone lesions reflecting infectious disease in general, and an increase in degenerative conditions of the spine, probably reflecting a lot of hard physical labor. "Life expectancy at birth in the pre-agricultural community was about twenty-six years," says Armelagos, "but in the post-agricultural community it was nineteen years."[71]

Got to get ourselves back to the Garden

But hang on. Doesn't this sound familiar to those of us who are Baby Boomers? It's that hippie "Back to the land" thing, isn't it?

Any guesses when the thesis here popularized by Diamond actually emerged?

Would "1960s" surprise you?

That was when the original studies of the Hazda and other foraging groups were undertaken. That was when the watershed "Man the Hunter" conference was held, 1966, just in time for the Summer of Love. At which, it seems, the entire field of anthropology wheeled on point to the premise that primitive man had it better than we do.

The times, of course, were a'changing. Civilization in general meant to those of us there at that time eternal war and slow radiation death from the inevitable atom bomb. People wanted to hear this: civilization was a dead end. And anthropologists probably more than anyone. They had given their life to the study of foraging societies. Why would they do this, if they did not hope or want to believe that such societies had something of value to tell us? Argue that primitive societies knew something of vital importance that we do not know, and suddenly it is a glorious, an influential, and a profitable thing to be an anthropologist.

And so, the Noble Savage's Affluent Society premise quickly came to be, says David Kaplan, "widely accepted by anthropologists"—the "enlightened anthropological view."[72] It has been ever since. Don't just ask Jared Diamond. Only recently, in 2015, Yuval Harari summed it up in his best-seller *Sapiens: A Brief History of Humankind.* "Rather than heralding a new era of easy living," Harari writes, "the Agricultural Revolution left farmers with lives generally more difficult and less satisfying than those of foragers. Hunter-gatherers spent their time in more stimulating and varied ways, and were less in danger of starvation and disease.... The average farmer worked harder than the average forager, and got a worse diet in return. The Agricultural Revolution was history's biggest fraud."[73]

Right. Got it. It was at about the same time that Indian culture got its latest big gust of prestige, and we started turning against the idea of assimilation. "America Needs Indians" was the slogan of Stewart Brand, one of Ken Kesey's original Merry Pranksters and the creator of the *Whole Earth Catalog.*

Let's look at the claims in turn.

First, with more than a hat-tip here to Karl Marx and his theories of economic evolution, it seems agriculture caused class divisions, and the birth of tyranny and social oppression. As Diamond puts it,

> Besides malnutrition, starvation, and epidemic diseases, farming helped bring another curse upon humanity: deep class divisions. Hunter-gatherers have little or no stored food, and no concentrated food sources, like an orchard or a herd of cows: they live off the wild plants and animals they obtain each day. Therefore, there can be no kings, no class of social parasites who grow fat on food seized from others. Only in a farming population could a healthy, non-producing elite set itself above the disease-ridden masses.[74]

There is a logical flaw apparent here. If only with agriculture was there enough excess food for anyone to devote their time to anything besides agriculture, how can it concurrently be true that people had more food, and acquired it more easily, before agriculture? As a matter of fact, surely Diamond's thesis that we chose agriculture so that we could have more children necessarily implies that, before agriculture, some children were starving. Isn't his thesis, then, self-contradictory?

And note, for now, the ominous implications of not storing food. What if Loblaw's isn't open?

Secondly, it takes a Marxist to suppose the division of labour is a bad thing, that it is necessarily "oppression." That's from *Das Kapital.* What about competitive advantage? If I am better at making shoes than you, and you are better at farming, aren't we both better off if I concentrate on shoes, and you on growing barley? Am

I oppressing you? Diamond's thesis that those not producing food are "parasites" requires a pretty strictly Marxist understanding of the world. Is food production the only thing of value to mankind? Is there nothing to be said for the existence, say, of some sort of government, to protect one's rights and goods from one's neighbour, or the tribe over the next hill? Only in Marxist theory: without economic oppression, in the communist phase following the dictatorship of the proletariat, there would no longer be any need for government.

It follows that there was no need for government before classes developed.

I guess it all follows if you accept Marx as gospel. For my part, however, I am of the conviction that he has been thoroughly disproven.

As do Marx and Engels, Diamond has to also fit the oppression of women in there somewhere. He notes that primitive New Guinea agriculturalists require their women to do all the heavy labour. "Women in agricultural societies were sometimes made beasts of burden. In New Guinea farming communities today I often see women staggering under loads of vegetables and firewood while the men walk empty-handed."[75] He argues that this demonstrates that women, in particular, were subjugated by the invention of agriculture.

But Diamond offers no control. Let us grant, as seems obvious, that the lot of women in primitive New Guinea agricultural societies is worse than that of Canadian women today. It sounds bad to us. It does not follow that it was worse than among hunter-gatherers. The proper comparison is with women in those societies, and Diamond offers no examples.

As it happens, we have a few. The observations of the early missionaries and explorers conform exactly to Diamond's—in describing practices among Canadian Indians. Here, too, women did all the heavy labour.

"Having few dogs for transport in that country, the women alone perform that labour which is allotted to beasts of burden in other countries," writes Alexander Mackenzie on observing the Athapaskans in 1789. "It is not uncommon whilst the men carry nothing but a gun, that their wives and daughters follow with such weighty burdens that if they lay them down they cannot replace them; nor will the men deign to perform the service of hoisting them on to their backs."[76]

The problem is, these were hunter-gatherers, not farmers.

Accordingly, obviously, the oppression of women was not because of agriculture.

One might, on the other hand, ask why it might be that women almost always did all the heavy labour in primitive societies. Surely it makes more sense for men, with greater upper body strength, to do so?

Here we perhaps get a clue to what Indians were doing with all that free time. Women doing hard labour was likely due to the constant warfare and petty banditry one is going to get without effective government. The men, being stronger, always needed their arms free in case of sudden attack.

The bare necessities

Did hunter-gatherers work less for their livelihood?

Perhaps. Primitive tribesmen seem not as busy as we aging former yuppies are, busily scribbling books ... if not idle to the extent Diamond would have us believe. The Sixties studies show that Kalahari Bushmen had a "work week ... of 2.4 days per adult."[77] Aborigines in Arnhem Land were clocked in at 15-20 hours per week.[78] Looking at all such studies, Marshall Sahlins,[79] choosing his words carefully, concluded that "[r]eports on hunters and gatherers of the ethnological present—specifically on those in marginal environments—suggest a mean of three to five hours per adult worker per day in food production."[80]

Okay; that sounds almost like a government job. But note, what is being measured is food production alone. Going out and hunting down a plump gazelle or picking mongongo nuts might take less time than accountancy, but it might involve a bit of food preparation as well, more than you need if you seize your food at the local Sobey's in exchange for bits of paper and pieces of shiny metal. When you add in butchering, peeling, processing, crushing with rocks, cooking on outdoor fires without the aid of microwaves, plus the maintenance of hunting tools, plus the commute to the hunting grounds, the total work week for the bushmen on the lowest of estimates, according to Kaplan, turns out to be between 6 and 7 eight-hour days (not counting child care).[81]

It is tough to get a fair comparison, because it is actually arbitrary what one includes in "work." The average Hottentot does not punch a time clock. By one attempted estimate, Kalahari residents spend 44.5 hours a week at their "job," if male, 40 hours if female. But a mainstream Canadian male spends, by the same rough measure, 40 hours at paid work, and then another 40 hours weekly taking care of business that must be taken care of although not in his job description.[82] Advantage, still, to the Indians and aborigines. Just not as much advantage as might appear at first.

Not tainted by knowledge of the Sixties debate, Gilbert Sproat, writing of the Nootka Indians of British Columbia in 1868, observed "In their own work, among themselves, I should not call these Ahts a very lazy people, though they have no regular occupation, and though, from the toiling Englishman's point of view, they are the reverse of industrious. They have a good deal to do in making house utensils, nets, canoes, paddles, weapons, and implements. The high chiefs, of course, are mere gentlemen at large. I have seen Indians hard at work on canoes in the woods at five o'clock on an autumn morning, a long way from their houses."[83]

Sproat continued, "When I first employed Indians at Alberni, the price of their labour was two blankets and rations of biscuits and molasses for a month's work for each man, if he worked the whole time. The Indians became very tired after labouring for ten days or a fortnight, and many forfeited the wages already earned, rather than endure longer the misery of regular labour."[84]

So, in sum, it seems that aboriginal life is not short of work, but the work tends to be less repetitive than modern factory work, and this matters. You get shots of adrenaline when your occupation is hunting. There is not nearly as much hormonal excitement in insurance appraising. The general impression that aborigines are idle is fed, no doubt, by the underlying and pre-existent general prejudice that they are lazy. Perhaps it is true; but perhaps we do not want to feed into that impression.

The Sixties studies of hunter-gatherers miss one further factor that would have been a matter of life and death for the earlier aboriginals. Modern hunter-gatherers have a government somewhere to keep relations with their neighbours on an even keel. Murder, theft, and cannibalism are punished. They might now, as ever, have to spend only 44.5 hours a week on food. But now, unlike then, they need spend no additional time on defense. In the real state of nature, as Hobbes, not to mention Darwin, points out, self-defense would have been an all-consuming occupation. Government, oppressive as Diamond may find it, can prevent adversaries from gutting you, stealing your food, or having you for lunch.

Hence, perhaps, the "idle" hours. That may be a new thing. Available only to modern hunter-gatherers who have a government to protect them.

The Paleolithic diet

Diamond, however, goes further. It is not just that Indians ate with less effort. They also had a healthier, more diverse diet.

> First, hunter-gatherers enjoyed a varied diet, while early farmers obtained most of their food from one or a few starchy crops. The farmers gained cheap calories at the cost of poor nutrition. ... Second, because of dependence on a limited number of crops, farmers ran the risk of starvation if one crop failed.[85]

Diamond makes much of the variety of available food sources: "It's almost inconceivable that Bushmen, who eat 75 or so wild plants, could die of starvation the way hundreds of thousands of Irish farmers and their families did during the potato famine of the 1840s."[86]

But wait a nanosecond. Those of us who tried it back in the Sixties, found that this "living off the land" idea usually did not work out nearly as well as it looked in *Mother Earth News*. Isn't scavenging a bit iffy, like dumpster diving? Early foragers may well have had more food sources than 19th century Hibernian rustics. But there does not seem to be anything making this limited variety a necessary feature of agriculture. A farmer might just as easily keep a vegetable garden, cows, and chickens for eggs, along with their main crop. What farmer, left unregulated, doesn't? Nothing even prevents him from, at a whim, shooting a passing wild duck or going fishing. He has, in effect, the hunter's food sources, plus his own. Hard to see how the additional food sources are a minus.

He need not, and a wise farmer does not, put all his land into a single crop, or even just a few. That's not even good for the land. It is bad farming.

In the case of the Irish, since you ask, the problem was political, not pastoral. The native Irish were permitted to farm only tiny plots of land, too small to sustain their families with anything but potatoes. Their food sources were limited by government regulation; any other crops were exported.

No. Surely common sense tells us that, while hunter-gatherers might have a more diverse diet, it is out of desperation. It is the agriculturalist who has a greater choice of what to eat. Hunters and gatherers do not get to decide. If it is a porcupine we find on today's hunt, it is porcupine for supper. And breakfast. And lunch. And dessert.

Fortunately, they come with toothpicks.

During the Sixties survey of foraging practices among the aborigines of Arnhem Land, anthropologists came upon a bit of a problem. The locals, defying the fiction of being in a pristine state, actually had access to charity food from mission stations. There they could get flour, rice, and sugar. And usually did. In order not to falsify their data, the anthropologists had to go to some lengths to convince the natives to abstain from these foods for the course of the experiment. By the fifth day, tired of the "traditional" diet, a significant proportion of the men wanted to drop out.[87]

The food was free; but it follows that many aboriginals, given their druthers, might trade a little work time for other diet options.

Kaplan at least hints at the issue: "In 1980 the nut crop was a good one, but Wilmsen indicates that it was barely touched because most people [Bushmen] preferred maize meal. Hitchcock and Ebert ... also note that there are foragers in the Nata region of the Kalahari who have access to mongongos [a kind of nut] but choose not to exploit them in any quantity, presumably because they 'do not taste good.'"[88]

But, the Noble Savagists here protest, the skeletal remains of ancient hunter-gatherers demonstrate that they had a healthier diet than early agriculturalists.

Sure. Given choices, people do not always make the best ones. Ask Adam and Eve. Ask your kid, when he wants more candy.

People will usually, given the choice, eat what they like. That will probably end up limiting their diet. Early farmers would have known little about nutrition. They just knew what they liked.

Probable result: an overall decline in food health. Not from scarcity, but from abundance.

Sproat writes, of his Nootka, "Twenty years ago, when few trading vessels visited the coast, the Ahts probably were restricted to a diet of fish, wild berries, and roots; but they now use also for food, flour, potatoes, rice, and molasses. This change of food, from what I saw of its effect on two tribes with whom I lived, has proved to be very injurious to their health."[89]

The notion that primitive societies were "affluent," absurd on its face, is made possible by the corollary that, like good Zen Buddhists, "they limited their wants." So they were affluent strictly in the sense of achieving bare subsistence with relatively little work.

One can see the mark of the Sixties here. Out of the rat race, no nine-to-five job, no materialist hangups, lots of free time for recreational drug use. Wish, meet fulfillment.

The hunger games

But there is another issue, and it is the most important. Can you count on said subsistence? Although food may (and may not) have taken little time to acquire, was there always food to be had? What about the odds of starvation?

In simple fact, nothing was more obvious to early visitors to these shores than the extreme material poverty of the Indians. Father Bressani speaks of "this almost unexampled poverty."[90] Bressani was a seventeenth-century Italian. Keep in mind, when you read such observations, that peasant life in the Italian countryside in the seventeenth century was not itself all skittles and Chianti.

Father LeJeune speaks of the state of Indian shelter. "If you go to visit them in their cabins, ... you will find there a miniature picture of Hell, — seeing nothing, ordinarily, but fire and smoke, and on every side naked bodies, black and half roasted, mingled pell mell with the dogs, which are held as dear as the children of the house, and share the beds, plates, and food of their masters. Everything is in a cloud of dust, and, if you go within, you will not reach the end of the cabin before you are completely befouled with soot, filth, and dirt."[91]

Fleas were an endemic problem, commented upon by almost every observer. Champlain laments, of life among the Micmac, "They have a great many fleas in summer, even in the fields. One day as we went out walking, we were beset by so many of them that we were obliged to change our clothes."[92] Lie down with dogs…

"Their clothing, which chiefly consists of deer-skins in the hair," writes Samuel Hearne, "makes them very subject to be lousy; but that is so far from being thought a disgrace, that the best among them amuse themselves with catching and eating these vermin; of which they are so fond, that the produce of a lousy head or garment affords them not only pleasing amusement, but a delicious repast."[93]

And so we come to the food. The Hurons had it better than most. "A little Indian corn boiled in water, and for the better fare of the country a little fish, rank with internal rottenness, or some powdered dried fish as the only seasoning, — this is the usual food and drink of the country; as something extra, a little bread made of their corn, baked under the cinders, without any leaven, in which they sometimes mix some beans or wild fruits; this is one of the great dainties of the country. Fresh fish and game are articles so rare that they are not worth mentioning."[94]

These were early semi-agriculturalists. It was worse for the wandering hunting tribes. "The roving Barbarians, before knowing the French, lived solely by hunting or fishing, and, through necessity, fasted more than half the year—… frequently lacking the means of preserving game or fish a long time, when these abounded, as they had no salt; while the smoke which they used in place of salt, was not adequate for preserving provisions a long time; whence they frequently died of hunger, or sometimes inflicted death out of pity."[95]

Among these Indians, Bressani writes, hunger is a near-constant companion. And Champlain witnesses to the same: "These people suffer so much from lack of food that they are sometimes obliged to live on certain shell-fish, and eat their dogs and the skins with which they clothe themselves against the cold."[96]

Champlain records an encounter with the Innu when Quebec had just been founded.

> On the 20th, some Indians appeared on the other side of the river, calling to us to go to their assistance, which was beyond our power, on account of the large amount of ice drifting in the river. Hunger pressed upon these poor wretches so severely that, not knowing what to do, they resolved, men, women, and children, to cross the river or die, hoping that I should assist them in their extreme want. Having accordingly made this resolve, the men and women took the children and embarked in their canoes,... we heard them crying out so that it excited intense pity, as before them there seemed nothing but death. ... [T]hey reached the shore with as much delight as they ever experienced, notwithstanding the great hunger from which they were suffering. They proceeded to our abode, so thin and haggard that they seemed like mere skeletons, most of them not being able to hold themselves up. I was astonished to see them, and observe the manner in which they had crossed, in view of their being so feeble and weak. I ordered some bread and beans to be given them. So great was their impatience to eat them, that they could not wait to have them cooked. I lent them also some bark, which other savages had given me, to cover their cabins. As they were making their cabin, they discovered a piece of carrion, which I had had thrown out nearly two months before to attract the foxes .... This carrion consisted of a sow and a dog, which had sustained all the rigors of the weather, hot and cold. When the weather was mild, it stank so badly that one could not go near it. Yet they seized it and carried it off to their cabin, where they forthwith devoured it half cooked. No meat ever seemed to them to taste better. I sent two or three men to warn them not to eat it, unless they wanted to die: as they approached their cabin, they smelt such a stench from this carrion half warmed up, each one of the Indians holding a piece in his hand, that they thought they should disgorge, and accordingly scarcely stopped at all. These poor wretches finished their repast.[97]

Father LeClercq writes of the Micmac:

> The months of January and February are for these barbarians, as a rule, a time of involuntary penitence and very rigorous fasting, which is also often very sad as well, in view of the cruel and horrible results which it causes among them. ... [T]hey are sometimes reduced to so great need that they

> have neither the strength nor the spirit to leave their wigwams in order to go seek in the woods the wherewithal for living. It is then impossible to behold without compassion the innocent children, who, being nothing more than skin and bone, exhibit clearly enough in their wholly emaciated faces and in their living skeletons, the cruel hunger which they are suffering through the negligence of their fathers and mothers, who find themselves obliged, along with their unhappy children, to eat curdled blood, scrapings of skin, old moccasins, and a thousand other things incompatible with the life of man. All this would be little if they did not come sometimes to other extremes far more affecting and horrible.
>
> ... [T]hey find themselves often reduced to extremities so great and so cruel that one cannot even hear of them without shuddering, and nature cannot endure them without horror. We have seen a sufficiently deplorable example thereof at the River of Sainte Croix, otherwise called Miramichis, in the month of January 1680, when our Indians consumed all their meat and their smoked fish much sooner than they had expected. Matters reached such a pass that, since the season was not yet suitable for hunting, nor the rivers in condition for fishing, they found themselves reduced to suffer all the worst that can be experienced in a famine, which resulted in their deaths to the number of forty or fifty. The French who were then at the Fort of Sainte Croix, aided them as much as they could at a juncture when the obligation to aid one's neighbour, whom the Gospel commands us to love as ourselves, appeared too obvious not to be discharged with all the compassion and the charity possible.[98]

Sproat writes of the Aht, "[S]ometimes ... they are in straits for want of food, when the fish do not appear until late in the spring. Becoming weak and thin, they blacken their faces to hide their altered looks."[99] Augustus Thompson, of the Moravian missions in Labrador, reports, "Seasons of famine have occurred... The winter of 1836-7, for instance, was characterized by extreme severity and destitution, when famished natives were compelled to eat the skin coverings of their tents, to feed on boots and the like. At another period of distress (1851), the missionaries distributed seventy thousand dried fish among the destitute of Okak alone; and, at that station, out of three hundred dogs only twenty survived."[100]

At Red River in the 1820s, Reverend John West reports one harsh winter a procession of Indians seeking help.

> [O]n leaving me two more families came to my residence in a state of starvation. Necessity had compelled them to eat their dogs, and they themselves were harnessed to their sledges, dragging them in a most wretched and emaciated condition. One of the men appeared to be reduced to the last stage of existence ...[101]
>
> The party were dreadfully distressed for provisions, and had actually collected at their tents the remains of a dog which had died, with part of the head of a horse, that had been starved to death in the severity of the winter, and which was the only part of the animal that was left by the wolves. The head of the dog was boiling in the kettle, and that of the horse was suspended over it, to receive the smoke of the fire in the preparation for cooking; while the children were busily employed in breaking some bones which they had picked up, with an axe, and which they were sucking in their raw state for their moisture. This was the suffering extremity not of lazy bad Indians, but of those who bore the character of good hunters, and were particularly careful of their families.
>
> An Indian with his wife on their arrival gave me to understand that they had been without food for twenty days, and had lost their three children by starvation. Their appearance was that of a melancholy dejection, and I had my suspicions excited at the time that they had eaten them. This was confirmed afterwards by the bones and hands of one of the children being found near some ashes at a place where they said they had encamped, and suffered their misery. It appears that two of their children died from want, whom they cooked and eat, and that they afterwards killed the other for a subsistence in their dire necessity. I asked this Indian, as I did the other, whether from having suffered so much, it was not far better to do as the white people did and cultivate the ground; he said, 'Yes;' and expressed a desire to do so if he could obtain tools, seed wheat and potatoes to plant.[102]

Among the Dene in the 1830's, Sir George Back's journal records: "October. — Starving Indians continued to arrive from every point of the compass, declaring that the animals had left the Barren Lands where they had hitherto been accustomed to feed at this season; and that the calamity was not confined to the Yellow Knives, but that the Chipewyans also were as forlorn and destitute as themselves."[103]

> December 16. — ... those who happened to be within a moderate distance fell back on the Fort, as the only chance of prolonging their existence; and we freely imparted the

> utmost we could spare. In vain did we endeavour to revive their drooping spirits, and excite them to action; the scourge was too heavy, and their exertions were entirely paralysed. No sooner had one party closed the door, than another, still more languid and distressed, feebly opened it, and confirmed by their half-famished looks and sunken eyes their heart-rending tale of suffering. .... A handful of mouldy pounded meat, which had been originally reserved for our dogs, was the most liberal allowance we could make to each; and this meal, unpalatable and unwholesome as it was, together with the customary presentation of the friendly pipe, was sufficient to efface for a moment the recollection of their sorrows, and even to light up their faces with a smile of hope.[104]

> Our hall was in a manner filled with invalids and other stupidly dejected beings, who, seated round the fire, occupied themselves in roasting and devouring small bits of their reindeer garments, which, even when entire, afforded them a very insufficient protection against a temperature … below the freezing point. The father torpid and despairing — the mother, with a hollow and sepulchral wail, vainly endeavouring to soothe the infant, which with unceasing moan clung to her shrivelled and exhausted breast — the passive child gazing vacantly around; such was one of the many groups that surrounded us.[105]

The Rev. Andrew Browning writes, of the Indians around Prince Albert, Saskatchewan, "The winter of 1868-9 was very severe, and the Indians suffered greatly from cold and hunger. A number of families made their way to the mission utterly destitute, and would have starved but for what the mission families could spare for them."[106] F. F. Payne reports of the winter of 1885-6 in Hudson Strait, "many of those about me were reduced to mere skeletons through starvation, and although they were helped as much as possible, several, it is to be feared, died not far from us. Some had eaten the skin covering of their bed and were only saved by an occasional seal being killed and by the few lemmings they could catch under the snow."[107]

Odd that the anthropologists seem never to have read these historical accounts. But that is the way with anthropologists. History is for historians; anthropologists rely on interviews and digs, not written texts. It is the arbitrary division of academic disciplines.

Yet it turns out that even the early Sixties studies themselves discovered much of the same among the Kalahari bushmen they observed; but they missed mentioning it in their published reports. Kaplan notes that during the legendary "Man the

Hunter" conference, Lora Marshall commented: "The !Kung we worked with are very thin and ... constantly expressed concern and anxiety about food." In 1986, Nancy Howell writes that "...the !Kung are very thin and complain often of hunger, at all times of the year."[108] Kaplan also quotes a 1989 piece by Harpending and Wandsnider who assert that "Lee's studies of the !Kung diet and caloric intake have generated a misleading belief among anthropologists and others that !Kung are well fed and under little or no nutritional stress."[109] "Konner and Shostak [quoted again by Wilmsen, 1989] are quite emphatic that nutritional stress and its health consequences among the !Kung are hardly in the eye of the beholder: deprivation of material things, including food, was a general recollection [of !Kung adults]."[110] "Periodic food shortages," Kaplan concludes, "have been observed among all recent hunters and gatherers."[111]

All of them. Famine is an inevitable feature of primitive life.

But this was not in accord with the Sixties zeitgeist. It was not what people wanted to hear. The Noble Savage archetype is powerful enough to overcome the evidence of our own eyes.

There is, contrary to popular and fuzzy hip thought, no "balance of nature." Nature usually follows a patternless pattern of boom and bust, one absurd extremity following another. A nice warm wet spring, and prey animals have a pup explosion… leading to a boom in predators, which then deplete the prey, causing a collapse in predator numbers as well. General starvation is a predictable part of the "great circle of life," for all species. A hunter-gatherer lifestyle locks one in to these natural cycles, leading to inevitable periods of mass death.

Sadly, some have even recently perished of the glamour of the Noble-Savage-Affluent-Society myth. Consider the now-celebrated case of Chris McCandless, 24 years old, who sought to disappear "Into the Wild" of Alaska. And died quickly of either poisoning from eating the wrong wild plant, or simple unadulterated starvation. Because he was a modern, this was worth a best-selling book. Had he been a pre-contact aboriginal, it would have been simply the human condition.

The 1960s Noble Savagist surveys, deliberately or not, did not account for any slow periods in the good old merry-go-round of life—slow periods that, in Canada, will come predictably and severely every winter, for perhaps the odd seven months or so.

In a Canadian winter, no fruit grows, no green shows. It's the meat aisle or nothing. Yet even most animals are in hibernation. And no birds sing.

This is when, according to the early French journal-keepers, Indian starvation almost always appeared. From November to May, with nothing green other than pine needles growing, food is limited to ice-fishing and a few non-hibernating animals. Not easy to find at the best of times. Not easy to run down and kill, especially without rifles.

Samuel de Champlain reports: "The savages who dwell here are few in number. During the winter, in the deepest snows, they hunt elks and other animals, on which they live most of the time. And, unless the snow is deep, they scarcely get rewarded for their pains, since they cannot capture anything except by a very great effort, which is the reason for their enduring and suffering much."[112]

Deep snow was the one thing that allowed them to overtake the prey, if they were equipped with snow shoes. The animals could get bogged down in the deep drifts.

From the Canadian perspective, the studies of tropical Bushmen and aborigines were always "best-case" scenarios. Anthropologists were among their subjects for only a few days or a few weeks, at the most abundant time of the year. As Kaplan notes, "Although carried out under less contrived conditions than the McCarthy-McArthur survey in Australia [even worse, note, in this regard], Lee's investigation [of the Bushmen] suffers from some of the same shortcomings: for example, to buttress his argument concerning Bushmen well-being, Lee would like to extrapolate his findings from one portion of the seasonal cycle to the entire cycle, even though he is aware of the significant difference between the dry season and the wet season. Between August and October, water is limited and food scarce. Lee's survey was done from July 6 to August 1."[113]

The tropics may be the only place where hunting and gathering is viable. It is not easy to starve there. Some kind of fruit is in season at all times of the year; the woods are thick with birdsong. There is never the ghostly silence of a Canadian winter.

Welfare and social security

The general material poverty of Indian culture led to other unhappy consequences.

As evidence that women in foraging societies supposedly had higher status, Diamond offers this consideration: "[N]omadic hunter-gatherers have to keep their children spaced at four-year intervals by infanticide and other means, since a mother must carry her toddler until it's old enough to keep up with the adults."[114]

Diamond to the contrary, this does not sound like a good thing. Better for women? Aren't a certain proportion of those dead children female? Or is it that children are not human? Or that humans are evil? To me it sounds like something we should all be glad to have put behind us.

The traditional Indian lifestyle, because of the severe food constraints, did not leave much reserve for the social safety net we have in modern Canada. Most kids, it seems, were killed as a matter of course. Estimates for infanticide of female children in traditional Canadian native cultures range from 50 to 80 percent.[115] The Inuit killed children by throwing them into the sea. The Yukon tribes, and the Dene, stuffed their mouths with grass and left them to die. Of the Tlingit, Livingston Jones writes, "Strangulation is the usual method of disposing of them. In former years they were taken to the woods, their mouths stuffed with moss or grass, and then they were thrown into a hole to die."[116] Such practices lasted into the 1930s and 40s, when contact with the mainstream culture, and welfare payments, ended them. As late as 1931, Knud Rasmussen recorded that among the Inuit/Eskimo 40 percent of female children were killed at birth.[117]

Father Jouvency reports of the Innu, "[T]he women, although naturally prolific, cannot, on account of their occupation in these labors [the hard physical work demanded of them], either bring forth fully-developed offspring, or properly nourish them after they have been brought forth; therefore they either suffer abortion [i.e., miscarriage], or forsake their new-born children, while engaged in carrying water, procuring wood and other tasks, so that scarcely one infant in thirty survives until youth."[118] Orphans, he reports, are routinely killed.[119]

Orphans and prospective infanticides became, therefore, for the Jesuits, a rich harvest of souls. Father Biard, working among the Micmac, notes, "I saw this girl, eight or nine years old, all benumbed and nothing but skin and bone. I asked the parents to give her to me to baptize. They answered that if I wished to have her they would give her up to me entirely. For to them she was no better than a dead dog. They spoke like this because they are accustomed to abandon altogether those whom they have once judged incurable."[120]

If it is not already obvious, the same fate would await the aged, or the merely ill of any age. No room for sentimentality here. "[I]t is the custom," the Relations report of the Indians about Port Royal, in Acadia, "when the Aoutmoins [shamans] have pronounced the malady or wound to be mortal, for the sick man to cease eating from that time on, nor do they give him anything more. But, donning his beautiful robe, he begins chanting his own death-song; after this, if he lingers too long, a great many pails of water are thrown over him to hasten his death, and sometimes he is buried half alive."[121]

John West, travelling in Manitoba, writes, "It was painful to see several Indian women in an infirm state of health and lame, continually begging for a little oatmeal, or picking *tripe de roche* for a subsistence, being unable to follow the tribe they belonged to; and, upon inquiry, I found that it was a common custom among the Chipewyans, to leave the aged, the infirm, and the sick, when supposed incapable of recovery, to perish for want! and that one-half of the aged probably die in this miserable condition!"[122]

"It cannot be forgotten, by those who have interested themselves in the history of the people of Igloolik," writes the explorer James Ross about the Eskimos/Inuit, "that the aged parent was neglected, and that the helpless or widowed females in particular, were not simply suffered to starve, but robbed of their little property."[123]

The modern notion that the Indians had special respect for their elders is, clearly, a myth. All very well to have somebody around who remembers the past, but that's a luxury one could not always afford. Samuel Hearne, speaking of the Dene, writes,

> Old age is the greatest calamity that can befall a Northern Indian; for when he is past labour, he is neglected, and treated with great disrespect, even by his own children. They not only serve him last at meals, but generally give him the coarsest and worst of the victuals: and such of the skins as they do not chuse to wear, are made up in the clumsiest manner into clothing for their aged parents; who, as they had in all probability, treated their fathers and mothers with the same neglect, in their turns, submitted patiently to their lot, even without a murmur, knowing it to be the common misfortune attendant on old age; so that they may be said to wait patiently for the melancholy hour when, being no longer capable of walking, they are to be left alone, to starve, and perish for want. This, however shocking and unnatural it may appear, is nevertheless so common, that, among those people, one half at least of the aged persons of both sexes absolutely die in this miserable condition.[124]

For all these sufferings, it is only too apparent, the greatest help was to live near the newly arrived Europeans. Jesuits would take your excess babies and old folks. The French in their fort would give you, in need, provisions and birch bark for building. They would always trade food for furs. "[T]hose who are situated near the sea," Bressani observes, "have, by the exchange of their beaver skins, provisions for some part of the year."[125]

It does not seem to have been terribly clear to these first-contact Indians that the Europeans were robbing them of their land and their happy, idyllic, affluent lifestyle. No doubt more recently the Arnhem Land aborigines have suffered the same confusion, in light of the free nourishment from the nefarious mission stations.

In sum, then, I hold the case to be proven: traditional Indian culture is markedly inferior to modern culture in its ability to do what must be one of the primary purposes of any culture: to provide for the material needs of its people. Yes, it might be that hunter-gatherers need to do less work for food. But this may not leave them idle, and they get less choice in what they eat, eat less, and face bad odds of starvation.

Score one for the racing rats

7 HEAD-SMASHED-IN-BUFFALO-JUMP AS ECOLOGICAL PARADIGM

They don't really jump so much as fall like a sack of wet cement.

I live not in myself, but I become,
Portion of that around me; and to me
High mountains are a feeling, but the hum
Of human cities torture. I can see
Nothing to loathe in Nature, save to be
A link reluctant in a fleshly chain,
Classed among creatures, when the soul can flee,
And with the sky, the peak, the heaving plain
Of ocean, or the stars, mingle, and not in vain.

—*Lord Byron, quoted by Grey Owl to begin* Men of the Last Frontier.

Disney's animated musical romance *Pocahontas* is of course not sound history. Everybody knows that, right?

On the other hand, it is no doubt an accurate measure of what the average modern Canadian or American actually believes, or is expected to believe, about Indian culture. If they did not believe it before, having all seen *Pocahontas* they probably believe it now.

It worked so well it was all done again, in blueface, as *Avatar*, and again broke the box office.

Pocahontas in its many iterations make the final and the most important historical justification for Indian cultural backwardness. Indian technology, it argues, was not undeveloped. It's just that they had an abiding respect for nature. They chose to live, voluntarily, in harmony with nature, preserving the natural balance, keeping everything they did "sustainable." They were and are ecological heroes.

Pocahontas the movie sets the scene by firmly contrasting European and Amerindian cultural values. The English seamen, boarding their ship at the London docks, all sing of discovering gold in the New World—life's goal is to them material wealth. They place this concern above trivialities like ethics or brotherly love.

> *I'm gonna get a pile of gold, build me a big house …*
> *and if any Indian tries to stop me, I'll blast him.*

As soon as they land in Virginia, and before they attend to such matters as building shelter or planting crops, they bring out the spades and start tearing apart the landscape.

Does this make sense? Why dig up a beach?

"Why, of course," explains blackhearted Governor Ratcliffe. "Let's not forget what the Spanish found when they came to the New World. Gold! Mountains of it! Why, for years they've been ravaging the New World of its most precious resources…. But now it's our turn!"

Not subtle. Spoken like a true cartoon. Let's "ravage" Mother Nature.

The film then cuts away to Pocahontas's Powhatan tribe, living their daily lives in the as-yet-undiscovered Virginia wilderness. They sing in chorus:

> *Seasons go and seasons come.*
> *Bring the corn and bear the fruit.*
> *By the waters sweet and clean*
> *Where the mighty sturgeon lives.*
> *Plant the squash and reap the bean.*
> *All the Earth our mother gives.*
> *Oh, Great Spirit, hear our song!*
> *Help us keep the ancient ways.*
> *Keep the sacred fire strong;*
> *Walk in balance all our days.*

Unlike the grubby Europeans, Indian culture obviously values the environment. The Earth is our mother; we do not dig her dugs. Our water is clean, and full of unmolested fish, and this is important to us. Why else would we have no factories? We keep to the balance of nature. Nature, of course, having a balance, like the scales of Justice. But Europeans, the boors, in contrast, an Indian shaman explains at the council fire—or rather the fire itself shows it, to demonstrate its objective truth—Europeans all "prowl the Earth like ravenous wolves … consuming everything in their path."

Not the good guys, then—or "The Three Little Pigs" was a damnable lie.

Later, Pocahontas accuses John Smith in song of believing, like all Europeans, that "the Earth is just a dead thing you can claim."

Which, actually, it is. Gaea hypothesis to the contrary. But not hard to tell whose side you ought to be on, kids. Dead things are yucky.

And not at all a racist thing to say about Europeans, of course, because an Indian says it. Free pass.

Pocahontas, in contrast, being Indian, is friend to all the little forest creatures. Her buddies and boon companions are a raccoon and a hummingbird. She keeps regular counsel with a willow tree. It seems terribly unlikely she would ever, for example, kill and eat anything.

And even the rocks and river are alive.

We all know of the Indian love for nature and the land; it is what being Indian is all about. Or rather, to be more accurate, what being a Noble Savage is all about. In popular culture it is a given. It is the very bedrock on which we see Indians as having a continuing interest, a perpetual ownership, in the land, despite having quit their "aboriginal claim" for due compensation one or several centuries ago. After all, they understand themselves to have a fiduciary responsibility to nature. It's their Mum.

To any Indian, we believe with a perfect faith, the land is sacred. You cannot change that. Open a new mine within 90 or 100 kilometres of an Indian reserve like Attawapiskat, and, morally at least, you owe them compensation. As well as compensation to Fort Albany and Kashechewan First Nations, somewhat farther away.

Not, of course, that Indians care a fig about money.

The Indian respect for nature is an ancient and venerable thing. It is as old as the sun and the stars, with us from the beginning of time. It comes with being "aboriginal." It means you belong to the land—and, as corollary, the land to you.

Great Indian conservationists

So, to make his ecological point, in his 1992 book *Earth in the Balance*, celebrated

Nobel laureate Al Gore quotes the speech of Squamish chief Seattle to US government representatives back in 1854. Aboriginal people, you see, are the established authorities on stewardship of natural resources.

The same speech was also cited, to the same purpose, in Environment Canada's 1990 "Green Plan."

It was read publicly at the original Earth Day.

Here is a common abridged version. It is useful in order to remember the First Nations view.

> The President in Washington sends word that he wishes to buy our land. But how can you buy or sell the sky? The land? The idea is strange to us. If we do not own the freshness of the air and the sparkle of the water, how can you buy them?

[So there you have it—any sale of Indian land is only nominal. They still own it. Forever. It is all Indian land. The necessary corollary is generally overlooked: How can the Indians own it either?]

> Every part of the earth is sacred to my people. Every shining pine needle, every sandy shore, every mist in the dark woods, every meadow, every humming insect. All are holy in the memory and experience of my people.
>
> We know the sap which courses through the trees as we know the blood that courses through our veins. We are part of the earth and it is part of us. The perfumed flowers are our sisters. The bear, the deer, the great eagle, these are our brothers. The rocky crests, the dew in the meadow, the body heat of the pony, and man all belong to the same family.
>
> The shining water that moves in the streams and rivers is not just water, but the blood of our ancestors. If we sell you our land, you must remember that it is sacred. Each glossy reflection in the clear waters of the lakes tells of events and memories in the life of my people. The water's murmur is the voice of my father's father.
>
> The rivers are our brothers. They quench our thirst. They carry our canoes and feed our children. So you must give the rivers the kindness that you would give any brother.
>
> If we sell you our land, remember that the air is precious to us, that the air shares its spirit with all the life that it supports. The wind that gave our grandfather his first breath

> also received his last sigh. The wind also gives our children the spirit of life. So if we sell our land, you must keep it apart and sacred, as a place where man can go to taste the wind that is sweetened by the meadow flowers.

[Prescient of him. He calls, back in 1854, for national parks.]

> Will you teach your children what we have taught our children? That the earth is our mother? What befalls the earth befalls all the sons of the earth.

[Say—I guess this should be taught in schools. And so it is.]

> This we know: the earth does not belong to man, man belongs to the earth. All things are connected like the blood that unites us all. Man did not weave the web of life, he is merely a strand in it. Whatever he does to the web, he does to himself.
>
> One thing we know: our God is also your God. The earth is precious to him and to harm the earth is to heap contempt on its creator.
>
> Your destiny is a mystery to us. What will happen when the buffalo are all slaughtered? The wild horses tamed? What will happen when the secret corners of the forest are heavy with the scent of many men and the view of the ripe hills is blotted with talking wires? Where will the thicket be? Gone! Where will the eagle be? Gone! And what is it to say goodbye to the swift pony and then hunt? The end of living and the beginning of survival.

[Always a lot of buffalo then around Seattle, I guess—on the West Coast? And the first transcontinental telegraph line was strung in 1861, seven years after Seattle spoke. He must have seen the plans. Getting suspicious yet?]

> When the last red man has vanished with this wilderness, and his memory is only the shadow of a cloud moving across the prairie, will these shores and forests still be here? Will there be any of the spirit of my people left?
>
> We love this earth as a newborn loves its mother's heartbeat. So, if we sell you our land, love it as we have loved it. Care for it, as we have cared for it. Hold in your mind the memory of the land as it is when you receive it. Preserve the land for all children, and love it, as God loves us.

> As we are part of the land, you too are part of the land. This earth is precious to us. It is also precious to you.
>
> One thing we know—there is only one God. No man, be he Red man or White man, can be apart. We are all brothers after all.

A stirring example, surely, of the legendary Indian gift for oratory. It puts a human face on nature. And that human face is Indian.

One can also see here where the Indian world shown in Disney's *Pocahontas* came from—almost complete in this one brief passage. Even fairly incidental imagery. "Every humming insect"? Okay, that doesn't work. Little girls might find bugs creepy. But "humming"? Let's make it a hummingbird. "We know the sap that courses through the trees like we know the blood that flows through our veins"? Okay, have her talk to a willow tree as if it is her grandmother. The wind received our grandfather's last sigh? So, Pocahontas's father says her mother's voice is always in the wind. "The bear, the deer, the eagle, are our brothers"? That almost sings. We're doing a musical. There has to be a song in that.

Great historical research.

There is much more evidence, across popular culture, of the Indian concern for nature and the land. In 1971, when the charity "Keep America Beautiful" wanted to put a face on the value of picking up after yourself, they turned to "Iron-Eyes Cody," Hollywood's go-to Indian actor, to shed tears on cue over littering. It became one of the best-known public service ads of all time.

The message was clear and simple: if you litter, you make an Indian cry.

And then there was the celebrated Canadian conservationist, Grey Owl. Grey Owl, as he himself eloquently advertised to the world, was an Indian, or perhaps, by our current classification, Métis, his father Scottish, his mother Apache. He took up the cause of the threatened beaver, and became internationally famous for it. He later expanded his purview to include nature preservation generally, and assumed free residence in Prince Albert National Park. Back in the early 1930s, he called for people to remember, much in the spirit of Chief Seattle, that "you belong to nature, and not it to you."

Perhaps you have heard of Grey Owl. And perhaps you have realized by now the problem with all these examples of Indian environmental advocacy. None of them came from actual Indians. They are expressions instead of the imaginary Noble Savage archetype.

Grey Owl was not Métis. He was an Englishman, born Archie Belaney, who ran away to Canada in his youth for romance and adventure. He was influenced by the English Romantic poets more than by anything in Indian culture. He begins his first book, *The Men of the Last Frontier*, the one that made his name, with a passage of nature-worship from Byron. His prose is lush in the Romantic style. He even commonly uses the very term "romantic" to describe the Canadian wilderness:

> This then is the Canada that lies back of your civilization, the wild, fierce land ... where Romance holds sway as it did when Canada was one vast hunting ground. This is the last stronghold of the Red Gods, the heritage of the born adventurer.... [I]t can become a land of wild, romantic beauty and adventure.
>
> Up beyond the wavering line of the Last Frontier lies ... a rich treasure-house, ... transformed by the cosmic sorcery of the infinite into a land of magic glades and spirit-haunted lakes, of undiscovered fortunes, and sunset dreams come true.
>
> This is the face of Nature, unchanged since it left the hands of its Maker, a soundless, endless river, flowing forever onward in the perpetual cycle which is the immutable law of the universe.[126]

Disney's Pocahontas would feel at home.

As would most children.

We all retain, whatever our age, a bit of the wondering child within. This Wild Romantic Canada must all have sounded awfully good to a little boy growing up in settled, prim, proper England. Almost like a childhood dream that could come true. Mr. Owl almost says as much as that.

It would, of course, and did, have the same appeal to other children on its day of publication, or to those unlucky children who had inadvertently grown to adulthood in Montreal, or London, or Toronto, or New York.

To Indians, born out in the bush? Maybe not so much. To those still eking an aboriginal living, perhaps, just another bloody day at the plant.

Belaney was also either clever, or lucky, to hit upon the beaver as his theme. He said it was a sacred animal to the Indians. It was not. But it was sacred to Canadians. Kill a beaver, and you are by sympathetic magic killing Canada. Good marketing.

"Iron-Eyes Cody," the much-beloved Indian icon who shed tears over shed paper, was revealed in 1996 by his sister to have been born Espera Oscar de Corti in Louisiana, son of Sicilian parents.

Perhaps, at least, they came from the untamed west of Sicily. Or maybe they lived near a cigar store.

There are one or two morals to be gathered here, before we mosey on. Obviously, there is no overall discrimination or prejudice against Indians. Quite the opposite: con men have found it useful to pretend to be Indians, to put themselves in Indian paint. The rest of us are prone, it seems, to give Indians the benefit of the doubt, to assume the pure-heartedness of their motives and the sincerity of their speech.

Ask the Kickapoo Medicine Company. Having assumed the challenge of selling actual snake oil, they hit upon the idea of declaring themselves Indians, and hiring Indian pitchmen. They became the dominant patent medicine company in 19th-century America. Until they were wiped out in the early twentieth century by the passing of food and drug laws.

Somebody should try this with used cars.

It is all a bit of a burden to real Indians. Kimberly Tallbear, actually Indian, writes:

> Too often non-Indians have been disappointed by my contemporary manner of dress and my inability to spout mystical-sounding ecological wisdom.[127]

Real life cannot measure up to the Hollywood conception.

Who knew? *Pocahontas* is a cartoon.

Then there is the great Chief Seattle. Seattle, at least, was a real Indian, and possibly even a real chief. Though perhaps not a reliable spokesman for traditional Indian spiritual values, himself being Catholic. This makes his reported assertion that "our God and your God are the same" a bit self-evident.

But Seattle never spoke those words. The famous speech was penned by a Texas scriptwriter named Ted Perry, for a 1972 television film funded by the Southern Baptist Convention. It expressed current Southern Baptist views, not traditional Indian views, on the environment.

Were they similar? God knows. The God we all share with the Southern Baptists.

Good thing we have written sources we can go back to and check. If all we had were oral traditions, we would probably all believe Chief Seattle actually said these things, and nobody would ever know differently. We would probably all accept that they are a fair précis of the ancient Indian faith.

And that is an obvious problem with Indian oral traditions. Indians themselves probably have no particular insight into traditional Indian culture. They get their information the same places we all do. I found Seattle's speech reproduced in total on a native web site.

As to the real Chief Seattle's real feelings on negotiating a treaty with the US government, it seems he was all for it. And his main concern seems to have been getting the US Army into the region to protect him and his people from enemies to the north.

More in the spirit of Tom Hobbes than of Al Gore.

Grey Owl's original cause was the fate of the beaver, as it existed beyond the Canadian coinage. In its service, he tells the romantic and moving history of the fur trade. Indeed, he calls it "one of the most romantic phases in the development of the North American Continent."[128] Romantic: high praise, coming from Grey Owl.

> Attracted by the rich spoils of the trade, other companies [other, that is, than the Hudson's Bay Company] sprang up. Jealousies ensued, and pitched battles between the trappers of rival factions were a common occurrence. Men fought, murdered, starved and froze to death, took perilous trips into unknown wildernesses, and braved the horrors of Indian warfare, lured on by the rich returns of the beaver trade.
>
> Men foreswore one another, cheated, murdered, robbed, and lied to gain possession of bales of these pelts, which could not have been more ardently fought for had each hair on them been composed of gold.
>
> The Indians, meanwhile, incensed at the wholesale slaughter of their sacred animal, inflamed by the sight of large bands of men fighting for something that belonged to none of them, took pay from either side, and swooped down on outgoing caravans, annihilating them utterly, and burning peltries valued at hundreds of thousands of dollars. Often, glad of a chance to strike a blow at the beaver man, the common enemy, they showed a proper regard for symmetry by also destroying the other party that had hired them, thus restoring the balance of Nature.[129]

Ah, the balance of nature! And Belaney's—sorry, Grey Owl's—avaricious Europeans sound marvellously similar to Disney's Governor Ratcliffe. The Indians, meanwhile, were nobly concerned only with the preservation of the Earth, their mother, and the proverbial, if ephemeral, "balance of nature."

In the real world, however, any Europeans employed by the fur trading companies did not trap much beaver. They were the fur traders. They bought the pelts with European manufactured goods.

Someone else was doing the trapping. Someone who had a great desire for European manufactured goods. And saw them as worth more than a few bucktoothed rodents.

Partisans of the two great trading companies, the Hudson's Bay Company and the North West Company, it is true, sometimes came to blows. It is just possible to make out in Grey Owl's narrative traces of the Pemmican War. It lasted nine years; twenty-two people were killed at the Battle of Seven Oaks. The conflict, however, was not between rival European trappers, and not over beaver pelts. It was between fur traders and farmers, over access to pemmican. The fur traders were mostly not European, but Métis—or Indian, as Grey Owl would have put it, just as Grey Owl represented himself to be.

The two companies amalgamated in 1821, ending the strife.

And while there was some conflict between the Métis of the North West Company and the Scottish settlers sponsored by Lord Selkirk's Hudson's Bay Company, it was dwarfed by earlier wars between Indians over the *castor canadensis* trade. There were the Beaver Wars, which raged across most of America east of the Mississippi, and in which a fair number of Indian "nations" were ethnically cleansed from the face of the earth. Fought over trapping grounds and trade routes for the commerce in pelts. With the Europeans mostly alarmed bystanders.

The tragedy of the commons

In the real, non-animated world that some of us inhabit, it has generally been Europeans like Belaney who spent troubled hours on wildlife conservation, or conservation of any other kind. Already in 1635, disturbed by the devastations to the beaver population from the skin trade, Father LeJeune, S.J., of Quebec proposes a solution. The French government should offer an incentive to the Indians to settle down to farming. Then, LeJeune says, "[b]eavers will greatly multiply. These animals are more prolific than our sheep in France, the females bearing as many as five or six every year; but, when the Savages find a lodge of them, they kill all, great and small, male and female. There is danger that they will finally exterminate the species in this Region, as has happened among the Hurons, who have not a single Beaver."[130]

Energetic exploitation of the beaver by the Mohawk had already led by 1640 to the virtual disappearance of the lovably patriotic rodent in their traditional lands, the Hudson and Mohawk valleys. Fortunately for the Mohawk, if unfortunately for the beaver, that tribe found itself closest to the Dutch trading posts. As a consequence, the Mohawk, with their new Dutch muskets, turned to conquering all of their neighbours who still had beaver to trap. The Cree, spreading from their original lands adjacent to the first Hudson's Bay Company posts, waged a similar "beaver war" across the Northwest.

The beaver population has since been restored. Thanks mostly to intervention by Canadian governments.

We see here an example of "the tragedy of the commons." When nobody owns a thing, it is in nobody's interest to conserve it. Even if every Indian in Canada individually wanted the beaver preserved, reducing their own take of this resource only meant handing it to their enemies. The more so since diverse Indian groups commonly hunted through the same lands, and were at constant war.

The Indians themselves understood this. William Cormack reports of the Micmac of Newfoundland, in 1822, "[t]hey are most anxious that King George, as they call His Majesty, should make a law to prevent the hunting of beavers in the spring season. They acknowledge the practice of hunting them then, and also that the practice will soon destroy them altogether, as the animals are then with young. But they cannot desist of their own accord, being by nature hunters."[131] There are advantages to having a government.

If real Indians ever really did share the conservationist views of Archie Belaney, Espera de Corti, Ted Perry, and Al Gore, they have good reason to celebrate the arrival of the Europeans.

Of course, it could be argued that, without a ready market for beaver furs among European haberdashers, the original pressure on the beaver population would never have occurred. Fair enough. By the same token, we are now callously exploiting China by buying their cheap manufactured goods. Not to mention Germany or Japan, by buying their cars and cameras. And why would it be that, by exchanging tools for furs, the Europeans were exploiting Indians, but by exchanging furs for tools, the Indians were not exploiting Europeans?

It works only if you assume that Indians have no free will. But then, that follows, it stands to reason, if they are a part of nature.

That is the seamy underside of the Noble Savage myth. It does not see Indians as human.

Even if Europeans could be blamed for once-low beaver populations, are beavers the only resource that could be lost by this "tragedy of the commons"? If the Indians wanted European manufactured goods, they were going to find something that the Europeans valued in order to trade for them. If it hadn't been the beaver, it would have been saskatoon berries, elk leather, wild rice, fiddleheads, jelly donuts, or something else. Same problem. And the same problem applies, in principle, to any and all resources in the Americas, pre-contact as much as post-contact. Simply because the Indians had no effective government.

Set and match for civilization. Nature needs it.

Où sont les bison d'antan?

To demonstrate, back up a step. Recall that, just like other Canadians, the Indians were originally from abroad. Up to about 12,000 or 13,000 years ago, by current estimates, there were no humans in the Americas past Alaska. In those days, the fossil record tells us, the Americas were about as rich in animal life as the Calgary Zoo. The forests and plains hosted giant ground sloths, six times bigger than a man; armadillos the size of Volkswagens: lions, sabre-tooth tigers, and Florida cave bears; cheetahs, mammoths, mastodons, elephants, camels, giant water rats, even large buzzard-like birds with four-metre wingspans.

But, within a thousand years of man's arrival, all had disappeared. Heck of a coincidence.

Most probably, they were hunted out. A bit too visible and a bit too visibly tasty. Almost every large mammal over two continents.

Conservation? What is this conservation of which you speak?

Of course, the buffalo did survive. Granted, they used to have a larger cousin, *bison latifrons*; he was hunted out. But, when the white man first came to the Great Plains, he witnessed vast herds of buffalo (aka, for no very good reason but to show your great learning, "bison") easily a million strong, blackening the terrain for as far as the Cinerama camera could see.

Horace Greeley writes, in 1859, on return from a journey west, "What strikes the stranger with most amazement is their immense numbers. I know a million is a great many, but I am confident we saw that number yesterday. Certainly, all we saw could not have stood on ten square miles of ground. Often, the country for miles on either hand seemed quite black with them."[132]

Within a few decades, they were almost gone. At the lowest point, around 1900, perhaps 500 survived.

This is usually blamed on the white men.

However, although the toll taken by white hunters was terrible, it was, in the words of one researcher, only the "coup de grâce." Fur traders, white and Indian, shipped 1,278,359 hides east annually at the peak of the industry, in 1872. There were an estimated 30 million buffalo—and undisturbed, a buffalo herd grows 20 percent per year.[133] This could not by itself have been the crucial factor.

Without any European involvement in the hunt, Dr. Dan Flores, the A. B. Hammond professor of Western history at the University of Montana, estimates, the final buffalo would have given up the ghost in about 1920[134] Instead, because Europeans were involved, we still have buffalo. Or bison, for that matter. In growing numbers.

As to their decline, we cannot be certain what the crucial factor was. Quite likely it had to do with the coming of the pony and the gun; newfangled Western technology, but mostly in Indian hands. It may also have had to do with the boom and bust cycle of always unbalanced nature. Alfred Crosby notes that, when De Soto crossed the American Southeast in the early 16th century, he saw no buffalo.[135] It might be that, in the centuries between Columbus and the founding of Columbus, Ohio, there was a buffalo baby boom, due perhaps to unusually good weather, perhaps to global warming, perhaps to a sudden decline in predator numbers—i.e., the Indians, decimated by epidemics. The subsequent decline of the buffalo may have been, at least in part, a return to the norm. Rapid expansion of the herds lured many Indian groups west for the easy living. Most of the tribes of the Plains, the Blackfoot, Assiniboine, and Plains Cree, seem to have been newcomers. As always happens, the predators overshot the mark, and prey numbers declined swiftly.

Behold the balance of nature. Dizzy yet?

Whatever really happened to the buffalo in the 19th century, the traditional Indian bison hunt does not stand as a model of conservationist principles. As any tourist knows who has visited Head-Smashed-In Buffalo Jump, the preferred technique was to stampede a herd over a cliff. Necessarily, inevitably, the Indians being nomadic and unable to store much food, there was great wastage. Reputedly, in some cases, faced with such abundance, some Indian groups did not clean their plates. They would at times cut out only the tongues, buffalo tongue being a special delicacy, and leave the rest of the carcasses to rot.

Early European visitors often commented on the wastefulness of the native practice. It offended their environmentalist sensibilities.

Many European observers were shocked by gourmandizing and by what struck them as subsequent "profligacy" or "indolence." At times, Indians used everything. But on occasions they did not, and the observers remarked upon "putrified carcasses," animals left untouched, or Indians who took only the best parts of the meat.[136]

Lewis and Clark describe such a buffalo hunt, from the days before the Plains tribes had firearms. Blame the two explorers for the creative spelling and grammar. Americans are like that.

> Today we passed on the Stard. [starboard] side the remains of a vast many mangled carcases of Buffalow which had been driven over a precipice of 120 feet by the Indians and perished; the water appeared to have washed away a part of this immence pile of slaughter and still their remained the fragments of at least a hundred carcases they created a most horrid stench. In this manner the Indians of the Missouri distroy vast herds of buffaloe at a stroke....[137]

The fire last time

And then there are the trees. The sweet embraceable trees. Grandmother Willow and the girls.

Real Indians apparently would be less likely to talk to them, or to hug them, than to burn them to ash.

"Many people believe that the first English to settle North America," the trade publication *Fire Management Today*, the sort of people who ought to know, summarizes, "found an ancient, impenetrable wilderness stretching uninterrupted from the shores of the Atlantic to the banks of the Mississippi. The popular view of a pristine wilderness inhabited by American Indians who left no trace on the land is rooted in the romantic notion of 'the forest primeval' promoted by such poets as Henry Wadsworth Longfellow. The romantic view entered the early conservation movement through the writings of Henry David Thoreau and others.... [T]here is '... some truth to one researcher's claim that most of the forests seen by the first settlers in America were in their first generation after one or another kind of major disturbance'."[138]

Setting the woods on fire was a convenient, if wasteful, hunting technique. Wildlife would flee the flames, and could be easily picked off by waiting hunters. "Indians burned large areas," *Fire Management Today* explains, "to force deer, elk, and bison into small unburned areas for easier hunting. Fire was also used to drive game over cliffs or into impoundments, narrow chutes, and rivers or lakes where the animals could be easily killed." Flames were used to drive buffalo off the cliffs. "Some tribes used a surround or circle fire to force rabbits and other game into small areas."[139]

Burning down the forest might also make it easier to gather wild berries or other edibles in the undergrowth. So why not? For the most part, you can't eat a tree. "[T]hey burned patches where flame could help them extract some resource—camas, deer, huckleberries, maize."[140]

Burning down the trees might also deprive an enemy of their hunting grounds. All's fair in the Indian code of war.

Pyne summarizes: "[M]uch burning resulted from malice, play, war, accident, escapes, and sheer fire littering. The land was peppered with human-inspired embers."[141]

Cormack, exploring the unknown Newfoundland interior in 1822, writes: "Many of the savannas exhibit proofs of being once wooded; and in some places with a much larger growth of trees than that at present in their vicinity. Roots of large trees, with portions of the trunks attached, and lying near, are sometimes seen occupying evidently the original savanna soil on which they grew, but are now partially, or wholly covered with savanna. Fires, originating with the Indians, and from lightning, have in many parts destroyed the forest; and it would seem that a century or more must elapse in this climate before a forest of the same magnitude of growth can be reproduced naturally on the savannas."[142] There were probably never more than 5,000 Beothuks in Newfoundland. But they left their ecological footprint on the landscape well enough.

It all met with European disapproval. Alexander Ross, Scottish settler and retired fur trader at Red River in the first half of the 19th century, complains of the wasteful use of natural resources by his Métis neighbours. They will, he says, occupy any unused land, log it out, and, once the timber is gone, simply move on to the next plot. "Thus," Ross laments, "the upper and best wooded part of the settlement has been entirely ruined, and rendered treeless."[143]

Further west, "White settlers, according to Langston, 'hated the fires that swept through the mountains, and usually saw the Indian burning practices as threatening the open pine [*pinus ponderosa*] forests they loved.'"[144]

"Wherever Europeans went," says Williams, "they generally stopped the Indians from burning.... Ironically, more forest exists today in some parts of North America than when the Europeans first arrived. As Pyne (1982) observed, 'The Great American Forest may be more a product of [European] settlement than a victim of it.'"[145]

Iron Eyes crying in the rain

Indians apparently were not overly concerned with pollution either. Sproat, on the West Coast, reports, "If the natives did not thus often move their quarters, their health would suffer from the putrid fish and other nastinesses that surround their camps, which the elements and the birds clear away during the time of non-occupation."[146]

> The outside ... is the worst, for the whole refuse of the camp is thrown there; and, not being offensive to the organs of the natives, is never removed. A pinch of snuff and a toothful of good brandy are very grateful to one who picks his way among the putrid fish and castaway mollusks that cover the ground.[147]

Of the Tlingit, Livingston Jones writes, "The sanitary conditions of nearly every native community are deplorable. Were it not that the beneficent tides flush the beaches twice every twenty-four hours nothing could have saved them from extinction years ago by some malignant epidemic produced by their own filth and carelessness."[148]

"Alaskans," writes Maturin Ballou, "have no idea of sewerage, or of the proper disposal of domestic refuse. All accumulations of this sort are thrown just outside the doors of their dwellings, to the right and left, anywhere, in fact, which is handiest. The stench which surrounds their cabins, under these circumstances, is almost unbearable by civilized people, and must be very unwholesome."[149]

As with trees, buffalo, trash, and beaver, so with any other resource. When the Jesuits arrived at Huronia in the early 17th century, they reported it stripped of game. The Huron diet was accordingly almost vegetarian, augmented by what fish they might catch or buy dried from the Algonquins.

The Indians generally did keep dogs, if not raccoons and hummingbirds, as pets. But again, their treatment of them often seemed inhumane to the Europeans. Father Biard describes a Micmac funeral ceremony, held, as was common, with the subject still alive. "The farewell and the mourning are finished by the slaughter of dogs, that the dying man may have forerunners in the other world."[150] The French Jesuit demanded that this stop. "I told him that … the slaughter of the dogs ... displeased me very much."[151]

French poodles, even then, probably had a better life.

John West writes, of the Plains tribes, "I have frequently witnessed the cruelty with which parents will sometimes amuse their children, by catching young birds or animals, that they may disjoint their limbs to make them struggle in a lingering death. And a child is often seen twisting the neck of a young duck or goose, under the laughing encouragements of the mother for hours together, before it is strangled."[152]

All this ugly reality unfortunately paints the Indians as far from proper ecologists or environmentalists, by modern Canadian standards. Indeed they were, but let's be fair. Even if they held fine conservationist sentiments, and even aside from the aforementioned tragedy of the commons, it is best to remember that ecology, contrary to popular belief, is an indulgence attractive and even available only to materially highly developed societies.

Long ago, as an undergraduate, I attended a lecture by Buckminster Fuller, he of the geodesic dome. Being an actual Sixties icon, like most actual Sixties icons, he had no truck nor trade with the Sixties mentality. He explained to the audience that technology is by itself and by definition the best conservation. To improve technology is to accomplish more with fewer resources. As civilization develops, we take out some of this advantage in more population; some of it in greater comfort; and some of it, as an investment in the future, by reducing our use of resources. Not a lot of whale oil in the streetlamps these days. Settle down to farm instead of hunt, and, like a charm, the same land that once supported one person can now support one hundred. Or, 1 percent of it can support one person, and 99 percent be returned to verdant wilderness, if that is what we prefer.

The traditional hunter-gatherer lifestyle of the Indians is by contrast ecologically disastrous. "Animal provisions seem always diminishing, and it is surprising what a vast expenditure of animal life is required to sustain even a very small population on meat only.... Altogether, with the sparsest of populations, there is an enormous expenditure of animal life every year in Mackenzie River for provisions. When to this is added the number of animals slaughtered for their fur, the total is very great. It is a country of death. It seems an instinct in an Indian to destroy every living animal he sees."[153]

Living at subsistence level concentrates one's mind mightily on the present day and the most basic needs. One is not putting anything in the environmental bank. One is less inclined to the luxury of holding a landscape intact and apart, as Ted Perry, aka Chief Seattle, would want, for uplifting strolls and purely aesthetic purposes. Nature indeed. Can one wear nature against the cold? Get rich, and then you can maybe afford to keep a deer park just for walking through.

Nature and chaos

And, in expecting Indians to worship "nature," are we not projecting an entirely European concept? Is it likely to have meant much to them without having read Emerson, Wordsworth, and Byron? Indeed, does it really mean much of anything anyway? Have any other cultures anywhere actually ever had a similar concept? I recall a Japanese friend in graduate school who regularly equated "nature" with the supposed English cognate "chaos."

Not quite the politically correct view.

Peter Coates tries to nail down a coherent meaning for the English word "nature." He gives five rather different senses, commonly confused:

1 – nature as a particular set of physical places, notably those parts of the world more or less unmodified by people.

This is the meaning in the phrase "unspoiled nature." It is what Parks Canada tends to prefer. It involves, note, the notion that people "spoil" things by their existence. Hard to say whether this idea might spontaneously occur to another culture, or why it would be entertained with favour.

If you create a new wilderness national park, and ban all people from it, and then a tree falls, does it make a sound?

2 – nature as all physical places and things, including those touched and untouched by people.

Nature in this sense more or less equates with the word "environment"; albeit only if properly used, which it usually is not. It is what is meant in the older term for science, "natural philosophy." This does not mean pondering virgin forests, but the postulated world as perceived through the five senses.

3 – nature as force or entity with religious qualities.

This meaning is captured in the phrase "Mother Nature" or the "laws of nature," which cause certain things to happen.

This is where the supposed "balance of nature," for example, comes in. Not to mention the modern ecological movement more or less as a whole. In other words, nature includes or is whatever is *not* natural in the sense of physical.

This tends to be the Romantic use. It is hard to see any logical connection here with the other senses of nature. Indeed, it seems to contradict them: nature is supernatural?

By now, surely it gets hard to see any underlying coherence.

4 – nature as an essence, for example in the phrase "human nature" to explain certain behaviours.

Here "nature" is whatever is not touched by reason and, more importantly, free will; whatever is not, in other words, voluntary. You can perhaps see the problem here with calling a group of people "natural."

5 – nature as the opposite of culture, so that it is everything that has nothing to do with humans.[154]

Sort of like Scarborough, Ontario. This is what my Japanese friend probably understood when he related nature to "chaos." Here, of course, calling a group of people "natural" is simply a polite way of saying they have no, or little, culture.

Is that too confusing? Too confusing, surely, to expect the same rather arbitrary congeries of meanings to occur independently, and be embraced, by pre-contact Indians.

Okay; so are Indians more natural in sense 5? Problem: to say so is really saying they have less culture. Might sound right to a modern Canadian, but might not have naturally—to coin a phrase—occurred to pre-contact aboriginals. It is simply another way of saying that Indian culture, Indian civilization, accomplished little.

If you see "nature" as the absence of man, this automatically requires you to see man as radically different from nature: "Only on the supposition that man is by nature rational and free do those human works which are the products of reason or the consequences of free choice does man seem to stand in sharp contrast to all other natural existences and effects of natural causes."[155]

In other words, no human being can actually be, by definition, subjectively "at one with nature," or "in tune with nature" in the full European sense. One can only see another human being, not oneself, as being "at one with nature," or "in tune with nature." And only because you see that person not as a separate conscious subject, but as an object. A thing, not a person.

Somewhat insulting to a real Indian.

If nature stands in distinction to reason and free will, implied at least in Coates's definition 4, to whatever extent Indians are more "natural" than Europeans, that means they are less rational and have less free will. Picturesque, perhaps, like an animal in the zoo, but would you want your daughter to marry one?

That would explain why the Europeans, and not the Indians, are considered responsible for the decline of the beaver population. And that would explain the eternal urge to protect and look after Indians, denying them any personal agency. They are not responsible enough to sell their own land, for example; they are, more recently, not to be held fully responsible if they commit crimes. They are not fully moral beings.

But for any individual, including an Indian, it is probably impossible subjectively to believe you do not have free will. One can only think that of others, by seeing them as objects. Purely natural beings.

All clear now? To call Indians "children of nature" or the original environmentalists is not just patently wrong; it is racist and dehumanizing.

It almost makes you want to go out and burn down a tree.

The "Noble Savage myth," the idea that Indian culture is somehow especially in tune with and at one with nature, requires a conflation of the different senses of "nature": the one which means "lack of culture," definition 5, with Coates's definition 3, nature as a religious entity; wrapped up with the idea of nature as a particular area of land, Coates's definition 1; giving the Indians a supposed sacred bond with the land. But these notions are only arbitrarily connected, and probably only in Western Romantic tradition.

They have nothing to do with Indian culture. Nor can they, as seeing oneself and one's own culture as natural would be self-contradictory

8 PLATO AMONG THE INDIANS

Wandering tribe in the state of nature. *Providence Lithograph Company.*

Perhaps in this neglected spot is laid
Some heart once pregnant with celestial fire;
Hands, that the rod of empire might have sway'd,
Or wak'd to ecstasy the living lyre.

But Knowledge to their eyes her ample page
Rich with the spoils of time did ne'er unroll;
Chill Penury repress'd their noble rage,
And froze the genial current of the soul.

Full many a gem of purest ray serene,
The dark unfathom'd caves of ocean bear:
Full many a flow'r is born to blush unseen,
And waste its sweetness on the desert air.

Some village-Hampden, that with dauntless breast
The little tyrant of his fields withstood;
Some mute inglorious Milton here may rest,
Some Cromwell guiltless of his country's blood.

□ *Gray, "Elegy Written in a Country Churchyard."*

Indians as Platonists

But what then are we to make of Indian culture? If its basic values are not ecological, what are they?

The Jesuits, of course, especially strained to know; philosophy was their stock and trade and butter and daily bread. They were here to engage the Indians in a philosophical discussion.

Father LeJeune gives us his understanding of the Indian concept of the soul:

> [T]he Savages persuade themselves that not only men and other animals, but also all other things, are endowed with souls, and that all the souls are immortal; they imagine the souls as shadows of the animate objects; never having heard of anything purely spiritual, they represent the soul of man as a dark and sombre image, or as a shadow of the man himself, attributing to it feet, hands, a mouth, a head, and all the other parts of the human body.[156]

So far, so Pocahontasy. Disney would concur. It does sound, at first hearing, like a sort of "worship" of "nature": all things, not just men, are endowed with souls.

To the Jesuits, of course, living before the English Romantic poets, it all sounded instead rather materialistic. The poor Indians seem never to have thought of anything beyond their five senses. Souls with feet and hands? Isn' t this just a childish confusion of the spiritual with the material? Indeed, told of the Supreme Being, the Indians would laugh and respond almost like modern atheists: how can these foreigners possibly believe in something they cannot see?

It sounded terrible to the Jesuits. It sounded great to the Romantics. But they were both basing this on the same misunderstanding.

One should notice a contradiction here. Can these Indians who object that they can't see God see the souls of beaver, or of trees? Necessarily not—unless they have some senses we don't have.

The same Jesuits report of the same Indians, "During the night, a woman who had gone out, returned, terribly frightened, crying out that she had heard the Manitou, or devil. At once all the camp was in a state of alarm, and every one, filled with fear, maintained a profound silence. I asked the cause of this fright, for I had not heard what the woman had said; *eca titou*, *eca titou*, they told me, Manitou, 'Keep still, keep still, it is the devil.'"[157]

Had she really heard the voice of a devil? Can you see or hear the devil? Can the Indians? Do you suppose she instead heard the sound of some forest creature, and mistook it for a supernatural sound? You mean forest-dwelling Indians would be unfamiliar with the usual sounds of the forest?

Yes, she heard something, and no, not with her physical ears—here is where the cultural confusion begins. You can "see" or "hear" in the imagination—literally, the "imaging faculty." We can see or hear spirits, for example, in our dreams. The Indians could not believe in the Christian God because they could not picture Him in their minds—at least not at that point. He was not vivid to them. They believed that beaver and trees, on the other hand, had spiritual forms because they obviously did: you can readily imagine a beaver or a tree. And there they are. What you see in such a case is a spiritual beaver, or a spiritual tree, not a physical one.

As matter-of-fact as can be.

To understand this way of thinking, it is first essential that you disabuse yourself of the prejudice, if you have it, that "imaginary" means "not real." That is debatable, if not simply arbitrary. To the Indians, the imagined was real, and the physical world was not, or was secondary, like a reflection on the surface of a pond. To us contemporary Canadians, ordinarily, it is the opposite.

Shanawdithit, last of the Beothuks, is a useful informant, for she was mostly untainted by European influences. A Mr. Gill recounts, "At times she fell into a melancholy mood, and would go off into the woods, as she would say to have a talk with her mother and sister. She generally came back singing and laughing, or talking aloud to herself. She would also frequently indulge in the same practice at night, and when asked what was the matter would reply, 'Nance talking to her mother and sister.' When told not to be foolish, that they were dead and she could not talk to them, she would say, 'a yes they here, me see them and talk to them.'"[158]

If this all sounds odd or unfamiliar or even stark mad, one has not read Plato—the founder, most aver, of Western philosophy. Plato held that the only reason we can recognize a beaver as a beaver when we see one, and not a tree or a dumpster, is because the varmint with the overbite corresponds to an "ideal form" of a beaver that pre-exists in our mind. That ideal of a beaver, then, to either Plato or Shanawdithit, is the real beaver. The transient and mortal beaver we see is only an individual, imperfect, reflection of it.

The whole thing is so plain to Plato that, when he first refers to the idea in his dialogues, he does not bother to explain or justify it. He takes it as given. Why would not the Canadian Indians?

This, I submit, is the understanding held by most human cultures that have ever existed: the forms in the imagination are real. The physical world, less so. It is an entirely sensible, even obvious, way of looking at the world. We experience mental things directly. We experience physical things only indirectly, through the intermediary of our eyes. Who's to say they correspond to any underlying reality? Perhaps only the ideal forms.

We would get a lot closer to understanding the traditional Indian view, then, if, instead of trying to make them into Romantic naturalists, we saw them as Platonic idealists.

If so, Indians did very much believe in things they could not see—see, that is, with the imperfect bodily organ called the eye. They believed ultimately only in things they saw in the mind. They did not trust in the physical world, except as a reflection, like seeing your distorted face mirrored in the ripples of a pond.

If there is one thing about traditional Indian culture that seems definite, to which all actual witnesses attest, it is that the Indians put great stock in dreams.

Champlain reports: "[T]hey believe that all their dreams are true; and, in fact, there are many who say that they have had visions and dreams about matters which actually come to pass or will do so."[159] Father Brébeuf concurs: "[D]reams, above all, have here great credit."[160] Francis Parkman writes: "Dreams were to the Indian a universal oracle."[161] Reverend Peter Jones, himself an Ojibway chief, explains: "Many of their traditions are founded on dreams, which will account for the numerous absurd stories current amongst them."[162] On the West Coast, Sproat observes: "[T]he belief ... in the reality of dreams, is strongly held by the natives.... An unlucky dream will stop a sale, a treaty, a fishing, hunting, or war expedition."[163] Father LeClercq sees the same among the Micmac: "Our Gaspesians are still so credulous about dreams that they yield easily to everything which their imagination or the Devil puts into their heads when sleeping; and this is so much the case among them that dreams will make them come to conclusions upon a given subject quite contrary to those which they had earlier formed."[164] Livingston Jones, among the Tlingit, writes: "The superstitious belief in the reality and truth of dreams has tremendous hold on the native mind. If a sick native dreams of one bewitching him, that one is positively regarded as a witch. If a husband dreams that his wife has been untrue to him, he believes that she has and gives her a sound whipping on the strength of it."[165]

Brébeuf:

> They have a faith in dreams which surpasses all belief; and if Christians were to put into execution all their divine inspirations with as much care as our Savages carry out their dreams, no doubt they would very soon become great Saints. They look upon their dreams as ordinances and irrevocable decrees, the execution of which it is not permitted without crime to delay. A Savage of our Village dreamed this winter, in his first sleep, that he ought straightway to make a feast; and immediately, night as it was, he arose, and came and awakened us to borrow one of our kettles.

> The dream is the oracle that all these poor Peoples consult and listen to, the Prophet which predicts to them future events, the Cassandra which warns them of misfortunes that threaten them, the usual Physician in their sicknesses, the Esculapius and Galen of the whole Country,—the most absolute master they have. If a Captain speaks one way and a dream another, the Captain might shout his head off in vain,—the dream is first obeyed. It is their Mercury in their journeys, their domestic Economy in their families. The dream often presides in their councils; traffic, fishing, and hunting are undertaken usually under its sanction, and almost as if only to satisfy it. They hold nothing so precious that they would not readily deprive themselves of it for the sake of a dream. If they have been successful in hunting, if they bring back their Canoes laden with fish, all this is at the discretion of a dream. A dream will take away from them sometimes their whole year's provisions. It prescribes their feasts, their dances, their songs, their games,—in a word, the dream does everything and is in truth the principal God of the Hurons. Moreover, let no one think I make herein an amplification or exaggeration at pleasure; the experience of five years, during which I have been studying the manners and usages of our Savages, compels me to speak in this way.[166]

Father Jouvency adds: "What each boy sees in his dreams, when his reason begins to develop, is to him thereafter a deity, whether it be a dog, a bear, or a bird. They often derive their principles of life and action from dreams; as, for example, if they dream that any person ought to be killed, they do not rest until they I have caught the man by stealth and slain him."[167]

In other words, dreams, which is to say, the world perceived by the imagination, had greater reality than the physical world. The *real* world was that seen in dreams, by the imagination. The physical or material world, nature, was only its reflection.

The Indians accordingly explained to Brébeuf and LeJeune that "souls are not like us, they do not see at all during the day, and see very clearly at night; their day is in the darkness of the night, and their night in the light of the day."[168] In other words, the soul wakes when the body is asleep. It is fully awake when dreaming.

This is also no doubt why, by common Indian custom, the traditional tales, the myths, are not to be told in summer months, but only during winter—in the dark part of the year, when the visible world is less with us.

And how else make sense of the Indian creation stories, those on the lines of "how the camel got its hump," "how the loon got its necklace," or "how the leopard got its spots"?

The Abenaki, for example, held that Glooscap, the creator and culture hero, once asked the woodchuck for the hairs on its belly, from which he wove a magical sack. And this is why, they conclude, woodchucks have bare bellies.

This makes no sense if they are speaking of any individual woodchuck. How could what one did affect all others? But it makes sense if we speak here of the imagined woodchuck, the ideal form from which each individual woodchuck is known; in Jungian jargon, the woodchuck archetype. What is true of the archetypal woodchuck must then be true of each individual woodchuck, to the extent that they are woodchucks.

The Indians patiently explained to Father LeJeune that "all animals, of every species, have an elder brother, who is, as it were, the source and origin of all individuals, and this elder brother is wonderfully great and powerful."[169] Parkman speaks of this animal ancestor as "its progenitor or king, who is supposed to exist somewhere, prodigious in size, though in shape and nature like his subjects." "The patron bird of the Crow phratry," explains Livingston Jones, "is not the small crow or raven which we see flying about, but a mammoth imaginary creature of that species possessed with great strength and full of cunning and wisdom."[170]

This amounts to a pretty clear statement of Platonic idealism. To say "ancestor," or "elder brother," or "king," is one way, absent any shared technical jargon, to speak of an archetype. The ideal is related to the physical rather as a father is related to a son, or a king to his subjects. Having all the powers of the imagination, the archetype has all the powers one can imagine. In a dream, a beaver can be any size, can survive any wound, can and properly does live forever.

Note that this is not a question of both the physical world and the world of the imagination being equally real. The physical world is reflection of the imagined world: the imagined beaver is the ancestor and king of the physical beaver.

"If any one, when asleep," reports Father LeJeune, "sees the elder or progenitor of some animals, he will have a fortunate chase; if he sees the elder of the Beavers, he will take Beavers; if he sees the elder of the Elks, he will take Elks, possessing the juniors through the favor of their senior whom he has seen in the dream. I asked them where these elder brothers were. 'We are not sure,' they answered me, 'but we think the elders of the birds are in the sky, and that the elders of the other animals are in the water.'"[171]

Plato, explaining where his ideal forms reside, says something similar. They exist apart from us, as if apart in physical space, but do not exist anywhere in physical space.

Air and water are natural symbols of the non-physical. They offer a minimum of physical attributes, what Aquinas calls "accidents": lacking form, lacking colour, lacking size, lacking number, lacking, if air, any apparent mass or weight, transparent, invisible, unseen.

The Indians, therefore, were the farthest thing from nature worshippers, in the Romantic Western sense. They did not believe that nature, in Coates's definition 2, the physical world, was real. They did not worship rocks because they believed they had spirits; they worshipped spirits, and barely saw the rock.

Nor would they, accordingly, see much point in conservation. It is not as if the beaver or the buffalo could ever cease to be. Imaginary forms are immortal. Do memories die? And, as long as anyone could ever continue to imagine beaver or bison, to remember them, presumably, their physical reflections would continue as well. If someone dreamt of a beaver, the next day a beaver would appear. Even if none did, it is not as if there were no more beaver. That was just not possible. The real beaver continued forever to be.

It is and has always been the Europeans or "whites," the creators of the concept of nature, who have deep faith and respect for the physical world. Western culture is almost the only culture anywhere that accepts the physical world as unequivocally real. Let alone being the only culture that believes God expresses himself through the physical creation. Making it important, if not sacred, and a worthy object of study and of conservation, even without the fashionable "Gaea" hypothesis. Hence the West, and not the American Indians, invented science, most technology, and, indeed, ecology and conservation.

If you do not believe the material world is real, you are not going to devote as much of your time and labour to improving your material condition. It would be a waste. One very good reason why Indian culture was undeveloped, and why Indians have always been materially poor.

Pocahontas Indiansplains

This means that *Pocahontas* the movie, in its contrast between Western and Indian values, gets everything just about upside down. The English sailors, on embarkation, indulge in fantasies about the New World: the streets are proverbially paved with gold; or at least the strand is.

> *On the beaches of Virginny*
> *There's diamonds like debris*
> *There silver rivers flow and gold*
> *You pick right off a tree.*

With a nugget for my Winnie
And another one for me.

That is not a description of the physical world as it is. That is a dream image. That is a classic fantasy.

Gold is, in turn, not significant as a material resource. It is a symbol, a marker or exchange for material wealth. It is an ideal form, an archetype.

The Indians, on the other hand, according to Disney, are supposedly more interested in sturgeon. In purely physical things. They are portrayed as materialists. To Disney, of course, that is a good thing.

Odd, then, that Cartier was able to interest the local Indians in trading useful skins for nothing more than shiny bits of broken glass. Or that Peter Stuyvesant was reputedly able to buy Manhattan for a few glass beads and trinkets.

As late as the Treaty of Fort Niagara, land was exchanged for "12 thousand blankets, 23,500 yards of cloth; 5,000 silver ear bobs; 75 dozen razors and 20 gross of jaw harps."[172] Some of that is useful, but what about the ear bobs? Or the jaw harps?

In negotiating the numbered treaties, Lieutenant-Governor Morris "learned of the great significance the Chiefs placed on the suits, flags and medals that they had requested. 'They asked that the Chiefs and head men, as in other treaties, should get an official suit of clothing, a flag, and a medal, which I promised,' Morris reported. He was particularly struck by the significance the leadership placed on the medals: 'Mawedopenais produced one of the medals given to the Red River Chiefs, said it was not silver, and they were ashamed to wear it, as it turned black, and then, with an air of great contempt, struck it with his knife.' As one observer recalled, 'The result was anything but the "true ring," and made every man ashamed of the petty meanness that had been practised.' Morris was equally moved: 'I stated that I would mention what he had said, and the manner in which he had spoken.' Mawedopenais had insisted that only silver medals 'shall be worthy of the high position our Mother the Queen occupies.'"[173] "The Indians attach great importance to them and I am constantly shewn the King George medals," Morris wrote back to Ottawa, "which have been handed down as objects of great value."[174]

To the materialist Europeans, these seemed things of little real value, in comparison to actual land that might be farmed or built upon. To the Indians, because these beads, medals, and bits of glass were rare and shiny, although of no practical use, they were of equivalent or greater value. Because they were symbols: things that sparked the imagination, prompted dreams. Worth the exchange of a few dead acres of dirt. "The ordinary native is as well satisfied," explains Livingston Jones, "with a brass pin studded with glass gems as with one of pure gold studded with diamonds. The glitter is the chief consideration"[175]

"Vanity is another Thlinget trait," Livingston Jones adds, revealing the usual European lack of interest in the imagination. "They are very fond of military uniforms, caps and badges. Not a few join the Salvation Army that they may wear its caps and uniforms. We know a certain chief who changed his clothes several times while the transient tourist steamer was lying at the wharf, in order to display his suits. He would appear at the steamer and parade around until he was satisfied that he had been observed in all of his finery. He had military suits bedecked with badges, priestly suits (Russian), and other remarkable garments, all mainly for show."[176]

Vanity, no doubt, just foolishness, to a European. But if the imagination is real, being able to pretend to be an Orthodox priest or an American general is something wonderful.

Berating Captain Smith as an ignorant European, Pocahontas sings,

> *You can own the Earth and still*
> *All you'll own is earth until*
> *You can paint*
> *With all the colours*
> *Of the wind.*

Fair criticism. The beauty of art matters. And beauty obviously mattered to the Indians, with their ear bobs and medals.

But where, pray tell, are all the lovely examples of Indian pre-contact painting? And what are all those pretty things hanging in the Louvre, the Prado, the Hermitage, and the Vatican Museums, over in boorish uncultured Europe?

> [T]he Savages are not acquainted with the art of painting.[177]

This is confused Western Romanticism, seeing an equation between nature and art. If the Indians were lovers of nature, they must also have been authorities on art. In fact, the Indians generally had little art. Their preoccupation with the imagination did not even give them that advantage.

Yes, man does not live by bread alone. Yet poverty, and Indian poverty, pre-contact, was not just material. It was spiritual. With no permanent structures, no fixed abode where artifacts might be housed, no writing, there was little way to preserve anything fine for future generations. The lack of writing was bad enough.

But for the most part, the Indians of Canada were nomadic. And, *sans* the wheel or any large domestic animals, what they could own was limited to what could be carried on their backs. Or rather, on the backs of the women, for the men needed to keep their arms free in case of sudden attack.

"Some of their traps or household goods are packed on dogs," writes George Dawson of the Kaska, "but the greater part of their impedimenta is carried by themselves on their backs, canoes being seldom employed. Elvers and lakes are crossed in summer by rafts made for the occasion. They generally bring in only the fine furs, as bearskins and common furs are too heavy to transport."[178] Except for the fishing tribes of the British Columbia coast, who could generally find sufficient food in place, Canadian Indians could not afford the luxury of any *objets d'art*.

That means no poetry, visual art, or music other than what could be passed on memory to memory. Any Indian expressions of the human spirit were simply lost and forgotten; generations came and went like wolves howling at the moon. Of numberless lives, we know almost nothing: a few ambiguous rock carvings, a few oral traditions of dubious authenticity. In the Far West, some totem poles not yet utterly defaced by time. Nothing for the young and restless soul, seeking meaning, seeking what life is all about, seeking a voice to speak to them. Nothing but the daily struggle for subsistence.

This is a profound cultural poverty.

When Wolfe approached the battlements of Quebec, it is claimed, he was reciting to himself Gray's "Elegy Written in a Country Churchyard." He would rather, Wolfe said, have written those lines than take Canada.

The burden of that poem is the tragedy that so many men die unheard, unknown, and forgotten. None of their thoughts recorded, it is as though their lives were never lived.

Gray, and Wolfe, were thinking of 17th-century Englishmen. But the lament is more poignant if applied to Canadian Indians. That is just what traditional Indian culture condemned every Indian who ever lived pre-contact to.

It is the deepest poverty known to man.

Of Shanawdithit, an observer said: "[W]hen a black lead pencil was put into her hand and a piece of white paper laid upon the table, she was in raptures. She made a few marks on the paper apparently to try the pencil; then in one flourish she drew a deer perfectly, and what is most surprising, she began at the tip of the tail."[179]

Perhaps most ironically, Pocahontas concludes her cartoon denunciation of Westerners by lecturing the foolish Englishman Smith on proper appreciation of cultural differences:

> *You think the only people who are people*
> *Are the people who look and think like you*
> *But if you walk the footsteps of a stranger*
> *You'll learn things you never knew you never knew.*

Yet who would have more experience of strangers and their ways, a young girl living in a small village, in a place with no roads nor horses nor wheels nor ships, or an English seaman who has, the film has established, "seen hundreds of new worlds"?

And does it sound as though cartoon Pocahontas herself has taken the trouble to grasp the possible differences between her experiences and Smith's?

Isn't there some rich irony here?

Pocahontas makes good points against Indian traditional culture.

9 THE WAR OF ALL AGAINST ALL

Huron versus Onondaga.

I remember the Sixties.

They say, of course, that if you remember the Sixties, you were not really there.

Nevertheless, I think we all agree that something happened. There was a tectonic shift in Western culture, running right along the San Andreas Fault and through Haight-Ashbury. There was some existential earthquake of major magnitude. Why?

There were many factors, no doubt; but let's not underrate The Bomb. In the Fifties and early Sixties, "The Bomb," as we then called it, was new. We lived in constant worry of thermonuclear war, and "mutual assured destruction." Eminent philosopher Bertrand Russell opined at the time that, all things considered, it was better to surrender to the Soviet Union right now than to run the risk of nuclear war, whoever won. North American cities, on the model of London in the Blitz, set up systems of air raid sirens. Everyone built a bomb shelter in their back yard. Even Diefenbaker had his Diefenbunker.

Now we are all more sanguine, perhaps without good reason. But back then everything smelled of sulphur and cordite. Add that recollections of the Second World War and its carnage were still fresh, Korea and Vietnam had quickly followed, and the First World War was within living memory. It all left a general impression that civilization, technology, and the grand sweep of history were herding us lambs to the abattoir. More civilization simply meant bloodier and more awful war year upon year, as nations got stronger and weapons more powerful, until, inevitably, the entire species was blown to subatomic particles. Along with every other species. George Orwell's *1984*, composed in 1948, accordingly forecast a future of constant war.

So if civilization and progress were a dead end, what was our alternative?

Enter, stage left, a familiar *dramatis persona*, a stock character of stage, screen, and bodice-ripper: the Noble Savage. We began to imagine, as Europeans traditionally do whenever Europe is at war, that North American Indians, untouched by civilization and its discontents, were a contrasting model of peace, tolerance, and general human happiness. *Little Big Man*, the Western released in 1970, outlined the basic narrative, although not in as extreme form as the notion of primal innocence later became. In that film, Indian war is shown as a sort of shadow play: victory consists in touching the enemy, then retreating unharmed. The poor, good-hearted Cheyenne in the movie are unable to comprehend the reality of modern war, and die like stoned lemmings. The European protagonist, as a boy, lands a punch on the chin of an Indian antagonist. The native lad, nonplussed, just stands there, not knowing how to respond. He knew nothing of fisticuffs.

Right. Nice life, if there is not an angel with a flaming sword blocking your way. This, the Noble Savage, is a handy myth that has been with us since the dawn of civilization, always ready for service in this way. What Steven Pinker calls "the anthropology of peace" quickly developed. "Margaret Mead, for example, described the Chambri of New Guinea as a sex-reversed culture because the men were adorned with makeup and curls, omitting the fact that they had to earn the right to these supposedly effeminate decorations by killing a member of an enemy tribe. Anthropologists who did not get with the program found themselves barred from the territories in which they had worked, denounced in manifestos by their professional societies, slapped with libel lawsuits, and even accused of genocide."[180]

Sadly, some of us have recently been rudely awakened from this Samoan holiday of the intellectuals by the archaeological record. As Pinker and Lawrence Keeley (*War Before Civilization*) have outlined in recent books, if wars in the 20th century had generated the same mortality rates as the typical wars among hunter-gatherer societies, by 2000 there would have been two billion dead.[181] In the close encounters characteristic of tribal combat, Keeley says, casualty rates run to 60 percent, against 1 percent among soldiers in a modern war. On average, tribal wars are 20 times deadlier than that set-to Hitler started. Nor were they as uncommon as modern war: *The Economist* estimates that two-thirds of hunter-gatherer societies worldwide are at war constantly, and 90 percent go to war at least once a year. Working from prehistoric skeletons, Pinker estimates that up to 60 percent of our hunter-gatherer ancestors died by violence. In the 20th century, the rate is 3 percent.[182]

This tendency to group violence, it seems, we inherit from our animal ancestors. Pinker cites observations of chimpanzees by Jane Goodall:

> When a group of male chimpanzees encounters a smaller group or a solitary individual from another community, they don't hoot and bristle, but take advantage of their numbers. If the stranger is a sexually receptive adolescent female, they may groom her and try to mate. If she is carrying an infant, they will often attack her and kill and eat the baby. And if they encounter a solitary male, or isolate one from a small group, they will go after him with murderous savagery. Two attackers will hold down the victim, and the others will beat him, bite off his toes and genitals, tear flesh from his body, twist his limbs, drink his blood, or rip out his trachea. In one community, the chimpanzees picked off every male in a neighboring one, an event that if it occurred among humans we would call genocide. Many of the attacks aren't triggered by chance encounters but are the outcome of border patrols in which a group of males quietly seek out and target any solitary male they spot. Killings can also occur within a community. A gang of males may kill a rival, and a strong female, aided by a male or another female, may kill a weaker one's offspring.[183]

Apparently, Canadian Indians were a touch on the pacifist side. Keeley's data from North America suggest that, among our First Nations, only 87 percent engaged in war at least once a year. That's 3 percent less bellicose than the norm.

A notable excavation at Crow Creek, South Dakota, uncovered the skeletons of 500 men, women, and children, all, by the marks on the bones, dead by violence, scalped, and mutilated, a century and a half before Columbus sailed. No polluting influence of European civilization here. This was 60 percent of the estimated population of that village. Mostly missing, interestingly, were the bones of young women. That might account for the other 40 percent—carried off for future considerations.

This should not come as a shock to anyone. It conforms well with the historical record, and the historical record has always been clear. When Columbus disembarked, he found the Indians of San Salvador on alert against raids from nearby islands. John Smith, kidnapped by the Powhatans, was debriefed on the local situation: "Hee [the chief] described ... upon the same Sea, a mighty Nation called Pocoughtronack, a fierce Nation that did eate men, and warred with the people of Moyaoncer and Pataromerke, Nations upon the toppe of the heade of the Bay, under his territories: where the yeare before they had slain an hundred."[184] The Stadacona Indians at Quebec boasted to Cartier on his first visit of a recent successful raid on their neighbours resulting in 200 deaths, out of a population of a couple of thousand. When Champlain came seventy years later, of course, all the Stadaconans, and even any trace of their language, were gone. As Champlain and his arquebusiers landed, the local Indians promptly tried to recruit them in their ongoing war with the Iroquois. Champlain reports, of the local Indians, "All the time they were with us, which was the most secure place for them, they did not cease to fear their enemies to such an extent that they often at night became alarmed while dreaming."[185]

Jesuit chroniclers, often first at the frontier, and trained scientific observers, also noted this state of perpetual war. Father Jouvency says of the Indians of New France generally, "They engage in war rashly and savagely, often with no cause, or upon a very slight pretext."[186] "One tribe hardly ever has intercourse with another, either distant or near, except such as may arise in the prosecution of offensive or defensive warfare."[187] Of the Algonquins and Iroquois, the early Jesuits explain, "There has always been war between these two nations, as there has been between the Souriquois [Micmac] and Armouchiquois [modern identity unknown; possibly wiped out by the Micmac]."[188]

Of the Neutrals of Southwest Ontario, the Jesuits record:

> These peoples of the neutral Nation are always at war with those of the Nation of fire, who are still farther distant from us. They went there last Summer to the number of two thousand, and attacked a village well protected by a palisade, and strongly defended by nine hundred warriors who withstood the assault. Finally, they carried it, after a siege of ten days; they killed many on the spot, and took eight hundred captives,—men, women, and children. After having burned seventy of the best warriors, they put out the eyes and girdled the mouths of all the old men, whom they afterward abandoned to their own guidance, in order that they might thus drag out a miserable life. Such is the scourge that depopulates all these countries; for their wars are but wars of extermination.[189]

Father Lafleche, at Red River in 1849, tells of a small band of Sioux who stumbled into a larger group of Saulteaux. Once the latter determined by their accent that they were Sioux, "five of the Sioux are riddled with bullets, two attempt to flee, one of whom falls dead a short distance away, while the other rends the air with his shrieks as he is slashed and carved alive with the Saulteaux daggers. He is immediately scalped while still full of life, his limbs cut off one after the other, and everyone eagerly seeks for possession of some part of his body to take home as a trophy.[190]

Of the Nootka of British Columbia, Gilbert Sproat writes in 1868: "a trifling cause, such as an unavenged or an imagined affront offered, it may have been, in the time of a preceding generation, is considered a sufficient pretext for an attack on another unsuspecting tribe. Arrangements for war are made secretly, and a declaration or notice of the intention to attack is not given.... The question never is whether the proposed war is just or unjust, but whether there is sufficient force, and what are the chances of success."[191]

Among the Dene, Sir John Richardson writes in 1850 that they were at constant war, and that "one-half the population of the banks of the Yukon has been cut off within the last twenty years."[192]

Samuel Hearne sought the Coppermine River with a group of Dene Indians in the early 1770s. But when they discovered an Eskimo encampment on the way, priorities changed. They insisted on first wiping it out in a night raid.

> By the time the Indians had made themselves thus completely frightful, it was near one o'clock in the morning of the seventeenth; when finding all the Esquimaux quiet in their tents, they rushed forth from their ambuscade, and fell on the poor unsuspecting creatures, unperceived till close at the very eves of their tents, when they soon began the bloody massacre, while I stood neuter in the rear.
>
> In a few seconds the horrible scene commenced; it was shocking beyond description; the poor unhappy victims were surprised in the midst of their sleep, and had neither time nor power to make any resistance; men, women, and children, in all upward of twenty, ran out of their tents stark naked, and endeavoured to make their escape; but the Indians having possession of all the landside, to no place could they fly for shelter....
>
> The shrieks and groans of the poor expiring wretches were truly dreadful; and my horror was much increased at seeing a young girl, seemingly about eighteen years of age, killed so near me, that when the first spear was stuck into her side she fell down at my feet, and twisted round my legs, so that it was with difficulty that I could disengage myself from her dying grasps. As two Indian men pursued this unfortunate victim, I solicited very hard for her life; but the murderers made no reply till they had stuck both their spears through her body, and transfixed her to the ground. They then looked me sternly in the face, and began to ridicule me, by asking if I wanted an Esquimaux wife; and paid not the smallest regard to the shrieks and agony of the poor wretch, who was twining round their spears like an eel! Indeed, after receiving much abusive language from them on the occasion,

> I was at length obliged to desire that they would be more expeditious in dispatching their victim out of her misery, otherwise I should be obliged, out of pity, to assist in the friendly office of putting an end to the existence of a fellow-creature who was so cruelly wounded. On this request being made, one of the Indians hastily drew his spear from the place where it was first lodged, and pierced it through her breast near the heart. The love of life, however, even in this most miserable state, was so predominant, that though this might justly be called the most merciful act that could be done for the poor creature, it seemed to be unwelcome, for though much exhausted by pain and loss of blood, she made several efforts to ward off the friendly blow. My situation and the terror of my mind at beholding this butchery, cannot easily be conceived, much less described; though I summed up all the fortitude I was master of on the occasion, it was with difficulty that I could refrain from tears; and I am confident that my features must have feelingly expressed how sincerely I was affected at the barbarous scene I then witnessed; even at this hour I cannot reflect on the transactions of that horrid day without shedding tears.[193]

At another time, the expedition came across the camp of an unfamiliar Indian tribe, "who were all so poor as not to have one gun among them." Not known enemies—strangers.

> The villains belonging to my crew were so far from administering to their relief, that they robbed them of almost every useful article in their possession; and to complete their cruelty, the men joined themselves in parties of six, eight, or ten in a gang, and dragged several of their young women to a little distance from their tents, where they not only ravished them, but otherwise ill-treated them, and that in so barbarous a manner, as to endanger the lives of one or two of them. Humanity on this, as well as on several other similar occasions during my residence among those wretches, prompted me to upbraid them with their barbarity; but so far were my remonstrances from having the desired effect, that they afterwards made no scruple of telling me in the plainest terms, that if any female relation of mine had been there, she should have been served in the same manner.[194]

There really was, in fairness to *Little Big Man*, a practice among some plains Indians of "coup counting," getting boasting rights by touching an enemy and retreating unharmed. However, this was in addition to, not instead of, more lethal war, with all the blood and gore and stuff. There is no question real Indians understood the difference. "Although military historians tend to reserve the concept of 'total war' for conflicts between modern industrial nations," Mark Van de Logt writes of these same tribes of the plains, "the term nevertheless most closely approaches the state of affairs between the Pawnees and the Sioux and Cheyennes."[195] "To take one another's scalps had been for ages the absorbing and favourite recreation of all these Western tribes," Francis Parkman agrees.[196] Horace Greeley writes, from the 19th century frontier, "[T]he Aarapaho chief, Left-Hand, assures me that his people were always at war with the Utes—at least, he has no recollection, no tradition, of a time when they were at peace."[197]

It is also true enough that Indians, as shown in *Little Big Man*, did not box. But a real Cheyenne would not have responded only with shocked passivity if struck with a right hook. Father Biard, in the Jesuit Relations, reports just such a circumstance: "[T]hey do not understand boxing at all. I have seen one of our little boys make a Savage, a foot taller than himself, fly before him; placing himself in the posture of a noble warrior, he placed his thumb over his fingers and said, 'Come on!'"

"However," the Jesuit adds, "when the Savage was able to catch him up by the waist, he made him cry for mercy."[198]

Nor was this non-stop aggression simply a matter of young men needing to prove their mettle, while life went on more or less as normal back home among the wigwams and longhouses. This, as Pinker, Keeley, and Van de Logt point out, was total war in a sense the world wars of the 20th century never were. "Noncombatants were legitimate targets," Van de Logt notes. "Indeed, the taking of a scalp of a woman or a child was considered honourable because it signified that the scalp taker had dared to enter the very heart of the enemy' s territory."[199] The object of any war was, ultimately, extermination of the enemy. They were, after all, as we have seen in an earlier chapter, not human.

The Indian way of war was familiar enough to early colonists. In the raid on Deerfield, Massachusetts, during Queen Anne's War in 1704, Joseph Bradley's wife was taken captive; she later gave birth to a child in captivity. The assembled Indians, mostly Abenaki, with a sprinkling of French soldiers, killed the child by throwing hot coals in its mouth when it cried.[200] They also killed Mercy Sheldon, age two, by dashing her brains out on the door-stone.[201] Mariah Carter, five years old, was killed because the Indians did not think her fit for the march of captives back to New France.[202] For that was their plan for prisoners: to bring them back to their villages along the St. Lawrence for either ransom or servitude. On the long trek with their human booty, they killed a nursing baby.[203] Soon after, in a fit of drunkenness, they killed a black servant.[204] A Mrs. Williams, who had recently given birth, was tomahawked when she fainted along the way.[205] Next day, they killed another infant and a girl of eleven.[206] Next day, they tomahawked another woman.

The day following, they slaughtered four more. Women and children were seemingly killed first, on the grounds that they were not strong enough to survive being taken as captives.

Indian women were apparently hardier, or more desirable as slaves. Or perhaps the standard procedure simply differed with the circumstances. When an assembled force of their enemies overwhelmed the Outagamies outside Detroit, according to Parkman, "The women and children were divided among the victorious hordes, and adopted or enslaved. To the men, no quarter was given. 'Our Indians amused themselves,' writes Dubuisson [the commander of the French forces], 'with shooting four or five of them every day.'"[207]

Nor do we have only European informants. Robert Nasruk Cleveland, Inuit, offered this reminiscence in 1965:

> The next morning the raiders attacked the camp and killed all the women and children remaining there.... After shoving sheefish into the vaginas of all the Indian women they had killed, the Noatakers took Kititigaagvaat and her baby, and retreated toward the upper Noatak River.... Finally, when they had almost reached home, the Noatakers gang-raped Kititigaagvaat and left her with her baby to die.... Some weeks later, the Kobuk caribou hunters returned home to find the rotting remains of their wives and children and vowed revenge. A year or two after that, they headed north to the upper Noatak to seek it. They soon located a large body of Nuataagmiut and secretly followed them. One morning the men in the Nuataagmiut camp spotted a large band of caribou and went off in pursuit. While they were gone, the Kobuk raiders killed every woman in the camp. Then they cut off their vulvas, strung them on a line, and headed quickly toward home.[208]

You want to charge Sir John A. with "cultural genocide"? This was real genocide. All Indian wars were genocidal. You may have heard of "the last of the Mohicans"? Blotted out by the Mohawk. Recall the Stadaconans who greeted Cartier? Gone, as noted, eighty years later. The Dorset people, "skraelings," who fought off the Vikings? Gone a few hundred years later; only archaeological evidence remains. The Pocumtuc, prior residents of the Deerfield of which we spoke? Wiped out by the Mohawk in the early 1660s. The Yellowknives from the region of Great Slave Lake and the Coppermine River, the largest tribe in the Northwest when Samuel Hearne passed through in 1774? Obliterated by the nearby Dogrib Indians in the early nineteenth century.[209]

In the Beaver Wars, the Iroquois Confederacy exterminated the Wenro by 1638, the Huron by 1649, the Neutrals by 1651, the Eries by 1656, and the Susquehannock by 1677. They drove the remnants of the Shawnee west past the Mississippi River.

"Before French or English influence had been felt in the interior of the continent," writes Francis Parkman, "a great part of North America was the frequent witness of scenes ... of horror. In the first half of the seventeenth century the whole country from Lake Superior to the Tennessee, and from the Alleghenies to the Mississippi, was ravaged by wars of extermination, in which tribes, large and powerful by Indian standards, perished, dwindled into feeble remnants, or were absorbed by other tribes and vanished from sight."[210]

In 1638, Jesuit missionaries were present to see the survivors of the Wenro straggle in to Huronia, their own villages and most of their people having been wiped out by the Iroquois: "Notwithstanding the help that could be given them [by the Hurons], the fatigue and inconveniences of such a voyage—of more than eighty leagues, made by over six hundred persons, of whom the majority were women and little children—were so great that many died on the way, and nearly all were sick when they arrived, or immediately afterwards."[211] Eleven years later, Jesuits were present when the same fate befell the Hurons. "[N]otwithstanding the many alms that we gave ... we could not prevent hundreds and hundreds of them from dying in the winter by hunger. In the summer, many had rather postponed death than prolonged life, by living either in the woods on a few bitter roots and wild fruits; or on the rocks, on some little fish.... It was a frightful thing to see, instead of men, dying skeletons, walking more like shadows of the dead than like bodies of the living; and feeding themselves on that which nature has most in abomination, — exhuming the corpses (which we buried with our own hands, the relatives of the dead often lacking the strength to do so), in order to nourish themselves therewith, and eat the leavings of foxes and dogs."[212]

Hobbes' goblins

As and before the Noble Savage strutted his hour upon the stage, there was another Indian known to Europeans, based more closely on actual encounters. Horace Greeley, the author of the adage "Go west, young man," himself went west, and wrote of his discovery of the untrammelled Indian. "I have learned to appreciate better than hitherto, and to make more allowance for, the dislike, aversion, contempt, wherewith Indians are usually regarded by their white neighbors, and have been since the days of the Puritans. It needs but little familiarity with the actual, palpable aborigines to convince any one that the poetic Indian—the Indian of Cooper and Longfellow—is only visible to the poet's eye."[213]

Thomas Hobbes, the originator of the idea of a "social contract," grew to young adulthood in the days that England, his homeland, was starting its first settlements at Jamestown and Plymouth Rock. Far from endorsing the Noble Savage image, Hobbes held that man in a state of nature lived a life that was, now proverbially, "nasty, brutish, and short." The state of nature was, as indeed Darwin later saw it, a "war of all against all." Government, then, was man's great escape from this hellish condition, to protect his rights to life, limb, and property against each stronger neighbour. To Hobbes, even the most authoritarian, undemocratic, autocratic, oppressive government was better than this awful possibility of a state of nature. "Hereby it is manifest," he writes in *Leviathan*, "that during the time men live without a common Power to keep them all in awe, they are in that condition which is called Warre; and such a warre, as is of every man, against every man."[214]

Where did Hobbes get such a misanthropic notion? Such a dark and sinister view of human nature?

As it happens, Hobbes is explicit:

> It may peradventure be thought, there was never such a time, nor condition of warre as this; and I believe it was never generally so, over all the world: but there are many places, where they live so now. For the savage people in many places of America, except the government of small Families, the concord whereof dependeth on naturall lust, have no government at all; and live at this day in that brutish manner, as I said before.[215]

Hobbes, in short, was informed by contemporary reports from the American colonies.

This state of eternal war explains, to Hobbes' thinking, why Indian society had remained so materially undeveloped.

> In such condition, there is no place for Industry; because the fruit thereof is uncertain; and consequently no Culture of the Earth; no Navigation, nor use of the commodities that may be imported by Sea; no commodious Building; no Instruments of moving, and removing such things as require much force; no Knowledge of the face of the Earth; no account of Time; no Arts; no Letters; no Society; and which is worst of all, continuall feare, and danger of violent death; And the life of man, solitary, poore, nasty, brutish, and short.[216]

This alone would be enough to ensure that Indian societies did not develop.

Although it is a bit of a tautology: they did not develop because they were politically undeveloped.

Interestingly, the Indians of America are ultimately responsible for our current system of government: not just, as has often been claimed, for parts of the US Constitution, but for parliamentary democracy, for the idea of popular sovereignty, and for the doctrine of human rights. Hobbes' defense of absolute monarchy has long fallen out of favour; guillotines are our answer to that. But his essential insight of the social contract was built upon by John Locke, and liberal democracy was the upshot. Government is a pact we make to protect our rights. As part of that pact, we retain essential sovereignty, and have a right to always be consulted.

But Indian society was not the model: it was the counter-example.

Living a life that was nasty, brutish, and short cannot have been nearly as much fun as it looks in the movies. But do not blame the Indians. They were its chief victims. In said state of nature, each group faced a problem. Without some overarching authority to enforce it, burying the tomahawk and seeking to live in peace with one's neighbours simply left one open to conquest, enslavement, and bloody murder. Everyone was a tiger with another tiger by the tail.

One Yanomama Indian of Amazonia lamented to a modern anthropologist, "We are tired of fighting. We don't want to kill anymore. But the others are treacherous and cannot be trusted."[217]

The original social contract

Enter, happily, the French, British, and then Canadian government with their treaties. For both the "white" authorities and the Indians, these were not primarily about land. The Indians, with no concept of land ownership, probably did not attach much importance to this; especially since they were still allowed to hunt as before. For the government, they were about "civilizing" the Indians, bringing a rogue element into the social contract. But for the Indians too, perhaps even more, they were primarily seen as general peace treaties.

Not so much peace treaties with the Canadian government, either: peace treaties among the Indian tribes, with the federal government, and the mighty Mounties, reassuringly there to preserve it.

Cree chief Sweetgrass sent an appeal for a treaty to Lieutenant-Governor Alexander Morris in 1871. He cites the need to learn farming, but also writes, "We made a peace this winter with the Blackfeet. Our young men are foolish, it may not last long. We want you to come and see us and to speak with us."[218] He "wanted the

Crown to protect his people against illicit American traders, and to act as an arbiter between Amerindian nations."[219] The Blackfeet, his antagonists, sent a similar message, calling for a treaty while complaining, *inter alia*, that "the Half-breeds [Métis] and Cree Indians in large Camps are hunting Buffalo, both summer and Winter in the very centre of our lands."[220]

For most Indians, writes Keith Smith, "the treaties were peace treaties. As Piikani (Peigan) elder Cecile Many Guns (aka Grassy Water) confirmed almost a century after the treaty signings, the intent was that there would be 'no more fighting between anyone, everybody will be friends.... Everybody will be in peace.'"[221]

"The Great Queen Mother, hearing of the sorrows of her children," Mistawasis of the Blackfeet orates during negotiations, "sent out the Red Coats.... [T]he cutthroats and criminals ... immediately abandoned their forts.... It was the power that stands behind those few Red Coats that those men feared and wasted no time in getting out when they could; the power that is represented in all the Queen's people, and we the children are counted as important as even the Governor who is her personal speaker. The Police are the Queen Mother's agents and have the same laws for whites as they have for the Indians. I have seen these things done and now the Blackfoot welcome these servants of the Queen Mother and invite her Governor for a treaty with them next year. I for one look to the Queen's law and her Red Coat servants to protect our people against the evils of the white man's firewater and to stop the senseless wars among our people."[222]

In negotiating, Alexander Morris, the governor general who settled most of the numbered treaties, told the Indians they "must live together like brothers with each other and the white man." "In this country, now, no man need be afraid. If a white man does wrong to an Indian, the Queen will punish them. [I]f the Indians prove he did wrong, he will be punished.... [A]nd it will be the same if the Indian does wrong to the white man. The red and white man must live together, and be good friends, and the Indians must live together like brothers with each other and the white man."[223]

A common rap against Locke's theories, and by extension against the philosophical undergirdings of liberal democracy and human rights, is that the original "social contract" is purely a theoretical construct; that at no actual moment in history did any group of people actually, literally, enter into any such contract, delegating some of their rights and powers to a government. It follows, then, if so, that governments are not legitimate. There was no deal.

Not so. We have just such a historical example: the Indians of Canada, signing the numbered treaties.

Perhaps the greatest peril of the current, wildly romantic notion of a noble native savage living in a garden paradise is that Indians themselves now get most of their notions of "traditional Indian culture" from the media. Such misinformation encourages the Indian young in particular to wish to return to a purely imaginary state. Such efforts cannot end well: even if it were possible to return to innocence after knowledge, to crawl back up into your mother's womb and suck your thumb forever—before Jamestown, in all likelihood, is only Jonestown.

This aspect of Indian culture, surely, the lack of general government, alone shows the undesirability of such a return: yet that is the supposed goal of most of our current policies. The word we often see is "de-colonization."

Do we really understand what we are asking for?

10 WANT SLAVES?

Another kind of Lincoln memorial.

A few years ago I lived in Al Ain, an oasis in the Arabian Desert. It has a large livestock market, probably serving most of the United Arab Emirates and the southeastern quarter of Saudi Arabia. This is the last potable water inland from the Indian Ocean before the barren desert begins. At that coast, dhows once arrived from Oman's African possessions, stretching south to Zanzibar. With slaves.

Into the 1950s, this livestock market was also the regional slave market. Slavery was outlawed in Saudi Arabia only in 1962.[224] It was outlawed in Oman in 1970.[225]

Slavery has been common in China, India, Africa, and the Muslim world throughout history. It is enshrined in the Code of Hammurabi, the world's first recorded set of laws.

Almost all past societies have found it not just useful, but necessary. After all, before our current bankruptcy laws, what were you going to do if someone got himself into more debt than he could repay? What were you going to do if you took prisoners of war, in a time when social organization was too weak to sustain prisons? Indeed, what were you going to do with ordinary criminals? You could cut off their heads. You could cut off their hands. You could cut off their noses. You could flog them. Or you could take it out in sweat.

It is no particular knock against traditional Indian culture, then, that they practised slavery. But it is worth mentioning because the common Noble Savage archetype sees the life of pre-contact Indians as sublimely free of social constraints. That is a fantasy. Freedom and equality are modern luxuries, hard fought and hard won.

And, to be honest, slavery as practised by the Canadian Indians does seem to have been a bit rougher and more enthusiastically engaged in than was strictly required.

I feel I need to belabour the point, because it is sometimes denied. The prestige of the Noble Savage is such that people often do not want to accept that slavery was a part of Indian society. This is political correctness, as opposed to truth. Not only was it present; a plausible argument can be made that it is from the Indian example that the modern European-American experiment with slavery emerges: the chattel slavery of the Southern plantations.

The evidence of slavery among the Indians comes early and often. Columbus encountered slaving almost immediately on landing: the locals of San Salvador made him understand that "people from other adjacent islands came with the intention of seizing them, and ... they defended themselves."[226] Captain John Smith, of Jamestown, speaking of Powhatan's tribe, observes that they made war, "not for lands and goods, but for women and children, whom they put not to death, but kept as captives, in which captivity they were made to do service."[227]

Europeans were also taken by Indians in slavery, from early colonial days. "Strachey, in *The Historie of Travaile into Virginia*, speaks of a story that he had heard from the Indians, concerning an Indian chief, Eyanoco by name, liv'ng somewhere to the south of Virginia, who had seven white slaves who had escaped from the massacre at Roanoke. These slaves the Indians employed in beating copper."[228] "Captain Hendrickson, in 1616, found three persons belonging to the Dutch West India Company, who were slaves of the Mohawk and Minquae, and who were traded to him for merchandise."[229] Almon Lauber cites more cases from early records.

The *Jesuit Relations* have many stories of Indian slaves. Father (Saint) Isaac Jogues was captured by the Iroquois and enslaved for about a year, until he was ransomed by the Dutch.[230] Father Bressani was enslaved by the Iroquois in 1644.[231] Jesuit Father Fremin encountered an Iroquois woman who owned twenty slaves.[232] LaJeune, in 1632, reports slaves among the Algonquin. Tonti found Iroquois slaves among the Huron and Ottawa.[233] Hennepin tells of an attempt by the Jesuits in 1681 to free some Ottawas who were slaves of the Iroquois.[234]

Almon Lauber writes:

> The statement has been made that no personal slavery ever existed among the Iroquois, that their captives were either killed or adopted as a part of the nation. Quite the contrary is true. They held both Indians and whites in personal slavery. They brought back from the Ohio country bands of captives, sometimes numbering three or four hundred. They preyed upon the Shawnee and carried them off into slavery. They captured and enslaved the Miami for whose redemption they

> were presented with quantities of beaver skin. These they received but failed to free the slaves. They brought home slaves from Maryland and the south, and from the land of the "Chat" (the Erie). It was the Iroquois (the Seneca), called by an early writer "Sonnagars," who enslaved captives taken from the tribes of Carolina and Florida.[235]

To the northwest, the group we politically correct sorts recently started calling "Dene" were formerly called, from the Cree, the Slaves or Slavey. That was their significance to the Cree, who regularly raided and subjugated them.

"In 1724," adds Lauber, "de Bourgmont found the Kansas Indians employing Padouca slaves."

> In a letter written at Quebec, October 1, 1740, the Marquis de Beauharnois speaks of the Huron bringing slaves from the Flathead and delivering them up to the Outaouac (Ottawa). La Verendrye, in 1741, was told by the Horse Indians that the Snake Indians had destroyed seventeen of their villages, killed the warriors and women, and carried off the girls and children as slaves.
>
> Of the Wisconsin tribes, the Ottawa and Sauk, at least, were in the habit of making captives of the Pawnee, Osage, Missouri, and even of the distant Mandan, whom they consigned to servitude. The Menominee did not usually engage in these distant wars, but they, and probably other tribes, had Pawnee slaves whom they purchased of the Ottawa, Sauk and others who had captured them.[236]

On the Western plains, according to Franchère, the Blackfeet, Crow, and other tribes "were accustomed to keep the women taken in war as slaves."[237]

The Indians of the Pacific Coast were especially energetic slavers. One-quarter to one-third of the resident population among northwest tribes were slaves—a proportion similar to the US South before the Civil War. "A full third of the large population of this coast are slaves of the most helpless and abject description" writes Hubert Bancroft in his *History of Alaska*.[238] When being taken over by the United States after the Alaska Purchase meant freedom for their slaves, the Tlingit crafted a totem pole with the figure of Abraham Lincoln at the top, to shame the government and demand compensation.[239]

"Beginning with the Tlingit," writes Frederick Hodge, "slavery as an institution, using the term in its strictest sense, existed among all the Northwest coast Indians as far as California.... The Northwest region, embracing the islands and coast occupied by the Tlingit and Haida, and the Chimmesyan, Chinookan, Wakashan, and Salishan tribes, formed the stronghold of the institution."[240]

Slavery among Alaskan natives was finally outlawed by court decision in 1886, two decades after the US Constitution prohibited it for other Americans. Instances of enslavement are still reported as late as 1903. The Queen Charlotte Islands, now renamed, with proper respect to the local Indian culture, Haida Gwaii ("Islands of the Haida"), have been described as "the great slave mart of the northwest coast."[241]

The Thompson Indians of British Columbia kept slaves until 1850.[242] In 1836, the Chinook Indians of the BC interior still kept slaves.[243] As of 1850, so did the Dene, according to Sir John Thompson. "Slavery was common among them, and all possessed slaves who could afford them."[244] Lauber concludes, "among the North American tribes, the custom of slave-holding was practically universal."[245]

The nature of Indian slavery

The slavery deniers often rely on a spurious distinction between "captive" and "slave." But even this does not hold up. The early French sources make it clear that being captured in war was not the only way one could become a slave. There were slaving raids. Iroquois expeditions could harvest three or four hundred captives at a time.[246] Of the Nootka, Gilbert Sproat writes, "Some of the smaller tribes at the north of the [Vancouver] Island are practically regarded as slave-breeding tribes, and are attacked periodically by stronger tribes, who make prisoners, and sell them as slaves."[247]

Ojibway slaves came from as far afield as Eskimo country.[248] This implies a pretty solid and widespread institution. There was, clearly, an established slave trade.

Just as elsewhere, debt was another route to enslavement.[249] "The Indians were inveterate gamblers," explains Lauber, "and when nothing else was left, both men and women not infrequently staked themselves to serve as slaves in case of loss."[250] In times of famine, parents might sell their children for food.[251]

And among the Tlingit, at least, slavery was hereditary: the children of slaves were born slaves.[252]

It was full-bore chattel slavery, not just a labour arrangement. Either in the Eastern Woodlands or the Northwest, the rights of the slave owner were absolute. He could as he wished to a slave, with no questions asked. "Their masters had absolute power over them and could beat them, sell them or kill them as they pleased."[253] "[O]wners of slaves vied with one another in the sacrifice of slaves. Slaves were property, and the owner who destroyed the most was considered the greatest man."[254] The Jesuit records report, of the Iroquois, "When a barbarian has split the head of his slave with a hatchet, he says, 'It is a dead dog—there is nothing to be done but to cast it upon the dung hill.'"[255]

Gilbert Sproat says that among the Nootka of the West Coast, "So complete is the power over slaves, and the indifference to human life among the Ahts, that an owner might bring half a dozen slaves out of his house and kill them publicly in a row without any notice being taken of the atrocity."[256]

Slaves might be ritually killed at a potlatch, usually by having their brains knocked out before the guests with an axe. They might be killed at the death of their master, to be available to him in the next life. Or, as a matter of routine, if they grew old or got sick.

The custom among the Iroquois was to give a captive to any family who had lost a relative in war. The family—generally the wife or mother—could have the captive tortured to death, adopt them as a family member with nearly full rights, or make use of the slave's labour for as long as they saw fit.

Father Joseph Poncet writes, of his own captivity: "I was given to a good old woman in place of a brother of hers, who had been captured or killed by those on our side. Nevertheless, my life was not yet safe; for that woman could have made me die in all the torments that could have been suggested by revenge."[257]

Among the Tlingit, the practice was to pull out one eye to identify a slave as property. The Indians of the US Southwest would cut the tendons of the ankle, or cut off part of a foot, to make escape difficult.[258]

A prominent Tlingit or Haida might own as many as fifty slaves.

> There were several events which demanded the sacrifice of slaves, and no one could tell when these events would take place. The erection of a house, the death of the owner, the death of any member of his household, an unusual feast, some occurrence to give shame to the owner, the mere gratification of his vanity, demanded the sacrifice of slaves.
>
> When a chief died, just as he was expiring several slaves were sacrificed near the door of his house. A chief was drowned in the treacherous waters of the Taku river. His body was not recovered, but at the spot where he was drowned two of his slaves were put to death and their bodies thrown into the river.

> We have seen in the village of Kluckwan a house where a slave was put into each foundation hole of its corners for the posts to rest upon. We were told that this was done to insure a good foundation. When a member of any chief's family was tattooed, or had an earlobe pierced for rings, the event was so important that a slave was sacrificed. If a high-caste man was given any great shame, he would sacrifice a slave or two to wipe out the shame. This showed how rich and important he was.[259]

Cultural appropriation

A question of at least equal interest is how slavery came to the American South. It was not, after all, commonly practised in Europe at the time, or much before, or ever after. The peculiar institution now commonly blamed on Europeans was not a traditional European vice. In fact, in all the world, in pre-modern times, there was only one notable, though only partial, exception to the general practice of slavery: Christian Europe. Moreover, it was ultimately Christian European reformers who had the practice ended, world-wide, over the last two or three centuries. Christianity seems uniquely incompatible with slavery.

This is the more notable because the ancient Romans had slaves, the ancient Greeks had slaves, and so did the ancient Egyptians and Mesopotamians. But almost as soon as Christianity became the established faith of the Roman Empire, the practice fell into disuse. While usually not prohibited outright, it did not fit with the Christian belief in the equality of man. Usury too was by Christianity banned, preventing people from falling into insurmountable debt. Prisoners of war came to be ransomed, or simply "paroled," released on giving their word of honour that they would not again take up arms. Where the practice of slavery persisted, Christianity assigned the enslaved person rights. According to the Church, no one, on principle, could ever be owned by another person; the master had only the right to their labour. In other words, the Christian practice, relatively rare as it was, was bonded servitude but not slavery according to *Merriam-Webster*'s strict definition: "the state of a person who is a chattel of another." John Chrysostom, church father, described slavery as "the fruit of covetousness, of degradation, of savagery ... the fruit of sin, [and] of [human] rebellion against ... our true Father."[260]

So why did slavery, and full chattel slavery, appear among Europeans in the New World?

Two clues: it surfaced very soon after Columbus landed in 1492 (possibly slightly earlier in the Canaries, which fell under Spanish control in 1495), and it appeared only in the Americas and in the African colonies. It was not generally accepted, even then, in Europe. "England was too pure an air for a slave to breathe in."

Ownership of people had to be expressly permitted by statute in the American colonies; it had no place in English common law.[261] It was legalized in Massachusetts in 1641, in Connecticut in 1650, in Virginia in 1661. It was, to our credit, expressly banned in Ontario (then Upper Canada) in 1793. Upper Canada was the first British colony to abolish slavery. It had no major local presence at the time, but Governor Simcoe wanted to prevent United Empire Loyalists from bringing in slaves as they emigrated from the new United States. Simcoe called slavery "an offense against Christianity."

The obvious suspicion is that Europeans were re-exposed to the idea of slavery by their travels, by contact with the Muslim world, with Africa, and with the American Indians, among all of whom it was common practice. "The finding of the same custom among the Indians themselves, make their carrying on of the practice quite natural," Lauber suggests.[262]

The first slaves held by Europeans in America were certainly native Indians. One can imagine how it came about. Indians, wishing to make a bargain, would have presented slaves as trade goods as a matter of course. When in Rome ... Later, they discovered a European interest in furs, but at first the native interest in European goods inevitably far exceeded their capacity, in their poverty, to offer anything of significant value in return. Columbus attests to an extreme thirst to trade among the Indians he first encounters: "for the longing to possess our things, and not having anything to give in return, they take what they can get."[263]

A few examples: "De Boucherville ... on his journey from the Illinois country to Canada, 1728-1729, took with him a little slave for the governor-general of Canada ... and was offered other slaves as gifts by the Indians whom he encountered."[264] "In 1684, the Indians offered Du Luth slaves to take the place of some assassinated Frenchmen. In 1724, the Indians at Detroit offered the French commander, by way of truce, two slaves for the same purpose."[265]

The taste acquired, the number of available native natives become too few, and the Irish, conquered and sold into servitude by the English, often took their place. Then Africans were acquired, hardier in warm climates—offered by other Africans eager to trade for European manufactures.

The Portuguese had explored the coast of Africa down to the Cape of Good Hope by the time Columbus reached Hispaniola. The local inhabitants of their colonies along the African coast, which they had established for ship resupply, all offered slaves.

At first the Portuguese had no use for them. Then Spanish and Portuguese Catholic missionaries began advocating accepting them, as the alternative was generally to see them put to death by the tribes who had captured them as spoils of war.[266] The same may have been true of Indian slaves. If the Iroquois saw no value in a captive as a slave, the unfortunate unemployed bondsman was tortured to kingdom come.

"It must be understood," notes Lauber, "that enslavement of captives in war was in itself a kindly act on the part of the captors.... Otherwise, the prisoners were tortured and killed as an expression of hatred, or as a means of obtaining revenge for injury."[267]

And so the modern European/American practice of slavery, bizarrely but honourably enough, may have begun as an act of mercy. Of course, this cannot excuse chattel slavery as it became; at most, a period of indenture might have been justified. But slavery was still probably better than the alternative. This was, in fact, the law among the Spanish: a non-Christian could not be enslaved unless doing so saved him from a probably worse fate.

When you hear demands for a return to traditional Indian culture, and the assertion that it was an idyllic existence tragically corrupted by European influence, keep in mind that some of the corrupt influence may have gone the other way. And many of those Noble Savages were not there just for the good times.

It is hard to see the advantage in reviving and supporting said culture in every detail.

Want slaves? Ask an Indian.

11 A FATE WORSE THAN DEATH

Jane McCrae's fiancée is presented with her scalp

General Sir Guy Carleton, sitting in his office at the Quebec Citadel in May, 1775, had a problem. A shot had just been heard round the world: 13 British colonies were in revolt.

Sir Guy was known for never betraying fear or concern. But he surely knew that Quebec, then a vast territory stretching from Labrador to St. Louis, was in peril. The rebellion was on his doorstep. Quebec, as a Catholic and Indian entity blocking the American colonists' expansion westward, was one of their grievances. Perhaps the chief grievance, although modern historians prefer to focus on the nobler-sounding issue of "no taxation without representation." Carleton had every reason to expect either invasion or insurrection, or both, and imminently.

In fact, the Yankees had already taken Fort Ticonderoga and Crown Point, defending the main land route north to Montreal; reinforcing the suspicion that Quebec was their main concern.

Carleton had only 800 regular soldiers under his command—to hold half a continent.

The French-speaking population of Quebec surely held no special affection for the Crown of England: of a different language and creed, they had been defeated on the Plains of Abraham only 12 years before. There was also a small English-speaking population, mostly in Montreal. But they came almost entirely from the Thirteen Colonies. They were already frustrated at being allowed mere equality with the French Catholics, and were more than likely to retain ties to their southern cousins.

Luckily for Carleton, at that moment two delegations of Indians arrived to offer their support: Algonquin-speakers from the west, and Iroquois from upstate New York, under the command of Guy Johnson, intrepid British Indian agent.

Carleton turned them both down.

He asked the Algonquins to go home and stay neutral. He asked the Iroquois to remain in Quebec, where they were less likely to be caught up in the troubles.

Carleton was a capable administrator as well as military man. These were early days, and positions had not hardened. The United States had not yet declared independence. Sir Guy had reason to hope that reconciliation between Britain and its errant colonists was still possible.

But unleash the Indians and, given their methods of war, the breach was likely to become irreparable.

Carleton was right. When, in 1776, the Continental Congress did decide for full sovereignty, their Declaration included, as one of their justifications for the parting of the ways, "He [George III] has excited domestic insurrections amongst us, and has endeavoured to bring on the inhabitants of our frontiers, the merciless Indian Savages, whose known rule of warfare, is an undistinguished destruction of all ages, sexes and conditions."

This was what Carleton had taken such great risks to avoid.

Unfortunately, already in 1775, two separate American armies did indeed invade Canada—again suggesting the primacy of this issue to the Continentals. It was a close run thing; Carleton held out behind the walls of Quebec City until the Royal Navy arrived with reinforcements in the spring. The Americans were then pushed back, and, in a clash just outside Montreal remembered as "The Affair of the Cedars"—they ran into the Iroquois warriors.

According to the American accounts, the Iroquois tortured and executed American prisoners.

> The evening after major Sherburne was taken the Indians killed and scalped 2 of his men. Afterwards at different times they killed 4, or 5 others, one of whom was of those who had surrendered on capitulation at the cedars and was killed the 8th. day after that surrender. One other (as was affirmed by his companion now in possession of the savages and who saw the act) was first shot so however as not to kill him and then roasted. Others were left exposed on an island, naked

> and perishing with cold and famine, in which state they were found by Genl. Arnold's detachment.[268]

The British denied this; they claimed that the sheer fear of Indian torture led the Americans to surrender prematurely, and they then alleged torture to excuse their cowardice.

Either way, the incident may have been the fuse and powder that, in rebel propagandists' hands, finally utterly alienated the colonials. That, or the claimed execution by Indians travelling with British General Burgoyne of lovely young colonist Jane McCrea—although again the Indians insisted she was killed by a stray bullet.

That's as may be. Still, it seems unnecessary to have scalped her.

The Indians may or may not have committed actual acts of savagery in these instances. But at a minimum, we see that they by this time had a solid reputation for such tactics. So solid that it was taken by the Americans, and Guy Carleton, as the rule.

And so we come to another rather disheartening element of Indian culture, one that we may not want to nurture and preserve. Yes, Indian war was constant. Yes, Indian ways of war produced staggering casualties. Yes, they recognized no rights of non-combatants. But, as *K-Tel* used to say, wait, there's more. They apparently had not signed the Geneva Convention. There was also the likelihood of torture if captured.

Please be advised: if you are "triggered" by anything at all, what follows may trigger you. The editor of this book left long quotations here unedited, he warns, because he, a grown man, could not stomach reading them. If your stomach is not stronger, I suggest that you avoid reading any quoted passages from here to the end of the chapter. Just read the intervening paragraphs for the argument.

Ready? Shall we carry on, then?

William Bradford, of the Mayflower Pilgrims, said of the Indians of Massachusetts, "Not being content only to kill and take away life, [they] delight to torment men in the most bloody manner that may be, flaying some alive with the shells of fishes, cutting off members and joints of others by piecemeal and broiling on the coals, eat collops of their flesh in their sight while they live."[269]

According to the early Jesuits, Indians in general believed that "those who go to war are the more fortunate in proportion as they are cruel toward their enemies."[270]

Father Jouvency writes in the Jesuit Relations:

> Those who have been captured and led off to their villages are first stripped of their clothing; then they savagely tear off their nails one by one with their teeth; then they bind them to stakes and beat them as long as they please. Next they release them from their bonds, and compel them to pass back and forth between a double row of men armed with thorns, clubs and instruments of iron. Finally, they kindle a fire about them, and roast the miserable creatures with slow heat. Sometimes they pierce the flesh of the muscles with red-hot plates and with spits, or cut it off and devour it, half-burned and dripping with gore and blood. Next they plant blazing torches all over the body, and especially in the gaping wounds; then, after scalping him they scatter ashes and live coals upon his naked head; then they tear the tendons of the arms and legs, lacerate them, or, after removing a little of the skin, leisurely cut them with a knife at the ankle and wrist. Often they compel the unhappy prisoner to walk through fire, or to eat, and thus entomb in a living sepulcher, pieces of his own flesh. Torture of this sort has been borne by not a few of the Fathers of the Society. Moreover, they prolong this torment throughout many days, and, in order that the poor victim may undergo fresh trials, intermit it for some time, until his vitality is entirely exhausted and he perishes. Then they tear the heart from the breast, roast it upon the coals, and, if the prisoner has bravely borne the bitterness of the torture, give it, seasoned with blood, to the boys, to be greedily eaten, in order, as they say, that the warlike youth may imbibe the heroic strength of the valiant man.... The rest of the crowd consume the corpse in a brutal feast.[271]

The Jesuit martyrs

Most famous among the victims of Iroquois torture were the "Jesuit martyrs," of whom every Canadian Catholic schoolboy knows. We have Father (Saint) Isaac Jogues's own description. Captured in a party heading by canoe from Quebec to Trois-Rivières, he recalls,

> They [the Iroquois] fell upon me with a mad fury, they belabored me with thrusts, and with blows from sticks and war-clubs, flinging me to the ground, half dead. When I began to breathe again, those who had not struck me, approaching, violently tore out my finger-nails; and then biting, one after another, the ends of my two forefingers, destitute of their nails caused me the sharpest pain, grinding

> and crushing them as if between two stones, even to the extent of causing splinters or little bones to protrude.[272]

"They treated the good René Goupil," he adds, "in the same way." This, it seems, was standard practice. Nothing personal.

The captives were then marched back to Iroquois territory, 13 days away. During this march, says Jogues,

> ...the pain of our wounds,—which, for not being dressed, became putrid even to the extent of breeding Worms,—caused us, in truth, much distress.[273]

On day eight, Jogues and his fellows were obliged for the first time to "run the gauntlet." He describes the procedure:

> [T]hey set up a stage on a hill; then, entering the woods, they seek sticks or thorns, according to their fancy. Being thus armed, they form in line,—a hundred on one side, and a hundred on the other,—and make us pass, all naked, along that way of fury and anguish; there is rivalry among them to discharge upon us the most and the heaviest blows.[274]

During the ordeal, Jogues passed out. To prolong the merriment, the Indians cared for him tenderly until he revived, then resumed the torture. At this point, Jogues relates,

> They burned one of my fingers, and crushed another with their teeth, and those which were already torn, they squeezed and twisted with a rage of Demons; they scratched my wounds with their nails; and, when strength failed me, they applied fire to my arms and thighs.[275]

"My companions," he again adds, "were treated very nearly as I was."

It was not, of course, only Europeans who suffered in this way. Most victims, we should recall, were Indians. "Among the Hurons," Jogues reports,

> ...the worst treated was that worthy and valiant Christian, Eustache. Having made him suffer like the others, they cut off both thumbs from his hands, and thrust through the incisions a pointed stick even to the elbow.[276]

During the 13-day march, the captives were not fed. If they could snatch any wild fruits or berries from the trees and bushes as they passed, that was their sustenance. Eventually, they came to another Iroquois village, at which they were required to again run the gauntlet. This village, being near a Dutch trading post, was equipped with iron bars for the beating. The Indians, Jogues says, aimed for the shins.

In all, says Jogues, "we spent three days and three nights in the sufferings" on this particular scaffold.[277] Then their captors paraded the prisoners around to neighbouring villages, each of which got a whack at them. During this time,

> One of those Barbarians having perceived that Guillaume Cousture, although he had his hands all torn, had not yet lost any of his fingers, [no doubt a regrettable oversight] seized his hand, striving to cut off his forefinger with a poor knife. But, as he could not succeed therein, he twisted it, and in tearing it he pulled a sinew out of the arm, the length of a span.[278]
>
> The young men thrust thorns or pointed sticks into our sores, scratching the ends of our fingers, deprived of their nails, and tearing them even to the quick flesh; and, in order to honor me above the others, they bound me to pieces of wood fastened crosswise. Consequently, my feet not being supported, the weight of my body inflicted upon me a gehenna, and a torture so keen that, after having suffered this torment about a quarter of an hour, I plainly felt that I was about to fall in a swoon from it.[279]

In normal circumstances, prisoners were tortured to death; this would properly have been the time to cut Jogues open and eat his heart out. But a council of the Iroquois decided the Frenchmen were worth more alive than dead, that they might be bartered back to the Europeans for trade goods. Jogues was held as a slave. Eventually, he was bought by a Dutch trader, and able to set sail for France.

In a few years he was back, volunteered for the Iroquois mission, and they finally finished the job.

There are many such stories in the *Jesuit Relations*. It seems too morbid to tell them all; the outlines of the torture are similar. We cannot pass on, however, without retelling for the sake of fellow Catholics the case of the other most celebrated Jesuit martyr, Father (Saint) Jean de Brébeuf. It is told by a Huron witness, confirmed later by wounds found on his charred body.

Martyrdom of Jean de Brébeuf.

The Iroquois, on seizing and immolating with much slaughter the Huron village in which a Jesuit mission was located, seized two priests, one of them Brébeuf,

> ...stripped them entirely naked, and fastened each to a post. They tied both of their hands together. They tore the nails

> from their fingers. They beat them with a shower of blows from cudgels, on the shoulders, the loins, the belly, the legs, and the face....

An Indian whom Brébeuf had catechized, now a captive slave of the Iroquois and no doubt hoping to improve his situation, a typical kapo, "baptized" the Jesuit mockingly three times with boiling water. Then they made their hatchets red hot in the fire, and applied them to his crotch and under his armpits. Next, they strung the tomahawks into a collar, and hung it around his neck.

Either the Jesuit redactor, Father Régnault, or the Huron reporter, explains of this particular torture,

> ...you see a man, bound naked to a post, who, having this collar on his neck, cannot tell what posture to take. For, if he lean forward, those above his shoulders weigh the more on him; if he lean back, those on his stomach make him suffer the same torment; if he keep erect, without leaning to one side or other, the burning ratchets, applied equally on both sides, give him a double torture.[280]

The torture is both physical and psychological.

"After that," our source resumes,

> ... they put on him a belt of bark, full of pitch and resin, and set fire to it, which roasted his whole body.... To prevent him from speaking more, they cut off his tongue, and both his upper and lower lips. After that, they set themselves to strip the flesh from his legs, thighs, and arms, to the very bone; and then put it to roast before his eyes, in order to eat it.[281]

By now, Father Brébeuf was visibly weakened almost to the point of death. His tormentors, seeing this, proceeded to the dénouement. They made him sit down on the ground;

> ...and, one of them, taking a knife, cut off the skin covering his skull. Another one of those barbarians ... made an opening in the upper part of his chest, and tore out his heart, which he roasted and ate. Others came to drink his blood, still warm, which they drank with both hands.[282]

Other tribes

You get the general idea of how these things proceeded. Both of our cases have involved Iroquois, but do not suppose the practice was limited to that tribe. Father Régnault, in reporting the death of Brébeuf, adds, "I have seen the same treatment given to Iroquois prisoners whom the Huron savages had taken in war."[283] The Jesuit Relations report of the Iroquet, a Huron band,

> … they carried off the victory, bringing back with them thirteen prisoners alive, whom they caused to suffer horrible tortures. They sent one of these prisoners to the Three Rivers. Oh God! what cruelty was not exercised upon this poor wretch, by the wives of those who a little while before had been killed in the country of the Hiroquois. Father Buteux has written me the whole tragic story, describing the barbarity of these tigers. Their fury seemed to me so horrible that I have not been able to set it down on paper….[284]

Champlain, returning from his first joint raid upon the Iroquois, observed similar tortures by Algonquins, Montagnais (Innu), and Etechemins. From Champlain's journal:

> [O]ur men kindled a fire; and, when it was well burning, they each took a brand, and burned this poor creature [an Iroquois captive] gradually, so as to make him suffer greater torment. Sometimes they stopped, and threw water on his back. Then they tore out his nails, and applied fire to the extremities of his fingers and private member. Afterwards, they flayed the top of his head, and had a kind of gum poured all hot upon it; then they pierced his arms near the wrists, and, drawing up the sinews with sticks, they tore them out by force; but, seeing that they could not get them, they cut them. This poor wretch uttered terrible cries, and it excited my pity to see him treated in this manner.… After his death, they were not yet satisfied, but opened him, and threw his entrails into the lake. Then they cut off his head, arms, and legs, which they scattered in different directions; keeping the scalp which they had flayed off, as they had done in the case of all the rest whom they had killed in the contest. They were guilty also of another monstrosity in taking his heart, cutting it into several pieces, and giving it to a brother of his to eat, as also to others of his companions.[285]

Next expedition, a new batch of prisoners was treated in the same manner:

> They took the prisoners to the border of the water, and fastened them perfectly upright to a stake. Then each came with a torch of birch bark, and burned them, now in this place, now in that. The poor wretches, feeling the fire, raised so loud a cry that it was something frightful to hear; and frightful indeed are the cruelties which these barbarians practice towards each other. After making them suffer

> greatly in this manner and burning them with the above-mentioned bark, taking some water, they threw it on their bodies to increase their suffering. Then they applied the fire anew, so that the skin fell from their bodies, they continuing to utter loud cries and exclamations, and dancing until the poor wretches fell dead on the spot. As soon as a body fell to the ground dead, they struck it violent blows with sticks, when they cut off the arms, legs, and other parts; and he was not regarded by them as manly, who did not cut off a piece of the flesh, and give it to the dogs. Such are the courtesies prisoners receive. As to the other prisoners, which remained in possession of the Algonquins and Montagnais, it was left to their wives and daughters to put them to death with their own hands; and, in such a matter, they do not show themselves less inhuman than the men, but even surpass them by far in cruelty; for they devise by their cunning more cruel punishments, in which they take pleasure, putting an end to their lives by the most extreme pains.[286]

Father Vimont describes the condition of a prisoner upon escaping from the Algonquins:

> [T]wo of the principal Savages led him to the Hospital, where he was received by the Nuns with great joy. They call the Surgeon; the whole ward was full of Savages, in order to see in what state his wounds were. He had all his nails torn out; matter was issuing from three fingers, quite recently cut, and the worms were swarming therein; he had one foot pierced through and through with a stick; he had both wrists of his hands tied, even to the bone, with cords; and his body was burned, and pierced with awls in sundry places. I was present at this sight; the first view made us chill with horror."[287]

Similar stories are recorded of other North American tribes. John Gyles, taken from his farm on the Saint John River (New Brunswick) in 1692, reports his own torture and that of his companions by the Malecites (Algonquin speakers of the Saint John Valley) in his *Memoirs of Odd Adventures, Strange Deliverances, etc.*, published in 1736. He writes,

> My unfortunate brother, who was taken with me, after about three years' captivity, deserted with another Englishman, who had been taken from Casco Bay, and was retaken by the Indians at New Harbor, and carried back to Penobscot fort. Here they were both tortured at a stake by fire, for some time; then their noses and ears were cut off, and they made

> to eat them. After this they were burnt to death at the stake.[288]

In 1689, Major Waldron of Dover, New Hampshire, suffered a similar fate.[289] Mary Rowlandson, captured in a raid on Lancaster, Massachusetts, by the Narragansett in 1675, told of a companion slowly burned to death with her infant child.[290] Mary Jemison, taken by Seneca in the 1750s, wrote

> ...we passed a Shawnee town, where I saw a number of heads, arms, legs, and other fragments of the bodies of some white people who had just been burned. The parts that remained were hanging on a pole, which was supported at each end by a crotch stick in the ground, and were roasted or burnt black as a coal.[291]

Robert Rogers was captured in a raid on Salmon Falls, New Hampshire, in 1690. "They dragged him out," writes Cotton Mather,

> ...stripped him, beat and pricked him, pushed him forward with the points of their swords, until they got back to the hill from whence he had escaped. It being almost night, they fastened him to a tree, with his hands behind him, then made themselves a supper, singing and dancing around him, roaring, and uttering great and many signs of joy, but with joy little enough to the poor creature who foresaw what all this tended to.
>
> The Indians next cut a parcel of wood, and bringing it into a plain place, they cut off the top of a small red-oak tree, leaving the trunk for a stake, whereunto they bound their sacrifice. They first made a great fire near this tree of death, and bringing Rogers unto it, bid him take his leave of his friends, which he did in a doleful manner, such as no pen, though made of a harpy's quill, were able to describe the dolor of it. They then allowed him a little time to make his prayers unto heaven, which he did with an extreme fervency and agony; whereupon they bound him to the stake, and brought the rest of the prisoners, with their arms tied each to the other, and seated them round the fire. This being done, they went behind the fire, and thrust it forwards upon the man with much laughter and shouting; and when the fire had burnt some time upon him, even till he was almost suffocated, they pulled away from him, to prolong his existence. They now resumed their dancing around him, and at every turn they did with their knives cut collops of his flesh out of his naked limbs, and throw them with his blood

> into his face. In this manner was their work continued until he expired.[292]

So too with the tribes of the plains. Gregory and Susan Michno, in their book *A Fate Worse Than Death*, restrict themselves to accounts from Texas—but describe torture by the Sioux, Blackfoot, Comanche, Arapaho, Cheyenne, Lakota, Shoshone, Bannock, Mojave, Yavapai, Crow, Kiowa, Kickapoo, Utes, and Chiricahua.

John West says of the Sioux of the Northwest:

> They fell upon four lodges belonging to the Saulteaux, who had encamped near Fond du Lac, Lake Superior, and which contained the wives and children of about twelve men, who were at that time absent a hunting; and immediately killed and scalped the whole party, except one woman and two or three of the children. With the most wanton and savage cruelty, they proceeded to put one of these little ones to death, by first turning him for a short time close before a fire, when they cut off one of his arms, and told him to run; and afterwards cruelly tortured him, with the other children, till he died.[293]

Jackson Johonnet was captured by the Kickapoo.

> The second day after we were taken, one of my companions, by the name of George Aikins, a native of Ireland, became so fraught with hunger and fatigue that he could proceed no further. A short council was immediately held among the Indians who guarded us, the result of which was that he should be put to death; this was no sooner determined on than a scene of torture began. The captain of the guard approached the wretched victim, who lay bound upon the ground, and with his knife made a circular incision on the skull; two others immediately pulled off the scalp; after this, each of them struck him on the head with their tomahawks; they then stripped him naked, stabbed him with their knives in every sensitive part of the body, and left him, weltering in blood, though not quite dead, a wretched victim of Indian rage and hellish barbarity.[294]

Scalping was the practice almost everywhere, and, contrary to revisionist legend, was not introduced to the Indians by the Dutch. John Wilson describes it among the Micmac:

> These Indians chain the unfortunate prisoner to a large thick tree, and bind his hands and his feet, then beginning from the middle of the cranium, they cut quite round towards the

> neck; this being done, they then tear off the skin, leaving the skull bare; an inflammation quickly follows, the patient fevers, and dies in the most exquisite tortures.[295]

Parkman tells of his conversation in 1846 with an Ogillallah chief who boasted of burning to death a member of the Snake tribe.[296]

The "captivity narrative," usually including accounts of torture, became a recognized genre of American literature, and reports stretch all the way from first contact up to the closing of the American frontier in the 1890s—when Mounties and Texas Rangers finally galloped onto the scene.

Why torture?

A part of the torture, apparently, was to mock the victim. This was not some solemn, if ghastly, religious ritual. It was entertainment. Jesuit witnesses write, of a Huron torture session:

> But ... what was most calculated in all this to plunge him [the victim] into despair, was their raillery, and the compliments they paid him when they approached to burn him. This one said to him, "Here, uncle, I must burn thee," and afterwards this uncle found himself changed into a canoe. "Come," said he, "let me calk and pitch my canoe, it is a beautiful new canoe which I lately traded for; I must stop all the water holes well," and meanwhile he was passing the brand all along his legs. Another one asked him, "Come, uncle, where do you prefer that I should burn you?" and this poor sufferer had to indicate some particular place. At this, another one came along and said, "For my part, I do not know anything about burning; it is a trade that I never practiced," and meantime his actions were more cruel than those of the others. In the midst of this heat, there were some who tried to make him believe that he was cold. "Ah, it is not right," said one, "that my uncle should be cold; I must warm thee." Another one added, "Now as my uncle has kindly deigned to come and die among the Hurons, I must make him a present, I must give him a hatchet," and with that he jeeringly applied to his feet a red-hot hatchet. Another one likewise made him a pair of stockings from old rags, which he afterwards set on fire; and often, after having made him utter loud cries, he asked him, "And now, uncle, hast thou had enough?" And when he replied, "*onna chouatan, onna,*" "Yes, nephew, it is enough, it is enough," these barbarians replied, "No, it is not enough," and continued to burn him at intervals, demanding of him every time if it was enough. They did not fail from time to time to give him something to

> eat, and to pour water into his mouth, to make him endure until morning.[297]

Not only prisoners of war were tortured. Anyone outside the tribe, apparently, was fair game, if a bit of good fun was required. "Last year, on the 19th of October," say the Relations,

> ...Abdon [a chief of the Upper Algonquins] with his troop, returning from the war, brought to the Three Rivers a prisoner who was not Hiroquois, but their neighbor and friend: behold them suddenly resolving to burn him. ...They pierce one foot of this poor man with a stick, and atrociously tear out his finger-nails,—he held out his hand and gave his fingers, as if he had felt nothing: they tie both his wrists with cords with running knots, and four young men pull and fasten the cords with all their might, tearing and removing the flesh of his arms even to the bones. The pain causes him to fall in a swoon; they cease to torture him, throw water upon him, and give him food, in order to revive him for the torments; the wood was already prepared for burning him, and the night of this tragedy was about to begin."

"But," the Jesuit chronicler reports happily, "at evening, by good fortune, there arrived a canoe from Quebec, with letters from Monsieur the Governor to Sieur des Rochers, who commands at the Three Rivers, — to the end that he should ransom and release the prisoner,—which he did with much difficulty, for rage and vengeance possessed the hearts of those Barbarians."[298]

Not just a river in Africa

Revisionist historians in recent years have cast doubts on just how widespread Indian torture was. Believing devoutly in the goodness of the Noble Savage, they argue that, "captivity narratives" having become a popular genre, there was an obvious incentive for authors to fake details to make them as lurid as possible. Sells more tabloids, after all. They also sometimes argue that we see here a clash of cultural values; no doubt the Indians similarly found some of our European ancestors' behaviour barbaric. Their final point is that such stories might have been useful as propaganda to justify settlers encroaching on Indian land.

These objections, I submit, do not hold up on close inspection. To deal with the last first, if the local Indians were not brutal, the settler reaction in inventing such blood-curdling stories would seem far over the top. Why would they be so set against Indians as to promote such slanders? If farming the land might conceivably have put a crimp in Indian hunting practices, Indians following their traditional hunting practices did not really much interfere with farming the land; especially for these early settlers. Having Indians nearby should, on the other hand, be useful, so long as they did not enslave or torture: for showing what local plants were edible, explaining how to survive the local winter, to trade for mutual profit, for extra farm labour during the harvest, and so forth. Land envy does not seen sufficient to account for the evidence.

Granted, once the Europeans and Indians were already at war, there might be cause to invent atrocity stories, just as they have been invented in European wars. But the need to take land from Indians does not account for them. And many of the atrocity stories are told of tribes with which the reporting parties were not at war.

The yellow journalism charge is on its face more plausible. But note that many of the accounts we selected are from early Jesuits and explorers, who already find the practice of torture widespread and in a variety of tribes. It is hard to believe that they, writing well before there was any established genre, are already playing to the cheap seats. Moreover, it challenges belief that men who have sacrificed everything to their faith—homeland, family, and life itself—would casually disregard one of its basic tenets, that one ought not bear false witness against one's neighbour.

Finally, there is the matter of physical evidence. It is fairly easy to see if a thumb really has been cut off, or if a heart is missing from a corpse. And, in many of these cases, it is not just one man's testimony: we have multiple witnesses, of good moral character.

It might also be observed that those who knew the Indians best, the earliest settlers and those on the frontier, were those most inclined to accept these stories. Detroit's inhabitants, at the time on the far frontier of settlement, wrote in 1811 this poetic resolution pleading for government protection from the Indians: "The tenderest infant, yet imbibing nutrition from the *mamilia* of maternal love, and the agonized mother herself, alike wait the stroke of the relentless tomahawk.... Nothing which breathes the breath of life is spared.... It is in the dead of night, in the darkness of the moon, in the howling of the [wolf] that the demoniac deed is done."[299] Academics now and those back home in Britain then are and were most likely to doubt the tales; not those in the best position to know.

Even were all this not so, the tales of torture are so universal, it lends credence on the simple principle that where there is a choking smoke, there is also apt to be a fire.

Cultural relativism

Most disturbing is the idea that this is simply a clash of cultural values, and Indians are entitled to their own morality whether we like it or not. Morality is absolute, or it does not exist. Just because you live in Nazi Germany does not make it okay to kill Jews.

Accordingly, cultures can be more or less moral, just as can individuals. Torture is immoral. To suggest it isn't is morally appalling.

There might be circumstances in which dire necessity might justify it, but even so, where is the dire necessity here? Torture was not used to extort information. It did not even have some ritual aspect. It was done for no immediate practical purpose whatever.

It is, I think, important to note one aspect of this torture ritual: all members of the tribe took part. Indeed, all members of the tribe seem to have been forced to take part. We see repeatedly an insistence that women and children, not just the brawny men, act as torturers.

Why might this be?

People who are caught in an objectively evil culture, I submit, always know that what they are doing is wrong. We all have a conscience, and morality is not subject to where you live. Were this not so, the Nuremberg Trials would have been illegitimate.

Accordingly, there is always a guilty conscience for individuals. There is therefore a natural eagerness to implicate others in any social crime: "Look–he's as bad as or worse than I am!" It is never tolerable for any member of the group to stand aloof. For this automatically appears as a condemnation of the act, and the consciences of the perpetrators cannot tolerate it.

At the same time, if you can implicate everyone in the crime from an early age, they are less likely to turn against the practice, or you, later. Doing so would force them to confront the fact that they themselves have done something wrong.

And so, guilt loves company.

We seem to see this in the account of Father Jogues. He reports,

> An old man takes my left hand and commands a captive Algonquin woman to cut one of my fingers; she turns away three or four times, unable to resolve upon this cruelty; finally, she has to obey, and cuts the thumb from my left hand; the same caresses are extended to the other prisoners.[300]

After this general cutting off of thumbs, a lesson for the little ones:

> [T]hey made us lie down on pieces of bark, binding us by the arms and the feet to four stakes fastened in the ground in the

> shape of Saint Andrew's Cross. The children, in order to learn the cruelty of their parents, threw coals and burning cinders on our stomachs,—taking pleasure in seeing us broil and roast.[301]

Among the Nootka, Sproat observes the same concern to implicate the young:

> Part of a day is given up to an instruction of those children who are to be initiated, and it is impressed upon them that the *Klooh-quahn-nah* must always be kept up, or evil will happen to the tribe. The tendency, no doubt, and probably the intention of this human sacrifice, and the whole celebration, is to destroy the natural human feeling against murder, and to form in the people generally, and especially in the rising generation, hardened and fierce hearts. They themselves say that their "hearts are bad," as long as it goes on. In the attendant ceremonies, their children are taught to look, without any sign of feeling, upon savage preparations for war, strange dances performed in hideous masks, and accompanied by unearthly noises, and occasionally, at least, upon the cruel destruction of human life. Although I have no direct evidence of the fact, I believe that part of the course of those to be initiated would be to view, howl over, and perhaps handle, or even stick their knives into the dead body of the victim, without showing any sign of pity or of horror.[302]

This is probably the worst thing about immoral cultures. They make it impossibly hard for any individual to remain moral. They forever present the good with ethical dilemmas; they tempt and groom for immorality. This is why they need to be rejected, claims of "cultural genocide" be damned.

Let us make one thing clear. It is crucially important to do so, because too many today are inclined to confuse race with culture. It is wrong to blame these atrocities on "the Indians," as individual human beings, or as a racial group, or assume any one of us would not behave about the same in similar circumstances. Indians were the victims as much as the torturers. A poisonous culture puts every individual in an impossible moral quandary. We have the example of Nazi Germany, where "civilized" Europeans behaved almost as badly. We have the famous Milgram experiment, in which American grad students acted as willing torturers so long as they thought they were being asked by someone in authority.[303]

It is certain some Indians disliked what they were asked to do. They knew it was wrong. Almost every account of torture also includes an account of one Indian or another secretly bringing aid or succor to the victim. Susannah Johnson, captured in a raid on Charlestown, New Hampshire, by the Abenaki in 1754, reports her

Indian captor eventually said, through her interpreter, "'I could not sleep last night ... She may have her child! I cannot withhold it from her any longer!'" And, with the returned child, she also gave clothing and several presents.[304]

Father Bressani, tortured by the Iroquois for months, was sometimes done a kindness when some Indian could be sure he was not seen. "When Bressani, tortured by the tightness of the cords that bound him, asked an Indian to loosen them, he would reply by mockery, if others were present; but if no one saw him, he usually complied."[305]

People do have a conscience.

The inclusion of such details also tends to discredit the claim that such stories were fabricated as anti-Indian propaganda.

Of course, it is also possible that only those captives lucky enough to find compassionate Indians survived to tell the tale.

In any group of people, there are some good and some bad, probably in about the same proportions. But just as people are not all good, neither are societies. As with Nazi Germany, or Sodom and Gomorrah, some societies can be utterly immoral. When a culture is bad, we fellow humans surely have the right and the responsibility to root it out.

The miracle of 1812

Just as Indian torture played a role in the American War of Independence, it seems to have been crucial, fortunately and unfortunately, in the sequel, the War of 1812.

It is an abiding mystery, on the numbers, how weak little Canada emerged from that conflict intact. The statistical advantage held by the Americans, after all, was overwhelming. The situation was little better than that outlined for Carleton's time. The United States had 7,500,000 residents; Canada had 500,000. Jefferson thought conquest would be "a mere matter of marching." Canadians still congratulate themselves on the remarkable "victory." That's victory, of course, in Canadian terms: for "victory," read "survival."

This time, unlike during the Revolutionary War, the British had no particular need to restrain their Indian allies. The rift with the Americans was already permanent.

And so, Tecumseh and his warriors were a major factor. Several of the most important British-Canadian victories were wrought from sheer American fear of being tortured by Indians.

Begin with Sir Isaac Brock's miracle of Detroit, almost the first action of the war. Hopelessly outnumbered by the Americans under General Hull, General Brock had the Indians parade in a circle outside the fort, passing repeatedly through a clearing into view, making their numbers appear larger. He then sent a note to his American adversary: "It is far from my intention to join in a war of extermination, but you must be aware, that the numerous body of Indians who have attached themselves to my troops, will be beyond control the moment the contest commences."[306]

That did it. After taking some time to ponder, but almost without a shot, General Hull struck his colours. A mixed group of 1,300 under Brock took prisoner 2,500 Americans, and their well-appointed fort, gateway to the upper lakes.

Similar scenarios played out elsewhere. On May 29, 1813, a boatload of American troops rowed out to Captain John Richardson, commanding a British warship on Lake Ontario, under a white flag. They petitioned to be allowed to surrender, Richardson reports, and "claim our protection as prisoners of war against the savages on the shore."[307] He noted that the Americans were all armed. And they were followed by a second boatload making the same request. In the summer of 1813, there were stories among the Americans of a raiding party that had been found "most shockingly butchered, their heads skinned, their hearts taken out and put in their mouths, their privates cut off and put in the places of their hearts."[308] You might say it was disheartening.

And then there was the Battle of Beaver Dams.

You have probably heard of Laura Secord, who walked her weary milk cow through 20 miles—sorry, 32 kilometres—of rough terrain to warn the British of an American attack?

Have you heard the rest of the story? Whom she reported to, and what he did with the information?

The officer's name was James FitzGibbon, as much as Secord a hero of Canadian history. FitzGibbon, forewarned, asked several hundred Mohawk in the area to wait in ambush. They waylaid the American column where the main road was flanked on either side with trees. The Indians were heavily outnumbered, but, hidden in the forest, the Americans could not fire on them effectively, and could not see how many there were. The sound of the war-whoops was terrifyingly effective on American morale.

FitzGibbon then marched his own scant band of regulars, in view, to block the American retreat. This was a brash and purely psychological move: although he did his best to mask their low numbers, had the Americans charged his line, they would have easily overwhelmed it.

But the bluff worked. The Americans now thought themselves surrounded and cut off.

FitzGibbon then cooly approached the Americans under flag of truce, and demanded surrender "in order to avoid unnecessary bloodshed," saying he "could not possibly control the Indians for more than another five minutes."[309] At this time, unknown to the Americans, the Mohawks were already withdrawing, feeling they could accomplish no more.

Nerves shattered, the American commander agreed to surrender if FitzGibbon would guarantee, on his honour as a British officer, they would not be harmed by the Indians. FitzGibbon dramatically promised, if necessary, "to give his life in their defense." With a force of 46 muskets, plus 250 Indian irregulars only loosely under his command, FitzGibbon accepted the surrender of 554 American officers and men, two cannon, two cars of ammunition, and the regimental colours.

Were American fears unfounded? Probably not. The Indians in these cases outnumbered the British. Accordingly, the British did not dare press hard any restraint on their allies, any more than the French could in their day. There are many credible reports of real Indian atrocities during this time, some of them given by British officers.

And that, perhaps, was really how and why little Canada survived the War of 1812.

One remarkable thing about Indian torture is how little practical justification for it there seems to have been. It was not done, like waterboarding or the Spanish Inquisition, to extract information. One can imagine that it might work as a force multiplier—if only one tribe did it. It seems to have been just that in the War of 1812. But that was only possible when there was a non-torturing party alongside, here the British regulars, to play "good cop." In inter-Indian conflict, this was not the case. The chance of torture after capture was just as likely then to convince opponents to fight to the last man and the last breath rather than surrender.

So Indian torture seems to have been done just for fun.

How did it happen that almost every Indian group seems to have done it?

Some people are bullies. You grew up with some of them, back in the state of nature that is childhood. Some kids love to tie tin cans to doggies' tails, throw cats to see if they land on their feet, or blow up frogs with firecrackers. A certain percentage of people everywhere are psychopaths. They find pleasure by inflicting pain.

In any small group lacking a solid government structure to prevent it, the bullies are likely to take control. They want it more than anyone else, and they lack restraints in achieving their desires.

Indian bands, as the early Jesuits observed, or as Jared Diamond would attest, lacked much government. They were "*sans roi, sans loi, sans foi.*" For the most part, all available rule was mob rule. "[T]hey have neither political organization, nor offices, nor dignities, nor any authority, for they only obey their Chief through good will toward him," writes Father LeJeune.[310]

"Good will," however, might not be the precise term. Consider Jack and the choir in the novel *Lord of the Flies.* All it takes is a small band of bullies ready to cooperate for mutual advantage. In this "state of nature," without effective government, there is no mechanism to stop the bullies from taking charge: no primogeniture, no democracy, no secret ballot, no first nor fourth estate. It will happen sooner or later, probably sooner. Once they have it, the bullies will take pains to implicate everyone else in their crimes, ensuring their preferences and their power are preserved.

Hence, hell on earth.

And perhaps for many in the afterlife as well.

It is sad to have to outline such features of traditional First Nations culture. But it seems necessary in the face of the current dogma that all cultures are equally good, with the apparent exception of mainstream Canadian culture, and Indian culture must, as much as possible, be preserved.

Some cultures are, on balance, bad cultures; and some ideas are bad ideas.

12 OF ANTHROPOPHAGY AND ANTHROPOLOGY; OF CANNIBALS AND KINGS

Aztec eats; from the Florentine codex.

It feels like piling on to mention that many Canadian Indian groups were cannibals. This is not, after all, like slavery, torture, and killing of captives, a matter of objective morality. Torturing and killing are certainly not proper. But, once you have done this much, are you adding anything by eating the body? Why let good meat go to waste?

Indignities to a corpse are, of course, an offence in Canadian law. Do not, I urge you, try this at home. Anyone who "improperly or indecently interferes with or offers any indignity to a dead human body or human remains, whether buried or not, is guilty of an indictable offence and liable to imprisonment for a term not exceeding five years." But the Canadian law is based at least in part on the Christian belief in the resurrection—the victim is going to need that body again one day. It should not be considered binding on other cultures. As an Algonquin patiently explained to a Jesuit who objected to sharing in the unspeakable feast, "You have French taste, I have Indian. This is good meat for me."[311] It does not take a sophomore's expensive education to hit upon the idea of cultural relativism.

So dwelling on Indian cannibalism looks only like trying to prejudice the reader against native Canadians, just because their customs are not ours. Sauce for the Canada goose may not be sauce for the European gander.

have denied it. If they find it important enough to address, then we must as well—if only to dispel disinformation. If you want to revive traditional Indian culture, strictly speaking, this is one thing you are buying into.

Bite me!

William Arens argued, back in 1979,[312] that there were no first-hand accounts of human flesh eating among American Indians, or indeed any other hunter-gatherers worldwide. There was, in other words, no solid proof, just rural legend. Accordingly, it should be understood as a slander against the native American "other" by chauvinistic Europeans: a justification—the familiar line—for taking native land and pressing the natives into slavery. Neil Whitehead calls the cannibalism rumours "imperial propaganda."[313]

This position became widely popular among academics, and, perhaps even more, in the mainstream media. I heard it stated authoritatively and often, and not long ago. How, after all, could savages be so ignoble?

As anyone who has read up to this point must realize, this was always an odd claim. We have already seen first-hand accounts of cannibalism after torture from the Jesuit missionaries. Columbus, as soon as he arrived in America, heard of such dining habits among nearby tribes—the very word "cannibal" is a corruption of the term used for themselves by the Carib Indians of the West Indies. Peter Martyr, who accompanied Columbus, writes:

> The wild and mischievous people called cannibals, or Caribs, accustomed to eat men's flesh ... molest them (the locals) exceedingly, invading their country, taking them captive, killing and eating them. Such children as they take they geld to make them fat, as we do cock chickens and young hogs, and eat them when they are well fed. Of such as they eat, they eat not the entrails and extreme parts, as hands, feet, arms, neck, and head. The other most fleshy parts they preserve in store as we do bacon. Yet do they abstain from eating women, and count it vile.[314]

Cortes recounts similar tales. Bernardo Diaz, who accompanied Cortes as a footsoldier in Mexico, writes of the Aztecs "eating human meat, just like we take cows from the butcher's shops, and they have in all towns thick wooden jail-houses, like cages, and in them they put many Indian men, women and boys to fatten, and being fattened they sacrificed and ate them."[315] This is corroborated by other chroniclers, including Diego Munoz Carmago, who describes in Mexico "public butcher's shops of human flesh, as if it were of cow or sheep."[316]

These certainly claim to be first-hand accounts. Are all Europeans liars?

Arens and others retort that in 1503, Queen Isabella of Spain declared that slavery could only be imposed on peoples who were arguably better off as slaves—for example, those who practiced cannibalism among themselves, and who might otherwise be eaten, if not ransomed by the Spanish. Spain, after all, was a Christian country; it nominally respected the Christian prohibition on slavery.

The main thrust of Isabella's proclamation was to prohibit enslavement of native Americans as a general principle. But it unfortunately gave European newcomers in Spanish-dominated lands a motive to allege cannibalism everywhere. As a result, Arens feels justified in ignoring such accounts.

However, he seems to ignore that similar reports are given by French sources, although the French at this time had no great involvement in any slave trade and were not subject to this Spanish law. Etienne Brûlé, the first European to view Lake Ontario, Lake Huron, and Lake Superior, was dissected and devoured by Huron colleagues in 1632, according to the Indians themselves.[317] In 1528, his crew watched helplessly just beyond gunshot as Giovanni Verrazzano, celebrated discoverer of most of the East Coast of America, was offed and devoured on Guadalupe, during what, for obvious reasons, was his last voyage.

There are many more first-hand accounts in the Jesuit Relations. Among our witnesses is Saint Isaac Jogues, no slaver, who reports a time when his Iroquois captors were about to execute him in revenge for one of their warriors who had gone missing. "Happily ... a messenger arrived, who brought news that that warrior and his comrades about whom they were anxious were returning victorious, bringing twenty Abnaquiois prisoners.... Behold them all joyful; they leave the poor Father; they burn, they flay, they roast, they eat those poor victims, with public rejoicings."[318] Later in his captivity, he reported, "a Huron, desiring to reconnoître them [the Iroquois], was killed by an arquebus shot, and eaten by those Cannibals."[319]

If the word of a saint were not enough, Jogues's account of Mohawk practices is corroborated in detail by the Dutch Reformed minister, Johannes Megapolensis, who lived in Fort Orange on the edge of Mohawk territory at the time. He is, Francis Parkman notes, "very explicit as to cannibalism." Everyone in the village, Megopolensis explains, eats the arms, buttocks, and trunk of the victim, but the head and heart, as special delicacies, are reserved for chiefs.[320] To Megapolensis, the Mohawks were allies; Jogues was the nominal enemy. The Protestant minister had no motive to condemn the Indians, or to make Jogues's sufferings seem worse than they were.

Jesuit Father Francesco-Giuseppe Bressani was also captured and tortured by the Iroquois, and reports the same things Father Jogues saw. He describes a night of agony inflicted on a captive Algonquin.

"The following morning they roasted him alive. Then, because I had baptized him, they brought all his members, one by one, into the cabin where I was. Before my eyes they skinned and ate the feet and hands. The husband of the mistress of the lodge threw at my feet the dead man's head, and left it there a long while."[321] Another Jesuit records, "a Savage, having perceived Father Buteux and me mingling with the others, came up to us and said, full of joy and satisfaction, '*Tapoue kouetakiou nigamouau*'; 'I shall really eat some Hiroquois.' ... [S]ome of the Savages, addressing us, told us that this Hiroquois was one of those who the year before had surprised and killed three of our Frenchmen; ... and they even dared to ask some of our French if they did not want to eat their share of him, since they had killed our Countrymen."[322] Father LeJeune writes, "I have shown in my former letters how vindictive the Savages are toward their enemies, with what fury and cruelty they treat them, eating them after they have made them suffer all that an incarnate fiend could invent. This fury is common to the women as well as to the men, and they even surpass the latter in this respect."[323]

An Algonquin woman, taken with her children by the Iroquois in 1641, gives an especially wrenching account: "They took our little children, placed them on spits, held them to a fire, and roasted them before our eyes.... They looked at us, and cried with all their might. Our hearts were broken when we saw them roasting, all naked, before a slow fire.... After they had put the poor little babes to death by fire, they drew them off the spit to which they were fastened, threw them into their kettles, boiled them, and ate them in our presence."[324]

"In nearly every instance," writes David Scheimann, "the Iroquois ate parts of the bodies of war prisoners who had been tortured to death."[325]

You eat what you are

Nor was cannibalism a practice only of the Six Nations Iroquois. It seems to have been indulged in by all sorts of Indian groups. When Father Jean de Brébeuf and associates visited Neutral territory to scout the evangelical possibilities, they were welcomed by one Indian with the observation, "I've had enough of the dark-colored flesh of our enemies.... I wish to know the taste of white meat, and I will eat yours."[326] Champlain says the Algonquin, returning from a raid on the Iroquois, "attached to sticks in the prows of their canoes ... a dead body cut into quarters, to eat in revenge, as they said."[327]

Of the Huron, their special charges, the Jesuit priests who knew them best wrote "ere the faith had given them more light than they possessed in infidelity, [they] would not have considered that they committed any sin in eating their enemies, any more than in killing them."[328] Father Brébeuf and his colleague Lalemant report the painfully protracted torture of an Iroquois prisoner in their village. In the final dénouement, "one cut off a foot, another a hand, and almost at the same time a third severed the head from the shoulders, throwing it into the crowd, where some one caught it to carry it to the Captain Ondessone, for whom it had been reserved, in order to make a feast therewith. As for the trunk, it remained at Arontaen, where a feast was made of it the same day."[329]

Francis Parkman notes similar culinary preferences among the Ottawa at the siege of Fort William Henry during the Seven Years War. "[T]he missionary met troops of Indians conducting several bands of English prisoners along the road that led through the forest from the camp of Lévis. Each of the captives was held by a cord made fast about the neck; and the sweat was starting from their brows in the extremity of their horror and distress.... He presently saw a large number of them [the Ottawa] squatted about a fire, before which meat was roasting on sticks stuck in the ground; and, approaching, he saw that it was the flesh of an Englishman, other parts of which were boiling in a kettle, while near by sat eight or ten of the prisoners, forced to see their comrade devoured."[330] Parkman gives his own source as Bougainville, *Journal de l'Expédition contre le Fort George*. Since this is a French author of some authority, and the incident reflects badly on the French and their allies, indeed on the correspondent who is unable to stop it, it is worthy of credence.

In a later incident during the same action, English prisoners are taken from a boat. "Three of the bodies were eaten on the spot."[331]

Turnabout being fair play, George Schuyler gives the following anecdote of the Nine Years' War (1690s): "The Indians after their natural barbarity did cut the enemies' dead to pieces, roasted them and eat them." Colden relates. "Major Schuyler, (as he told me himself) going among the Indians at that time, was invited to eat broth with them, which some of them had ready boiled, which he did, till they, putting the ladle into the kettle to take out more, brought out a Frenchman's hand, which put an end to his appetite."[332]

At the siege of Fort Detroit, during Pontiac's Rebellion, according to Parkman, the Ottawa tortured and killed forty-six British soldiers, after which they "fell upon their bodies, cut them in pieces, cooked, and ate them" within view of the fort.[333]

LaSalle, exploring the West, returned with similar tales of people-consumption. He describes a case in which the Cenis Indians had taken a captive, a woman from a neighbouring tribe. After elaborate torture, "At last, one of them gave her a stroke with a heavy club on the head, and another ran her stake several times into her body, with which she fell down dead on the spot. Then they cut that miserable victim into morsels, and obliged some slaves of that nation they had been long possessed of, to eat them."[334] Wasn't that a dainty dish to set before a king?

The "Nez Percé" (not the Pacific Northwest tribe identified by this name, but the Amikwa, of Lake Nipissing, later wiped out by the Iroquois) showed similar tastes. "On the eighth of June, the Captain of the Naiz percez, or Nation of the Beaver, which is three days journey from us, came to request one of our Frenchmen to spend the Summer with them, in a fort they had made from fear of the Aweatsiwaenrrhonon, or stinking tribe [the Winnebago—this is a typical example of an unflattering name given to a nearby band], who have broken the treaty of peace, and have killed two of their men, of whom they made a feast."[335]

Charles Darling writes, "according to Nadenltoc, Sitting Bull's band of Sioux Indians opened the breasts and devoured the hearts of the soldiers slain by them. The Creek and Blackfeet tribes are also said by Farrand, a missionary for fifteen years among them, to have eaten their prisoners on the field of battle."[336]

The first visitors to the Pacific Coast encountered man-eaters there as well. "Cook says that, upon his landing, the Nootka tribe brought to him for sale human skulls and hands not quite stripped of their flesh, which they made him understand they had eaten. Some of the bones also bore marks of having been on the fire."[337] Henry Coke speaks of Snake Indians eating dead bodies and killing their children for food.[338]

Among the Kwakiutl, there was a secret society known as the "Hamatsa"—a word that literally means "cannibals."

Did they mean it literally?

According to early missionaries, they did.

Garry Hogg, who collects a variety of such missionary reports in his 1958 book *Cannibalism and Human Sacrifice*, includes two accounts. One was near Fort Rupert, a Hudson's Bay Company post on the northern tip of Vancouver Island. Two missionary witnesses report. "A Kwakiutl shot and wounded a slave," they relate, "who ran away and collapsed on the beach at the water's edge. He was pursued by the tribesmen, including a group of the 'Bear Dancers' and Hamatsas. The slave's body was cut to pieces with knives while the Hamatsas squatted in a circle round them crying out their terrible cry: 'Hap! Hap! Hap! Hap!'" The two Europeans then "watched the Bear Dancers snatch up the flesh, warm and quivering, and growling like the Grizzly they represented, offer it to the Hamatsas in order of seniority."[339] On another occasion, "A Hamatsa demanded that [a] ... slave—this time a female—should dance for him. She stood a moment looking at him in terror, and said: 'I will dance. But do not get hungry. Do not eat me!' She had hardly finished speaking when her master, a fellow member of the tribe, split her skull open with an axe, and the Hamatsa thereupon began to eat her flesh."[340]

"These people are cannibals," writes Robert Haswell, of the Indians of the Northwest coast generally, "eating the flesh of their vanquished enemies, and frequently their slaves, whom they kill in cold blood. They have no hesitation in owning to the fact, and I myself have seen them eat human flesh."[341]

Soon after arriving as schoolteacher at Fort Simpson in the 1860s, William Duncan records in his journal:

> One morning I was called to witness a stir in the camp.... When I reached the gallery I saw hundreds of Tsimsheans sitting in their canoes, which they had just pushed away from the beach. I was told that the cannibal party were in search of a body to devour, and if they failed to find a dead one, it was probable they would seize the first living one that came in their way; so that all the people living near to the cannibals' house had taken to their canoes to escape being torn to pieces....
>
> These, then, are some of the things and scenes which occur in the day during the winter months, while the nights are taken up with amusements—singing and dancing.... The cannibal, on such occasions, is generally supplied with two, three, or four human bodies, which he tears to pieces before his audience. Several persons, either from bravado or as a charm, present their arms for him to bite. I have seen several whom he has thus bitten, and I hear two have died from the effects.[342]
>
> The other day we were called upon to witness a terrible scene: An old chief, in cool blood, ordered a slave to be dragged to the beach, murdered, and thrown into the water. His orders were quickly obeyed. The victim was a poor woman.... I did not see the murder, but, immediately after, I saw crowds of people running out of those houses near to where the corpse was thrown, and forming themselves into groups at a good distance away. This, I learnt, was from fear of what was to follow. Presently two bands of furious wretches appeared, each headed by a man in a state of nudity.... For some time they pretended to be seeking the body, and the instant they came where it lay they commenced screaming and rushing round it like so many angry wolves. Finally they seized it, dragged it out of the water, and laid it on the beach.... In a few minutes the crowd

> broke again in two, when each of the naked cannibals appeared with half of the body in his hands. Separating a few yards, they commenced, amid horrid yells, their still more horrid feast. The sight was too terrible to behold.[343]

Duncan also tells of a boy kidnapped and "torn to pieces by the mouths of a set of cannibals at a great feast."[344]

Hall Kelly, in his 1830 description of the Oregon country, identifies the Indians on the north side of the Juan de Fuca Strait—in British Columbia—as cannibals. Of those they took captive in war, he writes, in what sounds like an eyewitness account:

> One of these unhappy victims was sacrificed every moon, or as often as the occurrence of their festival days, in the following manner. A part, or the whole, of the slaves are collected at the sovereign chief's house, where they are compelled to join in the music and the dance. The inferior chiefs sing the war song, dance round the fire, throwing oil into it to make larger the flame. In the midst of this hellish mirth, the principal chief, dressed and painted in savage costume, and in the appearance of a ghostly demon, enters blindfolded; in this state he pursues the unhappy wretches, whose struggles and shrieks to escape his fearful hold create an awful moment of confusion, and thrill with horror the heart of stone; the fatal grasp is made; the knife is plunged into the heart and the infernal shout announces the silence of the devoted victim; it is immediately cut into pieces; a reeking parcel is given to each of the guests, who, like dogs, seize the quivering flesh, and while they devour it, the blood runs from the mouth warm as in the current of life.[345]

Among the Dene, in the Hospital of the Sacred Heart, writes Fr. Duchaussois in 1917, "they once had an old man who, in time of famine, had eaten his wife and his four children. He was in hospital, because feeble and paralysed, no longer able to go to the hunting grounds. The Infirmarian Sister spent a long time instructing him and preparing him for eternity. The day before his death, he called her, and said confidentially, 'If I had a little human flesh, I think it would do me good.'"[346]

Some Inuit too practised spirit cooking. Akpatok Island in Ungava Bay was known for the practice, until its inhabitants vacated the site and melded into the mainland population in 1900. Rather like Hannibal Lecter. An unidentified native group in Labrador is reported to have offered sailors human skulls, hands and feet with the flesh still on them in barter.[347]

Note that many of our eyewitness reports are from missionaries. Besides their being in closest contact with the Indians in their home territory, I submit that this is some evidence of their good moral character.

James White, in his *Handbook of Indians of Canada* (1913), writing before the days of political correctness, gives some sense of how widespread the practice was:

> Among the tribes which practised [cannibalism], in one or another of these forms, may be mentioned the Montagnais, and some of the tribes of Maine; the Algonkin, Armouchiquois, Micmac, and Iroquois; farther west the Assiniboine, Cree, Foxes, Miami, Ottawa, Chippewa, Illinois, Kickapoo, Sioux, and Winnebago; in the south the people who built the mounds in Florida, and the Tonkawa, Attacapa, Karankawa, Kiowa, Caddo, and Comanche ...; in the northwest and west portions of the continent, the Thlingchadinneh and other Athapascan tribes, the Tlingit, Heiltsuk, Kwakiutl, Tsimshian, Nootka, Siksika, some of the Californian tribes, and the Ute. There is also a tradition of the practice among the Hopi, and allusions to the custom among other tribes of Arizona and New Mexico. The Mohawk, and the Attacapa, Tonkawa, and other Texas tribes were known to their neighbours as "man-eaters."[348]

Quite the guest list. Is anyone forgotten?

No $#!+

Given the weight of evidence, denial of the practice is remarkable evidence again of how powerful the appeal of the Noble Savage archetype is: mighty enough to make anthropologists willfully ignore the record.

Granted, as previously noted, written texts are not often the stuff of anthropology; the field generally depends either on interviews with living people, or the archaeological remains. Which is to say, digging through other people's garbage.

Living Indians are adamant that none of their ancestors was ever a cannibal. And, as we all know, Indian accounts of Indian tradition never lie.

The archaeological record, however, lately did this academic orthodoxy in. In September 2000, *Nature* published a new study that included a chemical analysis on human feces found in an Anasazi Indian site from around 1250 AD. Feces—the sort of thing serious anthropologists could really sink their teeth into.

The analysis turned up myoglobin, a human protein which apparently could only come to be there from eating human tissue.[349]

The test, mind, was done in the first place because archaeological sites across the American Southwest featured human bones from which the flesh seemed to have been cut or torn off.

What is true of the one site is probably, per Occam's razor, true of the others generally: one explanation is better than many different ones for the same observed evidence.

It appears this bone-stripping was not some religious ritual for interring the dead. It was food preparation.

How common, then, was cannibalism? Rare, or well done?

The Noble Savage lobby now resorts to claiming it was an unusual practice with religious significance. God made them do it.

Unusual, no doubt; human flesh is usually dearly bought. Moose and muskrat are not nearly so good at fighting back. But just how unusual?

Usual enough that the Jesuit Father Raguéneau estimated offhand of the prominent Algonquin convert Le Berger that "he had eaten his share of more than fifty men."[350]

His First Confession must have been interesting.

Father Lalemant observes of the Huron, "they eat human flesh with as much appetite and more relish than hunters eat the meat of deer."[351] Father Vimont makes an almost identical comment: "When the supper was cooked, these wolves devoured their prey; one seized a thigh, another a breast; some sucked the marrow from the bones; others broke open the skulls, to extract the brains. In a word, they ate the flesh of men with as much appetite as, and with more pleasure than, hunters eat that of a Boar or of a Stag."[352]

Not exactly a steady diet, granted; but not a rare religious ritual in which the act of eating is minimal.

Something reserved for special occasions.

Like turkey

13 MOTHER RIGHT AND FATHER LEFT

Among some interior Salish and Kootenay, it was customary to flatten women's heads to make them more attractive. *Paul Kane*.

> *A hunting Indian one day called at a farm-house for some food. The good woman of the house began asking him all sorts of questions. At length she pointed to a shaking aspen tree, and asked the Indian, "What do you call that?"*
>
> *He replied, "Me call it woman's tongue."*
>
> *"Why do you call it woman's tongue?" was the next question.*
>
> *The Indian then said, "You see those leaves always shaking, never stand still; some call it woman's tongue."*
>
> *– Ojibway joke, retold by the Rev. Peter Jones, aka* Kahkewaquonaby[353]

The Noble Savage, in his politics, is clearly a man of the left. He is both a communist and a feminist.

For feminism has its own version of the Noble Savage myth. Once again, Canadian Indians figure prominently. It bears some consideration here.

In her 1972 book *Wonder Woman*, Gloria Steinem tells the tale:

> Once upon a time, [yes, she really begins like that] the many cultures of this world were all part of the gynocratic age. Paternity had not yet been discovered, and it was thought ... that women bore fruit like trees—when they were ripe. Childbirth was mysterious. It was vital. And it was envied. Women were worshiped because of it, were considered superior because of it.... Men were on the periphery—an

> interchangeable body of workers for, and worshipers of, the female center, the principle of life.[354]

Ah, the days of primordial innocence. Ah, the days of not knowing where babies come from. Ah, the days of fruit ripening on every tree. Among other marvellous things, women then were given far more freedom and respect. There was perfect equality, and, of course, in said perfect equality, women were worshiped and men were consigned to the periphery. Don't quibble—this is dream logic. Shut up. There was perfect peace, justice, equality and domination. There was no private property. Everything was shared as needed. Especially sex.

Then someone—doubtless not a woman—bit an apple. Writing was invented. Knowledge of good and evil, of conventional bourgeois ethics, came to be. And all happiness fled, like a snaking wisp of ganja smoke, like an old acetate reel on fire, like waking from a pleasant dream. We learned, in short, we were naked.

> The discovery of paternity, of sexual cause and childbirth effect, was as cataclysmic for society as, say, the discovery of fire or the shattering of the atom. Gradually, the idea of male ownership of children took hold....
>
> ... [W]omen gradually lost their freedom, mystery, and superior position. For five thousand years or more, the gynocratic age had flowered in peace and productivity. Slowly, in varying stages and in different parts of the world, the social order was painfully reversed. Women became the underclass, marked by their visible differences.[355]

It was and is an appealing bedtime story, ringing all the old romantic chimes of original innocence, while furthering a feminist agenda. An unkind observer, mind, might note the suspicious lack of evidence, and the odd coincidence that such female-dominated societies disappeared at the very point—the invention of writing—at which we might have hoped for some solid evidence. Rather like a map that marks, wherever there is undiscovered terrain, "There be dragons here." They must be here, after all, because we know there be dragons, and we find them nowhere else.

So too with Amazons.

One might also think, unworthily, that there be here perhaps a trace of wish fulfillment. Women were, Steinem suggests, the rightful mistresses of the universe, illegitimately deposed by those dirty, vile men. Like Scar in *The Lion King.*

What was Steinem's warrant for this idyll?

Swallowing Amazons

The first modern to seriously suggest the existence of a primordial matriarchy was the Swiss classical scholar Johann Bachofen, in 1861. He based his notion of prehistoric "Mother Right" on his interpretation of ancient myth, which he read as history. Astarte, Isis, Ceres as Earth Mother, Tiamat, that sort of thing.

Never mind that Greek mythology, or Semitic mythology, for that matter, as we know it, is fairly male-dominant: Zeus, Kronos, Apollo, Bull-El, Baal, Yahweh and the boys. Bachofen detected surviving traces, he believed, of an earlier layer.

It was tantalizing, but speculative. How historical, in the end, is myth? Did Daedalus really fashion working wings from wax and feathers? Do unicorns really lose their fierceness when resting their head in a virgin's lap?

Possibly not. Myths have their meanings, but they may not always be reportage.

There was one obvious test. If matriarchy really was the initial and natural order of mankind, some examples should remain today, among "primitive" people.

Enter, on cue, the trusty Canadian Indian. The proverbial, standby primitive for European purposes, and the most available subject of the then-dawning field of anthropology. Of course, the Indians must demonstrate this "Mother Right." Whether they like it or not.

And, happily, it turned out, on very first appearance, that they did.

The early and notable anthropologist Lewis Henry Morgan lived in Rochester, New York, in the old Seneca country. He therefore based his extensive research on the Iroquois. And, his researches soon revealed, the Iroquois were matrilineal. They traced descent in the female, rather than the male, line.

This, to contemporary thinkers, was a striking fact. It seemed proof that the Iroquois, along with the many other Indian tribes that shared this trait, were just such a matriarchy as Bachofen imagined.

Among those who quickly embraced and advanced this proof of primordial matriarchy was early feminist Matilda Gage, president of the National Woman Suffrage Association, colleague and collaborator of Elizabeth Cady Stanton. She wrote, in her popular book *Woman, Church, and State*:

> The famous Iroquois Indians, or Six Nations, showed alike in form of government, and in social life, reminiscences of the Matriarchate. The line of descent, feminine, was

> especially notable in all tribal relations such as the election of Chiefs, and the Council of Matrons, to which all disputed questions were referred for final adjudication. No sale of lands was valid without consent of the squaws....[356]

"A form of society existed at an early age known as the Matriarchate or Mother-rule," Gage explains with an air of authority, combining Bachofen's thesis with Morgan's. "Under the Matriarchate, except as son and inferior, man was not recognized in either of these great institutions, family, state or church. A father and husband as such, had no place either in the social, political or religious scheme; woman was ruler in each. The primal priest on earth, she was also supreme as goddess in heaven. The earliest semblance of the family is traceable to the relationship of mother and child alone."[357]

That sounds pretty definite. And, as one might expect of the Noble Savage, "never was justice more perfect," Gage assures us, "never civilization higher than under the Matriarchate."[358] Justice is achieved when female dominance is complete. No more of this nonsense about equality of the sexes. The human condition, it seems, has been on the skids ever since.

This matriarchate thesis helpfully added another huge battalion of the chattering classes to the lobby for Indian segregation and for preserving Indian culture. Gage herself was initiated into the Wolf clan, and fought like a Fury against American citizenship for the Iroquois. Whether that was pro- or anti-Indian, you decide.

Gage is clearly Steinem's authority on the matriarchate. All Steinem had to do was paraphrase.

Engels' angle

But to fully appreciate the influence of the Iroquois on modern feminism, we must cite a second authority: Karl Marx.

He and his co-author of *The Communist Manifesto*, Friedrich Engels, also read Morgan with interest.

Just like the feminists, the communists needed the Noble Savage archetype. Marx posited that all evil came from class oppression. It followed that, in a time when there were not yet classes, there must have been no oppression. Peace must have ruled the planet and love have steered the stars.

It was not just Morgan's research on the Iroquois that enthralled them. Morgan went on to propose a general theory of the development of the family in prehistoric times. In broad outline, it all began, he thought, with group sex, every tribal male "married" to every tribal female. Over time, with the material development of society, this shifted to monogamy. At the same time, tracing descent through the mother was replaced with descent through the father.

This fit well with Marx's own ideas. It was dialectical materialism, extended backwards into prehistory and drawing the institution of the family into its purview. Engels writes, "Morgan in his own way had discovered afresh in America the materialistic conception of history discovered by Marx forty years ago, and in his comparison of barbarism and civilization it had led him, in the main points, to the same conclusions as Marx."[359] If Morgan was right, this was an important confirmation of Marx. Even better, Morgan had found that Iroquois longhouses held all significant property in common. They were, in effect, a working communist society—with all the natural appeal to Marxists that a supposed matriarchy had to feminists.

And so, Engels, in a book-length endorsement of Morgan's ideas, heralded him as one of the great thinkers of the age, right up there with Darwin and Marx. Engels writes, "This rediscovery of the primitive matriarchal gens as the earlier stage of the patriarchal gens of civilized peoples has the same importance for anthropology as Darwin's theory of evolution has for biology and Marx's theory of surplus value for political economy"[360]—a view still held by modern Marxists.

It does not seem obviously required by their own purposes for Marx and Engels to also endorse the idea that Iroquois society, and all early society, was a matriarchy. Nevertheless, it was helpful: if differentiation of labour is the root of all evil, then any differentiation in the roles of men and women in the family must have been the original sin. And so, like Gage, Marx and Engels took Morgan's "discovery" of original matrilineal descent as proving matriarchy. Morgan buttressed Marx; and Bachofen buttressed Morgan. Put them all together, and you see the outlines of a solid new materialist science of human history. Inevitable human progress ensues.

Engels therefore concludes, "Communistic housekeeping ... means the supremacy of women in the house.... Among all savages and all barbarians of the lower and middle stages, and partly even of the upper stage, the position of women is not only free, but highly respected.... The communistic household ... is the material foundation of that supremacy of the women which was general in primitive times."[361]

Again we see the dream logic that equality requires the supremacy of women. But now Indians are lashed in not just to the matriarchy but to communism, adding another phalanx of intellectual footsoldiers to the Noble Savagists.

And Engels is right on the communism bit. Iroquois longhouses were indeed communist. Indian reservations are communist today. Nobody owns their house or land. This is, perhaps, one reason for their poverty. Nobody has collateral for a loan, nobody has the incentive to strive economically.

But this revelation seems less than earth-shattering. All families are naturally communist: from each according to their abilities, to each according to their needs, given that all parties are acting morally. Indian social order does not progress much beyond the family; tribes are small and interrelated. And, in the end, Indians simply lacked the social mechanisms to protect private property. Moreover, for most Indian tribes, being nomadic, it was not practical to own anything you could not carry on your back. When you are poor enough, private property is a moot point. Was this a good thing?

But it was all most useful for Engels and Marx. Not only was communism now demonstrably possible as a governmental system: it was revealed as the "natural" order of mankind.

"The overthrow of mother right," writes Engels, cementing the feminist alliance, "was the world historical defeat of the female sex. The man took command in the home also; the woman was degraded and reduced to servitude; she became the slave of his lust and a mere instrument for the production of children."[362] The first class distinction was between male and female; the first private property was the wife; and the first oppressive government was the monogamous family. "The modern family contains in germ not only slavery (*servitus*) but also serfdom, since from the beginning it is related to agricultural services. It contains in miniature all the contradictions which later extend throughout society and its state."[363]

One begins to understand where modern feminism comes from.

"Monogamous marriage," Engels explains, "comes on the scene as the subjugation of the one sex by the other, as the proclamation of a conflict between the sexes unknown throughout the whole previous prehistoric period. In an old unpublished manuscript written by Marx and myself in 1846 I find the words: 'The first division of labour is that between man and woman for the propagation of children.'"[364]

Children are the problem. The little miscreants.

> And today I can add: The first class antagonism that appears in history coincides with the development of the antagonism between man and woman in monogamous marriage, and the first class oppression coincides with that of the female sex by the male.[365]

So there you have it. Women are the long-suffering proletariat, and men the bloated, selfish, cigar-chomping bourgeoisie. Marriage is oppression, children are oppression; and the communist utopia temptingly promises free sex.

The second wave hits the fan

Feminism as originally conceived had achieved its goals by the 1920s. Women had the vote. Feminism's two most notable secondary goals, prohibition and eugenics, had also by then been generally enacted, at least for a time. The fact that neither turned out well is a separate issue; although that did tend to take the stuffing out of the movement for a generation or two.

Then, in the 1960s, the women's movement booted up again. Why? What had changed? What again made it seem necessary? What were the pressing new goals?

What devotees call "second wave" feminism was more or less single-handedly kickstarted, many say, by Betty Friedan's *The Feminine Mystique* in 1963.[366]

It is probably important to note that Friedan was a committed Marxist.

She did not reveal this at the time. Then, and ever after, Friedan was adamant that until she researched and wrote that book, she was a typical suburban housewife, with no interests beyond that station.

This self-representation has since been debunked, notably by Daniel Horowitz.[367] Friedan had for at least the previous quarter century been a devoted Stalinist and a frequent writer—an ideologue, in party terms—for Marxist publications.

Why the deception?

Friedan, after all, was virtually quoting Engels.

Engels writes "all that this Protestant monogamy achieves, taking the average of the best cases, is a conjugal partnership of leaden boredom, known as 'domestic bliss.'"[368]

Friedan begins *The Feminine Mystique*:

> The problem lay buried, unspoken, for many years in the minds of American women. It was a strange stirring, a sense of dissatisfaction, a yearning that women suffered in the middle of the 20th century in the United States. Each suburban wife struggled with it alone. As she made the beds, shopped for groceries … she was afraid to ask even of herself the silent question—"Is this all?"[369]

In the climate of the early Sixties, in America, it would not do to make this Marxist provenance plain. The House Committee on Un-American Activities was still in operation. Khrushchev had only recently openly denounced Stalin's misrule. If it were too easy to connect the red dots, Friedan no doubt knew, her project could not have gained popular acceptance. And where would the revolution be then?

Having read Engels, she, as a Marxist, doubtless saw feminism as an element of the class struggle. She was fighting to bring into being Engels's and Marx's communist dream. The monogamous family was the root of social oppression. Overthrow the family, and you have the classless utopia.

Or at least group sex, as per Morgan's theories, endorsed by Engels. Which might have sounded almost as good to the bored suburban housewife of the Fifties.

Or for that matter the repressed Victorian matron of the 1890s. Engels wrote in 1884; Gage wrote in 1893.

Gage dedicates her 1893 book "to all Christian women and men, of whatever creed or name who, bound by Church or State, have not dared to Think for Themselves." Christianity, or Christian ethics, was the ultimate enemy. Engels also turns up his nose at "conventional" morality, which he calls, ironically for a materialist, "philistine."[370] The term "liberated woman," popular in Friedan's day, had certain connotations connecting it with the contemporaneous "sexual revolution."

For non-Marxists in particular, this was probably the bait. Buy the concept that women have traditionally been oppressed, and, male or female, you get a blank cheque for unrestricted sex without responsibility.

Along with communism, matriarchy, and equality of an oddly female-dominant sort, this unspoken promise of lots of wild, filthy sex was also projected back on the poor unsuspecting Indians. In *Little Big Man*, for example: Dustin Hoffman, as Jack Crabb, adopted by the Cheyenne, gets multiple wives. In 1973's *Papillon*, a sojourn in an Indian village is made to look attractive by the conspicuous presence of the lovely, and barking naked, Zoraima. Being Indian becomes a protracted sexual fantasy in Leonard Cohen's 1966 novel *Beautiful Losers*:

> Catherine Tekakwitha, who are you? Are you (1656-1680)? Is that enough? Are you the Iroquois Virgin? Are you the Lily of the Shores of the Mohawk River? Can I love you in my own way? I am an old scholar, better-looking now than when I was young. That's what sitting on your ass does to your face. I've come after you, Catherine Tekakwitha. I want to know what goes on under that rosy blanket.[371]

Which is to say, in an odd way, that Canadian Indians are inadvertently responsible for feminism, the New Left, and the sexual revolution.

The evidence

But enough of that fantasy, for now, and back to the core concept of Indian matriarchy. In the end, how plausible was it?

Unfortunately for the feminists, and possibly for the Indians, it was codswallop.

Significantly, none of this supposed female dominance, or even equality, was visible to early European explorers and missionaries. They tended to report the reverse, and lament the cruelty with which, to their minds, the Indians treated their women.

The pale ones noted that, among Indians, women did all the hard and heavy work, rather like Marx's proletariat, while men lived idly, like Marx's capitalists. "[T]he women ... bear all the burdens and toil of life," says Father Biard.[372] "The care of household affairs, and whatever work there may be in the family," explains Father Jouvency, speaking of the Indians of New France generally, "are placed upon the women. They build and repair the wigwams, carry water and wood, and prepare the food; their duties and position are those of slaves, laborers and beasts of burden."[373] Champlain writes that Huron women "have almost the entire care of the house and work; ...The women harvest the corn, house it, prepare it for eating, and attend to household matters. Moreover they are expected to attend their husbands from place to place in the fields, filling the office of pack-mule in carrying the baggage, and to do a thousand other things. All the men do is to hunt for deer and other animals, fish, make their cabins, and go to war."[374] Samuel Hearne writes of the women of the Northwest, "the whole course of their lives is one continued scene of drudgery, *viz.* carrying and hauling heavy loads, dressing skins for clothing, curing their provisions, and practicing other necessary domestic duties which are required in a family, without enjoying the least diversion of any kind, or relaxation, on any occasion whatever; and except in the execution of those homely duties, in which they are always instructed from their infancy, their senses seem almost as dull and frigid as the zone they inhabit."[375]

As to the Iroquois specifically, Morgan's subjects, "Currently, two words are used by the Iroquois to refer to women," explains William Starna. "The first is *wenon'towisas*, 'women.' The other is *nyeosjishaekaye*, 'she'll do the hoeing.'"[376]

This apparent exploitation of the labouring female class ought, one might think, to be a fatal problem for a Marxist. But Engels brushes it aside. "The reports of travellers and missionaries..." he writes, "to the effect that women among savages and barbarians are overburdened with work in no way contradict what has been said. The division of labour between the two sexes is determined by quite other causes than by the position of woman in society."

> Among peoples where the women have to work far harder than we think suitable, there is often much more real respect for women than among our Europeans. The lady of civilization, surrounded by false homage and estranged from all real work, has an infinitely lower social position than the hard working woman of barbarism, who was regarded among her people as a real lady [*frowa*, *Frau*—mistress] and who was also such in status.[377]

So living off the fruits of another's labour is not, after all, the core issue determining social dominance. It has instead primarily to do with descent being reckoned in your line.

Surely another example of the tremendous enchanting power of the Noble Savage myth.

So with modern feminism. Traditionally, and more so with modern labour-saving devices in the home, men do all the dangerous, dirty, and dull work, while women get to spend most of the capital—80 percent, on average. Yet Friedan and modern feminists see men as masters, and women as exploited. It inverts the Marxist theory of labour and of surplus value. The traditional deference of men toward women in the West, and the advantages they are traditionally given, Engels informs us, are not in their interest, but a tool of their oppression.

As to Indians showing no "false homage" toward woman, if this means any chivalry or sentimentality toward the "fairer sex," Engels is right. Of their frequent bouts of starvation, Father LeJeune writes, regarding the Innu, "When they reach this point, they play, so to speak, at 'save himself who can'; throwing away their bark and baggage, deserting each other, and abandoning all interest in the common welfare, each one strives to find something for himself. Then the children, women, and for that matter all those who cannot hunt, die of cold and hunger."[378] None of this sentimental nonsense about "women and children first."

And none of this sentimental nonsense about "from each according to his abilities to each according to his needs." The real historical communism, it appears, is nothing more than survival of the fittest and grab what one can. Cooperation for common ends? That is the essence of a developed civilization.

Champlain, European bourgeois that he is, is offended, at one point, to find a Huron cutting off the finger of a female prisoner, to commence the traditional torture. "I interposed," the French philistine explains, "and reprimanded the chief,

Iroquet, representing to him that it was not the act of a warrior, as he declared himself to be, to conduct himself with cruelty towards women, who have no defense but their tears, and that one should treat them with humanity on account of their helplessness and weakness; and I told him that on the contrary this act would be deemed to proceed from a base and brutal courage, and that if he committed any more of these cruelties he would not give me heart to assist them or favor them in the war."[379]

Sexist pig.

This deference toward women is one of the things modern feminism had to fight hardest against at its inception. This was why "consciousness-raising sessions" were so often required. Friedanites had to convince doubting middle-class women that they were better off not having doors opened for them, not having their meals out paid for, not being allowed to pursue what interested them at home; better off punching a time clock, working for wages by the sweat of their brow, and so on.

There was probably less resistance from men.

By the logic of Sixties feminism, Iroquet was acting properly, and Champlain was a chauvinist.

Still, one wonders, in the face of actual finger amputation, whether they were right.

The peace-loving Iroquois

But let's assume our consciousness has been raised by the proper re-education sessions. Eliminating special privileges for women, and having them do hard labour, is elevating their status. Fine. Still, since we were speaking of war, we have another problem with the matriarchy hypothesis as it applies to the Iroquois.

As argued by both feminists and Marxists, the existence of a communist, matron-ruled state ought to guarantee general peace.

But rather than justice and equality, we have slavery. Rather than peace, we have constant war in its most extreme form.

The Iroquois, cited by Morgan as the prime example of a matriarchy, were one of the most violent and warlike societies known to man. So were the Spartans, for that matter; another reputed matriarchy.

What? Aren't women by nature nurturing and non-competitive? Isn't there no longer any reason to fight when there is no private property?

Gage barely flutters an eyelash.

> Although the reputation of the Iroquois as warriors appears most prominent in history, we nevertheless find their real principles to have been the true Matriarchal one of peace and industry. Driven from the northern portion of America by vindictive foes, compelled to take up arms in self-protection, yet the more peaceful occupations of hunting and agriculture were continually followed.[380]

So in fact the Iroquois were pacifists, forced against their will to conquer all their vindictive neighbours, enslave them, torture them, exterminate them, their children, and all their works, and take their land. This is proven by the fact that they continued nevertheless to eat.

Procrustes, would that thou wert living at this hour.

Goddess worship

There are further problems for the matriarchy hypothesis. One of the strongest structural supports of the thesis since Bachofen is that "primitive people" worshiped "The Goddess." You've probably heard the claim. "The Goddess" experienced a major spiritual revival in the Seventies, when Merlin Stone published *When God Was a Woman.*[381] This book restated the old Bachofen thesis, adding new support from archaeology.

Or actually, not that much support. Part of Stone's argument was that the physical evidence of matriarchy had been systematically destroyed by later patriarchists. As with most conspiracy theories, the very lack of evidence was taken as evidence. European digs, however, were at the time turning up clay figures of an obese woman—obviously, "The Goddess." From her tiny clay loins, the new subculture of "feminist spirituality" was born. Which form of worship probably involved a liberal use of mirrors.

In the digs at Catalhoyuk, from 1961 to '65, just when it seemed relevant, such chubby terracotta females did keep emerging. At that point, it looked like a lot were; although more recent, more extensive, excavation has yielded a proportion of about 3% of all in-site figurines.[382]

Even if the proportion were much larger, that this demonstrated general worship of "The Goddess" seems a rather thin stretch of the intellectual bubble gum. There is actually a strong tendency in many religions, including, to cite a random list, Buddhism, Judaism, Islam and Protestant Christianity, to avoid depictions of the supreme godhead in graven form. Anyone who was depicted, or depicted so often, would actually by that fact in most religions have been shown to be a lesser personage.

Even in religions that in principle love images, like Catholicism or Hinduism, counting figurines does not seem an accurate theological measure. If, five thousand years from now, one were to excavate a typical Catholic church, one might easily conclude, by the preponderance of statues, that Catholics too worshiped "The Goddess."

Indeed, if one excavated a modern site at random, one might conclude that modern North Americans worshiped a goddess named "Barbie."

More recent scholars have pointed out that the "goddess" figurines of Catalhoyuk are usually found in ancient garbage dumps; not the obvious place for an object of religious veneration. Moreover, they were made without pedestals, meaning they could not have been used for worship at an altar.[383]

Moreover, without first buying in to Marxist theory, which was largely what needed to be demonstrated, it is not immediately obvious that the sex assigned to divinity has anything to do with which sex is dominant in society. It helps a lot, in order to hold such a thesis, to already believe in dialectical materialism. You must assume that religion is only a social construct of the ruling class to serve political ends. A masculine god is therefore there to justify masculine rule, a feminine goddess to justify female dominance. One might argue, instead, even if God is a social construct, that the common Judaeo-Christian conception of God as masculine is a matter of preference given to female worshipers. If God is love, and God is a man, who will find God easier and more natural to love, men or women? And, if God is a man, by this equation, the soul of the worshiper is naturally female. So indeed it has been traditionally depicted in either the Greek, Jewish, or Christian traditions. See Song of Songs. Or Hindu tradition, for that matter. See the Krishna Gopala cycle.

If you walk into a Christian church today, you will see many more female than male faces in the pews. There is a reason for this.

But never mind all that. There is a certain Marxist tradition here that must be honoured. To a good Marxist, can Marx and Engels ever be wrong? Surely not; admit that, and the entire edifice of scientific socialism could soon be Ozymandian dust. And Engels, based on Bachofen, wrote, "the position of the goddesses in ... [Greek] mythology, as Marx points out, refers to an earlier period when the position of women was freer and more respected."[384] So the matter is settled. Doubt is no longer an option. We must simply move on from here.

Gage concurs. Her status among feminists may not be comparable to Engels among Marxists, but she makes up for that by striving to sound authoritative. "In all the oldest religions, equally with the Semitic cults, the feminine was recognized as a component and superior part of divinity, goddesses holding the supreme place."[385] It must be true; sooner or later the necessary evidence will appear.

But leave aside for now our terracotta figurines and our unimpeachable ideological authorities. Once again, the Indians and especially the Iroquois ought to be our test case. If they are a matriarchy, and if the mythological theory is correct, they ought to still worship "The Goddess" in historical times. Do they?

Unfortunately, on the available evidence, no. In 1883, working for the Smithsonian, the ethnographer Erminnie Smith made a systematic effort to collect examples of Iroquois mythology. She found them, invariably, insisting that they and their ancestors always worshiped the definitely male "Great Spirit."[386]

Being herself a woman, and not therefore inclined to male bias, Smith helpfully suggests that nevertheless, such oral traditions are not reliable. The beliefs among Iroquois in 1883 may not actually have been their traditional beliefs. They might have been influenced and altered by contact with the larger society.

> The "Great Spirit," so popularly and poetically known as the god of the red man, and the "Happy Hunting-ground," generally reported to be the Indian's idea of a future state, are both of them but their ready conception of the white man's God and Heaven. This is evident from a careful study of their past as gleaned from the numerous myths of their prehistoric existence.[387]

Fair enough. Of course these traditions could have been altered. A point worth noting, when it comes to considering oral traditions generally. We may need to come back to that.

George Dawson, writing of the Tahltan in the late 19th century, indeed sees no evidence of a belief in a supreme being: "Their religious belief was simply what their medicine-men might lay down for them from time to time, the idea of a Supreme Being, being very obscure, if not altogether wanting."[388] "We have been able to find no term in their language to indicate that they had any idea of a Supreme Being such as God," writes Livingston Jones of the Tlingit. "The term they now use to designate the Supreme Being is *De-ke* (up) *On-Kowa* (Chief); that is, the Chief-above (God). This word was evidently coined after they had learned, through the missionaries, about God."[389] Father Hennepin writes, of the tribes he encounters generally, across the North American continent, "I have met with some of them, who seem to acknowledge that there is one first Principle that made all things; but this makes but a slight Impression upon their Mind."[390]

Our best source again, especially about the Iroquois, would be the early Jesuits. They were the folks who best knew the Indians at first or early contact, and they were, naturally, intensely curious about just this, the pre-existing native religious beliefs. It was, after all, their field.

On their evidence, the Iroquois may indeed not have worshiped a Great Spirit. He does not seem to turn up in their inquiries. The most important Iroquois divinity may even have been female—the evidence on this seems to go both ways.

But if so, she may not have been a figure they, the Iroquois, wanted to emulate.

We do not have much from the Jesuits on Iroquois mythology proper; the Iroquois were at eternal war with the French. But the fathers lived long among the Hurons, and the Hurons were, culturally, an Iroquois offshoot.

"They say," reports Brébeuf, "that a certain woman named Eataentsic is the one who made earth and men." So there you are: a female creator goddess. "They give her an assistant, one named Jouskeha, whom they declare to be her little son, with whom she governs the world." Aha! The chief male deity is only her son and assistant. But Brébeuf continues, "This Jouskeha has care of the living, and of the things that concern life, and consequently they say that he is good. Eataentsic has care of souls, and, because they believe that she makes men die, they say that she is wicked."[391]

So that's a mixed bag. The creator is a goddess, and the top god seems to be her second banana. On the other hand, she's the devil incarnate. The myth does not seem to clearly argue for putting women in positions of power.

This seems not to have been the only Huron version of the creation story. Another informant gave a different legend to Father LeJeune:

> [H]is people believe that a certain Savage had received from Messou [apparently the same as Nanabozho or Nanabush, male, a commonly invoked creator god, or more accurately, the restorer of mankind after a universal flood] the gift of immortality in a little package, with a strict injunction not to open it; while he kept it closed he was immortal, but his wife, being curious and incredulous, wished to see what was inside this present; and having opened it, it all flew away, and since then the Savages have been subject to death.[392]

Father LeClercq finds a similar tale among the Micmac. A group of Indians had voyaged to the next world and retrieved inside a bag a soul that would instruct them in all useful things.

> Their hopes, however, were vain and useless, for the father, having entrusted the bag to the care of an Indian woman, in order to assist and to dance more freely at the public festivals which were made for his happy return, this woman had the curiosity to open it, and the soul escaped immediately and returned whence it had come.[393]

This sounds awkwardly like the Judaeo-Christian story of Adam and Eve, or the Greek tale of Deucalion and Pandora. In all, woman is ultimately responsible for evil. Not an ideal employment reference.

LeJeune relates of some Indians:

> [T]hey recognize a Manitou [spirit], whom we may call the devil. They regard him as the origin of evil; it is true that they do not attribute great malice to the Manitou, but to his wife, who is a real she-devil.... As to the wife of the Manitou, she is the cause of all the diseases which are in the world. It is she who kills men, otherwise they would not die; she feeds upon their flesh, gnawing them upon the inside, which causes them to become emaciated in their illnesses. She has a robe made of the most beautiful hair of the men and women whom she has killed....[394]

So female figures may be more prominent in Indian and in Iroquois mythology than in the Judaeo-Christian Bible. But this is not necessarily to women's credit.

Morgan's Iroquois

So much for Bachofen. Now, let us turn to the matriarchists' use of the field work of Morgan. Of course, Morgan might himself be wrong. But did he even claim to discover what they said he discovered? Did he actually show Iroquois society to be matriarchal?

Other than legal descent from Mom, Gage's and Engels's claims are actually not supported by what Morgan found.

It is not possible to trace Gage's references. They are vague: only the name of an author or, at most, a book, lacking page or edition. But her claim regarding the sale of lands is unlikely on the testimony of Morgan, who tells, for example, of the Iroquois defeating the Delaware Indians and "reducing them to the status of women." The Delaware later sold some of their land to the state, and the Iroquois insisted that this was not permissible, because they were women. Women had no right to buy or sell land.

"How came you to take upon you to sell land at all?" the Iroquois chiefs say. "We conquered you; we made women of you. You know you are women, and can no more sell land than women."[395]

This directly contradicts Gage's claim that "No sale of lands was valid without consent of the squaws."

As to Gage's "Council of Matrons," it appears nowhere in Morgan's work. The closest approach seems to be a comment that "As a general rule the [tribal] council was open to any private individual who desired to address it on a public question. Even the women were allowed to express their wishes and opinions through an orator of their own selection. But the decision was made by the council."

Even the women were allowed to give opinions! There's equality for you![396]

A great deal has been made by later commentators of a note Morgan includes from another source, which puts the case for the ascendancy of Iroquois women about as strongly as can be found anywhere, among those who knew the Iroquois. But this is, literally, a footnote. It is meant in context only to establish that divorce among the Iroquois was easy and frequent, not that the Iroquois were governed by their women.

Here is the note:

> The late Rev. A. Wright, for many years a missionary among the Senecas, wrote the author in 1873 on this subject as follows: "As to their family system, when occupying the old long-houses, it is probable that some one clan predominated, the women taking in husbands, however, from the other clans; and sometimes, for a novelty, some of their sons bringing in their young wives until they felt brave enough to leave their mothers. Usually, the female portion ruled the house, and were doubtless clannish enough about it. The stores were in common; but woe to the luckless husband or lover who was too shiftless to do his share of the providing. No matter how many children, or whatever goods he might have in the house, he might at any time be ordered to pick up his blanket and budge; and after such orders it would not be healthful for him to attempt to disobey. The house would be too hot for him; and, unless saved by the intercession of some aunt or grandmother, he must retreat to his own clan; or, as was often done, go and start a new matrimonial alliance in some other. The women were the great power among the clans, as everywhere else. They did not hesitate, when occasion required, 'to knock off the horns,' as it was technically called, from the head of a chief, and send him

> back to the ranks of the warriors. The original nomination of the chiefs also always rested with them."[397]

That sounds at first hearing pretty matriarchal.

But note that it is prefaced with the words "it is probable"; later, "doubtless"; and it is written at a time when the longhouse no longer existed. It is, in other words, speculation, not evidence.

The basic premise seems probable. Extended families among the Iroquois shared a longhouse. Since the membership in the extended family was decided by female descent, the greatest number of family members would presumably be of the one clan, and this would be the clan of the house's women; the men would be of mixed clans.

But, also interestingly, both Wright and Morgan say this was for some reason not always the case.

The rule seems not to have been that women ruled. It was only an assumption that the clan that held a majority would rule, through force of numbers and natural clannishness, and this would most often happen, because of the matrilineal inheritance, to be the clan of the women. Maybe; maybe not. Majority rule is not the way in which societies or families always reach decisions. By this same logic, a polygamous Muslim family would also be ruled by the women. Do we assume so?

Whichever partner was not of the dominant clan, naturally enough, would indeed surely be expected to leave the longhouse in case of divorce. Again, it was not a matter of the man having to leave, because he was the man; apparently sometimes it was the woman.

Nor would this have been such a vital issue, or such a significant female advantage. Nobody, recall, had personal possessions beyond what they could carry with them, and what was not grabbed by somebody else; and either man or woman had the automatic option of moving in to their own clan's longhouse.

The Morgan footnote claims one other notable female power. Women, as a group, apparently could overthrow a chief or sachem. Morgan quotes that without comment; but perhaps only because it is beyond the point he is trying to make. For it contradicts what he himself observes regarding tribal offices. He says that chiefs or sachems were overthrown by council or by popular vote.[398] Council was entirely male, and in popular vote both men and women participated. Women could not by themselves overthrow, or, indeed, serve as sachems or chiefs.

Again, the passage says women nominated chiefs. But according to Morgan, so, equally, could men; it was done by popular vote without distinction of sex, and in either case selection was subject to the approval of the all-male council.[399]

So all that is shown here, at most, is that women probably had among the Iroquois a limited franchise: they had voice (by proxy) and vote, but could not be elected to office. This was in advance of Canadian or American women's political rights in the days of Matilda Gage; but it does not look like a matriarchy by modern standards. Nor by the standards of Gloria Steinem or Matilda Gage.

Morgan's own ultimate conclusion on women's status among the Iroquois is rather bluntly stated in his study, *League of the Ho-De-No-Sau-Nee or Iroquois* (1901): "The Indian regarded woman as the inferior, the dependent, and the servant of man, and from nurture and habit, she actually considered herself to be so."[400] Pretty much in line with the early Jesuit missionaries, who actually did know the Iroquois in their longhouse days. Morgan further notes the historical position of the Delaware, as previously mentioned, being "reduced" to female status as the result of losing a war. That's "reduced," not "promoted." One rarely gets prizes for losing a war.

> A deputation of Iroquois chiefs went ... into the country of the Delawares, and having assembled the people in council, they degraded them from the rank of even a tributary nation. Having reproved them for their want of faith, they forbade them from ever after going out to war, divested them of all civil powers, and declared that they should henceforth be as women. This degradation they signified in the figurative way of putting upon them the *Gd-ka-ahj* or skirt of the female, and placing in their hands a corn-pounder, thus showing that their business ever after should be that of women.[401]

Morgan also reports, in passing, the lyrics of one Iroquois war song: "I am brave and intrepid. I do not fear death, nor any kind of torture. Those who fear them are cowards. They are less than women."[402]

Try that at an Ottawa cocktail party today.

Mother right

Never mind. Morgan nevertheless did clearly show that Iroquois society was matrilineal: descent was reckoned through the mother. Even with nothing else to grasp at, that was warrant enough, for those who badly needed to believe, that the Iroquois, and the Indians generally, were matriarchies. It had to be so. Evidence is so androcentric.

Engels, indeed, argued that all else necessarily followed from this fact. "[T]he exclusive recognition of the female parent ... means that the women—the mothers—are held in high respect."[403] "[T]his original position of the mothers, as the only certain parents of their children, secured for them, and thus for their whole sex, a higher social status than women have ever enjoyed since."[404]

Gage too considers this proof that women were dominant. "In a country where she is the head of the family, where she decides the descent and inheritance of her children, both in regard to property and place in society, in such a community, she certainly cannot be the servant of her husband, but at least must be his equal if not in many respects his superior."[405] This must be so, she argues, not unreasonably, because in the earliest forms of society, the family was the society. If the woman ruled the family, then she ruled society, by definition and by default. "Even under those forms of society where woman was undisputed head of the family, its very existence due to her, descent entirely in the female line, we still hear assertion that his [the man's] must have been the controlling political power," she scoffs. "But at that early period to which we trace the formation of the family, it was also the political unit."[406]

But Gage's argument omits an important step. Does descent in the female line by itself demonstrate that women ruled the family? Granted, women's clans probably dominated in a longhouse, and this may have given some *de facto* power. But don't women often rule in the home in any case? Haven't husbands since time immemorial been required to smoke on the porch, to not walk on the kitchen floor, to retire to the garage or basement to play with their toys? Was there more to it than this?

Descent or inheritance in the female line is rather a passive thing: it does not obviously mean that any living woman has any particular power over inheritance or descent. Or anything else.

Gage, perhaps revealing a sense of the weakness of her case, further asserts such useful facts as "When an Indian husband brought the products of the chase to the wigwam, his control over it ceased."[407] But doesn't this simply mean that women did the cooking?

Free love, or just cheap love?

The fact that most Indians traced their descent through the mother was also clear enough to Champlain and the first missionaries. But it never occurred to them that this was evidence of female status and control. Rather, they saw it as a simple practical necessity given general Indian lack of social organization. In hunter-gatherer tribes, there is no effective government, there are no written laws, there is no police force, there is little social control. It is hardly surprising if that produces a higher level of sexual promiscuity than in societies with more regulation—one might say, more civilization.

Given little marital fidelity, as a matter of practicality, one never really knew who anyone's father was; but one always knows the mother. To keep inheritance, insignificant as it might be, in the family line, notably the inheritance of offices; to avoid incest taboos and trace ancestry; descent had to be reckoned through the female.

And this is just how Morgan, along with Champlain and the Jesuits, understands it. Champlain writes of the Hurons (members, recall, of the Iroquois language and cultural group), that "when night comes the young women run from one cabin to another, as do also the young men on their part, going where it seems good to them, but always without any violence, referring the whole matter to the pleasure of the woman. Their mates will do likewise to their women-neighbors."[408] He reports one Indian woman approaching him too, but claims he rejected the offer.

Bourgeois prig.

Generally, according to Champlain, Huron marriage came after the birth of the first child. Taking a husband then became of practical importance.

Yet even after marriage the favourite game of musical longhouses did not end: "But while with this husband, she does not cease to give herself free rein, yet remains always at home, keeping up a good appearance."[409]

It follows, Champlain suggests delicately, that "the children which they have together, born from such a woman, cannot be sure of their legitimacy. Accordingly, in view of this uncertainty, it is their custom that the children never succeed to the property and honors of their fathers, there being doubt, as above indicated, as to their paternity."[410]

Father LeJeune gives the same explanation—making one suspect that this was the conscious understanding among the Indians themselves, offered to any European who inquired.

> Now, as these people are well aware of this corruption, they prefer to take the children of their sisters as heirs, rather than their own, or than those of their brothers, calling in question the fidelity of their wives, and being unable to doubt that these nephews come from their own blood.[411]

It makes as much sense given a low opinion as a high opinion of women. It may imply an assumption of female immorality.

This did not, however, apparently indicate an open endorsement of free love, at least for women. Too bad for hopeful fellow travellers. Morgan reports that among the Iroquois he interviewed, albeit a few centuries later, "adultery was punished by whipping; but the punishment was inflicted upon the woman alone, who was supposed to be the only offender." This whipping was public, before the whole tribe.[412] Among the Powhatan, Pocahontas's tribe, we are simply informed, "Adultry [sic] is most severely punished."[413]

Granted, divorce was easy. For the man. Samuel Hearne writes, from the Northwest,

> Divorces are pretty common among the Northern Indians; sometimes for incontinency, but more frequently for want of what they deem necessary accomplishments or for bad behaviour. This ceremony, in either case, consists of neither more nor less than a good drubbing, and turning the woman out of doors; telling her to go to her paramour, or relations, according to the nature of her crime.[414]

According to Francis Parkman, among the Sioux, women were physically mutilated for adultery.[415] And this was the practice not just with the Sioux. Father Savard, in his *Histoire du Canada*, tells of a Frenchman returning from the north shore of Lake Huron with reports of "several girls the end of whose noses had been cut off in accordance with the custom of the country for having made a breach in their honour."[416] Rev. Peter Jones reports the same punishment among the Mississauga in the 19th century.[417]

George Dawson says of the Tahltan of the West Coast,

> A man's female children are as much his property as his gun and he sells them to whom he pleases without consulting their feelings at all.... If ... the husband pays for his wife in full, the vendor is held strictly to his bargain in respect to supplying a wife, and should the first die and he have any more eligible daughters, one of these must take her place.... Thus, for instance, a man of fifty may buy a young wife of fifteen (a not uncommon occurrence) and pay for her in full. Ten years afterward the young wife may die, and if there be another unsold sister, that sister according to their laws, must take her place....[418]

Livingston Jones writes of the Tlingit, "Girls seldom have any choice in their own marriage, but act in obedience to the dictates of their relatives and the rules of the people. Often they do not see the men who are designed to become their husbands until they are wedded to them."[419]

> If a man casts off his wife, he is not held accountable. The wife goes to her people and little or nothing is done about it. It is considered such a disgrace for a wife to be cast off by a husband that she will endure the most brutal treatment, and sometimes even death itself, before she will leave him.[420]

> The sister of a certain chief known to us married one of a lower caste. The chief not only disowned her, but threatened to kill her for the disgrace. In earlier times a brother had the right to kill a sister who disgraced the family in any way.[421]

Free love?

Livingston Jones, a proper Victorian, writes: "If a young girl received the attentions of a young man as our girls do, it would shock the natives beyond measure, and would be considered a terrible disgrace. Every girl is carefully watched and restrained from making any approaches to men. Their law of modesty requires that no girl shall speak to a man, not even to her own brother."[422]

Among the Nootka, says Gilbert Sproat, "A girl who was known to have lost her virtue, lost with it one of her chances of a favourable marriage; and a chief, or man of high rank in an Aht tribe, would have put his daughter to death for such a lapse."[423]

Of the Beothuk of Newfoundland, Shanawdithit, last known survivor, reports that "her tribe were very strict about the moral law, and visited severe penalties on any one who transgressed. Burning alive at the stake being the fate of the adulterer, which was witnessed by the whole tribe who danced in a circle around the victim."[424]

John West reports the traditional punishment for adultery among the Micmac to have been stoning to death—but apparently only the woman.[425]

It is not, then, that the Iroquois, or Indians generally, endorsed free love. It is that they could not consistently enforce moral norms. After all, in the general course of Indian life, a husband was likely to be away a lot, on hunting trips or in war parties.

"They are very subject to jealousy," writes Alexander Mackenzie of the tribes of the Northwest, "and fatal consequences frequently result from the indulgence of that passion. But notwithstanding the vigilance and severity which is exercised by the husband, it seldom happens that a woman is without her favourite, who, in the absence of the husband, exacts the same submission, and practises the same tyranny."[426]

Of the Ute, Cyrus Thomas writes, "Polygamy, though common, was by no means universal; the marriage tie, however, weighed so lightly on Ute husbands that they did not hesitate to sell their wives into slavery for a few trinkets."[427]

In one way, it is true, women were valued more highly than men. Gilbert Sproat writes of the Aht, "Men formerly were preferred to women, but since the island has been colonized women have brought higher prices, owing to the encouragement given to prostitution among a young unmarried colonial population…."[428] Bishop Hills, in 1860, reports that Indian females were worth 40 to 60 pounds a head at Victoria.[429] Not 40 pounds a night. Forty pounds a head.

As slaves.

Of the Stone (Tsilhqot'in) Indians of British Columbia, West writes:

> It does not appear that chastity is much regarded among them. They take as many wives as they please, and part with them for a season, or permit others to cohabit with them in their own lodges for a time, for a gun, a horse, or some article they may wish to possess. They are known, however, to kill the woman, or cut off her ears or nose, if she be unfaithful without their knowledge or permission. All the lowest and most laborious drudgery is imposed upon her, and she is not permitted to eat till after her lord has finished his meal, who amidst the burdensome toil of life, and a desultory and precarious existence, will only condescend to carry his gun, take care of his horse, and hunt as want may compel him.[430]

What matriarchy really looks like

In one of the earliest reports from Acadia, speaking of the Micmac around Port Royal, Father Biard, S.J., writes of "the men having several wives and abandoning them to others, and the women only serving them as slaves, whom they strike and beat unmercifully, and who dare not complain; and after being half killed, if it so please the murderer, they must laugh and caress him."[431]

Sir George Back tells of one Yellowknife woman:

> Another day a middle-aged woman, with a girl about six years old, came to us in great consternation, seeking protection against a hunter, over whose gun she had unluckily stept during the night. On discovering what she had done, ..., she was so alarmed for the consequences of her crime, that, though attached to the man, she preferred flight to the chance of what his fury might inflict on her. However, after allowing a reasonable time for the evaporation of his

> passion, she returned; and as he had, fortunately for her, shot an animal with the same gun since the disaster, she was let off with a sound thrashing, and an admonition to be more careful for the future. This, according to Indian law, was most lenient, as the unhappy female guilty of such delinquency seldom or ever escapes with a slighter punishment than a slit nose, or a bit cut off the ears.[432]

Is this what matriarchy looks like? Is this what Matilda Gage and Betty Friedan are fighting for?

"The women, it is true, sometimes receive an unlucky blow from their husbands for misbehaviour, which occasions their death; but this is thought nothing of," explains Samuel Hearne.[433]

When a particularly attractive woman is kidnapped from another tribe,

> ...[M]y guide, Matonabbee, who at that time had no less than seven wives, all women grown, besides a young girl of eleven or twelve years old, would have put in for the prize ..., had not one of his wives made him ashamed of it, by telling him that he had already more wives than he could properly attend. This piece of satire, however true, proved fatal to the poor girl who dared to make so open a declaration; for the great man, Matonabbee, ... took it as such an affront, that he fell on her with both hands and feet, and bruised her to such a degree, that after lingering some time she died.[434]

Is this what matriarchy looks like?

In his 1912 book *Pioneers of Canada*, Sir Harry Johnson is on the whole favourable to the Indians. "One direction in which the Amerindians did not shine," he writes, however, "was in their treatment of women."

> This perhaps was worse than in other uncivilized races. Woman was very badly used, except perhaps for the first year of courtship and marriage.... [N]ot long after she had become a mother she sank into the position of a household drudge and beast of burden. For example, amongst the Beaver Indians, an Athapaskan tribe of the far north-west, it is related by Alexander Mackenzie that the women are permanently crippled and injured in physique by the hardships they have to undergo.... If food was scarce, the women went without before even the male slaves of the tribe were unprovided with food. Women might never eat in the society of males, not even if these males were slaves or prisoners of war. If food was very scarce, the husband as

> likely as not killed and ate a wife; perhaps did this before slaying and eating a valuable dog.... So terrible was the ill-treatment of the women in some tribes that these wretched beings sometimes committed suicide to end their tortures. Even in this, however, they were not let off lightly, for the Sioux men invented as a tenet of their religion the saying that "Women who hang themselves are the most miserable of all wretches in the other world."[435]

"The grossest faults of the Denes, when the missionaries came amongst them," writes Father P. Duchaussois in 1919, "were polygamy, and cruelty to women and children. They took pride only in their sons. When a Montagnais used a certain expression, it was only the circumstances of the case which could show whether he meant 'my daughter' or 'my dog.' Beating their wives every day, keeping them without food, and laying heavy loads upon their shoulders, and sometimes even killing little girls, were not considered in any way wrong."[436]

> The coming of the Sisters of Charity made a profound impression on the Indians. Its first good effect was the revolution in their ideas concerning women. The pagan women thought of themselves as nothing but born thralls, to be sometimes sold or lent or exchanged, and always despised. The dignity and the holiness of the "Daughters of Prayer" was a permanent lesson for them, and still more for the Red Men, who had been accustomed to treat wife and daughter, mother and grandmother, with contempt and cruelty.[437]

Rev. Peter Jones, a Mississauga Indian, writes:

> In accordance with the custom of all pagan nations, the Indian men look upon their women as an inferior race of beings, created for their use and convenience. They therefore treat them as menials, and impose on them all the drudgeries of a savage life, such as making the wigwam, providing fuel, planting and hoeing the Indian corn or maize, fetching the venison and bear's meat from the woods where the man shot it: in short, all the hard work falls upon the women; so that it may truly be said of them, that they are the slaves of their husbands.
>
> In the wigwam the men occupy the best places, leaving such parts as are most exposed to the inclemency of the weather to the poor women. In regard to their food, the women eat the coarsest parts of the meat, or what the men leave. When travelling the men always walk on before. It would be considered great presumption for the wife to walk by the

> side of her husband; she therefore keeps at a respectful distance. I have often seen the husband start with nothing but his gun or bow and arrows, while the poor wife, at some distance behind, would be seen bending under the weight of all their goods, often with a child packed in the midst of materials for building the wigwam. These burdens they carry about with them in all their journeying, which soon makes them decrepit. The men have an idea that it is unmanly and disgraceful for them to be seen doing anything which they imagine belongs to the women's department. I have scarcely ever seen anything like social intercourse between husband and wife, and it is remarkable that the women say very little in the presence of the men.[438]

Of the Micmac, Father LeClercq observes, "The women have no command among the Indians. They must needs obey the orders of their husbands. They have no rights in the councils, nor in the public feasts."[439]

Missing aboriginal women

In all of this, our European (and aboriginal) witnesses may have been unfair to Indian men. As we have mentioned previously, some of what looks like brutality towards women may have been made necessary by the state of constant war: men had to stay alert and always have their hands free in case of attack.

However, it also used to be a commonplace that showing respect for women was a mark of class and good breeding, which is to say, civilization; and, within a civilization, of better education and material prosperity.

Want to overturn it and go back to an imagined state of nature, with the Noble Savage?

You may not like what you get, Ms. Gage.

Cece Hodgson-McCauley, a status Indian, laments only recently to Northern News Service, "aboriginal people have always been mean, especially to their wives. A lot of jealousies, we all know horror stories."[440]

Catherine Brooks, director of a residence for aboriginal women in Toronto, reports a survey that found "Twenty-four per cent of the respondents to our questionnaire indicated that they know of deaths as a result of Aboriginal family violence, and 54 per cent… know of cases where a woman sustained injury which required medical treatment as a result of family violence but did not seek medical attention out of fear and shame."[441]

You may have heard of the unusually high number of missing and murdered aboriginal women. According to the National Inquiry into Missing and Murdered Indigenous Women and Girls:

> Aboriginal women in Canada report rates of violence, including domestic violence and sexual assault, 3.5 times higher than non-Aboriginal women.
>
> Young Aboriginal women are five times more likely than other Canadian women of the same age to die of violence. Between 1997 and 2000, the rate of homicide for Aboriginal women was almost seven times higher than the rate for non-Aboriginal women.[442]

The BBC reports:

> Women made up more than half of all indigenous suicides in 2015 in Ontario, compared with the non-aboriginal population where women made up just one quarter of all suicides. Between 2006 and 2015, the number of female suicides climbed 1.5 times faster in indigenous women than it did for non-indigenous women.[443]

As a response, said federal inquiry has been struck, at a budgeted cost of $53.8 million, plus $16.17 million for "family information liaison units."

Mightn't the problem be obvious? According to police records, 62 percent of these missing women were killed by a spouse or family member. Seventy percent were killed by "members of their own communities."[444]

And mightn't we be, in some measure, guilty of these women's deaths by seeking to preserve the reserve system and what we imagine we can of traditional Indian culture? A culture that is historically not well disposed toward women?

That, for example, sees the devil as female?

14 A POX ON BOTH YOUR LONGHOUSES

The poison dress: arsenic and old lace.

With gifts they shall be sent,
Gifts to the bride to spare their banishment,
Fine robings and a carcanet of gold.
Which raiment let her once but take, and fold
About her, a foul death that girl shall die
And all who touch her in her agony.
Such poison shall they drink, my robe and wreath!

—*Euripides,* Medea

As we all know, Europeans waged genocide on the Canadian Indians, by infecting them with smallpox.

Smallpox being no small thing. Until the WHO in 1980 declared it struck from the scarred face of the earth, it was one of the great terrors of humankind. Come down with the pox, and you had about a one in three chance of ceasing to be in physical form. Survive, and you may have been rendered blind. Avoid that too, and you certainly had the marks on your face. And it was highly contagious. So much for friends and loved ones.

It was especially lethal to the American Indians. Conventional wisdom says this is because they had not encountered it before and so had no immunity.

Here is how the Florentine Codex, compiled in 1569 from eyewitness accounts, describes the outbreak in Mexico after the Spanish conquest:

> Some it indeed covered [with pustules]; they spread everywhere, on one's face, on one's head, on one's chest, etc.

> Many died of it. No longer could they walk; they only lay in their homes, in their beds. No longer could they move, no longer could they bestir themselves, no longer could they raise themselves, no longer could they stretch themselves out face down, no longer could they stretch themselves out on their backs. And when they bestirred themselves, much did they cry out. There was much perishing. Like a covering were the pustules. Indeed many people died of them, and many just died of hunger. There was death from hunger; there was no one to take care of another; there was no one to attend to another.[445]

Jared Diamond says, in *Guns, Germs, and Steel*, that "the Indian population decline in the century or two following Columbus's arrival is estimated to have been as large as 95 percent."[446] "The impact of these epidemics was stunning," writes Elizabeth Fenn, "particularly in the first century of European contact. From a pre-Columbian population that may have been as high as twenty-five million, the population of central Mexico plummeted to only two million by 1600.... Farther north, a similar pattern emerged, delayed by three-quarters of a century, but dramatic nonetheless. The Pueblo Indians of New Mexico saw their numbers drop from as many as one hundred thousand in 1600 to forty thousand in 1638 and only seventeen thousand in 1680. To the southwest, in the desert province of Sonora, one Jesuit missionary believed that the native population had declined more than 90 percent by 1706."[447]

So too in Canada. The first outbreak witnessed by Europeans was at Tadoussac in 1616. The Jesuits record it passing through the Huron country in the 1630s: "[T]wo things occurred this year, which somewhat checked the progress of the gospel. The first was a pestilence, of unknown origin, which eight months ago spread through several villages, and caused the death of many. The divine providence even so dealt with us that we should not be exempt from the calamity. In fact, it almost began with us, or at least attacked both us and the savages at the same time. Of us who labor here,—six priests, and the four lay brothers then with us,—we saw seven confined to their beds at the same time, and near unto death."[448] Among the victims was the first native Canadian saint, Kateri Tekakwitha, who was left with impaired eyesight and a marred face.

This was one of the greatest calamities in recorded history. In a passive sense, the newly arriving Europeans can be blamed—they inadvertently brought the disease, they say, and other diseases, with them. Then again, if this is so, it could be argued that all of this was only a matter of time. The Americas could not have hoped to remain forever in a bubble. If Europeans had not come when they did, Chinese, Japanese, Polynesians, Africans, gypsies, Fuller brush salesmen, or Romanian Orthodox Jews eventually would. And the longer they took to get here, the worse the eventual outbreak would presumably be.

But there is a tradition that the Europeans were to blame for the scourge and the suffering in a more direct and literal way. It is, in fact, a matter of common knowledge on the political left, and among many Indians, that the smallpox was deliberately introduced and spread by the Europeans in order to pilfer Indian lands. That it was, in fact, genocide. A recent column in a local British Columbia newspaper assures readers, without attribution, that "on the west coast, explorers handed out blankets contaminated by smallpox."[449]

The Montreal *Gazette* several years ago featured in its *Arts* section a story on a travelling exhibit by Marianne Corless, on the motif of Hudson's Bay blankets with red Canadian maple leaves on them, pocked and bloody.

Subtlety was not involved.

> Artist Marianne Corless says while the blanket is steeped with national pride for the Canadian mainstream, some aboriginals view it as a grim reminder of the smallpox epidemic that ravaged their communities during the 1700s and 1800s—a dark consequence of the fur trade glossed over by history books but smouldering in native consciousness.
>
> "It is not something that is really well known," Corless said in an interview from Victoria, adding some natives believe infected Bay blankets helped spread the epidemic.
>
> Her multimedia art exhibit, titled *Further* ... is a blunt critique [sic—as is often the case, they are misusing the term "critique" to mean "criticism." It is the characteristic spoor of the pseudo-intellectual] of European colonialism and the fur trade.
>
> Wall hangings feature five Bay blankets and explore themes of exploitation, disease and death.
>
> In Blanket 1, a Bay blanket is transformed into a diseased Canadian flag. Hung striped side down, its central feature is a large maple leaf infected and bleeding with smallpox pustules.
>
> "... I was trying to determine for myself what it meant to be a Canadian, to have this as part of our history," Corless said, noting the Bay, established in 1670, was instrumental in exploring and settling Canada.[450]

Buffy Sainte-Marie included the smallpox blankets charge in her 1966 protest song, "My Country 'Tis of Thy People You're Dying":

> *Hear how the bargain was made for the West*
> *With her shivering children in zero degrees*
> *Blankets for your land, so the treaties attest*
> *Oh well, blankets for land is a bargain indeed*
> *And the blankets were those Uncle Sam had collected*
> *From smallpox-diseased dying soldiers that day*
> *And the tribes were wiped out and the history books censored*
> *A hundred years of your statesmen have felt*
> *It's better this way*

Nasty bunch, these Europeans.

The idea has become so much a cliché of popular culture that it can be alluded to in passing to add colour to a description. Everybody will get the reference. "Consider this passage from a recent mystery novel by an African-American woman," writes Adrienne Mayor. "'He held [the will and testament] gingerly, as though it were one of those smallpox blankets the early settlers gave to the Indians.'"[451]

There you are—established fact. Everybody knows.

A blanket indictment

So what is the historical record on this?

There are indeed many Indian sources for it. Vine Deloria writes, in *Custer Died for Your Sins*, "In the old days blankets infected with smallpox were given to the tribes in an effort to decimate them."[452]

William Warren's *History of the Ojibways, Based Upon Traditions and Oral Sources*, compiled in 1885, includes this passage:

> To make up ... for their misconduct, as well as to avert the evil consequences that might arise from it, the Pillagers [a subtribe of the Ojibways, named such by the Indians in recognition of one particular bad habit] on the ensuing spring, gathered a number of packs of beaver skins and sent a delegation headed by one of their principal men to the British fort at Mackinaw [near Sault Ste. Marie], to appease the ill-will of the whites, by returning an ample consideration for the goods which they had pillaged.
>
> The British commandant of the fort received the packs of beaver, and in return he assured the Pillagers of his good will and friendship towards them, and strengthened his words by giving their leader a medal, flag, coat, and bale of goods, at

> the same time requesting that he would not unfurl his flag, nor distribute his goods, until he arrived into his own country. With this injunction, the Pillager chief complied, till he landed at Fond du Lac, where, anxious to display the great consequence to which the medal and presents of the British had raised him in his own estimation, he formally called his followers to a council, and putting on his chief's coat, and unfurling his flag, he untied his bale of goods, and freely distributed to his fellows.
>
> Shortly after, he was taken suddenly sick, and retiring to the woods, he expired by himself, as the discovery of his remains afterwards indicated. All of those who had received a portion of the goods also fell sick, one after another, and died. The sickness became general, and spreading to different villages, its fearful ravages took off a large number of the tribe. It proved to be the smallpox, and many of the Ojibways believed, and it is a common saying to this day, that the white men purposely inflicted it on them by secreting bad medicine in the bale of goods, in punishment for the pillage which the Leech Lake band had committed on one of their traders.[453]

The Ottawa had similar traditions. Andrew Blackbird, an Ottawa writer, says in 1887:

> It was a notable fact that by this time [1763] the Ottawas were greatly reduced in numbers from what they were in former times, on account of the small-pox which they brought from Montreal during the French war with Great Britain. This small pox was sold to them shut up in a tin box, with the strict injunction not to open the box on their way homeward, but only when they should reach their country; and that this box contained something that would do them great good, and their people! The foolish people believed really there was something in the box supernatural, that would do them great good. Accordingly, after they reached home they opened the box; but behold there was another tin box inside, smaller. They took it out and opened the second box, and behold, still there was another box inside of the second box, smaller yet. So they kept on this way till they came to a very small box, which was not more than an inch long; and when they opened the last one they found nothing but mouldy particles in this last little box! They wondered very much what it was, and a great many closely inspected to try to find out what it meant. But alas, alas! pretty soon burst out a terrible sickness among them. The great Indian doctors themselves were taken sick and died. The tradition says it

> was indeed awful and terrible. Every one taken with it was sure to die. Lodge after lodge was totally vacated—nothing but the dead bodies lying here and there in their lodges—entire families being swept off with the ravages of this terrible disease. The whole coast of Arbor Croche ... was entirely depopulated....
>
> It is generally believed among the Indians of Arbor Croche that this wholesale murder of the Ottawas by this terrible disease sent by the British people, was actuated through hatred, and expressly to kill off the Ottawas and Chippewas because they were friends of the French Government or French King.[454]

An Indian author in South America already gives a smallpox-in-a-gift-box story very similar to the Ottawa tale as early as 1613. In it, Spaniards reportedly send a messenger in a black cloak with a gift for the Incan Emperor, a small locked case. He says his orders specify that "only the king should open it." When it is opened, its contents appear to be scraps of paper that blow away. Within days, multitudes die, covered with burning scabs.[455]

Smohalla, a prophet of the ghost dance on the West Coast, understood something similar:

> [T]he whites have caused us great suffering. Dr. Whitman many years ago made a long journey to the east to get a bottle of poison for us. He was gone about a year, and after he came back strong and terrible diseases broke out among us. The Indians killed Dr. Whitman, but it was too late. He had uncorked his bottle and all the air was poisoned.[456]

We have a more recent account of this pale perfidy from an "eyewitness" in Kevin Annett's book *Hidden from History*; although the disease here is tuberculosis, not smallpox:

> Reverend Pitts, the Alberni school principal, he forced me and eight other boys to eat this special food out of a different sort of can. It tasted really strange. And then all of us came down with tuberculosis. I was the only one to survive, 'cause my Dad broke into the school one night and got me out of there. All of the rest died from tuberculosis and they were never treated. Just left there to die. And their families were all told they had died of pneumonia. The plan was to kill us off in secret, you know. We all just began dying after eating that food.[457]

Adrienne Mayor collects other examples. All seem to have come originally from

Indian oral sources. "One oft-repeated tale concerned a trader who invited Indians to a peace parley but then gave them a keg of rum wrapped in a pox-infected flag, telling them not to unwrap it until they reached their village. Heagarty [writing in 1928] dates the incident to 1700 and identifies the man as a fur company agent in Minnesota."[458] "In northeast Montana, Indians believed that rival Métis tried to spread smallpox as they migrated west between 1860 and 1870."[459]

This is all suggestive. Where there is smoke, after all, there is usually fire.

But on occasion, where there is smoke there are only mirrors. There is a general problem with using Indian sources to make the case. It is not just that Indian traditions, being oral, are malleable over time and rely, by definition, on word of mouth at third and further hand. It is that, by the nature of things, Indians are not in a position to know.

If smallpox was spread among them by European subterfuge, they probably would not have been told this by the Europeans. All they have, necessarily, is suspicions. If the thing truly happened, the conclusive evidence must come from the Europeans themselves. We must have original, European, documentary sources.

We seem to get this from Ward Churchill, former head of Ethnic Studies at the University of Colorado.

Churchill reports that in early 1837, the commander of Fort Clark ordered a boatload of blankets shipped from a military smallpox infirmary in St. Louis. When the shipment arrived at Fort Clark on June 20, U.S. Army officers requested a parlay with Mandan Indians who lived next to the fort. At the parlay, army officers distributed the smallpox-infested blankets as gifts. When the Indians began to show signs of the illness, U.S. Army doctors did not impose quarantine, but instead told the Indians to scatter, so that the disease would become more widespread and kill more Indians. Meanwhile, the fort authorities hoarded smallpox vaccine in their storeroom, instead of using it to inoculate the Indians.[460]

That sounds pretty clear, detailed, and damning.

Churchill argues a similar case against John Smith. "There are several earlier cases, one involving Captain John Smith of Pocahontas fame. There's some pretty strong circumstantial evidence that Smith introduced smallpox among the Wampanoags as a means of clearing the way for the invaders."[461] "Mysteriously—the Indians had had close contact with Europeans for years without getting sick—epidemics broke out in the immediate aftermath of Smith's expedition."[462]

Unfortunately, these references do not pan out. After being publicly accused of falsifying his sources, Churchill was finally called before a disciplinary panel at his university, and dismissed for academic misconduct in 2007. On Churchill's claims against John Smith, the committee concluded that he "fabricated his account, because no evidence—not even circumstantial evidence—supports his claim."[463] Ouch. On events at Fort Clark, Churchill cites another historian, Russell Thornton.[464] Sadly, no one else seems to be able to find the assertion in Thornton's book. Thornton himself calls the Churchill story of events at Fort Clark and Fort Union "out-and-out fabrication."[465]

When he was challenged by the disciplinary panel, Churchill's ultimate response seems to have been "everybody knows": "[H]e made no effort to offer corroboration of anything other than the number of fatalities presented for the ensuing pandemic because he considered his account to be 'rather self-evident—such stories have been integral to native oral histories for centuries; I've heard them all my life.'"[466]

But the panel concluded that Churchill had not consulted any actual natives for their oral histories, either.

So Churchill's claims cannot be accepted to show that the smallpox blankets story is something more than an urban legend. It sounds as though Churchill's claims might themselves be urban legend.

But the truth is probably still struggling to get its boots on.

Fort Pitt: The smoking blanket

There is, to be fair, one definite documented irrefutable case of smallpox-infected blankets being given to North American Indians in order to knowingly spread the loathsome pox. It happened at Fort Pitt, in what is now Pittsburgh, in 1763, during Pontiac's Rebellion. The British military post was under siege by the Delaware Indians, and when two chiefs came to demand its surrender, they were sent away with gifts, two of which were blankets taken from the station's smallpox infirmary—the fort being itself in the throes of an epidemic at the time.

Of this there can be no doubt. We have letters between Jeffery Amherst, the general in command of British forces, and Colonel Henry Bouquet, commanding a relief column sent to the fort, calling for this to be done. We have the journal entry of militia captain William Trent, stating that blankets taken from the smallpox hospital were given to the two chiefs. And we have an invoice, submitted to British command by Levy, Trent, and Company, requesting reimbursement for two blankets and one silk handkerchief, "taken from people in the Hospital to Convey the Smallpox to the Indians."[467]

One strange anomaly: the correspondence between Amherst and Bouquet calling for the measure is dated to July, whereas the invoice, and Trent's journal entry, are from June, the previous month. The thing was done before it was ordered to be done?

If anything, however, this suggests that we are dealing with not just one incident; that the idea was, shall we say, "in the air," and so may have been acted upon on more than one occasion.

On the other hand, why then is there not more of a paper trail? If blankets were used at other times, why only here, in this instance, do we have an invoice? Above all else, the English are careful accountants.

Those who believe there was a general plan to eradicate the Indians argue that it would all naturally have been concealed, and never set down on paper, because it would have been beyond the pale of civilized behaviour.

But that argument cuts both ways: if it was indeed thought by Englishmen of the day to be unspeakable behaviour, does that not argue that they were unlikely to do it? If admitting having done it might get them into trouble, doesn't that mean it cannot have been sanctioned or standard policy?

In the absence of any such definite evidence, we can really never know whether the deed was ever done outside Fort Pitt. It might have been. But we cannot take the absence of evidence as evidence. That way paranoia lies.

Moreover, in the absence of said evidence, decency requires us to give the Europeans the benefit of the doubt, even if they happen to be us. For this is a serious charge, and obviously promotes hatred toward an identifiable group. Without evidence, should we think such a thing of our fellow man?

Was there, for that matter, really a Jewish conspiracy to poison the wells? An oddly similar charge, after all.

The evidence is about the same. Which is to say, little or none.

And there are other arguments that make the charge unlikely.

Germ theory was still at this time relatively unknown. It did not become the dominant explanation for disease until the 1890s. Charles Darwin, no slouch on the current science, wrote in *The Descent of Man*, in 1871, "It further appears, mysterious as is the fact, that the first meeting of distinct and separated people generates disease."[468] Odd, that. I wonder why? Even at that late date, Europeans did not understand the matter.

The then-current theory of infectious disease, established since Galen and classical times, was that it was spread by "miasma." Which is to say, "bad air."

By this theory, blankets could indeed spread smallpox. But it was not because they were infected with germs, viruses, bacteria, cootie bugs, or any other troublesome microorganisms. It was because of foul smells. In 1348, faced with the Black Death, a blue-ribbon panel from the University of Paris advised, "The present epidemic or pest comes directly from air corrupted in its substance." The solution, therefore, was to use incense or perfume, fragrance, which "hampers putrefaction of the air, and removes the stench of the air and the corruption [caused by] the stench."[469]

A medical text of 1824 explains:

> Infection is a febrific agent, produced by the decomposition of animal and vegetable substances. It usually exists in the state of a gas or miasma, and in this form occurs in filthy houses, ships, jails, hospitals, and cities; and also in marshes and fenny and low districts of country. Under the denominations of marsh or paludal miasmata, exhalations of the soil, vegeto-animal effluvium, malaria, human effluvia, febrile and putrid contagion, its various specific effects are detailed in the works of practical writers.[470]

If we did not know this already from our reading of history, it is fairly clear from his own journal that Ecuyer, commander at Fort Pitt, accepted the miasma theory: "We are so crowded in the fort that I fear disease, for in spite of all my care I cannot keep the place as clean as I should like; moreover, the small pox is among us."[471] General dirtiness and smelliness was the cause of disease.

It follows that, for the smallpox blankets scheme to work, the blankets given as gifts would have to be dirty enough that they probably smelled bad.

Now, what are the chances of palming such blankets off on Indians as either proper gifts or acceptable trade goods? Wouldn't they immediately seem, instead, highly suspect, a deliberate insult, or possibly even an attempt to spread disease? Should the Indians accept them, wouldn't they be likely to wash them before use, eliminating, by the traditional theory, their ability to transmit smallpox?

Even given the modern germ theory, infected clothing, like blankets, is a possible but not a likely means for transmitting smallpox. "There is a remote possibility," writes Robert Boyd, "of acquiring the disease through contact with virus-laden items of clothing, personal possessions, etc."[472] Note that word, "remote." The usual method is by sneezing, and inhaling the particles in the air.

If Amherst suggested it, and the commandant tried it, at Fort Pitt in 1763, perhaps then it was a desperate measure called for by a desperate situation. When the context is considered, a case can be made that the smallpox blanket gambit was, in this case, as justifiable as, or more justifiable than, dropping Little Boy on Hiroshima or Fat Man on Nagasaki. Perhaps wrong, but a matter about which reasonable men can disagree.

First off, the Indians were illegally at war, and had launched the conflict with a sneak attack, comparable to Pearl Harbor. There is a reason why Francis Parkman calls the action "the Conspiracy of Pontiac": not the war; not the rebellion—the "conspiracy." Immediately before the action began, the Indian belligerents had concluded a peace treaty with the English, and sworn their allegiance. The English had agreed in turn to ban for the present white settlement west of the Alleghenies. Among other matters, the Indians had consented to the existence of Fort Pitt. Then, without any declaration of hostilities, they descended on several British forts along the frontier, in surprise attacks relying heavily on the British not knowing they were at war. At Michilimackinac, the Indians pretended to play lacrosse before the fort. When the gates were opened to allow them to continue inside, they suddenly pulled out hatchets, attacked and massacred the garrison.

Not cricket, to the English mind.

As Lord Amherst says in correspondence, "they were contemptible for violating the most solemn promises of friendship, without the least provocation on our side."[473]

There were, of course, and no doubt, justifications from the Indian point of view; as there were for Pearl Harbor among the Japanese. Or for the events of 9/11, among the jihadists. But we need not go into them here. The point to be made is merely that, from the British vantage point, these people were not legitimate combatants. They were, to use the current term, terrorists.

Moreover, surrendering the fort to them under any circumstances probably did not look like a viable option. During the Seven Years' War, just concluded, there was an instructive incident, considered at the time a historic atrocity, already alluded to here. Montcalm, the French commander, had negotiated the surrender of the British Fort William Henry in (present) upstate New York. The garrison, by the terms of the surrender, were to be given full battle honours and paroled—permitted to leave without their weapons, but unmolested and with their colours flying. Nevertheless, as soon as they lay down their muskets and passed the safety of the fort's walls, the English column was fallen upon by Indian allies of the French. Many were massacred. Many were taken to be later tortured to death.

Some of them, by French reports, were eaten.

In similar fashion, at the siege of Detroit, in the same rebellion under Pontiac, a relief column was ambushed by the Ottawa. According to Francis Parkman, 46 British soldiers were then tortured and killed, after which the Indians "fell upon their bodies, cut them in pieces, cooked, and ate them."[474]

So this might have been war, Jim, but not war as we know it. The Indians recognized no rules of engagement; letting them take the fort might have had upsetting consequences for the civilians, including women and children, sheltering inside. Perhaps, just this once, despite all the moral and the practical concerns, smallpox blankets might be the way to go.

And the use of smallpox blankets in time of war, even if played by Queensberry rules, is a far cry from the usual accusation, that blankets were used to spread smallpox among the Indians as a genocidal strategy, to kill them off and take their land. That at least is not demonstrated by the Fort Pitt incident.

The question of motive: follow the money

Let us accept, though, that all Europeans are rascals. Even if it be so, as a matter of sheer self-interest, would the crackers have wanted to wipe out the Indians? Why?

As previously noted here, if you farm, the same acreage that once supported one hunter can now support a hundred straw-gnawing rustics. Therefore, from the perspective of the settlers, there was room enough for all in this beautiful new land. There was no cause for them to resent or kill the Indians to take their land. It was a simple matter of teaching the poor savages to farm.

If there was resentment, it could only have come from the other side.

Maybe they poisoned the tobacco.

Hey, wait. That fits.

On top of this, by the time any settlers had arrived in any part of North America, the pox and other diseases had already been through, and decimated the original hunter-gatherer population. "When Hernando de Soto became the first European conquistador to march through the southeastern United States, in 1540," Jared Diamond writes, "he came across Indian town sites abandoned two years earlier because the inhabitants had died in epidemics. These epidemics had been transmitted from coastal Indians infected by Spaniards visiting the coast."[475] When Captain Vancouver touched in at the West Coast in 1792, again, he found deserted villages. "The houses … did not seem to have been lately the residence of the

Indians. The habitations had now fallen into decay, their inside, as well as a small surrounding space that appeared to have been formerly occupied, were overrun with weeds; amongst which were found several human sculls, and other bones, promiscuously scattered about."[476] When Lewis and Clark ventured west of the Mississippi in 1806, "the world the explorers described to the American people was one that had already undergone momentous change. As their own journals indicated, Variola's [i.e., smallpox's] transit of the continent had preceded them by a full generation."[477]

Accordingly, even if the resident hunter-gatherers were perversely bound and determined to cleave to their inefficient traditional scavenging way of life, given the dramatic drop in population that had already happened, there was no reason for the early settlers to see advantage in killing off Indians to take their land. And, indeed, no economic reason for the Indians to object to the settlers.

Why then, given no intervening untoward incident, would the Europeans feel animosity toward the Indians? Just on the general ethical principle of being villainous?

The first Europeans to contact the Indians almost anywhere, in any case, were not settlers, but missionaries or fur traders. Fort Clark and Fort Union, for example, where Churchill says the U.S. Army distributed smallpox blankets, were fur trading posts, with no military presence. No U.S. Army, in fact. The missionaries were there to save Indian souls, a project that would not have been obviously advanced by giving them smallpox. The fur traders were there to do business. It is not in Wal-Mart's interest, nor in Amazon's, to kill either their customers or their suppliers in large numbers.

Accordingly, the interests of the earliest Europeans, contrary to the smallpox blankets myth, were very much on the side of doing whatever they could to keep any resident Indians alive, fit, and happy. And so indeed they thought. "[T]he Spanish," says Paul Hackett, "had begun quarantining ships to the New World almost from the start of contact, and by the 1780s had in place a set of regulations designed to prevent the disease from reaching Mexico City from elsewhere."[478] When Lewis and Clark struck overland, President Jefferson sent with them the new smallpox vaccine, first demonstrated by Jenner in London in 1796, to vaccinate any Indians they met against the scourge. Unfortunately, their supply of vaccine spoiled.[479] Still, it was a curious tactic, if the aim was to wipe the Indians out.

When a smallpox epidemic struck the northern prairies in the 1770s, the Hudson's Bay Company understood their interests well enough. It might be too late for the Indians of the interior, but at least they were going to do their best to protect the

Indians near the coast. Word came down from head office: "Should you find the disorder has attacked any of them [the local Indians], do all in your power for their preservation."[480] York Factory quickly imposed a quarantine to protect the [coast-dwelling] Cree Indians they referred to as the "home guard." Only Europeans were to meet trading parties from the interior, and well away from the fort.[481] The measure proved effective, too, until the American Revolution interposed. A French fleet appeared in Hudson Bay, in support of the Americans, and the Company was obliged to abandon its posts for the duration.

When they returned after the war, it was to bleached bones.

Not many years later, in 1837, the smallpox epidemic that Ward Churchill traces to Fort Union and Fort Clark on the upper Missouri struck the same area. By this time, Jenner had demonstrated vaccination, and over half a continent, the Hudson's Bay Company wheeled into action with near-military precision. Fortunately, London had already shipped and distributed cowpox-based vaccine against such a contingency.

Dr. William Todd, at Fort Pelly on the Assiniboine, among the first to detect the disease, began vaccinations by September 20. "Thereafter, he dispatched news of the epidemic and fresh supplies of vaccine to other districts including the Carlton, Ile à la Crosse, Chipewyan, and Edmonton Districts."[482] At Cumberland House, John Lewis vaccinated every Indian "that would submit to it." He sent supplies of vaccine onward to Moose Lake and Lac la Ronge. At Fort Francis/Rainy River, factor John Charles did likewise, as did York Factory, and Robert Wilson at Fort Severn.[483]

At Cumberland House, dying Indians were taken in, given food, shelter, and 24-hour care. The house journal tells a sad story:

> 15th Tuesday. Late in the Evening a Distressed Woman and her Child came here, these are all that is alive out of one Tent, and has not yet been ailing. The News she brings is still more and more alarming … the small pox rageing amongst them with its greatest fury, and carrying all before it, they chiefly Die within the third or fourth Night, and those that survive after that time are left to be devoured by the wild beasts.[484]

With these timely interventions, according to Hackett, "the progress of the epidemic was effectively stopped after only a very limited penetration into Canadian territory."[485] At the very time Ward Churchill claims fur trading posts in the United States were trying to kill the Indians with smallpox, traders above the Canadian border were doing all they could to protect Indians from the disease.

These Europeans should get together on strategy.

The first claim, though, is undocumented. The latter claim is thoroughly documented in Hudson's Bay Company records of the time. Those English are indeed fierce at accountancy.

And it makes Marianne Corless's claims about Hudson's Bay blankets most cruelly unjust to a company that deserves recognition for their good deeds.

An American fur trader, Edwin Denig, of Astor's American Fur Company, posted at Fort Union, gave his northern competitors due credit: "Another visitation of this malady happened in 1838, but owing to the good management of the Hudson's Bay Company most of the nation [the Cree] were preserved by introducing vaccine matter and persisting in its application for several years previous."[486]

Those advocates of the smallpox blanket legend who understand that fur traders, if they spread smallpox to the Indians, would be working against their self-interest, have offered a counter-claim: that, while Indians in general might have been of some use to the traders, it still made sense for them to kill off local Indians, in order to cut out the middleman. They might then get furs from tribes farther away at lower cost.

This thesis does not work either, for several reasons. First, there would be no way, once the disease had been unleashed, for the Europeans, from a distance, to arrange to limit it only to the Indians near the posts. By the nature of any trading network, these Indians would soon come in contact with the Indians trading with them from further afield, so that all could ultimately be infected. Second, the Hudson's Bay Company was always capable of setting up trading posts further inland. They had made a business decision, until challenged in this by the North West Company, to keep their operations at the coast, and leave to the Indians, who were better at it, the task of transporting furs. It would, in the end, have cost the company more than their markup to do it themselves. Third, the trading posts depended on the nearby Indians for more than just trade. They were needed labourers, security guards, and a source of food and supplies. "[T]he Homeguard Cree ... helped to supply the posts with provisions, and performed other critical tasks for the traders. The Homeguard Cree ... had a long history of hunting geese and caribou for the English, as well as transporting goods and mail between the posts."[487]

The HBC men therefore took special care to ensure the welfare of the Indians they referred to as their "home guard."

Many of the same considerations would have applied to the early settlers. John

Smith would have been a fool if he indeed wanted to wipe out the local Indians. But in fact, he was not so foolish. His own writings argue the value of Indians as available labourers, for newborn baby colonies that would, necessarily, for some time lack manpower. Who you gonna get to pick that cotton?

And, of course, any settler setting loose smallpox on the nearby Indians would have run a terrible risk of killing his own family. If smallpox was a greater threat to the Indians, an estimated 25 percent of the European population was also vulnerable at any given time. In Canada's last outbreak, at Windsor, Ontario, in 1924, the death rate among the unvaccinated was 71 percent—all Europeans. This would have been a far greater worry centuries earlier, when nobody understood well how smallpox was transmitted.

All this being so, and in the absence of evidence otherwise, Occam's Razor seems to favour urban or forest legend as the most likely source of the smallpox blanket tale. Given that no human agency was required, no human agency need be postulated.

The evidence from fairyland

There are obvious similarities here with known myth.

Not just of Jews poisoning wells. Note first the apparent, no doubt unconscious, allusion to the Trojan Horse: a pretended gift to destroy an enemy and take their land. Adrienne Mayor points out a closer parallel: the shirt of Nessos, secretly soaked in the poisonous blood of a centaur, given as a gift to his unsuspecting wife, that killed Herakles, the mighty man and archetypal Noble Savage. And Mayor points to other classical examples. Euripides tells of a poisoned dress sent by Medea to her rival Glauce. Several ancient authors describe a dress fashioned by Hephaestos for Harmonia, the daughter of his unfaithful wife Aphrodite. It brought misfortune to anyone wearing it. Mayor cites similar tales from India. Heck, there is the suffocating dress, the poisoned comb, and the poisoned apple, all gifts, in the story of Snow White.

In the Ottawa story of the box from Montreal, and the similar Peruvian story, Pandora's box comes to mind. What is more, as we have seen in a previous chapter of our present saga, there was a pre-existing Huron legend very like the Pandora story. The wife of Nanabozho, out of curiosity, opened a sealed box and unleashed death into the world.

There is even a well-known modern urban legend:

A girl attends her senior prom in a beautiful new dress. During the dance, she feels faint, and asks to go outside for some fresh air. Gradually she becomes seriously ill, retreats to the toilet, and is later found there dead. It turns out that the dress had belonged to a corpse. It had been used as a funeral dress, then returned to the store for a refund. The formaldehyde the dress had soaked up from the embalming process was enough to kill the new owner.[488]

This suggests that the basic motif of the poisoned gift/blanket lives in and resonates in the human imagination. It touches upon an archetype of some sort. It appears in dreams. It is therefore likely to recurrently occur to both Indians and whites even in the absence of anything of the sort actually happening.

Bernard De Voto remarks that the blanket story "has the quality of legend and reappears at Fort McKenzie [on the Missouri] and in fact, nearly everywhere else."[489] Of course, that might be evidence that it actually happened. But urban legends are prolific in just this way.

Like an urban legend, what seems to have been originally the Fort Pitt story can be readily found here and there assigned by authors instead to the Seven Years' War, to New England, to Florida, to Andrew Jackson instead of Amherst—just like an urban legend, always given new relevance by supposedly having happened nearby, to someone famous, or to a friend of a friend of a friend. It happened at some fort, right? What forts do we have around here? As I recollect, that must have been either Fort Clark or Fort Union.

The true and original Fort Pitt incident was cited, with moral condemnation, by Francis Parkman in his 1851 study *The Conspiracy of Pontiac*. He called it "shameful" and "detestable."[490] Parkman's histories were widely popular and influential for about the next century; my grandparents, otherwise not history buffs, had copies in their library. It could from there have slipped into the popular culture, melded in many minds with a pre-existing mythical landscape, and worked its glamour on the collective unconscious. So the pervasive legend we know today.

Would Indians too have heard of it? There is no need to suppose so to explain the appearance of the myth motif—but then again, why not? If they did not read the books themselves, they would have been in contact with European traders who, as frontiersmen aficionados of the old frontier, would probably have steeped themselves in Parkman's books as a matter of geek pride.

It would not have necessarily hurt their interests, either, to recount the tale. While it might discourage trade, it might also be a warning not to trust other traders, or not to cheat the speaker. Esther and Allen Stearn report one apparent instance. Fur trader James McDougall is quoted saying to a summoned gathering of locals, "You know the smallpox. Listen: I am the smallpox chief. In this bottle I have it confined. All I have to do is to pull the cork, send it forth among you, and you are dead men. But this is for my enemies and not my friends."[491] Another fur trader, the Stearns report, once threatened Pawnee Indians that if they didn't agree to certain conditions, "he would let the smallpox out of a bottle and destroy them."[492]

This threat of disease is a time-honoured technique of Indian shamans too: treat them well, pay their fee, or they will curse you with some pestilence. "Hence," explains Father LeJeune in the Jesuit Relations, "it arises that these sorcerers are greatly feared, and that one would not dare offend them, because they can, the people believe, kill men by their arts."[493]

Such an urban legend, if it is a legend, would naturally be given a greater heft among Indians than we might expect among Europeans. And this quite aside from the fact that all their traditions are oral, the medium in which urban legends naturally thrive. Indians considered what is imagined to be real, and what is merely seen by the eyes to be of dubious consequence. Accordingly, if anyone ever dreamt that the Europeans were giving out smallpox blankets, that would be the hidden truth, understood as such. If the physical evidence was not there, that was not important. Sooner or later, it would probably show up. If not, so much the worse for physical evidence.

Regarding the myth of the Ojibway concerning infection by a British flag and other trade goods, quoted above, our literary source discovered the Ojibway were also aware of a quite independent explanation for the epidemic.

> This [the deliberate infection] was a serious charge, and in order to ascertain if it was really entertained by the more enlightened and thinking portions of the tribe, I have made particular inquiries, and flatter myself that I have obtained from the intelligent old chief of the Pillagers, a truthful account of the manner in which the smallpox was, on this occasion, actually introduced among the Ojibways.
>
> A war party of Kenistenos [Cree], Assineboines [Assiniboines], and Ojibways, was once formed at the great Kenisteno village, which was at this time located on Dead River, near its outlet into the Red River of the North. They proceeded westward to the waters of the Ke-che-pe-gan-o, or Missouri River, till they came to a large village of the Gi-aucth-in-ne-wug (Gros Ventres), which they surrounded and attacked. Through some cause which they could not at first account for, the resistance made to their attack was feeble. This they soon overcame, and the warriors rushing forward to secure their scalps, discovered the lodges filled with dead bodies, and they could not withstand the stench arising

> therefrom. The party retreated, after securing the scalps of those whom they had killed....
>
> ... [O]n the fourth day, one of their number died, they threw away the fearful scalp, and proceeded homeward with quickened speed. Every day, however, their numbers decreased, as they fell sick and died. Out of the party, which must have numbered a considerable body of warriors, but four survived to return home to their village at Dead River. They brought with them the fatal disease that soon depopulated this great village.... The large village of Sandy Lake suffered severely, and it is said that its inhabitants became reduced to but seven wigwams."[494]

One of the peculiarities of the imagination is that, within its magical realm, two or more contradictory things can both be true. In a dream, one can be walking down a street in Budapest, turn the corner, and be in Oshawa. As the Red Queen explained to Alice, in Wonderland it is perfectly simple to believe six impossible things before breakfast. "Truth" has to do with "vividness," not physical evidence or consistency. Accordingly, the Ojibway can tell two stories of the plague's start, both "true." They prefer the one that makes a better story, that touches more on important mythic themes. Our interlocutor, a European, prefers the one that seems more probable in fact. Bit of a dullard, actually.

Moreover, since all events begin in the imagination, it is impossible to explain any death by natural causes. Father LeJeune writes, "I hardly ever see any of them die who does not think he has been bewitched."[495] Someone must be to blame. Samuel Hearne writes, "When any of the principal Northern Indians die, it is generally believed that they are conjured to death, either by some of their own countrymen, by some of the Southern Indians, or by some of the Esquimaux."[496]

Now, given the mass death of so many Indians, and with whites generally not dying, who is obviously to blame?

When smallpox struck Huronia in the 1630s, this assumption was an immediate problem for Father Brébeuf and the Jesuits in residence. "The second obstacle arose from the tales spread among the people by followers of the devil,—that our Frenchmen, and we in particular, were the cause of this pestilence, and that our sole purpose in coming to their country was to compass their destruction."[497]

There is another relevant incident in the *Jesuit Relations*: the French overhear charges by an Algonquin that "the French had bewitched a cloak." Challenged, the man tells the French that he had heard it from the Hurons. Among the Hurons, when challenged, "those of one village accused the inhabitants of another of originating these reports." Eventually, they all agree that it was the Innu, not present, who started the rumour. Moreover, it was also really the Innu who were trading in poisoned clothing.[498] Amity was restored.

When a bad thing happens, it is the natural tendency to find someone to blame. Hence there was, we suppose, a vast conspiracy to assassinate Kennedy. Hence AIDS came originally from a secret CIA lab in Africa, intended to wipe out all members of the negroid race. And the convenient people to blame are always those not present at the table or council fire: the other guy. Here the Innu, once the French are present; most naturally, for any North American Indians, the Europeans.

There are other similar stories in the *Jesuit Relations*:

> On the 3rd of the same month [May], some Savages who came to see us said they had been told that a European of Acadia had asserted that word would be sent to the French who are in this country, that they should bewitch all the rivers and the waters of these regions, in order to kill off all the original Savages. "In fact," said they, "we already perceive that the waters taste bitter." They entreated me earnestly, if the ships brought such a message, to prevent this misfortune, and to warn them of it. These poor people do not know to what cause to attribute the mortality among them.[499]
>
> These tribes believe that we poison and bewitch them, carrying this so far that some of them no longer use the kettles of the French. They say that we have infected the waters, and that the mists which issue thence kill them [it appears that the Indians, like the Europeans, and for that matter the Chinese, the Turks, and the Indians of India, accepted the miasma theory of disease. Meaning, not incidentally, that they would have refused or cleaned any offered dirty blankets]; that our houses are fatal to them; that we have with us a dead body, which serves us as black magic; that, to kill their children, some Frenchmen penetrated the horrid depths of the woods, taking with them the picture of a little child which we had pricked with the points of awls, and that therein lay the exact cause of their death.[500]

The report on Ward Churchill's research misconduct puts it well: "We understand the grief and anger that have long led some people to see the outbreak as deliberate and to want to pin blame for the tragedy upon a particular group. Professor Churchill forms part of that tradition."[501]

Frankly, I blame the Jews. And the bicycle riders.

Again, any natural human tendency to scapegoat the "other" for misfortune is amplified in the native context. As we have seen, these were xenophobic cultures. They were at almost constant war with their neighbours, and usually did not see them as human. Why wouldn't a neighbour be out to destroy them by any means available?

Gilbert Sproat, reporting from among the Nootka of Vancouver Island in the later 19th century, remarks on the automatic suspicion among the Indians towards anyone not of their tribe. "[H]is eye is ever on the watch against the hostility of others," Sproat observes. "His thought, when he comes in contact with any but the few who are within the circle of his bosom friends, is, 'How can I turn this person to my own account, and how can I defend myself from his design against me?' ... [H]e does not for a moment believe that he is sacrificing a confiding or honest person, but sets down all appearance of unguardedness either to folly or simulation."[502]

And now you want him to believe that, given the opportunity, the whites are not trying to kill him? Please. What kind of sucker do you take him for?

"The Indian's suspicion," Sproat again says, "prevents a ready gratitude, as he is prone to see, in apparent kindness extended to him, some under-current of selfish motive."[503] Trojan horses are assumed.

Xenophobia also makes the image of "contamination" by newcomers both powerful and inevitable in the mind's eye—if in this case also largely true (if the disease did come, inadvertently, from the foreigners). Hence, by a natural association, there is contamination by Western trade goods. Hence, contamination by probably the most ubiquitous Western trade good, the blanket. It was the one most basic need of every trading Canadian Indian, in terms of what the foreigners had on offer—bedding and protection against the cold.

It fits, of course, equally well with the Noble Savage archetype. The Noble Savage is contaminated by any contact with civilization. Wearing the offered blanket brings death to the world.

On top of all this, it is in the interest of many in authority over the Indians not to discourage the legend of the smallpox blanket. It keeps their clients, so to speak, on the reservation. It convinces them that it is a cruel, dangerous, world out there, and they need the continued services of their known and trusted leaders to protect them from the evil outsiders. Nor should they interact with such outlanders, and so perhaps learn otherwise from them.

Bad medicine

Surprisingly enough, recent research casts new doubt on even the claim that it was European contact that brought the awful plagues to the Indians.

Tuberculosis, long thought to have come with Columbus, has now been found in ancient Peruvian corpses. The new theory is that it was reintroduced several times to America over the millennia by infected seals.[504]

As to the pox, recent work by McMaster University's Ana Duggan on the DNA of a mummified corpse in Latvia traces the origin of all known smallpox to a common ancestor that emerged somewhere between 1588 and 1645—both dates after Columbus.[505] What those early American outbreaks were, heaven knows—but the earliest definitely documented smallpox outbreak in Europe is actually London in 1632.[506]

It is even possible that smallpox emerged first among the Indians, and spread from them to Europe. In either case, where the infection started is suddenly irrelevant: both populations ought equally to have lacked immunity. Why then the far worse death toll in America?

There is an additional conundrum or two to consider here. There is growing evidence that Europeans, and Asians, have been visiting American shores for some time; Columbus seems only to have been the first naïve fool to publicize the event. At a minimum, the voyages of Leif Eriksson are now undeniable. Why then, having presumably already been exposed to European and Asian diseases, did so many Indians succumb in the 16th, 17th, 18th, and 19th centuries?

And again, there seems to have been not just one smallpox epidemic. When de Soto passed through the Southwest in 1540, he already found it radically depopulated by some plague. Vancouver found the Northwest again only recently depopulated in 1792. Lewis and Clark, venturing north and west of the Mississippi, found the area recently depopulated in 1806. The same region was depopulated by smallpox again in Ward Churchill's outbreak in the 1830s; and the Northwest Coast again in the 19th century. Wherever and whenever Europeans ventured in North America, they seem to have found the area only recently depopulated by disease.

These repeated waves of plague were noticed during the course of his own missionary career by Father Giroux, stationed at Arctic Red River. He saw several measles epidemics pass through, "so that it might be supposed that the most susceptible had been weeded out, and yet the last epidemic (1903) killed about one fifth of the entire population of the Mackenzie Valley."[507]

It cannot, then, in the end, be the Europeans who are responsible, even inadvertently. There was something in Indian culture that left it vulnerable to frequent, devastating plagues. These might well have been periodically passing through, without benefit of European interference, for as long as there have been mortal men in the Americas. The "balance" of nature, again.

It is impossible to tell from Indian oral traditions: there is no way of knowing whether a tribal memory is really from a hundred or from ten thousand years ago, or taken entire from the imagination a few nights before. In diagnosing mortality from diseases, as opposed to violence, skeletal remains are relatively unhelpful.[508] But, for what little it is worth, Father LeClercq finds among the Micmac a tradition of devastating plagues long before the first Europeans arrived.[509]

Jared Diamond suggests that the Indian population was simply too sparse to nurse a virus. He presents this as a big plus for pre-agricultural life: "Epidemics couldn't take hold when populations were scattered in small bands that constantly shifted camp."[510] We know this much to be false from our quick glance at the history of the North American Indian. Obviously, they were capable of experiencing epidemics. Big time. But perhaps the sparse population did mean that, once a virus thundered through and practically everybody died, there were not enough survivors with the resultant antibodies to keep said antibodies in the population. Too few people experienced low-level exposure from them, a natural inoculation. It was the antibody that could not "take hold." Over a generation or so, therefore, all natural immunity was lost, as if the virus had never been known.

"For mobile groups," writes William Buckner, "infants, the elderly, and other vulnerable individuals have little opportunity to develop resistance to local pathogens. This may help explain why infant and child mortality among hunter-gatherers tends to be so high. Across hunter-gatherer societies, only about 57% of children born survive to the age of 15."[511]

"Studies of an epidemiologically similar viral disease, measles, among isolated island populations," explains Robert Boyd,

> …have demonstrated that the disease will die out (for lack of susceptibles) when the total population drops beneath approximately one-third of a million. Above that mark, the disease is always present, maintained by a regularly renewed pool of susceptibles among the newborn and young children without acquired immunity. The aboriginal fishing and gathering populations of the Pacific Northwest were apparently neither dense nor continuous enough to support the continual presence of smallpox. The disease therefore occurred only periodically, dependent upon, first of all,

> introduction from outside the region and, secondly, the presence of a pool of non-immune susceptibles in the resident population. These epidemiological requirements explain the very distinctive patterning of smallpox epidemics in the Pacific Northwest during the early contact period. Epidemics appeared every generation: in the late 1770s, 1801-02, 1836-38, and finally (in two separate areas) in 1853 and 1862-63.[512]

Yet population density among the Indians of the Northwest Coast was among the highest anywhere in North America. At the same time, as most Indian groups were in constant motion, should some virus appear, it would quickly be widely spread.

Very well, then: one more big advantage, surely, to settled agriculture and civilization over the traditional Indian lifestyle. You get to not die off in droves every generation or so.

There is also another possibility, although it feels unkind to mention it: knowing nothing of hygiene, having little technology, including little medical technology, the Indians had no idea of how to prevent the spread of disease or reduce its mortality.

Early Europeans are indeed regularly appalled by the general lack of wholesomeness of the traditional Indian lifestyle.

Father LeJeune writes, of the Innu,

> They are nearly all attacked by this disease [scrofula; a form of tuberculosis], when young, both on account of their filthy habits, and because they eat and drink indiscriminately with the sick. I have seen them a hundred times paddle about in the kettle containing our common drink; wash their hands in it; drink from it, thrusting in their heads, like the animals; and throw into it their leavings; for this is the custom of the Savages, to thrust sticks into it that are half-burned and covered with ashes; to dip therein their bark plates covered with grease, the fur of the Moose, and hair; and to dip water therefrom with kettles as black as the chimney; and after that, we all drank from this black broth, as if it were ambrosia. This is not all; they throw therein the bones that they have gnawed, then put water or snow in the kettle, let it boil, and behold their hippocras. One day some shoes, which had just been taken off, fell into our drink; they soaked there as long as they pleased, and were withdrawn without exciting any special attention, and then the water was drunk as if nothing whatever had happened.[513]

Father LeClercq laments, of the Micmac,

> They are filthy and vile in their wigwams, of which the approaches are filled with excrements, feathers, chips, shreds of skins, and very often with entrails of the animals or the fishes which they take in hunting or fishing. In their eating they wash their meat only very superficially before putting it upon the fire, and they never clean the kettle except the first time that they use it. Their clothes are all filthy, both outside and inside, and soaked with oil and grease, of which the stink often produces sickness of the stomach. They hunt for vermin before everybody, without turning aside even a little. They make it walk for fun upon their hands, and they eat it as if it were something good.... Finally, however calm it may be outside of the wigwam, there always prevails inside a very inconvenient wind, since these Indians let it go very freely, especially when they have eaten much moose....[514]
>
> ... They content themselves with removing simply the largest moose hairs, although the meat may have been dragged around the wigwam for five or six days, and the dogs also may have tasted it beforehand. They have no other tables than the flat ground, nor other napkins for wiping their hands than their moccasins, or their hair, on which they sedulously rub their hands.[515]

Livingston Jones writes of the Tlingit, in the 19th century:

> The natives travel about so much and are so careless about spreading diseases that when this loathsome disease breaks out it soon goes from one end of the country to the other. Their communal style of living and the unsanitary conditions of their villages highly favor it. For these reasons, when it breaks out fearful mortality results from it.[516]
>
> The natives have no knowledge of, and, apparently, no concern about, sanitation. Discarded garments and old shoes lying rotting in the moist soil; salmon skins and salmon flesh disintegrating; tin cans partially filled with stinking slush and half buried; rotten logs and decaying organic matter everywhere. Both inside and out we find everything conducive to the propagation of germs.[517]

Vilhjalmur Stefansson says, of the Inuit/Eskimo,

> The housekeeping methods ... are entirely unsuited for the log cabin, which soon becomes filthy and remains so. Eventually the germs of tuberculosis get into the house and obtain lodging in it. The members of the same family catch the disease, one from the other, and when the family has

> been nearly or quite exterminated by the scourge, another family moves in, for the building of a house is hard work and it is a convenient thing to find one ready for your occupancy; and so it is not only the family that built the house that suffers but there is also through the house a procession of other families moving from the wigwam to the graveyard.[518]

Stefansson follows many writers in supposing that the problem began when Indians ended their nomadic habits and moved into log houses. This seems more likely only an expression of the Noble Savage myth: any troubles must be from civilization. Accumulated dirt is not the critical factor in spreading illness: it is sharing utensils, bedding, food, bodily fluids. This would have been equally possible in a wigwam. Indeed, leaving aside the testimony of LeJeune and LeClercq, the annual reports of the Department of Indian Affairs note of the Indians of Northwestern Ontario, still "living in tents during the entire year," "entirely dependent upon hunting and fishing," that "tuberculosis is the great menace to their health."[519] Stale air need have little to do with it; although it might have worsened the symptoms.

So too Bishop Bompas, writing of the nomadic Indians of the Mackenzie Valley in the 1880s:

> One great blessing of the Arctic climate is the healthiness of it. Sickness is rare among the resident Europeans.... Let the consumptive patients be despatched to Mackenzie River for recovery, rather than to Madeira to die. It is singular, however, that this climate, healthful to the resident Europeans, does not conduce to good health among the native Indians. These are often consumptive, a tendency which seems due to a scrofulous constitution. Vicious and uncleanly habits, irregular diet, alternate gluttony and starvation, exposure and self-neglect, may also be among the causes of the Indian sickliness.[520]

Smallpox is now thankfully eradicated everywhere; but tuberculosis, and other diseases, are still unusually common on Indian reserves. This can no longer be because of low population densities. Nor can it be due to feast or famine, nor irregular diet. It must have something to do with either genetics or the Indian lifestyle.

This all goes against conventional wisdom, of course. It is not just that "everybody knows" the Europeans deliberately killed off the Indians with smallpox blankets. It is also that "everybody knows" Indians have special wisdom when it comes to natural health, to healing plants and so forth. They gave us, after all, Kickapoo patent medicines, didn't they? That, and tobacco? Wait—one out of two still isn't bad, is it? And peyote? Okay, never mind.

But Indian medical expertise is all an artifact of the Noble Savage myth. Of course, being at one with nature, they were supposed to have a special insight into nature's healing powers. Albeit diseases are a part of nature too. Even so, back on Earth, it stands to reason that the same factors that caused the Indians to lag in material technology would also cause them to lag in medical knowledge—which is, after all, a form of material technology.

Samuel Hearne writes of the Dene, "[T]he natives themselves never make use of any medicines of their own preparing."[521] Bishop Bompas agrees: "None of the Indians of Mackenzie River seem to have been acquainted with the use of plants or herbs for medicines. In their medicine making they used only the charms of drumming and singing. The Esquimaux, with the drumming and singing, combine an address as to an invisible spirit supposed to have power over the disease."[522] Alexander Mackenzie writes: "[T]heir only remedies consist in binding the temples, procuring perspiration, singing, and blowing on the sick person, or affected part."[523] Yes, the Indians of the Plains had their "medicine bundles" which they carried with them at all times. But what was in those bundles? Mostly good luck charms, not anything we would understand as medicine.[524]

This stands to reason: if you do not believe the physical world is real, all illness is spiritual in origin; the treatment should also be spiritual.

And there is an additional factor: when everyone is dying young from constant war and starvation in any case, it does not seem urgent, and one does not commonly have the time or available control groups to study the effects of any given practice on one's long-term health. Smoking, getting blind drunk, indiscriminate sex, peyote, or sharing spit.

By artificially preserving some part of traditional Indian culture, are we killing Indians?

15 LAST OF THE BEOTHUK

Shanawdithit.

> *"All gone widdun (asleep). Nance go widdun too, no more come Nance, run away, no more come."*
>
> *—Shanawdithit, "Nancy April," last known Beothuk*

Are there Beothuks?

You may think you know a little about the Beothuk, the aboriginal inhabitants of Newfoundland. And you may be right. More likely, you are wrong.

For we know almost nothing about the Beothuk. Much of what is recorded is contradictory. It is mostly oral, at second or subsequent hand, often originally from trappers and fisherfolk. Sailors' tales and legends. You know what they say about sailors' tales.

The perfect blank canvas on which to project the familiar Noble Savage, and a terrible genocide as a parable for the evils of civilization.

And so we feature the Beothuk here. This is, with the smallpox blankets, the other familiar Canadian genocide claim; the traditional proof that the aboriginals were unjustly treated. The European settlers, we are told, hunted them for sport, to the point of extermination. When challenged, in the inky pages of the *National Post*, with the claim that there was no genocide against Indians in Canada, Stephen Maher writes, "Not genocide? Ask the Beothuks." The Europeans, he points out, "drove [the Beothuk] away from the coast, into the forest and barrens, where the ones who did not starve to death were hunted like animals."[525]

But in fact, the British and the Newfoundland government were not even sure the Beothuk existed.

When, in the first decade of the seventeenth century, a company formed in London with the madcap notion of planting a colony in Newfoundland, the charter averred, "we being well assured that the same country adjoining to the aforesaid coastes, where our subjects use to fishe, remaineth so destitute and so desolate of inhabitants, that scarce any one salvage [savage] person hath in many years beene scene in the most parts thereof."[526] In 1640, when an English expedition to Newfoundland loaded manufactures in hopes of trading with Indians, they faced the objection, "if there be a trade there must be somebody supposed with whom to trade, and there be noe natives, upon the island."[527]

As late as 1793, the matter was still disputed: "It has been doubted whether there are any Newfoundland Indians or not."[528] Even if Indians have been very occasionally spotted, said Indians, being nomadic, might just as well have come from the mainland, and be only visiting.

In 1811, Lieutenant Buchan, following an expedition to Red Indian Lake in the dark interior, is able at last to assert, of these Red Indians, "it appears then that they are permanent inhabitants, and not occasional visitors."[529]

Within 20 years, he was wrong.

As of 1830, by our best present estimates, there were indeed no native Indians in Newfoundland.

At least, there have been no sightings since.

How could the English have developed genocidal designs against the Beothuk, when they were not sure they existed? You want to go out and exterminate unicorns? And, if the Beothuk population was so scant, why any drive to be rid of them? In order to take their land? For fishermen?

Official policy for many years was actually to prohibit settlement in Newfoundland, and to refuse to recognize land ownership by Europeans. The home government feared it would interfere with the fishing trade. As early as 1633, and in repeated statutes following, European residence in Newfoundland was forbidden by the British government. Ships were not to transport settlers, or leave any crew behind. Squatters who might nevertheless be there were forbidden to cut trees or build structures within six miles of the coast. Until the early 19th century land title was not recognized.[530]

And so, despite what you read in the papers, there was no genocide, intentional or even as collateral damage.

War, not genocide

You need not take my word for it. This is not controversial among historians. It is the consensus. Pick up Totten and Bartrop's *Dictionary of Genocide*. Turn to the entry for the Beothuk. "[T]he critical component of intent is absent. The British government did not pursue a policy aimed at the destruction of the Beothuk.... Modern day claims that the Beothuks were 'murdered for fun,' by the English settlers, who hunted them for 'sport' do the historical record less than justice and sow an unfortunate confusion in the mind of an unsuspecting public. Extinction came to the Beothuks of Newfoundland, but it did not come through genocide."[531] Or take J.R. Miller's recent treatment of the history of Indians in Canada, *Skyscrapers Hide the Heavens*: "Older notions that the Europeans somehow 'used' the Mi'kmaq against the Beothuk are invalid, as is the controversial charge that Europeans hunted Beothuk for 'sport'.... [T]hey were not systematically hunted down, nor were they the objects of a campaign of genocide.... Accusations of genocide in Newfoundland ... diminish Europeans' humanity by accusing them of actions they did not perform."[532]

Granted, in a few outports on the northeast coast, Beothuk Indians seem to have come into lethal conflict with fishermen. Sir Joseph Banks writes, in 1766, "Our people, who fish in these parts, live in a continual state of warfare with them, firing at them whenever they meet with them, and if they chance to find their houses or wigwams as they call them, plundering them immediately...."

This, however, he does not understand as hunting anybody down. This was war. And there were two sides in this war. He goes on to say, "They in return, look upon us in exactly the same light as we do them, killing our people whenever they get the advantage of them, and stealing or destroying their nets, wherever they find them."[533]

Has Banks not, at least, proven the existence of the Beothuk? Not quite; he is only reporting second hand, and conveying oral traditions. He adds, "So much for the Indians: if half of what I have written about them is true, it is more than I expect…."[534]

In 1768, Governor Palliser commissioned Lieutenant John Cartwright to head into the dark interior, to see if he could indeed find any local Indians, and if so to establish friendly relations. Cartwright too speaks of local conflict with the Beothuk, and blames the English fisherfolk.

> On the part of the English fishers, it is an inhumanity which sinks them far below the level of savages. The wantonness of their cruelties towards the poor wretches, has frequently been almost incredible. One well-known fact shall serve as a specimen. A small family of Indians being surprised in their wigwam, by a party of fishermen, they all tried to avoid if possible, the instant death that threatened them from the fire-arms of their enemies; when one woman, being unable to make her escape, yielded herself into their power. Seeing before her none but men, she might naturally have expected that her sex alone would have disarmed their cruelty; but to awaken in them still stronger motives to compassion, she pointed with an air of most moving entreaty to her prominent belly. Could all nature have produced another pleader of such eloquence as the infant there concealed? But this appeal, Oh, shame to humanity! was alas! in vain; for an instant stab, that ripped open her womb, laid her at the feet of those cowardly ruffians, where she expired in great agonies. Their brutal fury died not with its unhappy victim; for with impious hands they mutilated the dead body, so as to become a spectacle of the greatest horror. And that no aggravation of their crime might be wanting, they made, at their return home, their boasts of this exploit. Charity might even have prevailed in their favour, against their own report, and have construed their relation into an idle pretence only of wickedness, which, however, they were incapable of having in reality committed, had they not produced the hands of the murdered woman, which they displayed on the occasion as a trophy."[535]

That sounds pretty bad. And again from Cartwright:

> Some fishermen, as they doubled in their boat, a point of land, discovering a single defenceless woman with an infant on her shoulde rs, one of them instantly discharged at her a heavy load of swan shot, and lodged it in her loins. Unable now to sustain her burthen, she unwillingly put it down, and

> with difficulty crawled into the woods, holding her hand upon the mortal wound she had received, and without once taking off her eyes from the helpless object she had left behind her. In this dreadful situation she beheld her child ravished from her by her murderers, who carried it to their boat.... [B]ut what feeling, what mode of disgust has nature implanted in the human heart, to express its abhorrence of the wretch who can be so hardened to vice as to conceive that he is entitled to a reward for the commission of such bloody deeds! One of the very villains concerned in this capture of the child, supposing it a circumstance that would be acceptable to the Governor, actually came to the writer of these remarks at Toulinguet, to ask a gratuity for the share he had borne in the transaction.[536]

Cartwright continues:

> [S]urprises in their wigwams have generally proved fatal to them, and upon sudden accidental meetings it has been the usual practice of the fishermen to destroy them unprovoked, while the terrified Indians have attempted nothing but to make their escape, of which the two cases I have mentioned are shocking instances. The fishermen generally even take a brutal pleasure in boasting of these barbarities. He that has shot one Indian values himself more upon the fact than had he overcome a bear or wolf and fails not to speak of it with a brutal triumph, especially in the mad hours of drunkenness.[537]

One can certainly see, from this, where the story of genocide came from. It may, indeed, have come entirely from this government report, and the testimony of Cartwright. It seems damning enough.

But is it the whole story? Was the conflict so one-sided? Was it a matter of isolated incidents, or something widespread? And if we are relying on the report of one man, there remains the possibility that Cartwright is not in this a reliable narrator. He may not be fair to the fisherfolk, in putting all blame on them. He writes, after all, in the days of the romantic period, when to be young, as Wordsworth said, was very heaven. Never were savages nobler. Living in the innocence of nature, they could not themselves have been responsible for any sort of sinful act. Had they been, the fall would have followed, and they would already be Europeans.

They were necessarily as guiltless as the jaybirds or the bunny rabbits.

If he is so influenced, Cartwright may simply be assuming *a priori* that the Beothuks cannot have been guilty of any comparable fault. We have seen already how the myth of the Noble Savage can supersede the evidence, even evidence readily-available.

There is surely a certain whiff of classism in Cartwright's condemnation of the poor, poorly educated, lower-class fisherfolk. In telling the tale of the taking of the Beothuk child, Cartwright seems most upset at the fact that the orphaned child was put on display before the common riffraff.

And for money!

And so little money!

"The woman was shot in August 1768, and to complete the mockery of human misery, her child was the winter following, exposed as a curiosity to the rabble at Pool for two pence apiece."[538]

Rabble. Not an egalitarian sentiment. This sort of hoi polloi might even vote for Trump.

The fisherfolk, as Cartwright is apparently unaware or does not see fit to report, had their tales of Beothuk atrocities.

> An old man named George Wells, of Exploits Burnt Island, gave me the following information in 1886.... His great uncle on his mother's side, Rousell of New Bay, ... was killed by them while taking salmon out of his pound (weir) in New Bay River. The Indians hid in the bushes and shot him with arrows, wounding him very severely. He ran back towards his salmon house where he had a gun tailed, but he fell dead before reaching it.[539]
>
> They frequently lay in ambush for the fishermen and even used decoys, such as sea birds attached to long lines. When the fishermen approached and gave chase to the birds, in their boats the Indians would gradually draw their decoys towards the shore, in order to get the boats within reach of their arrows. They sometimes used "dumb arrows" all of wood, without any stone point, which by reason of their lightness fell short when fired off, thus leading the fishermen to believe they could approach nearer without running any risk, but when they did so they were met with a shower of well pointed and heavier arrows.[540]

Inspector Grimes of the Newfoundland Constabulary, a native of Notre Dame Bay, recalled a tale from his youth of "how a party of fishermen were attacked in their boat by the Indians and all killed except one man who managed to effect his escape with an arrow sticking in his neck behind the ear. In this plight he reached his home with the boat."[541]

Who started the fight? That, unfortunately, is lost in the Newfoundland fog. All of this happened where there was no law, and mostly beyond the reach of official records.

"I was informed by Henry Rousell, residing in Hall's Bay," reports Thomas Peyton, a prominent resident on the northeast coast, "that the first five men who attempted to make a settlement in that Bay were all killed by the Indians. A crew came up from Twillingate shortly afterwards and found their bodies with the heads cut off and stuck on poles."[542]

So according to the fishermen, it began with the Beothuk.

Earlier, indeed, there seems to have been conflict between the Beothuk and the French.

> On October l0th, 1610, the *Procureur* of St. Malo made complaint that in the preceding year many masters and sailors of vessels fishing in Newfoundland, had been killed by the savages, and presented a request to Court that the inhabitants of St. Malo be allowed to arm two vessels to make war upon the savages, so that they might be able to fish in safety. Permission was obtained, and St. Malo fishermen fitted out every year, one or more vessels for this purpose.... The custom was continued at least until 1635.[543]

"In the harbor of Les Oyes (?), (St Julien)" reports Sir David Kirke, writing in or about 1638,

> ...about eighty Indians assaulted a companie of French whilst they were pylinge up their fishinge, and slew seven of them; proceedinge a little further, killed nine more in the same manner, and clothinge sixteen of their company in the apparell of the slayne French, they went on the next day to the harbor of Petty Masters (Croc Harbor), and not being suspected by the French that were there, by reason of their habit, they surprised them at their work and killed twenty-one more. Soe, in two dayes having barbarously maymed thirty-seven, they returned home, as is their manner, in great triumph, with the heads of the slayne Frenchmen.[544]

Captain Wheeler, commander of an English convoy in 1684, attests, "The French ... are at utter variance with the Indians, who are numerous [*sic*?!], and so the French never reside in winter, and always have their arms by them."[545]

Given the general uncertainty, we cannot be sure these conflicts were with the Beothuks, as opposed to the Eskimo, Innu, or Micmac, any of whom might also have been passing through Newfoundland. But if there was early conflict between the Beothuk and the French, that is remarkable. The French had a knack for getting along with Indians. And the French got along well, specifically, with the Innu and the Micmac.

From the Beothuk perspective, no doubt, even if they fired first, it was within their natural rights to attack anyone trespassing on their lands. The Europeans were the trespassers. You can see their point.

But you can also see the point of view of a fisherman living alone on the northeast shore, unacknowledged by the government, far from the protections of urban life. He had no interest in taking anyone's territory. His interest was the sea nearby, which belonged to all, by common law, and he took no resources from the Beothuk. His concern was cod; the Beothuk did not fish for cod.[546] Yet the Beothuk were taking his few belongings; they were trying to kill him, his wife, and his children. There was no law to stop them. He had three choices: get out; lay down and die; or defend himself by vigilante action.

The government response

As to how widespread this sort of thing was, Cartwright's allegations of conflict between fishermen and Indians on the northeast coast seem to have been news to the government, away in St. John's. After all, they were still not sure the Beothuk existed. Had they had many reports of such encounters, they would not have been in such doubt. But once they heard Cartwright's report, the government was not sanguine. A committee of enquiry was struck□ wisely enough not relying on just one man's word□ and took testimony from, among others, Vice Admiral Edwards, governor from 1757 to 1759, and again 1789 to 90.

"He knew one instance, in 1758, of a murder committed by some Irish hunters on the north part of the island." Governor Edwards testified. "They fired into a wigwam, killed a woman with a child and brought away a girl of nine years old. Complaint was made to him by the Justices, and pains taken to catch the culprits, but without effect. The girl was brought home to England." If the miscreants had been caught, Edwards maintained, "he would have tried them at the Court of Oyer and Terminer." But "Mr Cartwright never made any complaints to him of the cruel treatment of the Indians by the inhabitants, and he knows of no other instance of it."[547]

However, the majestic cogs and lovely flywheels of government now began to turn, and entirely on behalf of the still semi-mythical Beothuk. Within the year of Cartwright's report, John Byron, the incumbent governor, issued a proclamation:

> WHEREAS it has been represented to the King, that the subjects residing in the said Island of Newfoundland, instead of cultivating such a friendly intercourse with the savages inhabiting that island as might be for their mutual benefit and advantage, do treat the said savages with the greatest inhumanity, and frequently destroy them without the least provocation or remorse. In order, therefore, to put a stop to such inhuman barbarity, and that the perpetrators of such atrocious crimes may be brought to due punishment, it is His Majesty's royal will and pleasure, that I do express his abhorrence of such inhuman barbarity, and I do strictly enjoin and require all His Majesty's subjects to live in amity and brotherly kindness with the native savages of the said island of Newfoundland. I do also require and command all officers and magistrates to use their utmost diligence to discover and apprehend all persons who may be guilty of murdering any of the said native Indians, in order that such offenders may be sent over to England, to be tried for such capital crimes as by the statute of 10 and 11 William III for encouraging the trade to Newfoundland is directed.
>
> Given under my hand,
>
> J. BYRON.[548]

Note that, by this proclamation, the killing of an Indian was not just to be prosecuted as murder might be in England; it amounted in practical terms to a more serious crime. It was to be tried in England. This made anyone charged with the murder, guilty or innocent, liable for the price of passage, and certainly bound to lose his meagre income for the extended time that journey would require. A significant burden for a fisherman in a Newfoundland outport.

The proclamation was re-issued by Commodore Robert Duff, governor in 1775, and again by Governor Montague, in 1776.[549] It was stiffened by later governors. In 1807, for example, Governor Holloway issued this proclamation:

> It having been represented to me that various acts of violence and inhuman cruelties, have been, at different times, committed by some of the people employed as Furriers [i.e., trappers], or otherwise, upon the Indians, the original Inhabitants of this Island, residing in the interior parts thereof, contrary to every principle of religion and humanity, and in direct violation of His Majesty's mild and beneficial Instructions to me respecting this poor defenceless tribe, I hereby issue this my Proclamation, warning all persons whatsoever, from being guilty of acts of cruelty, violence, outrage and robbery against them, and if any Person or

> Persons shall be found after this Proclamation, to act in violation of it, they will be punished to the utmost rigor of the law, the same as if it had been committed against myself, or any other of His Majesty's Subjects. And all those who may have any intercourse or trade with the said Indians, are hereby earnestly entreated to conduct themselves with peaceableness and mildness towards them, and use their utmost endeavours to live in kindness and friendship with them that they may be conciliated and induced to come among us as Brethren, when the public, as well as themselves, will be benefited by their being brought to a state of civilization, social order, and to a blessed knowledge of the Christian Religion. And I hereby offer a Reward of Fifty Pounds to such person or persons as shall be able to induce or persuade any of the male Tribe of Native Indians to attend them to the Town of St. John's, as also all expenses attending their journey or passage. The same Reward shall be paid to any person who shall give information of any murder committed upon the bodies of the aforesaid Indians and being proved upon the oath of one or more credible witnesses.
>
> I therefore call upon all Magistrates and other Officers of Justice, to promote to the utmost of their power, the intention of this Proclamation, by apprehending and bringing to justice all persons offending against the same.
>
> Given under my hand at Fort Townshend,
>
> St. John's, Newfoundland, the 30th July, 1807,
>
> J. HOLLOWAY.[550]

Governor Keats's proclamation in 1813 ended with these words:

> [I]f any of His Majesty's subjects, contrary to the expression of these, His Royal Highness's commands, shall so far forget themselves, and be so lost to the sacred duties of Religion and Hospitality, as to exercise any cruelty, or be guilty of any ill-treatment towards this inoffensive people, they may expect to be punished with the utmost rigour of the Law.[551]

So there you are. Not a lot of ambiguity. It all seems rather less than a plan by the Europeans to wipe out the Beothuk. A very cold, holstered, gun.

If anything, the government seems to have systematically taken the side of the Indians against the poor fishermen. One hopes that there was some official intention, even if unstated, to also prosecute and punish Beothuks who murdered fishermen. The possibility does not seem to have occurred to the officials. The fisherfolk are given no such assurance; no protection is offered. Noble savages, after all.

Note that these proclamations also gave the poor fishermen themselves material incentives to report any killing of Beothuks. All they needed was the word of one other credible witness. A significant incentive, if you are living at the bare subsistence level. Yet no reports ensued.

This surely indicates that the shooting of Beothuks was actually rather rare.

What conflict there was on the northeast coast simply demonstrates that the state of man in nature is, in Hobbes's phrase, a "war of all against all." People of the palest possible complexion, forced by the absence of government into such a situation as the Indians always lived with, must act just as Indians did.

George Cartwright, John Cartwright's brother, was asked by the commission of enquiry, "Had the Magistrates used any exertions to prevent those outrages?" Cartwright replied, "There are no Magistrates within that district, that he knew of...." "And being asked, whether the Magistrates resident within any of the other districts were capable of preventing these horrors if they exerted themselves for that purpose, he said, 'He does not believe they could, because they reside at too great a distance.'"[552]

"[S]uch has been the policy respecting this island," John Reeves, Newfoundland's Chief Justice, agreed, "that the residents for many years had little benefit of a regular government for themselves, and when they were so neglected, it is not to be wondered that the condition of the poor Indians was never mended."[553]

Who killed the Beothuk?

So, given that it was not genocide, who or what killed the Beothuk?

In the first instance, what we have here is a failure to communicate.

As noted before, European settlers had no cause to kill Indians. Just the reverse—Indians were valuable suppliers, advisors, labourers, and customers.

This was the attitude of the English authorities in Newfoundland from the start. They wanted a fur trade. When, early in the 1600s, the "Council and Company of the New-Found-Land Plantation" was formed for the purpose of colonization, among the articles of incorporation was that the company's ships were to carry, duty-free, "all other things necessary and for the use and desoine and trade with the people there, if any be inhabiting in that country or shall come out of other parts, there, to trade with the 'Plantation.' …"[554] It was almost their first thought. They stocked up with trade goods just on the off-chance, even though conventional wisdom held that there were no Indians in the area.

But to make this work, even if there are Indians, you need to establish communication, and make the locals understand that you want to trade.

In most places, this was not difficult. The Indians spontaneously offered to trade with Columbus almost as soon as he landed. Cartier's log entry of his first encounter with North American Indians reads, "Although we didn't understand each other's languages we managed to trade some of our belongings for some food."[555] When Perez first met the Indians of Canada's Pacific Coast, he notes, "They were glad to barter their dried fish, furs, wooden boxes, and images, mats of wool or hair, and other native products, particularly for knives and anything made of iron."[556] Ross, seeking the Northwest Passage, gave the first Eskimos he encountered iron hoops. He intended them as gifts, but the Eskimos insisted on exchanging them for their spears.[557]

This stands to reason. The Europeans had many things the Indians did not have, which would be to the Indians of immense value: iron tools, warm blankets, iron weapons, gunpowder; not to mention lovely beads, jaw harps, or distilled spirits. Normally and naturally, the impetus for trade came from the Indians.

But the Beothuk never offered. They instead stayed hidden.

What do you do, with a new tribe, if they do not initiate the offer? Even should you locate them, neither party speaks the other's language. In the case of the Beothuk, being an island people, rarely seen and obviously shy, to say the least, of outsiders, including other Indians, this was a conundrum. There were no nearby tribes with friendly relations who could interpret, or pass on to them any information.

Once Lieutenant Cartwright's expedition, in 1768, had confirmed definitely that local Indians existed, the authorities attempted to make contact. Aside from the material benefits to both Indians and themselves, this would bring the Beothuk, and the fishermen, within the protection of law.

One strategy, tried on several occasions, was to leave "gifts" in any abandoned Indian dwelling, or at places the Indians were thought to frequent.

But this may have been counterproductive.

It did not result, usually, in a trade, and never established a trading tradition. It might instead have reinforced an idea, among the Indians, that any European goods were free for the taking.

This idea would have been already fostered by the European ban on settlement. Without permanent residents, fishing parties were obliged to leave their shore stations, built for drying the catch, untended each winter. Anything left was open to any nearby Beothuk for the taking. Theft, to the mind of the Europeans. Perhaps free gifts, to the mind of the Beothuk. And, thus able to get European stuff without cost, there was that much less incentive among the Beothuk for commerce. Why buy a newspaper when you can read the news free on the Internet? If, on the other hand, the Indians did understand what they did as pilfering, they were likely to fear and avoid the English rather than trade, fearing retribution.

The next government idea was probably worse. Governor Holloway alludes to it in his edict. He offers a reward to anyone who can "induce or persuade" a Beothuk to accompany him to St. John's. This means, in effect, given the inability to communicate, to kidnap an Indian. The plan was to treat the captive well, show them all the impressive sights, then release him or her back to the tribe, to report on what a decent bunch of chaps the English were. Even when Sir John Guy set out in 1610, among his instructions were, "And we would have you to assay by all good means to capture one of the savages of the country and to intreate him well, and to keep him and teach him our language, that you may after obtayne a safe and free commerce with them, which are strong there."[558]

This involved one obvious difficulty: kidnapping, however well meant, is not necessarily seen as a friendly act. When tried, it almost always led to killing at least one Indian—all in "self-defence" while spiriting another off. Worse, kidnapped Indians had a nasty but remarkably persistent habit of dying of consumption in custody, making all the nice treatment, gifts, coaching in English, and attention a bit of a waste. And probably leaving the impression among surviving tribe members that they had been murdered.

Beothuk captives who did survive were also apparently afraid to return to their people. "Shanawdithit," according to a resolution of the Beothuk Institute, formed for the protection and assistance of the Beothuk race, "the surviving female of those who were captured four years ago, by some fishermen, will not now return to her tribe, for fear they should put her to death."[559] "She feared to return to her tribe, believing that the mere fact of her residing amongst the whites for a time, would make her an object of hatred to the Red men."[560] Demasduit, an earlier captive, when brought back inland, first would not get out of the boat, then declared "that she only wanted her child and that she would return with us."[561]

Perhaps life among the Europeans was just too wonderful. Or perhaps Demasduit was worried about her fate should she stay.

In 1808, Governor Holloway hit upon another idea: make a painting, showing Indians trading cheerfully with Europeans, and have it conveyed to the Beothuk, to plant the proper idea in their minds. A picture, after all, is worth several thousand words in a language they cannot understand.

A painting was therefore commissioned. A Lieutenant Spratt was sent to the Bay of Exploits "in order to attempt a communication with the native savages of the Island." With him he carried the painting "which represented an officer of the Royal Navy in full dress shaking hands with an Indian chief, and pointing to a party of seamen behind him who were laying some bales of goods at the feet of the chief. Behind the latter were some male and female Indians presenting furs to the officers. Further to the left were seen an European and an Indian mother looking with delight at their respective children of the same size, who were embracing one another. In the opposite corner a British tar was courting, in his way, an Indian beauty."[562]

Unfortunately, no Indians were found.

The painting reportedly was later hung at the court house in St. John's.

In 1810, burdened with gifts, Lieutenant David Buchan was sent by the governor to again attempt contact. He surprised a Beothuk camp, and seemed to make them understand his honourable intentions. At last, the desired commerce seemed at hand.

> [F]rom the utmost state of alarm they soon became curious, and examined our dress with great attention and surprise. They kindled a fire and presented us with venison steaks, and fat run into a solid cake, which they used with lean meat. Everything promised the utmost cordiality; knives, handkerchiefs, and other little articles were presented to them, and in return they offered us skins. I had to regret our utter ignorance of their language, and the presents at a distance of at least twelve miles occasioned me much embarrassment; I used every endeavour to make them understand my great desire that some of them should accompany us, to the place where our baggage was, and assist bringing up such things as we wore, which at last they seemed perfectly to comprehend. Three hours and a half having been employed in conciliatory endeavours, and every appearance of the greatest amity subsisting between us; and considering a longer tarry useless, without the means of convincing them farther of our friendship, giving them to

> understand that we were going, and indicating our intention to return, four of them signified that they would accompany us. James Butler, corporal, and Thomas Bouthland, private of marines, observing this, requested to be left behind in order to repair their snow shoes; and such was the confidence placed by my people in the natives that most of the party wished to be the individuals to remain among them. I was induced to comply with the first request from a motive of showing the natives a mutual confidence, and cautioning them to observe the utmost regularity of conduct, at 10 a.m., having myself again shook hands with all the natives, and expressed, in the best way I could, my intentions to be with them in the morning, we set out. They expressed satisfaction by signs on seeing that two of us were going to remain with them, and we left them accompanied by four of them.
>
> ... Being under the necessity of going single, in turning a point one of the Indians having loitered behind, took the opportunity, and set off with great speed calling out to his comrade to follow.... This incident was truly unfortunate, as we were nearly in sight of our fire place.... He had however, evidently some suspicions, as he had frequently come and looked eagerly in my face, as if to read my intentions.... In order to try the disposition of the remaining Indian he was made to understand that he was at liberty to go if he chose, but he showed no wish of this kind. At 3 p.m. we joined the rest of our party, when the Indian started at seeing so many more men; but this was of momentary duration, for he soon became pleased with all he saw; I made him a few presents and showed the articles which were to be taken up for his countrymen consisting of blankets, woollen wrappers, and shirts, beads, hatchets, knives and tin pots, thread, needles and fish hooks, with which he appeared much satisfied, and regaled himself with tea and broiled venison....

The journal continues:

> Friday the 25th of Jan. — ... At 7 a.m. set out leaving only eight of the party behind.... At 2 p.m. we arrived at the wigwams, when my apprehensions were unfortunately verified; they were left in confusion, nothing of consequence remaining in them but some deer skins.
>
> Saturday 26th Jan. — ... As soon as it was light the crew were put in motion, and placing an equal number of blankets, shirts and tin pots in each of the wigwams, I gave the Indian to understand that those articles were for the individuals who

> resided in them. Some more presents were given to him, also some articles attached to the red staff, all of which he seemed to comprehend. At 7 a.m. we left the place intending to return the Monday following. Seeing that the Indian came on, I signified my wish for him to go back; he however continued with us, sometimes running on a little before in a zigzag direction, keeping his eyes to the ice as having a trace to guide him, and once pointed to the westward, and laughed. Being now about two-thirds of a mile from the wigwams, he edged in suddenly, and for an instant halted; then took to speed [ran off]. We at this moment observed that he had stopped to look at a body lying on the ice, he was still within half a musket-shot, but as his destruction could answer no end, so it would have been equally vain to attempt pursuit; we soon lost sight of him in the haze. On coming up we recognised with horror the bodies of our two unfortunate companions lying about a hundred yards apart; that of the corporal being first, was pierced by one arrow in the back; three arrows had entered that of Bouthland. They were laid out straight with their feet towards the river, and backs upwards; their heads were off, and carried away, and no vestige of garments left. Several broken arrows lying about and a quantity of bread, which must have been emptied out of their knapsacks; very little blood was visible.[563]

Damn.

The naive plans of civilized men, destroyed by the logic of total war.

According to Shanawdithit's later memories, the tribe, left alone, had decided the Europeans must have gone to bring a larger contingent in order to wipe them out. Best to disappear. But first, kill the hostages so they cannot give any clues.

The Beothuk seem to bear most of the responsibility here. They were obviously xenophobic, even by Indian standards. In the jargon of postcolonialism, they saw all "others" as "subalterns." Several reports have it that, unlike all other Indians, they did not keep dogs. Might this suggest some kind of purity taboo?

In trying to establish friendly contact and amicable relations, what would you have done that the British did not do? The French, perhaps, would have sent in a few Jesuits to be tortured and killed, to demonstrate their good character. The English may have lacked such volunteers.

This was unlucky primarily for the Beothuk. With a fur trade, instead of dying out, they might have prospered. Besides cool swag of all kinds, and no longer being shot at, they might have acquired guns themselves for self-defense and the hunt. If this did not already ensure enough food at all times, furs could be bartered for more. Even if they had no furs to trade, it would have been in the European traders' self-interest, as we have seen elsewhere, to keep them alive in any extremity.

But there were even worse consequences of the Beothuk failure to trade. There were lots of good-looking fur bearing critters in Newfoundland: beaver, fox, marten. Their anti-free trade policy left a vacuum for others to fill.

And not just European trappers, although they too came into conflict with the Beothuk. The French founded a post at Placentia, on the south coast. The Micmac, familiar with the French and the fur trade, followed them. They began trapping in Newfoundland, and a thriving market in furs grew.

But they were now in contact with the Beothuk, who hated intruders, and in competition with them for resources. And the Micmac, trading with the Europeans, had guns. The Beothuk, not trading, had none.

Shanawdithit, the last of the Beothuks, was kidnapped from her family at about age 20. At that age, she had two gunshot wounds, one in the hand and one in the thigh. Both, according to her, were from Micmacs.

A neighbour relates that Shanawdithit, when living with Mr. Peyton on the northeast shore, "was greatly alarmed at the sight of two Micmacs who came once to visit him, and hid herself during their stay."[564] "According to Mr. Peyton, she exhibited the greatest antipathy to the Micmacs, more especially towards one Noel Boss, whom she so dreaded that whenever he, or even his dog made their appearance, she would run screeching with terror and cling to Mr P. [Peyton] for protection."[565]

We learn of a Micmac tradition that, at the beginning of the 17th century, just when firearms would have become available, "a great battle took place between the Micmacs and the Red Indians [Beothuks] at the head of Grand Pond (Lake), but as the former were then armed with guns they defeated the latter, and massacred every man, woman and child."[566]

Clearly, this was not a "Kumbaya" moment. These tribes were not friendly neighbours.

The Micmac like the Europeans felt they had grievances against the Beothuk. On meeting a Micmac in Bay of St George in 1818, one Lieutenant Chappell asked him for information on the legendary "red Indians," the Beothuk. Did they too, like the Catholic Micmac, worship God? "With a sneer of the most ineffable contempt, he replied. 'No; no look up to God: killee all men dat dem see, Red Indian no good.'"[567]

We need not, of course, accept that as the definitive word on the Beothuk. More like an indication of war of all against all.

Here too, the Beothuk hostility to outsiders did not serve them well. They apparently had the general reputation among their neighbours of being hostile and warlike. Worse, they were big, strong, athletic, and good at war; "invincible."[568] They regularly fought with the Eskimo/Inuit to their north, "whom they despised, and called the 'four paws,'"—i.e., brute beasts.[569] They also fought, according to Cartwright, with the "Canadians," probably the Innu. "These Indians [the Beothuk] are not only secluded thus from any communication with Europeans, but they are ... effectually cut off from the society of every other Indian people. The Canadians have generally a strong hunt that range the western coast of Newfoundland, between whom and these natives reigns so mortal an enmity ... that they never meet but a bloody combat ensues."[570]

So, as soon as the Beothuk's neighbours got firearms, they had a good idea of how best to use them.

It is not surprising, therefore, that the Beothuk were wiped out. The same happened to many other tribes, and over the same resource. Recall the Beaver Wars. Understand that there were probably at all times, or all historical times, few Beothuk. At their peak, there might have been one or two thousand. If they had been some animal species, this would probably have immediately qualified them as "endangered." Any slight environmental stress might at any time throw them into a demographic death spiral.

We care uniquely much about the case of the Beothuk, among so many so much less familiar, largely because they died out during the romantic period. Halcyon Noble Savage days. Romantics also love ruins, deserted places, and melancholy. The "melancholy of ruins," explains Sabrina Ferri in a recent essay on the period, "articulates a modern sensibility defined by the recognition of an irreparable rupture with the past and with nature."[571] Whatever. Here we get them all rolled up into one sad beautiful wistful legend.

One can almost taste and touch the sentiment in Cormack's account of his last expedition overland to find the Beothuk. It was this expedition, funded by the "Beothuk Institute" of which Cormack was founder and president, that established their ultimate non-existence. Coming across some picturesque empty wigwams, he meditates, almost in the tone of Gray's "Elegy,"

> We spent several melancholy days wandering on the borders of the east end of the lake, surveying the various remains of what we now contemplated to have been an unoffending and cruelly extirpated race. At several places, by the margin of the lake, small clusters of winter and summer wigwams in ruins.[572]

A perfect picturesque set piece; and civilization was the necessary villain.

Some, in the Romantic spirit of a Cormack, maintain that, even if they did not actually shoot them down like game, the Europeans were nevertheless willfully responsible for the Beothuk's demise. Settled civilization, after all, took their land, and drove them away from the coast into the "forests and barrens," as Maher puts it in the *National Post.* It left them with no means of subsistence.

Who, after all, could expect an Indian to support himself in a forest?

This too, however, is not a fair accusation.

Recall that European settlement was sparse, and officially prohibited, for most of Newfoundland history—almost until after the Beothuk died out. Recall that the Europeans doubted there even were aboriginal inhabitants.

If there were always so few, how could they have been crowded out?

Starvation does seem to have been an issue in the last days. When Shanawdithit was abducted, she was starving, her sister was starving, and their mother was starving. She testified that many others of her tribe had died recently of hunger: "In the second winter afterwards [i.e., after the Buchan expedition; either 1813 or 1816; dates here are confused in the source], twenty-two had died about the river Exploits, and in the vicinity of Green Bay: and the third year also numbers died of hardship and want."[573]

However, Shanawdithit was described as tall. "She seemed about 22 years of age.... Her complexion was swarthy, not unlike the Micmacs; her features were handsome; she was a tall fine figure and stood nearly six feet high, and such a beautiful set of teeth, I do not know that I ever saw in a human head."[574]

This accords with a general tradition that the Beothuk were robust.

"It has been customary on the part of fishermen and others to describe them as a race of gigantic stature and numerous instances are recorded to bear out this statement. Major George Cartwright, in speaking of the Indians he saw on an island in Dildo Run, says 'One of them appeared to be remarkably tall.'"[575] An anonymous writer in the *Liverpool Mercury*, present at the capture of Mary March (Demasduit), speaks of her husband, killed in the effort of capturing her, measuring six feet seven and a half inches. A man shot in Trinity Bay is described as a "huge savage," and another seen by one Mr. Richards in Notre Dame Bay was supposedly "seven feet tall."[576] Buchan, in his 1811 expedition, does not discover them to be as tall as advertised. But he does still report them as taller than the average European, and "extremely healthy and athletic."[577]

One does not reach immense stature, as a rule, if one has been malnourished as a child. Yet even in the final generation, Shanawdithit was tall; and, dying in her twenties, her childhood had ended only years before.

Accordingly, any lack of food must have been a recent phenomenon.

Indeed, when Cartwright ventured into the "barrens" in 1768, the word that most occurs to him is "abundance."

> In the winter it seems they reside chiefly on the banks of the Exploits, where they are enabled to procure a plentiful subsistence, as appeared by the abundance of horns and bones that lay scattered about their wigwams at the deer fences.... [T]he channel of the Exploits, stretching itself directly across the regular and constant track of the deer, must necessarily insure to them abundance of venison.[578]
>
> It will be readily admitted that a country intersected throughout with rivers and ponds and abounding with wood and marshy ground is well adapted for uncivilized life, and calculated for the vast herds of deer that annually visit it. This is proved by the incredible quantity of venison they had packed up, and there yet remained on the margin of the pond a vast number of carcases which must have been killed as the frost set in, many being frozen in the ice. The packs were nearly three feet in length, and in breadth and depth fifteen inches, closely packed with fat venison cleared of the bone, and in weight from 150 to 200 lbs....[579]

So there you are—like starving in aisle three at Mr. Grocer.

One might suppose or suggest that, even if the Europeans did not interfere with their traditional hunting grounds in the interior, the foreign presence on the coast ended their ability to gather fish and birds' eggs, their summer fare. There would be no obvious reason, of course, for the Europeans to interfere in their doing this; they did not seek those resources, for the most part, themselves. If this is the case to be made, much or most of the blame must still be put on Beothuk xenophobia.

But even so, even if they had, Cartwright observes:

> [W]hen we consider on the other hand that the two capes which form the bounds of their settlements are thirty leagues apart, that between them there is at least an island for every man in the largest of these computations [of Beothuk numbers], and that near twenty capacious bays and inlets deeply indent the intermediate part of the coast; we shall easily find shelter in the woods that overhang all these shores, for a much greater number of these savages, who have no temptation to expose themselves carelessly to sight.[580]

That does not sound too claustrophobic.

And it does not seem as though they really ever even needed to go to the coast.

Cormack, our romantic colleague from the Beothuk Institute, did his first transit of the interior in search of the Red Indians in 1822, the very time they were apparently starving to death. Even then, he found a natural abundance. Moreover, he made his transit in summer, supposedly the fallow period, when the Beothuk were supposedly forced to the coast to survive. Loss of that access, then, if they ever lost it, cannot have been the critical issue.

Although this was not their motive, Cormack and his Micmac companion prove the point by easily living off the land throughout their transit.

> [G]rouse, ... the indigenous game bird of the country, rose in coveys in every direction, and snipes from every marsh. The birds of passage, ducks and geese, were flying over us to and fro from their breeding places in the interior and the sea coast; tracks of deer, of wolves fearfully large, of bears, foxes, and martens, were seen everywhere.... [L]and berries were ripening, game birds were fledging, and beasts were emerging to prey upon each other. Everything animate or inanimate seemed to be our own. We consumed unsparingly our remaining provisions, confident that henceforward, ... the destruction of one creature would afford us nourishment and vigour for the destruction of others.
>
> One of the most striking features of the interior are the innumerable deer paths on the savannas. They are narrow and take directions as various as the winds, giving the whole country a chequered appearance. Of the millions of acres here, there is no one spot exceeding a few superficial yards that is not bounded on all sides by deer paths.... The paths tend from park to park through the intervening woods, in

> lines as established and deep beaten as cattle paths on an old grazing farm.[581]

His list of tasty and nutritious natural resources goes on—but this is enough to make the point. Otherwise we are going to start sounding like the Newfoundland and Labrador Department of Tourism. Here, at least, was the seeming abundance of Eden.

Cormack runs across no Beothuk, but does meet Micmacs and an Innu. Chatting with the Innu, native to Labrador, he learns the latter "had come to Newfoundland, hearing that it was a better hunting country than his own."[582]

Obviously, the Europeans were not critically infringing on the Beothuk hunting grounds. The game was better than in Labrador, good enough even in the off-season to attract other Indians from some distance.

So how did the Beothuk starve in the midst of this plenty?

Not that strange—the Huron starved in similar circumstances. Famine is a common consequence of war.

First, the Innu, the Micmac, and Cormack had one great advantage over the Beothuk in their pursuit of game: guns. What they saw, they could shoot. Lacking firearms, the Beothuk method for catching the caribou, their main winter food source, was labour-intensive: they built fencing, forcing the migrating caribou to a point where they could be killed as they forded a river. The typical fence was a half mile long, doubled and running parallel, and had to be six to ten feet high, so the caribou could not jump over to escape.

Once the Beothuk population, already small, dropped below a certain level, they might well no longer have the manpower to keep these fences in good repair.

Add to that the fact that Micmac or Innu might be anywhere, and a European trapper might be anywhere else, and any of them would shoot a Beothuk on sight, and it looks tricky to work outside, in groups, in the open.

Such long fencing could also be knocked down by an enemy at any point along its length.

This, in turn, could obviously happen very quickly. One winter without working caribou fencing could kill them all. Three such winters in succession almost certainly would.

Not that the Micmac or the Europeans needed to compete with the Beothuk for these food resources. Apparently there was plenty enough for all, even at this late date.

There is, however, one resource that Cormack, in his soulful wandering, found to be depleted. "The beaver.... Owing to the presence of the birch tree, ..., all the brooks and lakes in the basin of the interior have been formerly and many are still inhabited by beavers, but these have in many places been destroyed by Indians."[583] The Beothuk no doubt prized the beaver for food, but these significant depradations suggest, here as elsewhere, the fur trade.

The Beothuk were not trading in furs.

Had the Beothuk not traditionally attacked outsiders on sight, they could probably have survived. As they were not trading in furs, and there was food enough, the outside trappers had no cause otherwise to shoot them.

With smallpox blankets, the accepted moral has been that Indians should shy away from anything from the outside. They supposedly were and are better off keeping apart from the Europeans, staying segregated, encasing their traditional culture in amber, not mixing at cocktail parties. This is still the thrust of current Canadian policy regarding Canada's Indians, Métis, and Inuit. Integration bad; segregation good. Schools bad; reserves good.

Yet this is exactly what the Beothuk did, to the letter and the dot and the cross above. They are the perfect control, our case study in the recommended approach. They carefully avoided all contact with the filthy aliens and their filthy civilization, scrupulously preserved their culture just as it always had been, resisted any foreign intrusions.

How did that work out?

The Cree, who shamelessly consorted instead with the Hudson's Bay Company from the start, are now the largest aboriginal group in Canada.

The Iroquois, who traded with the Dutch and then the English, conquered territories as distant as Virginia and the Mississippi.

Where are the once "invincible" Beothuk?

They may, granted, by this approach of non-approach, have avoided smallpox. We will probably never know, since they lived and died alone. We do know their segregation did not save them from tuberculosis. Every captive taken from the interior seemed to have it. This was, historically, the second great scourge of Indians everywhere.

Not only did the Beothuk do all the "right" things; so did the helpful Europeans. They largely left the land and the Beothuk alone, prohibiting development or settlement. Just as many have proposed for more northerly lands today. For the sake of the Indians.

And how did that work out?

Instead of helping them prosper, these seem to have been the two essential factors causing the Beothuk to cease to be. Had there been settlement, there would have been law and law enforcement. No eternal war, with fishermen or with Micmac. Had there been communication and trade, the Beothuk would have had guns to protect themselves, guns to hunt the plentiful caribou, trade to support them, and neighbours to turn to in their hour of need.

Indians today might take a lesson here. Apartheid, aside from being immoral, does not work. Staying put in an imaginary past is no option.

If we do not learn from the Beothuks, they have died in vain. If we can learn from them, to at least that extent, their memory survives.

16 WHAT CULTURAL GENOCIDE DOES NOT LOOK LIKE

Man bites dog: a *Lu'lim* potlatch ceremony among the Aht.

"It is a strict law that bids us to dance."

- Chief O'waxalagalis of the Kwakiutl, to anthropologist Franz Boas

So there was, we discover, no genocide of the Indians, at least by Europeans or European Canadians.

But there was a "cultural genocide," wasn't there? A deliberate attempt to wipe out Indian culture?

No.

First of all, calling something "cultural genocide" is what they call in formal debating "prejudicial language." That is, making things sound bad by arbitrary selection of words. There is probably no such thing, properly speaking, as "cultural genocide." The suffix "-cide" means you killed someone or some living thing. You cannot, except metaphorically, kill a culture, any more than you can kill an ice cube. And even in this metaphorical sense, you probably cannot "kill" a culture, that is, make it cease to be, without killing everyone who knows about it. Changing it is not killing it; otherwise Canadian mainstream culture is murdered about every other year. By Pokémon Go, recently. It is a culture that is not constantly changing that is dead.

Granted, a culture can be suppressed.

My Irish ancestors knew something about that. Education in the Irish language was forbidden; practice of the Catholic religion was forbidden; the traditional Irish

Brehon law system was forbidden; the Irish could hold no responsible positions in their own government; and so forth. If the motive was not simple hate for the Irish, as it may have been, then it was to turn them into proper Englishmen—"nation-building." The Highland Scots culture was similarly suppressed by law. So, in a less systematic way, and more obviously out of practical considerations rather than hostility, were the cultures of Brittany, Languedoc, Catalonia, or the Basque Country, to name a few: collectively, the ancestors of perhaps most of today's Canadians.

Such cultural suppression has been a common experience even within the borders of Canada: for every new wave of immigrants from any non-English- or French-speaking country, compelled to swear an oath to some foreign Queen, and to learn an unfamiliar language, customs, and laws.

If the same thing happened to the Indians too, it would not be so shocking. It would be wrong to call it "genocide."

But it did not. Aren't Indians, in fact, the one group of Canadians, other than the French and English, to which it has not? The one minority group whose traditional culture has been supported, if unevenly, by governments?

Moreover, the suppression of specific elements of a culture is not necessarily bad. Cultures can and should change, when something better comes along. Cultures can include objectively immoral practices. To say so is, really, only to accept the doctrine of human rights: it was not okay to kill Jews in Nazi Germany, or Croats in Bosnia, or Tutsis in Rwanda, just because it was legal there and socially acceptable. We generally now agree, as a matter of international and of natural law, that in such cases, foreign intervention is not only justified, but morally required. Historical cultures or cultural practices that could justly have been suppressed might include: slavery in the antebellum US South, the Imperial Shintoism of Japan, apartheid in South Africa, Nazism and antisemitism in Germany, the exposure of unwanted infants in ancient Greece, the caste system in India, the seigniorial "right of first night," if it ever really existed. The Old Testament was not awfully keen on the Canaanite custom of child sacrifice, or on the hospitality of Sodom and Gomorrah, the cities of the plain.

Accordingly, we must allow that there might have been aspects of Canadian Indian cultures that ought rightly to have been ended or suppressed. And, as we have seen, there were: slavery, torture, constant war with neighbours, the exposure of the old, sick, or young if their care became a burden, extreme poverty, periodic starvation, misogyny, endemic disease, environmental pollution, that sort of thing.

But other than that, Mrs. Lincoln, aboriginal cultural practices no doubt ought to be preserved.

The missionary position

With apologies, let's leave aside for now the residential school system, to be dealt with later. It is too large and controversial a topic.

But aside, then, from the residential schools, the usual designated villain in the charge of cultural suppression is or are the missions. They forced the unhappy natives to give up their spiritual traditions and embrace Christianity. Douglas Todd, writing in the *Vancouver Sun*, blames the sad current state of Canadian Indians on the colonization of Canada by, as he puts it, "European missionaries and settlers."[584] If missionaries are not held solely to blame, they do get pride of place.

"The Christian churches," laments the Truth and Reconciliation Commission, "not only provided the moral justification for the colonization of other peoples' lands, but they also dispatched missionaries to the colonized nations in order to convert 'the heathen.' From the fifteenth century on, the Indigenous peoples of the world were the objects of a strategy of spiritual and cultural conquest."[585]

There is an immediate problem with this accusation. Religion tends to be voluntary. How did the evil Christians manage to force their ugly culture down the throats of the Noble Savages?

Easy enough, I suppose, if you accept the unspoken premise that the Indians, being purely natural beings, had no free will. But if you see them as unromantically human, with the ability and the right to make up their own minds, it is hard to fault the missionaries for spreading their good news—giving the data to make an informed choice.

True, it is also possible to force an outward change of religion by legal fiat. We have mentioned the outlawing of Catholicism in Ireland—and, indeed, across the United Kingdom, and in the Thirteen Colonies, for centuries. Similar bans, as often against Protestantism, were once found across Europe. And, of course, against Judaism.

But did it ever happen in Canada, and to the Indians? Canada was, in its early days, an oasis of religious tolerance, a reproach to old Europe, and indeed to the Thirteen Colonies. It was the first part of the British Empire in which Catholics were fully enfranchised. Attempts to establish the Anglican Church in Upper Canada as in England were early opposed and overthrown by the Methodists and Presbyterians.

It would seem odd if similar tolerance was not extended to the native people. To suppress their religion would have gone against Canadian traditions, traditions on which the nation was founded. Moreover, if government were going to back an effort to convert the heathen to the one true faith, which faith might that be? To pick one over another would have been hugely controversial, in a nation with no established church, and split about 50/50 between Protestant and Catholic.

So, was there ever any compulsion among Indians to become Christian? Was there ever any legal compulsion, more generally, for Indians to assimilate?

No. As early as 1760, in the capitulation of France after the Seven Years' War, the British Crown expressly guaranteed to the Indians their "liberty of religion."

Which meant they could "keep their missionaries."

They were, by this time, Catholic. And the missionaries were there at their desire, not the government's.

Those who make the charge of forced assimilation most often refer to the *Gradual Civilization Act*, passed by the Canadian Parliament in 1857, later supplanted by the *Indian Act*: formally, "An Act to Encourage the Gradual Civilization of the Indian Tribes." Kevin Annett calls it "the deliberate and persistent eradication of aboriginal people and their culture, and the conversion of any surviving native people to Christianity."[586]

That sounds like an attempt to assimilate, doesn't it?

At least, if you do not read the text.

In fact, it simply outlines the legal method by which a status Indian, if he wishes to, may leave his tribe and become a Canadian citizen. In doing so, he waives his treaty rights, and in return is given his own plot of land. The crucial wording is this: "Indians who may desire to avail themselves of this act." Such process was voluntary, at the request of the Indian. Assimilation was permitted, not required, by government.

And it was actually extremely difficult.

The emphasis of the act is not on the "encourage," but on the "gradual" part. To legally renounce Indian status, individuals had to undergo examination by an Indian agent or a local missionary, who were to certify that they could speak, read, and write either French or English tolerably well, were tolerably well educated, and were of good moral character.

One might suspect that the government did not really particularly want Indians to assimilate.

And why would they? For popular consumption, it might be wise to say that assimilation was the goal. But let the Indians assimilate, and an arm of government, with lots of good jobs and ample public funding, is gone.

The sorry truth is that, up to 1920, leaving aside women who assimilated through marriage, the easy route, only 250 status Indians ever managed to surrender their status and gain citizenship under the Act.[587]

Those crying cultural genocide next turn to the fact that specific elements of Indian culture have been banned. True. As we have seen in an earlier chapter, the Indians of the Pacific Northwest were upset when their traditional practice of slavery was ended by the US government. And any two tribes going to war today would probably draw down the Mounties well before it even got to the torture of prisoners.

Potlatch

Perhaps the best case for suppression of an Indian tradition on the grounds of prejudice, rather than morality and human rights, is the potlatch. In Canada, the *Indian Act* was modified in 1884 to prohibit traditional potlatch ceremonies among the Kwakiutl and other tribes in the Pacific Northwest. The sun dance (thirst dance) of the Plains Indians fell under the same prohibition. Keith Smith writes, in a *BC Open Textbook* project, referring to the potlatch and sun dance, "spiritual practices that were fundamental to personal and community identity and well-being … were targeted for suppression."[588]

In the third section of the *Indian Act*, signed into law on April 19, 1884, it was declared that:

> Every Indian or other person who engages in or assists in celebrating the Indian festival known as the "Potlatch" or in the Indian dance known as the "Tamanawas" is guilty of a misdemeanor, and liable to imprisonment for a term of not more than six nor less than two months in any gaol or other place of confinement; and every Indian or persons who encourages… an Indian to get up such a festival… shall be liable to the same punishment.

Even at the time, this seemed to many an unnecessary interference in Indian affairs. Potlatches were just big parties at which everyone exchanged lavish gifts, right? What's wrong with that? Isn't generosity a good thing? Should we outlaw Christmas?

But what exactly was a potlatch?

The original statute did not say. This made the ban in practice meaningless; it was never enforced. Anyone charged with holding a "potlatch" could simply claim that the ignorant pale-faced judge did not know Indian traditions, that whatever they did last Saturday night was not a "potlatch."

Accordingly, the relevant section was later rewritten as:

> Every Indian or other person who engages in, or assists in celebrating, or encourages, either directly or indirectly, another to celebrate, any Indian festival, dance or other ceremony of which the giving away or paying or giving back of money, goods or articles of any sort forms a part, or is a feature, whether such gift of money, goods or articles takes place before, at, or after the celebration of the same, and every Indian or other person who engages or assists in any celebration or dance of which the wounding or mutilation of the dead or living body of any human being or animal forms a part or is a feature, is guilty of an indictable offence and is liable to imprisonment for a term not exceeding six months and not less than two months; but nothing in this section shall be construed to prevent the holding of any agricultural show or exhibition or the giving of prizes for exhibits thereat.

This seems not much better. It looks like a badly written law. Theoretically, it would indeed ban Christmas, except on the grounds that it is not "Indian"; or baby showers. Country fairs must be given a special exemption. But it gives us an idea of what it is about the potlatch that troubled the authorities. If it involved cruelty to animals, mutilating people, or indignity to corpses, we might not welcome it in our neighbourhood.

There may have been valid objections even to the gift giving. Some in contact with the Indians, including Gilbert Sproat, argued that the ethic of the potlatch made it impossible for Indians to better themselves. As soon as they made more than their neighbours, they were socially obliged to give it away. There was, therefore, no incentive to strive, to take risks, no way for an enterprising individual to get ahead. As Sproat wrote to John A. Macdonald, "It is not possible that the Indians can acquire property, or can become industrious with any good result, while under the influence of … [the Potlatch]."[589]

If this was the issue, one cannot, at least, charge government authorities with hating or seeking harm to Indians. They at least saw themselves as acting in the Indians' interests.

However, J.B. McCullagh, Anglican missionary and opponent of the potlatch, protests that this is still not the real problem. He laments the wording of the ban for missing the point. In many potlatch ceremonies, he points out, goods were not given away. Instead, they were thrown into the nearest fire.

> There is ... liable to be considerable wanton (from our point of view) destruction of property if the friends of the chief ... take it into their heads to do him honor. This they do by making him presents of articles of clothing, etc., but instead of putting them in his hand they put them in the fire, where they are quickly consumed. The chief then and there makes return presents also putting them in the fire, amid rounds of applause.[590]

Keynesian economics and the classic "broken window" fallacy to the contrary, this does not seem to benefit materially even the community as a whole.

In another form of the ceremony, McCullagh says, the "*Unana*," housewares are broken throughout the village.

> The *Unana* is a crockery-breaking honor. The candidate having been artistically painted, kilted and feathered, is armed with a club, works himself up into a towering rage, and then proceeds on his mission of destruction, stepping like a high-mettled charger. Entering into each house he goes foaming around breaking basins, plates, lamps, or anything he sees, and having completed his tour makes a grand display of recompensing the owners.[591]

Dorothy Johansen, corroborating McCullagh, describes the destruction of property as a feature of some potlatches.

> In the potlatch, the host in effect challenged a guest chieftain to exceed him in his "power" to give away or to destroy goods. If the guest did not return 100 percent on the gifts received and destroy even more wealth in a bigger and better bonfire, he and his people lost face and so his "power" was diminished.[592]

James Deans writes,

> [A] man who feels injured by another will destroy a certain amount of property, then his adversary is compelled to do the same, else a stain of dishonor will rest upon him until he destroys the same amount of property—or, if he refuses to do so, all his lifetime. I have heard of a case in which a man fancied another man had in some way or other injured him;

> so in order, as he thought, to punish his adversary, he destroyed all the property he could spare. His adversary quickly responded by destroying double the amount, which the other was unable to do, and so the whole village laughed at him.[593]

And this when many Indians risked starvation.

We have not dealt yet with the reference, in the revised legislation, to the mutilation of animals. McCullagh explains:

> The *Lu'lim* is a dog-eating degree, when the candidate, having made himself sufficiently mad in the woods—naked and fasting for several days—joins the ceremonial dance and tears a dog to pieces with his teeth before the assembled company, after which he distributes as much property as he is able.[594]

Would Pocahontas's forest buddies Meeko and Flit approve?

Note too the reference in the legislation to the mutilation of humans. McCullagh again:

> The *Ulala* is a cannibal degree, that is to say, the eating of human flesh is its leading feature. It is not so bad as it used to be when slaves were killed, I am told, and dead bodies exhumed for the purpose. The modern method is to get together as much property as possible, fix the date for the dance, then disappear into the woods for a few days cloaked in a bearskin with a bellows-whistle under each arm, and then when the dance is on turn up in a fine frenzy and start in biting those present. On some the biter only leaves the marks of his teeth, from others he will draw blood, while perhaps from others, if he can afford it, he will tear a piece of flesh away. After this beastly fit of voluntary insanity ... he will distribute his property among those he has bitten according to the nature of the bite inflicted.[595]

Anthropologist Franz Boas, who did much of his work among the Kwakiutl, notes that during a potlatch, "any mistake made by a singer or dancer is considered opprobrious. At certain occasions the dancer who makes a mistake is killed."[596]

There may indeed be some human rights issues here.

Livingston Jones describes the potlatch among the Tlingit:

> Sometimes tribal jealousies brought on conflicts. The tribe defeated in a dancing contest became jealous of the victorious tribe. Slurs and insults followed until a fight was precipitated. Sometimes a dozen or more would fall before the feud was settled. The killing proceeded until those who had fallen on one side were equal in rank to those who had fallen on the other. When they were dancing and potlatching, if one side made one song more than the other it would cause a quarrel which usually ended in a bloody encounter.[597]

If McCullagh and the others are correct, then, the essential fault of the Ottawa legislators and bureaucrats was not an unwarranted interference with traditional native culture. It was at most a poor job of drafting legislation.

Sun dance

The issue is similar for the sun (thirst) dance, an annual ceremony among the Assiniboine, Crow, Gros Ventre, Plains Cree, Plains Ojibway, and Blackfoot, among others. It fell under the same prohibition, because it featured human mutilation.

The Reverend John McLean describes the preliminaries for a Blackfoot dance:

> As I stood outside the lodge, a young Indian friend of mine, went to an old medicine woman and presented his sacrifice to Natos [the sun god]. During the year he had gone on a horse-stealing expedition and as is customary on such occasions had prayed to Natos for protection and success, offering himself to his god if his prayers were answered. He had been successful and he now presented himself as a sacrifice. The old woman took his hand, held it toward the sun and prayed, then laying a finger on a block of wood she severed it with one blow from a knife and deer's horn scraper. She held the portion of the finger cut off toward the Sun and dedicated that to him as the young man's sacrifice.[598]

But the centrepiece of the sun dance was the "making of braves," an adolescent rite of passage. McLean describes its Blackfoot version:

> He lay down, and four men held him while a fifth made the incisions in his breast and back. Two places were marked in each breast denoting the position and width of each incision. This being done, the wooden skewers being in readiness, a double edged knife was held in the hand, the point touching the flesh, a small piece of wood was placed on the under side to receive the point of the knife when it had gone through, and the flesh was drawn out the desired length for the knife

> to pierce. A quick pressure and the incision was made, the piece of wood was removed, and the skewer inserted from the underside as the knife was being taken out. When the skewer was properly inserted, it was beaten down with the palm of the hand of the operator, that it might remain firmly in its place. This being done to each breast, with a single skewer for each, strong enough to tear away the flesh, and long enough to hold the lariats fastened to the top of the sacred pole, a double incision was made on the back of the left shoulder, to the skewer of which was fastened an Indian drum. The work being pronounced good by the persons engaged in the operation, the young man arose, and one of the operators fastened the lariats giving them two or three jerks to bring them into position.
>
> The young man went up to the sacred pole, and while his countenance was exceedingly pale, and his frame trembling with emotion, threw his arms around it, and prayed earnestly for strength to pass successfully through the trying ordeal. His prayer ended, he moved backward until the flesh was fully extended, and placing a small bone whistle in his mouth, he blew continuously upon it a series of short sharp sounds, while he threw himself backward, and danced until the flesh gave way and he fell. Previous to his tearing himself free from the lariats, he seized the drum with both hands and with a sudden pull tore the flesh on his back, dashing the drum to the ground amid the applause of the people. As he lay on the ground, the operators examined his wounds, cut off the flesh that was hanging loosely, and the ceremony was at an end.[599]

I think we can grant that these ceremonies were painful for those involved, and we ourselves might not want to participate. Still, an obvious question: why can't the Indians decide this for themselves? If they really want to maim and kill, between consenting adults, wasn't that their business?

Perhaps not. These were not adults, and consent is not certain. If young Somali women want to mutilate their genitals, after all, isn't that also their business? From the standpoint of the individual, especially a young individual, a Somali teenager or a Blackfoot "brave," how much is really voluntary, and how much is social pressure?

No representation without potlatch

McCullagh claims the call to outlaw the potlatch came at least in part from the Indians themselves, and from a majority. "[T]he civilized Indians," he claims, "wish to see the Potlatch abolished."[600] Yes, they could refuse to take part. But all rights within the tribe were assigned through potlatch. On potlatch depended any rights to hunting, fishing, and berrying territories. Without a potlatch, even the birth of a child was not acknowledged. Meaning your child was not a member of the tribe.

This is very different from Christmas after all. The giving of gifts at Christmas is voluntary, and ideally a pure expression of the personal virtue of generosity. The giving of gifts at potlatch, even leaving aside its other troubling aspects, was not really voluntary, but required to avoid definite and comprehensive penalties.

"If, after an Indian leaves the Confederacy to join a mission, the potlatch would let him alone all would be well," explains McCullagh. "But it does no such thing. If the man be a chief the potlatch immediately usurps his chieftainship, promotes another chief in his place, takes away his name and title, and ignores him. This is very hard for some men to bear, not so much because of the humiliation as because of the injustice."[601]

Legaic, a prominent chief among the Tsimshian, had to surrender his status in order to join a Christian mission in the 1860s, and reportedly suffered for it.

> Constant inducements were held out to him to return; and on one occasion he actually gave way. He gathered the Indians together, on the Metlakahtla beach, told them he could hold out no longer, and was going back to his old life.... In tears he shook the hand of each in turn, and then stepping alone into his canoe, paddled rapidly away from his weeping friends. He went a few miles along the coast, and then, as darkness came on, put the canoe ashore. The night was one of such misery, he afterwards said, as no words could describe. "A hundred deaths would not equal the sufferings of that night." On his knees he wept and prayed for pardon, and for strength to return; and next day he again appeared at Metlakahtla, to the joy of all.[602]

The only option was to leave the tribe completely, abandon your Indian identity, and assimilate with the mainstream, surrendering any treaty rights. If, that is, the government would let you—there were, remember, rigorous tests to pass. Few managed it. Without this, you were entirely on your own: an outcast.

The laws against potlatch and sun dances could be seen as much as meant to allow Indians not to assimilate as to encourage them to do so. They remove compelling reasons for leaving the reserve and cutting all ties.

Why couldn't a majority of Kwakiutl or Blackfoot or Cree have abolished the potlatch or the sun dance among themselves?

McCullagh claims the Indians tried:

> The civilized Indian finds himself in a majority of two to one on the Naas, and yet he cannot get a hearing. He has appealed vainly to the authorities to be relieved from the tyranny of the potlatch, but he has not been understood, and it has not been thought advisable to give him relief, hence it is that the potlatch in a modernized, though no less injurious form, is now becoming as it were a necessity among the civilized Nishgas.[603]

If a majority of the Indians opposed and refused to participate in potlatch, that just meant the remnant, however small, inherited all the tribe's titles, rights, offices, and land. It is as if a majority of elected members of parliament refused to take their seats—with no rules requiring a quorum. There was no mechanism, no authority, short of bloody revolution, to overthrow this tribal structure.

So it seems reasonable at least to say that this was not a matter of banning some Indian spiritual practice in support of Christian evangelization. McCullagh indeed insists that the potlatch is not religious in nature. "[I]t is not a religious rite or ceremony, even though there may seem to be a strain of ancestral worship in it; ... it is a systematized form of tribal government based upon the united suffrages of the clans."[604]

James Deans, writing in the *American Antiquarian* at the turn of the 19th century, not long after the potlatch ban went into effect, notes: "patlatches [sic] are time-honored festivals of our aborigines, and probably existed before the adoption of Christianity."[605] This passing reference suggests again that this was not a question of government suppressing some religion competing with Christianity. These Indians were already Christian when it was banned. For all anyone really knew, they were Christian when the potlatch practice began.

And to recap, even if the potlatch and the sun dance had indeed been religious, or at least, expressions of Indian "spirituality," there are circumstances in which a liberal democracy is justified in banning a religious practice. The British encountered two examples in India: the tradition of suttee, in which a widow was burned to death on her husband's pyre, and the Thuggi habit of strangling unsuspecting coach passengers as a human sacrifice.

Among the ethical monotheisms, Judaism, Christianity, and Islam, objectively immoral rites rarely if ever arise; it would go against the assumptions of the faith. But among shamanic or magical traditions, having no moral dimension, rites and religious practices could be unethical. They are simply technologies: purely scientific and objective, as it were. Did it rain, or not? Did you catch fish, or not?

For this reason, it would seem wise as a matter of public policy to distinguish, as we currently don't, between shamanism and religion. They are apples and oranges, pomegranates and plums.

One is entitled to freedom of religion; it is a human right, because it involves freedom of conscience. One does not obviously, on the other hand, have a human right to consult a crystal ball, curse someone with boils, or market love potions. Indeed, such things have often been illegal. They are not done out of moral obligation, and so no violation of conscience is involved in banning them.

"Religion" originally and literally means something like "binding"—as in committing oneself to a set of actions, a personal path of conduct. Shamanism is not, therefore, a "religion." One makes no commitments to anything to be a shamanist, although one may to be a shaman. One does not, moreover, sacrifice to pagan gods because the gods deserve it, but because they demand it, and may hurt you if you don't.

A law prohibiting the potlatch or the sun dance could therefore be seen as a gift to Indians. Now they have, or had, a legitimate excuse to not do it. The gods, if angry, could not properly fault them. They could go smite Sir John A. Macdonald.

Do Hindus resent the ban on suttee or on thuggery? I note that independent India has not reinstated them.

Father Lalemant, in the *Jesuit Relations*, gives some idea of the social pressure and fear behind such practices among the Huron:

> When a prisoner is burned, if the young men are turbulent thereat, some old man begins to exclaim and storm because they are risking the ruin of the country, saying that this is a matter of importance and that they do not behave seriously enough in it....
>
> In short, it is the strangest servitude and slavery that can be imagined; and never did galley slave so fear to fail in his duty as these peoples dread to fall short in the least detail of all their wretched ceremonies—for there would follow from this omission, not only the privation of what they were expecting, but even physical punishment, which the devil for this reason exercises upon these poor wretches. The more thoughtful among them freely admit their misery, and frankly say that the demons alone are the real masters of the country,—that it is they who regulate and decree everything, whether in dreams or otherwise; that they see this plainly, but that there is no remedy for it; that they have always lived in

> this way, and that there is no prospect or means of living differently,—in other words, that were any detail omitted all would be lost.[606]

Perhaps some aspects of such a culture might be better dispensed with. For all concerned.

Resolved, therefore, that with the possible exception of the residential schools, not yet examined, there was never any Canadian government action or intent to suppress Indian culture.

Indeed, why would there have been? Human nature works against it. If you are a bureaucrat in the Department of Indian Affairs, or any of its other incarnations, and you encourage the assimilation of Indians, you only reduce your own power and risk losing a good job. Better to keep them Indians, and keep them apart, so they remain within your charge.

One particularly blatant example: without any kind of legal warrant, quite against the supposed intent of the legislation, the bureaucrats of the Indian Department, in the later 19th century, began requiring that status Indians get a pass from their local Indian agent before leaving the reserve. This was strict apartheid. Moreover, it was in violation of treaty, which gave Indians the right to hunt or fish on Crown land. It was justified to the public by the Northwest Rebellion of 1885; but this was a retroactive justification. The pass system began before the rebellion took place.[607]

Saint Anne of the Micmacs.

Indians are Christian

Shocking as it seems to some, completely counter to the cultural genocide accusation, most Canadian Indians are and long have been Christian.

I once lived, too briefly, in Kamloops, home to the Kamloops (Tk'emlups) Indian reserve. With our young son, we attended the local Christmas parade. I was beginning to be annoyed by all the commercialism, when at last, the float presented by the local band appeared. They, and they alone, gave us a nativity scene—the only unambiguous reference in the whole parade to the religious meaning of the holiday. The Kamloops reserve also features a lovingly restored mission church, which has become a tourist attraction. St. Thomas Anglican is a similar landmark in Moose Factory, the Cree settlement on James Bay. The oldest surviving Protestant church in Ontario is Her Majesty's Royal Chapel of the Mohawks, in Brantford.

Real Indians are Christians. And often more devout than the average European Canadian.

There was of course some opposition when the first missionaries appeared. If no one else, the established shamans were sure to resent this intrusion into their market; Christians discouraged magical practices. But in relative terms, there was surprisingly little, considering that Indian cultures seem conservative and wary of the strange and new. In the words of one Jesuit, "the beliefs and superstitions of the savages are not very deeply rooted in their minds; ... they fall of themselves, and suddenly disappear, or are dissipated by the rays of the truths, entirely conformable to reason, that are proposed to them."[608]

No doubt the black-robes would say that; they cannot have been disinterested. However, of the Micmac around Port Royal, the Sieur de Poutrincourt, a somewhat more detached observer, also remarks: "they seemed to wish for nothing better than to enroll themselves under the banner of Jesus Christ."[609] The Micmac flag is dominated by a cross. Christianity is a part of their ethnic identity.

The Abenaki next door, not having been sent a missionary, Christianized themselves, and then walked all the way to Quebec to request one. Repeatedly.

> One *sagamo*, or chief, accompanied Meiaskwat to Quebec, and, after instruction, embraced the faith. Others followed his example, and in a few years each Abenaki village could count several Christians. At last two *sagamos* came on Assumption Day to ask for black-gowns to instruct the tribe.... Charmed by the happiness they had enjoyed, the Abenakis sent in September for their missionary, and again in the two following years; but were unable to obtain him, so

> limited was the number of missionaries for the stations then under their charge. In 1650, their assiduity and fervor was rewarded by success, and [Father] Druillettes set out with a party on the last day of August.[610]

Neighbouring Indian bands soon appealed for their own black-robe.

> Soon after beginning his labors here, [Father] Rale beheld a new tribe approach his mission. The Amalingans came to ascertain the truth of what they had heard. Struck by all that they saw at the mission, they solicited instruction, listened to his teaching, and embraced the faith when, at the next season, he visited their camp.[611]

Nor was this restricted to the Atlantic seaboard. It seems the usual thing. The *Jesuit Relations* report, "The Onnontaeronnon Iroquois invite us of their own accord, and solicit our coming by presents; they have assigned a place to us, and have described it to us as the finest spot in all those regions."[612] Hurons spread the gospel to the Neutrals: "Éstienne Totiri, of the village of St. Joseph, accompanied by one of his brothers, stopped in one of their villages nearer the frontier, and found ears so well disposed to listen to them that they had barely three or four hours at night for sleep."[613]

An Abenaki chief describes his conversion, in his own words:

> One day my canoe missed the route; I lost my path, and wandered a long way at random, until at last I landed near Quebec, in a great village of the Algonquins, where the black-gowns were teaching. Scarcely had I arrived, when one of them came to see me. I was loaded with furs, but the black-gown of France disdained to look at them: he spoke to me of the Great Spirit, of heaven, of hell, of the prayer, which is the only way to reach heaven. I heard him with pleasure, and was so delighted by his words, that I remained in the village near him. At last the prayer pleased me, and I asked to be instructed; I solicited baptism, and received it. Then I returned to the lodges of my tribe, and related all that had happened. All envied my happiness, and wished to partake it: they, too, went to the black-gown to be baptized.... Now I hold to the prayer of the French; I agree to it; I shall be faithful to it, even until the earth is burnt and destroyed.[614]

Not a lot of principled resistance there.

Nor was this a purely Catholic phenomenon. Protestant missionaries met with success at the same time in New England.

> Thirty years after … [Rev. John Eliot] … entered on his missionary work, twenty-four regular congregations had been gathered in Massachusetts, with the same number of native preachers [this circa 1675]; fifty years from the same date [circa 1696] there were thirty Indian churches, in some of which a native pastorate had been established, and three fourths of the whole Indian population ... were accounted Christians.[615]

At least one new congregation every two years; the main thing slowing Christianity's growth was a shortage of missionaries.

The Iroquois of the Six Nations who settled at Brantford after the American Revolution soon had a church build. But they had to wait over forty years for their first Anglican missionary. In the meantime, a service of readings was regularly conducted by the Mohawks themselves, and "such is their attachment to it, that numbers of the Mohawk and Oneida Indians regularly attend at every opening of the church." Others were busy translating the New Testament into their language.[616]

The Moravians found a similar welcome among the Labrador Eskimo/Inuit.

> In 1809, a small hymn-book and a few tracts were ready, which the converts, both in Greenland and Labrador, received with delight. One year later, a Harmony of the Gospels was in readiness. Eighteen hundred and twenty-one, the first jubilee of the mission, was signalized by the distribution of the entire New Testament in the vernacular. At once the poor people, without suggestion from any one, began to collect what they could, and forwarded the same to England as a thank-offering to the society which had bestowed so invaluable a treasure upon them.[617]

The Methodists were about as successful when they later evangelized the Ontario Ojibway (Mississauga): "The word of the Lord spread very rapidly from one tribe to another; so much so, that within a very few years [from 1823] fifteen Christian settlements were formed among those very people."[618]

The Reverend Peter Jones cites a newspaper report that the Salish of the West Coast "had arrived at some western towns, enquiring after the white man's religion, saying that ... they had come to ask for a missionary to tell their people the words of that good book." To do this they had, he claims, "travelled between two and three thousand miles on foot."[619] When a Catholic mission was set up at St. Eustache, Manitoba, in 1835, it soon entertained a delegation of Indians from the Rocky Mountains "come to enquire into the truth of what they had heard," that a priest "who spoke their own language like themselves was uttering words of an admirable wisdom." They had set out on February 20th, and arrived at the mission on the 2nd of June.[620]

Anglican missionary John West, visiting the Maritimes in the 1820s, laments that the Indians there were all Catholics. "He is a decided Roman Catholic," West complains of his Micmac host,

> ...as are all the Indians of the Province; and a circumstance occurred in the death of a child, while I was in the camp, which proved how strongly the Priests have entrenched them within the pale of their bigotry and dominion. I offered to bury the child, as they knew me to be a Priest, but they refused, with the remark, that it must be buried by their Priest; and the mother of the deceased child took the corpse upon her back, and carried it the distance of thirty miles to the French village of Sissaboo, where the Priest resided, for burial. I merely observed to Adelah, on this occasion, that I supposed Indians were all of the Roman Catholic religion, he said "yes," adding, "you know in England, Quakers, when born, all come little Quakers, so Indians, all come little Catholics."[621]

When Vilhjalmur Stefansson left the Arctic in September 1907, he counted six Christians in the entire Mackenzie District. When he returned ten months later, in July 1908, he says, "we found every man, woman, and child converted."[622]

Visiting a remote Eskimo settlement, Stefansson and his party find, "the local people inquired eagerly whether we had brought any new prayers with us." An Eskimo who knew a few was treated with the greatest respect. "During our entire stay he was much sought after and continually invited around to the various houses to eat and to teach the community new prayers."[623]

> The most prominent man of the village, Panniulak, had a large package of pictures concerning which he wanted my opinion. Most of them had evidently been clipped out of cheap American magazines and embraced subjects of all sorts. A considerable number were sacred pictures from the Old Masters, but not a few were pictures of actors and actresses of all nationalities. Panniulak said to me he understood fully that all the pictures where there was a circle around the head were pictures of Good Dead Men (which was his name for a saint). He knew further that some of those that did not wear a halo were Good Dead Men also, and he wanted my opinion on certain pictures as to whether they did or did not belong to this class.... It was an interested circle that watched me classify the pictures into two

> packages, on the basis of my idea of the comparative sanctity of the subject of each.[624]

Hearing that the old Tory government of Upper Canada, in one of the first of its "blue laws," had banned hunting on Sundays, the Ojibway Grand Council of 1840 lodged a protest with the Supervisor of Indian Affairs. It was not that their livelihood or traditional way of life might be threatened. It was not that they had a right to exemption from the game laws.

> Father,—Last winter an act was passed by the Parliament of this country for the preservation of game and for the better observance of the Sabbath day, imposing fines and penalties upon any person or persons shooting game on the Sabbath. It is our desire that our Great Father may be pleased to recommend that the said Act may be so amended as to impose the same fines and penalties upon any person or persons fishing on the Lord's Day.[625]

In Quebec, in the early 17th century, the Jesuits marvelled at the eagerness of their acolytes.

> [T]he desire of the savages, great and small, to learn the catechism and the prayers, often makes a chapel and a school of the sick ward as well as of our house at Sillery. They enter incessantly, and say: "Teach me; have me pray to God."[626]

Posted among the Abenaki, Father Druillettes reports,

> Their ardor was so great … for retaining the prayers or the truths that I taught them, that they spent the nights in repeating their lessons. The old men became pupils to their little children. The catechumens, very little versed in our science, were forced to play the doctor. Some would write their lessons after a fashion of their own, using a bit of charcoal for a pen, and a piece of bark instead of paper.... They carried away these papers with them, to study their lessons in the quiet of the night. Jealousy and emulation sprang up among them: the little ones vied with the older ones who should soonest learn his prayers; and those to whom I could not give all the time they asked me for, reproached me therefor.[627]

On a first visit to the Dene, Father Thibeault writes

> The zeal of these poor Indians to hear the word of God and learn how to serve him is extreme. Day and night they were busy repeating the prayers and instructions. Hence I left them with a knowledge of the Our Father, Hail Mary, the Creed, and the way of reciting the beads.... All understand

> and can explain the chief points of the Catholic Ladder. All those who could make themselves understood in Cree have gone to confession.[628]

We should all be such good Christians.

When Father Druillettes was obliged, by the traditional missionary rotation, to leave the Abenaki, they expressed much remorse. "A general grief prevailed. 'You grieve our minds to talk of your going, and the uncertainty of your return.' 'We must say,' said others, 'that Father Gabriel does not love us: he does not care, though we shall die, as he abandons us.'" On Druillettes's return, years later, "All the tribe were forthwith in motion, and, amid a volley of firearms, the chief embraced the missionary, crying: 'I see well that the Great Spirit, who rules in the heavens, deigns to look favorably on us, since he sends us back our patriarch.' Universal joy prevailed: men, women, children, all sought to express their happiness at the missionary's return. A banquet was spread in every cabin, and he was forced to visit all. 'We have you, at last,' they cried; 'you are our father, our patriarch, our countryman....We had thought of leaving this land to seek you, for many have died in your absence. We were losing all hopes of reaching heaven. Those whom you did instruct, performed all they had learnt, but their heart was weary, for it sought and could not find you.'"[629]

Despite all the anti-Christian sentiments they currently absorb from the popular culture, the media, the political left, and often from those who claim to speak in their behalf, Indians remain today more Christian than the general population. According to Census Canada, three out of four Canadian aboriginals list themselves as Christian.[630] For the population as a whole, that figure is 67.3 percent. Reginald Bibby, Canada's well-known sociologist of religion, finds that 54 percent of aboriginal teenagers say they trust in church and other religious leaders. For non-aboriginal teenagers, the figure is 39 percent. Among aboriginal teenagers, 78 percent believe in a creator God—eleven percentage points higher than the national average.[631]

Most actual Indians, it seems, do not buy the "cultural genocide" bit.

Christianity as the ark of Indian culture

The charge that the missionaries committed cultural crimes against the natives is actually deeply ironic. The Jesuits who first catechized most of the tribes of Eastern Canada were commonly accused in their own day, here as in other parts of the world, of "going native," of not doing their bit to introduce the Indians to European civilization. "[I]t was the reproach of the Jesuit missions," Francis Parkman writes, "that they left the savage a savage still, and asked little of him but the practice of certain rites and the passive acceptance of dogmas."[632] Instead of teaching the natives French, the Jesuits learned Indian languages. The Sieur de Cadillac objected that the Jesuits were not even converting fast enough. Rather than pushing their religion on the Indians, they commonly refused baptism until they were certain their charges were properly catechised, and understood what they were about.[633] Alexander Mackenzie makes a similar charge: "They habituated themselves to the savage life and naturalised themselves to the savage manners, and by thus becoming dependent, as it were, on the natives, they acquired their contempt rather than their veneration."[634]

Real missionaries had reasons not to assimilate the Indians to European culture. First, the more things they demanded that the Indians change about their existing culture, the harder a sell Christianity, their true concern, became. Why fuss? Why set up barriers? Who cares on which side one puts the fork or spoon for a formal meal? Second, the missionaries worried that introducing Indians wholesale to the European culture was dangerous to their morals—European culture was sadly not what it should be, and not an ideal example of the Christian life. Alcohol was an obvious concern. Governor Callières worried that "the Indian girls brought up at the Ursuline Convent led looser lives than the young squaws who had received no instruction."[635] Maybe so; or maybe another example of the Noble Savage myth. Had he really fully observed them in their wigwams in the woods? But Champigny agreed: "[A]ll intimacy of the Indians with the French is dangerous and corrupting to their morals."[636]

If true, perhaps this was culture shock. It would not be surprising. We probably know more about it today. Even any college freshman who moves away from home experiences a bit of it. Immersing oneself suddenly in an unfamiliar milieu, and discovering that so many old, assumed rules no longer apply, leads to a false sense of liberation, an impression that here there are no rules, that one can now do whatever one pleases. The experience must be particularly powerful in a conservative and communal society such as the Indians knew.

I submit, however, that the Jesuit prescription was wrong. The proof is that, many generations later, we still see the same culture shock, if culture shock it is, among Canadian aboriginals. Those with experience of living abroad know that the way to conquer the shock is not to wall oneself up in one' s room, not to hang out only with other expats—not to segregate yourself on a reserve. That is the way to prolong the misery indefinitely. The remedy is to make full contact with the new milieu, and, over time, begin to understand the underlying logic in its ways. The universe comes slowly back into focus, and the attractions of sitting in an expat bar grumbling and knocking back firewater grow less.

There was a third consideration pushing missionaries toward segregation over assimilation. Assume, if you like, that the missionaries were all scoundrels and hypocrites, had no morals, and looked out only for themselves. Even so, they had reason to resist the integration of their flocks. Keeping the Indians at arm's length from other Europeans increased their own power and influence. If the Indians could not speak French or English, and had little contact with other outsiders, the missionary became a vital advisor, intermediary, and interpreter for both Indians and the authorities.

Forced assimilation, then, was never the risk.

As for the fate of traditional Indian culture, if we really want to preserve it, the best thing to do is to recruit more Christian missionaries.

It is likely that, without the missionaries and their efforts, we would now know little or nothing about Indian culture. To evangelize, the first thing missionaries had to do was learn the Indian languages. To learn the Indian languages, one would create a written form, collect its vocabulary in writing, and analyse its grammar. No small benefit to the survival and propagation of any language: a dictionary and a formal grammar. The Abenaki dictionary compiled by Father Rale, for example, "has since been regarded as one of the most precious remains of the early philological labors on the Indian languages. The original is still preserved with the greatest care in the safe of the library of Harvard College….," writes John Shea, in the middle of the 19th century.[637] And Rale was not alone. Missionaries did the same thing everywhere, with every aboriginal language. LeClercq invented a writing system for Micmac. In Kamloops, Father Jean-Marie-Raphaël LeJeune created a syllabary for the Chinook language, and published the *Kamloops Wawa* newspaper, in Chinook. Methodist missionary James Evans invented Canadian Aboriginal Syllabics in 1840; they now supply a written form for a range of Indian languages.

Without this labour, many such languages would probably now be forgotten. With it, Indian cultures for the first time enter history in their own voice. For the first time, we have records of Indian ways, Indian affairs, Indian thought, and Indian literature, from the Indian point of view. Before it, we have little but bone fragments and ambiguous shards of stone.

The next thing missionaries naturally needed to do was collect any information about existing Indian spiritual beliefs. They had to understand the context: what concepts pre-existed, for example, and could be used in explaining Christianity? Did the Indians have a notion of the afterlife? Of the soul, and its immortality? Did they have an idea of a supreme being?

Accordingly, if today we still have some idea of what "traditional native spirituality" really is, if native spirituality continues to exist, this is mostly due to early Christian missions. Yes, there were also Indian oral traditions, but oral traditions are malleable and forgettable. Epidemics and wars, in a small population, might easily have wiped out anyone with the memory. European influence might have wiped out any interest in preserving these mental souvenirs for a generation or two, after which it would have been impossible to recover them.

"Native spirituality" as we know it today is really largely formed not from these records, but from elements of the pop culture, of "New Age" beliefs. But to that extent it is, like modern "paganism," really a back-formation from Christianity, a reaction to it. It is still due to Christianity. But then, to the extent that anything authentic endures, then this, too, is thanks to Christianity, to the records of early Christian missionaries. Either way, it is beloved child and creature of the Christian missions.

Discriminating against real Indians

Far from suppressing traditional Indian "spirituality," the Canadian prison service currently spends more money on "native spiritual services" than on all other faiths combined.[638] Yet this is for a tiny minority of a minority of prisoners. Four-fifths of Indian convicts call themselves Christians. Moreover, there are no specific and required Indian "spiritual" observances, no ministers, no organized religion. There is really no such faith in the wild—just a collection of magical practices and customs. So what's the money going for?

"Native spirituality" also has, unlike the monotheisms, no particular ethical content, and so no obvious value for rehabilitation.

Indians in prison are having an imaginary "traditional" Indian culture forced upon them, and it is not in their interest, in the interest of the public, or in the interest of culture. It is a slap in the face to real Indians, like thoughtfully supplying Irish prisoners with shrines to leprechauns.

17 YODA—NOT A REAL INDIAN. THOUGH HE MIGHT BE A LUTHERAN

Iroquois flying head.

A man of knowledge lives by acting, not by thinking about acting.
—Carlos Castaneda

There is no try. There is only do, or do not.
—Yoda

The revelation that most Indians are Christians may produce, for many who did not already know, some cognitive dissonance. After all, we all know any Indian elder is bubbling full of spiritual wisdom, popping koans like a Shaolin monk or a Jedi master. Much more profound than the spiritless routine of Christian church-going. Why, then, would the Indians take to Christianity? Why would they abandon a superior spiritual wisdom for an inferior?

But perhaps the first question should be: Where did this general awareness of deep Indian spirituality come from?

Like so much else, it mostly showed up in the Sixties. Noble Savage salad days again. It comes largely from several books by Carlos Castaneda, best-sellers through the late Sixties and early Seventies.

Castaneda was an anthropology grad student at UCLA. Prospecting for Indian herbs in the desert, he met Don Juan Matus, a Yaqui Indian medicine man, who accepted him as his disciple. Don Juan introduced him, through the use of peyote, jimson weed, and mescaline, to the awareness of a "separate reality" in which he could turn into a crow, fly, talk to coyotes, or jump off a cliff without being harmed. And, he gradually came to understand, these were not just hallucinations. Reality itself was an arbitrary construct; there was no objective truth. It was the story we chose to believe. It could, if one developed enough shamanic "power," be altered at will.

You can see how this would have gone over well back in the day. *Time* magazine declared Castaneda the "Godfather of the New Age"; *Salon* calls him "the literary embodiment of the Woodstock era." Much that we call "postmodernism" can be found here. And there is a good reason why Don Juan seems reminiscent of Yoda or Obi-Wan-Kenobi. George Lucas, creator of the *Star Wars* universe, claims to have been deeply influenced by the Don Juan books. Castaneda was Skywalker, Skywalker was Castaneda, in the Tatooine instead of the Sonoma desert, the apprentice Jedi knight.

But it was all originally to do with Indians.

The books, presented as legitimate anthropological field research, have given "native spirituality" its current prestige. Behind that dour exterior, those infinitely wise old Indians were hiding superpowers. They've probably been laughing at us all along.

This prestige is no doubt why the Canadian prison service currently pays more for native spiritual services than for all other faiths combined, for the benefit of 5 percent of prisoners who are nominally adherents of "native spirituality." Everyone has seen Star Wars.

This accepted as so, as said, the fact that most Indians are Christians becomes a puzzle.

And we have been able to discount the idea that this was done by compulsion. So how?

Jesuit trickery

It must have been some trick. For example, seeing the European wealth, perhaps they feigned conversion for material advantage. They are really all still secret pagans.

This is a charge often made against Christian missionaries. In China, the term is "rice Christians"—locals who allegedly converted to Christianity to get a daily dole of rice from the nearest mission.

This may sometimes have been true.

The French gave Indians converting to Catholicism one great material advantage: a firearm. They would not even sell or trade a firearm to a non-Christian Indian.

Convert, then, and you got a gun, for self-protection and for hunting. It could mean your life.

For the French government, this was not intended mostly as an incentive to convert. It was more a matter of wanting to get weapons into the hands of your allies and not your enemies.

Still, it might have served that purpose.

But if this was the motive, there is still a puzzle here. The Dutch and English in New York and on Hudson Bay had no such compunction. They would trade guns to anyone. As a result, Indians who allied with the French were at a serious disadvantage. Serious enough to have meant extinction to the Huron. And yet, most of the Indians preferred to deal with the French. When the French lost the Seven Years' War and had to leave North America, Pontiac was able to assemble a vast coalition of tribes to fight to have them return.

Firearms cannot have been the incentive. The French must have offered the Indians something more important than firearms. Something almost more important than life itself.

Father Brébeuf reports a Huron chief telling him, "Echon, I must speak to you frankly....The people of Ihonatiria said last year that they believed, in order to get tobacco."[639] A clear admission?

Maybe not. This was in reaction to the Jesuits announcing to the Indians that, as Christians, they would have to give up polygamy and other pleasures. It might not have been strictly true—more a matter of asserting that the Indians did not want a new religion that would deny them familiar pleasures.

After all, the Indians hardly needed the French to acquire tobacco. Nor does it seem a worthy exchange for switching religion. More like a metaphor chosen to express triviality.

Our Jesuit correspondents indeed reveal their concern with the possibility of conversion for gain in maintaining that this was at least not always so. "No one can say that this good neophyte," they report of one convert, "has enrolled himself under the standard of Jesus Christ out of worldly considerations.... [H]e has never asked, nor showed any inclination to get, anything from us.... We had neglected him for a long time, not even giving him anything to eat, or paying him much attention.... Indeed, he often said to Father Brébeuf, 'I became a Christian, not for the body, but for the soul.'"[640]

We cannot simply take the Jesuits' word on this. Honourable men, no doubt, but not disinterested parties. Whether true or not, they would want to believe that Indians were not converting for ulterior motives.

But note that Brébeuf and his catechumen here are strictly correct in terms of Catholic theology. Although it finds a place in some forms of Calvinism, there is no room in Catholicism for the "prosperity gospel." It would be bad theology for Catholics, and the Jesuits knew their theology. Even if some Jesuits wanted to falsify Catholic doctrine in order to attract converts—a meaningless achievement in theological terms—they would have risked entangling themselves in theological and logical incoherence. It is hard to make the idea of material rewards mesh with much in the gospel or the catechism. A shrewd Indian could have brought them up short.

Legaic, a Tsimshin convert of the 1860s, recorded addressing his tribe, seems to understand the theology well enough: "He then exhorted all to taste God's way, to give their hearts to Him, and to leave all their sins; and then endeavoured to show them what they had to expect if they did so—not temporal good, not health, long life, or ease or wealth, but God's favour here and happiness with God after death."[641]

Given that Catholicism expressly rejects material rewards, and promises its treasure "not in this world but the next," the hope of material advantage through one's religion probably, on the whole, would have worked against the missionaries, not for them. If Christianity does not promise toys and stuff, their rivals, the shamans with their traditional practices, did. As, indeed, does Castaneda's don Juan. Shamanism is mostly magical: do this dance, and you get rain. Use this herb, and you get a pretty wife. This charm helps with the seal hunt. The early Moravian missionaries lament, of the Eskimos/Inuit, "They could see no practical benefit from this new religion, which did not promise them any help in seal-fishing, or in building their kayaks."[642] "Do not speak to me about the soul," remarked one materialist Indian to Father LeJeune, "that is something that I give myself no anxiety about; it is this (showing his flesh) that I love, it is the body I cherish; as to the soul, I do not see it, let happen to it what will."[643]

It seems the spiritual message got through, but not on this basis.

And, even if imagined material benefit was behind the original conversion, this could not explain the continuing Indian loyalty to Christian ideals since. There would be no reason now to dissemble. The material incentives are all in the opposite direction. Look at the prison service.

Good timing

Another theory sometimes heard is that it was all dumb luck. The missionaries inadvertently brought the smallpox. The smallpox devastated Indian cultures, making many question established verities. The traditional shamans based much of their prestige on being able to cure illness. There is a reason why they are called "medicine men." Happening to be there when this void occurred, Christianity was able to benefit, even if it was really an inferior creed.

Elizabeth Fenn makes this claim.

> Repeated bouts of pestilence shattered native tribal organization, disrupted kinship ties, undermined Indian belief systems, and called into question the skills of traditional medical practitioners. The chaos made many Indians more receptive to the alternative religious and social structures offered by Catholic evangelicals when they moved into disease-ravaged regions.[644]

This seems superficially plausible as well. Father LeJeune claims, "These poor barbarians, perishing every day, say that there is no longer any real *Manitouisiou* [shaman] among them, that is to say, no genuine sorcerer."[645] The Jesuits record, of one Indian, "this poor barbarian did come to see ... [Governor Montmagny], and asked him why they were becoming visibly depopulated, and we, on the contrary, lived so long. 'It must be,' said he, 'that you know some secret for preserving your people, and that you have an intimate acquaintance with the Manitou.'"[646] Another delegation of Indians at Quebec say, "It must surely be, … that the God whom this Father announces to us, is powerful, since he so perfectly cures the greatest and the most contagious diseases,—which the Manitou or Genii, whom our sorcerers invoke, cannot do.'"[647]

"On the first day of July," Father LeJeune records,

> …a Captain of the petite nation of the Algonquins brought me letters stating that this Captain [chief] was coming down to Kebec to see the Captain of the French. 'He is considered,' said this Savage, 'a grand personage in our country; they say he is a great friend of the Sun, and that he gives letters which prevent one from dying, at least soon. I am going to ask him for some of them,' said he."[648]

Unlike the cargo cult/rice Christian notion, this was also reasonably in line with Christian traditions. One does not become a Christian for one's health; but Jesus went about healing the blind and lame. Healing is the most common type of miracle attributed to the Catholic saints. It is a traditional way for the Christian

God to manifest his power. It was one way the Holy Spirit did his work. So it was proper for the Jesuits themselves to promise that God would give health. "Two or three persons, having had recourse to the superstitions of the jugglers," one Jesuit reports, "died almost in their hands; and all those who addressed themselves to God were either cured or relieved in their diseases."[649] So too today: visit St. Joseph's Oratory in Montreal, or Lac Ste. Anne in Alberta, and count the discarded hearing aids and crutches on the wall.

Yet this factor may have been, for the early missionaries, a double-edged sword. After all, it was not likely to escape Indian notice that, wherever the black robes came, the smallpox seemed to come in their wake. Did this new religion cure disease, then, or did it cause it?

"I wish to say," writes one Jesuit,

> …that the savages have all the reasons which purely human argument can suggest to them, for having an aversion toward the faith, or rather, for rejecting it.... Since we have published the law of Jesus Christ in these regions, plagues have rushed in as in a throng. Contagious diseases, war, famine,—these are the tyrants that have sought to wrest the faith from the faithful, and that have caused it to be hated by the infidels. How many times have we been reproached that, wherever we set foot, death came in with us! How many times have they told us that they had never seen calamities like those which have appeared since we speak of Jesus Christ! "You tell us" (exclaim some) "that God is full of goodness; and then, when we give ourselves up to him, he massacres us. The Iroquois, our mortal enemies, do not believe in God, they do not love the prayers, they are more wicked than the demons,—and yet they prosper; and since we have forsaken the usages of our ancestors, they kill us, they massacre us, they burn us, they exterminate us, root and branch. What profit can there come to us from lending ear to the Gospel, since death and the faith nearly always march in company?" There are Christians who generously answer these complaints: "Though the faith should cause us to lose life, is it a great misfortune to leave the earth in order to be blest in heaven? If death and war slaughter the Christians, no more do they spare the infidels." "Yes, but," answer the others, "the Iroquois do not die, and yet they hold prayer in abomination. Before these innovations appeared in these regions, we lived as long as the Iroquois; but, since some have accepted prayer, one sees no more white heads,—we die at half age."[650]

"It is *la prière* that kills us," one Indian maintained to the Jesuits. "Your books and your strings of beads have bewitched the country. Before you came, we were happy and prosperous. You are magicians. Your charms kill our corn, and bring sickness and the Iroquois. Echon (Brébeuf) is a traitor among us, in league with our enemies."[651]

In 1844, on the lonely shores of Lake Winnepegosis, Father Jean-Edouard Darveau and his companions were shot dead by the Muskegong Indians on the charge that they and their teachings had brought a recent epidemic.[652]

"There is no human eloquence," laments another missionary, "which can persuade a people to embrace a religion which seems to have for companions only pestilence, war, and famine. It is God alone who causes the Faith to germinate, who preserves it, and who vivifies."[653]

So smallpox is unlikely to have been a critical factor leading to the general conversion. In any case, as with material prosperity, if the Indians were "tricked" into becoming Christians by seeing it as medicine (and granted that Christian prayer really may heal), why their continued commitment today?

We are left, then, with the likelihood that, to the minds of the Indians, who should know best, Christianity was simply a superior spiritual doctrine, a superior explanation of human existence, better than anything their traditions offered.

The real Don Juan

In order to understand this, it is probably helpful to know that Castaneda's Don Juan, the wise Yaqui shaman on whom our high opinion of "native spirituality" is mostly based, was a fictional character—no more real than Obi-Wan Kenobi. Castaneda was one more in a line of charlatans who saw that, by putting their claims in the mouth of an imaginary Indian, they gained credibility. Without this literary device, who was actually going to accept that Castaneda turned into a crow, or learned to fly? Yet they did in his day—up to and including his thesis committee at UCLA, and University of California Press. Indians, we instinctively believe, being uncorrupted by civilization, cannot lie.

In 1973, however, *Time* magazine discovered that most of Castaneda's public claims about his biography were false, and for no obvious reason. He had lied about his military service, his father's occupation, his age, his country of birth; possibly about his name. So others began to examine the details of his tales about Don Juan. While Don Juan supposedly presented "a Yaqui way of knowledge," and was strongly anti-Christian, it turned out that the real Yaquis were, so far as anyone could tell, Catholic. Unlike Don Juan, even in their pagan traditions, they did not use peyote or other psychoactive substances. In his 1980 piece "The Don Juan Papers," psychologist Richard de Mille tracks down Don Juan's spiritual sayings, and discovers they are generally taken more or less verbatim from familiar philosophers, spiritual writers, and anthropological literature. Either Don Juan spent a lot of time in a college library, or Castaneda did.

In one example, de Mille first quotes a passage by a mystic, Yogi Ramacharaka (himself really a Pennsylvania lawyer named William Walker Atkinson): "The Human Aura is seen by the psychic observer as a luminous cloud, egg-shaped, streaked by fine lines like stiff bristles standing out in all directions." In *A Separate Reality*, Don Juan says a "man looks like a human egg of circulating fibers. And his arms and legs are like luminous bristles bursting out in all directions."[654]

To be fair, Castaneda was probably justified by his own stated beliefs in claiming that his experiences with don Juan were real. After all, if we can all make our own reality, a fictional character is as real as you or I. Don't say we weren't warned.

But it would be wrong for the rest of us to suppose that Don Juan tells us anything about Indian culture we could not just make up ourselves.

He, and Castaneda's claimed experiences, have clear precedents in the European romantic tradition of the Noble Savage. Castaneda more or less casts himself as the hero in Matthew Arnold's Victorian poem "The Scholar Gipsy." The original setting is Oxford, not UCLA, and the savages are gypsies instead of Indians. But the basic narrative is otherwise the same:

And near me on the grass lies Glanvil's book—
Come, let me read the oft-read tale again!
The story of the Oxford scholar poor,
Of pregnant parts and quick inventive brain,
Who, tired of knocking at preferment's door,
One summer-morn forsook
His friends, and went to learn the gipsy-lore,
And roam'd the world with that wild brotherhood,
And came, as most men deem'd, to little good,
But came to Oxford and his friends no more.

But once, years after, in the country-lanes,
Two scholars, whom at college erst he knew,
Met him, and of his way of life enquired;
Whereat he answer'd, that the gipsy-crew,
His mates, had arts to rule as they desired
The workings of men's brains,
And they can bind them to what thoughts they will.
"And I," he said, "the secret of their art,

> *When fully learn'd, will to the world impart;*
> *But it needs heaven-sent moments for this skill."*

Arnold himself was working from an earlier legend, dating back at least to the seventeenth century.

Black Elk speaks

Castaneda was not alone. In 1932, the poet John Neihardt put out an "autobiography" of the Lakota Sioux shaman, Black Elk. When first published, it made few waves. But it was reissued in 1961, and found an eager public. Black Elk Speaks helped kick-start the Sixties. It was probably a model for Castaneda. It described Indian life as an idyll, destroyed by the coming of the white man. It was full of accounts of impressive visions and spiritual experiences, worthy of the best acid trip. Black Elk was heralded as a religious genius, a hero of the New Age, and the book as a "spiritual classic."[655]

The book ends with Black Elk lamenting the massacre at Wounded Knee:

> And so it was all over.
>
> I did not know then how much was ended. When I look back now from this high hill of my old age, I can still see the butchered women and children lying heaped and scattered all along the crooked gulch as plain as when I saw them with eyes still young. And I can see that something else was buried in the blizzard. A people's dream died there. It was a beautiful dream.[656]

Very poetic. But then, it was written by an accomplished poet.

Unlike Don Juan, Black Elk was a real person. This gives him a certain added credibility. But there are problems with the account of his life in Neihardt's book. For one thing, it shows him as a pagan shaman, a proponent of pre-Christian Sioux spirituality. The real Black Elk, or Nick Black Elk, as he was known to friends and family, was Catholic. And not just Catholic—a trained catechist and lay minister whose main fame among his fellow Sioux was as a Christian missionary, who brought hundreds to the faith. He is currently under consideration for Catholic sainthood.

Other Indians, and other Sioux, say they see little of actual Indian culture in Neihardt's book. And Black Elk seems to agree with them. He is on record twice in letters as objecting to it. He writes in 1934:

> I shake hands with my white friends. Listen, I speak some true words. A white man made a book and told what I had spoken of olden times, but the new times he left out. So I speak again, a last word. I am now an old man.... In the last thirty years I am different from what the white man wrote about me. I am a Christian ... I say the Apostle's Creed and I believe every word of it.

And in 1935:

> Three years ago in 1932 a white man named John G. Neihardt came up to my place whom I have never met before and asked me to make a story book with him.... He promised me that if he completed and publish [*sic*] this book he was to pay half of the price of each book. [He told me] he hasn't seen a cent from the book which we made. By this I know he was deceiving me about the whole business. I also asked to put at the end of the story that I was not a pagan but have converted into the Catholic Church in which I work as a catechist for more than 25 years. I've quit all these pagan works. But he didn't mention this. Cash talks.[657]

Nick Black Elk also never made the famous speech that ends the book.[658] That is apparently pure Neihardt.

Raymond DeMallie also catches Neihardt omitting elements of Black Elk's youthful visions that mark them as Christian, not pagan. The fact, for example, that the luminous figure he sees in a vision standing before a tree with arms outstretched has holes in his palms, and is the son of the Great Spirit.[659]

In short, much of the book, including its main thrust, is not true autobiography. It is the work of a European-American poet, working within the European romantic tradition, on Indian materials. It is a romantic legend. It is, in the words of its alleged subject, a "story book."

William Powers, Indian, writes, "My ... contention is that the book *Black Elk Speaks*, and the plethora of other books, articles, reviews, essays, songs, plays, and poetry, in fact, obscure Lakota religion rather than explain it. Further, I will argue that much of what passes as Lakota religion today is the product of the white man's imagination."[660]

Even Black Elk's pre-conversion visions, it seems, were not expressions of traditional beliefs. They were of the ghost dance, and the ghost dance, in turn, could best be described as poorly assimilated Christianity, heard still mostly at second remove.

This is the core message of the ghost dance faith, as acquired by James Mooney through luck and perseverance. It is a direct quote, translated by Mooney, from a confidential letter sent by the prophet Jack Wilson to the Arapaho and Cheyenne in Indian Territory:

> Do not tell the white people about this. Jesus is now upon the earth. He appears like a cloud. The dead are all alive again. I do not know when they will be here; maybe this fall or in the spring. When the time comes there will be no more sickness and everyone will be young again.[661]

It is a vision of the Second Coming.

Upaya

Real Indian religion, no relation to Castaneda's creed, and little relation to Neihardt's, might well have been just as far behind Europe as Indian material technology was. Why would it not be so? A resistance to the strange or new would have inhibited innovation in spiritual as much as material matters. The same need to focus on the daily struggle, on war and subsistence, would have drained away time for quiet meditation as much on spiritual as on material affairs. And the lack of writing would have been crucial. There is a reason why the great religions are so often and so tightly built around "The Book," around scripture. If you have the essence written down, you have a foundation on which to build generation by generation, as great minds come along. If all must be passed on orally, you have built on sand. You can retain, meditate on, and annotate no more from one generation to the next than can be stored in one human memory. General understanding cannot surpass the best understanding in each small tribe in each generation. If a spiritual genius arises, his contribution will be lost in two generations. Solutions found a hundred or a thousand years ago are likely to be unremembered today.

Time and again, when the Jesuits ask the Indian elders a difficult question about this or that aspect of their beliefs, they seem obliged to answer, "about this, our ancestors did not say; we do not know." There were, it seems, logical gaps in their traditions, fairly obvious questions left unanswered. If someone had somewhere once worked these out, the information was not passed on.

Christian cosmology, after two or three thousand recorded years of scholarship (counting the Jewish tradition), tested too in the rational fire of Greek philosophy, tends to be a rather complete, comprehensive, and defensible world view. It might easily have blown away traditional aboriginal understandings in any open debate.

In addition to this, there is the matter of "*upaya*." This is a Buddhist concept, and a useful one.

Ontology, or cosmology, is only the starting gun. Right. God exists. The next question: What are you going to do about it? Buddhism, usefully, understands religion not as a set of beliefs about the world, but primarily as "*upaya*," literally, "skillful means." Religion is spiritual technology—practical ways to achieve a full and true experience of the divine, and to live a life in accordance with this. God is not an abstract term on a page: he is a living person with whom one wants a living relationship.

The most common observation made regarding the pre-existing native religion by the first missionaries and explorers was that they, the Indians, did not seem to have any. There was a near-complete lack of rituals, votive objects, prayers, any physical or visible evidence of religious concerns—of spiritual technologies, of "*upaya*." "I cannot obtain the least insight into the religion of the Red Indians," writes John Cartwright of the Beothuk, "and have thought it very remarkable, that in a journey of about seventy miles through the heart of their winter country, not a single object should present itself that might be looked upon as intended for religious purposes or devoted to any superstitious practices of those people."[662] The Jesuits made similar observations of other tribes. "[T]hey have hardly any virtue or religion," writes Brébeuf of the Huron.[663] "[T]he savages have no definite religion," writes Father Biard of the Micmac.[664] "There is among them no system of religion, or care for it," writes Father Jouvency of the Algonquins.[665]

Father LeClercq writes, "The Gaspesians, if we except those who have received the faith of Jesus Christ with their baptism, have never really known any deity, since they have lived down to our own day without temples, priests, sacrifices, and any indication of religion. Thus, if one may judge of the past by the present, it is easy to infer that if they have worshipped any deity at all, they have shown him so little veneration and respect that they have been in reality indifferent and unfaithful in the matter of religion."[666]

"They had no temples," writes Livingston Jones of the Tlingit, "no religious assemblies, no representations of deity, in short, no rites or ceremonies that might properly be called religious, in early days. They were truly heathen."[667] Samuel Hearne writes that religion "has not as yet began to dawn among the Northern Indians; ... they, as well as their credulous neighbours, are utterly destitute of every idea of practical religion."[668]

Bishop Bompas makes such observations of the Eskimo/Inuit: "The Esquimaux have still a word for a world above, and acknowledge that a system of religion was known to their forefathers, but say they have forgotten it."[669]

Having rituals, symbols, sacraments, smoke and incense and bells and hymns and prayers and devotions, means more paths to the sacred. Christianity could in this regard have been as obviously technologically superior to traditional shamanism as the arquebus was to the bow and arrow. Or more so.

Bad trips

Castaneda's fictional Indian spirituality shares a superficial resemblance to real Indian world-views: like the Indians, Castaneda maintains that the real world is the world as imagined, not as sensed. But note a critical difference. Castaneda believes, with the New Age and postmodernism, that we can construct our own reality. With psychic "power," with The Force, we get, God-like, to choose for ourselves what is and is not real.

This is entirely different from the Indian experience. To Indians, one did not choose the dream—what you dreamt was real, and no more readily manipulated than the visible world. You did not get to be God here; you were obliged to obey. And this was almost as true of shamans as of laymen.

The source for Castaneda's doctrine that you get to choose what to believe is, again, not native Indian, but European. The most probable source is Martin Luther. Luther introduced the doctrine of *sola fide*—"salvation by faith alone." All very well if by "faith" Luther meant "trust." But *fide* is not always understood so. *Sola fide* implies, at least in some interpretations, "belief," in the sense that believing in the truth or reality of "A" instead of "B" is a moral act. Which is to say, it is a matter of free will.

If one chooses what one will believe, one chooses one's reality.

This is not how the imagination is experienced, or indeed how belief really works. We do not decide what we will dream. That is why the Indians considered the imagined world objective: it is not part of us, we did not make it, we cannot control it.

Nor does an honest man choose what to believe—he seeks truth, whatever it is, or seems to be.

Castaneda's separate reality looks appealing when you suppose it means you make your own reality: I choose not only to be able to fly, but also to have a million dollars in the bank. And, of course, to be dead handsome. And descended from Portuguese royalty. Immortal would be good, too.

But, as we discovered in the Sixties, not all trips are good trips. This, no doubt, is why there is not as much of a market for LSD any more.

Gilbert Sproat explains that for the Nootka, "Dreams are both good and bad, but oftener forebode evil than good. Almost equal to dreams in importance is the influence of omens. An eagle flying near the houses, the appearance of many seals, a watery moon, the presence of a white man, are the fancied causes of innumerable events; in fact, hardly a day passes in a native house without some fear being caused by dreams or omens. All the people live in constant apprehension of danger from the unseen world."[670]

This does not sound like so much fun. It sounds more like living in near-constant terror. "The turning of a leaf, the crawling of an insect, the cry of a bird, the creaking of a bough, might be to him the mystic symbol of weal or woe."[671]

LeClercq, who took shamanism seriously, said of the Micmac, "Our poor Gaspesians were formerly tormented by the Devil, who often beat them very cruelly, and even terrified them by hideous spectres and horrible phantoms to such an extent that, on some occasions, frightful carcasses have been seen to fall in the midst of their wigwams, a circumstance which caused to the Indians so much terror that sometimes they fell dead upon the spot."[672]

"The belief in the existence of evil spirits," writes Livingston Jones of the Tlingit,

> … is the foundation of shamanism. They propitiate and conjure with these imaginary evil spirits in order to purchase their good will, but they do not worship them. Shamanism is one grand effort to wrestle with these supposed evil spirits and obtain immunity from them. But their belief in the existence of spirits was never elevated into a religion.[673]

"Their aboriginal belief," writes Ballou, "is ... the propitiating of evil spirits by acceptable offerings."[674]

John West writes, of the Plains Indians, "Their general idea is, that they are more immediately under the influence of a powerful Evil Spirit. Experience has taught them this melancholy fact, in the trials, sufferings, afflictions, and multiform death which they undergo; and therefore their prayers are directed to him, when any severe calamity befalls them."[675]

You might call that a religion, but it is a joyless religion, a religion of servitude.

And it gets worse.

> His belief in the existence of evil and malignant spirits is the foundation for his belief in witchcraft. He regards them as

> not only capable of producing disease, but of sending other calamities. They may make a heavy storm swamp his canoe, cause him to be drowned, to be destroyed by bears, triumphed over by his foes, and in other ways do him untold harm.[676]
>
> It would be almost impossible to exaggerate the native's terror of witches. It is for this reason rather than for hardness of heart or delight in human sufferings, that they torture them. They deem nothing too cruel for them because they hold them responsible for all human sufferings and death itself.[677]
>
> The one settled on as the witch was generally some unimportant member of the community, an uncanny-looking creature, a slave, or some one who had the ill will of the doctor or the relatives of the patient. This was a very effective way of ridding one of his enemy.
>
> No one, not even the victim himself, thought of disputing the shaman's judgment. Whom he designated as the witch was believed by all to be such, and was immediately treated as such. A near relative of the witch usually took the initiative in the punishment.
>
> The victim was first reviled, reproached, brutally and shamefully treated, and subsequently put to death. No punishment was considered too cruel for a witch, and various means were devised for their torture. They were tied to stakes before the rising tide, and to stakes in the forests for wolves to devour; they were made to die from starvation, with food almost within their reach; their limbs were tied to their bodies and then they were thrown naked on a bed of thorns. In short, all kinds of exquisite tortures were applied to the miserable wretches.
>
> After the witch was left to die, no one would dare approach him, or in any way offer relief.
>
> The curse of the community would be on the head of the one who did.[678]

The Indian pantheon of supernatural beings includes many that would work well in a horror movie. The Abenaki had Atosis, a reptilian humanoid, who forces people to find a stick so that he can cook them on it. There was the Dzee-dzee-bon-da, so fearsome to look at that even he is terrified by his reflection in a still pond. There is M-ska-gwe-demoos, a moss-covered woman who lives in the swamp. She might turn into Maski-mon-gwe-zo-os, a giant toad who lures men and children into the depths of the bog, then drowns them. There is a vampire, the *tsi-noo*, whose heart is of ice, and who, having no soul, must eat the souls of others to survive.

The Algonquins had a version of the sasquatch, called Bagwajiwininiwag, an ape-like being larger than a man. They feared a flying skeleton called Bakaak, a giant horned panther called Mishibizhiw who caused unwary travellers to drown, and the notorious cannibal spirit of the woods, the Wendigo. Lakes generally entertained some sea monster. There is, for that matter, the sasquatch.

And so it goes, tribe by tribe. Fun, perhaps, for a Saturday matinee, but not fun to live with day to day.

Nor could the Indians turn to any trustworthy spiritual champion in times of peril. Chief among the gods, in the Eastern Woodlands was Nanabozho or Nanabush, the creator or restorer. He is, like the Greek gods, not a moral being. "[S]ometimes," writes Parkman, "he is a vain and treacherous imp."[679] The "good guys" in Indian legends are themselves, if not malicious, not ethical; they are "tricksters."

We have previously mentioned Father LeJeune's experience one dark and stormy night among the Innu. It is relevant here: "During the night, a woman who had gone out, returned, terribly frightened, crying out that she had heard the Manitou, or devil. At once all the camp was in a state of alarm, and every one, filled with fear, maintained a profound silence. I asked the cause of this fright, for I had not heard what the woman had said; *eca titou, eca titou*, they told me, Manitou, 'Keep still, keep still, it is the devil.'"[680]

Manitou, strictly speaking, means only "spirit." But spirits generally were among Indians beings to be feared. So many dragons, so few bold knights!

And here perhaps we see a critical advantage of Christianity.

"I began to laugh," LeJeune continues, speaking like a Christian jedi, "and rising to my feet, went out of the cabin; and to reassure them I called, in their language, the Manitou, crying in a loud voice that I was not afraid, and that he would not dare come where I was. Then, having made a few turns in our island, I reëntered, and said to them, 'Do not fear, the devil will not harm you as long as I am with you, for he fears those who believe in God; if you will believe in God, the devil will flee from you.' They were greatly astonished, and asked me if I was not afraid of him at all. I answered, to relieve them of their fears, that I was not afraid of a hundred of them; they began to laugh, and were gradually reassured."[681]

Christianity protects one from demons.

This should come as no surprise. It was a prominent feature of Christianity in first-century Judaea, too: the ability to cast out devils. See the New Testament.

> Jesus went up on a mountainside and called to him those he wanted, and they came to him. He appointed twelve that they might be with him and that he might send them out to preach and to have authority to drive out demons. (Mark 3: 13-5; NIV)

This may have been the feature that allowed Christianity to spread so quickly through the Roman Empire. Ramsay McMullen has called Christian exorcism "the chief instrument of conversion" throughout the ancient world.[682]

The omnipotent God is necessarily more powerful than other spiritual beings. Cleave to him, and you have nothing to fear from demons of the night. And, unlike even the nicer pagan gods, he cares for you. He would not treat you as a wanton boy might treat a fly.

"It is known that since they have been instructed in our holy mysteries," writes Father LeClercq, "especially those whom we have baptized, they are no more beaten or tormented by the Devil in the manner in which formerly they were before they had received the first and most necessary of our sacraments."[683]

This way madness lies

Modern psychiatrists would no doubt instead tell the Indians that these spirits of the night did not exist, were "only in their heads." That might work for some; but not likely for most Indians, who fully understood that the imagination was real. You cannot just will something not to exist. And saying ghouls are "unreal" sounds like whistling past the graveyard. "I don't believe in ghosts; because if I don't believe in them, they can't hurt me." Not terribly helpful. A child's logic.

It has been claimed that Indian medicine men regularly faked madness, to demonstrate their contact with the spiritual world. "The Neutral nation," writes Parkman, "was full of pretended madmen who raved about the villages, throwing firebrands, and making other displays of frenzy."[684]

But why assume they were pretending?

Two logical objections here: first, it requires assuming that other Indians were stupid and gullible, and could not tell real from faked madness. This is not plausible. Second, it assumes that psychiatric professionals too cannot tell real from feigned madness. For many years, up to the middle of the 20th century, the traditional Algonquin shamans, the *waabanowin*, were commonly put into mental hospitals by American mental health authorities.[685]

If this was not madness, I think we need to question whether we know what madness is.

Oxford defines "psychosis" as a state in which "contact is lost with external reality."[686] *Merriam-Webster* says it is a state in which you "believe things that are not true."[687] If for "external reality" or "truth" you read "physical reality," as I suspect most of us do, then any genuine Indian shaman was, in fact, by this measure, psychotic. When at his channeling trade, he was fully in the spirit world, the world of the imagination.

More generally, all Indians, in their traditional culture, were half-mad in modern Western terms.

This is not necessarily a good thing.

You can argue that traditional shamanic beliefs are actually superior to modern psychiatry. Some observers remark that Indians seem never to suffer what we would call mental illness. That would be a great cultural advantage. But this, surely, is because what we would call mental illness was defined by them instead as shamanic talent. Instead of being locked up and drugged to semi-consciousness, the native psychotic remained within the community, was respected, and had a means to support himself.

All to the good.

Except that, at the same time, he risked murder by anyone who suspected he had laid a curse on them.

Father LeCaron writes, in 1624, "If, indeed, these jugglers are not adroit in getting credit and turning their very blunders to account when the person dies or the enterprise fails in the desired success, the juggler is sometimes executed on the spot without any other formality."[688]

The best option here is not psychiatry, but Christianity. It is all very well to let psychotics be productively psychotic, but, as noted, this can often be terrifying and excruciatingly painful; both to the psychotic, and to those around him or her. Ask any schizophrenic. But it is not terribly helpful to tell the psychotic he is just imagining things, and drug him, and leave him incapacitated. That is an awful life sentence.

Unlike modern medicine, Christianity does not deny the traditional Indian world view, the reality of the imagination. Instead, it accepts it, but introduces a new spiritual technology that can protect from any harm.

We really ought to try it on psychosis generally.

In the meantime, the same impulse that causes people to prefer sanity over psychosis would lead Indians to embrace Christianity.

The quiet voice within

We must also deal with another possible motive, although it is controversial. Suppose, for a moment, that morality is not just culturally determined, or randomly chosen by each of us for ourselves as individuals. Suppose right and wrong are instead real things. Suppose there really is something wrong with killing and eating children, abandoning the old and infirm, slaughtering those who speak a different language, holding fellow humans as slaves, beating women, sustained torture, and the like.

Suppose moreover that God has given each of us a conscience that tells us so—call it the better angel of our nature. Suppose this conscience can trouble us from time to time, when we do these things.

One might then see an automatic, if also painful, call in the Indian heart to follow the moral precepts advocated by Christianity.

I know it sounds mad, but this is the motive actually given by most missionaries and converted Indians.

Peter Jones:

> I can affirm that the Indian in his natural state is not happy. He has his trials, afflictions, and fears: the worst passions of the human mind bear uncontrolled sway, entailing misery and woe. "There is no peace, saith my God, to the wicked." A civilized state, even without religion, is far preferable to paganism.[689]

Now, suppose all this is true, and that we are actively supporting and underwriting traditional Indian spirituality.

18 FREE PRIVATE SCHOOLS

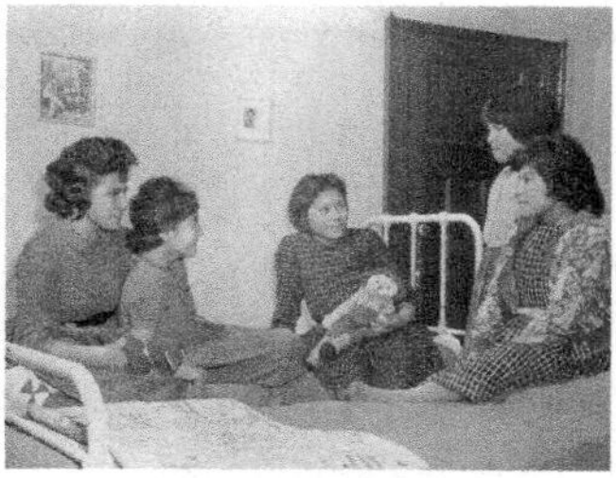

Dorm life.

Judge Sinclair has entered the court. Exhibit A for the charge of cultural genocide against Canadian Indians is now placed in evidence: the residential schools.

In 2008, the "Truth and Reconciliation" Commission was duly formed and funded to investigate this atrocity. Seven years and $60 million later, it writes, in its summary report, "Residential schooling was always more than simply an educational program; it was an integral part of a conscious policy of cultural genocide."[690]

The very first words of the report are:

> Canada's residential school system for Aboriginal children was an education system in name only for much of its existence. These residential schools were created for the purpose of separating Aboriginal children from their families, in order to minimize and weaken family ties and cultural linkages, and to indoctrinate children into a new culture—the culture of the legally dominant Euro-Christian Canadian society, led by Canada's first prime minister, Sir John A. Macdonald.[691]

The residential school system had "paternalistic and racist foundations."[692] "In Canada, residential schooling was closely linked to colonization and missionary crusades."[693] Irwin Cotler, as Justice Minister, called the residential schools "the single most harmful, disgraceful and racist act in our history." Kevin Annett, former United Church minister, says they "practised wholesale ethnic cleansing under the guise of education."[694]

Strong words. They must have been terrible. But exactly how?

Residential schools were an assault on aboriginal children

The first charge against them, historically speaking, is sexual abuse of the children. No doubt it happened. But this was the fault of individuals, not an intended feature of the system itself.

We cannot know how widespread it really was—such charges are by their nature usually one person's word against another's. Moreover, we are learning, if we did not already know, that such sexual abuse is a risk at schools everywhere. The unfortunate truth is that, if you are a pedophile or a sadist, classroom teaching is an ideal career—the second-best opportunity anywhere to pursue your hobby. More so in a remote residential school.

In 2004, the US Department of Education commissioned Charol Shakeshaft to survey the literature to determine how common sexual assault of students was in the US public school system. She cites studies estimating a range from 3.7 percent to 50.3 percent of all schoolchildren.[695]

There are apparently no figures available for private boarding schools.[696] However, logically, simply on the basis that their students are in school for more of the time, one would expect numbers for residential schools to be higher.

Based on claims filed by alleged victims, the rate for Canadian Indian residential schools—if all accusations are true—is 20 percent.[697]

This, bad as it might sound, falls within the known range for public day schools. In other words, there is no objective reason to think the Indian residential schools, despite their remote location, presented a unique problem in this regard. Or that Indian students would have been better off at some other kind of school, if they were going to attend school.

It is perhaps also worth pointing out, to cut through possible stereotypes of evil whites, that some proportion of assaults reported may be due not to staff, but to older students. See the tradition of "fagging" in British public schools.

"After 8:30 at night we were under no supervision," testifies ex-pupil Mary Carpenter, "and the world —the other world of the twilight took over. I am going to tell you about that. We were made by the senior and the stronger girls to drink urine and to go to bed, like a man and woman in bed. If we didn't we were beaten up."[698]

Many awful stories are also, indeed, related of staff. Most of the testimonies of "physical abuse" collected by the Truth and Reconciliation Commission seem pedestrian—apparently the schools used a leather strap much like the one used in the Catholic school I attended in Montreal, but administered with a witness present. An ominous-sounding "electric chair" reported by Kevin Annett ("Specially constructed torture chambers with permanent electric chairs")[699] turns out to have been intended for entertainment.[700] However, Mary Plamondon claims she once saw a student pushed down a flight of stairs.[701]

And there were staff like Arthur Plint, former supervisor of the Alberni Indian Residential School, who pleaded guilty in 1995 to sexual relations with 18 boys under his care, ranging in age from six to 13.[702]

But would most aboriginal children have been better off at home?

As we said, teaching is the second-best opportunity on earth for a pedophile or a sadist to ply their avocation. But if you are a pedophile, a sadist, or a bully, there is one even better situation: having your own kids at home. Ideally in a remote location. There is less supervision.

Bullying—bullying by adults—was the complaint among the dozen or so young Cree who threatened mass suicide not long ago at Attawapiskat Reserve. With a hint that this includes sexual assault.

"Something happened to me when I was a kid," said one 17-year-old girl when interviewed, "but I don't want to talk about it."[703]

More kids are molested or abused by family members than by teachers or strangers.

Because of their magnetic allure for pedophiles and sadists, it seems wise to run residential schools on religious lines, and seek teachers of religious commitment and good moral character. Hypocrisy is always a risk, but this is the obvious test. A vow of celibacy, as with Catholic religious, is an even higher bar.

Given this, the Indian residential schools, being religious institutions, may have done a better job of protecting their charges from sexual or emotional abuse than the typical private school, perhaps the typical public school, and probably the typical reserve. If there was still abuse, alas, this world is far from perfect.

And even if it were much more common than it seems to have been, sexual abuse of students would involve only a minority of students. Pedophilia is just not that common—perhaps 5 percent of adults are drawn to the practice. One study suggests 8.1 percent of the population has sadistic tendencies.[704] I would guess there is a great deal of overlap between the two. Sex with a small child seems inherently sadistic.

No; the schools, if they are to be properly demonized, must be demonized on other grounds.

And demonization seems the point. The mandate of the Truth and Reconciliation Commission did not allow for the possibility of finding the residential schools to be harmless or beneficial. It also proudly declared itself "victim-centred."[705] It heard almost solely from self-selected "victims," rather than trying anything so scientific as a survey. Few ex-staff were heard from. There was no cross-examination of witnesses; the commission apparently sharing the general prejudice that Indians and other aboriginals are incapable of telling a lie. Even if self-interest, such as receiving financial compensation, were involved.

It is striking, given the predetermined outcome, that the commission came up with so little. Perhaps to compensate, the summary report favours anecdotes that evoke the Nazi death camps. For example, there is surely an allusion to the crowded, windowless cattle cars of Eastern Europe (as well as a somewhat more appropriate allusion to the displacement of Southeastern US Indians to Oklahoma) in its accounts of leaving for residential school:

> Larry Beardy travelled by train from Churchill, Manitoba, to the Anglican residential school in Dauphin, Manitoba—a journey of 1,200 kilometres. As soon as they realized that they were leaving their parents behind, the younger children started crying. At every stop, the train took on more children and they would start to cry as well. "That train I want to call the train of tears."[706]

The first day of school is probably traumatic for most children. Surely more so if the school is residential. Still, we do not often see this as an argument for keeping children out of school, nor for seeing school as a holocaust. Lots of kids are sent to residential schools. Winston Churchill was, and he seemed to turn out okay. Franklin Roosevelt was, and he survived. Reference to a "train of tears" seems just a trifle over the top.

The Commission seems to relish the fact that children, on arrival at school, had their heads shaved. Just like inmates of the concentration camps. It was for "delousing"? Sure; that's what they said at Auschwitz.

> "When we arrived we had to register that we had arrived, then they took us to cut our hair." Bernice Jacks became very frightened when her hair was cut on her arrival at a school in the Northwest Territories. "I could see my hair falling. And I couldn't do nothing. And I was so afraid my mom … I wasn't thinking about myself. I was thinking about Mom. I

> say, 'Mom's gonna be really mad. And June is gonna be angry. And it's gonna be my fault.'"[707]

Campbell Papequash interprets this as a deliberate humiliation. "And after I was taken there they took off my clothes and then they deloused me. I didn't know what was happening but I learned about it later, that they were delousing me; 'the dirty, no-good-for-nothing savages, lousy.'"[708]

But children really do get head lice. The best way to protect against them spreading through the school is indeed to shave the kids' heads when they arrive. Head lice are not good company in a dorm.

Residential schools were an assault on aboriginal families

Another charge made in the Truth and Reconciliation Commission Report is that the existence of the residential schools was an insult to the abilities of Indians as parents. Didn't the presence of such schools imply that the government did not trust them to look after their own kids?

But, if there was a general concern among whites (as well as Indians) about the state of the Indian family, it would seem to be with some reason. "By 1960," the Commission itself reports, "the federal government estimated that 50% of the children in residential schools were there for child-welfare reasons."[709] "Some children had to stay in the schools year-round because it was thought there was no safe home to which they could return."[710] Shubenacadie, the one residential school in the Maritimes, was always primarily an orphanage. "In 1977, Aboriginal children accounted for 44% of the children in care in Alberta, 51% of the children in care in Saskatchewan, and 60% of the children in care in Manitoba."[711] Today, although aboriginals are only 4 percent of the Canadian population, half the children in foster care are aboriginal.[712]

So yes, there may have been concerns about Indian parenting.

This was an important reason for the original formation of the residential schools. "In February, 1884," writes Andrew Brown in 1895,

> ...the Rev. Hugh McKay was designated a missionary to the Indians of the North West ... and, after some exploring, found an opening among the Crees in the Qu'Appelle valley at Round Lake. He began in a small way to take a few starving and half-naked Indian children into the little log house that served him for bachelor quarters. He fed them, clothed them and taught them, and from this modest

> beginning has grown the circle of eight boarding industrial schools under the care of the Presbyterian Church.[713]

A Grey Nun writes from the Northwest in 1867,

> I must give you a few instances to show you what is the depth of the moral misery which we are called on to relieve. What I tell you will shock you to hear, as it sickens me to tell. It was a rather general custom of the savages in these countries to kill, and sometimes to eat, the orphan children, especially the little girls. Religion has made a great change in this respect, but infanticide is still by no means rare.
>
> A mother, looking with contempt on her newly-born daughter, will say, "Her father has deserted me; I am not going to feed her." So she will wrap up the little one in the skin of an animal, smother her, and throw her into the rubbish heap. Another mother, as she makes her way through a snow-field, will say, "My child's father is dead; who will now take care of it? I am hardly able to support myself." Thereupon she makes a hole in the snow, buries her child there, and passes on. There was a case of an Indian father who, in a time of sickness, lost his wife, and two or three of his children. There remained to him one child still in arms. For two or three days he carried the little fellow, then he left him hanging on the branch of a tree, and went his way. I have said more than enough to grieve you. Now you will quite understand that all these wretched people would rather have given their children to us than have killed them, or let them die.[714]

Father Duchaussois tells of two of the orphans taken in to the Grey Nuns' school, Gabriel and Rosalie:

> Gabriel … belonged to a pagan group of the Sekanais tribe, living near the Rocky Mountains, in the neighbourhood of Fort Nelson, in the northeast corner of British Columbia. He was about eight years of age when he saw his mother kill his father, and throw his little brother into the fire. He himself was saved from the same fate by his grandmother, who took him to a Sekanais named Barby, who had no children of his own. A few days later Barby's wife sickened and died. Barby after some incantations, thought the Spirit told him that the adopted child was the cause of his wife's death. Accordingly he left the boy alone, on the bank of the Nelson river, near his wife's grave, and he removed his tent to the opposite bank. He left the little boy without food or fire, and almost naked, and watching him across the river, he took deliberate

> aim at him with his gun, whenever he saw the boy wandering around the grave, or coming to the water to drink, or pulling up roots to satisfy his hunger. At the end of ten days, a Trader of the Hudson Bay Company at Fort Nelson, Boniface Laferty, who had been one of the first pupils of the Nuns at Fort Providence, was passing northwards to Fort Liard. He heard of the case from the little boy's grandmother. He told the two Indians whom he had with him to take the boy and hide him in a certain place, whilst he himself distracted the attention of the fierce Sekanais. The child, when found, was little more than a skeleton, on which vermin and mosquitoes had been trying to feast. He was left at Fort Liard, "for the Nuns," by Mr. Laferty, and he was taken to Providence, 300 miles away, by Father Le Guen, O.M.I.
>
> In the Orphanage there, Gabriel remained for two years, learning how to pray to the Great Spirit and His Divine Son. But Gabriel had brought lung disease from the Nelson river, and in spite of tender care, by day and by night, he died very young.
>
> The story of Rosalie is different..... Rosalie, when left an orphan at four years of age, went to live with her uncle. The Dog-Ribs are all Christians, so she was not killed....
>
> For a year Rosalie followed the camp, eating whatever she could find left over by others, and having for her only bed-clothes such odds and ends of peltry as were of no use to others. One night she felt she was getting frost-bitten, and she tried in vain to rekindle the dying embers in the hut. Next day, as she could not walk, she was taken away on a sledge, "for the Nuns." At Fort Rae, on the North Arm of Great Slave Lake, the Company's officer, with his pocket knife, cut off both her feet, and so saved her life to be baptized and educated.[715]

"It was not long," Robert Carney writes more blandly of pre-Confederation residential schools, "before these institutions and their counterparts at Red River were called upon to cope with increasing numbers of children who were bereft of one or both parents, or who needed medical treatment or special attention of one kind or another."[716]

The residential schools were apparently needed to protect many of the kids sent there; it may be tragic for many Indian children that they no longer exist. There is still, as we are all aware, an epidemic of alcohol and "substance" abuse in aboriginal communities. Less than half (49.6 percent) of aboriginal children are living with both parents.[717]

Cafeteria food was bad

Okay, so maybe the residential school was better than home in some ways. But, the Commission argues, the food was lousy. One Indian Affairs agent reports of one school, in 1897, "[t]he bill of fare is decidedly monotonous and makes no allowance for peculiarities of taste or constitution."[718] "A 1966 dietician's report on Yukon Hall in Whitehorse observed that although the Canada Food Guide requirements were being met, 'because of the appetite of this age group, the staff are finding 66¢ per day per student is limiting.' In 1969, an official at Coudert Hall in Whitehorse wrote, 'The $0.80 alloted [*sic*] per student for food is not sufficient. In the north we find prices sky high.' To cope with the problem, the residence sometimes had to buy 'less meat and served maccaroni [*sic*] products.' A November 1970 inspection of the Dauphin, Manitoba, school noted that the 'menu appears to be short of the recommended two servings of fruit per day.'"[719]

That's tough. Only one serving of fruit a day. In the northern winter. Still, rather weak tea in the historic annals of genocide. Anyone who has lived on a cafeteria meal plan probably has similar complaints. My plan in grad school regularly served boiled barley as the vegetable. That at an expensive private university in the US Northeast.

"Survivor" Gerald McLeod recalls with horror that at the Carcross school in the Yukon, "you would never see eggs, you know, for a couple of months. It was always mush. A lot of people didn't like eating liver. They had liver there that people couldn't eat, and they forced us to eat it."[720] I know just how he feels. I had a mother like that; and I hated liver too. Actually, weren't all mothers once like that?

If anything, the documentation the Truth and Reconciliation Commission has produced shows that the government took some interest in and trouble with the quality of food students were getting. If it was a bit sparse in current terms, it should be measured against what the students were likely to eat in those days if they stayed home. According to the native activists themselves, on reserve they were starving.

Ivan George remembers his father explaining why he had to go to residential school: "I can't provide for you, or nothing to feed you, clothes on your back, education."[721]

Nor do all former students complain about the food. "You know," says one, "I've heard a lot of people say that, you know, their experience in residential school, their meals were terrible. It wasn't so in Gordon's. Gordon's provided really good meals, a lot of times they were hot, good meals."[722] Dora Churchill, who went to St. Anthony's Residential School, Saskatchewan, in the 1950s, recalls, "There was a lot of food, we were practically forced to eat. Every day there was delicious fresh bread, porridge, peanut butter and lots of stew. I was a picky eater back then, and the food was always very good."[723]

Was Dora Churchill's experience the common one, or was it the tragic lack of a second serving of fruit? Without a decent survey, we can only guess.

Sexes were segregated

But bad food was not the worst of it. As part of their more general attempt to destroy Indian culture and the Indian family, we are told, the schools deliberately separated family members within the institution: brothers and sisters were not allowed to spend time together. One former student laments, "So even though I was there with my sister and I only seen her about four times in that year and we're in the same building in the same mission. They had a fence in the playground. Nobody was allowed near the fence. The boys played on this side, the girls played on the other side. Nobody was allowed to go to that fence there and talk to the girls through the fence or whatever, you can't."[724]

I'm sure it was all terribly traumatic. Just as must have been the practice among some West Coast tribes that a boy was never again to speak to his sister after age eight. Or among the Yellowknives, of whom Samuel Hearne writes, "From the early age of eight or nine years, they are prohibited by custom from joining in the most innocent amusements with children of the opposite sex."[725]

But the situation must also sound familiar to many who, like me, attended Catholic school. They often used to be segregated by sex. How many of us were deeply traumatized by this? Besides preventing early sexual experimentation, current studies suggest that separating the sexes for schooling improves academic results for both boys and girls. They are interested in different things. And probably, beyond a certain age, too interested in each other.

All drill and memory work

Never mind; the Truth and Reconciliation Commission goes on to argue that the schools provided, on the whole, a substandard education. The summary report laments:

> Much of what went on in the classroom was simply repetitious drill. A 1915 report on the Roman Catholic school on the Blood Reserve in Alberta noted, "The children's work was merely memory work and did not appear to be developing any deductive power, altogether too parrot like and lacking expression." A 1932 inspector's report from the Grayson, Saskatchewan, school suggests there had been

> little change. "The teaching as I saw it today was merely a question of memorizing and repeating a mass of, to the children, 'meaningless' facts."[726]

Anyone familiar with the history of education, however, will recognize these as the standard complaints by educational reformers of the day against schools generally. There is no reason to suppose that Indian residential schools stood out in this regard. And more recent educational reformers have called these assumptions into question. There is now a "back to basics" and "core knowledge" movement that argues we have gone astray by abandoning this approach. Standardized tests in basic skills are now all the rage.

If it was an inferior education, this is not evidence of it.

"Because the pay was so low," the Commission further laments, "many of the teachers lacked any qualification to teach.… In 1955, 55 (23%) of the 241 teachers in residential schools directly employed by Indian Affairs had no teacher's certificate. In 1969, Indian Affairs reported it was still paying its teachers less than they could make in provincial schools. 'As a result, there are about the same number of unqualified teachers, some 140, in federal schools [residential and non-residential] now, as ten years ago'"[727]

Sounds awful. But it would be interesting to compare those figures, on teacher qualifications, with those for Canadian public schools generally. The expectation that a teacher hold a degree became widespread in Canada only after the Second World War. Only 10 percent did in 1950.

Nobody, in any case, has ever clearly demonstrated that any formal "teaching qualification" produces better teachers. In fact, many private school principals will say their ability to ignore formal education credentials—public schools are required to prefer them—is a reason why they consistently get better results. They can concentrate instead on subject knowledge and teaching ability. Nor does pay seem to matter. Private schools in Canada also usually pay their teachers less, yet their students score better on standardized tests. The Finnish public system, a world-beater by many measures, pays its teachers less than most developed countries. A good teacher, it appears, does not do it for the money.

They might, on the other hand, do it out of religious commitment.

You had to go

The next charge raised against the residential schools is that they were compulsory. Doesn't that make them like jail, or, better, a concentration camp? "Where residential schools were the only option, children were often forcibly removed from their families, or their families were threatened with fines or prison if they failed to send their children."[728] Mounties might knock at the door to drag them off.

But wait. This, right or wrong, is the same law that applies to all Canadian children. Sending your child to school, and attending school, is compulsory; although some leeway has been granted recently for home schooling.

In fact, far from acting authoritarian, the government seems to have been relaxed about enforcing Indian school attendance. As of 1910, the government estimated that 45 percent of Indian children were not enrolled in any school anywhere.[729] As of 1920, Indian schools of all kinds had capacity for only half the eligible students.[730]

You can't hide genocide

Now we get to something more serious: an alleged high death rate among students. Something must have been wrong, very wrong, if kids were dying in droves. If they were not deliberately slaughtered, the living conditions must have been appalling. Thomas King, in his bestseller *The Inconvenient Indian*, calls the schools "death traps." He says that up to half of the 150,000 Indian children who attended died: "Up to 50 per cent of them lost their lives to disease, malnutrition, neglect and abuse—50 per cent. One in two."[731] That would be 75,000 little corpses.

King does not say where he gets his figure. But since his book won several literary prizes, and sold well, these numbers have probably entered the popular consciousness.

Kevin Annett, who has published a book based on "eyewitness accounts," many of them anonymous, alleges 50,000 deaths "literally and officially."[732] He too gives no reference for this count.

However, the number the Truth and Reconciliation Commission is able to verify is about 3,000. This might be an undercount; records, they say, are sketchy. Perhaps the real number is 4,000; perhaps even 6,000.

Perhaps. But that is a rate of 2 percent to 4 percent, not 50 percent.

If 2 percent still sounds high, this was in a day when childhood diseases were rampant and deadly: tuberculosis, polio, measles, scarlet fever, and so on. The Spanish flu epidemic of 1918-19, part of the period under study, alone produced a global death rate of 3-6 percent.

Canada as a whole did better than did the schools. In earlier years, the death rate at the residential schools was still 4.9 times higher than in the general Canadian population.[733] But here the best test would be, was it higher than among Indian children staying on the reserves? Clifton and Rubenstein note that the Commission makes no attempt to compare.[734] But the Commission's own observations suggest they know that the death rates were comparable.

The most common killer in both places seems to have been tuberculosis, a menace second only to smallpox among aboriginals generally. In the *Jesuit Relations*, Father LeJeune observes that it is widespread among the Indians of New France in the 17th century: "They are nearly all attacked by this disease, when young."[735]

"The tuberculosis health crisis in the schools," the Commission itself observes, "was part of a broader Aboriginal health crisis that was set in motion by colonial policies that separated Aboriginal people from their land, thereby disrupting their economies and their food supplies."[736] Whether this was indeed the cause—it seems unlikely to have already been true in the early days of New France—this passage admits that tuberculosis was a problem on the reserves as well as in the schools. "For Aboriginal children," they note elsewhere, "the relocation to residential schools was generally no healthier than their homes had been on the reserves."[737] No healthier. At worst, they say, the children were no worse off for being at school.

And really probably better off. In 1909, at government request, two physicians examined 243 Indian children awaiting admission to residential schools in Calgary. They reported that "in no instance was a child awaiting admission to school found free from tuberculosis; hence it was plain that infection was got in the home primarily."[738] A study of 175 school-age Indian children in Saskatchewan in 1922 reported that 93 percent showed evidence of tuberculous infection.[739] If the death rate in the schools was 4.9 times the national average, Dr. Peter Bryce cites figures showing that as of 1922, the rate of tuberculosis fatalities among status Indians on reserve was eight times the national average.[740]

To be fair, the rate of TB on reserve may have been less than the 93-100 percent reported in the Calgary and Saskatchewan tests of prospective students. For it was in the interest of parents, if able, to send their sickest children to residential school. While there was no cure for consumption, care at the schools was better than could be had on a distant reserve. Accordingly, best to bundle Junior off to school as fast as possible.

Doctors and dentists made regular visits to residential schools to treat sick children, something that might not have happened if they had been living in their home communities, or if they had been out on the land hunting and fishing with their parents.[741]

If, then, death rates at schools were high, it might be for the same reason that death rates are high in hospitals. The fact that they were 2 percent to 4 percent, and not close to 100 percent, is a credit to the level of care available.

Nevertheless, the government took action to prevent children from entering the schools sick. No doubt they were not keen on having the Indian Department take the responsibility; and they also had some responsibility to healthy students, who might then contract the disease by coming. They had to choose the priority for the schools: health care, or education.

Instead of closing schools or turning them into sanatoria, the government's major response to the health crisis was the negotiation in 1910 of a contract between Indian Affairs and the churches. This contract increased the grants to the schools and imposed a set of standards for diet and ventilation. The contract also required that students not be admitted "until, where practicable, a physician has reported that the child is in good health."[742]

But tuberculosis can remain for years in a dormant state—and x-rays in the early days were rare or did not exist. Many students probably came to school with undetected cases of the illness, which then spread.

Once effective treatment for tuberculosis was found, death rates at the schools declined to close to the national average.[743]

Meantime, residential schools may have helped keep the rate of infection down on the reserve as well. "A great improvement is observed" in sanitation in the home, notes the Department of Indian Affairs Annual Report for 1917, reviewing the problem of tuberculosis on reserve, "in the case of those Indians who have been trained at the boarding school, and it is hoped that in time their influence will bring about a radical change."[744]

Residential schools were an assault on aboriginal culture

So much for the gas chambers of the mind. But the main charge remains. It is, after all, for all it's worth, "cultural genocide." The residential schools, the Truth and Reconciliation Commission and almost everybody else maintains, were there to destroy Indian culture.

Notably, according to the reports, schools did this by preventing the students from speaking their own Indian languages.

Interestingly, however, although you will see this charge often, the Truth and

Reconciliation Commission, after its seven-year investigation, seems hesitant to make it—at least, it does not maintain that this was a systematic practice. Here is the statement they have produced:

> The government's hostile approach to Aboriginal languages was reiterated in numerous policy directives. In 1883, Indian Commissioner Edgar Dewdney instructed Battleford school principal Thomas Clarke that great attention was to be given "towards imparting a knowledge of the art of reading, writing and speaking the English language rather than that of Cree." In 1889, Deputy Minister of Indian Affairs Lawrence Vankoughnet informed Bishop Paul Durieu that in the new Cranbrook, British Columbia, school, mealtime conversations were to be "conducted exclusively in the English language." The principal was also to set a fixed time during which Aboriginal languages could be spoken. In 1890, Indian Commissioner Hayter Reed proposed, "At the most the native language is only to be used as a vehicle of teaching and should be discontinued as such as soon as practicable." English was to be the primary language of instruction, "even where French is taught." The Indian Affairs "Programme of Studies for Indian Schools" of 1893 advised, "Every effort must be made to induce pupils to speak English, and to teach them to understand it; unless they do the whole work of the teacher is likely to be wasted."[745]

None of these, presumably examples of the policy at its "worst," actually involves a ban on speaking Indian languages. Indian languages are to be used, if sparingly, in instruction, or time is to be set aside for them. The issue seems not to be speaking Indian languages, but making sure that pupils also speak English. Is that so bad? Does learning a new language make you lose your first one? If, in aid of this objective, in some situations use of the first language was forbidden, this is standard practice in language learning today, commonly found in any language centre. Immersion is simply thought to be the fastest way to acquire a new language.

According to former faculty, Indian languages were most often discouraged in residential schools that included children from different tribes, and so of different tongues. English was the lingua franca; using one's native language tended to be divisive, to lead to gangs and cabals, especially hurtful to vulnerable minorities. And as a practical matter, one would not be generally understood.

> Others had day populations and boarders from farther afield. Some served very scattered populations and were entirely residential; prohibitions against speaking Indian were more

> common at these, especially where the students came from different tribes historically at war with each other."[746]

Albert Fiddler, a "survivor," recalls the regime at his Beauval, Saskatchewan, school: "they only teach us how to pray in Cree in catechisms in the classroom, but not to talk to each other because it's un-polite for somebody that doesn't understand Cree."[747]

In other schools, faculty encouraged the use of native languages, sometimes against the opposition of parents.

"The French Oblates and Jesuits, among others, made it a practice to teach in the native tongues even in the face of pressure from the federal government, and, as the years passed, increasingly from native parents themselves, to teach the children in French or English."[748] Robert Carney reports that "[t]here is no evidence that native language use was prohibited in the classrooms or elsewhere in the Catholic residential schools of the time." For the first few grades, the native language was the sole language of instruction.[749] This is the continuation of a longtime Jesuit policy, remarked upon elsewhere. They were usually supportive of Indian culture. Their interests were religious; why carry water for one culture over another? Easier for one Jesuit to learn Dene than for 500 Dene to learn English.

In the Anglican school at Onion Lake (Saskatchewan), the children were taught to "read and write both Cree and English."[750] At the Churchill school, according to former student Alex Alikashuak, "there were no restrictions on the use of Aboriginal languages." "The only time, real time we spoke English was when we were in the classroom, or we're talking to one of the administration staff, or somebody from town that's not Inuit, but otherwise we, everybody spoke our language."[751]

"One of us worked as the Senior Boys' Supervisor in Stringer Hall, the Anglican residence in Inuvik, N.W.T., for the 1966-1967 school year," write Rodney Clifton and Hymie Rubenstein in the *National Post*, "and also lived in Old Sun, the Anglican Residential School on the Blackfoot Reserve (Siksika First Nation) in Southern Alberta, in the summer of 1966."

> In each of the two sex-segregated junior dormitories at Stringer Hall, there were four female supervisors, two young Inuk women and two older non-aboriginal women. Many of the young Inuit students did not speak English and the Inuk supervisors spoke to them in Inuktitut. None were punished for doing so.
>
> Virtually all of the Dene students spoke English as their second language, which was the only way they could

> communicate with English-speaking Inuit. Most of the supervisors, and especially the residential administrator and the matron, used Inuktitut words and facial expressions when communicating with the children, including the Dene and white children.[752]

Even where Indian languages were discouraged, this does not seem to have been strictly enforced or harshly punished; just what one might expect if it was done for purposes of efficient language learning. Donald Cardinal notes that, although speaking his native Cree was officially prohibited at his residential school, "he cannot remember ever being punished for it."[753] Rufus Goodstriker, who attended St. Paul's residential school in the 1940s, remembers, "We were supposed to speak English, but I spoke Blackfoot all the time anyway."[754]

"After a 1935 tour of Canada," the Truth and Reconciliation commissioners report, "Oblate Superior General Théodore Labouré expressed concern over the strict enforcement of prohibitions against speaking Aboriginal languages. In his opinion, 'The forbidding of children to speak Indian, even during recreation, was so strict in some of our schools that any lapse would be severely punished—to the point that children were led to consider it a serious offense.'"[755]

This is meant to condemn the schools. Yet the main point made is that speaking native languages was not a serious offense. Any administrators or teachers who acted otherwise were in violation of policy. And church authorities were taking action against it.

Cultural practices condemned

The Truth and Reconciliation Commission also takes some school administrators to task for objecting to the potlatch and the sun dance. It is no longer fashionable to be against the potlatch or the sun dance. But as we have seen, there were honourable reasons to be against both, on the basis not of some religious or cultural prejudice, but of human rights.

"Evelyn Kelman recalled that the principal at the Brocket, Alberta, school warned students that if they attended a Sun Dance that was to be held during the summer, they would be strapped on their return to school," writes the Commission. "In 1943, F.E. Anfield, the principal of the Alert Bay, British Columbia, school, wrote a letter encouraging former students not to participate in local Potlatches, implying that such ceremonies were based on outdated superstition, and led to impoverishment and family neglect."[756]

If this was a matter of cultural intolerance, and of wishing to suppress native culture, rather than concern for human rights, the schools and their administrators were not the parties at fault. Both the potlatch and the sun dance were illegal. Whatever you might think of the actual ceremonies, it is the duty of an educator in a government-funded school to teach his charges to obey the law.

"The missionaries who ran the schools," the summary report elsewhere states, "played prominent roles in the church-led campaigns ... to end traditional Aboriginal marriage practices."[757] To be clear, that would be marriage practices like polygamy, forced marriage, child marriage, casual divorce, and temporary marriage. The Jesuits were definitely not keen on this. It is hardly surprising to find Catholic religious schools, after all, teaching Catholic morality. Why else would you have a Catholic school?

On the whole, were the schools hostile to native culture? The answer is not clear, unless it is a clear no.

> Some schools even stimulated resistance to assimilative efforts and helped preserve and advance native culture. As one reviewer noted in her review of St. Mary's School in Mission and the Qu'Appelle Industrial School at Lebret, Saskatchewan, natives in these schools retained their own cultural institutions in the form of dancing groups and traditional gatherings. When St. Mary's closed in 1984, native dances by native staff were part of the chapel liturgy.[758]
>
> The Canadian Welfare Council's 1967 report on nine Saskatchewan residential schools described "an emphasis on relating course content to the Indian culture." ... By 1968 [*sic*; this was not new], the Roman Catholic school in Cardston was incorporating Blackfoot into its educational program. In some schools, Aboriginal teachers were brought in to teach dancing and singing.[759]

Rena Martinson, co-head of St. Phillips Anglican School in Fort George, Quebec, learned Cree, went with the students on seal hunts, and adopted four native children.[760] Oblate Father Antonio Duhaime, principal of Duck Lake Residential School from 1962 to 1968, and of St. Mary's School from 1968 to 1980, learned Blackfoot and was inducted as an honourary chief. He recalls the struggles he had with parents who wanted their children to learn English.

> The parents brought us their kids in September, and said "Father, I want my children to learn English" and now they're accusing us of forbidding them to speak their native languages. If some of the natives are successful today, they can thank the residential schools. No one else was interested in the Indian people back then.[761]

"Some school administrators and supervisors were aboriginals," reports one former student who went on to become staff.

> At Stringer Hall, for example, two of the six residential supervisors were Inuit women. Did aboriginal supervisors abuse the children under their care? Do both the children and the supervisors deserve compensation? Some children in residential schools were not aboriginals. I myself attended a United Church residential school in the early 1960's, and when I was a supervisor at Stringer Hall, about 12% of the 280 students were non-aboriginal. Children of school administrators, white trappers, missionaries and merchants attended these schools. If aboriginal people are going to receive compensation, do the non-aboriginal students also deserve compensation?[762]

After all, with all the emphasis in some schools on aboriginal culture, weren't the European students victims of "cultural genocide"?

Religious schools were religious schools

There is more than an undertone of hostility in the Truth and Reconciliation report toward these religious schools for actually teaching religion. It offends our contemporary secularism, it seems; but to make this charge against religious schools is absurd.

"The churches," the Commission complains, "placed a greater priority on religious commitment than on teaching ability."[763] "In the minds of some principals, religious training was the most valuable training the schools provided. In 1903, Brandon, Manitoba, principal T. Ferrier wrote that 'while it is very important that the Indian child should be educated, it is of more importance that he should build up a good clean character.'"[764]

Welcome to the traditional philosophy of education everywhere. This demand for moral character was a standard approach to choosing teachers at the time and at most times; especially, of course, in religious institutions. It is also highly defensible. What is education? What do you want the children to learn? Surely, for anyone with the slightest moral feeling, you are educating souls, just as Principal Ferrier understands. Even if a secular school, you are educating for good citizenship. You want before all else to impart good morals.

This was unambiguously the intent of all the posh private ("public") schools of old England. In *Tom Brown's Schooldays*, meditating on why he sends his son Tom off to Rugby, the old squire observes, "I don't care a straw for Greek particles, or the digamma; no more does his mother. What is he sent to school for? ... If he'll only turn out a brave, helpful, truth-telling Englishman, and a gentleman, and a Christian, that's all I want."[765]

Accordingly, moral awareness and good character is the most important quality in a teacher, the more so since he or she becomes a model to the students. Conversely, what could be more harmful than a teacher who is visibly immoral?

"The residential school system," the Truth and Reconciliation Commission complains, "was based on an assumption that European civilization and Christian religions were superior to Aboriginal culture."[766] "There was no moral imperative," the Commission lectures, "to impose Christianity on the Indigenous peoples of the world."[767] But of course there is such a moral imperative. If Christianity is truth, or indeed if science is truth, it is not an act of generosity to leave one's fellow man in darkness and ignorance. Especially when teaching them costs you, not them, money. Nor is it necessary to accept that Christianity is truth to understand that those who ran the residential schools were doing so in good faith: one only has to accept that they were not hypocrites, that they themselves believed that Christianity (or science, or human rights) was true.

Moreover, as we have seen, nobody imposed either Christianity or education on the Indians. It was they who demanded both.

This charge seems especially unfair when one considers the privations and personal sacrifices the early teachers and missionaries sometimes underwent in order to bring schooling to the Indians and Inuit. "There are no more arduous mission fields in the world," writes William Withrow in 1895, "than those among the native tribes of the great North-West."

> The devoted servant of the Cross goes forth to a region beyond the pale of civilization. He often suffers privation of the very necessaries of life. He is exposed to the rigour of an almost Arctic winter. He is cut off from human sympathy or congenial companionship. Communication with the great world is often maintained by infrequent and irregular mails, conveyed by long and tortuous canoe routes in summer or on dog-sleds in winter. The unvarnished tales of some of these missionaries lack no feature of heroic daring and apostolic zeal. But recently one, with his newly-wedded wife, a lady of much culture and refinement, travelled hundreds of miles by lake and river, often making toilsome portages, once in danger of their lives by the upsetting of their birch-bark canoe in an arrowy rapid. In midwinter the same intrepid missionary made a journey of several hundred miles in a dog-sled, sleeping in the snow with the thermometer forty, and

> even fifty, degrees below zero, in order to open a new mission among a pagan tribe.[768]

"With the conveniences which civilization has placed at the disposal of the modern wayfarer," writes Adrien Morice in 1910, "it is impossible to form a correct idea of the perils and fatigues such a voyage [to a Northwest mission] involved."

> Barring the dangers due to the wild hordes of Indians, constantly clashing with one another and ever ready for robbery and pillage, the missionary had many a time to ford swollen rivers with the water up to his neck, or swim across streams while clinging to the mane of his horse. And then who will adequately picture to himself the weariness of a six-month ride under the deadly rays of the sun, tempered by no other shelter or shadow than that afforded by one's horse, with improper food, numberless accidents and unmentionable hardships?[769]

If it was difficult for some Indian children to be separated from their families for most of the year, how difficult was this for their first European teachers?

Once at the mission, things were little better, according to Morice.

> The extent of the poverty common to all the northern posts was truly amazing. Even flour was then, and remained for many years afterwards, a veritable luxury in the north, many missionaries passing several years without tasting bread. If we consider that most of these hailed from France, where the daily diet is based on bread incomparably more than it is in America, we will better realize the intensity of their privations.
>
> As a rule, two sacks of flour were sent yearly to each mission, one of which was for the priests themselves, and the other for their engagé and his family. Nor should we forget that the missionaries were generally two, sometimes three, in a place. A few bags of pemmican, tough, stale and rancid from age, were added to this, and the fathers, in spite of their bodily exertions while building up their homes or appurtenances and toiling during their travels over several feet of snow, had to rely on the denizens of the lakes for their staple food.
>
> This was fish, annually caught in large quantities for themselves and their sleigh dogs. After having been cut open, and spread out by means of wooden spits, this was left to dry hanging from poles laid on scaffoldings. As a result of this treatment, it lost all the flavour it might have originally

> possessed, when, in course of time, the stench it emitted and the "animation" of which it became the theatre did not render it absolutely repulsive to anything but a famishing stomach. Famine was indeed a familiar experience with all the missionaries in the north, who usually made light of it, and replaced a missed meal by tightening their belts, as they would good-humouredly put it.
>
> If therefore we add these privations to the fatigues and discomfort of long voyages on foot, or, worse than all, on snowshoes (the inexpressible agony of which one must experience to properly appreciate it), we will understand why a publicist felt warranted in writing that "it is well known among all the religious Orders that the missions of Athabasca-Mackenzie are the most difficult and painful in the whole world, without excepting those of China, Corea and Japan."[770]

"In the 1960s, when I lived and worked in residential schools," recalls one former staffer, "it was the evangelistic calling for committed Christians similar to rebuilding houses following disasters in South America. Most residential school employees worked for very little pay, less recognition, and many sleepless nights."[771]

Another complaint from the Truth and Reconciliation Commission was that the residential schools cost so little.

This is proof that the Indian students were being shortchanged.

But this may not be the whole story. It may be instead that the government simply got a bargain by involving religious organizations. Inexpensive staff, to begin with. John West, proposing Indian schools in 1827, writes that instructors "would need a religious motive to cause them to persevere in their truly arduous task."[772] G. Kent Gooderham laments, of secular schools, "in most of our remote native communities, teacher recruitment and turn-over problems are endemic."[773] Good people are prepared to do much out of compassion and idealism that they would not do for money.

In addition, good-hearted religious people elsewhere were pouring money into the schools as an act of charity. "Most of the Protestant Indian boarding schools," writes Robert Carney of the pre-Confederation situation, "had access to four sources of support: government grants, band funds, contributions from the sponsoring churches and donations from philanthropic organizations, such as the New England Company."[774] Often, the religious body paid the capital cost of building the schools.[775] The Methodists paid half the salary for their teachers in

Ontario and Quebec.[776] Members of Catholic religious orders often taught for no more than room and board, having taken vows of poverty.[777]

Now, of course, the descendants of those religious people are being asked to pay reparations for their charity.

All cultures are equal

"Although, in most of their official pronouncements, government and church officials took the position that Aboriginal people could be civilized," the Truth and Reconciliation Commission continues, "it is clear that many believed that Aboriginal culture was inherently inferior."[778]

Of course, if you believe that Christianity is true, it follows that any teaching that disagrees with it is, to that extent, false. So some elements of Indian culture, inevitably, would not have been supported by the missionaries. Or, for that matter, some elements of mainstream Canadian culture.

It also seems reasonable if they supposed that getting your food by hunting and gathering was significantly less efficient than settled agriculture, that wheels and metals were useful things, and that total war was best avoided. If to them it seemed wrong to enslave, torture, or eat others. If it seemed improper to beat your wife, or cut off her nose. The schools and their teachers would probably have upheld all of these propositions.

After all, most Indians thought so too. And the Truth and Reconciliation report makes no attempt to disprove them. It instead dismisses any such claims out of hand, apparently on the basis of cultural relativism. All cultures are and must be understood to be equal in detail; perhaps, to finish the thought, because all values are themselves culturally determined.

"Residential schools," the Commission explains,

> ...were justified by arguments that they would assist Aboriginal people in making the leap to civilization. It is still argued by some that while residential schools may have been unpleasant, at least they helped Aboriginal people become civilized. This, it was said, was the price of progress. These views are not acceptable. They are based on a belief that societies can be ranked in value. In this ranking system, Aboriginal societies are described as primitive and savage. European societies judged themselves as having progressed to the top of the scale, and pronounced themselves civilized. This determination of whether a society could be termed "civilized" supposedly was made on the basis of such criteria

> as level of social organization, moral and ethical advancement, and technological achievement. In reality, it was a highly biased judgment, usually made by a powerful society about a less powerful one whose lands and resources it coveted and whose social and cultural differences it either misunderstood or feared.[779]

In so many words, as a flat assertion: the commission writes "there is no hierarchy of societies."[780]

Common sense and common experience say there is.

Technically, for example, to be civilized, you have to have cities. And writing. *Oxford* says civilization means "[t]he comfort and convenience of modern life, regarded as available only in towns and cities." *Merriam-Webster* defines it as "the stage of cultural development at which writing and the keeping of written records is attained." Tom Flanagan consults an archaeology textbook, and finds four essential ingredients: writing, cities, taxation, and monumental architecture.[781] Canadian Indians had none of these.

If all cultures are equal, and equally "civilized," the English word "civilized" no longer has any meaning. Even once you civilize, surely Montreal has more to offer, culturally, than Sudbury.

How many Indians today are content to do without metals, government, television, or the wheel?

Moreover, if there is no way to objectively judge different cultures, we face some troublesome issues. Do we have any right, then, to condemn what Hitler did, or to have hanged the poor Nazi defendants at Nuremberg? Weren't they simply following different cultural assumptions? And what if we build a bridge in India following the principles of Canadian mathematics, our own cultural values? Isn't it likely to fall down, the culture being different?

Only given this mad concept of cultural relativism does the charge make sense that the residential schools suppressed—instead of, say, nurtured and developed—Indian culture.

"Taken as a whole," the Commission complains, "the colonial process relied for its justification on the sheer presumption of taking a specific set of European beliefs and values and proclaiming them to be universal values that could be imposed upon the peoples of the world."[782]

Are there no absolute or universal values? Perhaps we should point out that this is what we are doing when we insist on universal human rights. Or the truth of science. Or mathematics. Or logic. Or morality.

Kill the man to save the Indian

At this point, someone will offer up some version of a quotation asserting that the residential schools were intended to "take the Indian out of the child," or to "kill the Indian to save the man." The quote is usually attributed to Duncan Campbell Scott, poet and longtime bureaucrat in the Department of Indian Affairs. So, for example, claims Kevin Annett ("Kill the Indian within the Indian").[783] Sometimes it is put instead in the mouth of Sir John A. Macdonald. Chief Justice Beverley McLachlin, in a speech to the fourth annual "Pluralism Lecture" of the Global Centre for Pluralism (pluralism, awkwardly, being possible only if you believe in the reality of mathematics), said of the residential schools that "[t]he objective was to 'take the Indian out of the child,' and thus to solve what John A. Macdonald referred to as the 'Indian problem.' 'Indianness' was not to be tolerated; rather it must be eliminated. In the buzzword of the day, assimilation—in the language of the 21st century, cultural genocide."[784]

Scott never said it. Macdonald never said it. The line is from General Richard H. Pratt, American Civil War hero, friend of the Indian, and founder of Carlisle College, Pennsylvania. He apparently thought this would, indeed, be a good idea: to take the Indian out of the child in order to save the man. And perhaps he was right, and perhaps he was wrong. But in the same speech, importantly, he insisted that all-Indian residential schools were not the way to do it.

"Indian schools are just as well calculated to keep the Indians intact as Indians," Pratt objects,

> … as Catholic schools are to keep the Catholics intact. Under our principles we have established the public school system, where people of all races may become unified in every way, and loyal to the government; but we do not gather the people of one nation into schools by themselves, and the people of another nation into schools by themselves, but we invite the youth of all peoples into all schools. We shall not succeed in Americanizing the Indian unless we take him in in exactly the same way.… Purely Indian schools say to the Indians: "You are Indians, and must remain Indians. You are not of the nation, and cannot become of the nation. We do not want you to become of the nation."[785]

Pratt wanted to abolish the "Indian school plants, ... with their fad systems"

> … giving us "whited sepulchres" in which we bury the race within itself. How far better for employees, pupils, and the government and quicker in every way, is the method urged on the department for years, to have Indian school teachers, and employees attend the State and County Conventions of school people in their localities, and go to the various special summer schools each year for added equipment, thus keeping them in touch with the best, and help the forwarding of Indian youth into the public schools.[786]

Yet, against this advice from Pratt, this was the path Macdonald and Scott chose for Canada—to keep the Indian in the man.

Pratt did not, mind, advocate leaving the Indian children on the reserve either. Pratt advised having them board with local families as they attended day schools in town. To be clear, this is an option the Truth and Reconciliation Committee rejects as "just as unhappy an experience" as residential schools.[787] They want Indian children to stay on the reserve.

To Pratt, the problem with the residential schools was exactly the opposite of what is usually alleged. It is not that they tried to assimilate the Indians, but that they prevented this from happening. They were segregated schools, separate and unequal, of the sort that Brown v. Board of Education and the US civil rights movement fought to end for American blacks. By their nature they preserved a sense of difference, including Indian cultural difference, whatever the particular content of that difference might be.

R.V. Sinclair makes the same point in the columns of the Ottawa press back in 1910:

> [It] is very doubtful indeed whether any attempt to educate Indian children apart from the children it is designed to make them resemble can be wise, because it is entirely incompatible with the proper intention to convert Indians into citizens at the earliest moment possible.… For that is to train Indian children as units of a separate population; to inculcate those very ideas of separation which directly conflict with the only sound idea, that of assimilation; to make them feel a difference whilst trying to extirpate difference, and to perpetuate the very things to which it is our reasonable and worthy object to completely put an end.[788]

The residential schools did not in fact teach what Indians needed to integrate into the wider culture; and they deliberately did not. Egerton Ryerson, influential as Ontario Schools Commissioner in their early years, argued that "such institutions should not give instruction in 'white man's trades,' but should concentrate instead on 'common school learnings and the acquisition of agricultural skills and knowledge.'"[789] They were not to join the mainstream as individuals, but go back and raise the Indian tribe as a group.

Father Duchaussois describes the teaching methods of the Grey Nuns in the Northwest as of 1917:

> Method of education—for the children of the woods—there was none. The Sister of Charity invented her own system, and its success is her praise. Well she knew that it would be not merely useless, but mischievous, to try to give a taste for the town life of the Palefaces to those who are destined to go back to the wigwam, to travel on snow shoes, and to use no other implement than the fishing net and the gun.[790]

Well intentioned. But perhaps the wrong choice.

They were not what the Indians wanted

Far from having been imposed on the Indians, it was the Indians who called for residential schools, very much on the model ultimately chosen. The European way of getting food, by tilling the land, was obviously superior, more secure and more productive, than hunting and scavenging. Periodic starvation is not fun. The Europeans knew how to farm; the Indians did not. Obviously, it would be of benefit to the Indians, and an act of generosity on the part of Europeans, to show the Indian children how.

"The second means of commending ourselves to the Savages, to induce them to receive our holy faith," explains Father LeJeune in the earliest years of New France,

> …would be to send a number of capable men to clear and cultivate the land, who, joining themselves with others who know the language, would work for the Savages, on condition that they would settle down, and themselves put their hands to the work, living in houses that would be built for their use; by this means becoming located, and seeing this miracle of charity in their behalf, they could be more easily instructed and won. While conversing this Winter with my Savages, I communicated to them this plan, assuring them that when I knew their language perfectly, I would help them cultivate the land if I could have some men, and if they wished to stop roving,—representing to them the wretchedness of their present way of living, and influencing them very perceptibly, for the time being. The Sorcerer, having heard me, turned toward his people and said, "See

> how boldly this black robe lies in our presence." I asked him why he thought I was lying. "Because," said he, "we never see in this world men so good as you say, who would take the trouble to help us without hope of reward, and to employ so many men to aid us without taking anything from us; if you should do that," he added, "you would secure the greater part of the Savages, and they would all believe in your words."[791]

In 1861, Rev. Peter Jones, Ojibway chief, writes, in question and answer format:

> Query No. 24. — Can you offer any suggestions for the improvement of the condition of the Indians?
>
> Answer No. 24. — I would most respectfully suggest—
> 1st.—The importance of establishing schools of industry as soon as possible, that there may be no further delay in bringing forward the present rising generation.[792]

"I am now trying to get the Wesleyan Missionary Committee in London," he writes from England in 1838,

> ...to establish a central manual labour school. They have given me encouragement to hope that they will take up the subject and put one in operation. I feel very anxious to see an institution of this kind established amongst us, for I am fully persuaded that our children will never be what they ought to be until they are taught to work and learn useful trades, as well as to learn to read and write.[793]

At a general council of the Ontario Ojibway in 1840, one of the items on the agenda, duly approved, was a request for schooling in the trades:

> Thirdly, To consider whether anything can be done to promote their civilization, forming manual labour schools, &c. Colonel Jarvis [Indian Commissioner] expressed his happiness to hear that the attention of the chiefs had been directed to this subject; ... and said that the Home Government was now considering what can be done for the central manual labour schools.[794]

Chief Jones was no outlier. Most of the Indian chiefs across Canada made this a priority in their dealings with government. Chief Joseph Brant of the Iroquois had been a student at Moore's Indian Charity School in Connecticut. "Though I was an unprofitable pupil in some respects," he writes, "yet my worldly affairs have been much benefited in the instruction there received...." Determined to acquire the same benefits for his people, he sent his son to London in 1822 to ask for residential schools in Canada.[795]

The Mohawk Institute, which he inspired, began taking residential students in 1834. Council minutes from 1844 show the band donating 200 acres for an additional facility to teach farming skills.[796]

Newly appointed as missionary to the Hudson's Bay Company in the 1820s, Rev. John West had no trouble collecting pupils for a proposed day school with billeting for students on a trip from York Factory to his posting at Red River. "[A]s the canoe was paddled from the shore, I considered that I bore a pledge from the Indian that many more children might be found, if an establishment were formed in British Christian sympathy, and British liberality for their education and support."[797]

At Treaty 3 negotiations, "Chief Ka-Katche-way of the Lac Seul band came forward to state his willingness to treat, but not without making additional demands for a schoolmaster, seed, agricultural implements, and cattle."[798] The same demand for schools was made by the Indians for each of the later numbered treaties.

William Duncan reports of putting up his school at Fort Simpson, British Columbia:

> Yesterday I spoke to a few on the subject, and all seemed heartily glad. One old chief said to me, "Cease being angry now," thinking, I suppose, my delay [in starting the school] was occasioned by anger. He assured me he would send his men to help. It was quite encouraging to see how earnestly they expressed their desire for me to proceed with the work, and I may safely say the feeling was universal.... About half-past six one of the Indians on the raft sprang to his feet, gave the word of starting, which is a peculiar kind of whoop, and he, with the few so inadequate to the work, determined to begin. At this I proceeded up the beach to the place for building upon, but what was my surprise when, on returning, I met upwards of forty Indians carrying wood. They all seemed to have moved in an instant, and sprung to the work with one heart. The enthusiasm they manifested was truly gladdening, and almost alarming. Amongst the number were several old men, who were doing more with their spirited looks and words than with their muscles. The whole camp seemed now excited. Encouraging words and pleasant looks greeted me on every side. Every one seemed in earnest, and the heavy blocks and beams began to move up the hill with amazing rapidity. When the Fort bell rang for breakfast they

> proposed to keep on. One old man said he would not eat till the work was done.... By three o'clock p.m. all was over, for which I was very glad, for the constant whooping, groaning, and bawling of the Indians, together with the difficulties of the work, from the great weight of the pieces and the bad road, kept me in constant fear.[799]

In 1896, the Methodist Church laments, of their Indian residential schools, "it is impossible to receive all the Indian youth who desire admission."[800]

From the beginning the Indians, unlike the Truth and Reconciliation Commission, also wanted these schools to be religious in nature. "An Indian chief, residing in the neighbourhood of Lake Simcoe," reports Rev. Peter Jones,

> ...came to solicit missionary aid. After unfolding their needy state, he observed that they did not wish the labours of the missionary for nothing. They would hunt deer, beaver, &c., and each one would lay aside some skins, and appropriate the avails of them to the support of the mission. As a demonstration of this generous disposition, and of their ardent desire to have their children instructed, the women stripped themselves of their nose and ear jewels, brooches, and breastplates, which had been given them by Government, and sent them to the missionary to purchase books for the school; and these were exhibited on the occasion, as an evidence of their devotion to this sacred cause.[801]

Jones elsewhere writes:

> Query No. 10. — What, in your opinion, is the best mode of promoting the moral, intellectual, and social improvement of the Indians?
>
> Answer No. 10. — The establishment of well-regulated schools of industry, and the congregating of the several scattered tribes into three or four settlements, which would be a great saving of expense to the Government and to missionary societies, at the same time it would afford greater facilities for their instruction in everything calculated to advance their general improvement.[802]

John West, visiting the Six Nations in 1827, writes,

> The chiefs of these heathen nations [meaning the bands near the Mohawks who had not yet Christianized] lately met in council, to deliberate on the subject of education, and particularly requested Mr. Brandt to use his influence with

> those who had encouraged and defrayed the expenses of educating the Mohawk children, to make known the wish of the different tribes, located with the Mohawks, and the Oneidas, to have their children educated in like manner.[803]

The Ojibwe (Ojibway) Grand Council of 1840 passed the following resolution, addressed to Colonel Jarvis as Chief Superintendent of Indian Affairs. Note that the desired education is specified as religious in character:

> Father,—It is our earnest desire that one or more manual labour schools should be established at some of our settlements for the religious education of our children, and at the same time to train them up in industrious and domestic habits. And we beg to state that if our Great Father would render assistance in the formation of such schools, we are willing ourselves to appropriate part of our land payments for these objects.[804]

During his negotiations of Treaties 3 through 6, Lieutenant-Governor Alexander Morris similarly reported a "universal demand" for teachers *and for missionaries.*[805]

Brant was appealing to London in the 1820s for such schools, Rev. Jones from the 1830s into the 1860s; the tribes of the Plains were asking for them in the 1820s, and negotiating for them in the 1880s and later. As late as the 1930s, Gerry Kelly, coordinator for the National Catholic Working Group on Native Residential Schools, reported the same demand: "In several cases, Indian bands asked the government to establish schools. In the 1930s, the Sechelt band near Vancouver lobbied the Oblates for such a school; some aboriginal communities wanted the schools so badly that they built them themselves."[806]

To be clear: the Indians wanted the schools. They wanted the schools to teach trades. They wanted the schools to be religious in character. And they wanted the schools to be residential.

"Gentlemen," again writes the Rev. Jones,

> … From the knowledge I have of the Indian character, and from personal observation, I have come to the conclusion that the system of education hitherto adopted in our common schools has been too inefficient. The children attend these schools from the houses of their parents, a number of whom are good pious Christians, but who, nevertheless, retain many of their old habits; consequently, the good instructions they receive at school are in a great measure neutralized at home. It is a notorious fact that the parents in general exercise little or no control over their

> children. Being thus left to follow their own wills, they too frequently wander about in the woods with their bows and arrows, or accompany their parents in their hunting excursions. Another evil arises from their not being trained to habits of industry, so that by the time they leave the schools they are greatly averse to work, and naturally adopt the same mode of life as their parents.
>
> Under these considerations, I am very anxious to see manual labour schools established among our people, that the children may be properly trained and educated to habits of industry. I see nothing to hinder the entire success of such a plan, and as [a] school in the Missouri country is answering the most sanguine expectations of its promoters, we may safely conclude that the same success would attend the like operations among our Indians. I am happy to inform you that all the Indians with whom I have conversed highly approve of the project. They are ready and willing to give up their children to the entire control and management of the teachers.... [807]

Far from showing a general resistance to sending children to the schools, the main complaint against them at a Centennial conference in 1967 seems to be that they are too popular: "Some parents were sending their children as young as four and five years old even though they were not supposed to send them until they were seven—so you could see what residential schools were doing to the parents at that time."[808] Of the Sitka Presbyterian residential school, across the Alaska border, Livingston Jones writes, "in no year in its history could it begin to receive all applicants for admission."[809]

The government was somewhat less keen on this residential model. It cost them, after all, more money than would day schools. "We can give school privileges to four or five young Indians for what one costs us at a boarding school," laments Samuel Blake in 1908; "or, to make a more sweeping calculation, we are spending to-day at least twice as much as could be profitably spent to give our whole Indian school population the facilities they actually need, even keeping in mind the need of a few boarding schools still, and this in spite of the fact that at the larger part of our day schools we provide a hot noonday lunch for the little people, and help out the parents in clothing them suitably for attendance."[810]

Accordingly, as early as 1949, the official government policy was actually to educate the Indians in provincial public schools wherever possible. Most Indians even then never went to the residential schools, and from that point there was an official plan to phase them out, on economic grounds.

The Catholic Church, too, seems to have preferred day schools.

> The educational programs of the Jesuits, who returned to Canada West in 1843 to assume responsibility for Roman Catholic Indian missions, challenged the prevailing view of Indian schooling. In areas of white settlement, they encouraged the admission of Indian children into the common public or separate day schools, where they would be instructed alongside white children. The Jesuit preference for day schools in their Indian missions became apparent in the 1840s at Wikwemikong, Walpole Island and Fort William, where they opened day schools and conducted them differently from the approach taken in Protestant Indian day and residential schools.[811]

Although there was support for residential schools from Protestant missionaries, and from such notables as Egerton Ryerson, the motive was not just to separate the children from their parental culture, but to ensure their attendance, given their parents' transient lifestyle.[812] This is the sole reason given by the Methodists in their memorandum of 1896: "It seems to be impossible to secure in the day-school on an Indian Reserve anything like a regular attendance."[813]

"Though the day school system is the ideal mechanism for the uplifting of the Indians," writes Anglican missionary John West in 1824, "we cannot yet wholly dispense with boarding schools because so many tribes still continue the nomadic or semi-nomadic habits which would require the continual moving of the day schools from place to place in order to keep near a sufficient number of families for their support."[814]

They were punishment for bad kids

Being able to send your children to a residential school sounds suspiciously like a privilege. Your kids got a free education; they were fed, clothed, and housed at no expense to you; and their existence did not interfere with your attempts to pursue your livelihood or personal interests. Better than free day care! It all looked too like the upper class British tradition of sending your children off to boarding school.

Probably aware of this vexing appearance, the Truth and Reconciliation Commission summary report takes the trouble to point out, without offering evidence, that the residential schools were modelled not after Harrow and Eton, but after English "Industrial Schools" for children convicted of begging or vagrancy. "The model for these residential schools for Aboriginal children, both in Canada and the United States, did not come from the private boarding schools to which members of the economic elites in Britain and Canada sent their children.

Instead, the model came from the reformatories and industrial schools that were being constructed in Europe and North America for the children of the urban poor."[815]

This is not true. Carney, writing well before the commissioners' report, dismisses this claim: "Contrary to what is claimed in some accounts of native schooling, aboriginal boarding schools were not modeled on another nineteenth century educational phenomenon, the industrial or reformatory school.... Misconceptions about the term 'industrial school' may be because of the several meanings given it in the nineteenth century."[816]

As a matter of record, the Canadian residential school system was modelled on the US Indian residential school system. This is clear from a government study in 1879 by Nicholas Flood Davin, *Report on Industrial Schools for Indians and Half-Breeds*. Davin was, by his own report, drawn to the residential model by the advice of American Cherokee leaders. Day schools, they told him, did not work "because the influence of the wigwam was stronger than the influence of the school." "[T]he chief thing to attend to in dealing with the less civilized or wholly barbarous tribes," they said, "was to separate the children from the parents."[817]

The American system, in turn, was founded on the model of the Carlisle Residential School in Pennsylvania. It "became a reference point" for the US Indian Department.[818]

Carlisle's curriculum was certainly different from that at Eton or Andover. But it did have its pretensions. In early days it competed on the gridiron against Harvard, Yale, Columbia, and other Ivy League schools. The school band played at presidential inaugurations and at the Paris World Exposition in 1900.

To be sure, the Canadian government was not prepared to fund the typical Indian school to the level of endowment Carlisle had; but this was the poster child, and the ideal.

Nor was Carlisle trying to "take the Indian out of the man." As we noted, its founder, General Pratt, maintained the opposite. Samuel Blake interviews its art teacher, Miss Angel DeCora, on her philosophy:

> The method of educating the Indian in the past was to attempt to transform him into a brown Caucasian within the space of five years, or a little more. The educators made every effort to convince the Indian that any custom or habit that was not familiar to the white man shewed savagery and degradation. A general attempt was made to bring him "up-to-date." The Indian who is so bound up in tribal laws and customs knew not where to make the distinction, not what

> of his natural instincts to discard, and the consequence was that he either became superficial and arrogant, and denied his race, or he grew dispirited and silent.
>
> … I have taken care to leave my pupils' creative faculty absolutely independent, and to let the pupil draw from his own mind, true to his own thought, and, as much as possible, true to his tribal method of symbolic design.[819]

If some former residential school students remember their experiences with loathing, so do some Etonians or Upper Canada College graduates. Witness the movie *If…*, George Orwell's memoir "Such, Such Were the Joys," or James FitzGerald's book on Upper Canada College, *Old Boys.* At the same time, as with Rugby, Selwyn House, or Brébeuf, many former students remember the residential schools with fondness.

> The nuns taught us so much. I only remember one nun who was very strict and one nun who made us pray too much. In every society you have people with personalities that are on the bad side. But, I can swear on the Bible that my time in the convent was good. We ate three meals a day, not fancy but nourishing, a lot of recreation, every winter they built us a big slide and we would have fun sliding and we went on many picnics in summer time and in the winter we would go for hay rides, sleighs pulled by oxen.[820]
>
> We set rabbit snares and ate rabbit. They had pemmican.... They taught us how to knit stockings for ourselves, to do fancy beading for moccasins and to do quill work, from two quills up to 12 quills. We learned to make our own dresses, they taught how to cook and bake and clean.[821]
>
> As a journalist since 1979, I've heard people credit residential schools with the foundation for learning that allowed them to pursue successful academic careers.… Others tell of being introduced to skills that became lifelong careers, and still others, like my mother, talk of being introduced to a faith that guided the rest of their lives.…[822]

Canadian playwright Tomson Highway, Cree, has good memories.

> "All we hear is the negative stuff, nobody's interested in the positive, the joy in that school. Nine of the happiest years of my life I spent it at that school. I learned your language, for God's sake. Have you learned my language? No, so who's the privileged one and who is underprivileged?"

> "You may have heard stories from 7,000 witnesses in the process that were negative," he adds. "But what you haven't heard are the 7,000 reports that were positive stories. There are many very successful people today that went to those schools and have brilliant careers and are very functional people, very happy people like myself. I have a thriving international career, and it wouldn't have happened without that school."[823]

So does Ethel Blondin-Andrew, the first aboriginal woman to serve in the federal cabinet, who attended Grandin College in Fort Smith. She says the school "saved" her.[824]

Livingston Jones gives excerpts from letters written by Tlingit children attending residential school in Alaska, circa 1914.

Mary Kadashan, Chilkat, writes:

> . . . Young people have good times during their school days, but we young people go to school, not only to have a good time, but to learn what is right, and to do good, and to talk English. We are here in school so that we may have better lives when we go away from here. So we must not idle away our time, but we must work, and use our time well. We must try to learn all we can to tell our companions, who have not been to school, about this good life. I try to keep it. I shall never forget it. This is the most precious time of our life. So we must keep it in our head.

Johnnie Johnson writes:

> ... My father is dead, so I have no home. My sister says "Don't anywhere go you, just in mission stay you." My sister says when five years gone next five year's more I'll stay. I am trying to get to the Third reader. I hard study me my second Reader. I am a little boy, but I just try to know something more so good man me.

Fanny Phillips writes:

> . . . The first opportunity the native girl has is her schooling.... Here we are instructed by our teachers about housekeeping, sewing, cooking and dressmaking; all these things help us to make our living. . . . A young lady may be useful in many ways. She may be used as a school-teacher in the government schools, or as a nurse to help to stamp out the consumption from among our own people. We have several cases of girls who have done this and are making a success. There is no

> nobler work for a girl than that of improving the conditions of a home, for on the home depends the advancement of the people. Surely education and instruction has brought about a marked change in our homes and mode of living.[825]

They might sound stilted, coached, but these are not puff pieces to encourage the donors. These were first printed in the *Boston Alaskan*, a local secular paper in Boston, Alaska.

Father Duchaussois describes a banquet celebrating the golden jubilee of the Sacred Heart School on the shores of Lake Athabasca in 1917:

> Nearly all those Indians were old pupils of the Sisters, and it was very consoling to hear how they spoke of their youthful days in the Convent. Good old grandmother Bouvier was quite proud to tell that it was her children who were the first pupils of the Nuns at Fort Providence. She herself sang and danced for us. Her son, John Baptist, having been taught English and French by the Nuns, held an important position at the Fort, in the service of the Hudson's Bay Company. He is now pensioned off. In our festive gathering, he made a speech, and proposed the health of the Mother General, telling of all the good done to the Indian people by her devoted Nuns, those who have gone to their reward, and those who have come to fill the void left by their departure.[826]

When, then, the government sought to close the residential schools, Indians objected. "Having concluded that it was far too expensive to provide residential schooling to these students," the Truth and Reconciliation Commission explains, "Indian Affairs began to look for alternatives..... From 1945–46 to 1954–55, the number of First Nations students in Indian Affairs day schools increased from 9,532 to 17,947. In 1949, the Special Joint Committee of the Senate and House of Commons Appointed to Examine and Consider The Indian Act recommended 'that wherever and whenever possible Indian children should be educated in association with other children.' In 1951, the Indian Act was amended to allow the federal government to enter into agreements with provincial governments and school boards to have First Nations students educated in public schools."[827]

But "When the government revised the Indian Act in the 1940s and 1950s, some bands, along with regional and national Indigenous organizations, wanted to maintain schools in their communities.... In the 1960s, when the government decided to close certain schools, some Indian bands pleaded to have them remain open."[828]

This was the case, for example, for the venerable Mohawk Institute in Brantford, Ontario. The local band wanted it to stay open, on the grounds that many "successful members of Six Nations passed though the Institute."[829] In the summer of 1970, hearing that the Blue Quills residential school was to be shuttered and their children sent to a local public school, Indian parents took the measure of occupying the school. "It was estimated that over 1,000 people participated in the sit-in, with rarely fewer than 200 people being at the school on any given day."[830] Instead of being closed, the school was handed over to the local band to operate.

The real value of residential schools

Why now, after wanting them so badly for so long, have Canadian Indians generally turned against the residential schools?

One reason is surely that the schools are a useful scapegoat.

If things go wrong on the reserve, if someone drinks too much, or hurts his kids, or beats his wife, if folks are poor, if money goes missing, if someone gets caught in a crime, the residential schools are there to take the blame, avoiding the need to assign individual responsibility and preserving community solidarity. Everybody wins, except the unseen other.

This works well enough, it seems, despite the awkward fact that areas that never had a residential school, like Labrador or New Brunswick, have the same problems among native people in the same degree as areas that did. Indeed, at their most prevalent, only 30 percent of native children ever went to residential schools. Can you tell the difference?

One other good reason for the scapegoating is, sadly, there is money in it. Under an agreement reached in 2005, the federal government set up a $1.9 billion fund to pay out an average of $24,000 to anyone who had attended a residential school. Anyone claiming specific abuse can still sue for more. More money is being shovelled in from the various churches who ran the schools.

That's a good deal more than thirty pieces of silver.

And the advantages of scapegoating the residential schools are more than just financial.

On April 1, 2016, Alain Bellemare was sentenced in a Quebec court for torturing a five-year-old girl, inflicting 25 third-degree burns with a cigarette and two more with a lighter. He then left the child without medical attention. Some burns were on the face, some on her genitals. She survived, but will be scarred for life.

Bellemare was given a 15-month sentence.

The prosecution asked for four years, which seems little enough.

The judge reduced the sentence on the grounds that Bellemare was an aboriginal who had suffered from the experience of residential schools.[831]

So how long did Bellemare spend in residential schools?

He never went.

Neither had anyone in his immediate family.

His grandparents had.

The ghastly effects of the residential schools now linger unto the third generation, stripping the poor Indian of responsibility for his acts.

This would, of course, not be credible if Indians were understood as sentient beings like the rest of us, with free will and able to think for themselves. But the Noble Savage archetype does not permit that notion.

The judge probably felt he was striking a blow for native people. This is myopic, even leaving aside the eternal dependency it implies for Canadian Indians. Had there been poor conditions for aboriginal children in residential schools three generations ago, that is past. Aboriginal children being tortured today is a present problem we can do something about, and judge Guy Lambert arguably aided and abetted rather than discouraging it.

Judge Lambert's authority was the Criminal Code of Canada, which, in section 718.2e, inserted in 1996, instructs judges that "all available sanctions, other than imprisonment, that are reasonable in the circumstances and consistent with the harm done to victims or to the community should be considered for all offenders, with particular attention to the circumstances of Aboriginal offenders."

Lambert's broad interpretation of section 716.2e depends, in turn, on the case of Jamie Gladue, back in 1999. Ms. Gladue, suspecting her common-law husband of an affair, stabbed him to death.

She was sentenced to three years, and out in six months.

A higher court then scolded the judge for an "overly narrow" interpretation of section 716.2e. Gladue had been treated too harshly; 716.2e should be applied to reduce jail time for aboriginals even in the most serious of crimes.

Every time a Canadian Indian or Eskimo is convicted, there now must be a "Gladue Report," giving any available rationale for a more lenient sentence.

This provision of the Criminal Code, and the way it has been used by the courts, is of course a violation of equal treatment before the law.

Still, surely it makes the Indian Residential School system terribly useful for some.

19 NO LAND WAS STOLEN FROM THE INDIANS

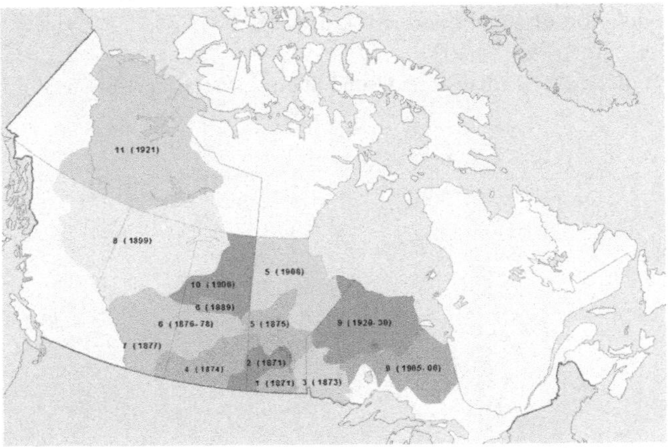

The Numbered Treaties. *Wikimedia Commons*: https://commons.wikimedia.org/wiki/File:Numbered-Treaties-Map.svg

Okay, so there was no genocide of the Indians, and no cultural genocide.

Still, we took their land. Their land was stolen, right? It is "politically insensitive (if not offensive) to celebrate and memorialize all Canadian prime ministers … on land that traditionally belongs to the … Anishnaube and Haudenausanee peoples …," as they say.

The summary report of the Truth and Reconciliation Commission makes the standard claim, for those drooling alien troglodytes who have not heard it: "The mere presence of Indigenous people in these newly colonized lands blocked settler access to the land. To gain control of the land of Indigenous people, colonists negotiated Treaties, waged wars of extinction, eliminated traditional landholding practices, disrupted families, and imposed a political and spiritual order that came complete with new values and cultural practices."[832]

However, the idea that the land was stolen is almost the opposite of the truth.

Did the Indians own land?

To begin with, as outrageous as it might first sound, consider: Did the Indians really own any land?

They were transient, and passed through the land indifferently without cultivating it. We do not recognize ownership of the air, or of the sea. "[E]veryone may enjoy them, but he has no exclusive rights to them...."[833] Was the Indian use of land so different?

Property ownership means "[t]he right and interest which a man has in lands and chattels to the exclusion of others."[834] Indian tribes did not maintain or recognize, on the whole, exclusive rights to any land. Different tribes often passed through and hunted the same territory—sometimes resisted, sometimes not.

There is another important legal principle involved in the concept of property. "Property is not a thing," explains the Federal Court of Appeal in *Manrell v. Canada*, 2003, "but a right, or better, a collection of rights (over things) enforceable against others."[835]

Problem: with no government, no Indian band had any enforceable rights over any lands, except what they could maintain day to day by the strength of their own strong right arm.

Duhaime's Law Dictionary says: "Property and law were born and die together. Before laws were made, there was no property. Take away laws and property ceases."[836] "Before laws were written and enforced, property had no relevance."[837]

As both a legal and a practical matter, therefore, no Indian tribes owned any property in Canada until the British Imperial government, or before it the French, marched in with the ability and intent to create and enforce such rights.

In 1516, Thomas More explains that the inhabitants of his imaginary ideal society Utopia "account it a very just cause of war for a nation to hinder others from possessing a part of that soil of which they make no use, but which is suffered to lie idle and uncultivated, since every man has, by the law of nature, a right to such a waste portion of the earth as is necessary for his subsistence."[838] This would seem to justify Europeans taking any land they needed for their own sustenance that Indians did not have under cultivation. As More wrote this well before England had colonies in the New World, it cannot have been self-serving. And, since More is a saint of the Catholic church, his views on morality do carry a certain weight.

Indeed, to anyone familiar with Catholic moral teaching, this argument should sound familiar. It is a part of Catholic social teaching that each man has a right to what he needs for his sustenance, and this supersedes another's property rights. If a poor European needed that land, then, and the Indians were not using it, or not using it as intensively as they might, he had a natural right to it.

John Locke, the father of our liberal democratic governmental system, the philosophical founder of the modern doctrine of equality and human rights, also weighed in on the issue, in favour of a European right to uncultivated land. His argument is extensive. He begins with the premise that the earth is man's common legacy. Each man, however, owns his own labour. If, therefore, a man improves a piece of land by his labour, he has established ownership over it.

> He has removed the item from the common state that nature has placed it in, and through this labour the item has had annexed to it something that excludes the common right of other men: for this labour is unquestionably the property of the labourer, so no other man can have a right to anything the labour is joined to—at least where there is enough, and as good, left in common for others.[839]

According to Locke, taking over unimproved land did not really mean taking anything from the Indians. It was, rather, giving them something:

> [H]e who appropriates land to himself by his labour, does not lessen, but increase the common stock of mankind: for the provisions serving to the support of human life, produced by one acre of inclosed and cultivated land, are (to speak much within compass) ten times more than those which are yielded by an acre of land of an equal richness lying waste in common. And therefore he that incloses land, and has a greater plenty of the conveniencies of life from ten acres, than he could have from an hundred left to nature, may truly be said to give ninety acres to mankind: for his labour now supplies him with provisions out of ten acres, which were but the product of an hundred lying in common.[840]

Before 1763, the concept of Indian land title was irregularly dealt with. Sometimes treaties were made calling only for "peace and friendship," not mentioning land. Sometimes a payment was made for the land used by settlers.

In New England, writes William Hubbard:

> They [the colonists] were also encouraged in making these scattered settlements by the general friendly disposition of the Natives, who freely sold their lands, for which a valuable consideration was paid, without acception [*sic*], where a claim was made. The Indians perceived their interest in admitting their English neighbors, as they furnished them with means of much easier sustenance and the utmost care was taken by the several governments of the united colonies, to prevent every occasion of distrust.[841]

The British Peace and Friendship Treaty with the Micmacs in 1760, on the other hand, says only that the Indians "do acknowledge the jurisdiction and Dominion of His Majesty George the Second over the Territories of Nova Scotia or Accadia and we do make submission to His Majesty in the most perfect, ample and solemn manner." They promise that "they shall not molest any of His Majesty's subjects or their dependents, in their settlements already made or to be hereafter made or in carrying on their Commerce or in any thing whatever within the Province of His said Majesty or elsewhere."[842]

It is a simple adhesion to the social contract, with the benefits it provides: "if any Quarrel or Misunderstanding shall happen between myself and the English or between them and any of my tribe, neither I, nor they shall take any private satisfaction or Revenge, but we will apply for redress according to the Laws established in His said Majesty's Dominions."

Settlers were for the most part not competing with the Indians for resources. They were farming, not hunting. And their presence was advantageous: Europeans had manufactured goods to trade, could ally to protect local Indians from their enemies, and had many useful things they could teach the local tribes. When the hunt was not successful, the Europeans had stores of food they could barter; and if the European crops failed, they could barter food from the Indians.

Accordingly, rather than "stealing the land," they were in a symbiotic relationship. Father LeJeune, writing in 1634, advocates more settlement specifically for the Indians' benefit. "I think that they would soon become good Christians, if people would come and inhabit their country, which they are for the most part desirous of."[843] Nasty, brutish, and short wears thin after a few millennia.

Champlain makes almost the same observation: "I believe they have no law among them, nor know what it is to worship and pray to God, and that most of them live like brute beasts; and I think they would speedily be brought to be good Christians, if their country were colonised, which most of them would like."[844]

There was no lack of land to be had. As Francis Parkman describes the scene,

> Ascending the St. Lawrence, it was seldom that the sight of a human form gave relief to the loneliness.... Ascending farther, all was solitude, except at Three Rivers, a noted place of trade, where a few Algonquins of the tribe called Atticamegues might possibly be seen.... At Montreal, there was no human life, save during a brief space in early summer, when the shore swarmed with savages who had come to the yearly trade....[845]

Given Canada's vast spaces, had the Indian population remained the size it was at contact, the relation today could still be symbiotic. It would theoretically still be possible to live by the old ways, if anyone wanted to. Eighty-five percent of Ontario is still Crown land, unsettled and uncultivated; for Canada as a whole, the figure is 89 percent.

But why would anyone want to? The choice was poverty or plenty. And there was room for all and for many more starving people from Europe, if the Indians too adopted the more efficient and secure European means of producing food. One clear motive for the treaties was helping the Indians transition to this new, technically superior, method of living. This is part of Father LeJeune's, and Champlain's, early rationale for settlement.

> Now, with the assistance of a few good, industrious men, it would be easy to locate a few families, especially as some of them have already spoken to me about it, thus of themselves becoming accustomed, little by little, to extract something from the earth.[846]

A gift of the Crown

Still, rather than just move in, the British authorities chose, in the Royal Proclamation of 1763, to formally recognize aboriginal land rights. They then negotiated treaties to purchase clear title at an agreed-upon price.

From either a legal or military point of view, this was unnecessary. As 19th-century BC Chief Justice Sir Matthew Begbie advised a group of West Coast Indians who had murdered some sailors to take their gear,

> [I]f the white men intended to do harm to the Indians, the whites could destroy them off the face of the earth. The whites could send up one man-of-war, which could easily, and without landing a man, destroy all their houses and canoes and property, and drive them naked and helpless into the woods to starve.... In one year the white men could destroy all the Indians on the coast without losing a man.[847]

Probably true.

But, to their credit, the authorities, both English and French, instead saw the Indians as fellow souls, sons of Adam, hence subjects deserving full protection of law.

It was not in the interests of the Indians to remain in a state of constant war, among themselves or with European settlers. Nor, of course, was it in the interests of the settlers. If it was general war, the settlers would inevitably eventually win. But this was not white against red. This was order against mayhem. This was ending a Mad Max environment, an endless turf war among rival gangs.

Such was the duty of any government to attempt.

The notion of Indian land ownership, and compensation for any land used, was a useful legal premise to draw the Indians into the social contract. They gained property rights in return for recognizing law and government. The value of rule of law was made immediately apparent: it gave them stuff.

Ideally, they then settled down and became prosperous farmers and responsible citizens.

The 1763 Royal Proclamation read:

> And whereas it is just and reasonable, and essential to our Interest, and the Security of our Colonies, that the several Nations or Tribes of Indians with whom We are connected, and who live under our Protection, should not be molested or disturbed in the Possession of such Parts of Our Dominions and Territories as, not having been ceded to or purchased by Us, are reserved to them, or any of them, as their Hunting Grounds.—We do therefore, with the Advice of our Privy Council, declare it to be our Royal Will and Pleasure, that no Governor or Commander in Chief in any of our Colonies of Quebec, East Florida, or West Florida, do presume, upon any Pretence whatever, to grant Warrants of Survey, or pass any Patents for Lands beyond the Bounds of their respective Governments, as described in their Commissions: as also that no Governor or Commander in Chief in any of our other Colonies or Plantations in America do presume for the present, and until our further Pleasure be known, to grant Warrants of Survey, or pass Patents for any Lands beyond the Heads or Sources of any of the Rivers which fall into the Atlantic Ocean from the West and North West, or upon any Lands whatever, which, not having been ceded to or purchased by Us as aforesaid, are reserved to the said Indians, or any of them.
>
> And We do further declare it to be Our Royal Will and Pleasure, for the present as aforesaid, to reserve under our Sovereignty, Protection, and Dominion, for the use of the said Indians, all the Lands and Territories not included within the Limits of Our said Three new Governments [Quebec and the two Floridas], or within the Limits of the

> Territory granted to the Hudson's Bay Company, as also all the Lands and Territories lying to the Westward of the Sources of the Rivers which fall into the Sea from the West and North West as aforesaid.
>
> And We do hereby strictly forbid, on Pain of our Displeasure, all our loving Subjects from making any Purchases or Settlements whatever, or taking Possession of any of the Lands above reserved, without our especial leave and Licence for that Purpose first obtained.

The recent Truth and Reconciliation Commission Report writes, "The Royal Proclamation, in effect, ruled that any future transfer of 'Indian' land would take the form of a Treaty between sovereigns."[848] "The Numbered Treaties and the Pre-Confederation Treaties, reached between the Crown and sovereign First Nations, were the equivalent of international treaties. Treating them as anything less reflects a colonialist attitude and ignores the viewpoint of the Aboriginal negotiators."[849]

This is plainly false. The Royal Proclamation makes clear that there is only one sovereign over all Indian lands: "to reserve under our Sovereignty, Protection, and Dominion, for the use of the said Indians, all the Lands and Territories not included within the Limits of Our said Three new Governments."

In signing treaties with the Crown, Indians were assenting to this and waiving claims to sovereignty. In return, they were given a payment, on the premise of yielding land claims. Moreover, their "ownership" right was strictly a question of the lands being "reserved" for them at the King's "Royal Will and Pleasure," with the implied right to change his will and pleasure at any time; "until our further Pleasure be known." These were, in other words, limited property rights bestowed by and subject to the king and his government. Limited, for one thing, to hunting rights—use of land as their "hunting grounds." Limited also in another vital sense: they could not legally sell their land interests to anyone but the government. In other words, ultimately the land belonged not to them, but to the King. Even the reserves they were given are not, technically, their own land, but land held by the Crown for their use. The text of the Indian Act defines a reserve as a "tract of land, the legal title to which is vested in Her Majesty, that has been set apart by Her Majesty for the use and benefit of a band."

Not incidentally, this act of relative generosity toward the Indians, in acknowledging land rights, became one of the causes of the American Revolution.

Negotiating the Treaty of Niagara in 1764, a general peace between Britain and 24 Indian tribes after the Seven Years' War, the British made certain the Indians understood the Royal Proclamation. This, from the English perspective, was the main purpose of the pact. "It must not be forgotten that the terms of the Royal Proclamation were explained to, and accepted by, Indigenous leaders during the negotiation of the Treaty of Niagara of 1764."[850] This was the social contract. The Indians thereby accepted the sovereignty of the British Crown, and so the rule of law.

Addressing the Indians assembled to negotiate Treaty 8, before saying anything about land, Lieutenant-Governor David Laird made his main purpose clear:

> The Queen wants all the whites, half-breeds and Indians to be at peace with one another, and to shake hands when they meet. The Queen's laws must be obeyed all over the country, both by the whites and the Indians. It is not alone that we wish to prevent Indians from molesting the whites, it is also to prevent the whites from molesting or doing harm to the Indians. The Queen's soldiers are just as much for the protection of the Indians as for the white man.

The land deal was a means to this end. "One thing Indians must understand, that if they do not make a treaty they must obey the laws of the land—that will be just the same whether you make a treaty or not; the laws must be obeyed."

The land offered them was represented as a gift from the Queen:

> [A]s the Queen wishes the Indians to have lands of their own, we will give one square mile, or 640 acres, to each family of five. In return for this the Government expects that the Indians will not interfere with or molest any miner, traveller or settler. We expect you to be good friends with everyone, and shake hands with all you meet. If any whites molest you in any way, shoot your dogs or horses, or do you any harm, you have only to report the matter to the police, and they will see that justice is done to you. There may be some things we have not mentioned, but these can be mentioned later on.... The Queen owns the country, but is willing to acknowledge the Indians' claims, and offers them terms as an offset to all of them.[851]

The government was not buying land from the Indians. It was buying peace, order, and rule of law, by offering them land.

It is asserted by the Alberta Chiefs in their 1970 *Red Paper* as an article of faith that the treaties were about land. "The purpose of the Dominion in making the Treaties was to acquire the land of the Indians. The yielding up of most of their land was clearly the most important undertaking to which the Indians agreed in signing a treaty contract."[852]

This is not true. Lieutenant-Governor Alexander Morris, negotiating numbered Treaties 3 through 6, assigned a reserve and other benefits typical of these treaties to a group of Sioux who had no conceivable historic "land claims," having only moved up from the United States a dozen years earlier. They were given the same deal as other Indians who did traditionally live in the area, for nothing but a promise to keep the peace. Because they, as much as any other Indian group, were capable of breaking it.

> As these Sioux had been living on the British side for twelve years, Morris promised them a reserve near Portage la Prairie, and promised to forward their requests for agricultural implements along to Ottawa. In exchange, he "impressed upon them the necessity for their being orderly and quiet, told them that they must on no account trouble the settlers or the other Indians, and must go at once on to their reserve lands—all which they promised."[853]

Delgamuukw

That entire legal apple cart seems now to have been upset by the 2007 Supreme Court of Canada *Delgamuukw* decision.[854] Chief Justice Lamer, writing the majority decision for the court, argued that, at the time that British or Canadian jurisdiction commenced, Indians already here had what amounted to "squatters' rights" in common law. Hence, aboriginal land title.

But there is a problem with the court's logic. In common law, squatters' rights require proof that the party in possession has heretofore exercised exclusive use of the land: "proof of non-permissive use which is actual, open and notorious, exclusive, adverse, and continuous for the statutory period." This is almost never true of any Indian band, not even excepting the semi-settled Iroquoians in the East: nomadic, they naturally travelled through shared territories. None of the "numbered treaties" signed across the Canadian Prairies, for example, was with only one Indian group. It was whoever happened to be in the neighbourhood.

Moreover, the common law principle of "squatter's rights" actually argues against Indian ownership. The principle on which a squatter gains rights is that cultivating land, as Locke argued, establishes ownership. In *Finley v. Yuba Water County District*, 1979, the California Court of Appeal wrote, "As to adverse possession, its underlying philosophy is basically that land use has historically been favored over disuse, and that therefore he who uses land is preferred in the law to he who does not, even though the latter is the rightful owner."[855] In his book *Principles of Property Law*, Bruce Ziff explains that "[t]he penalty for non-use (of land) is tantamount to private expropriation by a squatter without compensation."[856]

Accordingly, even if Canadian Indians did once hold ownership rights, by common law those rights would have lapsed 5 to 20 years after the land was first cultivated, and are now in the hands of whoever cultivated the lands, their heirs or assigns.

Nevertheless, we now have a new concept of "aboriginal land title" as an inherent right, rather than one bestowed by law. It remains to be seen how it will play out. It is hard to see it ending well: a huge proportion of the Canadian population, after all, has a right to be considered "non-status Indians," and therefore to have unextinguished land title, and money owing from the rest of the population, mostly more recent immigrants. At a minimum, it is going to be a lot of well-paid work for a lot of lawyers and bureaucrats, largely at public expense. What percentage of a given patch of land belongs to the Haudenausanee, and what percentage to the Neutrals or the Anishnaube, and what percentage of the present owner's blood is any or either, and who owes how much to whom?

But even if you accept the *Delgamuukw* premise, land has not been stolen. Recognized land title has always been negotiated and compensated for. It was never seized in war, at least by the Europeans in Canada. Some land rights have only recently been recognized, not to say given, and the necessary treaties are accordingly now in the works. It does look a bit like a giveaway to a group on grounds of ethnicity; perhaps a pilfering of tax dollars; but there is obviously no attempt to steal anything from Indians.

What about the treaties already signed, usually long ago? Were they, as is sometimes alleged, swindles, in which the naïve Indians were not properly compensated? Was it a sharp practice of Peter Stuyvesant to, famously, buy Manhattan for $24 in baubles and beads?

No. Land values rise. If the deals were unfair, why was it usually the Indians, and not the Europeans, who pushed for the treaties? Must we assume that Indians are just too stupid to manage their own affairs?

"It bears reminding that Amerindians were the first to take the initiative in making treaty, and not the Canadian government," writes Talbot.[857] "The Plains Cree west of Manitoba, especially, had for some time been lobbying for a treaty.... Macdonald had not been keen on extending the responsibilities of the cash-strapped government. He preferred to wait for the demand for settlement to increase before making any treaty."[858] "[M]any chiefs and councillors were anxious to sign treaties with the Crown so as to establish a relative stability and secure a new means for survival."[859]

In 1871, Cree Chief Sweetgrass petitioned the government in these words:

> Great Father, I shake hands with you, and bid you welcome..... Our country is getting ruined of fur-bearing animals.... We want cattle, tools, agricultural implements and assistance in everything when we come to settle—our country is no longer able to support us.... We have had great starvation the past winter, and the small-pox took away many of our people.... We want you to stop the Americans from coming to trade on our lands.... We invite you to come and see us and to speak with us.[860]

It was not a question of the traditional Indian way of making a living becoming no longer viable because of an influx of settlers. At this point, there had not yet been an influx of settlers. It was, as Sweetgrass says, because the supply of fur-bearing animals was running out. The Cree had become accustomed to making their living trapping and selling to the Hudson's Bay Company. That was what was no longer viable, because of over-trapping.

A band from Norway House explained, during talks for Treaty Number 5, that they had come "to escape from starvation and cannibalism and to adopt the means employed by the white man to preserve life, by disturbing the soil and raising food out of the ground."[861]

Other Indian bands sought the commission out, in hopes of making a deal:

> On their journey home, the Colville [a steamer bearing the treaty commissioners] encountered another group at Dog Head Point, where the Commissioners were again greeted with a *feu de joie*. The Amerindians, led by Thickfoot, had caught wind of the Commissioners' mission, and "had been waiting to see us." They were anxious to sign the treaty: "Thickfoot said he had cattle and would like to have a place assigned to his people on the main shore, where they could live by farming and fishing. We suggested Fisher River to them, which they approved of. Eventually we decided on paying these Indians—took Thickfoot's adhesion to the treaty." The meeting ended cordially. "Thickfoot expressed gratitude for the kindness of the Government, and his belief that Indians of the various Islands and of Jack Head Point would cheerfully accept the Queen's benevolence and settle on a reserve."[862]

Both the Indians and the Canadian government understood the treaties as something done primarily for the benefit of the Indians. It was a matter of "the Queen's benevolence." Without treaties, they were only too likely to starve. But then, they had always been periodically likely to starve. Without treaties, too, they were likely to get shot, or to lose their lands, in endless war.

Social contract? Where do I sign up?

Sharp practices

Did the Indians understand what they were signing away? This is the common argument from many who say they were cheated: they did not understand the treaties as the whites did.

"The Aboriginal view of the treaties was very different," explains the Royal Commission on Aboriginal Peoples. "They believed what the king's men told them, that the marks scratched on parchment captured the essence of their talks. They were angered and dismayed to discover later that what had been pledged in words, leader to leader, was not recorded accurately."[863]

"Many Aboriginal people say that the written version of treaties fails to reflect crucial verbal agreements reached by negotiators," says the 1996 Royal Commission on Aboriginal Peoples.[864]

One natural problem was that the Indians were illiterate, there being no standard written forms of Indian languages. And few of them spoke English, the language in which the treaties were written. So it seems on the surface entirely possible that in the treaties they waived rights they had no intention to waive. You can understand that they would feel cheated if this was the case.

In fact, there was a real problem of this sort with Numbered Treaties 1 and 2.

> The earliest treaty implementation challenge that [Lieutenant-Governor Alexander] Morris had to face involved the so-called "outside promises" of Treaties 1 and 2, signed in 1871. The "outside promises" consisted of a series of items that the Amerindian leadership insisted had been included in the negotiations with Archibald and Simpson, but had not been written down in the treaty texts. The root of the miscommunication lay between the then-Lieutenant-Governor and the interpreter, the latter apparently having promised more than what was said. Even more, Archibald and Simpson [the chief government negotiator] had made different promises. As a result, Amerindians party to the treaty had begun to voice strong complaint by late 1872 that the treaty as they understood it was not being fulfilled.[865]

But this would seem to be the exception that proves the rule. This sort of thing, when it did happen, was quickly and easily detected. It took all of one year. The treaties were then reopened and renegotiated at Indian request. Having discovered the risks, negotiators were accordingly doubly careful in later talks to make everything transparent.

This government reaction also shows that there was never an intent to mislead.

That, after all, would have been counter-productive, given the true intention of the treaties. It was not, once again, to get Indian land. It was to establish peace and mutual trust.

Morris's biographer maintains that the Lieutenant-Governor "knew that anything spoken of in the slightest way as a promise would be taken as writ by the Chiefs. Throughout all of the proceedings, from Treaties 3 through 6, Morris was careful to avoid statements on which he knew he would not be able to deliver."[866]

At Treaty 6, Indians were allowed to select their own interpreter, at government expense, to ensure that they got the full story.[867] Erasmus, the Indian interpreter, kept his own notes of treaty negotiations. This becomes an added proof that there was no trickery. "With a few notable exceptions, Erasmus's recollection of the proceedings was significantly consistent with that reported by Morris and recorded by his secretary, Dr. A. G. Jackes."[868]

A similar practice was followed in renegotiating Treaties 1 and 2:

> As at Treaty 6, he had his own interpreters and interpreters selected by the Amerindians read out the written settlement of the outside promises clearly. Morris was careful to personally write up the new terms, in part to finalize the agreement, but also to ensure that a record would be available to hold the government and future administrators to account.[869]

To ensure that the Indians knew exactly what was in the document, Morris also gave them their own copies of the text. If they could not read them themselves, they could get a trusted translator to check and confirm terms at any time.

> [W]e have had the treaty written out, and we are ready to have it signed, and we will leave ... with any Chief you may select ... a copy written out on skin that cannot be rubbed out and put up in a tin box, so that it cannot be wet, so that you can keep it among yourselves so that when we are dead our children will know what was written.[870]
>
> As at previous treaties, the signing of Treaty 6 ended in ceremony. After each of the signings at Forts Carlton and Pitt, Morris provided the Chiefs with medals, representing and commemorating the agreement, uniforms and flags,

> which afforded recognition for the Chiefs and Councillors as officers of the Crown, and copies of the treaty, so that the promises made would not be "rubbed out."[871]

"In my language, there is no word for 'surrender'," argued Chief Francois Paulette of the Treaty 8 Tribal Council to the Royal Commission on Aboriginal Peoples, 1996. "There is no word. I cannot describe 'surrender' to you in my language, so how do you expect my people to [have] put their X on 'surrender'?"[872]

If so, it seems Paulette's native language is radically deficient. English, according to *Roget's*, has twenty-eight synonyms for the word, in the specific sense of giving up a right. In a pinch, the English word "give" would probably do. Is Paulette saying Dogrib has no word meaning "give"? If not, what does this say about Dogrib culture?

Surely Paulette means "surrender" in the specific sense of "admitting defeat in war." Which is not the sense used here.

One claim often heard today is that Indians believed they were only giving up rights to the land "to the depth of a plough." That is, they were allowing the Europeans only the agricultural use of land that remained theirs. So—they retain mineral rights.

Not that traditional Indian culture had much if any use for minerals.

The question of mineral rights actually did come up at Treaty 3 negotiations, and Alexander Morris made clear that tribes did not retain mineral rights outside their reserve. "He ... told the Saulteaux that they would have mineral rights on their reserve lands, but not on Crown land."[873]

When the cession of title was part of the treaty terms, treaty language went the full monty to ensure that this cession was absolute. The Treaty of Niagara surrenders title:

> … together with all the hereditaments and appurtenances to the same belonging or in anywise appertaining, and also all our estate Right, Title, property, possession, claim or demand in law or equity in or to the same or any part thereof. To released and confirmed and aforesaid with the hereditaments and appurtenances thereunto belonging unto our said Sovereign Lord King George the Third. His heirs and successors and to and for his and their own proper use & behoof forever.

In the numbered treaties, the standard phrase used is "do hereby cede, release, surrender and yield up to the Government of the Dominion of Canada, for Her Majesty the Queen, and Her successors forever, all their rights, titles and privileges whatsoever, to the lands included within the following limits."

Hard to read mineral rights out of that.

The Douglas treaties in British Columbia included this boilerplate:

> [The Indians] ... do consent to surrender, entirely and for ever, to James Douglas, the agent of the Hudson's Bay Company in Vancouver Island, that is to say, for the Governor, Deputy Governor, and Committee of the same, the whole of the lands.... It is understood, ..., that the land itself, with these small exceptions, becomes the entire property of the white people for ever.[874]

The 1850 Robinson Treaty with the Ojibway of Lake Superior reads:

> ... the said chiefs and principal men do freely, fully and voluntarily surrender, cede, grant and convey unto Her Majesty, Her heirs and successors forever, all their right, title and interest in the whole of the territory above described, save and except the reservations set forth in the schedule hereunto annexed.

Another common claim is that the Indians were shunted off to reserves on undesirable land. Again, this is not true. They had first choice of land, before the bulk of settlers arrived. Peter Robinson records, of the Ontario treaties he negotiated, "In allowing the Indians to retain reservations of land for their own use I was governed by the fact that they in most cases asked for such tracts as they had heretofore been in the habit of using for purposes of residence and cultivation, and by securing these to them."[875] In negotiating the numbered treaties, Indians were told "they might have their land where they chose, not interfering with existing occupants."[876]

Oral traditions

Along with its assertion of inherent aboriginal title, the Supreme Court's *Delgamuukw* decision introduced another wrinkle to Canadian aboriginal affairs. Chief Justice Lamer wrote:

> Notwithstanding the challenges created by the use of oral histories as proof of historical facts, the laws of evidence must be adapted in order that this type of evidence can be accommodated and placed on an equal footing with the

> types of historical evidence that courts are familiar with, which largely consists of historical documents.

The ruling here does not refer directly to treaties and treaty rights. But the implications would seem to be broad, and ominous. This could open everything up. What if the descendants of the Indians who signed a treaty now claim an oral tradition that their ancestors agreed to something quite different? All the government can offer to prove its case are its pathetic signed written texts. Lamer seems to argue that any Indian oral claims must now be taken as just as authoritative. Texts carefully preserved on indelible animal skin in sealed tin boxes be damned.

In a later case, Chief Justice Beverley McLachlin has ruled, "In determining the usefulness and reliability of oral histories, judges must resist facile assumptions based on Eurocentric traditions of gathering and passing on historical facts."[877]

In another case (*Tsilhqotin Nation v. B.C.*), Justice Vickers of the BC Supreme Court has written, "I propose to take this entire body of evidence [oral history and legends] into account and to the extent that I am able, consider it from the Aboriginal perspective."

Those who have read thus far regarding the aboriginal perspective should see a problem. The traditional Indian perspective takes no particular interest in factuality. If you dream a thing, for example, it is so.

If you dream that white men owe you a million dollars, then …

This is not going to be easy to litigate, and it seems unlikely to end in anything like justice.

Indian oral traditions are, in common law terms, hearsay evidence. There are good reasons why hearsay evidence is not admitted in court: it is rumour, and has undergone all the processes that lead to legend, urban or otherwise. It does not allow for cross-examination. It is obviously possible for anyone presenting oral evidence in their own behalf to simply alter it to help their case; all that is preventing this is personal integrity. It's like asking a suspect if he committed the crime, and accepting his response.

Sadly, the modern Canadian bench seems to have bought the Noble Savage myth that Indians, being innocent natural beings without consciousness, cannot lie.

Early settlers and missionaries, crippled in their shrivelled imaginations by actually knowing Indians as humans, thought differently.

The Indians themselves fully understood and understand written records to be superior to their own oral traditions. The *Jesuit Relations* record an instructive incident:

> "Consider, you people," said he [an Indian chief], "whether you wish to help us, according to the promise made to us by the late Monsieur de Champlain."
>
> Thereupon Monsieur the Governor asked sieur Olivier and sieur Nicolet, who were present, if it were true that Monsieur de Champlain had made this promise.... Now, as I was present at that assembly, I begged Monsieur the Governor to let me answer the Savages; this being granted to me, I told them that they were forgetting part of what had been decided at that meeting. They replied that they had not the use of the pen, as we had, to preserve upon paper the remembrance of what was discussed among them.[878]

And so it goes.

You know what they say about shit hitting the fan?

I think this is one of those newfangled wind turbines.

20 THE INDIAN OF THE IMAGINATION

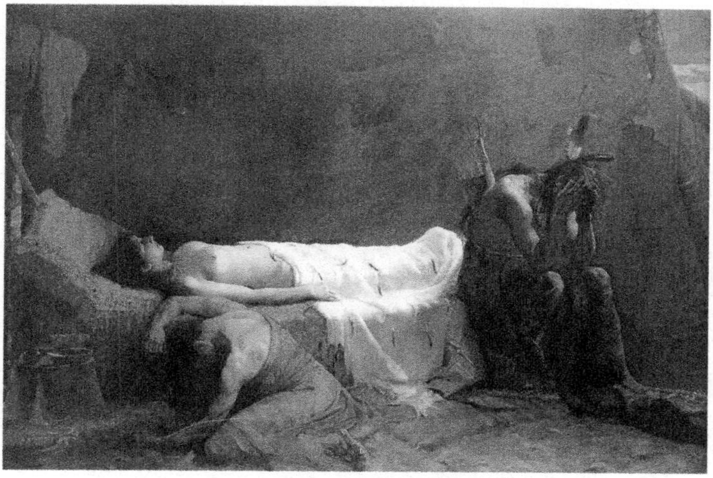

Longfellow's Minnehaha, dying poetically and clothed more or less as nature made her. *Dodge.*

The Red Rose Maiden

By the Metabichouan Falls there sat
An Indian Princess fair;
Red were her lips, dark were her eyes,
Glossy her long black hair.
A warrior passed the foaming Falls
Of the Algonquin tribe.
He said: "Sweet maiden fair as morn
And bright as dewdrops on the corn
Come, be a warrior's bride."

"Come with me to my forest home,"
Cried the Algonquin bold;
"Of ermine, gold and wampum bead
I'll give thee wealth untold."
"Great Chief," she said. "that cannot be,
I love a warrior true;
He went to chase the moose and deer,
And I must wait to meet him here;
I cannot go with you."

"Thou wilt not come," the chieftain said

"Oh, lovely star of morn?
Then thou must be a wild red rose
And grow amongst the corn."
The warrior true came from the chase
To meet the maiden fair
Beside the Metabichouan Falls.
He heard the wind and loon's wild call;
The maiden was not there.

Sadly he sat by council fires
Whilst others danced with glee;
A voice kept calling night and morn.
"Oh, come and set me free;
In lonely wilds, bound by a spell,
I wait and watch for you.
Then haste through dell and over hill,
A wild red rose is waiting still
Her warrior brave and true."

He searched through dell, by lake and stream,
O'er plain and mountain high;
He found her when his form was bent.
And dimmed his eagle eye.
"How can I free thee, love," he cried.
"And give thy soul sweet rest?"
"Just pluck one leaf and break the spell."
He plucked the leaf, the maiden fell
Upon the warrior's breast.

Her hair was white as driven snow.
And sparkled with the dew;
She waited there so many moons
Her warrior good and true.
They met beside the sea of Death,
When life's short race was run;
Then through the portals of the west
They went to join the good and blest
Beyond the setting sun.

—*Martha Craig (Princess Ye-wa-ga-no-nee),* Legends of the North Land.

The Indian prejudice

In the 2016 American League playoff series, the Toronto Blue Jays faced the Cleveland Indians at home.

Inevitably, someone□ the architect Douglas Cardinal□ appealed to the Canadian and Ontario Human Rights Commissions to prohibit use of the visitor team's name in Canada. Nor were they to wear their uniforms, display their logo, or show their mascot. All were offensive to First Nations.

For even if there was no genocide against the Indians, and no cultural genocide, and nobody stole their land, at the very least, there has always been a general prejudice against them. Everyone hates Indians. Right?

In support of the proposed ban, a "meme" from the National Congress of American Indians circulated the Internet suggesting that "Indians" as a team name was offensive just as it would be offensive to call a team "the New York Jews," or "the San Francisco Chinamen."[879] Why should "the Cleveland Indians" be different?

Why, indeed?

And why is it different from the Minnesota Vikings, the Boston Celtics, the New York Knicks, the New York Yankees, the Montreal Canadiens, the Vancouver Canucks, the Queen's Golden Gaels, the Airdrie Irish, the Laurentian Voyageurs, or the Notre Dame Fighting Irish? All are similarly ethnic.

Truth is, teams everywhere want to name themselves after Indians. We have the Edmonton Eskimos, the Atlanta Braves, the Chicago Blackhawks, the Kansas City Chiefs, the Washington Redskins, the Florida State Seminoles, and so on. Even European teams take Indian names. The Exeter Chiefs play rugby in England. The Malmo Redhawks play hockey in Sweden.

Yet nobody anywhere, except maybe Yeshiva University, seems to have wanted to name a team after Jews or Chinese. And even though so many of the top athletes in basketball or football are African-American, nobody outside the old black leagues seems to have thought to name a team the Negroes, or Nubians, or Zulus. When one team in the old coloured baseball leagues sought wider fan support, they named themselves … the Cuban Giants. To gain acceptance, black athletes pretended to be Cuban. Or Native American.

Pure business, folks. If you name a team the Indians, people like them and want to support them. If you name a team the Jews or the Chinamen or the Negroes, people sit on their hands or stay home. They do not identify.

In other words, there is a general popular prejudice against the Jews or Chinese or blacks, but in favour of Indians. The surest proof that a group is not being discriminated against, is that it is used as the name of a sports team. That means people want to cheer it.

Douglas Cardinal was not protesting discrimination. He was pulling rank.

This, of course, flies in the face of the common conception. Every right thinker thinks Indians have been oppressed throughout history. Haven't they always been discriminated against? Haven't they always been despised, spat upon, looked down upon as "bloodthirsty savages"—at least until recent, more enlightened times? Wasn't the only good Indian once a dead Indian?

Nope. This is all a part of the Noble Savage myth. Beginning with that quotation, "The only good Indian is a dead Indian." It was attributed to General Philip Sheridan by his opponents, in order to discredit him. He denied ever saying anything like it. Nobody has ever endorsed the sentiment.

One has to believe white folks are bigots. As C.L. Sonnichsen puts it, not quite felicitously, "If the Apache is a gentleman of distinguished culture, the white man is a savage."[880] Sonnichsen misuses the term "savage" here—he means scoundrel, someone morally evil. But if you believe in the myth of the "Noble Savage," you must as necessary corollary believe that civilization and civilized man is bad. If the state of nature is a state of grace, evil arrives with and derives from civilization, from the development of a sophisticated culture. So it must be that civilization is oppressive of the natural man. The innocent Indian must have been hard done by. Somehow, but systematically.

The bloodthirsty Indian and the Noble Savage

Rather than simply claim that everyone discriminates against Indians, more sophisticated analyses go so far as to admit that there are two stereotypes of the North American Indian: the "bloodthirsty savage," and the "Noble Savage."[881] Both, however, the wise will understand, are equally wrong. Truth is always found judiciously in the middle between any two extremes. Lacy Cotton laments "the swinging pendulum of popular opinion concerning American Natives, and how that opinion always reached for one extreme or the other."[882]

That sounds balanced and enlightened.

It is not. It is sophomoric and simple-minded. Sometimes, when opinions differ, it is because one party is right, and the other party is wrong. Amazingly, it seems that this needs to be said.

It ought to count for something that the "Noble Savage" is usually the Indian encountered in fiction, whereas the "bloodthirsty savage" is the one found in eyewitness accounts.

Only one of them is a literary stereotype.

The common thesis in "culture studies," tiresomely repeated, is that Western civilization, being evil and greedy, has invented a slander against the Indians in order to steal their land. "The creation of a mythological West," Charalambos Vrasidas explains, "justified the seizure of land and the genocide of the Natives."[883]

Think of the villain Ratcliffe in Disney's *Pocahontas*, digging the beach for gold. Same level of analysis.

The whole idea that the "whites" stole the Indian land is probably a necessary part of the Edenic Noble Savage myth: it is part of the concept of the Golden Age that it is irreparably lost.

Never mind that, as we have noted, the white settlers had no need to steal land from the Indians. Never mind that there is still adequate uncultivated land around Attawapiskat and points north to continue the traditional Indian way of life, if anyone were mad enough to try.

The romantic legend also requires that in the past, white people despised the Indians on grounds of pure uninformed prejudice, but now, we, present company, are more enlightened. Part of this is the principle that, ideally, the designated scapegoat must never be part of present company. It is therefore always safest to scapegoat the dead.

But beyond this, a rejection of "civilization" is a rejection of tradition. A rejection of tradition is a rejection of the wisdom of our ancestors, in favour of the spontaneous urges of the now. If civilization is evil, the counsel of our ancestors is evil, for that is what civilization is.

We, on the other hand, being at least capable of acting in and of the moment, can make some claim to spontaneity and innocence. So we good guys are on the side of the Indians. We are, secretly, Indians ourselves.

Keats represented civilization as the voices of the dead in his romantic study, "La Belle Dame Sans Merci." The narrator's fantasy of unfettered romantic love is arrested by an interfering conscience personified as:

> *… pale kings and princes too,*
> *Pale warriors, death-pale were they all;*
> *They cried—"La Belle Dame sans Merci*
> *Hath thee in thrall!"*

I saw their starved lips in the gloam,
With horrid warning gapèd wide,
And I awoke and found me here,
On the cold hill's side.

That's your civilization, if you are a Rousseauvian romantic. A bunch of old fogies ruining the party.

In Keats's poem, the proper response is ambiguous. But to any romantic, of course, the wiser path is to ignore the voices of social propriety, in favour of the love of the moment. You get the girl.

Some may object that the aboriginals themselves have and had a great respect for the wisdom of their ancestors: the "elders."

It is not clear that they did. Many tribes seem to have been inclined, instead, to abandon the old and infirm to starve. A sense of one's history is only worth so much.

But even if they had honoured grey heads—that would only show that they too, like most men everywhere, saw the value of civilization: that they were not themselves romantics. Yet as a practical matter they were crippled in their desire for culture, if they had one, by the lack of any system of writing. Their knowledge of their own traditions, and their ability to build on them, was limited to living memory.

The golden age

The Noble Savage myth seems to be as old as the oldest sustained narrative known to man, the *Epic of Gilgamesh*, circa 1200 BC: Enkidu, Gilgamesh's BFF, is a wild man of the forests who comes to rescue mankind from, apparently, excessive government. A visually similar horned figure, usually termed "The Lord of the Beasts," turns up on seals of the ancient Indus Valley civilization from circa 2500 BC. Similar prehistoric figures have been excavated across the Middle East and as far north as Denmark.

The world has ever been too much with us modern men.

And then there is the fairy lore of northern Europe. Consider: the fairy is a fundamentally similar image to our popular idea of the Canadian Indian. Fairies are usually said by the legends to be remnants of an aboriginal race, the previous inhabitants of the given land. This is true, for example, of the Tuatha Dé Danann of Ireland. Like Indians, they are said to be found in remote, wild places; like Indians, they are "nature spirits." The Indian maiden image is also cognate to the

Greek nymphs, dryads, and naiads.

It all has to do, as well, with the "Golden Age," a time in everyone's remote past. In this Golden Age, according to Hesiod, men

> … lived like gods without sorrow of heart, remote and free from toil and grief: miserable age rested not on them; but with legs and arms never failing they made merry with feasting beyond the reach of all devils. When they died, it was as though they were overcome with sleep, and they had all good things; for the fruitful earth unforced bare them fruit abundantly and without stint. They dwelt in ease and peace.[884]

The *Mahabharata*, the chief epic of India, nurses the same cosmic fantasy:

> Men neither bought nor sold; there were no poor and no rich; there was no need to labour, because all that men required was obtained by the power of will; the chief virtue was the abandonment of all worldly desires. The Krita Yuga was without disease; there was no lessening with the years; there was no hatred or vanity, or evil thought whatsoever; no sorrow, no fear. All mankind could attain to supreme blessedness.[885]

Engels or Matilda Gage could not have said it better.

The myth of the noble savage is every man's yearning for a simpler life in the midst of the restraining requirements of existence with others. We each indulge it, spontaneously, when we feel nostalgia for our youth, a supposedly simpler, happier time.

That's how many of us remember childhood. J.M. Barrie had reason to locate a tribe of Indians in Never Never Land, as neighbours to the Lost Boys who have chosen never to grow up.

But this Golden Age, if a fair reflection of childhood for some, is unlikely to be a fair reflection of history.

In the extensive gardens of the Palace of Versailles, Marie Antoinette maintained "*le Petit Hameau*," "the Little Hamlet." A mock farm, complete with cows and hens, there she would sometimes withdraw to dress as a shepherdess and play at the simple, happy peasant life.

Korean royalty had a similar setup in their palace, Changdeokgung. It is a universal fantasy.

Alexander Pope wrote in his "Essay on Man" (1734):

> *Lo, the poor Indian! whose untutor'd mind*
> *Sees God in clouds, or hears him in the wind;*
> *His soul proud Science never taught to stray*
> *Far as the solar walk or milky way;*
> *Yet simple Nature to his hope has giv'n,*
> *Behind the cloud-topp'd hill, a humbler heav'n;*
> *Some safer world in depth of woods embrac'd,*
> *Some happier island in the wat'ry waste,*
> *Where slaves once more their native land behold,*
> *No fiends torment, no Christians thirst for gold!*
> *To be, contents his natural desire;*
> *He asks no angel's wing, no seraph's fire:*
> *But thinks, admitted to that equal sky,*
> *His faithful dog shall bear him company.*[886]

Same place, isn't it? Eden; the Golden Age.

In the 18th century, this was the most famous take on the American Indian in all of English literature. And we plainly see here the Noble Savage as already the dominant view, even before the romantics. While Pope, a Catholic, does understand the Indian as lacking vital knowledge, the savage lives in general contentment, "to be" satisfying his "natural desires." Unlike Christians, who "thirst for gold!" So there, Governor Ratcliffe!

This, unfortunately, we know from missionary accounts to be untrue: Mr. Lo Indian was often tormented by fiends, discontented, and valued shiny trinkets. But it fits with the Garden of Eden / Golden Age image.

It also reveals just how condescending the "Noble Savage" idea is toward actual Indians. Innocence is not itself a virtue, any more than ignorance. It is simply a state of never having exercised free will. It more or less amounts to calling Indians stupid.

On French shores in the 18th century, similarly, and importantly for Canadian perceptions, there was Rousseau, the great proponent of the state of nature; and before him, Montaigne. "He [Rousseau] explained that all men when in the state of nature were essentially good, with untainted intuitions and inclinations. But to be civilized was to be corrupted and made unhappy by experiences in society. Gaining knowledge through tuitions enforced unnatural behavior on the natural man and removed him from his more natural, and therefore good, inclinations.... American

Indians, then, became an ultimate example of man uncorrupted and unfettered by civilization, a concept that countered the beliefs surrounding original sin and reinforced that all men were, at their core, good."[887]

One might add Freud to the mix. Civilization, according to Dr. Freud, represses our natural instincts, and repression of our natural instincts causes us to go mad. See *Civilization and Its Discontents*. Therefore—free sex is a moral right. Civilization is the axis of evil.

One can see the allure of the argument quite apart from its possible truthfulness. Everybody, in the abstract, would prefer to follow their instincts. Pleasure is pleasurable. The only problem is everyone else doing likewise. Damn society!

Feminism, too, drinks deep of this joy juice of the Kickapoo: all tradition, all established social norms, are of the evil patriarchy, Pluto, there to oppress women, who represent in contrast unblemished nature. All virginal Indian princesses, all of them. Therefore—free sex is a moral right. Civilization is the axis of evil.

One can see again why church-run residential schools are often chief villain in the piece. They teach original sin! They deny our original innocence! They oppose free sex!

The Indian princess

The epitome of the noble savage is the cult of the Indian princess: Pocahontas, Sacajawea, Tiger Lily, Leonard Cohen's mental image of Kateri Tekakwitha, Land O'Lakes butter's or Mazola corn oil's Indian maiden, and so on and on. The Indian princess is La Belle Dame sans Merci, image of, in the end, the passion of the moment, the eternal child, free love. She is found classically in Kore, Persephone, the maiden daughter of Mother Nature. She is the mad possibility of unbridled instinct, raw sexual passion, emotion without pale reason, including and consummately symbolized by carnal union, without the restraints imposed by polite society. Adam and Eve without the fig leaves, snakes and angels be damned.

The idea that the residential schools were harmful to Indian children is part of the same myth: the schools were, symbolically, the imposition of civilization on these pure children of the woodlands, these vestal Indian maidens. The white man is Pluto, rich, selfish, and cruel; the residential school is his dark realm of Hades, to which the helpless maiden is abducted.

The American as Indian

Now let us pass to the specifically North American Noble Savagist tradition.

The Transcendentalists, American romantics, of course embraced the idea of original innocence. Emerson encouraged all to "seek the Aboriginal Self" in his essay "Self Reliance." "This self supposedly existed inside all men and listened not to the tuitions taught by society, but to the natural instincts of the soul."[888]

Plainly put, Indians have always been venerated in American, Canadian, and European culture, so long as that culture has found itself in a comfortable drawing room, far away from the real frontier. They are not now, and have not been, discriminated against; the usual discrimination has been in their favour.

African Americans for many years wanted nothing so much as an end to segregation, and to fit in to mainstream society. Indians saw the same proposal, offered to themselves, as a demotion.

So, no doubt, would the Queen of England.

If they have nevertheless been at times described as bloodthirsty savages, this can most easily be explained, Occam avers, not by prejudice, but by the fact that they were, at times, bloodthirsty savages.

Here are some savages of the traditional literary sort:

> Slowly the ship comes in, nearer and nearer the little wharf. Now, with a heavy swash of water and a boom, she touches; out jump her sailors to fasten her ropes.
>
> But hark! what noise is that? It is the Indian war-whoop. And see! down rush the Indians themselves, yelling and brandishing their tomahawks. In an instant they have boarded the vessel. Down into the hold they go, yelling and whooping at every step.
>
> The terrified sailors stand back aghast. Out they come again, lugging with them their heavy chests of tea.
>
> Still they yell and whoop; and over go the chests into the dark water below.
>
> And now, when every chest is gone, suddenly the Indians grow very quiet; they come off from the deck; and, orderly, take their stand upon the wharf; then do we see that they were not Indians at all. They were only men of Boston disguised.[889]

Sound familiar? Recognize the scene?

Many of us have heard the tale, of the first stirrings of the American War of Independence.

But did you ever wonder why the disaffected colonials dressed up as Indians?

For the same reason the Cleveland baseball team does.

Americans in general, and Canadians as much, far from seeing the Indians as despicable others, have always identified with them. True or not, almost everyone's family believes they have Indian blood. The Europeans were the bad guys. As for us colonials, nobody here but us innocent, freedom-loving Indians. At least in some part of our still-girlish hearts.

"The Mohawk image," Donald Grinde and Bruce Johansen conclude in their book *Exemplar of Liberty: Native America and the Evolution of Democracy*, "was emerging as a revolutionary symbol of liberty in the new land, long before Uncle Sam came along. The resort to Indian guise was not seen only in Boston, but at similar protests up and down the Atlantic coast. One unit of the Sons of Liberty called themselves the 'Mohawk River Indians.'" Mock Indians burned the British ship *Gaspee* in June of 1772. Some anti-British proclamations distributed by the patriotic groups were signed "The Mohawks."[890]

Notice the eagle on the Great Seal of the United States—arguably an Indian symbol. And note the arrows he holds in his left talon. Are they Indian inspired? Why not a sword?

I don't know: flip a coin.

Wait—isn't that an old Indian-head penny? No, my mistake. It's an Indian-head nickel. Right where, in monarchies, the queen's or king's head would appear.

Visiting the fledgling United States in the 1820s, Englishman John West had the term "Yankee" explained to him. The Americans believed it was the name of a tribe of Indians "who were overcome by the first settlers, to whom the vanquished chief gave the name, that it might not become extinct."[891] Americans, in other words, were the heirs of the Indians.

The etymology is probably wrong; but the myth was and remains strong.

In October 1988, the US Congress passed *Concurrent Resolution 331*, to formally recognize the influence of the Iroquois Constitution (the Great Law of Peace) upon the American Constitution and Bill of Rights. This seems dubious; if you read accounts of the (oral) Iroquois constitution, it is hard to see anything that resembles the US Constitution. But it is something everyone wants to believe. It makes Americans, again, the heirs of the Indians.

With this perhaps comes American "freedom," freedom from the commands of Keats's pale kings and princes, from the stodgy baggage of the "Old World." The British are the oppressively moral bourgeois, the Americans the free and noble savages.

Canadians, of course, demur. North of 49 Americans are seen as Americans see Europeans. Canadians are the true inheritors of the Indians. Were we not the *coureurs du bois* who lived among the tribes? Were we not the allies of Tecumseh and Brant? Did we not give sanctuary to Sitting Bull? If we live in the West, was not Louis Riel our founder? If we live in Quebec, did we not grow up adoring the Indian maiden Kateri Tekakwitha?

The founding myth

There are two great American founding myths. Both involve native people. One is the story of the first Thanksgiving, of concord between the new settlers and the native people, the natives passing on their wisdom to their spiritual successors.

The other is the story of Pocahontas.

Here it is as related in a 19th century children's history book:

> Two large stones were placed in front of Powhatan and Smith was pinioned, dragged to the stones, and his head placed upon them, while the warriors who were to carry out the sentence brandished their clubs for the fatal blow. One of the daughters of Powhatan, named Matoa, or Pocahontas, sixteen or eighteen years old, sprang from her father's side, clasped Smith in her arms, and laid her head upon his. Powhatan, savage as he was, and full of anger against the English, melted at the sight. He ordered that the prisoner should be released, and sent him with a message of friendship to Jamestown.[892]

And from the early 20th century, another version:

> The prisoner's arms were tied behind him. His head was laid on the stone. An Indian brave stood ready with his war club. The club was raised to strike. A scream was heard, and in rushed Pocahontas and threw herself on the captive.
>
> "Kill me," she cried, "kill me, but you shall not kill him."
>
> The Indian did not dare to strike. He would have killed his chief's beloved daughter. The heart of the Indian chief was touched. Of all his children, he loved her best.[893]

There is slim evidence that the scene actually happened. If it did, Pocahontas must not have been more than 10 or 12 years old, making a romantic attachment rather unsightly. But it is cherished, because it says something important about the natural man, or natural woman: that she is innately good, that her most basic instinct is love. And that she promises good, spontaneous, unfettered sex. Trouble only comes with growing up. Those meddlesome adults!

We want that to be true. It reflects well on all of us. The archetype of the Indian princess, the Pocahontas myth, keeps our hope alive.

Ever since the time of John Smith, it has been a mark of nobility in Virginia to claim descent from Pocahontas. Charles Dudley Warner, in 1881, writes of "the natural pride of the descendants of this dusky princess who have been ennobled by the smallest rivulet of her red blood."[894] Two American first ladies claim such ancestry: Edith (Woodrow) Wilson and Nancy Reagan.

In North America, in short, to be Indian is to be of noble lineage. Johnny Cash and Jessica Alba were publicly disappointed to discover they had no Indian ancestry, contrary to their family traditions. Elvis always believed he did. Elizabeth Warren knows she does, because she has high cheekbones.

There is a third American foundation myth. Less well known, perhaps, but much like the other two. It is the story of the Lost Roanoke Colony, and Virginia Dare. Dare was in one sense the original American—the first "white" child born on US soil. She disappeared, with the rest of her colony, in one of history's great mysteries. The persistent tradition, however, is that she was adopted by the Indians, and became—of course—an Indian princess.

In Canada, this desire for an Indian identity has been expressed recently by John Ralston Saul's essays arguing that Canada is a "Métis nation." As a result of this heritage, "Canada's founding rationale and ongoing purpose in the world is to serve as a bulwark against the American steamroller of technology, capitalism and individualism."[895]

We hosers are the Noble Savages; the Americans represent the evils of plutocracy. Saul argues that the "single greatest failure of the Canadian experiment, so far, has been our inability to normalize—that is, to internalize consciously—the First Nations as the senior founding pillar of our civilization." To Saul, "single-payer health care, environmental protectionism, peacekeeping, soft power diplomacy, even the egalitarian elements of the Charter of Rights and Freedoms—these all ... bear the unmistakable stamp of aboriginal ideas and influences." All the virtues of the Canadian personality are owed to the country's Métis character; our "desire for harmony and balance, our preference for diversity, inclusion and complexity, our renewed interest in egalitarianism—all are emanations of our aboriginal soul."[896]

Remarkable how like the Americans we are, then. Odd, though, that we evolved to so many opposite conclusions based our shared Indian heritage. To Americans, being Indian means individualism and personal freedom. To Saul, it means communitarianism, and keeping everyone equal.

Put an Indian face on it, and any ideology at all sounds nobler.

Sacajawea is another American legend of the aboriginal princess. She gets to be on the dollar coin, after all, like the Queen; although she is of course not the first Indian to feature on the coinage. She is credited with guiding Lewis and Clark to the Pacific.

This is probably not true. According to the expedition's records, she gave directions in only a few cases. Her principal value to the expedition was apparently her mere presence, because it suggested to the various native groups the peaceful intent of the expedition.

Nevertheless, her part has been lionized because it fits with the desired American archetype of the good and wise Indian princess, especially as a founder figure.

The literary Indian

The Noble Savage and the Indian princess myth continue to play out through American literature.

The American Indian was, notes Lacy Cotton, idealized in this fashion "most notably in literature during the nineteenth century, including in James Fenimore Cooper's *Leatherstocking Tales*, with its noble descriptions of chief Chingachgook and his son Uncas, Herman Melville's *Moby Dick*, featuring Queequeg, and Daniel Defoe's *Robinson Crusoe* [*sic*—not of the 19th century], containing Crusoe's companion, Friday."[897]

Not to mention Chief Bromden in *One Flew over the Cuckoo's Nest*, Chief Dan George in *Little Big Man*, or Nobody in the Jarmusch film *Dead Man*. Magic Indians are everywhere.

The first American bestseller had an Indian in its title: James Fenimore Cooper's *Last of the Mohicans*, 1826. And the eponymous Indian was certainly of the Noble Savage tribe—literally a noble in Indian terms, the son of a chief and last of his line.

"Uncas ... clearly demonstrates a noble and chivalrous nature toward Cora Munro, his unrequited love," writes William Starna. "He dies stoically and with honor at the hands of Magua after Cora is killed by another Huron."[898]

Nor is *Last of the Mohicans* Cooper's only depiction of savage nobility. "James Fenimore Cooper was well known," writes Lacy Cotton, "for his sympathetic opinion of Native Americans in his writing."[899]

> Cooper's *The Pioneers* (1823), ... is set in the twilight of rural 18th century central New York where the frontier has now moved West beyond them; the beautiful wilderness replaced by orderly farms. Cooper's "civilization," however, is prone to irrational, sinful destruction of nature. The townsfolk's slaughter of the wild animals is well beyond any safety or economic justification. In one scene, the hero character of Natty Bumppo, whose legendary wilderness skills and attitudes were honed through his intimate contact with nature and Indians, is appalled at their employment of a cannon to bring down a massive flock of migrating pigeons. Bumppo criticizes the "wasty ways" of so-called civilization and says it's a sin to kill more than one can eat. Meanwhile, the noble Indians struggle to understand and accept the "order" imposed on them in the form of strict hunting laws.[900]

Unlike his hero Natty Bumppo, Cooper had little intimate contact with nature or Indians. "[T]he closest Cooper ever got to the vanishing wilderness was Scarsdale."[901] This no doubt helped his characterization immeasurably.

> Chingachgook is first introduced (in the arrangement of the book order) in *The Deerslayer* (1841) as Natty Bumppo's traveling companion and adopted brother. His presence is representative of nature, and natural living, and he is often contrasted against the actions of other white characters like Harry March. One of the most poignant scenes in the novel takes place in chapter thirty-two, where Natty Bumppo stands between two trails, that to the garrison, and that to the village of the Delawares. Waiting in one direction are Chingachgook and Hist-Oh!-Hist, and in the other, Judith, Captain Warley, and the settlement troops. Natty Bumppo is faced with the choice of moving on into the wilderness with the Indians or devoting himself to Judith and leading a domestic, civilized life with her. Ultimately, he chooses to go with Chingachgook and Hist-Oh!-Hist, metaphorically rejecting white civilization and choosing the life of the Noble Savage for himself as well.[902]

This is the mother road, the Main Street of America, Frost's road less travelled, which forever leads to the frontier. The "Last Mohican" of the book title may not actually be Uncas. For Natty Bumppo too is a Mohican, and survives him. He is Uncas's adopted uncle, Chingachgook's adopted brother, and he has symbolically chosen the Indian way. The "Last of the Mohicans," the heir to the Indian line, may be understood to be the American frontiersman. The cowboy. Indianness is the ultimate Americanness.

The Noble Savage has thus remained at the noble and savage heart of American literature.

In 1826, actor Edwin Forrest took out an advertisement in the *New York Critic* newspaper offering $500 "to the author of the best tragedy, in five acts, of which the hero … shall be an aboriginal of this country." The winner was *Metamora; or the Last of the Wampanoags*. It became the first American stage sensation. Broadway began here.

Down in Greenwich Village, Washington Irving was another loyal acolyte of the Noble Savage. In "Traits of Indian Character," 1819-20, he wrote,

> The current opinion of the Indian character …. is too apt to be formed from the miserable hordes which infest the frontiers and hang on the skirts of the settlements. These are too commonly composed of degenerate beings, corrupted and enfeebled by the vices of society without being benefited by its civilization…. Poverty, repining and hopeless poverty, a canker of the mind unknown in savage life, corrodes their spirits and blights every free and noble quality of their natures.[903]

Noble—nature. Note the automatic juxtaposition. Of course, there can be no poverty in nature.

"How different was their state," he continues,

> … while yet the undisputed lords of the soil! Their wants were few, and the means of gratification within their reach. They saw everyone around them sharing the same lot, enduring the same hardships, feeding on the same aliments, arrayed in the same rude garments. No roof then rose but was open to the homeless stranger; no smoke curled among the trees but he was welcome to sit down by its fire and join the hunter in his repast. "For," says an old historian of New England, "their life is so void of care, and they are so loving also that they make use of those things they enjoy as common goods, and are therein so compassionate that rather than one should starve through want, they would starve all; thus they pass their time merrily, not regarding our pomp,

> but are better content with their own, which some men esteem so meanly of." Such were the Indians while in the pride and energy of their primitive natures they resembled those wild plants which thrive best in the shades of the forest but shrink from the hand of cultivation and perish beneath the influence of the sun.[904]

Cruel civilization crushes these innocent wild blossoms of the forest.

Irving presents this, even in 1819, as the modern revisionist view of the Indians. Yet he is able to quote the same view already from an "old historian." Being a new and revolutionary view is part of the myth, not the reality. But neither Irving nor his original source in old New England, I warrant, lived near any actual Indians following the tribal life. They were not common even in those days in either Manhattan or Cambridge.

In a sense, however, Irving is right; the period not long before his own was dominated by the "captivity narrative," which usually told of Indian cruelty to European captives. But there is a crucial difference: captivity narratives at least claimed to be non-fiction. The authors of the original captivity narratives were supposedly writing from personal experience. Irving's Indians were literary inventions, known only from books; and literary Indians have always been noble.

There was also a backlash to Irving's and Cooper's depiction of the Native American. Some then, living beyond the Alleghenies, still had knowledge of real Indians outside the settled pale. The vanguard of this backlash was the less-well-remembered novel *Nick of the Woods*, published by Robert Bird in in 1837. Its Indians were more savage than noble, at least in the eyes of Bird's protagonist.

However, this was not an established literary convention of the time: rather, according to his preface, Bird wrote the book specifically in rebuttal of Cooper.

"At the period when *Nick of the Woods* was written," Bird explains,

> … the genius of Chateaubriand and of Cooper had thrown a poetical illusion over the Indian character; and the red men were presented—almost stereotyped in the popular mind—as the embodiments of grand and tender sentiment—a new style of the beau-ideal—brave, gentle, loving, refined, honourable, romantic personages—nature's nobles, the chivalry of the forest.[905]

Bird did not wish to malign Indians, he says, but simply to paint a more realistic portrait.

> It may be submitted that such are not the lineaments of the race—that they never were the lineaments of any race existing in an uncivilised state—indeed, could not be—and that such conceptions as Atala and Uncas are beautiful unrealities and fictions merely, as imaginary and contrary to nature as the shepherd swains of the old pastoral school of rhyme and romance; at all events, that one does not find beings of this class, or any thing in the slightest degree resembling them, among the tribes now known to travellers and legislators.[906]

"The Indian is doubtless a gentleman," Bird continues;

> ... but he is a gentleman who wears a very dirty shirt, and lives a very miserable life, having nothing to employ him or keep him alive except the pleasures of the chase and of the scalp-hunt—which we dignify with the name of war. The writer [Bird himself] differed from his critical friends, and from many philanthropists, in believing the Indian to be capable—perfectly capable, where restraint assists the work of friendly instruction—of civilisation: the Choctaws and Cherokees, and the ancient Mexicans and Peruvians, prove it; but, in his natural barbaric state, he is a barbarian—and it is not possible he could be anything else. The purposes of the author, in his book, confined him to real Indians. He drew them as, in his judgment, they existed—and as, according to all observation, they still exist wherever not softened by cultivation,—ignorant, violent, debased, brutal; he drew them, too, as they appeared, and still appear, in war—or the scalp-hunt—when all the worst deformities of the savage temperament receive their strongest and fiercest development.[907]

Bird, note, says he does not believe that Indians are inferior or depraved. They simply behaved as their unfortunate condition, a war of all against all, required of them. It is the romantics, he insists, who see Indians as inferior, as bestial.

Bird was condemned for this assertion and this depiction at the time, and has been condemned for it ever since. This may be why he is less well remembered than Irving or Cooper.

His preface goes on to say:

> Having, therefore, no other, and certainly no worse, desire than to make his delineations in this regard as correct and true to nature as he could, it was with no little surprise he [the author, Bird] found himself taken to account by some of

> the critical gentry, on the charge of entertaining the inhumane design of influencing the passions of his countrymen against the remnant of an unfortunate race, with a view of excusing the wrongs done to it by the whites, if not of actually hastening the period of that "final destruction" which it pleases so many men, against all probability, if not against all possibility, to predict as a certain future event.[908]

This prediction of the Indian's inevitable disappearance, of course, has not come to pass: Bird, not Cooper or Irving, has proven prescient here. The idea of the extinction of the Indian is a part of the Noble Savage myth. Eden and the Golden Age, like childhood, must by their nature be lost forever in order to be truly romantic and real to the imagination; just as Swift's Lilliput or Brobdingnag or Barrie's Never Never Land must not be found on any conventional maps. The Noble Savagists cannot, in the end, as Bird rightly saw, allow the Indian into the modern world. Indians must forever be picturesquely dying, or already dead.

This is a vital reason why, for the sake of real Indians, we must all become aware of the Noble Savage myth. It sounds flattering, but it is not good for Indians.

Bird does not say that Indians are evil, but he draws a portrait of a fictional protagonist who does. A not-uncommon sentiment, Bird maintains, among those who had dealt with real wild Indians before the cruel influence of civilization blasted these innocent forest flowers.

"No one conversant with the history of border affairs," Bird writes,

> … can fail to recollect some one or more instances of solitary men, bereaved fathers or orphaned sons, the sole survivors, sometimes, of exterminated households, who remained only to devote themselves to lives of vengeance; and "Indian-hating" (which implied the fullest indulgence of a rancorous animosity no blood could appease) was so far from being an uncommon passion in some particular districts, that it was thought to have infected, occasionally, persons, otherwise of good repute, who ranged the woods, intent on private adventures, which they were careful to conceal from the public eye.[909]

"The author remembers," said author continues,

> … in the published journal of an old traveller … who visited the region of the upper Ohio towards the close of the last century [the 18th], an observation on this subject, which made too deep an impression to be easily forgotten. It was stated, as the consequence of the Indian atrocities, that such

> were the extent and depth of the vindictive feeling throughout the community, that it was suspected in some cases to have reached men whose faith was opposed to warfare and bloodshed.[910]

Nevertheless, his seems to have been a rare and futile kick against the pricks already by the early 19th century.

Like the first really popular American play, and the first really popular American novel, the first musical score published in America was about Indians, and presented from the Indian perspective: "The Death Song of an Indian Chief," released in March 1791 in the *Massachusetts Magazine*.[911]

It was always the proper business of Indians to be romantically dying.

"Romanticizing the Indian dominated western fiction and poetry between 1800 and 1830," writes Lacy Cotton. "Titles such as *Frontier Maid; or, the Fall of Wyoming* (1819); *Logan, an Indian Tale* (1821); *The Land of Powhatten* (1821); and *Ontwa, Son of the Forest* (1822), all portrayed dramatically idealized Indians that fit into the Noble Savage definition..... By 1830 the theater was dominated by 'Indian' plays, that heavily featured the Noble Savage motif.... [O]n stage in 1893 was Belasco and Fyles's play, 'The Girl I Left Behind Me,' which victimized [*sic*] innocent Indians at the hands of corrupt white culture."[912]

More accurately stated, it portrayed Indians as victimized by corrupt white culture.

So too in Canada. Adam Kidd, in 1830 Montreal, published the long poem "The Huron Chief," including the lines

> *Undisturbed as the wild deer that strays o'er the mountain,*
> *Or lily that sleeps in its calm liquid bed,*
> *In that arbour of green, by the gush of the fountain,*
> *Oft, oft has my Huron there pillowed his head.*
> *But the hand of the white man has brought desolation—*[913]

Duncan Campbell Scott, Confederation poet, is often criticized for showing traditional Indian life as harsh; he was with the Bureau of Indian Affairs, and knew something of real Indians. Nevertheless, his poetry also shows elements of the Noble Savage myth. In "On the Way to the Mission," he tells the story of a lone Indian shot dead by Europeans, the "whitemen servants of greed," in order to steal his sled-load of furs.

And then there are Grey Owl, Pauline Johnson, and Emily Carr, aka "Klee Wyck." Johnson declared herself a native princess, and recited in stage-Indian dress. Farley Mowat made his literary reputation with *People of the Deer* (1952), about the

Eskimo/Inuit. It was sympathetic to the native people, critical of the government, the Hudson's Bay Company, and Western civilization generally. "It's the story," explains Craig MacBride in the *Toronto Review of Books*, "of white people disrupting and ruining Indigenous culture."[914] Highly marketable. Unfortunately, charges are that Mowat made most of his stuff up. "Mowat came under tremendous fire from the Federal Government who disputed Mowat's accuracy on a grand scale," writes David Towler. Mowat's response was, "It matters little whether things happened as they are said to have happened.... Never let the facts stand in the way of the truth"[915]

In Canada, claiming to be Indian or an adopted Indian has always been a good career move in the arts.

In 1911, the *Dallas Morning News* and the Associated Press favourably reviewed a book of that year, titled *The Indian Book*, by William John-Hopkins. AP praises it for its "multi-layered view of the Mandan Indians," saying that "the author makes the simple life of these primitive people vividly human, and the child forms a sympathetic and humane conception of this vanishing race, altogether different from his usual picture of the paint-daubed scalper."[916]

But this "usual picture" of a "paint-daubed scalper" seems always to have been unusual. The vanishing race living at peace with nature is the literary norm.

Pop goes the Indian

Without citing evidence, the "TV Tropes" web site (tvtropes.org), explains that "[i]n the era of the 'Revisionist Western' [the era in which we now live], fiction often attempts to provide a more diverse and historically accurate view of violence by and against Native Americans." The prior norm, however, was supposedly ahistorically anti-Indian. Clarence Lowrey writes, in 1960, "the entertainment industry pictures Indians as savage, dirty, uncultured and, sometimes, inhuman."[917]

"When film was invented," explains Charalambos Vrasidas, "Native Americans were shown on screen, riding horses, screaming, killing, and scalping people."[918]

"One of the main problems with the earlier Westerns," agrees a movie site, "is that they painted the Native Americans into the stereotypical savage who was only out to rape, pillage, and murder the white man."[919] "Before the movies added sound," this account continues, "Native Americans in films ... were always shown with scowls, while wearing war paint, showing that they were ready to kill at any time, or that they were less than the whites and that the Indians had need to be helped with everything having to do with the white way of life."

Hmm. Does that sound like Tonto as you remember him?

And didn't we all grow up not just with the righteous Tonto, and Pocahontas, and the Pilgrims and the friendly Indians sharing the first Thanksgiving, and Sacajawea guiding Lewis and Clark across the continent, but also with Tiger Lily, Indian princess, the true and loyal friend to Peter Pan? And, if of a certain unspeakable age, with Princess Summerfall Winterspring and Chief Thunderthud on the Howdy Doody Show?

How bloodthirsty was all that?

Throughout the 19th and into the 20th centuries, one of the most popular forms of entertainment throughout North America was the medicine show. Indians here too were shown to the rubes in an entirely favourable light. The success of the enterprise depended, after all, on the general prejudice that Indians could not dissemble. "The Noble Savage's determining features," notes Cotton in another context, "included a harmony with nature coupled with a moral innocence and inability to lie."[920] Accordingly, if they said a patent medicine worked, it must work.

Were little white children once taught to see the Indians as bloodthirsty savages? Here is how an Ontario schoolbook of 1879 introduces them: "They were bold and cunning, generous to their friends, but bitterly revengeful to their foes." Just like fairies. "There were, however, some great chiefs among them, who were noted for their love of the people, their honesty, and their kindness to enemies."[921]

Said chiefs are not identified; we are left to speculate. Perhaps they mean Tecumseh, described in another Canadian schoolbook as "a brave Indian who helped the Canadians to fight against their enemies. He was ... tall and very handsome ... very brave and very wise."[922]

The same book instructs kids in how to play Indian games, and how to make their own war bonnet out of chicken feathers.

Of course, Canadian kids did once play that notoriously racist old game of cowboys and Indians. But consider: in order for it to work, roughly half of the tykes must have wanted to be Indians.

The first dime novel ever was *Malaeska, the Indian Wife of a White Hunter* (1860). Its vision of Indian life, as first presented to the reader, is romantic enough:

> … wigwams might be seen through a vista in the wood. One or two were built even on the edge of the clearing; the grass was much trampled around them, and three or four half-naked Indian children lay rolling upon it, laughing, shouting,

> and flinging up their limbs in the pleasant morning air. One young Indian woman was also frolicking among them, tossing an infant in her arms, caroling and playing with it. Her laugh was musical as a bird song, and as she darted to and fro, now into the forest and then out into the sunshine, her long hair glowed like the wing of a raven, and her motion was graceful as an untamed gazelle. They could see that the child, too, was very beautiful, even from the distance.[923]

Like a bird, or an untamed gazelle: Malaeska is the familiar innocent and good-hearted Indian princess, an imagined avatar of the purity of nature. "[H]er untutored heart, rich in its natural affections, had no aim, no object, but what centered in the love she bore her white husband. The feelings which in civilized life are scattered over a thousand objects, were, in her bosom, centered in one single being; he supplied the place of all the high aspirations—of all the passions and sentiments which are fostered into strength by society."[924] Pure of heart, in other words; but, as the story progresses, tragically ruined by contact with the evil Europeans and their civilized ways.

The same motif is reprised in *The Frontier Angel* (1861), its topic an Indian maiden's "suffering and devotion." This was followed by *King Barnaby or The Maidens of the Forest: A Romance of the Micmacs* (1861). *Oonomoo the Huron* appeared in 1862, plus a romance, *Ahmo's Plot, or The Governor's Indian Child*, based on the premise that Count Frontenac took an Indian wife; the daughter, of course, of a chief, an Indian princess. *Laughing Eyes*, in 1863, reverses the stock situation: it has a European woman falling in love with an Indian prince. *Mahaska, the Indian Princess* (1863) relates the further adventures of Frontenac's half-Indian daughter, her mother having died "of a broken heart, as we see forest birds perish in their cages."

Obviously, the fallout from the residential schools was not the first time we conceived the idea that exposure to European civilization was harmful to native people.

The Indian Princess was followed, logically enough, by *The Indian Queen*, supposedly the story of Mahaska become the Queen of the Seneca. In 1869, *Border Avengers, or The White Prophetess of the Delawares*, announced an upcoming series on *Wenona, the Giant Chief of St. Regis*, including *Silent Slayer, or The Maid of Montreal*, and *Despard the Spy, or the Fall of Montreal.* Despard, a European, was the villain. Wenona, a Mohawk, was of course the hero.

Over time, the frontier of romance, to remain plausible, had to shuffle west. *The Lone Chief or the Trappers of the Saskatchewan* (1873) tells of Chief Blackbird. It is a tale that "awakens our warmest admiration"; its heroine a "strangely beautiful" Cree girl. This was soon followed by *Old Bear Paw the Trapper King, or The Love of a*

Blackfoot Queen.

Indian princesses apparently everywhere populated the West. Assuredly, if you live west of the Lake of the Isles, you are descended from one.

Cowboys and Indians

Cowboys jumped to dime novels from the Wild West Show, as a new character who might be of interest to the same audience who enjoyed reading about Indians. And the Wild West Show itself, as popular entertainment, followed more or less the same evolution. The first Wild West shows, organized by artist George Catlin to tour the United States and Europe, featured only Indians. Buffalo Bill Cody had the idea of adding "cowboys," Europeans who lived on the frontier and adopted Indian ways. While the Indians were spectacle enough in themselves, by doing this, he could add displays of trick shooting, horsemanship, roping, and other talents more readily found among the pool of European-Americans. Visiting Europe, the "cowboys" made a show of sleeping outdoors, as did the Indian performers. They were, after all, children of nature.

In 1887, Henry Nash Smith, Beadle Dime Novels editor, hit upon the idea of the cowboy hero to augment the traditional Indian. He published a fictionalized biography of the real star of Buffalo Bill's Wild West Show, Buck Taylor (William Levi Taylor). The literary Taylor, the first cowboy, reveals his true lineage in his origin story: he is captured by the Comanches, then freed by an Indian friend. He is thus born again as an adopted Indian, in the mold of Natty Bumppo.

Contrary to pop culture history, the fictional cowboy was never the enemy of the Indian. He was his cultural brother. For both of them, the natural enemy was the settler. Both literary stock characters stood for freedom against encroaching settlement, which is to say, civilization. Both were noble, with their supposed unwritten codes of honour. Both were nomadic. Both must be understood, following the Eden convention, as citizens of the lost golden age, always riding off into the sunset, the last of their kind, or even already extinct; beings of a more perfect past of the imagination.

The Old West is dead; and it always was. Innocence by its nature, like virginity, like childhood, must always be under dire threat; and one is only aware of it once one has lost it. We grow up. Damn.

The Indian and the cowboy, therefore, are brothers in arms, like Uncas and Natty Bumppo, like Tonto and the Lone Ranger, like McMurphy and Chief Bromden, like Nobody and William Blake. If cowboys sometimes fought with Indians too, this was the Indian way. Cowboys also fought with cowboys, and Indians fought with Indians. It was the logic of the free life beyond the policeman's beat and the long arm's reach; and it was, in fictional form, as much fun as any Tom and Jerry cartoon.

The Western genre truly came into its own with the book-length yarns of Zane Grey. And, like his predecessors, Grey was a faithful fan of the Noble Savage. "His respectful treatment of Indians," boasts the Zane Grey's West Society web page (http://www.zgws.org/), "was ahead of its time."

Yep. Always was, always is, always will be.

"In his 1910 novel, *Heritage of the Desert*," writes Lacy Cotton, "Grey idealizes the Navajo people, particularly the Chief Eschtah."[925] "Grey represents the Indians as noble, handsome, and dignified."[926] The book, Grey's first Western, also features a half-Indian maiden as love interest. She is the granddaughter of the chief—an Indian princess.

Grey later wrote *The Vanishing American*, obviously sympathetic to the eternally dying Indians. Indeed, Grey claimed Indian ancestry, and his byline often included the phrase "the blood of Indian chiefs flows in his veins."

The Vanishing American was later made into what may have been the first Technicolor movie.

The Vanishing American features "lecherous and greedy ministers" who "oppose noble and good Indians that honor the nation by participating in World War I."[927] "This pattern of victimizing [*sic*—Cotton again means portraying him as a victim] the Noble Savage continues in Grey's novel, *The Rainbow Trail* (1915). In this story, yet another Indian maiden, named Glen Naspa, is seduced and assaulted by a white missionary."[928]

Sound familiar? The missionary is the inevitable stage villain in the Noble Savage saga; because he introduces the concept of sin.

In the same novel, "Shefford ... discovers [an] Indian woman in her home, having died in childbirth, and his guilt over the tragedy leads him to feel something of the white man's burden of crime toward the Indian weighing upon his soul."[929] "Grey," Cotton adds, "was not the only author to use this method of victimizing [*sic*] an Indian woman and orchestrating her death as a metaphor for the ruthless cruelty of white culture."[930]

"The roots of this imagery," Cotton goes on, "can be traced back as far as the 1890s, when David Belasco and Franklin Fyles wrote the play 'The Girl I Left

Behind Me.' This story of an Indian uprising involves a maiden named Fawn Afraid, whose involvement with white culture ultimately leads to her death."[931]

"Fawn Afraid"?

But Cotton is wrong here. The imagery of the innocent Indian maiden being destroyed by contact with white culture is not from some one play in the 19th century. It is an essential element of the Indian princess myth, going back to Kore/Persephone. We have already seen it many times.

The popularity of the cowboy has, of course, spread beyond North America. When the Americans occupied Germany after World War II, they were amused to find the Germans too wrapped up in the romance of the old frontier—as they remain today.

This is largely due to Karl May, probably the most popular novelist in the German language, who specialized in "Western" stories.

On May's frontier, as in the early dime novels, the central hero is an Indian, not a cowboy: Minnetou, the "wise chief of the Apaches." "Old Shatterhand," the cowboy, is, like Bumppo or the Lone Ranger, his "blood brother."

According to Anthony Grafton, writing in the *New Republic*, May always depicted Native Americans as "innocent victims of white law-breakers." May had much that was unflattering to say about Jews, Irish, Chinese, blacks, and Armenians; but never about Native Americans.

Why were Indians special?

"His readers longed to escape from an industrialized capitalist society," posits Grafton, "an escape which May offered."[932] The Noble Savage, again. A poor man's Petit Hameau.

Karl May and his Western yarns were special favourites of Adolf Hitler. "Hitler ... recommended the books to his generals and had special editions distributed to soldiers at the front, praising Winnetou as an example of 'tactical finesse and circumspection.'"[933] "The fate of Native Americans in the United States was used during the world wars for anti-American propaganda," writes Frederic Morton in the *New York Times*. "The National Socialists in particular tried to use May's popularity and his work for their purposes."[934]

This should not surprise us. The cult of the Noble Savage always had Fascist overtones. Like Nazism, it was a worship of nature and the natural man. Like Nazism, it believed in a mystic oneness of the "volk" with the land and landscape.

As with Nazism, foreigners were a threat. Foreigners were not pure. The evil forces of heterodoxy were easily transferred by the Nazis from May's encroaching European plutocratic civilization to the cosmopolitan, bourgeois Jews.

Germans, of course, were innocent Indians. Just like Americans and Canadians.

The Indian goes Hollywood

What about the movies? What about Hollywood? Surely here, at least, the racist stereotype of the bloodthirsty savage descending on the helpless wagon train ruled unchallenged?

So at least we are often told. "One of the main problems with the earlier Westerns is that they painted the Native Americans into the stereotypical savage who was only out to rape, pillage, and murder the white man."[935] Up until *Little Big Man*, or *Dances with Wolves*, wasn't the story always at the very least told from the point of view of the Europeans?

Anyone is free to believe that. So long as they have never seen a Hollywood Western.

Canadian Sidney Olcott founds the genre with *The Red Man's Way* (1907), the romantic story of Indian princess "Dove Eye," with no European characters.

The Red Man's View, 1909, by D.W. Griffith, is also told from the Indian perspective. According to a review of the time, the film is about "the helpless Indian race as it has been forced to recede before the advancing white, ... full of poetic sentiment."[936]

The full film is available for view at the Internet Archive.[937]

White people are the villains, and D.W. Griffith is rarely subtle about such things. They repeatedly drive the Indians off their land. And, of course, abduct a defenceless Indian princess.

The year 1910 also brought *White Fawn's Devotion*, by Indian director James Young Deer, with an almost entirely Indian cast, "in which the Indian wife White Fawn rescues her white husband from certain death by throwing herself over him."[938]

Sound familiar?

Olcott's 1910 efforts included *Her Indian Mother*, and *White Man's Money, The Red Man's Curse*, a story of "[t]he influence of the white upon the redskins."[939] As usual, all evil enters creation with the coming of civilization.

A classic treatment of the prototypical Pocahontas also appeared in 1910, and a second version in 1911. In 1912 came *The Heart of an Indian Maiden*[940] and *The Invaders*[941]—said invaders, of course, being Europeans. In the latter film, according to *IMDB*, "the U.S. Army and the Indians sign a peace treaty. However, a group of surveyors trespass on the Indians' land and violate the treaty. The army refuses to listen to the Indians' complaints, and the surveyors are killed by the Indians." *Internet Archive* describes it as "[a] relatively sensitive story of a broken treaty between Native American tribes and the US by encroaching railroad men."

Also in 1912 came D.W. Griffith's *A Temporary Truce*: "three malicious drunks have just killed an Indian, solely to amuse themselves. When Jim abducts the prospector's wife, and takes her to a remote place, he soon afterwards encounters a party of angry braves seeking revenge."[942]

Yes, you see fights between cowboys and Indians—but the cowboys are always at fault.

D.W. Griffith's *The Battle of Elderbush Gulch* (1913)[943] is sometimes cited as an example of the "bloodthirsty savage" sort of Indian. But the Indians' offence in the film is not great. Hungry, and not realizing this is taboo among whites, they try to eat a couple of dogs, and are shot dead for it. A battle ensues.

Who here is being portrayed as bloodthirsty?

One might expect that a film called *The Indian Wars Refought* (1914), filmed with the cooperation of the US government, might offer a more balanced account, if not an outright paean to the US Army.

We will never know. The film was suppressed, says *Wikipedia*, by the US government, and all copies are lost. Reputedly, this was because it turned out to be too pro-Indian and anti-US Army, heading into a period of wartime censorship.[944]

In 1922, Canada produced what is commonly credited as the first feature-length documentary film. That would be *Nanook of the North*, a sympathetic portrayal of the life of an Inuit/Eskimo hunter. Roger Ebert calls it "alone in its stark regard for the courage and ingenuity of its heroes."[945] Another "revisionist" view of aboriginals—as they all are. Nor was this the first Canadian film about the Inuit. The short subject *The Way of the Eskimo* was released in 1910. "The plot was slender, but the scenes portrayed the life of the frozen north with great fidelity and vigour, showing the Eskimo fishing through the ice, and hunting the polar bear and walrus by his primitive methods. A valuable polar bear was sacrificed in the desire for realism."[946]

Buster Keaton anted in in 1922, with a send-up of the genre, *The Paleface*. In the by-now-familiar formula, the Great Western Oil Company has stolen Indian lands, and has ordered the natives to leave. Keaton shows up, is made chief, and leads them in the fight against the evil Europeans. Inevitably, he meets an Indian maiden, marries her, and remains with the tribe.[947]

They Died With Their Boots On (1941) again tells the story of the Indian Wars, culminating in the Battle of Little Big Horn. As always, white men are at fault: "The battle against Chief Crazy Horse is portrayed as a crooked deal between politicians and a corporation that wants the land Custer promised to the Indians." "A letter left behind by Custer, now considered his dying declaration, names the culprits and absolves the Native Americans of all responsibility; Custer has won his final campaign."[948] It has to be so; if the Indians were guilty of anything, it would not be a satisfactory ending to an American audience.

Custer is cast, improbably, as a passionate defender of Native American rights. He tries to send an English soldier away from the last stand, saying that this is an American fight ... "The only real Americans in this merry old parish are on the other side of the hill with feathers in their hair," remarks the Englishman. "You're probably right about that," Custer replies, thoughtfully.[949]

Sitting Bull (1954) was the first Western in CinemaScope, featuring Iron-Eyes Cody as Crazy Horse. Again, it was filmed from the Indian point of view.

> Chief Sitting Bull of the Sioux tribe is forced by the Indian-hating General Custer to react with violence, resulting in the famous Last Stand at Little Bighorn. Parrish [a US cavalry soldier, focus of the story], a friend to the Sioux, tries to prevent the bloodshed, but is court-martialed for "collaborating" with the enemy. Sitting Bull, however, manages to intercede with President Grant on Parrish's behalf.[950]

"When the white man wins," this cinematic Sitting Bull complains, "you call it a victory; when the Indian wins, you call it a massacre."

This is the eternal lament of the Hollywood Indian; but there never seems to have been a prior time during which everyone called the one a victory, or the other a massacre. It is simply part of the Noble Savage myth.

There was nothing new or transgressive about *Dances with Wolves*. It had the same plot, more or less, as every Western ever made.

It is always possible, I suppose, that some day, someone actually will make an anti-

Indian movie. Or write an anti-Indian novel.

If so, it will probably be a scandal.

21 TRUTH AND RECONCILIATION–THE PARODY

Penobscot Indians coming to town.

History repeats itself, first as tragedy, second as farce.

— Karl Marx

Truth and reconciliation: those sound like good things. Who could be against either? Even better, the phrase refers to the successful process in South Africa of getting past the fearsome wounds of apartheid. Who's against Nelson Mandela?

So, if you want to put something over on people, call it truth and reconciliation.

Hey, let's strike a commission!

Confucius once said the chief task of government is making sure words mean what they are supposed to mean. It is too easy and too common to disguise something disreputable through a misuse of words to make it sound good. Virtually any sort of mischief may follow. That is the path to all bad policy.

The first distortion here is to associate the issue of residential schools with the issue covered by the commission of the same name in South Africa. The main thrust of the criticism of the residential schools is that the residential schools were not sufficiently committed to apartheid. They treated Indian children too much like other Canadians. This is a newly invented crime called "cultural genocide."

If apartheid was wrong, if Nelson Mandela and the South African Truth and Reconciliation Commission were right, then the residential schools, to the extent that this charge is true, were a good thing. Justice Sinclair and his commission are defending the views of P.W. Botha and Eugene Terreblanche, of Bull Connor and Orval Faubus, that minorities must be kept apart from the mainstream. Bantustans now, bantustans tomorrow, bantustans forever.

Truth

Then there is the word "truth" in its title.

The Canadian Commission is mostly here to demonize the residential schools. That it would find the residential schools an abomination was a foregone conclusion. It gives its mandate as "a sincere indication and acknowledgment of the injustices and harms experienced by Aboriginal people and the need for continued healing."[951] It is part of the Indian Residential Schools Settlement Agreement. The IRSSA already had declared the residential schools an atrocity. Payouts had begun. What if this more recent commission had found nothing?

As it is, what they found with which to accuse the schools seems tepid.

The Commission does not seem confident that it even knows what the word "truth" means, or whether the word has any fixed meaning. One witness, quoted in the summary report, asks the Commission, "When you talk about truth, whose truth are you talking about?" This is considered by the report "a critical question"—as opposed to a nonsensical one, as if there could be conflicting "truths." This is a tacit assertion that there is no objective truth. The meaning of "truth" seems up for grabs. Perhaps we can each invent our own.

The Commission responds, "by truth, we mean not only the truth revealed in government and church residential school documents, but also the truth of lived experiences as told to us by Survivors and others in their statements to this Commission."[952] It could be worse, I suppose. At least they accept official documents. That constrains them. Elsewhere, they proudly call their view "victim-centered."[953] This presupposes that all charges are true; the case is prejudged in favour of the prosecution.

This is not the way truth is discovered, in, for example, a scientific experiment or a court of law.

Whatever self-declared "survivors" say is to be taken as so. No cross-checking, no cross-examination, and no commitment to hear both sides. By such standards, there is no such thing as a lie.

Nor is lying the only danger. We are dealing here, in witness statements, with childhood memories of long ago. Old memories are unreliable. Children's memories are unreliable. Memories from childhood long ago are doubly unreliable. In a 1995 experiment, Elizabeth Loftis and Jacqueline Pickrell convinced subjects to falsely remember being lost in a mall in childhood.[954] "Since the original demonstration, experimenters have successfully implanted false memories for a wide range of events, including a religious ceremony (Pezdek et al. 1997), a hot air balloon ride (Wade et al. 2002), and a hospitalization (Hyman et al. 1995)."[955]

Some may recall the spate of recovered memories of childhood abuse in the 1980s and 90s, and the widespread "Satanic cult" frenzy. At one point most of the town of Martensville, Saskatchewan, was in the dock for supposed child abuse. Children testified that they had been driven to "the devil's church" in the country where they were forced to drink urine and eat feces. One child claimed that an axe handle had been forced into his penis. Another claimed one adult had cut off a child' s nipple and eaten it.[956]

Soon similar charges arose in Saskatoon:

> The children had stated that the Klassens and many other adults had forced them to consume blood, drink urine, and eat human eyeballs and feces. They were compelled to eat a neighbor's newborn baby who had been skinned, barbecued in the backyard, and buried.... They were forced to engage in sexual acts with both dogs and flying bats.[957]

Sixteen adults were arrested and charged with 70 counts. One pled guilty, in exchange for charges being dropped against others. Three more were convicted.

Two more adults were convicted in Martensville.

And then the belated revelation of "false memory syndrome."

It turns out to be easy to convince people they have memories of childhood events that never happened. It was, after all, on the testimony of children that the famous Salem witches were hanged.

Quite literally, the Truth and Reconciliation Commission is set up as a classic witch hunt.

But never mind. If I believe I am Napoleon, then, I am Napoleon. If I believe I was tortured, then I was tortured. That is my truth.

The reliance on "victim" testimony is probably a backhanded admission by the Commission that the residential schools were not that bad. They almost as much as admit by this selection of evidence that, had they stuck with objective facts and cross-examination, they would have been forced to a politically incorrect conclusion. The absence nevertheless of anything really salacious suggests that the residential schools were actually pretty well run.

Reconciliation

As for "reconciliation," the second claim in their title, the Commission attempted the opposite: its mandate as noted was to stress the damage supposedly done by the residential schools. It is an enterprise almost certain to stir up ill feelings between Indians and "whites." For example, it interviewed self-declared survivors and not, or rarely, those responsible for running the schools. This is an inversion of the methodology of the South African Commission, which interviewed mostly those responsible for apartheid, to hear their side. In return, they were granted immunity.

That would have been the reconciliation part.

The Commission writes:

> We call upon the federal, provincial, territorial, and Aboriginal governments to acknowledge that the current state of Aboriginal health in Canada is a direct result of previous Canadian government policies, including residential schools, and to recognize and implement the health-care rights of Aboriginal people as identified in international law, constitutional law, and under the Treaties.[958]

This is scapegoating. Aboriginal people already get free, and tax-free, health care. The only objective here seems to be to have the government consent to the claim that Indians have been badly treated. The public declaration that it has been so, true or false, then becomes the evidence that it is so.

> We call upon the Parliament of Canada, in consultation and collaboration with Aboriginal peoples, to enact legislation to establish a National Council for Reconciliation. The legislation would establish the council as an independent, national, oversight body with membership jointly appointed by the Government of Canada and national Aboriginal

> organizations, and consisting of Aboriginal and non-Aboriginal members.[959]

Note the significance of a permanent body in charge of reconciliation. Necessarily, this assumes reconciliation would never actually happen.

So what is the point of the exercise?

Its chief role would be to hand out pork to well-heeled buddies:

> We call upon the Government of Canada to provide multi-year funding for the National Council for Reconciliation to ensure that it has the financial, human, and technical resources required to conduct its work, including the endowment of a National Reconciliation Trust to advance the cause of reconciliation.[960]

With this public money, it will "[d]evelop and implement a multi-year National Action Plan for Reconciliation, which includes research and policy development, public education programs, and resources."[961]

Action plan. Great word, "action." Ideal for referring to inaction you want to get paid for.

The Commission insists on seeing Indian groups as fundamentally apart, independently sovereign, not Canadian. That might still be reconciliation, but does not obviously sound like reconciliation. More like an estranged couple still cohabiting. When the Thirteen Colonies to our south demanded independent sovereignty, there was a patch of bad feeling. It was even worse when the Southern states separated from them in 1860. Things were not immediately amicable when Croatia, Bosnia, or Kosovo separated from Yugoslavia, or when Pakistan split from India.

> We call upon the Government of Canada, on behalf of all Canadians, to jointly develop with Aboriginal peoples a Royal Proclamation of Reconciliation to be issued by the Crown. The proclamation would build on the Royal Proclamation of 1763 and the Treaty of Niagara of 1764, and reaffirm the nation-to-nation relationship between Aboriginal peoples and the Crown. The proclamation would include, but not be limited to, ...[962]

The government, representing "all Canadians," is to work jointly with aboriginal peoples, as a separate body, nation to nation. Indians, then, are not Canadians.

Indians probably do have a right to sovereignty in international law. Since the

Treaty of Versailles, we have all endorsed the notion of a right to self-determination of peoples; that is, of racial or ethnic groups. But let's be clear: said sovereignty is not now the case. There is no existing nation-to-nation relationship. The Royal Proclamation of 1763 and the Treaty of Niagara were not, as here claimed, treaties between sovereign nations. The Royal Proclamation made it plain that all sovereignty over North American soil resided in the British Crown, and the Indian bands were the King's subjects. Now, with patriation, sovereignty resides with the Crown in right of Canada. One might say there is a government-to-government relationship, but it is like the relationship between a national and a provincial or municipal government, not a foreign power.

Nevertheless, the Commission inconsistently demands that any and every body they can think of, in and outside Canada, must:

> Repudiate concepts used to justify European sovereignty over Indigenous lands and peoples...[963]

Strictly speaking, this demand is treason.

If Indians want to proclaim sovereignty, as we say, they have that right, but it must be negotiated and follow some agreed legal procedure.

Like Brexit, we could have Creexit, Inuexit, and so on. We could make a new deal acceptable to both sides, if possible. We could let the tribes run their own affairs on their reserves, and lots of luck to them, once they have assumed their share of the national debt and assets.

But they could not then, surely, expect any continuing transfer of monies from Canada to the reserves, in welfare payments, school costs, health costs, the financing of band governments, and so on and so forth. And why then should a Canadian National Council for Reconciliation, or any Canadian tax money, be involved?

Considering the possibility only to dismiss it, the Hawthorn report in 1966 wrote: "Indian bands in Canada, even the largest, are far too limited in population and resources to achieve anything approaching self-sufficiency. Their level of economic development depends essentially on their relationship with, and participation in, the external White-controlled economy."[964] A sovereign reserve would probably quickly starve.

It is also contradictory for the Truth and Reconciliation Commission to, on the one hand, insist on Indian sovereignty and separateness, and on the other, demand more cash from Ottawa to laud and commemorate "the Indian contribution to Canada":

> We call upon the federal, provincial, and territorial governments, in consultation and collaboration with Survivors, Aboriginal peoples, and educators, to: i. Make age-appropriate curriculum on residential schools, Treaties, and Aboriginal peoples' historical and contemporary contributions to Canada a mandatory education requirement for Kindergarten to Grade Twelve students.[965]
>
> … Developing and implementing Kindergarten to Grade Twelve curriculum and learning resources on Aboriginal peoples in Canadian history, and the history and legacy of residential schools.[966]
>
> Revising the policies, criteria, and practices of the National Program of Historical Commemoration to integrate Indigenous history, heritage values, and memory practices into Canada's national heritage and history.[967]
>
> Developing and implementing a national heritage plan and strategy for commemorating residential school sites, the history and legacy of residential schools, and the contributions of Aboriginal peoples to Canada's history.[968]
>
> We call upon the federal government, in collaboration with Aboriginal peoples, and the Canadian Museums Association to mark the 150th anniversary of Canadian Confederation in 2017 by establishing a dedicated national funding program for commemoration projects on the theme of reconciliation.[969]

Nice cake. I wonder if I can eat it now, then save it for later?

There is another logical contradiction here. Why it is that, if the Canadian government teaches Indian children about the majority culture, it is cultural genocide; but if the Indians teach majority children about Indian culture, it is simple justice? Even when at the other guy's expense?

It should be noted here as well that Canadian schoolchildren do currently learn about Indian cultures. "First Nations" is cited 175 times, for example, in the Ontario curriculum guidelines for Social Studies, grades 1-8—almost once per page. Not to mention "Métis" and "Inuit," which are also cited frequently. Indians seem always to have been a popular topic in the schools—far beyond what might be warranted by their proportion of the Canadian population.[970] But apparently we need more of the same.

Indigenous history is also already integrated into the National Program of

Historical Commemoration, probably also in great demographic disproportion to the Indian percentage of the Canadian population. This is the sort of thing that could not continue if the various Indian bands become sovereign nations.

Helping the poor Indians

Another false claim is the implicit one that the Commission is intended for the betterment of aboriginals. It is hard to find anything in the recommendations of the report that unambiguously does that. Rather, the thrust of most of its "calls to action" is to expand government bureaucracy. Whether that is better or worse for Indians is certainly debatable. Many would argue that Canadian Indians have been choking on bureaucracy since roughly 1763.

The commissioners are, in the end, well-paid office workers of the professional class, and they are acting, in the end, toward the betterment of their class, not Indians. They want more power for commissioners, bureaucrats, lawyers, and professionals. This by happenstance includes some aboriginals—the band leaders, for example, who are in effect career bureaucrats.

This begins with getting paid work with the Truth and Reconciliation Commission, which ran for seven years; just a year short of America's participation in Vietnam. Or rather, it began much earlier, with the Royal Commission on Aboriginal People, struck in 1996, leading to the release in 1998 of the federal government's Aboriginal Action Plan, which called for the settlement agreement, which called in turn for the current commission, which now calls for a new commission to be struck, the "National Council for Reconciliation."

A great deal of money spent, over 20 years, on commissions, and with no end in sight. As opposed to, say, giving that money, needed or not, deserved or not, to actual ordinary Indians.

If you say you are giving money to Indians, people think it is a good idea. As we have seen, everyone loves Indians. So let's say it is for the Indians. But it goes to civil servants and professionals.

Helping the poor orphans

Widows and orphans; everyone wants to help widows and orphans too. Say it is for Indian widows and orphans.

From the Commission's "calls to action":

> Requiring that all child-welfare decision makers consider the impact of the residential school experience on children and their caregivers.[971]

> We call upon the federal government to enact Aboriginal child-welfare legislation that establishes national standards for Aboriginal child apprehension and custody cases and includes principles that: ... Require all child-welfare agencies and courts to take the residential school legacy into account in their decision making.[972]

More forms for bureaucrats to jockey; another layer added to the child-welfare bureaucracy. In real terms, tax money taken away from abused children, and put instead in the pockets of bureaucrats.

> We call upon the federal government, in collaboration with the provinces and territories, to prepare and publish annual reports on the number of Aboriginal children … who are in care, compared with non-Aboriginal children, as well as the reasons for apprehension, the total spending on preventive and care services by child-welfare agencies, and the effectiveness of various interventions.[973]

> We call upon the federal, provincial, territorial, and Aboriginal governments to commit to reducing the number of Aboriginal children in care by: … ii. Providing adequate resources to enable Aboriginal communities and child-welfare organizations to keep Aboriginal families together where it is safe to do so, and to keep children in culturally appropriate environments, regardless of where they reside.[974]

> iii. Establish, as an important priority, a requirement that placements of Aboriginal children into temporary and permanent care be culturally appropriate.[975]

Money ostensibly going to orphans again going to bureaucrats. In the meantime, new regulations would ensure that fewer children are adopted, and more orphans stay orphans.

Why is taking children away from their families and putting them in residential schools wrong, yet keeping children in orphanages instead of placing them in a family is right?

Helping the poor children

The Commission report calls for the abolition of the "spanking law":

> We call upon the Government of Canada to repeal Section 43 of the Criminal Code of Canada.[976]

Section 43 allows parents and teachers to administer physical punishment, so long as it is commensurate with the offense:

> Every schoolteacher, parent or person standing in the place of a parent is justified in using force by way of correction toward a pupil or child, as the case may be, who is under his care, if the force does not exceed what is reasonable under the circumstances.

What does this have to do with aboriginals? Nothing—the law applies to all Canadians. One could argue that repeal might benefit all children; it might not. Either way, it is beyond the remit of the Truth and Reconciliation Commission. But its repeal gives lots more power to government and social workers. It gives them the power to seize more children, and subverts the family as a rival authority.

Helping the sick and infirm

From the report's "Calls to Action":

> We call upon the federal government, in consultation with Aboriginal peoples, to establish measurable goals to identify and close the gaps in health outcomes between Aboriginal and non-Aboriginal communities, and to publish annual progress reports and assess longterm trends. Such efforts would focus on indicators such as: infant mortality, maternal health, suicide, mental health, addictions, life expectancy, birth rates, infant and child health issues, chronic diseases, illness and injury incidence, and the availability of appropriate health services.[977]

More pencils pushed across big oak desks, and tax money supposedly going to care of the sick really going to bureaucrats.

The problem here seems obvious: reserve life is unhealthy. So what is this new commission going to study? If we know there is a gap in health outcomes between aboriginals and other Canadians, why do we still need to "identify" it? Perhaps because the real solution, while obvious, is not politically correct, so we must forever strike more commissions to find a new one.

> Ensure the retention of Aboriginal health-care providers in Aboriginal communities.[978]

> We call upon all levels of government to: … Increase the number of Aboriginal professionals working in the health-care field.[979]

Why should it matter to the average aboriginal whether the local dentist is Dene or Danish? That is, unless we are saying that only aboriginal doctors are competent to treat aboriginals. That would imply some radical racial differences.

The only possible excuse for it is as a kind of "affirmative action": racial discrimination in hiring. But this is racial discrimination to favour already highly-paid health-care professionals, at the cost of the ordinary Indian patients needing care. Who, the merit principle being thrown out the window, are no longer getting the best treatment available for the money spent.

Yet even on this basis, of helping well-off Indians, it seems short-sighted. If this demand is sound, this would equally be a good reason for "white" hospitals to refuse to employ Indians, wouldn't it? What could they know about treating Europeans?

Surely such thinking loses aboriginals more opportunities than it gains. There are more jobs in mainstream hospitals than on reserves.

> We call upon the federal government to provide sustainable funding for existing and new Aboriginal healing centres to address the physical, mental, emotional, and spiritual harms caused by residential schools, and to ensure that the funding of healing centres in Nunavut and the Northwest Territories is a priority.
>
> We call upon those who can effect change within the Canadian health-care system to recognize the value of Aboriginal healing practices and use them in the treatment of Aboriginal patients in collaboration with Aboriginal healers and Elders where requested by Aboriginal patients.[980]

If there is good evidence that "Aboriginal healing" works, it is criminal to withhold it from the rest of the population and offer it only to aboriginals. If there is no such good evidence, this is throwing public money away. Supposed to benefit Indians, it is benefitting no one but the practitioners.

Helping those in prison

Convicted criminals may not be such a sympathetic group, but they have their popular constituency. Visiting those in prison is, after all, a recognized corporal work of mercy.

The Commission demands:

> We call upon the federal, provincial, and territorial governments to provide sufficient and stable funding to implement and evaluate community sanctions that will provide realistic alternatives to imprisonment for Aboriginal offenders and respond to the underlying causes of offending.[981]
>
> We call upon federal, provincial, and territorial governments to commit to eliminating the overrepresentation of Aboriginal people in custody over the next decade, and to issue detailed annual reports that monitor and evaluate progress in doing so.[982]
>
> We call upon the federal, provincial, territorial, and Aboriginal governments to commit to eliminating the overrepresentation of Aboriginal youth in custody over the next decade.[983]

Reducing the punishment for crime might give an advantage to aboriginal criminals. But, even if racial discrimination in the administration of justice is justice, even if you are supposed to be judged not on what you did but on who you are, does that help aboriginals? The usual victims of Indian crime are also Indians. The guilty here simply get a better deal at the cost of the innocent. It is a vicious circle: the more aboriginals commit crimes, the less likely for aboriginals to be incarcerated for crime, and so the greater incentive for aboriginals to commit crime. Reduce the deterrent, and you are likely to increase the rate of crime—if imprisonment has any deterrent value in the first place.

And conditions on the reserves probably spin out of control—or even more out of control.

Who really benefits? Again, bureaucrats and professionals. The one ready tool government has to prevent crimes is the penal system. Here, it is called on to avoid the penal system. Lots of work for committees of bureaucrats proposing ways to do the impossible. Such committee work would almost of necessity become permanent. That's the great thing about making problems insoluble. Better yet, this one should make matters worse, calling for more strenuous government involvement in future.

This proposal also helpfully denies any agency to the individual. The individual is not to be held accountable for his or her acts; that is our basic premise here. This encourages a culture of dependency. Just what the Indians always needed, right? Just what they have been lacking until now?

But bureaucrats then get handsomely paid to mind your own business.

> In keeping with the United Nations Declaration on the Rights of Indigenous Peoples, we call upon the federal government, in collaboration with Aboriginal organizations, to fund the establishment of Indigenous law institutes for the development, use, and understanding of Indigenous laws and access to justice in accordance with the unique cultures of Aboriginal peoples in Canada.[984]

This is calling two separate legal systems: one for Indians, and one for "whites."

The inalienable truth that "all men are created equal" is the cornerstone of our concept of human rights, or indeed of morality generally (as in, "do unto others"). In legal terms, what we mean is equal protection under the law. There must not be different laws or penalties based on race, creed, or colour. The same crime must have the same penalty no matter who you happen to be.

This is just what the Truth and Reconciliation Commission rejects: it wants apartheid in the application of the law.

Aside from the violation of human rights, the money for setting up and running these Indigenous law institutes would of course go almost entirely into salaries for high-paid professionals, academics and administrators. After that, lots more work for lawyers and court officials, navigating those two separate legal systems; or rather, given that there are dozens of distinct aboriginal cultures in Canada, dozens of separate legal systems. Wealthy lawyers whose children no doubt might otherwise be starving.

To insist, on the other hand, as we traditionally do, on one law for all is not discriminatory towards Indian traditions. If Indians among themselves wish to observe their own traditional laws, they are at liberty, like the rest of us, to do so. This is called a contract. It can be done either on or off the reserve. As it is done now by Jews, or Catholics, or other groups who have their own traditional bodies of law.

New hope for the dead

> We call upon the parties engaged in the work of documenting, maintaining, commemorating, and protecting residential school cemeteries to adopt strategies in accordance with the following principles: … The Aboriginal community most affected shall lead the development of such strategies.[985]

More money to Indian bands, under the control of band leaders. But with no tangible payoff for any living Indians. And the dead would probably benefit more from prayer than from paperwork.

Helping the unemployed

> Ensure that Aboriginal peoples have equitable access to jobs, training, and education opportunities in the corporate sector, and that Aboriginal communities gain long-term sustainable benefits from economic development projects.[986]

The surest way to help real Indians is to help them find employment. This gives them not only the money for a better life, but independence, self-respect, and the ability to manage their own affairs: an independence that was once the essence of Indian life.

However, the best way to do this is probably to do nothing. The free market unfettered should ensure that employment is equitable. If company A insists on employing less-competent staff based on race or any other factor, company B gains a competitive advantage. Company A declines; company B takes over. Besides being inequitable, unjust, enforcing any hiring policies against this principle makes all companies less competitive. If they do not have a captive market, they probably go bust. If they do have a captive market, this additional cost of doing business will most probably be passed on to consumers; or to employees in lower wages. Consumers will pull out, employees will pull out, investors will pull out, businesses will shut down, and aboriginals, along with the rest of us, lose jobs and services. Any such regulation also raises the bar for entering the market, reducing competition and making discrimination more likely.

Such programs might help a few Indians, who get jobs they otherwise would not. It would probably harm more Indians, who pay more for products or lose jobs they might have gotten. Or are paid less then they might have been without this added cost of doing business.

And this does not account for money spent on "training and education opportunities" for said aboriginal workers, or for the money spent enforcing any "affirmative action" program. This is all money going, in the first instance, into the pockets of well-paid professionals, with only theoretical long-term benefits for ordinary Indians.

And this still deals only with the first half of the Commission's statement, calling for government programs to ensure aboriginal access to jobs. The second half, calling for payouts to aboriginal communities in return for allowing projects to proceed, is worse. The money the developers of new projects might otherwise pay to Indian employees simply goes instead to band leaders. If the financial demands by the band leaders are too high, projects do not proceed, and Indians lose jobs.

Wishing to find anything in the Commission's recommendations that would actually be in the interest of ordinary Indians, advocates might point to the claim by the Commission that Indians have special rights to natural resources:

> We call upon the corporate sector in Canada to adopt the United Nations Declaration on the Rights of Indigenous Peoples as a reconciliation framework and to apply its principles, norms, and standards to corporate policy and core operational activities involving Indigenous peoples and their lands and resources. This would include, but not be limited to, the following: … Commit to meaningful consultation, building respectful relationships, and obtaining the free, prior, and informed consent of Indigenous peoples before proceeding with economic development projects.[987]

As things stand, Indian bands have full control of land and resources on their reserves. Corporations need the informed consent of the owners before proceeding with projects, just as on any private land. So what is the commission talking about here?

If no treaty has been signed, lands over which the Indian tribes have some theoretical legal claim since the *Delgamuukw* decision? If so, it makes sense that they be consulted, but it is prejudicial to refer here to "their land and resources." Or to suggest that their informed consent must be obtained, as opposed to being desirable.

Or are the commissioners claiming Indian control of land and resources they signed off on by treaty generations ago, on the Noble Savage premise that Indians are forever "one with the land"?

Either way, it is wrong to think that this helps Indians. It adds another level of bureaucracy to be satisfied and to be paid off, and another tax on economic development, especially in areas near reserves where Indians live and might get jobs. The extra work, and most or all of the money, will go to lawyers and bureaucrats; possibly to bands, to be administered by band leaders. In the meantime, places Indians live will thereby remain underdeveloped. Fewer jobs, less money, less opportunity. It is not as if the developers of the resources would otherwise just walk off with the money as excess profit: the free market, in theory, ensures that cannot happen. If one proprietor tries to take out too much as profit, another proprietor just walks off with his customers due to lower prices. By the same principle, if developers must pay off nearby bands and bureaucrats in order to develop, the cost of the product goes up, and the jobs may migrate elsewhere, away from ordinary working Indians.

On February 6, 2017, DeBeers announced that it was shelving all plans to extend the life of the Victor diamond mine in Northern Ontario. The mine will close. This is because it was unable in the end to negotiate "approval" from the Attawapiskat First Nation Reserve band leadership, 90 kilometres away. Attawapiskat: you have probably heard the name. This is the remote Northern Ontario aboriginal community that has been in the news for years about its supposedly terrible poverty, the lack of decent housing, the mass suicide of youth.[988]

Aren't these the very ordinary Indians who could use some money and some work?

And yes, the diamond mine was not on reserve lands. It was on public land fully ceded by terms of Treaty Nine back in 1905.

Seems as though we ought to change policy, not double down.

> We call upon the federal government to develop with Aboriginal groups a joint strategy to eliminate educational and employment gaps between Aboriginal and non-Aboriginal Canadians.[989]

Again, money shown on the budget spreadsheet as going to education and jobs is really going to bureaucrats, blackening stacks of paper no one will read. How does one eliminate such education and employment gaps? Can government do it? Even if it can, is it the best instrument? Might individual Indians be better placed in this regard?

Helping starving students

Everyone wants to help youth, and everyone is in favour of education. So this should be in the mix somewhere.

> We call upon the federal government to prepare and publish annual reports comparing funding for the education of First Nations children on and off reserves, as well as educational and income attainments of Aboriginal peoples in Canada compared with non-Aboriginal people.[990]

Money supposedly for education here again goes instead to more bureaucrats. Not to classroom facilities, classroom teachers, pencils, laptops, libraries, or books, for either Indian or non-Indian kids. The money goes into annual reports. Detailed annual reports kept on the basis of race.

> Provide the necessary funding to post-secondary institutions to educate teachers on how to integrate Indigenous knowledge and teaching methods into classrooms.[991]

Here at least there is indeed money for education. But education at a high level, as far as possible, it would seem, from the needs of ordinary Indians. The money would go to professors, high-level teachers, to teach teachers to teach. Tail, meet dog. Dog, meet tail. Now bite hard.

Are such indigenous teaching methods and aboriginal knowledge of any real value to students? The same argument holds as with aboriginal health care: if they work, there is no excuse for excluding them from the non-aboriginal schools. If they do not, there is no excuse for employing them in the aboriginal schools.

> Establish senior-level positions in government at the assistant deputy minister level or higher dedicated to Aboriginal content in education.[992]

"Or higher." My guess is, ordinary Indians need not apply.

> We call on the federal government to draft new Aboriginal education legislation with the full participation and informed consent of Aboriginal peoples. The new legislation would include a commitment to sufficient funding and would incorporate the following principles: … Providing sufficient funding to close identified educational achievement gaps within one generation. …Improving education attainment levels and success rates.[993]

This is another usefully impossible demand: to close educational achievement gaps within one generation. For one thing, this "one generation" arbitrarily excludes any consideration of either the Indian family or the reserve culture as possible factors. It must all somehow be the fault of the schools, and the only option offered for improving it is to spend more money. Because it cannot be done, it ensures that the same demand can be remade, generation after generation, with higher and higher levels of funding, keeping everyone gainlessly employed figuring out random things to do.

> Provide the necessary funding to Aboriginal schools to utilize Indigenous knowledge and teaching methods in classrooms.[994]

> Developing culturally appropriate curricula.[995]

> We call upon the federal, provincial, territorial, and Aboriginal governments to develop culturally appropriate parenting programs for Aboriginal families.[996]
>
> We call upon the federal, provincial, territorial, and Aboriginal governments to develop culturally appropriate early childhood education programs for Aboriginal families.[997]

A call for separate aboriginal schools? Shall they be residential? This assumes and requires a continuing apartheid. And Indians are not to learn about any culture other than their own? Is this going to close the employment gap the commission laments?

It is colonialist, too, to suggest that aboriginal people, if they want this, cannot do it for themselves. We do not expect the government to create culturally appropriate materials for Mormons, Portuguese Canadians, Jews, Highland Scots, or any other ethnic group. Are we saying Indians are not competent to manage their own culture? How did they ever manage before they had the "white man" to do this for them?

> Ensuring that social workers and others who conduct child-welfare investigations are properly educated and trained about the history and impacts of residential schools.
>
> Ensuring that social workers and others who conduct child-welfare investigations are properly educated and trained about the potential for Aboriginal communities and families to provide more appropriate solutions to family healing.[998]
>
> Provide cultural competency training for all healthcare professionals.[999]
>
> We call upon medical and nursing schools in Canada to require all students to take a course dealing with Aboriginal health issues, including the history and legacy of residential schools, the United Nations Declaration on the Rights of Indigenous Peoples, Treaties and Aboriginal rights, and Indigenous teachings and practices. This will require skills-based training in intercultural competency, conflict resolution, human rights, and anti-racism.[1000]
>
> We call upon federal, provincial, territorial, and municipal governments to provide education to public servants on the history of Aboriginal peoples, including the history and legacy of residential schools, the United Nations Declaration on the Rights of Indigenous Peoples, Treaties and Aboriginal

> rights, Indigenous law, and Aboriginal–Crown relations. This will require skills based training in intercultural competency, conflict resolution, human rights, and anti-racism.[1001]
>
> We call upon Canadian journalism programs and media schools to require education for all students on the history of Aboriginal peoples, including the history and legacy of residential schools, the United Nations Declaration on the Rights of Indigenous Peoples, Treaties and Aboriginal rights, Indigenous law, and Aboriginal–Crown relations.[1002]
>
> Provide education for [corporate] management and staff on the history of Aboriginal peoples, including the history and legacy of residential schools, the United Nations Declaration on the Rights of Indigenous Peoples, Treaties and Aboriginal rights, Indigenous law, and Aboriginal–Crown relations. This will require skills based training in intercultural competency, conflict resolution, human rights, and anti-racism.[1003]
>
> We call upon the Federation of Law Societies of Canada to ensure that lawyers receive appropriate cultural competency training, which includes the history and legacy of residential schools, the United Nations Declaration on the Rights of Indigenous Peoples, Treaties and Aboriginal rights, Indigenous law, and Aboriginal–Crown relations. This will require skills-based training in intercultural competency, conflict resolution, human rights, and anti-racism.
>
> We call upon law schools in Canada to require all law students to take a course in Aboriginal people and the law, which includes the history and legacy of residential schools, the United Nations Declaration on the Rights of Indigenous Peoples, Treaties and Aboriginal rights, Indigenous law, and Aboriginal–Crown relations. This will require skills-based training in intercultural competency, conflict resolution, human rights, and antiracism.[1004]

Cumulatively, this must mean a massive expenditure of public funds. But again, if there is any obvious benefit here to anyone, it remains within the professions. There is extra work, and presumably more funding, for social workers, doctors, nurses, public servants, journalists, corporate managers, lawyers, and the professors to teach them. But at the same time, this work and this funding actually takes them away from anything that might directly benefit Indians or anyone else. For, it seems, purposes of indoctrination.

It is ironic, but typical of the territory, that these re-education and self-criticism sessions are said to include a segment on "anti-racism." Because nothing could be more racist than the assumptions of the Commission report as a whole. Here is an unusually fine example of Confucius's warning: if you want to get away with racism, you call it anti-racism. The report insists on the radical difference between aboriginal and other Canadians, and insists at every point on unequal treatment.

> We call upon the federal government, through the Social Sciences and Humanities Research Council, and in collaboration with Aboriginal peoples, post-secondary institutions and educators, and the National Centre for Truth and Reconciliation and its partner institutions, to establish a national research program with multi-year funding to advance understanding of reconciliation.[1005]

More gravy for another station along the gravy line: academics. Lots of time in meetings and jobs with the vague term "liaising" in the description. Still nothing for Indians, unless they happen also to be academics or bureaucrats.

Note again the usefulness of the word "reconciliation." That sounds good, but how does one actually research "reconciliation"? You might get funding for practically anything.

Or only for politically correct things. "Reconciliation" might be a euphemism for political correctness.

Helping underprivileged Indian languages

The Commission is fierce on the need to nurture native languages, out of the pockets, of course, by and large, of English and French speakers.

> We call upon the federal government to enact an Aboriginal Languages Act that incorporates the following principles: … Aboriginal languages are a fundamental and valued element of Canadian culture and society, and there is an urgency to preserve them.
>
> The federal government has a responsibility to provide sufficient funds for Aboriginal-language revitalization and preservation.[1006]
>
> Protecting the right to Aboriginal languages, including the teaching of Aboriginal languages as credit courses.[1007]
>
> We call upon post-secondary institutions to create university and college degree and diploma programs in Aboriginal languages.[1008]

What, in the end, is language, and what is its value to mankind? It is a tool for communication. It follows, therefore, that the value of a language is directly proportional to the number of people with whom you can communicate using it. For English, that would be about one billion. For French, about 300 million. For most aboriginal languages, a few thousand. Most or all of whom also speak English or French. In the words of Cree MP Romeo Saganash, speaking recently in the House of Commons, "All Indigenous people in Canada speak one official language or the other, English or French."[1009]

To be fair, of course, we also need here to count the dead: written language allows them too to speak with us. It preserves our past.

Very well. Add that in. For English or French, we have ponderous libraries of writings dating back perhaps a thousand years. The US Library of Congress holds 120 million volumes. For Indian languages, by contrast, maybe a hundred years, maybe two hundred, of written materials, and not in any quantity. Virtually all of which are also available in English or French. Indeed, there is far more information available even on Indian culture in English or French than in any Indian languages.

In sum, sentiment aside, it is probably against the best interests of any individual who does not already know it to spend much time learning an aboriginal language. Lead young aboriginals down this primrose path, and you are leading them away from their own best chances in life. I suppose it opens up an easy major for a few aboriginals who already speak the languages fluently. But that is still a primrose path. Get their degree, and how do they use it? Teaching others to teach others so they can teach others a skill of value only to teach it to others? Looks like a Ponzi scheme.

> We call upon the federal government to acknowledge that Aboriginal rights include Aboriginal language rights.[1010]

Everyone has the natural right to speak their language. This is not an aboriginal right. This is freedom of speech (available everywhere except Quebec). But aboriginals, or anyone else, do not have a right to government services in their language, or to government subsidy of their language. And that is surely what is meant here.

> Aboriginal language rights are reinforced by the Treaties.[1011]

Aboriginal "language rights" are not in any treaty. The Commission probably put this in precisely because they know it is not true. Now, anyone can cite the Commission report in an attempt to make this wild assertion stick. "According to the Truth and Reconciliation Commission ..."

As a practical matter, a demand for government services in native languages is not especially sane. There are 54 Indian languages in Canada today, plus 20 Eskimo dialects.[1012] That's 74 "official languages," added to English and French, with an average of fewer than 4,000 speakers each. For comparison, the United Nations has six official languages. To provide services in all, the civil service would need to grow exponentially. No, exponentially squared. For the sake of a few thousand speakers, most if not all of whom can also speak English or French. Besides benefiting so few so little at so much cost, how probable is it to find speakers of all these languages who are competent to do the government jobs?

And how would this be fair to the speakers of the many other languages spoken in Canada, many (indeed, virtually all) with more speakers and a larger literature?

> We call upon the federal government to appoint, in consultation with Aboriginal groups, an Aboriginal Languages Commissioner. The commissioner should help promote Aboriginal languages and report on the adequacy of federal funding of Aboriginal-languages initiatives.[1013]

Nice job for some bureaucrat; probably a full department of bureaucrats, doing nothing of any use to anyone.

But so long as Indians are encouraged to stay in their own linguistic ghettos, unable to speak with their neighbours or potential employers, there will be lots of good jobs for bureaucrats and band leaders taking care and control of them and making money in their stead.

Standing for justice

> Reconcile Aboriginal and Crown constitutional and legal orders to ensure that Aboriginal peoples are full partners in Confederation, including the recognition and integration of Indigenous laws and legal traditions in negotiation and implementation processes involving Treaties, land claims, and other constructive agreements.[1014]

This suggests a parity between Canadian law—even the Canadian constitution—and rules ("laws," if you must) set by aboriginal bands. This directly abrogates the social contract established in 1763. We cannot all make our own laws. And one group cannot be privileged over another in this regard, or you are creating a ruling class.

Even if this were not so, there is a further problem: the notion of an indigenous legal tradition is a myth. There are no written records, which is to say, no clear laws or precedents; all is hearsay. There was, before the British or French, no effective government, even at the tribal level, with perhaps the exception of the Iroquois Confederacy. In practice, it would be the law and the legal traditions of Canada and the English-speaking world, the common law, Magna Carta, the Charter of Rights and Freedoms, the Constitution, plus the Roman and Napoleonic Codes for Quebec, against the desires of any given Indian chief.

This would give Indian chiefs dictatorial powers, over other Indians and to some extent over the rest of us as well.

Indians would suffer most. In practice, each band leadership could operate as they wished outside the law and outside the Charter of Rights: the law on that reserve is anything they say it is. They could not be prosecuted, no matter what they did. Already, even now, according to Jean Allard,

> Reserves are, in effect, lawless societies. There are some superficial rules regarding administration, but there are no rules comparable to those for municipalities under provincial municipal acts. Whatever chief and council decide are the rules they want, those are the rules they implement. Ordinary Indians have few means to defend themselves against the arbitrary acts of chief and council. Since they are too often destitute and have very little mobility, they are trapped. They cannot even appeal to the Canadian Human Rights Commission for help, a right extended to all other Canadians, since the Indian Act is exempt.[1015]

Of course, it has so far never occurred to anybody that a government composed of Noble Savages could violate anybody's rights.

Helping the young

> We call upon the federal government to establish multiyear funding for community-based youth organizations to deliver programs on reconciliation, and establish a national network to share information and best practices.[1016]

It almost sounds like this money would go to young people. But would it? Not necessarily. They would presumably be provided "programs on reconciliation." What does that mean? Is it of any value or any interest to them? Might it actually be harangues on how evil the "white man" is? Is that to their benefit?

Or is it to the benefit of bureaucrats who thereby keep them on the plantation—er, reserve—forever, afraid of the outside world? Isn't the money in any case really going to the bureaucrats or academics employed to give these programs? From which Indian youth derive no definite benefit?

And some of this money, perhaps most of it, would be spent on "sharing information and best practices" among bureaucrats.

> We call upon the federal government to ensure that national sports policies, programs, and initiatives are inclusive of Aboriginal peoples, including, but not limited to, establishing: … In collaboration with provincial and territorial governments, stable funding for, and access to, community sports programs that reflect the diverse cultures and traditional sporting activities of Aboriginal peoples.[1017]

Equity for aboriginal athletes sounds good. But this is really the opposite. Special funding for traditional aboriginal sports? Unlike, say, hockey, football, kayaking, canoeing, tobogganing, or lacrosse, all of which have aboriginal roots? This is artificially pushing young aboriginals into a sports ghetto, while denying them their true heritage.

Segregation in sports might be a way to short-change Indians for funding, or a way to short-change "whites." But it has no other obvious purpose; nobody's culture suffers by playing a new sport. It does offer opportunities for graft, and keeps young Indians thinking of themselves as different and dependent. And imagining they cannot compete with whites on the proverbial level playing field. A novel idea, considering the many successful Canadian aboriginal athletes.

Many of the Commission's demands imply cultural relativism worse than this. For example,

> An elite athlete development program for Aboriginal athletes. … Programs for coaches, trainers, and sports officials that are culturally relevant for Aboriginal peoples.[1018]

When you play baseball or judo, does it make a big difference whether you are Dogrib or Japanese? While the provision of such courses might make a cushy job for someone, is it really going to do anything for any kid on the sandlot?

Helping indigenous peoples generally

> We call upon the federal government to provide funding to the Canadian Museums Association to undertake, in collaboration with Aboriginal peoples, a national review of museum policies and best practices to determine the level of compliance with the United Nations Declaration on the Rights of Indigenous Peoples and to make recommendations.[1019]

More make-work for bureaucrats and academics, surely. More thick reports, no other action specified. And God forbid such actions occur: a federal government censorship of museums?

The Commission is especially keen on the United Nations Declaration on the Rights of Indigenous Peoples.

> We call upon federal, provincial, territorial, and municipal governments to fully adopt and implement the United Nations Declaration on the Rights of Indigenous Peoples as the framework for reconciliation.[1020]
>
> Adopt and implement the United Nations Declaration on the Rights of Indigenous Peoples as the framework for reconciliation.[1021]
>
> Full adoption and implementation of the United Nations Declaration on the Rights of Indigenous Peoples as the framework for reconciliation.[1022]
>
> We call upon the church parties to the Settlement Agreement, and all other faith groups and interfaith social justice groups in Canada who have not already done so, to formally adopt and comply with the principles, norms, and standards of the United Nations Declaration on the Rights of Indigenous Peoples as a framework for reconciliation.
>
> Engaging in ongoing public dialogue and actions to support the United Nations Declaration on the Rights of Indigenous Peoples.
>
> Issuing a statement no later than March 31, 2016, from all religious denominations and faith groups, as to how they will implement the United Nations Declaration on the Rights of Indigenous Peoples.[1023]

As the current Liberal government, previously enthusiastic, has now admitted, fully implementing the UN Declaration on the Rights of Indigenous Peoples is not possible in a democracy, without overturning the democracy. The Declaration has other problems, but the insurmountable obstacle is this passage:

> Article 19: States shall consult and cooperate in good faith with the indigenous peoples concerned through their own representative institutions in order to obtain their free, prior and informed consent before adopting and implementing legislative or administrative measures that may affect them.

Any law passed by any Canadian government almost necessarily affects Indians, just as it does other Canadians. This article theoretically gives aboriginals a veto over all legislation. Canada would become an oligarchy, no longer a democracy, with aboriginals as a ruling class.

This might indeed be of advantage to Indians, although injurious to everyone else. Nevertheless, it is of most obvious benefit to tribal leaders, career bureaucrats, who would be the ones, according to the Declaration, actually exercising power in the name of Indians.

Indeed, it is unclear whether the non-native national government could legitimately place any restrictions on how indigenous groups managed their "own representative institutions." Accordingly, the tribal leaders with ultimate control over Canadian legislation might not have been fairly and openly elected even by Indians. And there is no reason to suppose they would have the interests of the ordinary Indian as their priority.

In support of traditional Indian spirituality

Aside from the family and the electorate, there is another possible rival source of power to be kicked to the curb by the bureaucrats: that most venerable of voluntary associations, the church. It must submit.

> We call upon church parties to the Settlement Agreement, in collaboration with Survivors and representatives of Aboriginal organizations, to establish permanent funding to Aboriginal people for:
>
> Community-controlled healing and reconciliation projects.
>
> Community-controlled culture and language revitalization projects.
>
> Community-controlled education and relationship building projects.
>
> Regional dialogues for Indigenous spiritual leaders and youth to discuss Indigenous spirituality, self-determination, and reconciliation.[1024]

This would mean, in the first place, that money donated in charity to one church and one religious doctrine must be handed over instead to promote a different "religion." How proper is that? What about freedom of conscience? And not really to a religion at all—note the phrase "community-controlled." That means the money is to be handed to the band leadership, the civil power, not to any genuinely religious figures. To the bureaucrats running the Indian "communities," who are in practice free to say what Indian "spirituality" is or is not as it suits them.

Is this to the benefit of ordinary Indians? No; most Indians, are Christians. They are paying for this, but not benefiting from it. Nor is their community, which is Christian. "Community-controlled" means the churches will have no say in how the money is spent. There will be no accountability to any outside party. The money will be controlled and spent by the band leaders.

> We call upon all levels of government that provide public funds to denominational schools to require such schools to provide an education on comparative religious studies, which must include a segment on Aboriginal spiritual beliefs and practices developed in collaboration with Aboriginal Elders.[1025]

The point of having a denominational school is to teach your children about your religion. This demand requires them instead to teach the beliefs of other religions. It is a direct attack on religious freedom. Bureaucrats—"Aboriginal Elders" and others—are to be given final say on the content of all religious education. And it is not as though aboriginal "elders" count as genuine authorities even on Indian spiritual traditions. They are free to make up anything they like, as it suits them, unconstrained by any scripture or church structure. In traditional Indian culture, indeed, "elders" were never held to have any special spiritual knowledge.

> We call upon leaders of the church parties to the Settlement Agreement and all other faiths, in collaboration with Indigenous spiritual leaders, Survivors, schools of theology, seminaries, and other religious training centres, to develop and teach curriculum for all student clergy, and all clergy and staff who work in Aboriginal communities, on the need to respect Indigenous spirituality in its own right, the history and legacy of residential schools and the roles of the church parties in that system, the history and legacy of religious conflict in Aboriginal families and communities, and the responsibility that churches have to mitigate such conflicts and prevent spiritual violence.[1026]

"Spiritual violence"? That's even better than "cultural genocide." *Oxford* says violence means "behaviour involving physical force intended to hurt, damage, or kill someone or something." *Merriam-Webster* says violence means "the use of physical force to harm someone, to damage property, etc." Physical force; although Webster does accept its metaphoric use ("as if"). "Spiritual violence" is a contradiction in terms, like "cold heat," "dry liquid," or "dark light." Presumably what the Commission means is disagreeing with someone—but only with some government functionary or Indian leader. This cannot work otherwise: both parties to any disagreement would then be equally guilty of this crime of "spiritual violence," making the charge impossible.

In other words, no more freedom of thought, or speech, or religion.

Most remarkable is this demand placed specifically on the Catholic Church:

> We call upon the Pope to issue an apology to Survivors, their families, and communities for the Roman Catholic Church's role in the spiritual, cultural, emotional, physical, and sexual abuse of First Nations, Inuit, and Métis children in Catholic-run residential schools. We call for that apology to be similar to the 2010 apology issued to Irish victims of abuse and to occur within one year of the issuing of this Report and to be delivered by the Pope in Canada.[1027]

"Spiritual abuse"? Let's just leave that one hanging there.

But nothing is now to be beyond the government's reach: its writ now extends over the mountains to Rome and to the hereafter. Even if an apology were warranted, why would it matter materially where the apology was made, or when? Whom does that benefit? Only the bureaucrats, in showing to all their sovereignty over the Catholic Church. The Catholic Church in particular is the great enemy. It must be brought to heel and humiliation, presumably, precisely because it is so influential among ordinary Indians. It rivals, perhaps supersedes, the bureaucrats in its influence among Indians. This prestige must be destroyed.

A good reason, not incidentally, for the attack on the residential schools. Band leaders as a class have a vested interest in trying to discredit the church. As did Henry VIII.

In support of residential schools

Had we not yet slipped into parody, there's more.

> We call upon the federal, provincial, and territorial governments to recognize as a high priority the need to address and prevent Fetal Alcohol Spectrum Disorder (FASD), and to develop, in collaboration with Aboriginal people, FASD preventive programs that can be delivered in a culturally appropriate manner.
>
> We call upon the federal, provincial, and territorial governments to work with Aboriginal communities to provide culturally relevant services to inmates on issues such as substance abuse, family and domestic violence, and overcoming the experience of having been sexually abused.[1028]

> We call upon the federal government to develop a national plan to collect and publish data on the criminal victimization of Aboriginal people, including data related to homicide and family violence victimization.[1029]

Do the commissioners not realize they here give powerful evidence that the residential schools were a blessing, not a curse, and that abolishing them was bad for Indians? They are admitting that alcoholic parents are a special problem for aboriginal children. Granted that, in the matter of fetal alcohol spectrum disorder, the worst damage is already done by the time of birth, even after birth, an alcoholic mother is not a happy thing to grow up with. The commissioners are admitting further a special problem in aboriginal communities with substance abuse, family and domestic violence, and sexual abuse. Surely the poor children might be better off elsewhere, at last for a part of their childhoods.

As to helping Indians with alcohol and addiction problems, nothing else has proven as effective as the AA program. Formal studies are ambiguous on this, but the testimony of former alcoholics is overwhelming; the program has accordingly been widely imitated by other groups. AA is faith-based. Yet the Commission wants to reduce the role of religion, and objects to the faith-based nature of the residential schools.

> We call upon the federal government, in consultation with Aboriginal organizations, to appoint a public inquiry into the causes of, and remedies for, the disproportionate victimization of Aboriginal women and girls. The inquiry's mandate would include: i. Investigation into missing and murdered Aboriginal women and girls. ii. Links to the intergenerational legacy of residential schools.[1030]

There is no plausible link between the disappearance of aboriginal women and the residential schools generations ago. The obvious link is to a failure of the Indian family, to which the residential schools were a response. No problem; the Commission simply mandates the government to find one. Among other concerns, such as its impossibility, this is the classic colonial attitude: everything is left up to the "white man," and he is expected to be able to work magic.

For the settlement of the land question

More magic:

> We call upon the Government of Canada, provincial and territorial governments, and the courts to adopt the following legal principles: … Aboriginal title claims are accepted once the Aboriginal claimant has established

> occupation over a particular territory at a particular point in time.[1031]

As worded, this suggests that, if someone of "aboriginal" status, however legally defined, can prove they once visited Niagara Falls, they own Niagara Falls.

This sounds like a major handout for aboriginals, but in practice probably not. It cannot rationally be applied, even if limited to aboriginals, because aboriginal claims would conflict. The impossibility of this criterion instead offers endless work to lawyers to try to determine what it really means.

In support of the neighbourhoods where bureaucrats live

> We call upon the federal government, in collaboration with Survivors and their organizations, and other parties to the Settlement Agreement, to commission and install a publicly accessible, highly visible, Residential Schools National Monument in the city of Ottawa to honour Survivors and all the children who were lost to their families and communities.[1032]

> We call upon provincial and territorial governments, in collaboration with Survivors and their organizations, and other parties to the Settlement Agreement, to commission and install a publicly accessible, highly visible, Residential Schools Monument in each capital city to honour Survivors and all the children who were lost to their families and communities.[1033]

Somehow, this strikes me at least as mere symbolism, rather than something of real value to Indians. In every capital city—even in provinces that had no residential schools?

Perhaps such public sculptures would be decorative. Perhaps they would be good for tourism. Even so, they are not being erected where Indians congregate, are they? They are to be erected where bureaucrats congregate, perhaps to provide a little shaded green space for their kids to play in. Rather than helping Indians in any tangible way, they seem intended to institutionalize the culture of grievance, in an effort to ensure that reconciliation not occur; and to offer employment to more committees to commission the art.

Instead of burying the hatchet, the Committee wants hatchets attractively displayed everywhere.

And, last but not least:

> We call upon the Government of Canada to replace the Oath of Citizenship with the following: "I swear (or affirm) that I will be faithful and bear true allegiance to Her Majesty Queen Elizabeth II, Queen of Canada, Her Heirs and Successors, and that I will faithfully observe the laws of Canada including Treaties with Indigenous Peoples, and fulfill my duties as a Canadian citizen."[1034]

No words suffice.

Legally, this is meaningless, since individual citizens are not signatory to any treaties. Nor does it do anything material to help any Indians. Perhaps it might appeal to their pride, in getting a call-out in the Oath of Citizenship. But if this is important to them, they obviously have too few real problems to contend with. Life must be pretty good.

Of course, this recommendation, or demand, has already been implemented by the present Liberal government. Awkwardly, they are pledged to implement all the Commission's recommendations.[1035] And this last one, perhaps the craziest one of all, is easiest to implement. It costs nothing but Canada' s dignity. It just makes us look thoroughly silly to any new immigrants.

But at least it's a good gag. Not everything the Commission has proposed is so funny.

22 ATTAWAPISKAT AND THE HEALING POWERS OF U-HAUL

Government: The poor Indian's friend.

> *It may be concluded safely that the poetic or picture Indian, the man of Nature equipped with the finest ideas of our own later culture, has never existed. Hiawatha, with the beautiful mind given him by Longfellow, does not live, in fact. Railway companies, for profit, officials for effect, and civilized Indians, who wish to take for their ancestors attributed reputation, have tried to keep such a picture before the public. It never was a true one. Poets, romance writers, tourists who engage unoccupied Indians as paddlers, and a few ignorant people have spread false notions.... Indians are just the same as other Canadians. They are in our professions, our trades, and our own occupations, and numbers reside in our communities.*
>
> —R. *Sinclair,* Canadian Indians[1036]

It has been a long time since I liked Jean Chrétien. Long ago, he was fun to listen to, and seemed to speak from the heart. Then he became prime minister, and never spoke an honest word again. But like Bill Clinton, or Pierre Trudeau, he is better out of office.

The old Chrétien is back. He is freer again to say what he thinks.

Eleven young people in the remote Cree community of Attawapiskat were overheard in April 2016 planning a joint suicide.

This electrified the country. Rallies and marches in support of the Indians of

Attawapiskat were held as far afield as Victoria. The Commons went into a five-hour emergency debate. Never say the general public does not care about Indians! In the debate, Chrétien was excoriated for suggesting to an interviewer that it might be best for some young residents of Attawapiskat to move, "like anybody else."[1037]

Good God. What a racist. Suggesting that Indians are "like anybody else"!

Niki Ashton, the NDP critic for Indian Affairs, accused Chrétien of being an "assimilationist." "First Nations people and many people who work in solidarity with First Nations people," she said, "know that these views are unacceptable."[1038]

Stewart Phillip, Grand Chief of the Union of British Columbia Indian Chiefs, agreed. "We're not bison. We shouldn't be herded around on the whims of a racist nation."[1039]

There is irony here. Evidently, by preserving the reserve system, we are doing nothing to preserve Indian culture.

This refusal to move for opportunity is the very opposite of traditional Indian culture.

The Cree were once nomadic. They moved their encampments about every two weeks. They spread over a few centuries from an original base near Hudson Bay to as far west as Peace River. On the plains, they indeed wandered about just like the bison—for they were hunting the bison as their source of subsistence.

All of this, apparently, has been forgotten. By the Indians. By the "elders." Even by the provincial chiefs.

The Hawthorn report found in 1966 that Indians are generally now less inclined than European Canadians to move for employment:

> Indians in some areas tend to be less mobile than Whites, more reluctant to leave their reserves permanently, or for extended periods of time for employment elsewhere. Unless a plant, a business or industrial centre is within commuting distance of a reserve or band community, therefore, the majority, for this and other reasons, fails to take advantage of the employment opportunities available.[1040]

The next most obvious characteristic of traditional Cree, and Indian, culture, was the lack of law and government: "*sans loi, sans roi, sans foi.*" The only government was local, and chiefs ruled mostly by personality and persuasion. As Jean Allard puts it,

> A chief did not order his people to follow his wishes. He advised them of his plans, and if people disagreed with him, they were free to make their own decisions about whether to follow him or join a different tribe. It was an effective check and balance on the power of leaders.[1041]

This too is now gone. Nothing could be more different than the ponderous excess of government found on a reserve. And everyone is trapped by their legal band membership. So that now the Attawapiskat Cree are expecting government in Ottawa to handle their problem for them.

This is the alien culture that has been instilled in Canadian Indians.

R. Sinclair lamented in 1910, "whatever the Indian may initiate, whatever he may undertake, there is not one single matter that is not dependent for its outcome on the whim of some official at Ottawa."[1042] And it is not just that federal bureaucracy and bureaucrats are omnipresent; all government funding funnels through the band council, with almost no private enterprise possible. Government, federal or local, is the only game in town.

Yet the proposals for improvement are always to add more government: more federal government initiatives, or a stronger band government. The Royal Commission of 1996, for example, called for two new government departments and two new cabinet ministers, both devoted to aboriginals: Minister for Aboriginal Relations, and Minister of Indian and Inuit Services.[1043] This recommendation was duly implemented by the Trudeau government in August, 2017.

Ashton of the tribe of the New Democrats sees the problem as entirely the fault of people with white skin. She is partly right; whites more than Indians invented this "Indian" culture. What even Indians think is Indian culture today owes more to Rousseau, Longfellow, Castaneda, Hollywood, and the Whole Earth Catalog than to any distant ancestors. But her solution is wrong. She feels the "whites" must pull out their wallets again to assuage their guilt.

This is doubling down. This is what we have always done. This is colonialism. It preserves and intensifies the notion that Indians have no free will, and can do nothing for themselves. Everything comes from the white man.

The band chiefs like the idea. Isadore Day's solution, as a band leader, is to hand unlimited money to band leaders, and ask no questions. "Nothing can change significantly until governments stop controlling the flow of money going to troubled First Nations."[1044]

The Truth and Reconciliation Commission more or less agrees: we need more public money—even if most of it would get nowhere near a reserve.

More bureaucratic control, more accountability to the federal government, as the Conservative party has recently advocated, is fiscally advisable, and would probably save some tax dollars. But more government is still not the answer to too much government. That includes more government money for local Indian government. But that includes more government money for more government paperwork to better account for the government money.

You see how easy it is to just keep going around in circles on this.

And it is not just the chiefs or the Ottawa bureaucrats. You can't blame only them. Everyone aboriginal has grown accustomed to the game: you go limp and get taken care of. A group of Attawapiskat teenagers, in response to public attention in the wake of the suicide crisis, have drawn up a list of new facilities they feel they need in the community to convince them not to kill themselves. They want a clean swimming pool, a movie theatre with six screens, a casino, and a meeting with the prime minister.[1045]

If the same money were just given to them, instead of used to build fun stuff, they would probably be better off. But they would then have to make decisions and shoulder responsibilities. It's more obviously pleasant and less stressful to open gifts.

The government has already built a grade school, a high school, a hospital. The young people's list of what they already have includes a local radio station, a gym, an arena, a soccer field, a baseball field, a skating rink. For a population of 2,000.

My wife comes from the Philippines, by world standards a middle income, not a poor, country. Any Filipino town of under 2,000 with those facilities would think they had died and gone to the better place. Yet Filipinos, on the whole, are not killing themselves. They seem to be happy.

This is typical of reserves. When the Quebec Innu community of Uashat mak Mani-Utenam had a similar problem with youth suicide, the coroner noted frankly that this was "despite numerous resources."[1046]

The poverty problem

This makes claims that it is all about poverty improbable.

Yet in their 1970 *Red Paper*, the Chiefs of Alberta stated unambiguously that poverty is the issue:

> The basic problem, in all its varying degrees of intensity, which is confronted by all reserves and their peoples, is that of poverty with all its relevant symptoms— unemployment, inadequate education, overcrowded and deteriorating housing, crime, alcohol, and drug abuse, sub-standard preventive medicine and resultant disease, apathy, frustration, moral decay, destruction of the family and community units and total alienation from society.[1047]

This sounds right to most people. It fits with a certain type of Marxist theory, for one thing. Although a Marxist friend insists that this sort of "welfare liberalism" is not really Marx at all; that Marx had contempt for the unemployed and for government handouts. Be that as it may; it is simple to understand, and seems simple to deal with: just send money. It suits bureaucrats, who get to dole out the money. And it works well for band chiefs, who receive it.

And, as of 2006, median income for aboriginals was officially 30 percent lower than for other Canadians.[1048]

But does poverty cause alcoholism, despair, and poor education; or might alcoholism, despair, and poor education cause poverty?

The poverty problem on reserves may also still be exaggerated. Beyond the community facilities they often have available, the income figures we see that suggest poverty are often on top of whatever their traditional way of life might bring in. A traditional hunter-gatherer way of life is still about as viable as it ever was for most residents of remote reserves. Because no commerce is often involved, and no money changes hands, none of that—everything they would have had before the "white men" came—shows in the official stats.

> Aboriginal people in rural communities and on reserve have non-monetary sources of income that are not captured in the census, such as food from gardening/farming and hunting/trapping. For example, the value of a moose—which would provide an average of 150 kilograms of usable meat—cannot be estimated in dollars because governments made selling wild game meat illegal.
>
> Information on this point is limited. However, a study of the Mitchikabibikok Inik (Algonquins of Barrière Lake) is informative. The study, conducted in the early 1990s, found that ... in a given year, the land provided the community with 60,000 kgs of edible meat (780 kgs per household and 130 kgs per person). On average each household harvested meat at a value of $6,623. Families burned an average of 10.5 face cords of wood, which gives a fuel value of $4,800. In

> addition, non-meat resources from the bush added at least $845 per household. The estimated value of goods taken by the Algonquin economy was $575,245 a year from the land base.[1049]

It seems possible that, adding in the federal perks and the wilderness resources, aboriginal people are actually doing about as well financially as anyone else.

If not, it is worth remembering that most Indians could expect a better life materially by simply moving from the reserves to where more jobs can be found. Most of the present population of Attawapiskat is on welfare. Yet, as Hawthorn has noted, many do not move. "Unless a plant, a business or industrial centre is within commuting distance of a reserve or band community, ... the majority ... fails to take advantage of the employment opportunities available."[1050]

And how can merely being poor hold a people back for generations? Most immigrants to Canada in the last three centuries arrived poor. The Irish of the famine, the Scots of the Highland clearances, the Poles, the Ukrainians, the "displaced persons" from the postwar period. And yet their descendants now are mostly doing well.

So the problem on the reserves is not poverty, and more money is not going to solve it. Jean Allard observes that since the government White Paper was presented in 1969, "[t]he budget for Indian Affairs has swelled dramatically, yet the problems faced by Canadian Indians today remain much the same as in 1969, and, in some cases, are worse."[1051] In 1978, Jack Beaver, an independent consultant, himself aboriginal, issued a semi-official report, originally commissioned by the Department of Indian Affairs and the National Indian Brotherhood, speaking of a "crisis of social breakdown" that was far worse than could be accounted for by "underdevelopment." "The tragedy," he added, "is that there is no evidence of improvement in this intolerable condition in spite of increasing Government expenditures."[1052]

The idea is also often heard that remote reserves should be given ownership of natural resources in order to be "self-funding." This would suit the Indian bureaucracy very well—it would end all accountability. But it would do nothing good for ordinary Indians. The proof is that some reserves have significant resource revenue now, and their situation is often no better than others.

> Samson Reserve near Edmonton sits on one of the largest oil and gas fields in the country; it accounts for 75 per cent of total oil and gas production on Canada's reserves. In 1996, band revenue was nearly $100 million, about half of it funding from the federal and provincial governments. The communal resources of the reserve are, in theory, to be

> shared among the more than 5,000 members of the band, but that is not what happens.... Nearly 80 per cent of the 5,100 on the reserve are on welfare, and the unemployment rate is estimated at 85 per cent....[1053]
>
> Living conditions on the oil-rich reserve are not appreciably different from those on Canada's most impoverished reserves. Samson has the same high unemployment and the same social breakdown—as betrayed by extensive welfare dependency, many vandalized buildings, an epidemic of alcohol and drug abuse, and high teenage suicide rates.[1054]

Money does not buy happiness, after all, and man does not live by bread alone. Even if Indians get a lot of money, we are probably still left with a broken society: single parenthood, child abuse and neglect, youth suicide, crime, "bullying," alcoholism and substance abuse, and illnesses such as diabetes and tuberculosis. It still sounds grim to be a Canadian Indian, especially a young Canadian Indian.

But of course, the government will spend more money. Spending more money is always the best solution—for government. Eighteen highly paid mental-health professionals were flown in to Attawapiskat, and put on 24-hour call, in response to the 11 threatened suicides. These highly paid professionals will probably do nothing to benefit the Cree: their presence does not address the underlying problem, they will soon be gone and the problems will stay, and it is arguable whether the "mental health" system ever helps anybody. But a lot of money will be spent, and will be seen to be spent. That achieves the goal. And the Cree kids are being given lots of attention and maybe stuff. They may try this suicide thing again.

The cycle of dependency continues.

Taking the man out of the Indian

Ashton of the NDP properly points out that the real problem is paternalism.

"[T]his didn't just happen," she explains. "In fact, the trauma that is apparent through suicide crises across Canada is the direct result of our history of colonization and decades of racist policies passed through this House."[1055]

All, then, was done by the white man. So, he must do more of the same. Colonization is the problem, so more colonization is the solution. Can't beat the logic. Ever.

Reserve Indians themselves regularly complain about not being given their own choices. They have long resented the dependency. That seems to be a core issue for them.

"[W]asn't there always a Whiteman around somewhere in the picture always waiting for the chance to supply his superior ideas?" asked Marie Baker at the National Conference on Indian and Northern Education, Saskatoon, 1967.

> "Those poor Indians need me." The full implications of this assumption show that in reinforcing this stereotype image, the Whiteman has of the Indian, Whiteman believes the Native is completely dependent on Whiteman.[1056]

Exactly. Except that the stereotype is at least as deeply ingrained in the Indians. Like a dog chasing its tail, or rather, like one of Pavlov' s pups at the sound of the bell, they keep asking for more government. And is it better to be dependent on the band council than the "Whiteman," just because their skin is the same tone as yours?

Although no special fan of either white people as such or residential schools, Buffy Sainte-Marie, Cree singer/songwriter, seems to make the same point in a March 2017 interview:

> People are still under the impression that, and put this in quotes, "our Indians" belong to the colonial administration and that's the way life has been for us. To decolonize you have to get rid of the basic assumption that indigenous people are somehow to be classed with the flora and the fauna.... [T]hat is sometimes how we have been treated.[1057]

That is what Attawapiskat is—a colony, where the inhabitants are kept apart, cared for by others, and allowed no responsibility over their lives. They live there in a human zoo, or a human nature preserve.

Phil Fontaine, longtime national chief of the Assembly of First Nations, makes the same complaint in a 2009 interview: "We want to be real contributors to Canada's prosperity. We never ever wanted to be dependent on someone else. Any suggestion that we are happy with our current situation is so completely wrong."

Unfortunately, he spoils it by calling for more government money: "there is no question," he is paraphrased by the reporter, "that the federal government must spend more money to address the serious problems in First Nations communities."[1058]

Ashton says the Indian Act is the root of the problem: "a piece of legislation that is the symbol of colonialism." "This piece of legislation and the way it is imposed on First Nations is deeply connected to the oppression that exists today."[1059]

"The Indian Act is the problem," agrees Ontario Regional Chief Isadore Day.[1060]

"[The Indian Act] has … deprived us of our independence, our dignity, our self-respect and our responsibility," agrees Katherine June Delisle of Kahnewake.[1061]

Funny, that. Chrétien, the man whom they now revile, was the great opponent of the Indian Act. His second cabinet portfolio was as Minister of Indian Affairs and Northern Development. He took the brief so much to heart that he and his wife adopted an eighteen-month old Inuit/Eskimo boy—an act of kindness and humanity that would probably not be permitted to a "white" family today. This was part of the "Sixties scoop," for which government and the rest of us are now being asked to pay reparations. Race-based adoption seems hardly in the interests of Indian orphans; but the individual needy Indian must always, it seems, be sacrificed.

Chrétien was the sponsor of the infamous proposal, in the 1969 Indian Affairs *White Paper*, to end the Indian Act and make Indians full Canadian citizens.

The Indian leadership rose to oppose it. The Chiefs of Alberta published their *Red Paper*, which declared plainly, "We reject the *White Paper* Proposal that the Indian Act be repealed. It is neither possible nor desirable to eliminate the Indian Act."[1062]

They wanted Indian status, and they wanted reserves. "We reject this proposal to abolish the Indian Affairs Branch. There will always be a continuing need for an Indian Affairs Branch."[1063]

This can mean one or both of only two things. Either Indians themselves are torn between two conflicting impulses, the one for autonomy, the other for security; or the government and the "Whiteman" is just serving as a useful scapegoat. They want to get rid of the Indian Act; they do not want to get rid of the Indian Act. The whites are blamed for the Indian Act, and blamed for trying to end it. They are faulted for paternalism and asked for more paternalism. They are asked for schools, then blamed for schools. Indians need to be consulted, but are not to be considered responsible for their own decisions.

Given this vicious circle, reconciliation is not possible.

And it is up to Indians, not whites, to change things.

In the case of Attawapiskat, Chrétien's advice is obviously sound. Attawapiskat is remote—one of the world's most remote communities. There are no jobs; there is 70 percent unemployment. Vegetables, fruit, building materials, and just about everything else must be flown in at high expense; even on welfare, you would be better off elsewhere. Professionals, teachers, doctors, nurses, dentists, opticians, pharmacists consider it a hardship post; few want to come and fewer want to stay.

Nothing but life is cheap.

And, did I mention, it is damned cold? Just a little to the north, the ground is permanently frozen; trees cannot grow.

Why wouldn't anyone counsel or consider moving? Is suicide really better?

Isn't this assumption itself an example of a truly pathetic helplessness?

It is to this that a policy of paternalism has reduced the Indians.

R. Sinclair laments, in 1910:

> It is a singular fact that whilst we are annually spending large sums of money under the pretext of making our Indians a responsible, self-dependent people, and half of them, or more, have in spite of adverse legislation become just as well able to manage their individual business as other people do, the laws of Canada should deprive them of the right to do what they choose with nearly everything they acquire by their own personal industry.
>
> Yet such is the outcome of Canadian legislation. Intended formerly to protect a semi-savage people against the rapacity of unprincipled persons, and perhaps in some remote parts still beneficial [this, mind you, was in 1910], its operation upon those who have long since ceased to need any such protection is not only absurd but actually and actively vicious. It prevents most of the Indians of Canada from enjoying those rights and the safeguards of those rights which every free man is entitled to enjoy in any free country.[1064]
>
> A Government department has been formed to deal with Indian affairs. A bureaucracy of officials, whose interest it is to assume the whole management of Indian affairs, is constantly, by legislation promoted by themselves ... drawing the reins of control tighter and tighter, assuming functions or duties which formerly the Indian exercised himself.[1065]

General Pratt, founder of the Carlisle Indian School, was similarly critical of the situation below the Medicine Line:

> For many years the United States has been absolute in its control over the Indians. It has segregated them remote from any participation in our affairs, and has enforced the dominance and poverty of opportunity of their old tribal life.

> The government has gone so far as to command and control all their resources and assume all responsibility for their special support, education and industrial training, requiring it to be mostly in the environments of this exclusive, tribal life and has always influenced them back into continuing that life. They have been imperiously kept from all large contact with our American civilization and only allowed such civilizing influences as trickled to them through a constantly changing, and varying purposed, ill-informed and inadequate oversight.[1066]

Jack Beaver, in his 1979 report, writes:

> [Indian Affairs] has taken on the exclusive control over the definition and purported satisfaction of almost all the basic human needs (healing, teaching, provision of food and shelter, burying the dead) to the point that it prevents or inhibits the natural competence of the people to provide for themselves.... The effect of the policies of the Government of Canada has been to impose the consumption of standard products (nurses, teachers, welfare officers, frame houses, and undertakers) that only the Government can provide. This in turn has created a deep-rooted dependency on the very commodities and services that Indian Affairs, Health and Welfare, and others deem to be "in the public good."[1067]

Chrétien's 1969 *White Paper* argues:

> The result of Crown ownership and the Indian Act has been to tie the Indian people to a land system that lacks flexibility and inhibits development. If an Indian band wishes to gain income by leasing its land, it has to do so through a cumbersome system involving the Government as trustee. It cannot mortgage reserve land to finance development on its own initiative. Indian people do not have control of their lands except as the Government allows....[1068]

The 1970 *Red Paper* from Alberta's chiefs, while objecting to the *White Paper*, actually makes the same complaint:

> The whole spirit of the Indian Act is paternalism. The Act provides that: "...The Minister may ... authorize use of lands for schools or burial grounds ... authorize surveys and subdivisions ... determine and direct the construction of roads ... issue certificates of possession ... direct an Indian person or the tribe to compensate another Indian ... call a referendum ... appoint executors of wills ... declare the will of an Indian to be void ... issue temporary permits for the

> taking of sand, gravel, clay and other non-metallic substances upon or under lands in a reserve … make expenditures out of the revenues of the tribe to assist sick, aged, or destitute Indians of the tribe and provide for the burial of deceased indigent members … etc. etc. etc."
>
> As one example, under Section 32 [of the Indian Act], an Indian rancher might spend four days and 100 miles of driving to obtain authority to sell a calf, obtain permission to receive the proceeds and cash the cheque![1069]

And yet, these same chiefs opposed repealing the Indian Act.

Many of the problems we see on reserves look like problems of the family: child abuse, lack of educational attainment, the disappearance of young women, teenage suicide, teenage crime, alcoholism, substance abuse.

This is a known result of relying on government money and handouts, instead of on employment. As Daniel Patrick Moynihan pointed out in the 1960s, families on welfare tend to fall apart.[1070] A reliance on welfare removes the husband and father from any clear family role. Given no purpose in the family or in life, and told in effect that he is not responsible for his wife or kids, why try anything? Why not just go out and get drunk? Why not have sex with any woman who consents? Or, for that matter, doesn't? With no financial power, how else maintain your family position, should you hang around, but by physical force?

Granted, a good man should rise above all that. But why make it so hard? Indians are human, after all.

This is a problem shared by the poor in Canada everywhere; it is hard to see a complete fix without somehow fixing welfare. We do not, after all, want to see women and children starve any more than did Sir John A. But it is several steps further down the slippery slope for Indian men: even if employed, their families don't need them for housing, health care, or to pay for college. Everyone gets everything laid on, by government and the band, for being Indian. Indian men are systematically humiliated.

Consider: in refusing Indians the right to sell their land, we put them in the position in which the Iroquois put the Delaware, when, to their own minds, they reduced them to "women": they could no longer dispose of land.

And, of course, we deny them thereby the possibility of building equity or raising capital for any enterprise. Ensuring their eternal dependence on government.

Why did we do something so perverse?

Unfortunately, the myth of the Noble Savage was influential in 1763, as it remains today. It probably began with the determination, in the Royal Proclamation of 1763, to deal with Indians always as corporate entities, tribes, not individuals. Indians were really not full human beings capable of making their own responsible decisions. Like children, they had to be protected by the Great White Father.

The upshot was, they had no rights. Any more, as Buffy Sainte-Marie says, than porcupines in a game reserve.

Realizing in the postwar years that they had in fact groomed Indians on reserves to perpetual dependency, Canadian governments made a fatal mistake. They determined to reverse policy: from now on, just as the chiefs advised, Indians would get to run their own affairs, and Ottawa would mostly just send money. That, after all, was what "the Indians" were calling for. The Alberta Chiefs, in their *Red Paper*, described the proper role of the Department of Indian Affairs as to "channel federal funds to the tribes or to the provincial association depending on circumstances."[1071]

This only replaced paternalism from Ottawa with paternalism from the local band leadership.

In fact, according to Jean Allard, it was worse than that. Not wanting to seem to dictate to the Indians, the politicians pulled back—and left everything to the bureaucrats. Now there was not only no control or oversight by the Indians—there was also no control by the wider public. "In the absence of government policy on Canadian Indians, the Indian Affairs bureaucracy and the designated Indian political organizations, both amply serviced by consultants of all kinds, have been running the show."[1072]

And it is getting worse, not better. The 1996 Royal Commission even wants welfare payments to go to the band instead of the individual, to be doled out to the intended recipient at the band's discretion. "We think Aboriginal communities should be able to use the money now earmarked for individual welfare payments as an instrument of broader economic development…. Aboriginal communities or nations could take charge of the funds their residents now receive for social assistance."[1073]

So long as Indians are relying on government money, the paternalism is still present, and men are still devalued. However, there is something to be said for the Guaranteed Annual Income idea, being promoted by Senator Hugh Segal and others. The idea is that it is better to give the poor money than to provide free services. They know their own needs best, and it allows them some decision-making power. So it seems preferable, so long as we are still sending cash, to send the cash to individual Indians rather than asking the band to care for them. It is at least a step on the road to self-sufficiency. Why not use Canadian indigenous people as our test of the GAI concept?

Herding unicorns

Nor is the problem that traditional Indian culture has been insufficiently nurtured or respected or protected. Everyone loves Indian culture, or this thing they think is Indian culture. Everyone laps it up, in their movies and their dime novels and their New Age workshops and their comic books. Absolutely nothing has been done in this country, until the recent fad of multiculturalism, to preserve traditional Jewish or Irish or Lebanese culture. Yet these groups have survived the trauma well enough.

But while the Armenians or the Italians or the Germans have by and large, in all that is not useful or essential to their conscience, sought to assimilate, more or less everything we have done "for" the Indians has tended to preserve or create difference from the mainstream.

Let's look briefly at the real post-contact history of the Canadian Indian. It is hardly a history of forced assimilation.

To begin with, it was not in the interest of the fur trade, Canada's first great industry, to see Indians assimilate. If they did, if they settled down to farm, the trading companies would lose their supply of furs. The Hudson's Bay Company and its peers, therefore, did not go out of their way to encourage the process.

"The chief officers," writes Father Lacombe, missionary to the Northwest,

> … sometimes looked on our arrival and our work with a jealous eye. In addition to this they felt that their policy was being interfered with—that policy of preventing the entrance of civilization and of retaining the ancien régime. We were received and tolerated, but it was because they could not do otherwise.[1074]

Father Morice echoes the point:

> [T]he great commercial corporation scarcely relished the idea of seeing missions, ... established within its vast dominions.… [I]ts directing body had voted an order of the day whereby it was decided that "neither the Protestant nor the Catholic missionaries would be encouraged or assisted in extending their labours beyond the limits of the [Red River] colony without its special consent."[1075]

So much for having a foreign religion forced upon them.

As for the Canadian bureaucracy that succeeded the fur traders, it is written plainly enough on page 273 of the Indian Department's *Blue Book* for 1908, as for other years: "It was never the policy nor the end and aim of the endeavor to transform the Indian into a white man."[1076] The 1966 Hawthorn Report observes, "Reserves, according to the theory of the time, were to be kept free from the influence of the modern industrial world."[1077] For many years, on their own initiative and without legal warrant, even in violation of treaty, the bureaucrats of Indian Affairs prohibited natives from leaving their reserves without a permit. Although segregation might not have been their reason for doing this—it was supposedly to avoid clashes during and after the North West Rebellion—assimilation was the last thing this was promoting.

"Many of those charged with fixing the problem are too busy profiting by it" laments Frank Busch, a modern Indian entrepreneur.[1078] Rubenstein and Clifton decry "the profitable 'Indian industry,' a loose coalition of like-minded and self-serving people and groups, aboriginal and non-aboriginal, whose positions, status and livelihoods would be adversely affected if indigenous people ever achieved the same life-chance outcomes as other Canadians."[1079] Allard writes "the impoverished Indians living in Third World conditions are essential to the continued existence of the multitude of consultants, program analysts, researchers, administrators and managers who swell the ranks of the bureaucracy. These are largely middle class professionals who have families to support and households to maintain. They are part of the Canadian economy. If Indian Affairs was successful in addressing the needs of its clients, its raison d'être would cease. All those people who make up the bureaucracy would find themselves unemployed."[1080]

The residential schools did not, as charged, attempt to assimilate the Indians. The very notion of a separate Indian school system, as opposed to having Indian children attend regular schools with everyone else, was apartheid, and ideal for preserving their separateness. Far from "taking the Indian out of the man," and teaching Indians as if they were whites, according to Claire Hutchings,

> [f]ollowing the ideas of Sifton and others like him, the academic goals of these schools were "dumbed down." As Campbell Scott stated at the time, they didn't want students that were "made too smart for the Indian villages": "To this end the curriculum in residential schools has been simplified and the practical instruction given is such as may be immediately of use to the pupil when he returns to the reserve after leaving school."[1081]

Deputy Minister of Indian Affairs James Smart argued in 1898: "To educate children above the possibilities of their station, and create a distaste for what is certain to be their environment in life would be not only a waste of money but doing them an injury instead of conferring a benefit upon them."[1082]

Their "station"? Unless it is assumed that Indians are mentally inferior to whites, why are they not entitled to the same educational opportunities, and the same station? This was a system designed to entrap them on reserves.

The Hawthorn Report, in 1966, notes:

> With the earlier policy, the Indian was expected to be born, live and die on his reserve. There was no question of his leaving. The reserve was his refuge and salvation. Under these circumstances, the little education extended to the Indians was felt to be adequate to assure their economic and social welfare within the limits of the reserve. To be able to read, write and count, to know how to utilize and preserve the environment, to possess some notion of hygiene, this was felt sufficient for life on the reserve. Academic knowledge as such was not considered important.[1083]

Note here the assumption that Indians needed to be taught about preserving the environment. They were not yet natural romantics, as they supposedly are today, thanks to Chief Pseudo-Seattle and the New Age.

Nor did the missionaries, counter to the standard and unjust accusation, practice "cultural imperialism" or "cultural genocide." As serious Christians, they inevitably considered themselves "in the world but not of it"; they felt no special allegiance to the majority culture, which was, after all, the kingdom of this world. Most often, for all that they disapproved of many elements of Indian tradition, they saw themselves as a bulwark for the native people against the evils of the mainstream as well.

Even had they been driven by sheer self-interest, their self-interest was to keep the Indians apart. This increased their own importance and influence, with both the Indians and the government, as mediators, advisers, and interpreters.

Jesuits are not dumb.

And there was not going to be much argument from band leaders. Preserving Indian segregation is also in their interest. Governments dealing only directly with them, and not with individual Indians, increased and still increases their wealth and power. They have become feudal lords. Are they going to overturn their own privileges? Can we expect Louis XVI to help storm Versailles?

The general population has always considered all this reasonable, and has never raised the uproar that it ought, because it all meshes with the Noble Savage myth. Of course, Indians must not ever be released into the real world. That would destroy their innocence. They might get hit by a car or something. They must be taken care of, like the charming imaginary forest creatures they are. They, and their idyllic cartoon culture, must be protected from civilization; civilization is dirty and evil. And they are not supposed to be doing well, in the midst of it all.

The Noble Savage's burden

Chrétien, who with his background knows the problem better than most, summarizes the issue as he sees it: "they are traditional.... They are nostalgic about the past when they were going hunting and fishing...."[1084]

It is not that traditional Indian culture is conservative, traditionalist, isolationist; although it was. It is that the myth of the Noble Savage is conservative. It is founded on a nostalgia for an imagined past. Too many Indians are trapped in it, and feel a false moral imperative to walk backwards into the Never Never Land of childhood dreams. Breaking that imaginary bond is no easy thing. G. Kent Gooderham suggests, of the Indian dilemma as he sees it, "passing [as white] leaves a sense of betrayal of a social legacy."[1085] That is the burden of the Noble Savage.

Lord Savage, though noble, dare not leave his estate. Contact with the outside is poison; so says the legend. But staying keeps him soaked in a destructive cult of nostalgia, reinforces this fantasy Kool-Aid, driving him to drugs, drink, violence, despair or death.

Many aboriginals have probably, within their own psyche, in the darkness of their nights, influenced as much as the rest of us by popular culture, been caught in this double bind. If they succeed, if they are at peace in the world, if they do anything by and for themselves, if they strive to make things better, they have betrayed their heritage. They have let everyone down.

They are supposed to be poor, disconsolate, depressed, and nostalgic for a perfect but lost past: our collective childhood.

They have left only one choice. They can buy into the myth, lament that their heritage has been taken from them, and play dead. That is the easy road. Or else the logic of the romantic legend leaves them only the painful alternative of walking away from their Indian identity, denying they were ever Indian. Because Indianness has been defined as incompatible with life in the modern world.

That is an unfair choice. By seeking to artificially sustain an unsustainable imaginary culture, we are killing both Indians and any real Indian traditions of value that remain.

Anyone can see from the anguish of Attawapiskat that the current situation of Canadian Indians on reserve is not good.

In Quebec, according to government sources, "the death rate among Aboriginal children is triple the death rate among non-Aboriginal children, diabetes is two or three times more common, Aboriginal children are three to five times more likely to experience poverty, neglect, and abandonment, nearly half of families are single-parent, one out of four adults is unemployed, and rates of tuberculosis are high."[1086] Naomi Riley cites similar numbers for the United States: "Involvement in gang activity is more prevalent among Native Americans than it is among Latinos and African Americans. Native American women report being raped two and half times as often as the national average. The rate of child abuse among Native Americans is twice as high as the national average."[1087]

The Assembly of First Nations offers this list of laments:

> One in four children in First Nation communities live in poverty. That's almost double the national average.
>
> Suicide rates among First Nation youth are five to seven times higher than among young non-Aboriginal Canadians.
>
> The life expectancy of First Nation citizens is five to seven years less than non-Aboriginal Canadians and infant mortality rates are 1.5 times higher.
>
> Tuberculosis rates among First Nation citizens living on-reserve are 31 times the national average.
>
> A First Nation youth is more likely to end up in jail than to graduate high school.
>
> First Nation children, on average, receive 22% less funding for child welfare services than other Canadian children. [Not mentioned, but surely at least as worrisome, is the fact that far more Indian kids are in care.]
>
> There are almost 600 unresolved cases of missing and murdered Aboriginal women in Canada.[1088]

Menno Boldt, writing in 1993, cited the following:

> Indian suicide rates are unmatched in any other population in the world; their life expectancy is ten years less than for all Canadians; they experience epidemics of tuberculosis that do not occur in any other part of Canadian society; their rate of infant mortality is 2.5 times the Canadian rate; the number of children "in care" is 6 times the Canadian rate; their incidence of alcoholism is 13 times the Canadian rate; their rate of foetal alcohol syndrome is between 15 and 20 times the Canadian rate; their rate of incarceration is 5 times the Canadian rate; the death rate for Indians under the age of 35 is 3 times the Canadian rate; their rate of unemployment stands at 70 per cent on most reserves; 80 per cent live under the "poverty line."[1089]

It sounds awful. And no, as we have seen, this is not all somehow due to "poverty."

But wait. Before we go further, is all this really true, of Indians generally?

Probably not.

Remember, many Canadians, perhaps 50 to 75 percent, have Indian blood. They are your neighbours. They might be you. They are not appearing in any of those figures. They are in the statistics for non-aboriginal Canadians. They are so far as we can tell doing well.

So it is specifically those who continue to identify as Indians, and especially those on reserves, who are doing poorly. Those who have carefully preserved their supposed Indian cultural identity as Noble Savages.

On the one hand, this is our proof that Indians are perfectly able to assimilate. They have, and they are. On the other, this is our clear proof that they are better off if they do.

If that is not enough evidence, consider this: self-identified "Métis"—at least half-integrated, and *sans* reserves—do better than Indians or Inuit/Eskimos on almost any measure, while Indians and Inuit, with widely different original cultures and genetic makeup, do almost the same.

Identifying with an imaginary culture is a failing strategy. Obviously. Klingons, hobbits, and Jedi knights are probably doing poorly too. Most of them live in their Mum's basement playing computer games.

Nor is assimilation really the issue. That has already happened. Preserving or letting go of traditional culture is not the issue. We have little to no idea what of traditional Indian culture remains; and neither do the Indians. Nothing was written down. Not that what we know of traditional Indian culture tends to recommend it as a viable and a proper way of life.

What we have now is a distinct "Indian" culture, but a new one. What we have is a dependent culture, a permanent underclass, developed over the last one or two hundred years. It is, in many ways—notably in its dependency and its bureaucracy—the very opposite of traditional Indian culture.

It is the romantic allure of the Noble Savage, not assimilation nor retention of traditional ways, that holds Indians back. It is dysfunctional on its face. You cannot live on rainbows. For many who bought in heavily, the Sixties did not end well, either. Even the romantic poets had a knack for addiction, insanity, and dying young.

Depression, staying blind drunk, sudden rage, and suicide are the only rational responses.

Reserves and reservations

The first suggestion the young people of Attawapiskat came up with in their brainstorming session for making things better was not actually more government money, but to "Stand up against bullying and etc."[1090]

"And etc."?

Are they being coy? Is there something here they are afraid to make explicit?

When interviewed, one 17-year-old was a little more forthcoming. She said the bullying was not from other kids, but from adults. That should raise flags: a reserve is not a happy social environment.

> "Something happened to me when I was a kid," she added, "but I don't want to talk about it."[1091]

It looks as though for some, perhaps most, of the kids who were thinking of self-termination, the real issue was child abuse.

This is also the opinion of Susan Aglukark, the Inuit singer/songwriter. She told Canadian Press in an interview she believed child sex abuse is the "root cause of the youth suicide crisis that has been ravaging remote northern outposts in recent years, such as the Attawapiskat and Wapekeka First Nations in northern Ontario." She herself was sexually abused as a child, and she says this is the common experience in aboriginal communities.[1092]

Pity, then, that we've done away with the residential schools. There goes the obvious option for escape.

Ending the reserves was a recommendation of Chrétien's 1969 *White Paper.* They are the very essence of segregation. Pierre Trudeau called them "ghettos." Were camps for Japanese-Canadians a good idea?

Some have argued that the sheer absence of private property on reserves explains the general despair, disorder, and disrepair found there. Involuntary "communist" societies have always failed world-wide. Why should we expect any different on James Bay?

R. Sinclair writes:

> No Indian has an understood, defined interest in the land that his band owns, nor in that which he occupies. He has not property, subject to his disposal, even the right to use the land he occupies. Worse still, he has no real property in the buildings he erects, in the fences he constructs, in the wells he digs, in the drains he makes, in the garden he enriches, in anything he does to improve such land, nor in any chattels or things he possesses, if these happen to be on a reserve.[1093]

One can see how this might limit one's ambitions.

"An Indian annuitant," Sinclair complains,

> … cannot with his annuity money purchase anything that he can dispose of, or give title to, no matter how necessitous his circumstances may be, or how advantageous it might be for him to complete such arrangement as he might desire to enter upon. The Indian when he wishes to deal with the white man is found by the latter so involved in the technicalities, prohibitions and exemptions of the Indian Act and its multifarious amendments that he is absolutely prevented from doing business or transacting even the most ordinary affairs that daily, as a matter of course, are the ordinary incidents of life in the experience of other citizens…. [T]he effect of the Indian Act and its administration has been to deprive the Indian of initiative, ambition, self-reliance and every other factor that goes to make a man and citizen, to drive him and his race into a corner and permanently accentuate the differences between two peoples.[1094]

All the problems reported of native people seem to be worst on reserves. Riley says in *The New Trail of Tears*, "an estimated one out of every four girls and one out of every six boys in Indian country is molested before the age of 18.... Violent crime on the country's 310 reservations is on average about 2.5 times as high as the national average."[1095]

The absence of private property is not the only problem. It causes others. A reserve is also, and perhaps inevitably, a little oasis of totalitarianism, reinforcing dependency. When nobody owns anything, the government owns everything. All money is under the control of the federal government or the local council.

"Since there is no real separation between politics and administration on reserves," writes Jean Allard,

> ...everything on a reserve that is in any way related to band administration is politicized. Whoever is elected is in control of just about everything on a reserve.... Chiefs, councils and their allies—who make up the ruling elite—exercise power and control over the lives of people who live on reserves that is unheard of in a democratic country. They control everything: from who gets the on-reserve jobs to who gets plumbing repairs. The ruling elite exercises total control while the impoverished class is voiceless and powerless.[1096]

Leona Freed, national president of the First Nations Accountability Coalition, complains that "[i]f a band member opposes the chief and council, all services are cut off. They are chased off the reserve.... There is abuse of authority and intimidation tactics...."[1097] "If you oppose [Chief and council]," she wrote, "you get your tires slashed, the contents of your house destroyed, your pets murdered, your children are apprehended by their child care agency ... you can lose your job, and if you are on welfare, you can lose that, too."[1098]

Elections on most reserves are now nominally democratic, thanks to federal government requirements. But no real democracy can operate under these conditions. "Democracy cannot be adequately served," says Allard, "where the same elected officials running for office are also in control of the election machinery."[1099] Since the government holds all power, anyone known to be in dissent risks losing home and livelihood. Perks of all sorts can be doled out to supporters, and even the returning officer is a local band hire. It would take an exceptionally honest band leader and council not to take advantage. How then dares opposition organize?

Although not all reserves are remote, some are. This makes it that much harder for Indians to find work. This is not a magic solution: the Hawthorn Report discovered that, even in reserves located close to jobs and population centres, most Indians tend to be unemployed or underemployed.[1100] But it would help if they did feel more inclined to move. As they once did.

Behind the buckskin curtain

There is another problem with the reserves, and with trying to preserve their essentially communist nature. Perfect social equality in material goods may not imply the peaceful sharing community that Engels and others envision.

"As far as could be seen," writes F.F. Payne of the Inuit/Eskimo of Hudson Strait in the late 19th century,

> … it seemed to be the general belief that all property, especially in the way of food, belonged to everybody in common and therefore, if you held more than another it was only because you or your family were physically strong enough to protect it. Few men of course would steal from one another when food was plentiful, thereby making enemies for themselves, but, when food is scarce, might is right, and all make note of the position of their neighbors' caches before the winter's snow covers them.[1101]

Sir George Back notes, "the Indian considers, and perhaps rightly, that he is only obeying the natural impulse of self-preservation, in laying forcible hands on whatever falls within his reach."[1102]

Father LeJeune writes, of his experience with the Huron:

> With all these fine qualities, the Savages have another, more annoying than those of which we have spoken, but not so wicked; it is their importunity toward strangers.… [I]f they know our dinner hour, they come purposely to get something to eat. They ask continually, and with such incessant urgency, that you would say that they are always holding you by the throat. If you show them anything whatever, however little it may be adapted to their use, they will say, "Dost thou love it? Give it to me." ... [T]hey would not give you the value of an obole, if they did not expect, so to speak, to get back a pistole; for they are ungrateful in the highest degree.

He offers this extreme example:

> We have kept here and fed for a long time our sick Savage, who came and threw himself into our arms in order to die a Christian, … on his account, his children brought a little elk meat, and they were asked what they wished in exchange, for the presents of the Savages are always bargains. They asked

> some wine and gunpowder, and were told that we could not give them these things; but that, if they wished something else that we had, we would give it to them very gladly. A good meal was given them, and finally they carried back their meat, since we did not give them what they asked for.... From this sample, judge of the whole piece.[1103]

This is not a reflection on Indian character. This is a reflection on Indian culture. This is what real communism looks like; you are going to see this sort of thing in any society in which the right to private property is not recognized.

The syllogism works like this: You have something. I do not. I want it. You have no greater right to it than I. Therefore, if you keep it and do not give it to me, you are doing me an injustice.

Since tribal life lacks the legal structures to protect private property, this is a feature of tribal life. And Father LeJeune is wrong to think Indians act differently among themselves. Samuel Hearne writes, "They are forever pleading poverty, even among themselves; and when they visit the Factory, there is not one of them who has not a thousand wants."[1104]

Livingston Jones reports of the Tlingit:

> The most absurd claims are made for money. A native who owned an interest in a well-paying gold mine was hounded for money by a woman, on the ground that she and her people used to fish in the stream near the gold mine. Another woman insisted on a man paying her some money because at one time she prayed (so she claimed) for the superintendent of the Training School to take his sister into the school. She urged that it was owing to her prayer that the sister was taken in, and the girl's education was, therefore, due to her. For this reason she claimed that the brother should pay her some money.[1105]

This is not about Indian culture in particular, either. The same things are said by anthropologists of the equally tribal African Bushmen.

> [T]he pervasive occurrence of "demand-sharing" (see Peterson 1993) may act as a disincentive to increased effort. Everyone who has worked among the Bushmen has commented upon the continual dunning and constant pressures to share that go on. Here is Patricia Draper (1978:45): "The give and take of tangibles and intangibles goes on in the midst of a high level of bickering. Until one learns the cultural meaning of this continual verbal assault,

> the outsider wonders how the !Kung can stand to live with each other ...." People continually dun the Europeans and especially the European anthropologists since unlike most Europeans, the anthropologists speak !Kung. In the early months of my own field work I despaired of ever getting away from continual harassment. As my knowledge of !Kung increased, I learned that the !Kung are equally merciless in dunning each other. Both Wiessner (1982:79) and Marshall (1968:94) have commented on the fact that the persistent pressures to share have led the !Kung to limit their work effort, since in working harder they would likely expose themselves to demands to share the fruits of their additional labors.[1106]

Similar observations have been made by anthropologists observing Australian aborigines.[1107]

In the absence of any property rights, peace and security for each individual, such as it is, also depends on keeping the rest of the tribe content. Anyone who has more than the next guy is immediately in danger: there is little to prevent the others from just taking it. So, the pressures to "share" are enormous. We have seen this dynamic in the potlatch.

Hawthorn observed of Canadian Indians in 1966, "the temporarily successful individual whose 'family and kinfolk move in on him and eat and drink him out of house and home' has become a widely quoted item in the folklore about Indians."[1108]

It becomes important, therefore, in reservation culture, always to appear poorer than the next chap. Otherwise, you are going to lose what you have. But if you can make yourself out as poorer, he has to give you his stuff.

This is the opposite of a work incentive. You would have to be a fool to work hard.

"When two parties of ... Indians meet," Samuel Hearne says of the Chipewyan,

> ... the ceremonies which pass between them are quite different from those made use of in Europe on similar occasions; for when they advance within twenty or thirty yards of each other, they make a full halt, and in general sit or lie down on the ground, and do not speak, for some minutes. At length one of them, generally an elderly man, if any be in company, breaks silence, by acquainting the other party with every misfortune that has befallen him and his companions from the last time they had seen or heard of each other; and also of all deaths and other calamities that

> have befallen any other Indians during the same period, at least as many particulars as have come to his knowledge.
>
> When the first has finished his oration, another aged orator, (if there be any) belonging to the other party relates, in like manner, all the bad news that has come to his knowledge; and both parties never fail to plead poverty and famine on all occasions.[1109]

It is a competition to convince the other that you are worse off than he is.

Hearne tells of an encounter with a visiting group of Indians. The Europeans, not knowing the protocol, nor how communism works, of course do not follow it. They come in looking prosperous.

> [A] committee of them entered my tent. The ringleader seated himself on my left-hand. They first begged me to lend them my skipertogan to fill a pipe of tobacco. After smoking two or three pipes, they asked me for several articles which I had not, and among others for a pack of cards; but on my answering that I had not any of the articles they mentioned, one of them put his hand on my baggage, and asked if it was mine. Before I could answer in the affirmative, he and the rest of his companions (six in number) had all my treasure spread on the ground. One took one thing, and another another, till at last nothing was left but the empty bag, which they permitted me to keep. At length, considering that, though I was going to the Factory, I should want a knife to cut my victuals, an awl to mend my shoes, and a needle to mend my other clothing, they readily gave me these articles, though not without making me understand that I ought to look upon it as a great favour. Finding them possessed of so much generosity, I ventured to solicit them for my razors; but thinking that one would be sufficient to shave me during my passage home, they made no scruple to keep the other; luckily they chose the worst. To complete their generosity, they permitted me to take as much soap as I thought would be sufficient to wash and shave me during the remainder of my journey to the Factory.[1110]

This was nothing personal, nor was it aimed at Europeans in particular; the Indians travelling with Hearne were treated the same way.

Hearne reports such behaviour as the norm. "[T]he Northern Indians are so covetous, and pay so little regard to private property as to take every advantage of bodily strength to rob their neighbours, not only of their goods, but of their wives," he writes.[1111]

> It has ever been the custom among those people for the men to wrestle for any woman to whom they are attached; and, of course, the strongest party always carries off the prize. A weak man, unless he be a good hunter and well-beloved, is seldom permitted to keep a wife that a stronger man thinks worth his notice: for at any time when the wives of those strong wrestlers are heavy-laden either with furs or provisions, they make no scruple of tearing any other man's wife from his bosom, and making her bear a part of his luggage. This custom prevails throughout all their tribes, and causes a great spirit of emulation among their youth, who are upon all occasions, from their childhood, trying their strength and skill in wrestling. This enables them to protect their property, and particularly their wives, from the hands of those powerful ravishers; some of whom make almost a livelihood by taking what they please from the weaker parties, without making them any return. Indeed, it is represented as an act of great generosity, if they condescend to make an unequal exchange; as, in general, abuse and insult are the only return for the loss which is sustained.[1112]

This is the one feature of traditional Indian culture that is apparently carefully preserved on our reserves, if in a muted form. On them all major property is held in common: this retains the basic structure.

This "demand-sharing" may be the "adult bullying" described by the youth of Attawapiskat. The group pulls down any individual who stands out.

Investigating possible malfeasance on the Stoney Reserve, Alberta Provincial Court Judge John Reilly found that "[i]n my attempts to find people who would be interested in participating in a justice committee, victim assistance, and sentencing circles, I have been told over and over again that people are afraid to participate because of repercussions. This fear, and intimidation and violence, appear to be a dominant part of life on this reserve.... Residents of the reserve describe it to me as a 'prison without bars', and a 'welfare ghetto.'"[1113]

Mary Baker, at the 1967 National Conference on Indian and Northern Education, opposed too much education for fellow Indians on the grounds that "Indians just may find out that their own educated offspring, their sons and daughters, are even more anti-Indian than the most ignorant, insensitive Whiteman."[1114]

Why would that be?

Perhaps because, if you stand apart as better educated, better paid, smarter, more moral, or more successful, your life on reserve becomes intolerable. In order to safely achieve, Indians may find themselves forced to leave the reserve, to leave their native milieu—those who are strong enough and brave enough to do so. Writing in 1966, Hawthorn laments that "[a] high proportion of Indian students who complete their high school education and take special vocational, technical or professional training, leave their home reserve permanently."[1115]

Aside from holding Indians back from adventuring anything, peer pressure and the ethic of "demand-sharing" could contribute to the constant complaints of having been "cheated" by treaty and by the "white man." Tribal life is a training ground for envy and for begging. Demands for more money may never end. So long as another Canadian has anything some Indian does not, by these tribal mores, the other Canadian is obliged to hand it over.

The urgent need not to rock the boat among your neighbours on reserve may also make it awkward to attribute any fault to a fellow tribe member. Hence the need, when bad things happen, for the white man to be available as scapegoat. If it is not the residential schools, it will be something else.

Have no illusions: given these social norms, reconciliation will never come.

Catch-22

We are faced, however, with a double bind. Anything we do *for* the Indians makes the problem worse. Anything given to the Indians is itself a part of the problem. It reinforces the dependency. Yet, given their dependency, they are not motivated to do anything for themselves. Even a thing so simple as to move away.

Moreover, the Canadian government is limited in what it can do by treaty. It has treaty obligations, now enshrined as well in the Canadian constitution. A treaty cannot be unilaterally changed. Whatever is done, the affected Indians must agree.

As of 1970 and their response to the *White Paper*, the Indians have chosen continued dependency. And left themselves no hope.

Or have they?

At that time, before, and ever since, it has been the Indian *chiefs* who have chosen dependency: the provincial band leaderships, and later the Assembly of First Nations, the AFN. They have continued to speak for all Indians.

They unfortunately have a vested interest.

Their power in this regard is in itself a creation of the Canadian government. At treaty negotiations, the Canadian commissioners required the Indian tribes to select a leader who would speak for them all. Negotiating Treaty 1 at Fort Garry in 1871, Lieutenant-Governor Archibald advised the assembled Indians,

> As the Queen has made her choice of a chief to represent her, you must, on your part, point out to us the chiefs you wish to represent you, as the persons you have faith in.
>
> Mr. Simpson cannot talk to all your braves and people, but when he talks to chiefs who have your confidence he is talking to you all, and when he hears the voice of one of your chiefs whom you name he will hear the voice of you all. It is for you to say who shall talk for you, and also who shall be your chief men. Let them be good Indians, who know your wishes and whom you have faith in.[1116]

The chief selected was then treated as if a civil servant and a representative to the Indians of the federal government. His special status was enshrined in the treaties. Ever since, he has been in effect a government functionary.

His pre-eminent position, the office of Indian chief or band leader as we now know it, was a creation of the treaty process. In most traditional Indian groups, leadership was more casual, situation by situation, depending on personal prestige. Individuals generally had the option to refuse to go along or follow some new leader almost issue be issue. It was a free market in leadership; but no longer.

Moreover, according to Jean Allard, himself Métis, the Assembly of First Nations is itself not necessarily responsive even to the band leadership. It was more or less arbitrarily recognized at first by the federal government as the voice of Canada's Indians, and then given all the public money, solidifying its position and forcing Indians to conform to its dictates.

In 1973, Allard says, the federal government hired an outside consultant to evaluate whether the National Indian Brotherhood, predecessor to the AFN, in fact did represent the average Indian. He identified two weaknesses in both the provincial and national associations:

> 1. The Associations are not directly accountable to those whom they hold they represent since the people cannot effectively withdraw support.
>
> 2. Credence is lent by specific recognition by Government through such funding that such Organizations do in fact represent the people.[1117]

"This silencing of people," Allard goes on to say, "is further entrenched because dissenters cannot withdraw their support of Indian political leaders by withdrawing their financial support: all financial support comes from Indian Affairs and other government departments."[1118] This leads to "a form of totalitarianism whereby the rights of the individual are denied in the name of an allegedly infallible leadership."[1119]

It is perhaps time the government began talking to all the "braves and people," to use Archibald's phrase.

The government has a ledger of all treaty Indians, in which each new birth is recorded. Instead of dealing with band leadership, all dealings henceforth could be with individuals, who can then decide for themselves and spend the money as they see fit.

They might choose to fund a band organization with the power to levy taxes, as other Canadians do with municipal governments. They might choose to combine to preserve shared cultural traditions. They might not. But they would be taking responsibility for themselves at last. They would at last have their freedom, and their chance to make decisions for themselves.

Necessarily, enfranchisement and full equal citizenship for Canadian Indians must come on an individual basis, as they assume personal responsibility. This is something that cannot be done for them as a group.

In a backhanded way, the Alberta chiefs pinpointed the problem in their 1970 *Red Paper*: "Freedom," they argue, "depends on having financial and social security first."[1120]

They used this premise to ask for more money for the Indian bands and reserves. "The immediate problem before us, therefore, is to enable the bands to achieve basic, financial and social security where they live now, and it is crucial that they do so as a community."[1121]

Wrong about that last clause. If their argument is valid, and it is, it applies equally to Indians as individuals. Unless they individually have financial and social security, they do not have freedom. They cannot remain subject to the paternalistic control of the band leadership—"the community."

Calls to action

The reserves must be broken up.

I believe the government has the power to do this already, individual by individual. According to the original Indian Act, should an individual Indian qualify for, and request, enfranchisement, "[t]he Superintendent-General may give him a suitable allotment of land from the lands belonging to the band of which he is a member." The government might make this more attractive by offering enfranchisement on demand, and allowing some form of intermediate "enfranchisement" which involves only separating from the reserve. It might not automatically require the individual to surrender other rights accorded by treaty or by aboriginal status.

This is only a partial solution, but it may be a *sine qua non* for anything more: to get the individual out of a poisonous milieu and beginning to do things for him- or herself.

Another approach could be to recognize the band and its assets as a corporation, in which all current band members hold shares. The band as a corporation might then be prohibited from alienating property, as at present; but each individual would be free to sell his share, or borrow against its value, thereby walking away from the reserve, if he or she chose, with a fair share of its assets; or, if they preferred, mortgaging to get the capital for a business.

This could be relatively profitable for the bands themselves: beyond the value of the land and buildings, many people, as we have seen, want to think of themselves as Indians, and might be prepared to pay for official band membership as some people now buy British peerages. And, after all, we all officially insist that being Indian should not be a matter of race, but of self-identity.

Stockholders could then set up the bylaws of their corporation more or less as they see fit, to preserve or promote their concept of their culture: just as can the Oddfellows or the Foresters. No government need do it for them. But then, if any individual does not like the terms, or some new rule, he can also walk away without crippling financial loss.

Sure, some Indians might foolishly sell off their membership for too little money, and regret it later. That is the risk you take when you manage your own affairs. It is an adult problem.

Beyond breaking up the reserves, we must open a friendly path to happy monoculturalism. This is necessary, first, for the well-being of the Indians. It is necessary, second, because preserving two different forms of citizenship is anathema to our belief in human equality.

It will be very difficult emotionally for individual Indians to take the steps to become full, equal citizens. While being treated like animals is frustrating and infuriating, at the same time, the idea of being left to fend for yourself must be terrifying. So many or most might indefinitely demand the present system of childlike, but secure, dependency.

Many Indians will also suppose that loss of Indian status is against their self-interest: that legally, they are now given superior status, and lots of free stuff. That was the tone of the 1970 *Red Paper*. This is superficially true, but in the long run, false. The proof is in the numbers: those who persist in their official Indian status are simply and plainly not doing as well over time as those who have not. And to insist on being Other is probably to insist on others seeing you as not as fully human as themselves. There is something to be said for human dignity.

This is without necessarily disputing the claim that elements of real Indian culture are useful and admirable. It should go without saying that such elements have mostly already been integrated into the mainstream Canadian culture. People given their own head are unlikely to reject what is useful or attractive, once made aware of it. We heterodox Canadians have from Indian and Eskimo/Inuit sources the canoe; the toboggan; lacrosse; the kayak; the parka; part or most of hockey and football. As most of us learn at some point in school, we have from native North American sources a wide range of our traditional foods: corn, potatoes, tomatoes, beans, peppers, chocolate, pumpkins, turkey, cranberries, wild rice, peanuts, popcorn, maple syrup. Imagine Canada without maple syrup, or canoes, or turkey, or poutine, or ketchup chips. Imagine Canada without hockey. Imagine Canada without the name Canada, for that matter.

One might wonder parenthetically why, when, as we have pointed out, it produced little other technology, Indian culture gave us so many edible plants.

Simple: necessity here is the mother of invention. We who always have enough to eat fall into our settled tastes, and rarely explore. Did you know, for example, dear reader, that crabgrass and dandelions are delicious and full of good nutrition?

But when you are starving, you are likely to try anything. Some of it doesn't kill you.

But as to Canadian culture, John Ralston Saul is essentially right: Canadian culture is a Métis culture. Canadian (and American) culture is what Indian culture evolved to become, by assimilating anything useful from Europe, as Europeans in turn assimilated what was useful from America. To be a real and not a cartoon Indian is simply to be a Canadian or an American.

For real Indians, therefore, joining the mainstream is no betrayal of their heritage. It is their heritage.

The Canadian government should probably not, the recent fad of "multiculturalism" to the contrary, be promoting any culture but Canadian culture. It is the job of a government to promote unity, amity, and a common core of shared values. If Indians themselves want to promote their separateness, that is fine; but funding should come from themselves.

Nor should the government be multiplying advantages to retaining Indian status. The goal should be as it was held to be at the beginning of the treaty process, to gradually phase Indian status out. It was meant as an aid to transition, not a permanent dependent state. Canada is not a nation based on race. Yes, we must honour treaties, but we should not add new benefits making permanent Indian legal status more attractive.

This has certainly been the case to date. It seems like being kind to "poor" Indians, but the bald statistics show it is not.

New treaties might have to be signed, thanks to recent Supreme Court rulings. This is unhelpful. It is a retrograde step. But at least any new treaties should, as a matter of simple equity, offer essentially the same terms as previous ones. Otherwise, you are favouring some Indians over others, and unfairly punishing those who agreed to terms earlier. This was indeed a core principle during the negotiation of the Numbered Treaties: no one group of Indians could be given a significantly better deal than the others.

According to the Numbered Treaties, although they vary in details, acceding Indians are generally entitled to a school or teacher on each reserve (Treaty 1, 2, 3, 7), $3 annually per person (Treaty 1, 2), or $5 annually per person (Treaty 3), $1,500 per band per year in hunting and fishing supplies (Treaty 3), and so on. Chiefs are to be paid $25 a year and get a new suit of clothes every three. Treaty 6 specifies help in case of famine, and a medicine chest on each reserve.

Honouring this indefinitely would not be much help to Indians, but also would not break the federal budget, or amount to an insurmountable temptation to remain dependent on government. Especially if it is given, as it originally was, *in lieu* of any regular social assistance. This would surely be too severe; but it could at least deducted from them.

Or perhaps it is not too severe. Nobody would starve. If anyone genuinely needed help, they could get it promptly: by turning in their Indian card and renouncing Indian status. And, as a matter of course, leaving the reserve.

This works to encourage Indian initiative either way. To be Indian then would be a declaration of independence. If Indian culture is viable, this should be a good test.

But these originally modest provisions have been gradually reinterpreted over the years to mean large-scale ongoing financial support.

The Royal Commission of 1996 argues, for example, that "the $5 annual treaty money—a gift commemorating the agreement in Aboriginal eyes, a form of rent for use of the land in European eyes—was a significant sum in its time. Or, to take another example, the promise of a medicine chest for those who signed Treaty 6 was a commitment to provide the best health care available at that time."[1122]

This is not true. The annuity was not understood by the government as rent, since the Indians had surrendered all rights in the land. It was understood as assistance to starving Indians. And, while $5 per annum was indeed a more significant sum in 1873, when Treaty 3 was signed, just how significant? *EH.net* provides a calculator. Depending which measure you use, it reports, "In 2015, the relative value of $5.00 [US] from 1873 ranges from $93.00 to $10,200.00."[1123]

Given the premise that the money was intended to help provide for the Indians' basic needs, the relevant measure is probably purchasing power. That would put the current equivalent amount according to *EH.net* at $103 per year.

Or take the median figure: $5,146.50. Jean Allard comes up with almost the same figure, based on relative value of Manitoba farmland in 1875 and today.[1124] That is a lot less than Indians now receive from the government.

Nor was promising a chest of medicines a commitment to provide "the best health care available at that time." At that time, there were doctors, nurses, hospitals, pharmacists, and surgeons. The government declined to provide them, as they were too expensive. They agreed to a cabinet of common medicines. Yet this article in one treaty is now expanded to mean free health care of all kinds.

The promise of a teacher or a school, originally apparently intended to give knowledge of basic trades, agriculture, or husbandry, has similarly been expanded to "[t]he provision of education of all types and levels to all Indian people at the expense of the Federal government."[1125]

And so, let us honour the treaties as written and intended, until all Indians, one by one, are ready to care for themselves. Let us honour them, instead of something new and strange we have now substituted. Scrupulously honoured, as written, they would not be so destructive of Indian enterprise.

Some provisions, it is true, cannot be honoured any longer, and perhaps should not be. Originally, Indian status meant waiving the franchise; a significant sacrifice. It is only logical: if Indians are not competent to care for themselves in modern society, then, as with children, they are not competent to participate or serve in government.

Another original provision in most treaties was the prohibition of alcohol; this remains in the treaty texts. This too makes some sense on the same basis, just as it is appropriate for those not yet of age. And this provision was almost everywhere included at the request of the Indians themselves. But the Supreme Court has made this part of the treaties legally impossible to enforce. This part of the treaties, for better or for worse, has been unilaterally abrogated by the "white man."

In sum, we see over time to have systematically removed all the disadvantages of separate and dependent Indian status, while adding advantages.

Were you wondering about that Indian card?

As it has been dealt, it's a joker. Played from the bottom of the deck.

ABOUT THE AUTHOR

Stephen K. Roney is a Canadian writer, editor, and college instructor, now semi-retired. He is a past president of the Editors' Association of Canada ("Editors Canada"). You may have seen his commentary in *Report* Newsmagazine, the Toronto *Star*, *Catholic Insight*, or in several dozen other publications in Canada and abroad.

CONNECT

This book has a *Facebook* page. Visit, like, and follow for updates on the issues and for many colour illustrations relating to the matters and the history discussed here.

Click, like, follow: https://www.facebook.com/playingtheindiancard/

Visit the author's long-running blog at odsblog.blogspot.com. Subscribe and follow!

"Favourite" the author at Smashwords:
https://www.smashwords.com/profile/view/sroneykor

ENDNOTES

[1] https://www.change.org/p/wilfrid-laurier-university-stop-the-statue-project

[2] Simona Chiose, "Wilfrid Laurier University to Reconsider Plan for Prime Ministers' Statues," *Globe & Mail*, Oct. 21, 2015.

[3] https://www.insidehighered.com/news/2015/07/08/what-should-educators-make-spray-painting-campus-statues-and-symbols-old-south

[4] Derrick O'Keefe, "Canada 150: Against liberal revisionism and false consensus," Medium.com

[5] Charges are per Timothy J. Stanley, "John A. Macdonald's Aryan Canada: Aboriginal Genocide and Chinese Exclusion," *Active History*, July 30, 2015.

[6] "He [George III] ... has endeavoured to bring on the inhabitants of our frontiers, the merciless Indian Savages whose known rule of warfare, is an undistinguished destruction of all ages, sexes and conditions."

[7] Tristin Hopper, "Sure, John A. Macdonald was a racist, colonizer and misogynist—but so were most Canadians back then," *National Post*, January 10, 2015.

[8] D. J. Hall, *From Treaties to Reserves*, Kingston: McGill/Queen's University Press, 2015, p. 75.

[9] "How do we judge Sir John A. Macdonald for starving Indigenous people?" *Rabble*, January 30, 2015.

[10] Bill Curry, "Aboriginals in Canada face 'Third World'-level risk of tuberculosis," *Globe & Mail*, March 10, 2010.

[11] *Facts Respecting Indian Administration in the North-West*. Ottawa: Indian Affairs Branch, 1886, p. 38.

[12] *Ibid*, p. 6.

[13] Robert Talbot, *Alexander Morris: His Intellectual and Political Life and the Numbered Treaties*, Ottawa: U of O Press, 2007, p. 157.

[14] Gilbert Elliot, Earl of Minto, "The Recent Rebellion in North-West Canada," *The Nineteenth Century*, Aug. 1885, v. 18, no. 102, p. 314.

[15] Theresa Gowanlock and Theresa Delaney, *Two Months in the Camp of Big Bear*. Parkdale, ON: *Times*, 1885, p. 100.

[16] William Cameron, *Blood Red the Sun*, Edmonton: Hurtig, 1977, p. 36.

[17] J. J. Curran, "Debate on Louis Riel," Ottawa: *Hansard*, 1886, pp. 8-9.

[18] Robert J. Talbot, *Negotiating the Numbered Treaties*, Saskatoon: Purich Press, 2009, p. 144; Alexander Morris, *The Treaties of Canada*, Toronto: Willing and Williamson, 1880, p. 224.

[19] Tom Flanagan, *First Nations: Second Thoughts*, McGill-Queen's Press, 2000, 2nd edition, 2008, p. 18.

[20] Rev. Andrew Brown, *The Indians of Western Canada*, Toronto: Presbyterian Church in Canada, 1895, p. 13.

[21] Erwan Chartier-Le Floch, "Les Bretons au Canada," *Le Telegramme*, April 6, 2014; http://www.letelegramme.fr/histoire/les-bretons-au-canada-06-04-2014-10111102.php

[22] *Jesuit Relations* 1, p. 161.

[23] *Ibid.*, p. 171.

[24] Peter Jones, *History of the Ojebway Indians*, London: Wesleyan Missionary Society, 1861, p. 39.

[25] Marc Stengel, "The Diffusionists Have Landed," *The Atlantic*, January 2000.

[26] Joseph Brean, "CBC under fire for documentary that says first humans to colonize New World sailed from Europe," *National Post*, January 11, 2018.

[27] Fr. Chrestien LeClercq, *New Relation of Gaspesia*, Toronto: Champlain Society, 1910, pp. 85-6.

[28] John West, *The Substance of a Journal During a Residence at the Red River Colony*, London: L.B. Seeley, 1827, p. 132.

[29] Jesse Kline, "Killing Aboriginals with Our Kindness," *National Post*, May 14, 2013.

[30] Royal Commission on Aboriginal Peoples, *People to People, Nation to Nation: Highlights from the Report of the Royal Commission on Aboriginal Peoples*. Ottawa: 1996.

[31]Truth and Reconciliation Commission, *The Survivors Speak*, Ottawa: 2015, p. 7.

[32] With thanks to Cy Strom for this insight. See, for example, http://www.britishmuseum.org/research/collection_online/collection_object_details/collection_image_gallery.aspx?assetId=30526001&objectId=951898&partId=1

[33] Charles Mair, *Through the Mackenzie Basin: A Narrative of the Athabasca and Peace River Treaty Expedition of 1899,* London: Simpkin Marshall, 1908, pp. 62-3.

[34] P. H. Bryce, *The Story of a National Crime*, Ottawa: James Hope, 1922, p. 2.

[35] Lewis H. Morgan, *The League of the Iroquois*, NY: Dodd Mead, 1922. Appendix B, p. 277.

[36] *Ibid.*, p. 269.

[37] Richard Pratt, *Drastic Facts about our Indians and our Indian System.* Berkeley, CA: Daily Gazette, 1917, p. 3.

[38] *The Jesuits in North America in the Seventeenth Century*, Boston: Little, Brown, 1912, pp. 321-2.

[39] *Wikipedia*, "Genetic history of indigenous peoples of the Americas."

[40]Graeme Hamilton, "Mikinaks call themselves Quebec's newest aboriginal group," *National Post*, July 7, 2016.

[41] Royal Commission on Aboriginal Peoples, *People to People, Nation to Nation: Highlights from the Report of the Royal Commission on Aboriginal Peoples*. Ottawa: 1996.

[42] e.g. Indian Chiefs of Alberta, *Citizens Plus* (Red Paper), Edmonton: 1970, p. 196.

[43] Ives Goddard, "I am a Redskin," *Native American Studies* 19:2, 2005.

[44] "*cupientes occidentales, et meridionales Indos*," Paul III, *Sublimis Deus*, 1537.

[45] https://en.oxforddictionaries.com/definition/us/nation

[46] http://www.webster-dictionary.org/definition/nation

[47] Jared Diamond, *Guns, Germs, and Steel*, NY: Vintage, 1997, Kindle edition, loc. 628-9.

[48] https://www.merriam-webster.com/dictionary/primitive

[49] https://en.oxforddictionaries.com/definition/us/primitive

[50] Peter Jones, *History of the Ojebway Indians*. London: Wesleyan Missionary Society, 1861, p.32.

[51] Ojibway elders, quoted by Peter Jones, *op cit.*, p. 31.

[52] Augustus C. Thompson, *Moravian Missions*, NY: Charles Scribner's Sons, 1883, p. 232.

[53] "First Nation teen told not to wear 'Got Land?' shirt at school," *CBC*, January 14, 2014.

[54] http://www.smalldeadanimals.com/2014/01/got-land.html

[55] Jared Diamond, *Guns, Germs, and Steel*, NY: Vintage, 1997, p. 577.

[56] "The Iroquois ... made it [pottery] in smaller quantities and in a limited number of forms; but the Non-horticultural Indians, who were in the Status

of savagery, such as the Athapascans, the tribes of California and of the valley of Columbia were ignorant of its use." Lewis Morgan, *Ancient Society*, Chicago: Charles H. Kerr & Co., n.d., p. 13.

[57] Diamond, *op. cit.*, p. 389.

[58] William Cormack, after a trip to the interior of Newfoundland in 1822, quoted in James Howley, *The Beothuks or Red Indians: The Aboriginal Inhabitants of Newfoundland*, Cambridge: 1915, p. 155.

[59] http://www.muskoxfarm.org/

[60] Diamond, *op. cit.*, p. 391.

[61] Christopher Columbus, Journal of the First Voyage, 12th of October.

[62] *Relations* 31, pp. 221-3.

[63] *Relations* 16, p. 199.

[64] *Canada Press*, May 10, 2017.

[65] Chantelle Bellrichard, "Canada Council for the Arts confronts cultural appropriation in 'post-Truth and Reconciliation era,'" *CBC*, September 8, 2017.

[66] Michael Davis, "Indigenous Peoples and Intellectual Property Rights," Research Paper 20, Parliament of Australia, 1996-7.

[67] Jared Diamond, "The Worst Mistake in the History of the Human Race," *Discovery* Magazine, May, 1987, pp. 95-8.

[68] *Ibid.*, p. 98.

[69] *Ibid.*, p. 95.

[70] *Ibid.*, p. 96.

[71] *Ibid.*, p. 97.

[72] David Kaplan, "The Darker Side of the Original Affluent Society" *Journal of Anthropological Research*, 56:3, Autumn, 2000, pp. 301, 303.

[73] Yuval Harari, *Sapiens: A Brief History of Humankind,* London: Random House, 2011, p. 72.

[74] Diamond, *op. cit.*, p. 97.

[75] *Ibid.*, p. 98.

[76] quoted in Sir Harry Johnston, *Pioneers in Canada*, London: Blackie and Son, 1912.

[77] Lee, *The !Kung San. Men, Women, and Work in a Foraging Society*, Cambridge: Cambridge U. Press, 1979, pp. 250-80.

[78] Kaplan, *op cit.*, p. 303.

[79] Marshall Sahlins, *Stone Age Economics*. New York: de Gruyter, 1972, p. 34.

[80] Kaplan, *op. cit.*, p. 303.

[81] Kaplan, *op. cit.*; http://www.rachellaudan.com/2016/01/was-the-agricultural-revolution-a-terrible-mistake.html

[82] Kaplan, op. cit., p. 308.

[83] Gilbert Sproat, *Scenes and Studies of Savage Life*, London: Smith, Elder, 1868, p. 52.

[84] *Ibid.*, p. 52.

[85] Diamond, *op. cit.,* p. 97.

[86] *Ibid.*, p. 97.

[87] Kaplan, *op. cit.*, p. 306.

[88] *Ibid.*, p. 311.

[89] Sproat, *op. cit*, p. 53.

[90] *Jesuit Relations* 39, p. 246.

[91] *Relations* 17, p. 13.

[92] Champlain, *Voyages* 1, Ch. 14.

[93] Hearne, *A Journey from Prince of Wales's Fort in Hudson's Bay to the Northern Ocean in the Years 1769, 1770, 1771, and 1772*. Toronto: The Champlain Society, 1911; originally published 1795, p. 312.

[94] Father LeJeune, *Relations* 17, p. 15.

[95] Father Bressani, *Relations* 39, p. 243.

[96] Champlain, *Voyages* 2, Ch. 4.

[97] Champlain, *Voyages* 2, Ch. 5.

[98] LeClercq, *New Relation of Gaspesia*, Toronto: Champlain Society, 1910. Original French edition 1691, pp. 110-112.

[99] Sproat, *op. cit.*, p 53.

[100] Augustus Thompson, *Moravian Missions*, New York: Charles Scribner's Sons, 1883, p. 231.

[101] John West, *The Substance of a Journal During a Residence at the Red River Colony*, London: L.B. Seeley, 1827, p. 126.

[102] *Ibid.*, pp. 127-9.

[103] Sir George Back, *Narrative of the Arctic Land Expedition to the Mouth of the Great Fish River, and Along the Shores of the Arctic Ocean in the Years 1833, 1834, and 1835*, London: John Murray, 1836, p. 194.

[104] *Ibid.*, pp. 209, 210.

[105] *Ibid.*, p. 218.

[106] Andrew Browning, *The Indians of Western Canada*, Toronto: Presbyterian Church in Canada, 1895, p. 10.

[107] F. F. Payne, "A Few Notes upon the Eskimo of Cape Prince of Wales," Toronto: Meteorological Office, 1889, pp. 359-60.

[108] Nancy Howell, "Feedback and Buffers in Relation to Scarcity and Abundance: Studies of Hunter-Gatherer Populations," *The State of Population Theory*, ed. D. Coleman and R. Schofield. New York: Basil Blackwell, 1986.

[109] Kaplan, *op. cit.*, p. 309, quoting Wilmsen, 1989.

[110] Kaplan, *op. cit.*, p. 309.

[111] Kaplan, *op. cit.*, p. 321; S. Eaton, M. Shostak, and M. Konner, *The Paleolithic Prescription*. New York: Harper and Row, 1988.

[112] Champlain, *Voyages* 1, Ch. 6.

[113] Kaplan, *op. cit.*, p. 307.

[114] Diamond, *op. cit.*, p. 98.

[115] Carmel Schrire, William Steiger, "A Matter of Life and Death: An Investigation into the Practice of Female Infanticide in the Arctic," *Man: the Journal of the Royal Anthropological Society* 9: 162, 1974.

[116] Livingston Jones, *A Study of the Thlingits of Alaska*. NY: Revell, 1914, p. 45.

[117] Knut Rasmussen, *The Netsilik Eskimos, Social Life and Spiritual Culture*. Copenhagen: Gyldendal, 1931.

[118] *Relations* 1, p. 255-7.

[119] *Relations* 1, p. 259.

[120] *Relations* 2, p. 13.

[121] *Relations* 1, p. 167.

[122] West, op. cit., p. 187.

[123] James Ross, *Narrative of a Second Voyage in Search of a North-West Passage*, London: Webster, 1835, p. 5.

[124] Hearne, *op. cit.*, pp. 326-7.

[125] *Relations* 39, p. 243.

[126] Grey Owl, *Men of the Last Frontier*, New York: Scribner's, 1932, pp. 43-4.

[127] Kimberly Tallbear, "Shepard Krech's *The Ecological Indian*: One Indian's Perspective," *The Ecological Indian Review*, IIRM Publications, Sept. 2000.

[128] Grey Owl, *op. cit.*, p. 144.

[129] *Ibid.*, pp. 144-5.

[130] *Relations* 8, p. 55.

[131] quo James Howley, *The Beothuks or Red Indians: The Aboriginal Inhabitants of Newfoundland*, Cambridge: 1915, p. 152.

[132] Horace Greeley, *An Overland Journey from New York to San Francisco in the Summer of 1859*, NY: Saxton, Barker, 1860, p. 87.

[133] Andrew Isenberg, in E. Douglas Branch, *The Hunting of the Buffalo*, Lincoln, Nebraska: University of Nebraska Press, 1962, p. xiii.

[134] "Historians Revisit Slaughter on the Plains," *NY Times*, November 16, 1999.

[135] Alfred Crosby, *Ecological Imperialism,* Cambridge: Cambridge U. Press, 2015, p. 213.

[136] Shepard Krech, "Buffalo Tales: The Near-Extermination of the American Bison," National Humanities Center, http://nationalhumanitiescenter.org/tserve/nattrans/ntecoindian/essays/buffalo.htm

[137] Lewis and Clark, *Journals*, May 29, 1805.

[138] 60:3, Summer, 2000. sidebar; unattributed.

[139] Gerald Williams, "Introduction to Aboriginal Fire Use in North America," *Fire Management Today*, 60:3, Summer, 2000.

[140] Stephen Pyne, "Where Have All the Fires Gone?" *Fire Management Today*, 60:3, Summer, 2000.

[141] *Ibid.*

[142] James Howley, *op. cit.*, p. 145.

[143] Alexander Ross, *The Red River Settlement*, London: Smith, Elder, 1856, p. 199.

[144] Gerald Williams, "Reintroducing Indian-Type Fires: Implications for Land Management," *Fire Management Today*, 60:3, Summer, 2000, p. 40.

[145] *Ibid.*

[146] Gilbert Sproat, *Scenes and Studies of Savage Life*, London: Elder, 1868, p. 38.

[147] *Ibid*. p. 42.

[148] Livingston Jones, *A Study of the Thlingits of Alaska*. NY: Revell, 1914, p. 67.

[149] Maturin Ballou, *Ballou's Alaska,* Boston: Houghton Mifflin, 1896, p. 195.

[150] *Relations* 2, p. 15.

[151] *Ibid.*, p. 17.

[152] John West, *The Substance of a Journal during a Residence at the Red River Colony,* London: L.B. Seeley, 1827, pp. 153-4.

[153] William Bompas, *Diocese of Mackenzie River,* London: Society for Promoting Christian Knowledge, 1888, pp.100-1.

[154] definitions from Peter Coates, *Nature: Western Attitudes Since Ancient Times,* Cambridge: Polity Press, 1998, pp. 3–10.

[155] Mortimer J. Adler, *The Great Ideas*, NY: Macmillan, 1992, p. 561.

[156] *Relations* 7, pp. 173-5.

[157] Father LeJeune, *Relations* 7, p. 83.

[158] James Howley, *The Beothuks or Red Indians: The Aboriginal Inhabitants of Newfoundland*, Cambridge: 1915, p. 181.

[159] Champlain, *Voyages*, 2, Ch. 4.

[160] *Relations* 8, p. 119.

[161] Parkman, *The Jesuits in North America in the Seventeenth Century*, Boston: Little, Brown, 1879, p. 55.

[162] Peter Jones, *History of the Ojebway Indians*. London: Wesleyan Missionary Society, 1861, p. 36.

[163] Gilbert Sproat, *Scenes and Studies of Savage Life*, London: Elder, 1868, p. 175.

[164] Chrestien LeClercq, *New Relations of Gaspesia*, Toronto: Champlain Society, 1910, p. 227.

[165] Livingston Jones, *A Study of the Thlingits of Alaska*. NY: Revell, 1914, p. 166.

[166] Brébeuf, *Jesuit Relations* 10, p. 167-9.

[167] *Relations* 1, p. 285.

[168] *Relations* 6, p. 177.

[169] *Relations* 6, p. 159.

[170] Livingston Jones, *op. cit.*, p. 235.

[171] *Relations* 6, p. 157

[172] *Wikipedia.*

[173] Alexander Morris, *The Treaties of Canada*, Toronto: Willing and Williamson, 1880, p. 74; Robert Talbot, *Negotiating the Numbered Treaties*, Vancouver: UBC Press, 2009, p. 107.

[174] Talbot, *op. cit.*, pp. 185-6, note.

[175] Livingston Jones, *op. cit.,* p. 67-8.

[176] *Ibid.*, p. 93.

[177] *Relations* 12, p. 213.

[178] George Dawson, "Notes on the Indian Tribes of the Yukon District," Geological Survey of Canada, 1887, p. 11.

[179] Howley, *op. cit.*, p. 171.

[180] Steven Pinker, *The Better Angels of Our Nature*, NY: Penguin, 2011, p. 80.

[181] Spengler, "The fraud of primitive authenticity," *Asia Times Online,* July 4, 2006, citing Nicholas Wade.

[182] Pinker, "A History of Violence: Edge Master Class 2011," Edge.org.

[183] Pinker, *The Better Angels of Our Nature*, p. 71.

[184] John Smith, *A True Relation of Such Occurrences and Accidents of Note as Hath Hapned in Virginia*, 1608, p. 49.

[185] Champlain, *Voyages*, 2, Ch. 4.

[186] *Jesuit Relations* 1, p. 267.

[187] *Relations* 2, p. 199.

[188] *Relations* 1, p. 103.

[189] *Relations* 27, pp. 23-5.

[190] Adrien Morice, *History of the Catholic Church in Western Canada*, Toronto: Musson, 1910, p. 236.

[191] Gilbert Sproat, *Scenes and Studies of Savage Life*, London: Smith, Elder, 1868, pp. 186-7.

[192] Cyrus Thomas, *Indians of North America in Historic Times*, Philadelphia: George Barrie and Sons, 1903, p. 358.

[193] Samuel Hearne, *A Journey from Prince of Wales's Fort in Hudson's Bay to the Northern Ocean in the Years 1769, 1770, 1771, and 1772*. Toronto: The Champlain Society, 1911; originally published 1795, pp. 179-80.

[194] *Ibid.*, pp. 281-2.

[195] Mark Van de Logt, *War Party in Blue. Pawnee Scouts in the US Army*. Norman, OK: University of Oklahoma Press, 2012. p. 35.

[196] Francis Parkman, *A Half Century of Conflict*, 2, Boston: Little, Brown, 1905, p. 21, speaking of the Outagami, Winnebago, Sacs, Sioux, and Illinois.

[197] Horace Greeley, *An Overland Journey from New York to San Francisco in the Summer of 1859*, NY: Saxton, Barker, & Co, 1860, p. 52.

[198] *Relations* 3, p. 91.

[199] Van de Logt, *op. cit.*, p. 35.

[200] Francis Parkman, *A Half Century of Conflict*, 1, Boston: Little, Brown 1894, p. 91.

[201] *Ibid.*, p. 115.

[202] *Ibid.*, p. 117.

[203] *Ibid.*, p. 123.

[204] *Ibid.*, p. 124.

[205] *Ibid.*, p. 126.

[206] *Ibid.*, p. 126.

[207] *Ibid.*, p. 497.

[208] Pinker, *The Better Angels of Our Nature*, pp. 82-3.

[209] Keeley, *War before Civilization*, Oxford: Oxford University Press, 1996, pp. 67-9.

[210] Parkman, *A Half Century of Conflict*, 1, pp. 498-9.

[211] Fr. LeJeune, *Jesuit Relations* 17, p. 25.

[212] *Relations* 40, p. 47.

[213] Horace Greeley, *op. cit.*, pp. 152-3.

[214] Hobbes, *Leviathan*, ch. 13.

[215] *Ibid.*

[216] *Ibid.*

[217] Pinker, *The Better Angels of Our Nature*, p. 84.

[218] Alexander Morris, *The Treaties of Canada with the Indians of Manitoba and the NorthWest Territories* 1880; reprint, Saskatoon, Fifth House, 1991, pp. 170-171.

[219] Robert Talbot, *Alexander Morris: His Intellectual and Political Life and the Numbered Treaties*, Ottawa: U of O, 2007, p. 134.

[220] Treaty 7 Elders and Tribal Council. *The True Spirit and Original Intent of Treaty 7* Montreal: McGill-Queen's University Press, 1995, pp. 276-277.

[221] Keith Smith, "Living with Treaties," *Canadian History: Post-Confederation*, John Douglas Belshaw, ed. BC Open Textbooks. Unpaginated.

[222] Talbot, *op. cit.*, 151-2.

[223] Morris, *op. cit.*, p. 109.

[224] Guy Nixon, *Slavery in the West*, Bloomington, IN: Xlibris, 2011, p. 13.

[225] Robert Spencer, "Slavery, Christianity, and Islam," *First Things*, 2.4.08.

[226] Columbus, *Journal of the First Voyage*, 12th of October.

[227] Samuel Purchas, *Purchas His Pilgrimes*, 1625, edition of 1908, 4, pp. 1699-1700.

[228] Almon Lauber, "Indian Slavery in Colonial Times," Columbia University Ph.D. Thesis, 1913, p. 46, note; citing Hakluyt Society Publications, 6, p. 26.

[229] Samuel Hazard, *Annals of Pennsylvania*, Philadelphia: Hazard and Mitchell, 1850, p. 7.

[230] *Jesuit Relations* 31, p. 91.

[231] *Relations* 26, p. 49.

[232] *Relations* 54, p. 93.

[233] Lauber, *op. cit.*, p. 28.

[234] "Hennepin's Narrative," in John Shea, *Discovery and Exploration of the Mississippi Valley*, NY: Effingham Maynard, 1890, p. 144.

[235] Lauber, *op. cit.*, p. 29.

[236] *Ibid.*, p. 32.

[237] "Franchère's Narrative," in Reuben Thwaites, *Early Western Travels*, 23, Cleveland: A.H. Clark, 1904, p. 118.

[238] Hubert Bancroft, *History of Alaska,* San Francisco: Bancroft, 1886, p. 711.

[239] Nixon, *op. cit.*, p. 50; http://www.classicalvalues.com/archives/2007/07/they_wouldnt_li.html

[240] Frederick Hodge, *Handbook of American Indians North of Mexico*, Bureau of American Ethnology, Bulletin 30, pt. ii, p. 598.

[241] Hubert Bancroft, *History of the Northwest Coast*, 2, San Francisco: Bancroft, 1884, pp. 647-649.

[242] James Teit, "The Thompson Indians of British Columbia," *Memoirs of the American Museum of Natural History*, NY: 1903-21, pp. 269, 290.

[243] Cyrus Thomas, *Indians of North America in Historic Times*, Philadelphia: George Barrie and Sons, 1903, p. 369.

[244] *Ibid.*, p. 359.

[245] Lauber, *op. cit.*, pp. 45, 48.

[246] *Ibid.*, p. 29.

[247] Gilbert Sproat, *Scenes and Studies in Savage Life*, London: Smith, Elder, 1868, pp. 91-5.

[248] *Relations* 30, p. 133.

[249] *Relations* 16, p. 199.

[250] Lauber, *op. cit.*, p. 26.

[251] *Ibid.*, p. 26.

[252] Livingston Jones, *A Study of the Thlingits of Alaska*. NY: Revell 1914, p. 116.

[253] *Ibid.*, p. 113.

[254] *Ibid.*, p. 93.

[255] *Relations* 43, p. 295.

[256] Sproat, *op. cit.*, pp. 91-5.

[257] *Relations* 40, p. 135.

[258] Lauber, *op. cit.* p. 41.

[259] Jones, *op. cit.*, pp. 117-8.

[260] (Saint) John Chrysostom, *Homily to the Ephesians* 22.1.

[261] https://en.wikipedia.org/wiki/Somerset_v_Stewart

[262] Lauber, *op cit.*, p. 46.

[263] Columbus, *op. cit.*, 13th of October.

[264] Lauber, *op, cit.*, p. 32.

[265] *Ibid.*, p. 38.

[266] Nixon, *op. cit.*, p. 11.

[267] Lauber, *op. cit.*, p. 40.

[268] *sic*; "Major Sherburne's Testimony on the Affair at the Cedars," 17 June 1776.

[269] Steven Pinker, *The Better Angels of Our Nature*, NY: Penguin, 2011, p. 81.

[270] *Jesuit Relations* 31, p. 29.

[271] *Relations* 1, p. 269-73.

[272] *Relations* 31, p. 25.

[273] *Ibid.*, p. 27.

[274] *Ibid.*, p. 29.

[275] *Ibid.*, p. 31-3.

[276] *Ibid.*, p. 33.

[277] *Relations* 31, p. 43.

[278] *Ibid.*, p. 45.

[279] *Ibid.*, p. 47.

[280] *Relations* 34, pp. 25-7.

[281] *Ibid.*, pp. 27-9.

[282] *Ibid.*, pp. 29.

[283] *Ibid.*, p. 31.

[284] *Relations* 12, p. 179-81.

[285] Champlain, *Voyages* 2, ch. 10.

[286] *Ibid.*

[287] *Relations* 24, p. 181.

[288] Samuel Drake, *Tragedies of the Wilderness*, Boston: Antiquarian Bookstore, 1844, p. 83.

[289] Albert Alden, *Indian Anecdotes and Barbarities*, Barre, NH: Gazette, 1837, p. 8-9.

[290] Mary Rowlandson, *Narrative of the Captivity and Restoration of Mrs. Mary Rowlandson*, 1682, Fourth Remove.

[291] James E. Seaver, *The Life and Times of Mary Jemison,* 1824, ch. 3.

[292] Samuel Drake, *op. cit.*, p. 110.

---

[293] John West, *Substance of a Journal During a Residence at Red River*, London: L.B. Seeley, 1824, p. 88.

[294] Joseph Pritts, *Incidents of Border Life*, Lancaster, PA: J. Pritts, 1841, p. 184.

[295] John Wilson, *A Genuine Narrative of the Transactions in Nova Scotia Since the Settlement June 1749, till August the 5th, 1751*, London, n.d., p. 14.

[296] Parkman, *The Jesuits in North America*, p. 211.

[297] *Relations* 13, pp. 43-77.

[298] *Relations* 24, p. 191.

[299] Resolution of a Detroit public meeting, December 8, 1811, quoted in Alan Taylor, *The Civil War of 1812*, NY: Vintage, 2011, Kindle edition, loc. 3985.

[300] *Relations* 31, p. 41.

[301] *Ibid.*, p. 43.

[302] Gilbert Sproat, *Scenes and Studies of Savage Life,* London: Smith, Elder, 1868, p. 157.

[303] https://en.wikipedia.org/wiki/Milgram_experiment

[304] Susannah Johnson, *Narrative of the Captivity of Mrs. Johnson*, Windsor, VT: Pomroy, 1834, p. 56.

[305] Parkman, *The Jesuits in North America*, p. 216.

[306] Taylor, *op. cit.*, loc. 3250.

[307] *Ibid.*, loc. 3968.

[308] *Ibid.*, loc. 4011.

[309] Mary FitzGibbon, *A Veteran of the War of 1812*, Toronto: W. Briggs, 1894, p 87.

[310] *Relations* 6, p. 229.

[311] Francis Parkman, *Montcalm and Wolfe*, vol. 1, Boston: Little, Brown, 1884, p. 497.

[312] William Arens, *The Man-Eating Myth,* Oxford: Oxford U. Press, 1979.

[313] Neil Whitehead, "Carib Cannibalism: The Historical Evidence," *Journal de la Societe des Americanistes*, 70:1, 1984.

[314] Charles F. Thuing, *Cannibalism in North America*, Cambridge, Mass., 1883, p. 32.

[315] Díaz del Castillo, *The Conquest of New Spain* [*Historia verdadera de la conquista de Nueva España*], c. 1568. Hakluyt Society edition, trans. Alfred Maudslay, London: 1909, p. 289.

[316] Diego Muñoz Camargo, *Historia de Tlaxcala,* c. 1585, Mexico City: 1892 edition, p. 153.

[317] Consul Willshire Butterfield, *History of Brûlé's Discoveries and Explorations*, Cleveland: Helman Taylor, 1898, p. 120. Original source Recollet Friar Gabriel Sagard, *Histoire du Canada*, 1636.

[318] *Jesuit Relations* 31, p. 83.

[319] *Ibid*., p. 173.

[320] Francis Parkman, *The Jesuits in North America in the Seventeenth Century*, Boston: Little, Brown, 1912, p. 199; his source is Megapolensis, *A Short Account of the Mohawk Indians*, 1644.

[321] Fr. Bressani, second letter, August 31, 1644; in Horace Kephart, *Captives among the Indians*, New York: Outing, 1915.

[322] *Relations* 8, pp. 21-3.

[323] *Relations* 6, p. 243.

[324] Fr. Vimont, *Relations* 22, p. 253.

[325] David Scheimann, "Adoption or Entrée," Ohio University, https://www.ohio.edu/orgs/glass/vol/1/14.htm

[326] Parkman, *The Jesuits in North America in the Seventeenth Century,* p. 147.

[327] Champlain, *Voyages* 2, p. 184.

[328] *Relations* 35, p. 87.

[329] *Relations* 13, pp. 43-77.

[330] Parkman, *Montcalm and Wolfe*, vol. 1, p. 482-3. Parkman gives his source as Bougainville, *Journal de l'Expedition contre le Fort George*.

[331] Parkman, *Montcalm and Wolfe*, vol. 1, p. 484.

[332] George Schuyler, *Colonial New York*, NY: Scribner's, 1885, p. 40.

[333] Parkman, *The Conspiracy of Pontiac*, London: Macmillan, 1885, p. 202, note.

[334] B.F. French, *Historical Collections of Louisiana*, NY: Wiley and Putnam, 1846, p. 160.

[335] Father (Saint) Jean de Brébeuf, *Relations* 10, p. 81.

[336] Charles Darling, *Anthropophagy*, Utica, NY: T. J. Griffiths, 1886, p. 43.

[337] Thuing, *op. cit.*, p. 3.

[338] Henry Coke, *A Ride over the Rocky Mountains*, London: Richard Bentley, 1852, p. 275.

[339] Garry Hogg, *Cannibalism and Human Sacrifice*, NY: Citadel Press, 1966, pp. 70-2; London: Robert Hale, 1958, p. 67.

[340] *Ibid.*

[341] Robert Haswell, *A Voyage Round the World on Board the Ship 'Columbia Hediviva' and Sloop 'Washington,' in 1787-9*, B. L. Eddy, 1896; Sept. 1787.

[342] Eugene Stock, *Metlakahtla and the North Pacific Mission,* London: Church Missionary Society, 1880, p. 6.

[343] *Ibid.*, p. 24.

[344] *Ibid,* p. 56.

[345] Cyrus Thomas, *Indians of North America in Historic Times,* Philadelphia: George Barrie and Sons, 1903, p 391-2.

[346] Pierre Duchaussois, *The Grey Nuns in the Far North,* Toronto: McClelland and Stewart, 1917, p. 126.

[347] Darling, *op. cit.*, p. 39.

[348] James White, Handbook of Indians of Canada, Ottawa: C.H. Parmalee, 1913, p. 77.

[349] Richard Marlar, et al., "Biochemical Evidence of Cannibalism at a Prehistoric Puebloan Site in Southwestern Colorado," *Nature* 407, 7 September 2000, pp. 74-78.

[350] *Relations* 35, pp. 43-48, quoted by Parkman, *The Jesuits in North America*, p. 244.

[351] *Relations* 35, p. 166.

[352] *Relations* 22, p. 251-3.

[353] Peter Jones, *History of the Ojebway Indians,* London: Wesleyan Missionary Society, 1861, p. 205-206.

[354] Gloria Steinem, *Wonder Woman*, NY: Holt, Rinehart and Winston, 1972.

[355] *Ibid.*

[356] Matilda Gage, *Woman, Church, and State*, NY: The Truth Seeker Co., 1893, pp. 17-8.

[357] *Ibid.*, p. 13.

[358] *Ibid.*, p. 15.

[359] Friedrich Engels, *The Origin of the Family, Private Property, and the State,* Zurich: 1884, p. 4.

[360] *Ibid.*, p. 11.

[361] *Ibid.*, p. 55.

[362] *Ibid.*, p. 65.

[363] *Ibid.*, p. 66.

[364] *Ibid.*, p. 35.

[365] *Ibid.*, p. 75.

[366] Betty Friedan, *The Feminine Mystique*, NY: W.W. Norton, 1963.

[367] Daniel Horowitz, *Betty Friedan and the Making of the Feminine Mystique,* Boston: U Mass Press, 1998.

[368] Engels, *op. cit.*, p. 81.

[369] Friedan, *op. cit.*, p. 15.

[370] Engels, *op. cit.*, p. 18.

[371] Leonard Cohen, *Beautiful Losers*, Toronto: McClelland & Stewart, 1966, p. 1.

[372] *Jesuit Relations* 2, p. 21.

[373] *Relations* 1, p. 255.

[374] Champlain, *Voyages*, NY: Scribner, 1908, Voyage of 1615, p. 319.

[375] Samuel Hearne, *A Journey from Prince of Wales's Fort in Hudson's Bay to the Northern Ocean in the Years 1769, 1770, 1771, and 1772.* Toronto: The Champlain Society, 1911; originally published 1795, pp. 319-20.

[376] William Starna, "Cooper's Indians: A Critique," in *James Fenimore Cooper: His Country and His Art*, Papers from the 1979 Conference at State University College of New York, Oneonta and Cooperstown. George A. Test, ed., pp. 63-76.

[377] Engels, *op. cit.*, p. 56.

[378] *Relations* 7, p. 47.

[379] Champlain, *Voyages*, Voyage of 1615, p. 290.

[380] Gage, *op. cit.*, p. 19.

[381] Merlin Stone, *When God Was a Woman*, NY: Houghton Mifflin, 1976.

[382] Carolyn Nakamura and Lynn Meskell, "Articulate Bodies: Forms and Figures at Çatalhöyük," *Journal of Archaeological Method and Theory* 16, 2009, pp. 205–230; p. 206.

[383] Nakamura and Meskell, *op. cit.*

[384] Engels, *op. cit.*, p. 71.

[385] Gage, *op. cit.*, p. 16.

[386] Erminnie Smith, *Myths of the Iroquois*, Washington: Government Printing Office, 1883, p. 51.

[387] *Ibid.*, pp. 52-3.

[388] George Dawson, *Notes on the Indian Tribes of the Yukon District and Adjacent Portions of Northern British Columbia*, Ottawa: Geological Survey of Canada, 1887, p. 8.

[389] Livingston Jones, *A Study of the Thlingits of Alaska*. NY: Revell 1914, p. 236.

[390] Louis Hennepin, *A New Discovery of a Vast Country in America. Extending above Four Thousand Miles, between New France and New Mexico*, 2, London: 1698, pp. 460, 466.

[391] *Relations* 8, p. 115.

[392] *Relations* 6, p. 157.

[393] Chrestien LeClercq, *New Relations of Gaspesia*, Toronto: Champlain Society, 1910, p. 213.

[394] *Relations* 6, p. 173.

[395] Lewis Morgan, *League of the Ho-dé-no-sau-nee or Iroquois*, NY: Dodd, Mead, 1904, p. 328.

[396] Morgan, *Ancient Society*, London: Macmillan, 1877, p. 119.

[397] *Ibid.*, p. 464.

[398] Morgan, League of the Iroquois, p. 83.

[399] Morgan, *op. cit.*, p. 66.

[400] Morgan, *op. cit.*, p. 314.

[401] *Ibid.*, p. 328.

[402] *Ibid.*, p. 259.

[403] Engels, *op. cit.*, p. 55.

[404] *Ibid.*, p. 11.

[405] Gage, *op. cit.*, p. 14, note.

[406] *Ibid.*, p. 15.

[407] *Ibid.*, p. 18.

[408] Champlain, *Voyages*, Voyage of 1615, p. 320.

[409] *Ibid.*

[410] *Ibid.*

[411] Father LeJeune, *Relations* 6, p. 253.

[412] Morgan, *League of the Iroquois*, p. 32.

[413] H. C. Porter, *The Inconsistent Savage: England and the North American Indian, 1500-1600*, London: Duckworth, 1979, p. 398.

[414] Hearne, *op. cit.*, p. 303.

[415] Francis Parkman, *The Jesuits in North America in the Seventeenth Century*, Boston: Little, Brown, 1912, p. 17.

[416] Consul Willshire Butterfield, *History of Brûlé's Discoveries and Explorations*, Cleveland: Helman-Taylor, 1898, p. 167.

[417] Peter Jones, *op. cit.*, p. 80.

[418] Dawson, *op. cit.*, p. 8.

[419] Livingston Jones, *op. cit.*, pp. 125-6.

[420] *Ibid.*, p. 127.

[421] *Ibid.*, p. 59.

[422] *Ibid.*, pp. 125-6.

[423] Gilbert Sproat, *Scenes and Studies in Savage Life*, London: Smith, Elder, 1868, p. 95.

[424] James Howley, *The Beothuks or Red Indians: The Aboriginal Inhabitants of Newfoundland*, Cambridge: Cambridge University Press, 1915, p. 181; memories of a Mr. Gill.

[425] John West, *Journal of a Mission to the Indians of the British Provinces of New Brunswick and Nova Scotia*, London, L.B. Seeley, 1827, p. 253.

[426] Alexander Mackenzie, *Voyages from Montreal on the River St. Laurence, through the Continent of North America, to the Rrozen and Pacific Oceans; in the Years 1789 and 1793*, London: R. Noble, 1801, p. 22.

[427] Cyrus Thomas, *Indians of North America in Historic Times*, Philadelphia: George Barrie and Sons, 1903, p. 373.

[428] Sproat, *op. cit.*, pp. 91-5.

[429] Eugene Stock, *Metlakahtla and the North Pacific Mission,* London: Church Missionary Society, 1880, p. 19.

[430] John West, *The Substance of a Journal During a Residence at the Red River Colony, British North America in the Years 1820, 1821, 1822, 1823.* London: L.B. Seeley, 1824, p. 39.

[431] *Relations* 1, p. 171.

[432] George Back, *Narrative of the Arctic Land Expedition to the Mouth of the Great Fish River, and Along the Shores of the Arctic Ocean in the Years 1833, 1834, and 1835,* London: John Murray, 1836, pp. 213-4.

[433] Samuel Hearne, *op. cit.*, p. 144.

[434] *Ibid.*, pp. 265-6.

[435] Sir Harry Johnston, *Pioneers in Canada*, London: Blackie and Son, 1919, pp. 170-1.

[436] Pierre Duchaussois, *The Grey Nuns in the Far North,* Toronto: McClelland and Stewart, 1919, p. 70.

[437] *Ibid.*, pp. 232-3.

[438] Peter Jones, *op. cit.*, p. 60.

[439] LeClercq, *op. cit.*, p. 239.

[440] C. Hodgson-McCauley, "Positive stories from residential school," *Northern News Service*, December 3, 2012.

[441] Royal Commission on Aboriginal Peoples, *People to People, Nation to Nation: Highlights from the Report of the Royal Commission on Aboriginal Peoples*. Ottawa: 1996.

[442] Background, *National Inquiry into Missing and Murdered Indigenous Women and Girls,* http://www.mmiwg-ffada.ca/en/background/

[443] Robin Levinson-King, "Teen Suicide on the Rise among Canadian Girls," *BBC News*, Toronto, March 13, 2017.

[444] Douglas Quan, "Most murdered and missing aboriginal women victims of indigenous perpetrators: RCMP," *National Post*, April 13, 2015.

[445] Florentine Codex, 12, "The Conquest of Mexico," Arthur Anderson and Charles Dibble, trans.

[446] Jared Diamond, *Guns, Germs, and Steel*, NY: Vintage, 1997, p. 500.

[447] Elizabeth Fenn, *Pox Americana*, NY: Hill and Wang, 2001, p. 142.

[448] Brébeuf, *Jesuit Relations* 11, p. 11.

[449] I said it was without attribution.

[450] Rita Trichur, Montreal *Gazette*, May 25, 2004.

[451] Adrienne Mayor, "The Nessus Shirt in the New World," *Journal of American Folklore* 108: 427, Winter, 1995, pp. 54-77.

[452] Vine Deloria, *Custer Died for Your Sins: An Indian Manifesto.* London: Macmillan, 1970, p. 54.

[453] William Warren, *History of the Ojibways, Based Upon Traditions and Oral Sources,* St. Paul: Minnesota Historical Society, 1885, pp. 220-221.

[454] Andrew Blackbird, *History of the Ottawa and Chippewa Indians of Michigan,* Ypsilanti MI: The Ypsilanti Job Printing House, 1887, pp. 9-10.

[455] Mayor, *op. cit.*, p. 59

[456] James Mooney, *The Ghost Dance Religion and the Sioux Outbreak of 1890*, Washington: Government Printing Office, 1896, p. 724.

[457] "Testimony of William Sport to IHRAAM officers, Port Alberni, BC, March 31, 1998"; in Kevin Annett, *Hidden from History,* Vancouver: The Truth Commission into Genocide in Canada, 2001, p. 17.

[458] Mayor, *op. cit.*, p. 59.

[459] *Ibid.*, p. 60.

[460] Thomas Brown, *Did the U.S. Army Distribute Smallpox Blankets to Indians?* Ann Arbor, MI: MPublishing, University of Michigan Library, 2006, p. 100.

[461] Churchill, "An American Holocaust? The Structure of Denial," *Socialism and Democracy* 17, 2003.

[462] " 'Nits Make Lice': The Extermination of North American Indians, 1607-1996," in *A Little Matter of Genocide: Holocaust and Denial in the Americas, 1492 to the Present.* San Francisco: City Lights Books, 2001, p. 169.

[463] M. Wesson, R. Clinton, J. Limon, M. McIntosh, M. Radelet. "Report of the Investigative Committee of the Standing Committee on Research Misconduct at the University of Colorado at Boulder concerning Allegations of Academic Misconduct against Professor Ward Churchill." May 6, 2006, p. 38.

[464] Russell Thornton, *American Indian Holocaust and Survival: A Population History since 1492.* Norman OK: University of Oklahoma Press, 1987.

[465] Kevin Vaughan, "Shifting facts amid a tide of contention: Sources cited don't back other smallpox claims by Churchill," *Rocky Mountain News*, June 6, 2005.

[466] "Report of the Investigative Committee," p. 67.

[467] Philip Ranlet, "The British, the Indians, and Smallpox: What Actually Happened at Fort Pitt in 1763?" *Pennsylvania History* 64: 3, Summer 2000, pp. 427-441.

[468] Charles Darwin, *The Descent of Man*, NY: Appleton & Co., 1871, p. 230.

[469] Carl S. Sterner, "A Brief History of Miasmic Theory," 2007, www.carlsterner.com.

[470] Joseph Smith, *Elements of the Etiology and Philosophy of Epidemics*, NY: J. & J. Harper, 1824, p. 43.

[471] Elizabeth Fenn, "Biological Warfare in Eighteenth-Century North America," *Journal of American History* 86: 4, March, 2000, pp. 1552-1580.

[472] Robert Boyd, "Smallpox in the Pacific Northwest." *BC Studies* 101, Spring, 1994, p. 6.

[473] Philip Ranlet, "The British, the Indians, and Smallpox: What Actually Happened at Fort Pitt in 1763?" *Pennsylvania History* 67:3, Summer, 2000, p. 430.

[474] Francis Parkman, *The Conspiracy of Pontiac*, London: Macmillan, 1885, p. 202, note.

[475] Diamond, *Guns, Germs, and Steel*, p. 498.

[476] George Vancouver, *A Voyage of Discovery to the North Pacific Ocean*, 2, 1798, pp. 229-230.

[477] Elizabeth Fenn, *Pox Americana*, p. 259.

[478] Paul Hackett, "Averting Disaster: The Hudson's Bay Company and Smallpox in Western Canada in the Late Eighteenth and Early Nineteenth Centuries," *Bulletin of the History of Medicine*, February, 2004, p. 579, p. 584.

[479] *Ibid.*, p. 589.

[480] Hackett, *op.cit.*, p. 586, quoting HBC records.

[481] *Ibid.*, p. 586.

[482] *Ibid.*, p. 599.

[483] *Ibid.*, pp. 600-601.

[484] C. Stuart Houston and Stan Houston, "The First Smallpox Epidemic on the Canadian Plains: In the Fur-Traders' Words," *Canadian Journal of Infectious Diseases* 11:2, March/April 2000, 112-115.

[485] Hackett, *op. cit.*, p. 601.

[486] John C. Ewers, *Five Indian Tribes on the Upper Missouri: Sioux, Arickaras, Assiniboines, Crees, Crows* Norman: University of Oklahoma Press, 1961, p. 115; Hackett, op. cit., p. 595.

[487] Hackett, *op. cit.*, p. 580.

[488] http://urbanlegends.about.com/od/horrors/fl/The-Poison-Dress.htm; http://www.snopes.com/horrors/poison/dress.asp; Jan Brunvand, *Encyclopedia of Urban Legends*, Santa Barbara: ABC-CLIO, 2012, p. 494; or just ask at the corner.

[489] De Voto, *Across the Wide Missouri*, Boston: Houghton Mifflin, 1947, quoted by Mayor, *op. cit.*, p. 60.

[490] Parkman, *op. cit.*, pp. 38-42.

[491] Esther Stearn, Allen Stearn, *The Effect of Smallpox on the Destiny of the Amerindian,* Minneapolis: University of Minnesota, 1945, pp. 13-20.

[492] *Ibid.*, pp. 73-94, 97.

[493] *Relations* 12, pp. 5-7.

[494] Warren, *op. cit.*, pp. 260-2.

[495] *Jesuit Relations* 12, p. 155.

[496] Samuel Hearne, *A Journey from Prince of Wales's Fort in Hudson's Bay to the Northern Ocean in the Years 1769, 1770, 1771, and 1772.* Toronto: The Champlain Society, 1911; originally published 1795, p. 321.

[497] Brébeuf, *Relations* 11, p. 11.

[498] *Relations* 12, p. 245.

[499] *Relations* 12, p. 167.

[500] *Relations* 12, p. 235.

[501] "Report of the Investigative Committee."

[502] Gilbert Sproat, *Scenes and Studies of Savage Life*, London: Smith, Elder, 1868, p. 161.

[503] *Ibid.*, p. 165.

[504] Kirsten Bos, et al, "Pre-Columbian Mycobacterial Genomes Reveal Seals as a Source of New World Human Tuberculosis," *Nature* 514, 23 October 2014, pp. 494–497.

[505] Ana Duggan, et al, "17th Century Variola Virus Reveals the Recent History of Smallpox," *Current Biology*, 26:24, Dec. 19, 2016, pp. 3407–3412.

[506] *Ibid.*, p. 3411.

[507] Vilhjalmur Stefansson, *My Life with the Eskimo*, New York: Macmillan, 1913, p. 26.

[508] Debra Martin and Alan Goodman, "Health Conditions before Columbus: Paleopathology of Native North Americans," *Western Journal of Medicine*, January 2002, 176:1, pp. 65–68.

[509] Chrestien LeClercq, *New Relations of Gaspesia*, Toronto: The Champlain Society, 1910, pp. 146-7, p. 165.

[510] Jared Diamond, "The Worst Mistake in the History of the Human Race," *Discovery* Magazine, May, 1987, p. 90.

[511] William Buckner, "Romanticising the Hunter Gatherer," *Quillette*, December 16, 2017.

[512] Robert Boyd, "Smallpox in the Pacific Northwest: The First Epidemics," *BC Studies* 101, Spring 1994, p. 7.

[513] *Relations* 6, p. 261-3.

[514] LeClercq, *op. cit.*, p. 253.

[515] *Ibid.*, p. 121.

[516] Livingston Jones, *A Study of the Thlingits of Alaska*. NY: Revell, 1914, p. 223.

[517] *Ibid.*, p 225.

[518] Vilhjalmur Stefansson, *My Life with the Eskimo*, New York: Macmillan, 1913, p. 23.

[519] *Annual Report*. Ottawa: Department of Indian Affairs, 1917, p. 31.

[520] William Bompas, *Diocese of Mackenzie River,* London: Society for Promoting Christian Knowledge, 1888, p. 75-6.

[521] Hearne, *op. cit.*, p. 321.

[522] Bompas, *op. cit.*, p. 93.

[523] Alexander Mackenzie, *Voyages from Montreal Through the Continent of North America to the Frozen and Pacific Oceans in 1789 and 1793*, NY: New Amsterdam Book Company, 1902, p. 24.

[524] see William Wildshut, *Crow Indian Medicine Bundles*, NY: Museum of the American Indian, 1975.

[525] Stephen Maher, *National Post*, June 11, 2015.

[526] James Howley, *The Beothuks or Red Indians: The Aboriginal Inhabitants of Newfoundland*, Cambridge: 1915, p. 14. Howley took the trouble to collect

in this one volume all written references to the Beothuks from the period of their actual existence, and living memory of it.

[527] Henry Kirke, *The First English Conquest of Canada,* London: Sampson, Low, Marsden, 1908, p. 139; quoted by Howley, *op. cit.*, p. 23.

[528] "Commission of Enquiry into the Trade with Newfoundland," 1793, Howley, *op. cit.*, p. 54.

[529] Howley, *op. cit.*, p. 85.

[530] Government of Canada, *Newfoundland: An Introduction to Canada's Newest Province*, Ottawa, 1950, pp. 15-41; Daniel Prowse, *A History of Newfoundland*, London: Eyre and Spottiswoode, 1895, p. 143.

[531] Samuel Totten and Paul Bartrop, *Dictionary of Genocide*, Westport, CT: Greenwood, 2008, p. 39.

[532] J. R. Miller, *Skyscrapers Hide the Heavens*, Toronto: U of T Press, 1989, p. 114.

[533] Joseph Banks, *Journal of Sir Joseph Banks*, 1766; Howley, *op. cit.*, p. 28.

[534] *Ibid.*

[535] John Cartwright, "Remarks on the Situation of the Red Indians," in Howley, *op. cit.*, p. 34.

[536] Cartwright; Howley, *op. cit.*, p. 34-5.

[537] Cartwright; Howley, *op. cit.,* p. 36.

[538] Cartwright; Howley, *op. cit.*, p. 35.

[539] Howley, *op. cit.*, p. 270.

[540] *Ibid.*

[541] *Ibid.*, p. 273.

[542] *Ibid.*, p. 282.

[543] *Ibid.*, p. 22.

[544] Henry Kirke, *op. cit.*, p. 140; Howley, *op. cit.*, p. 23.

[545] Howley, *op. cit.*, p. 24.

[546] Ingeborg Marshall, *History and Ethnography of the Beothuk*, Kingston: McGill-Queen's Press, 1996. p. 20; quoting Crignon.

[547] Howley, *op. cit.*, p. 54.

[548] *Ibid.*, p. 45.

[549] *Ibid.*, p. 45.

[550] *Ibid.*, pp. 64-5.

[551] *Ibid.*, p. 91.

[552] "Commission of Enquiry into the Trade with Newfoundland," Howley, *op. cit.*, p. 51.

[553] *Ibid.*, pp. 54-5.

[554] Howley, *op. cit.*, p. 14.

[555] Cartier, *Journal of the First Voyage*, June 1, 1534.

[556] Perez, *Voyage up the Northwest Coast*, 1773; in Hubert Bancroft, *History of the Northwest Coast*, 1, San Francisco, A.L. Bancroft, 1884, p. 154.

[557] James Ross, *Narrative of a Second Voyage in Search of a Northwest Passage*. London: Webster, 1835, p. 245.

[558] Prowse, *op. cit.*, p. 96.

[559] William Cormack; Howley, *op. cit.*, p. 184.

[560] *Ibid.*, p. 221.

[561] David Buchan, "Report of Second Expedition"; Howley, *op. cit.*, p. 121.

[562] Howley, *op. cit.*, p. 68.

[563] "Narrative of Lieut. Buchan's Journey up the Exploits River in Search of the Red Indians in the Winter of 1810-1811"; Howley, *op. cit.*, pp. 77-80.

[564] J. Beete Jukes, *Excursions in and about Newfoundland*. London: John Murray, 1842; Howley, *op. cit.*, p. 26.

[565] "Extract of a disputation from R. A. Tucker, Esq. Administering to the Government of Newfoundland, to R. Horton, Esq., 1825"; Howley, *op. cit.*, p. 176.

[566] Howley, *op. cit.*, p. 269-70.

[567] Edward Chappell, *The Voyage of the* Rosamond, London: J. Mawman, 1818; quoted Howley, *op. cit.*, p. 288.

[568] William Cormack, 1822; Howley, *op. cit.*, p. 142.

[569] Howley, *op. cit.*, p. 270.

[570] John Cartwright; quoted by Howley, *op. cit.*, p. 35.

[571] Sabrina Ferri, "Time in Ruins: Melancholy and Modernity in the Pre-Romantic Natural Picturesque," *Italian Studies* 69:2, June 22, 2014, pp. 204-230.

[572] quoted by Howley, *op. cit.*, p. 192.

[573] Howley, *op. cit.*, p. 227.

[574] *Diary of Reverend William Wilson;* quoted by Howley, *op. cit.*, p. 260.

[575] Howley, *op. cit.*, p. 257.

[576] *Ibid.*, pp. 257-8.

[577] *Ibid.*, p. 86.

[578] John Cartwright; Howley, *op. cit.*, p. 33.

[579] *Ibid.*, p. 86.

[580] *Ibid.*, p. 38.

[581] Cormack; Howley, *op. cit.*, pp. 139-141.

[582] *Ibid.*, p. 148.

[583] *Ibid.*, p. 142.

[584] Douglas Todd, "Aboriginals Surprisingly Loyal to Christianity," *Vancouver Sun*, August 28, 2009.

[585] Truth and Reconciliation Commission, *Honouring the Truth, Reconciling for the Future,* Ottawa: 2015, p. 48.

[586] Kevin Annett, *Hidden from History*, Vancouver: The Truth Commission into Genocide in Canada, 2001, p. 12.

[587] Truth and Reconciliation Commission, *Honouring the Truth, Reconciling for the Future*, p. 54.

[588] Keith Smith, "Living with Treaties," in *Canadian History: Post-Confederation*, ed. John Douglas Belshaw. BC Open Textbooks, 2015; unpaginated.

[589] Douglas Cole and Ira Chaikin. *An Iron Hand upon the People: The Law Against the Potlatch on the Northwest Coast.* Seattle: University of Washington Press, 1990, p. 15.

[590] James McCullagh, "The Indian Potlatch," substance of a paper read before the C.M.S. Annual Conference, Metlakatla, B.C., 1899, p. 14.

[591] *Ibid.*, p. 12.

[592] Dorothy Johansen, *Empire of the Columbia: A History of the Pacific Northwest*, 2nd ed., New York: Harper & Row, 1967, pp. 7–8.

[593] James Deans, "When Patlatches Are Observed," *The American Antiquarian and Oriental Journal* 18, 1896, p. 331.

[594] McCullagh, *op cit.*, p. 11.

[595] *Ibid.*

[596] Franz Boas, "On Certain Songs and Dances of the Kwakuitl of British Columbia," *Journal of American Folklore* 1, April, 1888, p. 51.

[597] Livingston Jones, *A Study of the Thlingits of Alaska*. NY: Revell, 1914, p. 115.

[598] John McLean, "The Blackfoot Sun Dance," *Proceedings of the Canadian Institute* 151, 1889, p. 235.

[599] Clark Wissler, "The Sun Dance of the Blackfoot Indians," *Anthropological Papers of the American Museum of Natural History*, 16:3, 1918, p. 264; McLean, *op. cit.*, pp. 5-6.

[600] McCullagh, *op. cit.*, p. 12.

[601] *Ibid.*, p. 16.

[602] Eugene Stock, *Metlakahtla and the North Pacific Mission*. London: Church Missionary Society, 1880, p. 51.

[603] McCullagh, *op. cit.*, p. 17.

[604] *Ibid.*, p. 2.

[605] Deans, *op. cit.*, p. 331.

[606] Lalemant, *Jesuit Relations* 17, p. 159.

[607] Keith Smith, *Liberalism, Surveillance and Resistance*, Athabasca, AB: Athabasca University Press, 2009, pp. 60-7.

[608] *Jesuit Relations* 16, p. 198.

[609] *Relations* 1, p. 69.

[610] John Shea, *Catholic Missions to the Indian Tribes of the United States*, NY, 1857, p. 136, p. 138.

[611] *Ibid.*, p. 144.

[612] *Relations* 40, p. 219.

[613] *Relations* 27, p. 19.

[614] Shea, *op. cit.*, p. 146-7.

[615] Augustus Thompson, *Moravian Missions*. New York: Charles Scribner's Sons 1883, pp. 274-5.

[616] John West, *Journal of a Mission to the Indians of the British Provinces of New Brunswick and Nova Scotia*, London, L. B. Seeley, 1827, p. 278.

[617] Thompson, *op. cit.*, p. 235.

[618] Rev. Peter Jones [Kahkewāquonāby], *History of the Ojebway Indians; With Special Reference to Their Conversion to Christianity*. London: Wesleyan Methodist Missionary Society, 1861, p. 4.

[619] *Ibid.*, pp. 226-7.

[620] Adrien Morice, *History of the Catholic Church in Western Canada*, Toronto: Musson, 1910, pp. 142-3.

[621] West, *op. cit.*, pp. 246-7.

[622] Vilhjalmur Stefansson, *My Life with the Eskimo*, New York: Macmillan, 1913, p. 38.

[623] *Ibid*, p. 81.

[624] *Ibid.*, p. 82.

[625] Peter Jones, *op. cit.*, p. 128.

[626] *Relations* 24, p. 185.

[627] *Relations* 38, p. 25.

[628] Morice, *op. cit.*, p. 199.

[629] Shea, *op. cit.*, p. 139.

[630] Douglas Todd, "Aboriginals Surprisingly Loyal to Christianity," *Vancouver Sun*, August 28, 2009.

[631] Todd, *op. cit.*; citing Reginald Bibby, *The Emerging Millennials,* Project Canada, 2009.

[632] Francis Parkman, *A Half Century of Conflict*, 1, Boston: Little, Brown, 1896, p. 50.

[633] *Ibid.*, p. 52.

[634] quoted in William Bompas, *Diocese of Mackenzie River,* London: Society for Promoting Christian Knowledge, 1888, pp. 34-5.

[635] Parkman, *op. cit.*, p. 53.

[636] *Ibid.*, p. 54.

[637] Shea, *op. cit.*, pp. 144-5.

[638] Marie-Danielle Smith, "Prisons Pay More for Native Spiritual Services than All Other Faiths Combined," *National Post*, June 8, 2016.

[639] *Jesuit Relations* 13, p. 169.

[640] *Relations* 12, p. 257-9.

641 Eugene Stock, *Metlakahtla and the North Pacific Mission.* London: Church Missionary Society, 1880, p. 52. Emphasis in original.

642 Augustus Thompson, *Moravian Missions.* New York: Charles Scribner's Sons 1883, p. 232-3.

643 Father LeJeune, *Relations* 12, pp. 131-3.

644 Elizabeth Fenn, *Pox Americana*, NY: Hill & Wang, 2002, p. 142.

645 *Relations* 12, p. 7.

646 *Relations* 12, p. 183.

647 *Relations* 31, p. 199-201.

648 *Relations* 12, p. 181-3.

649 *Relations* 31, p. 197.

650 *Relations* 25, p. 33-5.

651 Francis Parkman, *The Jesuits in North America in the Seventeenth Century,* Boston: Little, Brown, 1912, p. 272.

652 Adrien Morice, *History of the Catholic Church in Western Canada*, Toronto: Musson, 1910, pp. 179-80.

653 *Relations* 31, p. 239.

654 Robert Marshall, "The Dark Legacy of Carlos Castaneda," *Salon* magazine, Apr. 12, 2007.

655 Christopher Dodson, "Black Elk: Native American & Catholic," *New Oxford Review*, April, 1995.

656 Neihardt, *Black Elk Speaks,* NY: William Morrow, 1932, p. 276.

657 Michael Steltenkamp, *Black Elk, Holy Man of the Oglala,* Norman, OK: University of Oklahoma Press, 1993, pp. 82-3, 85.

658 Alan R. Velie, "Black Elk Speaks, Sort Of: The Shaping of an Indian Autobiography," *Revue LISA/LISA e-journal*, 2:4, 2004, pp. 147-161.

659 Matthew Milliner, "An American Virgil," *First Things*, Sept. 2, 2015.

660 William Powers, "When Black Elk Speaks, Everyone Listens," *Social Text* 24, 1990, pp. 43-56.

661 James Mooney, *The Ghost-dance Religion and the Sioux Outbreak of 1890,* Washington: US Government Printing Office, 1896, p. 791.

662 Captain John Cartwright, 1768. Quoted by James Howley, *The Beothuks or Red Indians: The Aboriginal Inhabitants of Newfoundland*, p. 39.

663 *Relations* 10, p. 115.

664 *Relations* 2, p. 7.

665 *Relations* 1, p. 285.

666 Chrestien LeClercq, *New Relations of Gaspesia*, Toronto: The Champlain Society, 1910, p. 165.

667 Livingston Jones, *A Study of the Thlingits of Alaska*. NY: Revell, 1914, p. 231.

668 John West, *The Substance of a Journal During a Residence at the Red River Colony,* London: L.B. Seeley, 1827, p. 169.

669 William Bompas, *Diocese of Mackenzie River,* London: Society for Promoting Christian Knowledge, 1888, p. 99.

670 Gilbert Sproat, *Scenes and Studies of Savage Life*, London: Smith, Elder, 1868, p. 175.

671 Parkman, *The Jesuits in North America*, p. 55.

672 LeClercq, *op. cit.*, p. 224.

673 Livingston Jones, *op. cit.*, p. 232.

674 Livingston Jones, *op. cit.*, p. 232.

675 John West, *op. cit.*, p. 134.

676 Livingston Jones, *op. cit.*, p. 162.

677 *Ibid.*, p. 157.

678 *Ibid.*, pp. 156-7.

679 Parkman, *op. cit.*, p. 45.

680 *Relations* 7, p. 83.

681 *Ibid.*, p. 85.

682 Ramsay McMullen, *Christianizing the Roman Empire*. New Haven: Yale University Press, 1984, p 27.

683 LeClercq, *op. cit.*, pp. 224-5.

684 Parkman, *op. cit.*, p. 80.

685 Christopher Vacsey, *Traditional Ojibwa Religion and its Historical Changes*, Philadelphia: American Philosophical Society, 1983.

686 https://en.oxforddictionaries.com/definition/us/psychosis

687 https://www.merriam-webster.com/dictionary/psychosis

688 LeClercq, *First Establishment of the Faith in New France*, 1, NY: J. G. Shea, 1881, p. 219.

[689] Rev. Peter Jones [Kahkewāquonāby], *History of the Ojebway Indians; With Special Reference to Their Conversion to Christianity*. London: Wesleyan Methodist Missionary Society, 1861, p. 93.

[690] Truth and Reconciliation Commission, *Honouring the Truth, Reconciling for the Future*, Ottawa: 2015, p. 55.

[691] *Ibid.*, p. v.

[692] *Ibid.*, p. vi.

[693] *Ibid.*, p. 50.

[694] Kevin Annett, *Hidden from History,* Vancouver: The Truth Commission into Genocide in Canada, 2001, p. 12.

[695] Charol Shakeshaft, *Educator Sexual Misconduct: A Synthesis of Existing Literature*, Washington: Policy and Program Studies Service, US Department of Education, 2004, p. 20.

[696] Jonathan Saltzman, et al., "Private Schools, Painful Secrets," *Boston Globe*, June 5, 2016.

[697] Tim Naumetz, "One in Five Students Suffered Sexual Abuse at Residential Schools, Figures Indicate," *Globe & Mai*l, Jan, 17, 2009.

[698] Mary Carpenter, *National Conference on Indian and Northern Education*, Saskatoon, 1967, p. 48.

[699] Annett, *op. cit.*, p. 30.

[700] Truth and Reconciliation Commission, *The Survivors Speak*, Ottawa: 2015, p. 143.

[701] *Ibid.*, pp. 143-4.

[702] Susan Lazaruk, "77-year-old Pedophile Sentenced to 11 Years," *Windspeaker*, 13:2, 1995.

[703] Mark Gollom, "Additional Mental Health Workers Being Sent to Remote Northern Ontario Community," *CBC News*, Apr 12, 2016.

[704] J. Reich, "Prevalence and Characteristics of Sadistic Personality Disorder in an Outpatient Veterans Population." *Psychiatry Res.* Sept., 1993, 48:3, pp. 267-76.

[705] Truth and Reconciliation Commission, *They Came for the Children*, Ottawa: 2012, p. 89.

[706] Truth and Reconciliation Commission, *Honouring the Truth, Reconciling for the Future*, pp. 37-8.

[707] *Ibid.*, p. 38.

[708] *Ibid.*

[709] *Ibid.*, p. 68.

[710] *Ibid.*, p. 72.

[711] *Ibid.*, p. 69.

[712] *APTN National News,* May 8, 2013.

[713] Andrew Brown, *The Indians of Western Canada*, Toronto: Presbyterian Church in Canada, 1895, p. 20.

[714] Pierre Duchaussois, *The Grey Nuns in the Far North*, Toronto: McClelland & Stewart, 1917, pp. 119-20.

[715] *Ibid.*, pp. 121-3.

[716] Robert Carney, "Aboriginal Residential Schools before Confederation: The Early Experience," *CCHA Historical Studies* 61, 1995, p. 38.

[717] *APTN National News,* May 8, 2013.

[718] Truth and Reconciliation Committee, *Honouring the Truth, Reconciling for the Future*, p. 89.

[719] *Ibid.*, pp. 90-1.

[720] Truth and Reconciliation Commission, *The Survivors Speak*, p.73.

[721] *Ibid.*, p. 19.

[722] *Ibid.*, p. 77.

[723] Thomas Thorner and Thor Frohn-Nielsen, *A Country Nourished on Self-Doubt*, U of T Press, 2010, p. 400.

[724] "14 First-Hand Stories Underlining How Residential Schools Tried to 'Get Rid' of Indigenous Cultures," *PressProgress*, Dec. 15, 2016. http://pressprogress.ca/14_first_hand_stories_underlining_how_residential_schools_tried_to_get_rid_of_indigenous_cultures/

[725] Samuel Hearne, *A Journey from Prince of Wales's Fort in Hudson's Bay to the Northern Ocean in the Years 1769, 1770, 1771, and 1772*. Toronto: The Champlain Society, 1911; originally published 1795; p. 302.

[726] Truth and Reconciliation Commission, *Honouring the Truth, Reconciling for the Future*, p. 72.

[727] *Ibid.*, p. 73.

[728] *Wikipedia*, "Canadian Indian residential school system."

[729] Truth and Reconciliation Commission, *They Came for the Children*, p. 17.

[730] *Ibid.*

[731] Thomas King, *The Inconvenient Indian: A Curious Account of Native People in North America* Minneapolis: U. of Minnesota Press, 2013, p. 120.

[732] Kevin Annett, *op. cit.*, p. 6, p. 20.

[733] Truth and Reconciliation Commission, *Honouring the Truth, Reconciling for the Future*, p. 93.

[734] Hymie Rubenstein, Rodney Clifton, "Debunking the Half-Truths and Exaggerations in the Truth and Reconciliation Report," *National Post*, June 4, 2015.

[735] *Jesuit Relations* 6, pp. 261-3.

[736] Truth and Reconciliation Commission, *Honouring the Truth, Reconciling for the Future*, p. 93.

[737] *Ibid.*, p. 95.

[738] Peter Bryce, *The Story of a National Crime*, Ottawa: James Hope, 1922, p. 14.

[739] *Ibid.*

[740] *Ibid.*, p. 11.

[741] Rodney Clifton, "Residential Schools Story More Complicated," *Frontier Centre*, May 1, 2003.

[742] Truth and Reconciliation Commission, *Honouring the Truth, Reconciling for the Future*, p. 99.

[743] *Ibid.*, p. 93.

[744] *Annual Report*, Ottawa: Department of Indian Affairs, 1917, p. 30.

[745] Truth and Reconciliation Commission, *Honouring the Truth, Reconciling for the Future*, p. 80.

[746] Patrick Donnelly, "Scapegoating the Indian Residential Schools," *Alberta Report Newsmagazine*, Jan. 26, 1998, 25:6, p. 6.

[747] Truth and Reconciliation Commission, *The Survivors Speak*, p. 54.

[748] J. Fraser Field, "The Other Side of the Residential School Question," *Vancouver Sun*, Dec. 5, 1996.

[749] Carney, *op. cit.*, p. 36.

[750] Truth and Reconciliation Commission, *Honouring the Truth, Reconciling for the Future*, p. 83.

[751] *Ibid.*

[752] Clifton and Rubenstein, *op. cit.*

[753] Donnelly, *op. cit.*

[754] *Ibid.*

[755] Truth and Reconciliation Commission, *Honouring the Truth, Reconciling for the Future*, pp. 80-1.

[756] *Ibid.*, p. 83.

[757] Truth and Reconciliation Commission, *Honouring the Truth, Reconciling for the Future*, p. 4.

[758] Field, *op. cit.*

[759] Truth and Reconciliation Commission, *Honouring the Truth, Reconciling for the Future*, p. 83.

[760] Garett Williams, "Woman Honoured for Positive Impact at Residential School," Kenora *Daily Miner & News*, December 21, 2010.

[761] Donnelly, *op. cit.*

[762] Clifton, *op. cit.*

[763] Truth and Reconciliation Commission, *Honouring the Truth, Reconciling for the Future*, p. 73.

[764] *Ibid.*, p. 73.

[765] Thomas Hughes, *Tom Brown at Rugby*, Boston: Ginn, 1900, pp. 76-7.

[766] Truth and Reconciliation Commission, *Honouring the Truth, Reconciling for the Future*, p. 4.

[767] *Ibid.*, p. 53.

[768] William Withrow, *The Native Races of North America*, Toronto: Methodist Mission Rooms, 1895, p. 49.

[769] Adrien Morice, *History of the Catholic Church in Western Canada*, Toronto: Musson, 1910, pp. 166-7.

[770] *Ibid.*, p. 286.

[771] Clifton, *op. cit.*

[772] John West, *A Journal of a Mission to the British Provinces of New Brunswick and Nova Scotia*, London: Seeley, p. 248.

[773] G. Kent Gooderham, "Bilingual Education for Indians and Inuits: The Canadian Experience," paper presented at the Annual Meeting of the American Anthropological Association, Mexico City, November 1971, p. 7.

[774] Carney, *op. cit.*, p. 28.

[775] Augustin Brabant, *Vancouver Island and Its Missions*, NY: Messenger of the Sacred Heart Press, 1900, p. 88.

[776] "Memorandum Respecting Indian Institutes and Boarding Schools in Ontario, Manitoba, the North-West and British Columbia." Toronto: Methodist Church, 1896, p. 4.

[777] Truth and Reconciliation Commission, *They Came for the Children*, p. 74.

[778] Truth and Reconciliation Commission, *Honouring the Truth, Reconciling for the Future*, pp. 4-5.

[779] Truth and Reconciliation Commission, *They Came for the Children*, p. 3.

[780] Truth and Reconciliation Commission, *Honouring the Truth, Reconciling for the Future*, p. 49.

[781] Tom Flanagan, *First Nations: Second Thoughts*, McGill-Queen's Press, 2000, 2nd edition, 2008, p. 32.

[782] Truth and Reconciliation Commission, *Honouring the Truth, Reconciling for the Future*, p. 53.

[783] Annett, *op. cit.*, p. 26.

[784] Beverley McLachlin, "Reconciling Unity and Diversity in the Modern Era: Tolerance and Intolerance," Aga Khan Museum, Toronto, May 28, 2015.

[785] Richard Pratt, *Official Report of the Nineteenth Annual Conference of Charities and Correction*, 1892, pp. 46–59. Reprinted in Pratt, "The Advantages of Mingling Indians with Whites," *Americanizing the American Indians: Writings by the "Friends of the Indian" 1880-1900* Cambridge, Mass.: Harvard University Press, 1973, pp. 260–271.

[786] Richard Pratt, *Drastic Facts about Our Indians and Our Indian System*, Berkeley, CA: *Daily Gazette*, 1917, p. 19.

[787] Truth and Reconciliation Commission, *The Survivors Speak*, p. 131.

[788] R.V. Sinclair, First Letter, August 18, 1910, in *Canadian Indians*, Ottawa: Thornburn & Abbott, 1910.

[789] Carney, *op. cit.*, p. 27.

[790] Duchaussois, *op. cit.*, pp. 235-6.

[791] *Jesuit Relations* 6, p. 143-5.

[792] Peter Jones [Kahkewāquonāby], *History of the Ojebway Indians; With Special Reference to Their Conversion to Christianity*. London: Wesleyan Methodist Missionary Society, 1861, pp. 242-3.

[793] *Ibid.*, p. 264.

[794] *Ibid.*, p. 115.

[795] Carney, *op. cit.*, p. 23.

[796] https://deyoyonwatheh.blogspot.ca/2016/04/lies-about-genocide-and-other-alleged.html

[797] John West, *The Substance of a Journal During a Residence at the Red River Colony, British North America in the Years 1820, 1821, 1822, 1823.* London: L. B. Seeley, 1824, p. 14.

[798] Robert Talbot, *Alexander Morris: His Intellectual and Political Life and the Numbered Treaties*, Ottawa: U of O Press, 2007, pp. 97-8.

[799] Eugene Stock, *Metlakahtla and the North Pacific Mission.* London: Church Missionary Society, 1880, pp. 24-5.

[800] "Memorandum Respecting Indian Institutes and Boarding Schools in Ontario, Manitoba, the North-West and British Columbia." Toronto: Methodist Church, 1896, p. 1.

[801] Peter Jones, *op. cit.*, p. 202.

[802] *Ibid.*, p. 115.

[803] West, *op. cit.*, pp. 289-90.

[804] Peter Jones, *op. cit.*, p. 127.

[805] Talbot, *op. cit.*, p. 157.

[806] J. Fraser Field, *op. cit.*

[807] Peter Jones, *op. cit.*, p. 276-7.

[808] Mrs. Hattie Fergusson, National Conference on Indian and Northern Education, Saskatoon, 1967, p. 35.

[809] Livingston Jones, *A Study of the Thlingits of Alaska.* NY: Revell, 1914, p. 247.

[810] Samuel Blake, *The Call of the Red Man*, Toronto: Bryant Press, 1908, p. 9.

[811] Carney, *op. cit.*, p. 27.

[812] *Ibid.*, p. 35.

[813] "Memorandum Respecting Indian Institutes and Boarding Schools in Ontario, Manitoba, the North-West and British Columbia," p. 1.

[814] West, *op. cit.*, p. 6.

[815] Truth and Reconciliation Commission, *Honouring the Truth, Reconciling for the Future*, p. 59.

[816] Carney, *op. cit.*, p. 38.

[817] John Milloy, *A National Crime: The Canadian Government and the Residential School System, 1879 to 1986*, Winnipeg: U of Manitoba Press, 1999, p. 8.

[818] *Ibid.*, p. 13.

[819] Blake, *op. cit.*, p. 18.

[820] Cece Hodgson-McCauley, "Positive Stories from Residential School," *Northern News Service*, December 3, 2012.

[821] *Ibid.*

[822] Richard Wagamese, "The Good Side of the Residential School Story is Valid, Too," Calgary *Herald*/Vancouver *Sun*, May 12, 2008.

[823] Joshua Ostroff, "Tomson Highway Has a Surprisingly Positive Take on Residential Schools," *Huffington Post*, December 15, 2015.

[824] Truth and Reconciliation Commission, *They Came for the Children*, p. 49.

[825] Livingston Jones, *op. cit.*, pp. 241-242.

[826] Duchaussois, *op. cit.*, pp. 140-1.

[827] Truth and Reconciliation Commission, *Honouring the Truth, Reconciling for the Future*, p. 68.

[828] *Wikipedia*, "Canadian Indian Residential School System."

[829] Truth and Reconciliation Commission, *Final Report Volume 1: The History*, p. 93.

[830] Truth and Reconciliation Commission, *Honouring the Truth, Reconciling for the Future*, p. 70.

[831] Graeme Hamilton, "'Collateral Victim' of Residential Schools Gets 15 Months for Burning Child 27 Times with Cigarette, Lighter," *National Post*, April 6, 2016.

[832] Truth and Reconciliation Commission, *Honouring the Truth, Reconciling for the Future*, Ottawa: 2015, p. 45.

[833] John Bouvier, *A Law Dictionary*, 2, Philadelphia: Childs & Peterson, 1856, p. 394.

[834] *Ibid.*

[835] http://www.canlii.org/en/ca/fca/doc/2003/2003fca128/2003fca128.html

[836] Jeremy Bentham, *Principles of the Civil Code*, London: Bowring, 1843.

[837] http://www.duhaime.org/LegalDictionary/P/Property.aspx

[838] Thomas More, *Utopia*, 1516, "Of Their Traffic." Note that More here is specifically discussing the matter of establishing colonies on a neighbouring continent.

[839] John Locke, *Second Treatise of Government*, 1690, article 27.

[840] *Ibid.*, article 36.

[841] William Hubbard, *A Narrative of the Indian Wars in New England, 1677*, Boston: Boyle, 1775, p. vii.

[842] https://www.aadnc-aandc.gc.ca/eng/1100100028596/1100100028597

[843] Father LeJeune, *Jesuit Relations* 6, p 147-9.

[844] Champlain, *Voyages*, 1, 1603, p. 117.

[845] Francis Parkman, *The Jesuits in North America in the Seventeenth Century*, Boston: Little, Brown, 1912, p. 7.

[846] Father LeJeune, *Jesuit Relations* 6, p. 147-9.

[847] Eugene Stock, *Metlakahtla and the North Pacific Mission.* London: Church Missionary Society, 1880, p. 58.

[848] Truth and Reconciliation Commission, *Honouring the Truth, Reconciling for the Future*, p. 55.

[849] Truth and Reconciliation Commission, *The Survivors Speak*, Ottawa: 2015, p. 7.

[850] Truth and Reconciliation Commission, *Honouring the Truth, Reconciling for the Future,* p. 248.

[851] Charles Mair, *Through the Mackenzie Basin: A Narrative of the Athabasca and Peace River Treaty Expedition of 1899* Toronto: W. Briggs, 1908, pp. 56-9.

[852] Indian Chiefs of Alberta, *Citizens Plus* ("Red Paper"), Edmonton: 1970, p. 214.

[853] Robert Talbot, *Alexander Morris: His Intellectual and Political Life and the Numbered Treaties*, Ottawa: U of O Press, 2007, p. 175.

[854] http://www.canlii.org/en/ca/scc/doc/1997/1997canlii302/1997canlii302.html

[855] *Finley v. Yuba County Water Dist.* [160 Cal. Rprt. 423], 1979.

[856] Bruce Ziff, *Principles of Property Law*, Toronto: Carswell, 1993, p. 95.

[857] Talbot, *op. cit.*, p. 79.

[858] *Ibid.*, p. 108.

[859] *Ibid.*, p. 79.

[860] David Arnot, *Statement of Treaty Issues*, Ottawa: Office of the Treaty Commissioner, 1998, p. 23; Talbot, *op. cit.*, p. 79.

[861] Talbot, *op. cit.*, p. 125.

[862] Alexander Morris, *The Treaties of Canada*, Toronto: Willing and Williamson, 1880, pp. 150-151.

[863] Royal Commission on Aboriginal People, *People to People, Nation to Nation: Highlights from the Report of the Royal Commission on Aboriginal Peoples*, Ottawa, 1996.

[864] Royal Commission on Aboriginal Peoples, *op. cit.*

[865] Talbot, *op. cit.*, pp. 179-80.

[866] Talbot, *op. cit.*, p. 147.

[867] *Ibid.*, p. 150.

[868] *Ibid.*, p. 133.

[869] *Ibid.*, p. 194.

[870] Morris, *op. cit.*, pp. 122-123.

[871] *Ibid.*, p. 208; Talbot, *op. cit.*, p. 154.

[872] Royal Commission on Aboriginal People, *op. cit.*

[873] Talbot, *op. cit.*, p. 100.

[874] Teechamitsa Treaty, 1850.

[875] Peter Robinson, in Morris, *op. cit.*, p. 19.

[876] Morris, *op. cit.*, p. 34.

[877] Beverley McLachlin, *Mitchell v. M.N.R.*, 2001; Bruce Granville Miller, *Oral History on Trial*, Vancouver: UBC Press, 2011.

[878] *Jesuit Relations* 12, p. 161.

[879] "Racism of Sports Logos Put Into Context by American Indian Group," CBS Cleveland/AP, October 8, 2013.

[880] C.L. Sonnichsen, *From Hopalong to Hud,* College Station: Texas A&M University Press, 1978, p. 65.

[881] See, for example, Kenneth Melichar, "The Filmic Indian and Cultural Tourism," M.A. thesis, University of Georgia, 2009.

[882] Lacy Cotton, "American Indian Stereotypes in Early Western Literature and the Lasting Influence on American Culture," M.A. thesis, Baylor, 2008, p. 37.

[883] Charalambos Vrasidas, "The White Man's Indian: Stereotypes in Film and Beyond," *VisionQuest: Journeys toward Visual Literacy*. Selected Readings from the Annual Conference of the International Visual Literacy Association, Cheyenne, Wyoming, October, 1996, p. 65.

[884] Hesiod, *Works and Days*, ll. 109-120.

[885] *The Mahabharata of Krishna-Dwaipayana*, book 3, part 2, section 148.

[886] Alexander Pope, *An Essay on Man*, Epistle 1, III.

[887] Cotton, *op cit.*, p. 30.

[888] *Ibid.*

[889] Mara Pratt, *American History Stories*, 2, Boston: Educational Publishing Company, 1908, pp. 30-31.

[890] Donald Grinde and Bruce Johansen, *Exemplar of Liberty: Native America and the Evolution of Democracy,* LA: UCLA, 1991, chapter 7.

[891] John West, *Journal of a Mission to the British Provinces of New Brunswick and Nova Scotia,* London: Seeley, 1827, p. 222.

[892] Henry Mann, *The Land We Live In: The Story of Our Country*, NY: *Christian Herald*, 1896, pp. 36-7.

[893] Albert Blaisdell and Francis Ball, *The Child's Book of American History*, Boston: Little, Brown, and Company, 1923, pp. 32-3.

[894] Charles Dudley Warner, *The Story of Pocahontas*, Kindle edition, p.1.

[895] Andrew Potter, "Are We a Métis Nation?" *Literary Review of Canada*, April, 2009.

[896] *Ibid.*

[897] *Ibid.*

[898] William A. Starna, "Cooper's Indians: A Critique," originally published in *James Fenimore Cooper: His Country and His Art*, Papers from the 1979 Conference at State University College of New York, Oneonta and Cooperstown. George A. Test, ed., pp. 63-76.

[899] *Ibid.*, p. 65.

[900] *Ibid.*

[901] William Wilson, *An Incomplete Education*, NY: Ballantyne, 1986, p. 8.

[902] Cotton, *op. cit.*, p. 43-44.

[903] Washington Irving, "Traits of Indian Character," *The Sketch-Book of Geoffrey Crayon*, NY: Putnam, 1864.

[904] *Ibid.*

[905] Robert Bird, *Nick of the Woods*, NY: J. W. Lovell, 1852, p. iv.

[906] *Ibid.*

[907] *Ibid.*, pp. iv-v

[908] *Ibid.*, p. v.

[909] *Ibid.*, p. vi.

[910] *Ibid.*, pp. vi-vii.

[911] Cotton, *op. cit.*, p. 5.

[912] *Ibid.*, p. 6.

[913] Adam Kidd, *The Huron Chief and Other Poems*, Montreal: *Herald and New Gazette*, 1830.

[914] Craig MacBride, "Farley Mowat's *People of the Deer*," *Toronto Review of Books,* March 15, 2013.

[915] John David Towler, "Literature and Social Criticism: A Case Study of Canadian Author Farley Mowat," M.A. Thesis, Vermont College of Norwich University, 1989, p. 31.

[916] Cotton, *op. cit.*, p. 41.

[917] Clarence Lowrey, *The Invasion of America*, Lumberton, NC: Heritage Printers, 1962, preface.

[918] Vrasidas, *op. cit.*, p. 65.

[919] Clay Upton, "Stereotyping Indians in Film," *Clio's Eye*, December, 2012; http://clioseye.sfasu.edu/Archives/Main%20Archives/Stereotyping%20Indians%20in%20Film%209Upton).htm

[920] Cotton, *op. cit.*, p. 30.

[921] J. Frith Jeffers, *History of Canada*, Toronto: Canadian Publishing Company, 1879, p. 4.

[922] D. J. Dickie, *All about Indians*, Toronto: J. M. Dent, 1926, p. 49.

[923] Anne Stephens, *Malaeska: The Indian Wife of a White Hunter,* London: Routledge, 1860, p. 10.

[924] *Ibid.*, pp. 31-32.

[925] Cotton, *op. cit.*, p. 4.

[926] Ron Scheer, "Zane Grey, *Heritage of the Desert*," *Buddies in the Saddle*, Nov. 22, 2010.

[927] Cotton, *op. cit.*, p. 51.

[928] *Ibid.*, p. 48.

[929] *Ibid.*, pp. 48-9.

[930] *Ibid.*, p. 49.

[931] *Ibid.*

[932] Grafton, "Mein Buch," *The New Republic*, December, 2008.

[933] *Ibid.*

[934] Frederic Morton, "Tales of the Grand Teutons: Karl May among the Indians," *The New York Times*, 4 January 1987.

[935] Upton, *op. cit.*

[936] *NY Mirror*, quoted in Thomas Cripps, *Hollywood's High Noon: Moviemaking and Society before Television*, Baltimore: Johns Hopkins University Press, 1997, p. 27.

[937] *Internet Archive*, https://archive.org/details/TheRedMansView_201401

[938] *"Indian Pictures": Film Portrayals of Native Americans in the Silent Era*, http://jannasoeder.wixsite.com/silent-natives/white-fawns-devotion-1910; *Internet Archive*, https://archive.org/details/white_fawn_1910

[939] Peter Morris, *Embattled Shadows: A History of Canadian Cinema, 1895-1939,* Kingston: McGill-Queen's University Press, 1978, p. 40.

[940] *YouTube*: https://youtu.be/-kVKKEEiJR0

[941] *Internet Archive*, https://archive.org/details/the_invaders_1912

[942] *IMDB*; *Internet Archive*, https://archive.org/details/PreviewATemporaryTruce

[943] *Internet Archive*, https://archive.org/details/TheBattleOfElderbushGulch

[944] *Ibid.*, pp. 31-32.

[945] Roger Ebert, "Nanook of the North [1922]," *Chicago Sun Times*, Sept. 25, 2009.

[946] Peter Morris, *op. cit.*, p. 41.

[947] *Internet Archive*, https://archive.org/details/ThePaleface

[948] *Wikipedia,* "They Died with their Boots On."

[949] Alex von Tunzelmann, "*They Died with Their Boots On*: Overdressed, Overblown and So Over," *The Guardian*, Feb. 12, 2009.

---

[950] *IMDB*; Jim Beaver, http://www.imdb.com/title/tt0047501/plotsummary?ref_=tt_stry_pl

[951] Truth and Reconciliation Commission, *They Came for the Children*, Ottawa: 2012, p. 89.

[952] Truth and Reconciliation Commission, *Honouring the Truth, Reconciling for the Future*, Ottawa: 2015, p. 12.

[953] Truth and Reconciliation Commission, *They Came for the Children*, p. 89.

[954] Elizabeth Loftis and Jacqueline Pickrell, "The Formation of False Memories," *Psychiatric Annals* 25:12, Dec. 1995, pp. 720-5.

[955] Henry Roediger and Elizabeth Marsh, "False Memory," *Scholarpedia*, 4 (8):3858, 2009. See also Julia Shaw, *The Memory Illusion: Remembering, Forgetting, and the Science of False Memory*, NY: Random House, 2016.

[956] "The 'Martensville Nightmare' Ritual Abuse Case," *ReligiousTolerance.org*, http://www.religioustolerance.org/ra_marte.htm

[957] "The Scandal of the Century," *ReligiousTolerance.org*, http://www.religioustolerance.org/ra_reddeer.htm

[958] Truth and Reconciliation Commission, *Honouring the Truth, Reconciling for the Future*, p. 170.

[959] *Ibid.*, p. 328.

[960] *Ibid.*, p. 218.

[961] *Ibid.*, p. 328.

[962] *Ibid.*, p. 199.

[963] *Ibid.*, p. 200.

[964] H. B. Hawthorn, ed., *A Survey of the Contemporary Indians of Canada*, 1, Ottawa: Indian Affairs Branch, 1966, p. 27.

[965] *Ibid.*, p. 238.

[966] *Ibid.*

[967] *Ibid.*, p. 291.

[968] *Ibid.*, p. 334.

[969] *Ibid.*, p. 232.

[970] *The Ontario Curriculum Social Studies Grades 1 to 6, History and Geography Grades 7 and 8*, Toronto: Ontario Public Service, 2013.

[971] Truth and Reconciliation Commission, *Honouring the Truth, Reconciling for the Future*, p. 140.

[972] *Ibid.*, p. 143.

[973] *Ibid.*, p. 140.

[974] *Ibid.*, p. 319.

[975] *Ibid.*, p. 320.

[976] *Ibid.*

[977] *Ibid.*, p., 322.

[978] *Ibid.*, p. 323.

[979] *Ibid.*, p. 322.

[980] *Ibid.*, p. 163.

[981] *Ibid.*, p. 173.

[982] *Ibid.*, p. 324.

[983] *Ibid.*, p. 178.

[984] *Ibid.*, p. 207.

[985] *Ibid.*, p. 263.

[986] *Ibid.*, p. 337.

[987] *Ibid.*, p., 322.

[988] "De Beers Shelves Diamond Mine Expansion in Northern Ontario after Failing to Win Attawapiskat's Support," *Reuters*, Feb. 6, 2017.

[989] Truth and Reconciliation Commission, *Honouring the Truth, Reconciling for the Future,* p. 147.

[990] *Ibid.*, p. 148.

[991] *Ibid.*, p. 238.

[992] *Ibid.*

[993] *Ibid.*, pp. 320-1.

[994] *Ibid.*, p. 238.

[995] *Ibid.*, p. 149.

[996] *Ibid.*, p. 144.

[997] *Ibid.*, p. 152.

[998] *Ibid.*, p. 319.

[999] *Ibid.*, p. 323.

[1000] *Ibid.*, p. 164.

[1001] *Ibid.*, pp. 329-30.

[1002] *Ibid.*, p. 335.

[1003] *Ibid.*, p.337.

[1004] *Ibid.*, p. 168.

[1005] *Ibid.*, p. 242.

[1006] *Ibid.*, p. 321.

[1007] *Ibid.*, p. 149.

[1008] *Ibid.*, p. 157.

[1009] Chris Selley, "Indigenous MP opposes fellow New Democrats on official bilingualism for Supreme Court," *National Post*, November 10, 2017.

[1010] Truth and Reconciliation Commission, *Honouring the Truth, Reconciling for the Future,* p. 321.

[1011] *Ibid.*, p. 156.

[1012] G. Kent Gooderham, "Bilingual Education for Indians and Inuit: The Canadian Experience," Paper presented at the Annual Meeting of the American Anthropological Association, Mexico City, November 1971.

[1013] Truth and Reconciliation Commission, *Honouring the Truth, Reconciling for the Future,* p. 321.

[1014] *Ibid.*, p. 199.

[1015] Jean Allard, "The Road to Freedom: Big Bear's Treaty," *Inroads* 11, June 2002, pp. 110 – 271; p. 148.

[1016] Truth and Reconciliation Commission, *Honouring the Truth, Reconciling for the Future*, p. 245.

[1017] *Ibid.*, p. 300.

[1018] *Ibid.*

[1019] *Ibid.*, p. 252.

[1020] *Ibid.*, p. 325.

[1021] *Ibid.*, p. 326.

[1022] *Ibid.*

[1023] *Ibid.*, p. 327.

[1024] *Ibid.*, p. 330.

[1025] *Ibid.*, p. 331.

[1026] *Ibid.*, p. 232.

[1027] *Ibid.*, p. 330.

[1028] *Ibid.*, p. 324.

[1029] *Ibid.*, p. 325.

[1030] *Ibid.*

[1031] *Ibid.*, p. 215.

[1032] *Ibid.*, pp. 334-5.

[1033] *Ibid.*, p. 335.

[1034] *Ibid.*, p. 345.

[1035] https://www.liberal.ca/realchange/truth-and-reconciliation-2/

[1036] R. Sinclair, *Canadian Indians*, Ottawa: Thorburn & Abbott, 1911, Letter No. 8, October 12th, 1910.

[1037] Susana Mas, "Jean Chrétien's Comments on Attawapiskat Criticized in Commons," *CBC News*, Apr 13, 2016.

[1038] *Ibid.*

[1039] Bruce Hutchinson, "'We're not bison,' Grand Chief Says to Suggestion First Nations People Leave Troubled Reserves Like Attawapiskat," *National Post*, April 15, 2016.

[1040] H. B. Hawthorn, ed., *A Survey of the Contemporary Indians of Canada*, 1, Ottawa: Indian Affairs Branch, 1966, p. 54.

[1041] Jean Allard, "The Road to Freedom: Big Bear's Treaty," *Inroads* 11, June 2002, pp. 110 – 271; p. 120.

[1042] Sinclair, *op. cit.*, quoting an editorial in the Boston *Evening Standard* of August 28, 1910.

[1043] Royal Commission on Aboriginal Peoples, *People to People, Nation to Nation: Highlights from the Report of the Royal Commission on Aboriginal Peoples*. Ottawa: 1996.

[1044] Canadian Press, "Jean Chrétien's Solution for Struggling Attawapiskat Reserve: They Should Move," *National Post*, April 12, 2016.

[1045] Kristy Woudstra, "Attawapiskat Crisis: Teens Reveal What Their Community Needs," *Huffington Post Canada*, April 13, 2016.

[1046] Canadian Press, "'Apartheid System': Five Suicides in Quebec Indigenous Communities Were Avoidable, Coroner Says," *National Post*, Jan. 15, 2017.

1047 Indian Chiefs of Alberta, *Citizens Plus* ("Red Paper"), Edmonton: 1970, p. 224.

1048 Daniel Wilson and David Macdonald, "The Income Gap Between Aboriginal Peoples and the Rest of Canada," *Canadian Centre for Policy Alternatives*, 2010, p. 3.

1049 Daniel Wilson and David Macdonald, *op. cit.*, p. 12.

1050 Hawthorn, *op. cit.*, p. 54.

1051 Allard, *op. cit.*, p. 129.

1052 *Ibid.*, p. 136; Jack Beaver, *To Have What is One's Own*, National Indian Socio-Economic Development Committee. 1979, pp. 22-23.

1053 Allard, *op. cit.*, pp. 144-5.

1054 Allard, *op. cit.*, p. 145; P. Cheney, "How money has cursed Alberta's Samson Cree," *The Globe & Mail,* 28 October 1998.

1055 Mas, *op. cit.*

1056 Marie Baker, *National Conference on Indian and Northern Education*, Saskatoon, 1967, p. 54.

1057 Joshua Ostroff, "Buffy Sainte-Marie on the 'North American Holocaust' and Why Canada Needs to Decolonize," *Huffington Post Canada*, March 30, 2017.

1058 "Living conditions for First Nations 'unacceptable': Fontaine," *CBC News*, Feb 06, 2007.

1059 Mas, *op. cit.*

1060 Hutchinson, *op. cit.*

1061 Royal Commission on Aboriginal Peoples, *People to People, Nation to Nation: Highlights from the Report of the Royal Commission on Aboriginal Peoples*. Ottawa: 1996.

1062 Indian Chiefs of Alberta, *op. cit.*, p. 200.

1063 *Ibid.*, p. 206.

1064 Sinclair, *op. cit.*, Letter No. 5, Sept. 17th, 1910.

1065 Sinclair, *op. cit.*, quoting editorial in Boston *Evening Transcript* of August 28th, 1910.

1066 Richard Pratt, *Drastic Facts about our Indians and our Indian System*, Berkeley, CA: *Daily Gazette*, 1917, p. 5.

1067 Jack Beaver, *op. cit.*, pp. 26-7.

[1068] Department of Indian Affairs and Northern Development, *Statement of the Government of Canada on Indian Policy* ("White Paper"), 1969.

[1069] Indian Chiefs of Alberta, *op. cit.*, pp. 200-1.

[1070] Daniel Patrick Moynihan, *The Negro Family: The Case for National Action*, US Department of Labor, 1965.

[1071] Indian Chiefs of Alberta, *op. cit.*, p. 207.

[1072] Allard, *op. cit.*, p. 129.

[1073] Royal Commission on Aboriginal Peoples, *op. cit.*

[1074] Katherine Hughes, *Father Lacombe, The Black-Robe Voyageur*, NY: Moffat, Yard, 1911, p. 57.

[1075] Adrien Morice, *History of the Catholic Church in Western Canada*, Toronto: Musson, 1910, p. 158.

[1076] R. Sinclair, *op. cit.*, Letter No. 10, Nov. 1, 1910; *Annual Report of the Department of Indian Affairs,* Ottawa: 1908, p. 273.

[1077] H. B. Hawthorn, ed., *A Survey of the Contemporary Indians of Canada*, 2, Ottawa: Indian Affairs Branch, 1966, p. 30.

[1078] Frank Busch, "Is This the Solution to Native Poverty?" *Huffington Post Canada*, August 13, 2013.

[1079] Hymie Rubenstein and Rodney Clifton, "Truth and Reconciliation Report Tells a 'Skewed and Partial Story' of Residential Schools," *National Post*, June 22, 2015.

[1080] Allard, *op. cit.*, p 137.

[1081] Claire Hutchings, "Canada's First Nations: A Legacy of Institutional Racism," *Tolerance.cz*, http://www.tolerance.cz/courses/papers/hutchin.htm

[1082] Truth and Reconciliation Commission, *They Came for the Children*, Ottawa: 2012, p. 12.

[1083] Hawthorn, *A Survey of the Contemporary Indians of Canada*, 2, pp. 22-3.

[1084] Mas, *op. cit.*

[1085] G. Kent Gooderham, "Bilingual Education for Indians and Inuit: The Canadian Experience," *Annual Meeting of the American Anthropological Association*, Mexico City, Nov., 1971.

[1086] *AFNQL*, 2007; *Réseau de recherche en santé des populations du Québec*, 2008; *Health Canada*, 2003; *FNQLHSSC*, 2006.

[1087] Naomi Riley, *The New Trail of Tears*, NY: Encounter Books, 2016, location 89, Kindle version.

[1088] Assembly of First Nations, "Fact Sheet—Quality of Life of First Nations," June, 2011.

[1089] Menno Bolt, *Surviving as Indians*, Toronto: University of Toronto Press, 1993, p.15.

[1090] Woudstra, *op. cit.*

[1091] Mark Gollom, "Additional Mental Health Workers Being Sent to Remote Northern Ontario Community," *CBC News*, April 12, 2016.

[1092] Kristy Kirkup, "Inuit Artist Susan Aglakark Says Sex Abuse is at the Root of Indigenous Suicide Crisis," *CP*, Feb. 5, 2017.

[1093] Sinclair, *op. cit.*, Letter number 5.

[1094] Sinclair, *op. cit.*, quoting an editorial in the Boston *Evening Transcript* of August 28th, 1910.

[1095] Riley, *op. cit.*, location 89.

[1096] Allard, *op. cit.*, pp. 130-1.

[1097] Leona Freed, quoted in S. Alberts, "Self-Government is Self-Destruction, Native Group Says," *National Post*, March 3, 1999.

[1098] Leona Freed, "Calling for Accountability," First Nations Accountability Coalition brief to the Senate Standing Committee on Aboriginal Affairs, January 28, 1999; Allard, *op. cit.*, p. 158.

[1099] *Ibid.* p. 132.

[1100] Hawthorn, *A Survey of the Contemporary Indians of Canada*, 1, p. 54.

[1101] F. F. Payne, "A Few Notes upon the Eskimo of Cape Prince of Wales, Hudson's Strait," *Proceedings of the American Association for the Advancement of Science*, 1889, p. 358.

[1102] Sir George Back, *Narrative of the Arctic Land Expedition to the Mouth of the Great Fish River, and Along the Shores of the Arctic Ocean in the Years 1833, 1834, and 1835*, London: John Murray, 1836, p. 194-5.

[1103] Fr. LeJeune, *Relations* 6, pp. 257-9.

[1104] Samuel Hearne, *A Journey from Prince of Wales's Fort in Hudson's Bay to the Northern Ocean in the Years 1769, 1770, 1771, and 1772.* Toronto: The Champlain Society, 1911; originally published 1795; p. 299.

[1105] Livingston Jones, *A Study of the Thlingits of Alaska,* NY: Revell, 1914, pp. 96-7.

[1106] David Kaplan, "The Darker Side of the 'Original Affluent Society'," *Journal of Anthropological Research*, 56:3, Autumn, 2000, p. 315.

[1107] Jon Altman, "A Genealogy of Demand-Sharing: From Pure Anthropology to Public Policy," in Y. Musharbash and M. Barber, eds., *Ethnography and the Production of Anthropological Knowledge: Essays in Honour of Nicolas Peterson*, ANU Press, Canberra, pp. 187-200.

[1108] Hawthorn, *A Survey of the Contemporary Indians of Canada*, 1, p. 57.

[1109] Hearne, *op cit.*, p. 317.

[1110] *Ibid.*, p. 97.

[1111] *Ibid.*, p. 144.

[1112] *Ibid.*, pp. 141-2.

[1113] Allard, *op. cit.*, p. 149.

[1114] Baker, *op. cit.*, p. 55.

[1115] Hawthorn, *op. cit.*, p. 181.

[1116] Alexander Morris, *The Treaties of Canada*, Toronto: Willing & Williamson, 1880, p. 30.

[1117] Jean Allard, *op. cit.*, p. 128; Canada, Report to R. Connelly, Assistant Deputy Minister, Indian Affairs, Ottawa: Department of Indian Affairs, 1973.

[1118] Allard, *op. cit.*, p. 128.

[1119] *Ibid.*, p. 129.

[1120] Indian Chiefs of Alberta, *op. cit.*, p. 204.

[1121] *Ibid.*

[1122] Royal Commission on Aboriginal Peoples, *op. cit.*

[1123] https://www.measuringworth.com/uscompare/relativevalue.php

[1124] Allard, *op. cit.*, p. 166.

[1125] Indian Chiefs of Alberta, *op. cit.*, p. 195.

Made in the USA
Monee, IL
03 July 2020

35713854R00266